TH

THE BABURNAMA

MEMOIRS OF BABUR, PRINCE AND EMPEROR

Translated, edited, and annotated by

Wheeler M. Thackston

Introduction by Salman Rushdie

THE MODERN LIBRARY

NEW YORK

2002 Modern Library Paperback Edition

Translation/main text and notes copyright © 1996 by the Smithsonian Institution
Introduction copyright © 2002 by Salman Rushdie

This work was originally published in slightly different form in 1996 by
Oxford University Press. This edition published by arrangement with
Smithsonian Institution, Freer Gallery of Art, Arthur M. Sackler Gallery.

LIBRARY OF CONGRESS CATALOGING-IN-PUBLICATION DATA
Babur, Emperor of Hindustan, 1483–1530.
[Baburnamah. English]
The Baburnama: memoirs of Babur, prince and emperor /
translated, edited, and annotated by Wheeler M. Thackston.
p. cm.
Originally published: Washington, D.C.: Freer Gallery of Art:
Arthur M. Sackler Gallery, Smithsonian Institution, 1996.
Includes bibliographical references and index.
ISBN 978-0-375-76137-9 (trade pbk.)
1. Babur, Emperor of Hindustan, 1483-1530. 2. Mogul Empire.
3. Mogul Empire—Kings and rulers—Biography.
I. Thackston, W. M. (Wheeler McIntosh), 1944– II. Title.

DS461.1 .B23213 2002
954.02'52—dc21 2002019644

Modern Library website address: www.modernlibrary.com

Printed in the United States of America

FRONTISPIECE: *Babur Receives a Courtier,* attributed to Farrukh Beg. From a
Baburnama of Zahiruddin Muhammad Babur, Lahore, dated 1589. Opaque
watercolor and gold on paper. Arthur M. Sackler Gallery, Smithsonian
Institution; Purchase—Smithsonian Unrestricted Trust Funds, Smithsonian
Collections Acquisition Program, and Dr. Arthur M. Sackler, S1986.230.

Contents

THE BABURNAMA

INTRODUCTION

Salman Rushdie

Zahiruddin Muhammad Babur (1483–1530), the founder of the Mughal Empire in India, is best remembered for three things: the story of his death, the controversy over his mosque, and the extraordinary reputation of the *Baburnama*, his book.

I first heard the legend of Babur's death when I was still a boy. His son and heir, Humayun, was ill, the story went. His fever rose and the court's doctors despaired of saving him. Then Babur, after consulting a mystic, walked three times round Humayun's bed and offered himself to God in his son's place. Whereupon Humayun strengthened and recovered, and Babur weakened and—on December 21, 1530—died. This story struck me with an almost mythic force. I remember having been horrified by Abraham's unnatural readiness to sacrifice his allegedly beloved son—Isaac according to the Old Testament, but Ismail in the Muslim version. Was that what the love of God made fathers willing to do? It was enough to make one regard one's own parent with a somewhat worried eye. Babur's story served as an antidote. Here the love of God was used to make possible the opposite and somehow more "natural" sacrifice: the father dying that the child might live. Babur and Humayun's story lodged deep within me as the paradigmatic tale of fatherly love.

These days, Babur's name is still associated with legends, but of a different and more controversial kind. The Babri Masjid, the mosque he built in Ayodhya, a city in what was once the kingdom of Awadh (Oudh) and is now the heartland state of Uttar Pradesh, was demolished in 1992 by Hindu extremists who believed that it had been built on the ruins of a Hindu temple sacred to the mythic hero of the Ramayana, Lord Ram (or Rama) himself; a temple, moreover, which had been constructed to mark the site of the *Ramjanmabhoomi*—the actual birthplace of the hero-god.

"Ayodhya" was indeed the name of Ram's city, whence he set forth to rescue his beloved Sita from her abductor, Lord Ravan. But there's little reason to believe that modern-day Ayodhya stands on the same site as the Ramayana's fabled realm. And, at the risk of rousing the ire of militant Hindus, there is no real proof that the mythological Lord Ram, an incarnation of the great god Vishnu, was a historical personage at all. Even the simplest facts remain in doubt; archaeologists disagree about the site, and as to it being the "real" Ramjanmabhoomi, that's about as likely as Christ being born in modern Bethlehem's Manger Square. (It is also pointed out that many Hindu temples in India are built over the ruins of Buddhist shrines.)

All these doubts and caveats are swept aside by the zealots' wrath. Babur, the bloodthirsty slayer of infidels, the devoted destroyer of temples, is in their eyes guilty as charged, and all India's Muslims are indirectly tainted by his crime. (There's a Hindu nationalist view that India is a country of many peoples: Hindus, Sikhs, Parsis, Buddhists, Jains, Christians—and Mughals.) They claim, moreover, that the Babri Masjid is only the first of the mosques on their hit list. In Mathura, they allege, another mosque stands on the demolished birthplace of another divinity—another incarnation of Vishnu, actually—Lord Krishna, he of the milkmaids and the lustrous blue skin.

The autobiography that is Babur's third and most enduring claim to fame is inconveniently silent—or, in the opinion of his more strident critics, conveniently so—on the time Babar spent in and around the Ayodhya region. In all surviving manuscripts there's a five-month gap between April and September 1528, the period during which Babur was in Oudh, and during which the Babri Masjid was built. Thus there's no proof that anything at all was demolished to build the mosque; or, alternatively, that it wasn't. In our paranoid age it's perhaps necessary to point out that there's nothing suspicious about this gap. Four hundred and seventy-plus years is a long time. Things get lost in four and a half centuries; sometimes the things (Thomas Kyd's *Hamlet*, for example) that we most want to find.

A man's character can get blurred by the passage of time. Where facts are insufficient, what fills the space is interpretation. Take two recent depictions of a single scene from the Emperor's life: the temporary capture in the Punjab of the founder of Sikhism, Guru Nanak, by Babur's conquering army. The critic N. S. Rajaram, a deconstructionist of Indian "secularist myths," an apologist for the destruction of the Babri Masjid, and in general no fan of Babur's, writes that "in his *Babur Vani,* Nanak denounced him in no uncertain terms, giving a vivid account of Babur's vandalism in Aimanabad." Against this, Amitav Ghosh tells us in a recent essay that Sikhs "have long cherished a story, preserved in their scriptural tradition, about an encounter between Babur and the founder of their faith, Guru Nanak.... Learning of a miracle performed by the Guru, Babur visited him in prison. Such was the presence of the Guru that Babur is said to have fallen at his feet, with the cry: 'On the face of this faqir one sees God himself.' "

Ghosh concedes that Sikhs became "dedicated adversaries of the Mughal state in the 17th century," but argues powerfully that the flowering of Hinduism, including the Vaishnavite development of the theology and sacred geography of Krishna-worship, which took place in northern India under Babur and his successors, would have been impossible in a climate of persecution. "Hinduism would scarcely be recognizable today," Ghosh writes, "if Vaishnavism had been actively suppressed in the 16th century: other devotional forms may have taken its place, but we cannot know what those would have been. It is a simple fact that contemporary Hinduism as a living practice would not be what it is if it were not for the devotional practices initiated under Mughal rule. The sad irony of the assault on the Babri mosque is that the Hindu fanatics who attacked it destroyed a symbol of the very accommodations that made their own beliefs possible."

Rajaram argues back, with almost equal force, that Babur "was more than ordinarily ruthless. He pursued to the limit the concept of Jihad—a total war for the annihilation of his adversaries as prescribed by Islam of which he was a practitioner. He was a product of his age and his environment, and that is exactly how we must see him. Whitewashing his blood-soaked record to turn him into a figure of chivalry and a prince charming is an exercise in juvenile fantasy. Babur saw ruthlessness as a virtue, and terror as a useful tactical tool. In this he was a true descendant of Timur and Genghis Khan—both of whom were his ancestors. Guru Nanak's eyewitness account gives a better picture of Babur and his methods than almost any modern history book. The same holds true for the *Baburnama:* it is a primary source of great importance that goes to demolish romantic tales about him." (Somewhat coarsely, Rajaram reminds us that the phrase *Babur ki aulad,* "offspring of Babur," is a common term of abuse leveled at Indian Muslims.)

How contemporary this dispute sounds! Today, once again, we are tossed between Islam's apologists and detractors. In part because of these modern disagreements, those who would defend India's Muslims against the accusations of Hindu nationalists naturally stress the civilization and tolerance of Mughal Islam. As many writers have said, the dynasty Babur founded—his true *aulad*—was noted for its polytheistic inclusiveness. At the height of the Mughal Empire, Babur's grandson Akbar went so far as to invent a new creed—the *Din-i-Illahi*—that sought to be a fusion of all that was best in Indian spirituality. Against this, however, it's argued that the last of the so-called Grand Mughals, Aurangzeb, did his iconoclastic best to undo his predecessors' good work, rampaging across the country destroying temples. (Some of India's most precious antiquities, such as the temple complex at Khajuraho, survive only because in Aurangzeb's time these extraordinary edifices with their famous erotic carvings had faded from prominence and weren't marked on his maps.)

Who, then, was Babur—scholar or barbarian, nature-loving poet or terror-inspiring warlord? The answer is to be found in the *Baburnama,* and it's an uncomfortable one: he was both. It could be said that the struggle taking place within Islam in our own era, the struggle which has, I believe, been a feature of the history of Islam from its beginnings to the present day—between conservatism and progressivism, between Islam's male-dominated, aggressive, ruthless aspect and its gentler, deeply sophisticated culture of books, philosophers, musicians, and artists, that same, contradictory doubleness which modern commentators have found so hard to understand, was, in the case of Babur, an internal conflict. Both Baburs are real, and perhaps the strangest thing about the *Baburnama* is that they do not seem to be at odds with each other. When the book's author looks inward and reflects, he is often melancholy; but the dark clouds that gather over him do not seem to be the product of a storm within. Mostly, they have to do with his sense of loss. The first Mughal Emperor of India was also an exile and a homesick man. His soul pined for what we would now call Afghanistan.

Afghanistan's new significance in the world after September 11, 2001, changes the way we now read the *Baburnama*. Hitherto, the book's Indian section has been of most interest, with its firsthand account of the birth of an empire that lasted 200 years, until the British supplanted it. But suddenly it is the work's "Afghan" beginnings that fascinate us. Place names from Konduz to Kabul, made newly familiar by the bulletins of a modern war, leap out at us. The ancient treacheries of the region's warlords seem to have things to teach us about the power struggles of today. Babur is fascinatingly frank about all of this. (It's plain that in his time the best response to the death of a parent was to dive for cover and plot one's siblings' deaths, knowing that those siblings would be filled with similarly loving thoughts about you.)

Yet this treacherous land was the place Babur loved. Read him on Kabul, "a petty little province," and vivid detail enlivens his simple declaratory sentences. "At the end of the canal is an area called Gulkana, a secluded, cozy spot where much debauchery is indulged in." The *Baburnama*, not unattractively, finds sex and booze wherever it goes. "Kabul wine is intoxicating. The wine from the slopes of Khwaja Khawand Sa'id mountain is known for being strong." Tropical and cold-weather fruits are eulogized, melons are disparaged, meadows are praised for being free of flies while others are flyblown and to be avoided. Mountain roads and passes, which became the subjects of nightly analyses on the world's media during the recent battles against the Taliban and Al-Qaida forces, are here meticulously described. Muskrats scuttle and partridges rise. A world leaps into view.

In India, which he so famously disliked, his powers of description grow, if anything, stronger. Sometimes he succumbs to fantasy. "It is said that . . . there are elephants ten yards tall." Usually, however, he confines his remarks to what he has seen with his own eyes. "[Rhinoceroses] wield their horns in an amazing way. . . . During one hunt a page named Maqsud had his horse thrown a spear length by one. Thereafter he was nicknamed Rhinoceros Maqsud." He describes the cows, the monkeys, the birds, the fruits of India; but in spite of his evident respect for the "excellent" system of numbering and the "wonderful" systems of weights and measures, he can't resist going on to the attack. "Hindustan is a place of little charm. There is no beauty in its people.... The arts and crafts have no harmony or symmetry.... There is no ice.... There are no baths." He likes the monsoon, but not the humidity. He likes the winter, but not the dust. The summer isn't as hot as it is in Balkh and Kandahar, and that's a plus. He admires the "craftsmen and practitioners of every trade." But what he likes most is the wealth. "The one nice aspect of Hindustan is that it is a large country with lots of gold and money."

The contradictions in Babur's personality are well illustrated by his account of the conquest of Chanderi in 1528. First comes a bloodthirsty description of the killing of many "infidels" and the apparent mass suicide of two or three hundred more. ("[T]hey killed each other almost to the last by having one man hold a sword while the others willingly bent their necks.... A tower of infidels' skulls was erected on the hill on the northwest side of Chanderi.") Then, just three sentences later, we get this: "Chanderi is a superb place. All around the area are many flowing streams.... The lake ... is renowned throughout Hindustan for its good, sweet water. It is truly a nice little lake...."

The Western thinker whom Babur most resembles is his contemporary, the Florentine Niccolò Machiavelli. In both men, a cold appreciation of the necessities of power, of what would today be called *realpolitik*, is combined with a deeply cultured and literary nature, not to mention the love, often to excess, of wine and women. Of course, Babur actually was a prince, not simply the author of *The Prince*, and could practice what he preached; while Machiavelli, the natural republican, the survivor of torture, was by far the more troubled spirit of the pair. Yet both these unwilling exiles were, as writers, blessed, or perhaps cursed, with a clear-sightedness that looks amoral; as truth so often does.

The *Baburnama*, the first autobiography in Islamic literature, was originally written in Chaghatay Turkish, the language of Babur's ancestor Temur-i-Lang, "lame Temur," better known in the West as Tamerlane. Wheeler M. Thackston's translation replaces the inadequate Beveridge version, and is so fluently readable, and so thoroughly backed up by the detailed scholarship of Thackston's many annotations, as to feel definitive. From Thackston's notes we learn about much that Babur leaves unsaid—about, for example, Persian verse forms such as the qasida and the ghazal; or peaked Mongolian caps; or the place in the heavens of the star Canopus. He is not afraid to argue with Babur. When Babur speculates that the name of a province, Lamghan, is derived from the Islamic version of the name of Noah, "Lamkan," Thackston ripostes: "He is quite mistaken in this, for the -ghan and -qan endings on so many toponyms in the area are of Iranian origin." Babur should feel well pleased to have so unsubmissive a translator and editor. A great translation can unveil—can, literally, dis-cover—a great book; and in Thackston's translation, one of the classic works of world literature arrives in English like a marvelous discovery.

———

SALMAN RUSHDIE is the author of eight novels, including *Fury* and *Midnight's Children,* four works of nonfiction, and a collection of stories. He has been awarded numerous prizes, including the Booker Prize and the Booker of the Bookers. His work has been translated into thirty-seven languages. His most recent book is the essay collection *Step Across This Line.*

TRANSLATOR'S PREFACE

Zahiruddin Muhammad Babur (1483–1530),[1] born prince of Fergana in Transoxiana (modern Uzbekistan and Tajikistan), was a scion of the dynasty that had reigned undisputed throughout eastern Iran and Central Asia since the time of its progenitor, Amir Temür (1336–1405).[2] Occupying the sovereign throne of Samarkand at the age of twelve, Babur emerged as a Timurid ruler when there were too many claimants to too few thrones. Driven from his homeland, he spent a lifetime winning kingdoms and losing a few along the way, gradually moving south from modern Uzbekistan and Tajikistan, through Afghanistan, to the Indian subcontinent. Successively becoming monarch of Kabul and emperor of Hindustan, Babur expanded the boundaries of the Timurid cultural sphere and founded, in 1526, what was to become the great Mughal Empire of India, whose last reigning sovereign, the twenty-third of his line, was exiled from Delhi in 1858. A figure of consequence in world history, Babur not only made his mark on the historical record but also left a written account of his life.

Said to "rank with the Confessions of St. Augustine and Rousseau, and the Memoirs of Gibbon and Newton,"[3] Babur's memoirs are the first—and until relatively recent times, the only—true autobiography in Islamic literature. Although the biographical sketch had long been an integral part of the literary legacy, and biographical dictionaries for various classes and professions abounded, the autobiography as we know it was unheard of when Babur decided to keep a written record of his life.[4] We have no way of knowing what prompted Babur to write his open, frank, and occasionally quite intimate memoirs, and aside from the few internal references to the work as a "history" and his stated determination to be absolutely truthful and unbiased in his record, he gives no hint of his motivation or inspiration:

> I have not written all this to complain: I have simply written the truth. I do not intend by what I have written to compliment myself: I have simply set down exactly what happened. Since I have made it a point in this history to write the truth of every matter and to set down no more than the reality of every event, as a consequence I have reported every good and evil I have seen of father and brother and set down the actuality of every fault and virtue of relative and stranger. May the reader excuse me; may the listener take me not to task.[5]

Babur made an unusual decision to keep a record of his life, but the language in which he chose to keep it was even more uncommon. Opting not to write in Persian, the universal language of culture and literature of his time and place, he kept his memoirs in Chaghatay Turkish, the Timurids' spoken language—indeed of the whole Turco-Mongolian world at the time.[6] Poets and writers had sporadically dabbled in Chaghatay from the beginning of the Timurid period, and under the patronage of Babur's elder contemporaries in Herat, Sultan-Husayn Mirza and Mir Ali-Sher Nawa'i, Chaghatay poetry enjoyed a short-lived florescence at the end of the fifteenth century; but Chaghatay never threatened Persian as the dominant language of culture, and little expository or narrative prose had ever been written in Chaghatay, even in Herat. To this day the *Baburnama*[7] is one of the longest examples of sustained narrative prose in the language, as the attempts to turn Chaghatay into a viable literary vehicle turned out to be a "flash in the pan," doomed by the turn of events that swept the Timurids from Iran and Central Asia. Ironically, Timurid rule was overwhelmed by two dynasties that were also Turkic: from the west came the Safavids (1501–1732) and their predominantly Turcoman supporters, and from the north the Turco-Mongolian Uzbeks. Since the Safavids' primary cultural identification was with Iran, their cultural language was Persian; and even though their home language remained Turkish throughout the dynasty's long history, their Turkish was the western dialect of the Turcomans of eastern Anatolia and Azerbaijan and not the eastern, Chaghatay dialect of the Timurids. The Uzbeks, suffering from a cultural inferiority complex, concentrated their efforts on the cultivation of Persian, mainly by importing talent, both voluntary and involuntary, from Timurid Herat and had little time or inclination for patronage of their own Turkish language.

HISTORY OF THE TEXT
AND TRANSLATIONS

From internal evidence and references to sections of the manuscript that no longer exist it is clear that the memoirs were originally much more extensive than they are now. The gaps in the text as we have it today, particularly the two large lacunae that span from 1508 to 1519 (between fols. 216b–217) and from 1520 to 1525 (at the end of Part 2, in fol. 251b), are likely the result of loss of quires during a storm (see fol. 376b). Several comments show that Babur was reworking parts of his memoirs in 935 (1528–29), the last year for which there is an entry, and he died the following year, in 1530. That Babur's son and successor, Humayun, knew Chaghatay well and read his father's memoirs there is no question. Babur corresponded with him in that language, correcting his spelling and commenting on his style (see fol. 349b). It is not unlikely that Humayun's son and successor, Akbar, also knew Chaghatay, for Akbar was only fourteen years old when Humayun died in 1556, and the young emperor was raised by the regent, Bayram Khan, a Turcoman of eastern Anatolian and Azerbaijani origin whose father and grandfather had joined Babur's service.[8] Bayram Khan wrote poetry in Chaghatay and Persian, and his son, Abdul-Rahim Khankhanan, was fluent in Persian, Chaghatay, and Hindi and composed poetry in all three languages.[9] During Akbar's long reign, however, Chaghatay was on the wane, as was the Central Asian Timurid character of Babur's empire, and the dominant Persian language and Persianate culture of the subcontinent rapidly drove the Central Asian Turkic element into oblivion.

It is difficult to imagine that many at the Mughal court could read a book in Chaghatay by the end of Akbar's long reign (1556–1605). One of the few who could, Abdul-Rahim Khankhanan, translated the

Baburnama into Persian and presented it to Akbar in 1589, aptly after Akbar had visited Babur's tomb in Kabul.[10] It is almost certain that the khankhanan used Babur's own text to translate the work into Persian.[11] Afterward, the Chaghatay original disappeared, last seen in the imperial library sometime between 1628 and 1638 by one of the historians of Shahjahan's reign (1628–57).[12] Many copies of the Persian translation were produced, however, some of them lavishly illustrated by artists in the imperial Mughal workshops.[13]

EUROPEAN INTEREST
IN THE BABURNAMA

British interest in the *Baburnama* began, predictably enough, in India. Around 1805 an English translation of the memoirs was started by John Leyden, who worked from an imperfect Chaghatay text he had found either at Fort William College in Calcutta or in the collection of Mountstuart Elphinstone, the British Resident at Nagpur from 1804 to 1808. Unable to locate a Persian translation in Bengal, Leyden was provided with one by William Erskine, who had had a copy made in Bombay of a manuscript of the Persian translation. Several years after Leyden's death in 1811, the work he had done was sent to Erskine, who had also begun a translation, but from the Persian alone. Encouraged to continue by Elphinstone, then the Resident at Poona, and by other officers of the British East India Company, Erskine attempted to reconcile Leyden's translation from the Chaghatay and adapt it to his own translation from the Persian. In the end he rejected Leyden's attempts (although he would give him first billing in the published version) and in 1816 completed his translation, based exclusively on the Persian translation. Late in the game Elphinstone had sent him a copy of a Chaghatay text he had acquired in Peshawar in 1810. "The discovery of this valuable manuscript," Erskine wrote, "reduced me, though heartily sick of the task, to the necessity of commencing my work once more." Erskine, however, had little knowledge of Chaghatay and could not have used it to make significant changes in his translation. His, the first translation into a modern European language, appeared in print ten years after its completion, in 1826.[14]

Erskine had worked exclusively from the khankhanan's Persian translation. The Persian, however, is so faithful to the syntax of the original that the language is, at best, enigmatic and, at worst, incomprehensible. "Though simple and concise," Erskine relates, "a close adherence to the idioms and forms of expression of the Tûrki original, joined to a want of distinctness in the use of the relatives, often renders the meaning extremely obscure, and makes it difficult to discover the connexion of the different members of the sentence."[15] It is certainly a tribute to the translator's ability that he was able to produce a readable and fairly accurate rendering. The English, however, is couched in a style that is much more elevated than the original (and now quite dated)—a flaw for which the translator cannot be blamed, working as he was at second hand from the Persian translation, which by default is more literary than the original, to which he did not have access.

On the Central Asian and Russian fronts, a manuscript of the Chaghatay text, purportedly copied in Bukhara in 1714 from a manuscript produced in 1709, was sold to a member of a Czarist mission to Turkistan in 1721. That copy was brought back to the Russian Foreign Ministry in 1725, where it was copied in 1737 by a Russian orientalist, Georg Jacob Kehr, who made a garbled Latin translation. Kehr's Chaghatay text was used by Nikolai Ilminski to produce, in 1857 in Kazan, the first printed version of the memoirs in Chaghatay,[16] from which the French turkologist Abel Pavet de Courteille made a French translation that appeared in 1871,[17] the first to have been made from what was then considered to be the original Chaghatay text. In the meanwhile, however, the manuscript—if there ever was such a manuscript—from which the Bukhara copy had been made disappeared and has yet to be rediscovered.

In 1900 another Chaghatay text was found in Hyderabad, Deccan, by a British orientalist, Henry Beveridge. The manuscript, which had belonged to Sir Salar Jang of Hyderabad, was published in facsimile in 1905 as the first volume in the "great text" series founded as a memorial to the scholar of Turkish literature E. J. W. Gibb.[18] Comparison between the Kehr-Ilminski and Hyderabad texts reveals that the Kehr-Ilminski version, though in general agreement with the Hyderabad text for roughly the first half of the manuscript, is thereafter a retranslation into Chaghatay from a Persian translation. One can speculate that the Bukhara copy had been made from a partial Turkish text in Central Asia (Babur mentions sending a copy to Khwaja Kalan in Kabul [fol. 363], and it is known that Muhammad-Husayn Mirza Dughlat had a copy), and the Persian was used to complete the copy by retranslating the missing portions into Turkish. The Hyderabad text, on the other hand, is, as determined by close comparison with the Persian translation, absolutely authentic and has only minor omissions caused by haplography and a few copyist errors. The manuscript is not dated, but it is probably from the late seventeenth or early eighteenth century—certainly before 1739, when Delhi was sacked by Nadir Shah, and the Mughal imperial library, which undoubtedly housed Babur's own original text (or texts), was dispersed. To date, the manuscript from which the Hyderabad copy was made, if it still exists, has not come to light. The Hyderabad text of the *Baburnama* was translated into English by Annette Beveridge, Henry Beveridge's wife. Her translation appeared in four fascicules from 1912 to 1921.

After the introduction of the Chaghatay text, the translator's job was made more complex. Much of the bizarre syntax and wording of the Persian was explained by the Chaghatay, but that language was little known and not well understood at the time. Annette Beveridge was timid in her approach, opting for a literal, almost word-for-word rendering of the Chaghatay—much as the khankhanan had done when he turned the work into Persian, but for a very different reason. Insofar as is known, although there had been a great deal of translation from Persian into various sorts of Turkish over the centuries, there was no precedent at all for the translation of Turkish into Persian. The khankhanan must have chosen as a model the type of translation with which he was most familiar, that is, the interlinear translation of Koranic Arabic to Persian and/or Turkish. In those translations every word is translated verbatim, without much regard for the syntax of the target language.

Beveridge's translation, on the other hand, reads like a student's effort—all the words have been looked up in the dictionary and put together in a meaningful fashion but without certainty as to the force or nuance of the original. She also chose to reproduce the repetitiousness of the original and, far worse, to retain a one-for-one correspondence between Turkish and English words. This was a conscious decision on her part, for she dwells on it in her introduction and faults her predecessors for doing otherwise, insisting on "strict observance of Babur's limits of vocabulary, effected by allotting to one Turki word one English equivalent, thus excluding synonyms for which Turki has little use because not shrinking [*sic*] from the repeated word."[19] To be sure, the lexicon of Chaghatay is not large, far smaller than Persian. Nonetheless, the same word used in different contexts does convey different shades of meaning to a native speaker. It is a grave mistake for a translator to insist on such a one-to-one correspondence in translation, particularly in the case of modern English, the vast lexicon and abundant synonyms of which have rendered repetition irritating to the reader. A sixteenth-century reader of Chaghatay would have found nothing strange or vexing about the constant repetition of a word or phrase, but the same sort of repetition in English gives the text an unwarranted coloration. Babur, for example, qualifies practically every adjective with *khaylî*, "very," the retention of which in English has been deemed unnecessary because the sense of that feeble adverb can be better conveyed by a slightly more forceful adjective. Beveridge also followed the khankhanan into translating Chaghatay syntax verbatim, producing phrases such as "it was stopped" for *tüshüldi*, when what is meant is "we stopped" or "one dismounted" (the French impersonal construction *on s'est arrêté* comes closer to capturing the Chaghatay).[20] A literal reproduction of alien syntax is a mistake in any translation. Beveridge even tried to reproduce the etymological history of Chaghatay in English. It is quite true that the three main lexical constituents of Chaghatay—native Turkic, sophisticated Persian, and learned Arabic—can be fairly equated on a general level with Anglo-Saxon, Norman French, and Greco-Latin elements in English, but when it comes to individual lexical items the equation does not necessarily hold, and it is wrong to burden oneself with such a programmatic approach to translation.

Babur's Chaghatay is fluid, idiomatic, and colloquial—"written in a simple, unaffected and yet very pure style" is Mirza Haydar's assessment.[21] Babur writes in his native tongue, a language that had little or no literary pretensions, and his style is devoid of the sumptuous Persianate artifice and literary contrivance, with its penchant for rhyming synonyms and seemingly endless parallel constructions, that characterize the Chaghatay prose of Sultan-Husayn Mirza and Ali-Sher Nawa'i.[22] In the present translation every effort has been made, however, to preserve the flavor of the original but to couch it in modern English, without straying across the thin line that separates a nonliteral translation from one that has abandoned the original in favor of a free rendering, bearing in mind that it is impossible to reproduce in English, with its centuries of literature, the ambiance of a book written in a language with few, if any, literary antecedents, like Chaghatay.

ORGANIZATION OF THE BOOK

The memoirs as we have them today, which are assumed to be as Babur left them, are easily divisible into three fairly equal parts, all of which maintain the chronological arrangement, typical of its time, by year of the Hegira calendar, not by topic. While the narrative proceeds strictly chronologically in the larger framework, Babur does, however, jump back in time when he introduces individuals and their antecedents, sometimes two or three generations. He also on occasion stops the narrative to give what he calls the "recent history" of a locality, which may go back many scores of years. I have added annotations to flesh out from Babur's story the customs, manners, and history of events and to introduce them to the general reader.

The first part, which deals with Babur's early life from the time he was proclaimed ruler in Khodzhent in 899 (1494) at the age of twelve until he left Transoxiana in 908 (1503), has obviously been carefully worked, rewritten, and edited by Babur. Historical background material has been inserted in its proper place, and persons are identified.[23] The narrative flows nicely, and the prose is well thought out.

The second part, Kabul, from 910 (1504) through 926 (1520), has also been edited, more or less to the same extent as the first part. It also contains the two large gaps in the text, one from just after the beginning of 914 (May 1508) until the beginning of 925 (January 1519), and the other from just after the beginning of 926 (December 1519) through the end of 931 (October 1525).

The third part, from the beginning of 932 (1525) to the end of the text as it breaks off in midsentence at the beginning of 936 (September 1529), is still in the form of a rough draft. Large parts look as though Babur copied them directly from a diary with the intention of returning to edit and annotate—a chance he never got.

The Hyderabad manuscript gives most of the year headings, and those that it lacks are supplied by the Persian translation. Although topical subheadings were common in Persian historical works in Babur's time, he did not use them; I have inserted all subheadings in this translation to organize and therefore ease the reading of what is otherwise continuous text. The folio numbers of the Hyderabad manuscript are included within square brackets in this translation; the *b* after the folio number refers to a verso page.

Dates in the original texts are given, of course, in Hegira years and months. In the translation all Hegira dates are followed by the corresponding Western (that is, Julian) date in square brackets. The full corresponding Julian year is given (e.g., 1526–27 for A.H. 932), unless the exact part of the year is known (e.g., in which case only 1526 might be cited). Western dates have been calculated through the most reliable conversion tables and computer programs, but, as is usual in these conversions, the days of the week do not always coincide. For instance, Babur records "Wednesday the thirteenth of Dhu'l-Qaʿda" in 932. That date converts to August 21, 1526, but, according to the tables, in 1526 the twenty-first of August fell on Tuesday, not Wednesday. There seems to be no way to reconcile these discrepancies, and the days of the week have therefore been left as Babur wrote them, on the assumption that he knew better than a modern conversion table what day of the week it actually was.

Babur has preserved a great deal of the history of his period not found in any other sources. Khwandamir, author of *Habib al-siyar,* and Muhammad-Haydar Mirza Dughlat, author of the *Tarikh-i Rashidi,* were reliable contemporary historians and knew Babur personally (Muhammad-Haydar Mirza was also Babur's first cousin on his mother's side). Both authors used Babur's memoirs as a primary source for their own reports, and, insofar as they treat the same material as Babur does, they corroborate his data.

Many beautifully illustrated *Baburnama*s were produced by the Mughals from the end of the sixteenth century through the seventeenth. Although some of these manuscripts contain exceptionally fine examples of Mughal book painting, they have the disadvantage of showing figures as contemporary Mughals in contemporary Indian settings and thus illustrate later generations' conceptions of Babur more than they illustrate Babur himself. We have chosen rather to use as illustrations paintings that are as closely contemporary as possible with Babur, and objects of the sort that Babur may well have possessed—in some cases, actually did possess. Landscapes speak for themselves, as little has changed.

NAMES AND TITLES OCCURRING IN THE BABURNAMA

For the reader the greatest challenge lies not in the language but, as E. M. Forster observed of the *Baburnama,* in the onslaught of unfamiliar names of people and places: "Those awful Oriental names! They welter from start to finish. Sometimes twenty new ones occur on a page and never recur. Among humans there are not only the Turki descendants of Tamerlane and the Moghul descendants of Genghis Khan, all royal, and mostly in motion; long lists of their nobles are given also."[24] In common with historians of the period, Babur indeed peppers his accounts with a large number of names. In part, he had a desire to memorialize his comrades and subordinates, as well as his foes, who exhibited remarkable bravery and skill on the battlefield or performed outstanding service in some other arena. On the other hand, there was a tendency in Muslim historiography to legitimize a historical account with all the known names of the persons involved, regardless of how insignificant their roles may have been. The seemingly least important of characters—messengers, gatekeepers, grooms—are often identified by name, even though they appear no more than once. For major characters, little can be done to remedy the unfortunate similarity between, for example, Babur's father's brothers, Sultan-Ahmad Mirza and Sultan-Mahmud Mirza, and his mother's brothers, Sultan-Ahmad Khan and Sultan-Mahmud Khan; but genealogical charts are provided to alleviate some of the confusion of mirzas and begs, and a short note here on common titles may help the reader.

The Timurids, the descendants of Amir Temür, all bear the title Mirza, a shortened form of *amirzada,* "offspring of the Amir," and, in the Turkish fashion, the title follows the proper name. Female Timurids have the title Begim, "my lady." Thus Babur is Babur *Mirza,* his father is Umar-Shaykh *Mirza,* his aunt is Payanda Sultan *Begim.* Autonomous rulers of the House of Timur, in addition to their hereditary title of Mirza, are styled Padishah. Babur, for instance, formally changed his title from mirza to padishah (see fol. 215).

Descendants of Genghis Khan have the title Khan following their name, as Babur's uncle, Sultan-Mahmud *Khan,* and his grandfather, Yunus *Khan.* Female Genghisids have the title Khanïm, as Babur's mother, Qutlugh Nigar *Khanïm.* In the Hindustan section, where Babur encounters the Afghan nobility of the Delhi sultanate, they too bear the hereditary title of khan, although they are not Genghisid by any means. Uzbek rulers bear the Khan title, as Muhammad *Khan* Shaybani. Uzbek princes bear the title Sultan after their names, such as Temür *Sultan* and Mahdi *Sultan.*

Turkic tribal and military lords bear the title Beg, "lord." Tajiks (Persians) schooled in Muslim institutions of higher learning, many holding important positions in the bureaucracy, have the title Mawlana (Arabic, "our lord"), often shortened to Mulla, before their names. High-ranking Sufis bear the title Khwaja before their given names. Sayyids (descendants of the Prophet Muhammad) may have the title Amir, sometimes shortened to Mir, before their names instead of Sayyid.

In this translation, diacritical marks, meaningless to those who do not know Persian and superfluous for those who do, have been dispensed with in spelling. Only the umlaut for Turkish words has been retained (*ö* and *ü* as in German; *ä* for the *a* of "cat," as opposed to *a,* like the *o* in "cot"; and *ï,* like the Russian *y* and close to the *io* in "nation"). The *q* is pronounced like a *k,* but the point of articulation is farther back in the throat.

THE GEOGRAPHY OF THE BABURNAMA

Geographically, most of the regions that formed Babur's world—modern Uzbekistan, Tajikistan, Afghanistan, northern Pakistan, and India—are unfamiliar, even to specialists. E. M. Forster again complains, tongue in cheek:

> Geography is equally trying; as Babur scuttles over the earth a mist of streams, and villages, and mountains arises, from the Jaxartes, in the centre of Asia, to the Nerbudda, in the centre of India. Was this where the man with the melon fell overboard? Or is it the raft where half of us took spirits and the rest *bhang,* and quarrelled in consequence? We can't be sure. Is that an elephant? If so, we must have left Afghanistan. No:

we must be in Ferghana again; it's a yak. We never know where we were last, though Agra stands out as the curtain falls, and behind it, as a tomb against the skyline, Kabul. Lists of flowers, fruits, handwritings, head-dresses.... We who are not scholars may grow tired.[25]

The unfamiliarity of place-names will certainly plague the reader, although the flow of geography in the memoirs proceeds, with Babur, from Transoxiana to Kabul to India, and there is little backtracking with which to deal. Everyone has heard of Samarkand, but few could place it on a map; by virtue of recent events, all know that Kabul is the capital of Afghanistan, but Herat, the fashion capital of the eastern Islamic world in the fifteenth century, does not loom large in the modern consciousness. Fortunately Babur's landscape has not changed appreciably over the last five hundred years, and the majority of the places he mentions still exist. Maps are provided for each of the three sections of the book, and place-names are spelled in their generally accepted modern versions, with a few reservations.[26] Not all places have been located. This may be for either of two reasons. First—and, except for the Hindustan section, the more likely of the two—is distortion in the manuscripts. Arabic script, for all its beauty, is extremely liable to miscopying, and the more unfamiliar the word (particularly place-names), the more likelihood there is that a copyist will garble it beyond recognition. This is especially true for a work like the *Baburnama*, copied in India but dealing with faraway places in Central Asia with strange-sounding names the copyists had never heard. No wonder Kassan is usually turned into the much more familiar Kashan, and Pskent and Beshkent are confounded. The second reason—the one that is much more likely in Hindustan—is that the place no longer exists. It is impossible to locate places that were too small and insignificant for inclusion into medieval geographical works and have since changed their names or ceased to exist. Whereas the topology of Central Asia and Afghanistan has proven fairly constant over the last five hundred years, the rivers of India have often shifted their courses and carried away innumerable villages, including, it seems, some of those Babur mentions.

Given the lists of fruits and flowers, guest lists for parties, and yes, the lists of nobles who participated in battles, somewhere in the memoirs even scholars will come across sections they find tiresome. The reader may skip or skim at will; but the totality of the memoirs as Babur left them is given unabridged, for only in their totality do they give us a picture—indeed the only such written portrayal that exists today—of a sixteenth-century individual, a ruling prince at that, with his likes and dislikes, temperament, struggles, successes and failures, from a world that has long since vanished.

A keen archer and horseman, and fond of swimming, the martial arts, music, and poetry, Babur has left an incredibly detailed record of his life and not a few insights into his thoughts, his strategy, and his dealings with his commanders and subordinates. "This prince was adorned with various virtues, and clad with numberless good qualities, above all of which bravery and humanity had the ascendant."[27] Known to history primarily as the progenitor of the "Grand Mughals" of India, Babur was, ironically, a man of whom it has been said that "nothing in his life was Indian, except, possibly, the leaving of it."[28] In fact, Babur found everything about the subcontinent, other than its riches, distasteful. A Timurid prince accustomed to the society of Transoxiana and the beautiful landscape and climate of Kabul, he disapproved of almost everything he saw in Hindustan and longed to return to his beloved Kabul, a trip he made only posthumously.

CHRONOLOGY

Year	Begins On	Folio	Events of Significance
888	February 9, 1483		Babur born on February 14, 1483

PART ONE: FERGANA AND TRANSOXIANA

Year	Begins On	Folio	Events of Significance
899	October 12, 1493	1b	*Baburnama* begins with death of Umar-Shaykh Mirza; death of Sultan-Ahmad Mirza; Sultan-Mahmud Mirza succeeds his brother in Samarkand
900	October 2, 1494	24a	Death of Sultan-Mahmud Mirza; the Battle of Isfara; visit to Sultan-Mahmud Khan (Ulugh Khan) in Shahrukhiyya
901	September 21, 1495	32b	Sultan-Husayn Mirza besieges Hissar; the Tarkhan Revolt in Samarkand; Babur and Sultan-Ali Mirza lay a short siege to Samarkand
902	September 9, 1496	38b	Second siege of Samarkand
903	August 30, 1497	42b	Babur occupies Samarkand for 100 days.
904	August 19, 1498	58a	Babur goes to Pishagar; Margilan is recovered; Andizhan is recovered.

905	August 8, 1499	66a	Campaign against Sultan-Ahmad Tambal; Mady is taken; Khusrawshah murders Baysunghur Mirza; Babur's first marriage, to Ayisha Sultan Begim; Sultan-Ali Mirza yields Samarkand to Shaybani Khan
906	July 28, 1500	80a	Second conquest of Samarkand; loses the Battle of Sar-i-Pul to the Uzbeks; besieged in Samarkand
907	July 17, 1501	94b	Babur abandons Samarkand; goes to Ulugh Khan in Tashkent.
908	July 7, 1502	101a	Kichik Khan comes to Tashkent; the khans' expedition against Sultan-Ahmad Tambal in Andizhan; Babur's hand-to-hand combat with Tambal.
909	June 26, 1503	(—)	

PART TWO: KABUL

910	June 14, 1504	120a	Babur takes Kabul.
911	June 4, 1505	156b	Raids on Turcoman Hazaras; Sultan-Husayn Mirza dies
912	May 24, 1506	183a	Babur goes to Herat; returns to Kabul through the snow; rebellion in Kabul
913	May 13, 1507	203a	The Uzbeks take Herat; Battle of Kandahar; Hindustan campaign planned; marriage to Ma'suma Sultan Begim; birth of Humayun
914	May 2, 1508	215b	Moghul rebellion
915	April 21, 1509	(—)	Ulugh Khan put to death in Khodzhent by Muhammad Khan Shaybani

916	April 10, 1510	(—)	Battle of Merv (Dec. 2, 1510): Muhammad Khan Shaybani is defeated by Shah Ismail and killed; the Safavids occupy Herat
917	March 31, 1511	(—)	Babur defeats Hamza Sultan and Mahdi Sultan at Hissar; Babur retakes Transoxiana (Oct. 1511).
918	March 19, 1512	(—)	Temür Sultan and Ubaydullah Khan recapture Transoxiana from Babur, who retreats to Hissar after the Battle of Köl-i-Malik (April 1512); Battle of Gizhduvan (Nov. 12, 1512), in which the Safavids are defeated by the Uzbeks, Amir Najm II is killed, and Babur flees.
919	March 9, 1513	(—)	Babur in Badakhshan
920	February 26, 1514	(—)	
921	February 15, 1515	(—)	Nasir Mirza dies.
922	February 5, 1516	(—)	Babur's son Askari is born.
923	January 24, 1517	(—)	
924	January 13, 1518	(—)	Campaign in the territories northeast of Kabul is initiated.
925	January 3, 1519	216b	Bajaur is taken; first foray into Hindustan, Bhera, etc.; Babur's son Hindal is born.
926	December 23, 1519	248b	Excursion to Laghman. Kandahar is besieged.
927	December 12, 1520	(—)	
928	December 1, 1521	(—)	Babur besieges Shuja' Beg in Kandahar; negotiations with the Safavid general Durmïsh Khan; Babur withdraws and then takes Kandahar.

929	November 20, 1522	(—)	Babur's daughter Gulbadan is born.
930	November 10, 1523	(—)	Fourth foray into Hindustan, against Dipalpur (Jan. 1524)
931	October 29, 1524	(—)	

PART THREE: HINDUSTAN

932	October 18, 1525	251b	Fifth expedition to Hindustan; Battle of Panipat (April 20, 1526), defeat of Sultan Ibrahim and entrance into Delhi
933	October 8, 1526	302a	Battle of Khanua (March 17, 1527), defeat of Rana Sanga and the Rajput coalition
934	September 27, 1527	331a	Conquest of Chanderi
935	September 15, 1528	339a	End of memoirs, August 1529
936	September 5, 1529	382a	
937	August 25, 1530		Babur dies 6 Jumada I 937 (Dec. 26, 1530)

THE GENGHISID AND TIMURID:
BACKGROUND OF IRAN AND
CENTRAL ASIA

The Mongol invasion of the thirteenth century changed the face of Central Asia and Iran forever and issued in a new social and political reality. Sweeping across Eurasia and eliminating all who stood in their path, the Mongols struck terror in the hearts of their foes. Yet, despite the carnage and destruction the unstoppable hordes wrought, an era of great artistic and literary endeavor was born in Iran during the aftermath of the invasion as the Mongol overlords settled down and became assimilated to their new environment. Their patronage of Persianate culture eclipsed all that had come before. Book illustration, incorporating techniques from as far afield as China and Byzantium, was reestablished, and literary figures and poets flourished and were lavishly recompensed.

Politically the Mongols bequeathed to the whole of Central Asia, Iran, and the Eurasian steppe a structure, which continued for many centuries, of a ruling post-Mongol elite whose base of power rested on Turkic tribes whose territories were interlinked with the pockets of settled populations within a vast area. The spoken language shared by all the Turco-Mongolians throughout the area was Turkish; the religion was Islam, administered by a Persian-speaking, Arabic-educated clerical class; and the political organization hearkened back to the steppe-nomadic system of patronage introduced by Genghis Khan.

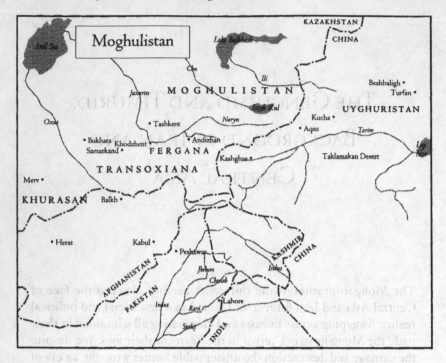

Even as the centralizing power of the Mongol Ilkhanids in Iran (1256–1353) faded and gave way to smaller successor states, such as the Jalayirids in Baghdad and Azerbaijan (1336–1432), the Qaraqoyunlu Turcomans in Azerbaijan and Iraq (1380–1468), the Aqqoyunlu Turcomans in eastern Anatolia and Azerbaijan (1378–1508), the Injus and Muzaffarids in Shiraz (1314–93), and the Karts in Herat (ca. 1260–1381), the post-Mongol rulers continued to patronize a highly refined and lively literary and artistic production, particularly the arts of the book—illustration, illumination, and calligraphy.

THE TIMURIDS

The whole panoply of post-Mongol Iranian cultural sophistication was inherited by the Timurids (1370–1506), who extended the scope of the Turco-Iranian world into their Central Asian homeland. The progenitor of the Timurids, Amir Temür (1336–1405), grew up in Kish (Shahrisabz), not far from Samarkand and Bukhara, the main cities of Central Asia and ancient outposts of Persianate civilization. A member of the ruling Barlas clan, Amir Temür gained ascendancy within Central Asia, consolidated his power, and then set out on a program of world conquest. From these expeditions Amir Temür sent back to his capital, Samarkand, artists and artisans from every land he conquered—Iran, Anatolia, Syria, and India, creating in Central Asia an opulent and cosmopolitan center for the arts, particularly architecture.

Throughout the fifteenth century, Amir Temür's successors in Samarkand and Herat reveled in an "imperial sumptuousness" reflected in painting, architecture, literature, and the plastic arts. Under their aegis cultural artifacts that dazzle the eye and impress the beholder—in fact, some of the most splendid examples of Persian art ever produced—were created. They were calculated to reinforce the notion that imperial splendor equals legitimacy. Timurid titles, which began with the modest *amir* (commander), swelled, generally proportionally with their loss of territory, to the most grandiose imperial Persian titles. Finally, the Timurids succeeded so well in securing legitimacy in eastern Iran and Central Asia that by the end of the fifteenth century they had supplanted the descendants of Genghis as legitimate rulers. Their end came only when another expanding confederation of Turco-Mongolians led by khans of Genghisid descent, the Uzbeks, took advantage of the internal weakness and disorganization of the Timurids and seized what was left of their territories. The successors to the Timurids simply adopted the regalia and paraphernalia of Timurid sovereignty.

To a large extent the Timurids' success was owed to the cultural sophistication of the many princes of the dynasty, all of whom were highly educated and well trained in the arts of the battlefield, and to their intimate knowledge of their subjects, settled and tribal, with whom they never really lost touch. The princely educational system, a legacy of the Turco-Mongolians that worked so well that it was later adopted wholesale by the Safavids, at once removed a young prince from the influence of the intrigue-ridden court and forged political alliances often useful later on. For his education a Timurid prince was

REGNAL DATES OF THE TIMURIDS

AMIR TEMÜR, R. 1370–1405

In Samarkand	*In Herat*
Khalil-Sultan 1405	Shahrukh 1405–47
(Shahrukh 1405–47[1])	
Ulughbeg Mirza 1447–49	Abu'l-Qasim Babur 1447–57
Abdul-Latif Mirza 1449–50	Shah-Mahmud 1457–59
Abdullah Mirza 1450–51	
Sultan-Abusa'id Mirza 1451–69	Sultan-Abusa'id Mirza 1459–69
Sultan-Ahmad Mirza 1469–94	Yadgar-Muhammad 1470
Sultan-Mahmud Mirza 1494–95	Sultan-Husayn Mirza 1470–1506
Baysunghur, Sultan-Ali, Babur	Badi'uzzaman Mirza 1506–07
Uzbek conquest 1500	Uzbek conquest 1507

turned over at a young age to a noble, often a relative on the mother's side, who became the prince's *atäkä,* or *beg atäkä,* a surrogate father, responsible for overall upbringing and training in the martial arts and in princely conduct. Normally a prince was taken to his atäkä's territory for his education, as Babur's youngest brother, Nasir Mirza, was in Kassan with his atäkä, Ways Laghari, when Umar-Shaykh Mirza died. Babur gives almost no information on his own infancy and early childhood, but he does mention that his first atäkä was Shaykh Mazid Beg. At an early age princes were usually given governorships under supervision, and Babur was appointed governor of Andizhan, probably around the age of ten or eleven. When he went there in his official capacity as child governor, Baba-Qulï was assigned as his *eshik-aqasï,* "gate-lord," the noble who controlled access to the prince's court and who served in lieu of an atäkä.

In addition to the education provided by the atäkä, a prince's religious, moral, and academic education was undertaken by a prominent figure in the religious hierarchy, usually a Sufi shaikh. In Babur's case we assume that that aspect of his education was supervised by Khwaja

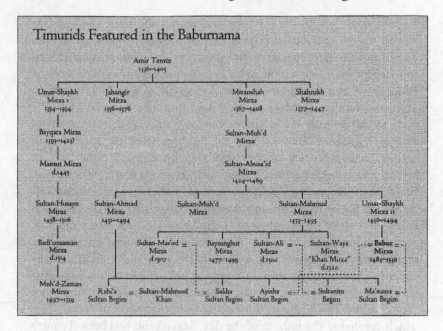

Timurids Featured in the Baburnama

Mawlana Qazi, a disciple of Khwaja Ubaydullah Ahrar, the great Naqshbandi shaikh of Samarkand, for Babur speaks of him with great respect (fol. 54) and mentions (fol. 189b) that when he was an adolescent, the khwaja had kept him so religiously pure that he would not have taken a drink of wine even if it had occurred to him to want to.

Removed to a provincial seat as governor, even at a young age, Timurid princes not only learned the ways and customs of their urban and settled subjects but also—and perhaps more importantly—gained invaluable experience dealing with the Turco-Mongolian tribal peoples.

TURCO·MONGOLIAN
AND PERSIANATE SOCIETY

In Transoxiana and Cisoxiana (Khurasan and what is now Afghanistan) the Timurids inherited from the Mongols a bifurcated society—Turco-Mongolian and Persianate, two peoples existing side by side who had divided the responsibilities of government and rule into the military and civilian along ethnic lines. The military was exclusively Turco-Mongolian, and the civilian was exclusively Persian.

The Persians—or, to use the terms current at the time, the Sarts, or Tajiks[2]—were the settled populations of villages, towns, and cities. They were the bureaucrats, merchants, artisans, peasants, and clergy, and, except for a few remote areas like the inaccessible reaches of the Hindu Kush and the Pamirs, they spoke Persian or a dialect thereof. In Transoxiana, the region of Central Asia from the river Oxus northward to the steppe, the ancient cities of Samarkand, the capital of Transoxiana since Temür's day, and Bukhara were the major urban centers and nurturers of Persianate civilization. To the east of Samarkand lay the Fergana Valley, with its seven towns, Khodzhent, Isfara, Margilan, Akhsi, Andizhan, Kassan, and Osh. The Fergana Valley, where Babur was born, on the edge of Moghulistan to the east and north, and the eastern gateway to the great Central Asian cities of Samarkand and Bukhara, was also steeped in Timurid culture even though its population was a mix of Turks and Tajiks. South of the Oxus to the east was Kabul, the outpost link to the Indian subcontinent; and to the west lay the vast province of Khurasan and the other capital of the Timurids, the flourishing and urbane city of Herat, from which emanated the fashion of the day. Samarkand had been Temür's capital, but his son and successor, Shahrukh (r. 1405–47), established his seat in Herat, which remained the main center of the Timurids' synthesis of Turco-Persian culture throughout the fifteenth century.

Outside the towns and villages, the Turco-Mongolian component of society was tribal and transhumant—or seminomadic in the sense that they were highly mobile, migrating from lowland winter pastures (*qïshlagh*) to highland summer pastures (*yaylagh*). In large part the geography of Central Asia, with its few fertile valleys surrounded by forbidding mountain ranges, favored the nomadic element. Much of the area is arid plain and grassy steppe, unsuited for agriculture but ideal for the grazing of animals. Even within the fertile agricultural regions like the Fergana and Zeravshan (Kohak) valleys there are large areas of low-lying marshland that serve as wintering places for tribal herdsmen who take their flocks and herds up to the grassy mountain slopes in summer.

Turco-Mongolian society was a steppe aristocracy, with tribal chiefs (*noyan, amir, beg*) and braves (*bahadur*) at the top, followed by the free men who became liege men (*nökär*) to the nobles, and finally common tribesmen and slaves. Organized into clans and tribes who formed confederations, some fairly permanent and others quite ephemeral, all these groups were linked together by hereditary bonds of personal, not institutional, loyalty, and they all shared an abhorrence of the settled life and a disdain for settled people. The Turco-Mongolians were the soldiers, and the army was organized hierarchically, very much like the tribal population from which it was almost exclusively drawn:[3] at the top were generals of ten thousand (*tümän begi*), followed by commanders of a thousand (*ming begi*), captains of a hundred (*yüz begi*), and squad leaders of ten ordinary soldiers. Overall, the army was organized into left wing (*jawunghar*), center (*qol*), and right wing (*baraun-ghar*). Positions in each of the three divisions were handed down hereditarily, unchanged from Genghis Khan's time, as Babur mentions:[4] "Among the Moghuls the arrangement of the army is exactly as Genghis Khan left it. Right wing, left wing, center—from father to son they remain where they were assigned" (fol. 100b).

The genesis of the Chaghatayid Turco-Mongolians lay with Genghis Khan's second son, Chaghatay, or Jaghatai, who inherited the Issyk-Kul region, the basin of the Ili River southeast of Lake Balkhash, and the eastern portion of the steppes of the Chu and Talas rivers, with Kashghar and Transoxiana as dependencies. Beshbaligh, Turfan, and Kucha, the territory of yet another Turkish-speaking people, the Uyghurs, were added later. The various peoples within this vast territory, the middle part of Genghis Khan's empire, constituted the *ulus* (nation) of Chaghatay. Unlike their kinsmen to the east, the house of Kublai in China, and to the west, the house of Hülägü in Persia, the Chaghatayids did not assimilate to the ruling traditions of ancient empires, for the territory in which they found themselves really had no established legacy of urban administration. While the rulers of the Yuan dynasty (1279–1368) became Sons of Heaven in the Chinese mold, and the Ilkhanids became sultans in the Iranian fashion, the khans of the Ulus Chaghatay became Turks, the peoples among whom they dwelt.

Around the beginning of the fourteenth century the Chaghatayids nominally converted to Islam, although, since they surrounded themselves with the trappings of their quasi-Buddhist, quasi-shamanistic past, the wilder elements in the east continued to appear half-pagan to the fervent Muslim populations of Samarkand and Bukhara, who called them Moghuls.[5] Babur reflects the same attitude of the civilized urbanite toward the uncivilized steppe peoples in his descriptions of Moghuls—even of his uncle Sultan-Ahmad Khan, the khan of eastern Moghulistan, whose tent "looked like a robber's den—melons and grapes and horse trappings strewn all over" (fol. 108b). The historian Muhammad-Haydar Mirza Dughlat (1499–1551) says of the Moghuls: "Most of [them] had never possessed or even lived in a village—nay, had never even seen cultivation. They were as wild as the beasts of the mountains."[6] In Babur's time the Moghuls spoke Turkish—it is extremely unlikely that many of them knew Mongolian at all[7]—and the descendants of the original Mongol tribes and garrisons that had come into the area were indistinguishable from their neighboring Turkic tribesmen.

Moghulistan had become a recognizable entity shortly after 1340, when the Chaghatayid khanate split into two branches, one in Transoxiana under Qazan Khan (ca. 1343–46), whose descendants fell into a position subordinate to Turkic tribal lords of the sort typified by Amir Temür, and the other in "Moghulistan," the region of the Talas and Chu rivers, Issyk-Kul, the Ili, Ebi Nor, and Manas, where a Chaghatayid, Tughlugh-Temür (r. 1347–63), was set up as khan by the chiefs of the powerful Dughlat clan. After a long and stormy period of succession, few details of which are known with any degree of certainty, upon the death of Ways Khan in 1429 the lords of Moghulistan divided over the succession of his sons, Yunus Khan and Esän-Buqa Khan. Esän-Buqa's party won the day, and Yunus, the elder brother, was forced to take refuge with the Timurid Ulughbeg Mirza in Samarkand, later spending many years in Shiraz. In 1456 the Timurid Sultan-Abusa'id Mirza summoned Yunus Khan from exile, recognized him as khan of Moghulistan, and sent him off equipped to win his fortune against his brother. Despite the recognition Yunus Khan gained in western Moghulistan, Esän-Buqa continued to rule as khan in eastern Moghulistan until his death in 1462. Esän-Buqa was succeeded by his son and grandson, but with the murder of the grandson in 1472, Yunus Khan became the sole ruler of all Moghulistan.

Today, with the Silk Route only a memory, and overland trade having dwindled to almost nothing, the area that was encompassed by Moghulistan has become a backwater, but at the end of the fifteenth century the educated elite were still very much in contact with the major centers of Persianate Timurid culture. Yunus Khan spent many

years at a Timurid court in Shiraz and maintained his Persianate manners even after his return to Moghulistan. The following observation
made by a religious dignitary to Muhammad-Haydar Mirza Dughlat,
who, incidentally, was writing his *History of the Moghuls of Central Asia* in
Persian in eastern Moghulistan while his cousin Babur was writing in
Turkish in Kabul and Delhi, shows the extent of Yunus Khan's Per-
sianization:

> I had heard that Yunus Khán was a Moghul, and I concluded that he
> was a beardless man, with the ways and manners of any other Turk of
> the desert. But when I saw him, I found he was a person of elegant de-
> portment, with a full beard and a Tájik face, and such refined speech
> and manner, as is seldom to be found even in a Tájik.[8]

Indeed, given the extraordinarily unified culture that had been produced by a century of Turco-Persian Timurid rule, the educated elite
from Chinese Turkistan to Constantinople, regardless of ethnicity,
communicated on a learned level in one language, Persian, read the
same classics of Persian literature, and participated in one Persianate
culture. To have been reared in Persianate culture meant primarily a
knowledge of Persian and a respectable knowledge and appreciation
of the classics of poetry, as well as some ability to compose. Babur's father, Umar-Shaykh Mirza, is a good example. Although he spent most
of his time trying to extend his territory at the expense of his brothers,
father-in-law, and brother-in-law, according to Babur he often turned
to the *Shahnama*, the great epic of Iranian kingship by Firdawsi, and
read Rumi's *Mathnawi* and the *Khamsas* of Nizami and Amir Khusraw.
Babur also credits him with a "poetic stamp," meaning an ability to
compose poetry, but he did not often compose, unlike his brother,
Sultan-Mahmud Mirza, who composed so much, Babur comments
(fol. 26), that his poetry probably would have been better if he had
composed less. Under the pen name Adili, Babur's cousin Baysunghur
Mirza composed poetry that was renowned in its day, and Babur too,
like many of the Timurids of Herat, left a collection of poetry. When
he began to be serious about composition and needed advice on tech-
nical aspects of rhyme and meter, he consulted his mother's brother,
Sultan-Mahmud Khan, who he assumed, as a matter of course, would
be conversant with such matters. It turned out that the khan did not

have the answers Babur needed, but Babur's assumption that any educated man would know the technicalities of poetry is indicative of the
culture. Even when these Turks composed poetry in Chaghatay Turkish, as Babur and Ali-Sher Nawa'i did, they were really composing in
Persian, for the entire canon of Chaghatay poetry is calqued on Persian. The meters, conventions, references, and stock themes are taken
directly, with no change or alteration, from the accumulated corpus of
Persian poetry.

On his father's side Babur's great-great-grandfather, Amir Temür,
made world-renowned conquests ranging from India to Anatolia. His
extraordinary power notwithstanding, during Temür's lifetime
Genghisid legitimacy was unquestioned, and he was careful to rule
through a puppet Genghisid khan, as many of his predecessors in the
Ulus Chaghatay had done before him. After Temür's death, however,
the Timurids ruled in their own right in Khurasan and Transoxiana,
without the benefit of Genghisid legitimization. In fact, by the end of
the fifteenth century, in a curious replay of history, the Timurids had
taken the role of the Genghisids as de jure rulers, and Turkic warlords
used Timurid princes like Babur and his brother Jahangir to legitimize
their de facto rule of provinces. Just how far the relationship between
the Timurids and Genghisids had been reversed from what it once was
is well illustrated by the words Sultan-Abusa'id Mirza addressed to
Yunus Khan before he sent him into Moghulistan:

> Since I have ascended the throne, my power is so absolute that I have
> no need of a Khán; so now I have divested you of the garments of
> poverty and, having clothed you in princely robes, am sending you
> back to your native country on the following conditions: For the future
> you must not follow the example of your ancestors and say, "Amir
> Timur and the race of Amir Timur are our vassals, and have been for
> generations." For although it was formerly so, things have changed
> now, and I am *pádisháh* in my own right; thus, now if you are going to
> be my vassal, you must bear the name of "servitor" and do away with
> the name of "friend."[9]

This speech notwithstanding, Sultan-Abusa'id and Yunus Khan were
generally on extremely good terms, and Yunus Khan married three of
his daughters to three of Sultan-Abusa'id's sons. Mihr Nigar Khanïm

was married to Sultan-Ahmad Mirza; Sultan Nigar Khanïm to Sultan-Mahmud Mirza; and Qutlugh Nigar Khanïm to Umar-Shaykh Mirza, and from that union came Babur.

Sultan-Abusaʿid Mirza, Temür's grandson and Babur's grandfather, was the last Timurid to hold both Khurasan and Transoxiana, and while he ruled from Herat, he followed Genghis Khan's and Temür's examples by parceling out sections of his empire to his sons: Samarkand and Bukhara to Sultan-Ahmad Mirza; the Fergana Valley to Umar-Shaykh Mirza, Babur's father; Kabul to Ulughbeg Mirza; Badakhshan to Ababakr Mirza; and Garmser-Kandahar to Sultan-Murad Mirza. After Sultan-Abusaʿid's death on an ill-fated campaign to Azerbaijan in 1469, Samarkand remained in Sultan-Ahmad Mirza's hands until his death in 1494. It was then held by his brother, Sultan-Mahmud Mirza, for a short time until he died early in 1495. Thereafter Sultan-Mahmud's sons and Babur squabbled over possession of the capital and finally lost it altogether to the Uzbeks.

After Sultan-Abusaʿid's death, the other great Timurid city, Herat, the capital of Khurasan, was taken first in 1470 by Yadgar-Muhammad Mirza, a distant cousin of Babur's from another branch of the Timurid House, and three months later by Sultan-Husayn Mirza (d. 1506), an equally distant relative from yet another branch of the Timurids. Under Sultan-Husayn Mirza, Herat reached its cultural apex, as poets, artists, and courtiers were lavishly patronized. "I really wanted to see Herat," says Babur, "which had no equal in all the world and which during Sultan-Husayn Mirza's reign had been adorned and decorated ten, nay twenty times over" (fol. 188). This same much-impressed young provincial says of the city he visited in 1506: "Sultan-Husayn Mirza's time was marvelous. Khurasan, especially the city of Herat, was filled with people of talent and extraordinary persons. Everyone who had an occupation was determined to execute his job to perfection" (fols. 177–177b).

The heyday of Herat did not last long beyond Sultan-Husayn Mirza's reign. After his death in 1506, rivalries among the surviving sons and the powerful influences of tribal factions combined to prevent the election of a single prince to the throne, and the unheard-of compromise of a joint kingship shared by Badiʿuzzaman Mirza and Muzaffar-Husayn Mirza further weakened the already strained resources of the relatively small territory actually under Timurid control. Ultrarefined and sophisticated, these princes were incapable of mustering their forces to confront the encroaching Uzbeks, who had already taken Transoxiana and driven Babur from the throne of Samarkand to take refuge at a safe distance from the Uzbeks in Kabul. In May 1507, Herat too fell to the Uzbeks, completing the Uzbek conquest of Transoxiana and Khurasan that had begun some years earlier. With the fall of Herat, the only remaining ruling member of the Timurid dynasty was Babur in the picturesque but poverty-stricken Kabul. Precisely because Kabul was so poor and provided such a meagre income, Babur and his officers made periodic raids on the upper subcontinent in the area then known as Afghanistan, now the Northwest Frontier Province of Pakistan. With increasing success, the assaults penetrated deeper and deeper into the subcontinent and into the heart of the territory ruled by the Lodis of Delhi. Finally, Babur engaged Sultan Ibrahim Lodi at the Battle of Panipat on April 20, 1526, and gained the victory. His defeat the following year of the Rajput coalition led by Rana Sanga completed his nominal takeover of Hindustan, although the job of consolidating the vast territory he had won was far from over.

History has conspired to rob Babur not only of his fame as a Central Asian and sovereign over the kingdom of Kabul for much longer than he was in the subcontinent, but also of his primary identity as a Timurid by labeling him and his successors as "Mughals"—that is, Moghuls, or Mongols—an appellation that would not have pleased him in the least. In India the dynasty always called itself Gurkani, after Temür's title Gurkân, the Persianized form of the Mongolian *kürägän,* "son-in-law," a title he assumed after his marriage to a Genghisid princess. Nonetheless, Europeans, recognizing that there was some connection between Babur's house and the Mongols but ignorant of the precise relationship, dubbed the dynasty with some variant of the misnomer Moghul (Mogol, Mogul, Maghol, etc.) and made the name synonymous with greatness.

When Babur established himself in India, he had with him his Turco-Mongolian officers and soldiers from Central Asia, and the type of dynastic rule he envisioned would have been a replica of the Timurid model he had known all his life. Babur died, however, at the young age of forty-seven in 1530 and was succeeded by his son Humayun, who was driven from the subcontinent by the Sur Afghans in

1540. Humayun took refuge with Shah Tahmasp of Iran, with whose help he mounted a successful campaign in 1555 to regain his throne. When Humayun returned from Iran, he brought with him a host of Iranians, and the overtly Central Asian and Turkic elements of Babur's time rapidly faded away. At the height of the empire, under Jahangir and Shahjahan in the seventeenth century, the cultural synthesis was predominantly Persianate fused with Rajput elements, but the Timurid basis of the Moghul aesthetic, the culture brought to India by Babur and transplanted there, blossomed, in various combinations with elements both native to India and imported from Safavid Iran, and flourished for centuries.

PART ONE

FERGANA AND TRANSOXIANA

The history opens with the accidental death of Babur's father, Umar-Shaykh Mirza, in Akhsi on the Jaxartes River, in the province of Fergana. Umar-Shaykh, with his constant predations, had been a thorn in the side of his brother, Sultan-Ahmad Mirza, the padishah of Samarkand, and of his brother-in-law, Sultan-Mahmud Khan, the khan of Moghulistan. Just before Umar-Shaykh died, the two had formed an alliance against him and were proceeding from opposite directions to catch him in a pincers movement. As the threat advanced, Umar-Shaykh's officers and advisers, fearing that the coalition would capture the twelve-year-old Prince Babur, rallied around him in Andizhan, proclaimed him king, and prepared to defend the city against attack.

WMT

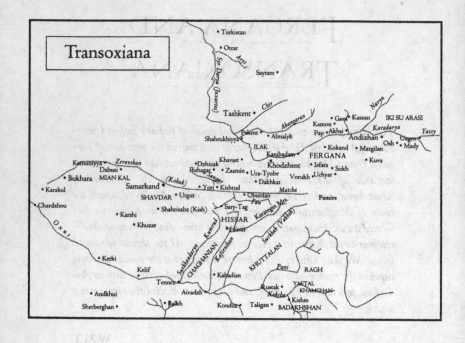

In the month of Ramadan in the year 899 [June 1494], in the province of Fergana, in my twelfth year I became king.

A DESCRIPTION OF FERGANA

The province of Fergana is in the fifth clime, situated on the edge of the civilized world.[1] To the east is Kashghar, to the west Samarkand, and to the south the mountains that border Badakhshan. To the north, although formerly there were cities like Almalyk, Almatu, and Yangi—which is called Otrar in books—because the Moghuls and Uzbeks passed there, there is no longer any civilization.[2]

It is a smallish province. Grain and fruit are plentiful. All around are mountains, except on the western side, that is, in Samarkand and Khodzhent, where there are none. So, aside from that direction, foreign enemies cannot penetrate.

The Jaxartes River, which is known as the Khodzhent River, [2] comes from the northeast, goes straight through the province, and flows to the west.[3] As it passes on the northern side of Khodzhent and the southern side of Fanakat, which is now known as Shahrukhiyya, it turns again to the north and goes in the direction of Turkistan. Far below Turkistan City the river sinks completely into the sand; it flows into no other body of water.

There are seven towns in Fergana, five to the south of the Jaxartes and two to the north. Of the towns on the southern side, (1) one is Andizhan, the capital of Fergana, located in the middle of the province. Grain and fruit are plentiful there, and the melons and grapes are excellent. During the melon season in the fall it is customary not even to sell them at the melon patches. No pears are better than those from Andizhan. In all of Transoxiana, after the Samarkand and Kish[4] fortresses, no fortress is larger than that in Andizhan. It has three gates, with the citadel located on the south side. Nine water channels enter it; amazingly, the water does not come out anywhere. Around the perimeter of the fortress, on the outer side of the moat, is a gravel highway, which separates the fortress from the surrounding agricultural area.

Game and sporting birds are plentiful in Andizhan. The pheasants [2b] get extremely fat, and it is said that not even four people can finish eating a stew made from just one.

The people are Turks. Among the city folk and merchants, there is no one who does not know Turkish. The people's pronunciation is like the literary language since the works of Mir Ali-Sher Nawa'i,[5] although he was raised in Herat, are in this language. Among the people there is much beauty. Khwaja Yusuf, who is famous for music, was from Andizhan.[6] The air is unwholesome, and in the autumn the inflammation of the eyes, called *aqrab* by physicians, is rampant.

(2) Another southern town in Fergana is Osh. It is four leagues[7] to the southeast of Andizhan, somewhat more to the east than the south. Its climate is good, running water is abundant, and the spring season is beautiful. There are many sayings about the excellence of Osh. On the southeastern side of the Osh fortress is a well-proportioned mountain

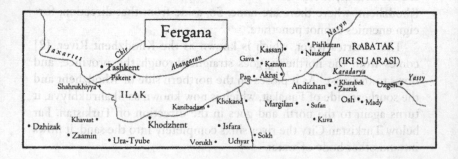

called Bara Koh, where, on its summit, Sultan-Mahmud Khan built a pavilion. Farther down, on a spur of the same mountain, I had a porticoed pavilion built in 902 [1496–97]. Although the former is higher up, mine is situated much better because it overlooks the whole town and outskirts below. [3]

The Andizhan River passes through the area around Osh and goes on to Andizhan. On both its banks are gardens, all of which overlook the river. The violets are beautiful, there is running water, and in the spring, when many tulips and roses blossom, it is quite nice.

On the lower slopes of Bara Koh, between the town and the mountain, is the Gemini Mosque. From the direction of the mountain flows a large main irrigation canal. Below the outer courtyard of the mosque is a delightful, shady field of clover, where every traveler and wayfarer stops to rest. It is a joke on the part of the urchins of Osh to pour water from the canal on anyone who falls asleep there.

Toward the end of Umar-Shaykh Mirza's time a stone with red and white variegations was found on Bara Koh. Knife handles, belt buckles, and other items are made of this beautiful stone. In all of Fergana Province no town has air as good as that in Osh.

(3) Another town is Margilan, seven leagues west of Andizhan, where the pomegranates and apricots are superb. One type of pomegranate, called "big seed," the sweetness of which has something of the taste of an overripe apricot, could be preferred to pomegranates from Simnan. [3b] A type, from which the stone is removed and stuffed with almond paste and then dried, is called *subhani*. It is really delicious. The game in Margilan is good; white deer may be found nearby. The people are Sarts.[8] They are a feisty people, ready with their fists. The custom of exorcism is widespread throughout Transoxiana, and most of the renowned exorcists of Samarkand and Bukhara are Margilanis. The author of the *Hidaya* was from a Margilan village called Rishtan.[9]

(4) Another is Isfara, located in the hills nine leagues to the southwest of Margilan. It has running water and pleasant gardens. The area has many fruit trees, but most of its gardens are almond groves. The people are all Sarts and speak Persian. One league to the south of Isfara, nestled among the hills, is Mirror Rock. Approximately ten yards long and in some places as high as a man and in others as low as a person's waist, the boulder reflects like a mirror. The Isfara region consists of four hill divisions, namely Isfara, Vorukh, Sokh, and Uchyar. When

Shaybani Khan and Sultan-Mahmud Khan defeated Alacha Khan and took Tashkent and Shahrukhiyya, I came to the Sokh [4] and Uchyar hills, where I stayed for nearly a year in deprivation before setting out for Kabul.[10]

(5) Another is Khodzhent, one of the cities of antiquity, twenty-five leagues west of Andizhan. From Khodzhent to Samarkand is another twenty-five leagues. Both Shaykh Maslahat and Khwaja Kamal were from Khodzhent.[11] Its fruits, especially the pomegranates, are famous for their excellence: the saying goes, "Apples of Samarkand and pomegranates of Khodzhent." Today, however, the pomegranates from Margilan are much better. The fortress is situated on high ground, with the Jaxartes River about an arrow shot away, flowing to the north. To the north of the river is a mountain called Manoghal.[12]

It is said that turquoise and other types of mines are located in the mountain. Many snakes are also found there, and the game and birds around Khodzhent are quite good; white deer, buck and doe, pheasant and hare are abundant. But the air is unwholesome and causes much eye inflammation in the autumn, a condition that is said to affect even sparrows. Apparently the bad air is caused by the mountain to the north.

One of Khodzhent's dependencies is Kanibadam,[13] five or six leagues east of Khodzhent. Although it is not actually a town, it is a rather nice little hamlet. The almonds, for which Kanibadam is named, are exceptional, [4b] and are exported to Hormuz and Hindustan.

Between Khodzhent and Kanibadam is a desert wilderness called Ha Darwesh. There, a fierce wind always blows east toward Margilan and west to Khodzhent. It is said that several dervishes encountered the wind there and, unable to find each other, cried out, "Hey, dervish!" over and over until they all perished. From that time, the place has been called Ha Darwesh.

The towns to the north of the Jaxartes River are the following.

(1) One is Akhsi, nine leagues west of Andizhan. In books it is written Akhsikat, as the poet Asiruddin is called Asiruddin Akhsikati.[14] Next to Andizhan it is the largest town in Fergana, and Umar-Shaykh Mirza made it his capital. Below the fortress, which is situated atop a high cliff, flows the Jaxartes; instead of a moat, the fortress is surrounded by deep ravines. Umar-Shaykh Mirza, once or twice had

other ravines made farther out. In all of Fergana no other such strong fortress exists. [5] The agricultural area is located a league away. The proverb, "Where is the village and where are the trees?" is certainly often said of Akhsi. The melons there are excellent. One type, called *mirtimuri*, is not known anywhere else in the world. The melons of Bukhara are famous, too, but when I took Samarkand, I had melons brought from Akhsi and Bukhara and had them cut open in a gathering; the one from Akhsi was incomparable. The game and birds there are very good as well. From the river toward Akhsi is wilderness where white deer are plentiful. On the Andizhan side is forest where buck and doe, pheasant and hare are found in abundance, and are exceptionally fat.

(2) The other is Kassan. A rather small town, it lies to the north of Akhsi. Just as the river at Andizhan comes from Osh, at Akhsi it comes from Kassan. It is a place with good air. Because all the riverbanks are covered with pleasant gardens, they call it Postin Besh Barah.[15] The people of Osh and Kassan have a rivalry over who has the better climate.

In the mountains surrounding the province of Fergana are excellent summer pasturelands. Spiraea trees—with red bark—are found in these mountains and nowhere else. [5b] From them are made staffs, whip handles, bird cages, and arrows. It is a very, very fine tree, which people carry to faraway places for good luck. In some books it is written that there is belladonna in the mountains, although it has not been heard of in these times. A plant in the Yeti Kent mountains,[16] which the people there call *ayïq otï,* is claimed to have the properties of mandrake. It most likely is the mandrake, but they call it by the other name. Turquoise and iron mines are also in the mountains.

The income of Fergana Province, if justly managed, will maintain three to four thousand men.[17]

Since Umar-Shaykh Mirza was a *padishah*[18] of exalted ambition with great claims, he was always bent on territorial expansion. Several times he led his army against Samarkand: sometimes he was defeated, and sometimes he returned disappointed. Several times also he invited his father-in-law, Yunus Khan, who was a descendant of Genghis Khan's second son, Chaghatay Khan, and was at that time the khan of the Moghul nation in Chaghatay Khan's territory. Each time Umar-Shaykh Mirza brought in Yunus Khan, he gave him lands. But Yunus

Khan did not always agree with Umar-Shaykh Mirza's ambitions, [6] sometimes owing to Umar-Shaykh Mirza's misconduct and at other times to the rebelliousness of the Moghul nation,[19] so Yunus Khan, unable to remain in the province, left for Moghulistan. The last time he brought in Yunus Khan, he gave him Tashkent, a province at that time under Umar-Shaykh Mirza's control. (In books Tashkent is called Shash and Chach, from which derives the "Chachi" bow.[20]) From that date[21] until 908 [1503] the territory of Tashkent and Shahrukhiyya was under the control of the Chaghatayid khans.

At that date the khanate of the Moghul nation was held by Yunus Khan's eldest son, my maternal uncle Sultan-Mahmud Khan. Umar-Shaykh Mirza's elder brother, the padishah of Samarkand, Sultan-Ahmad Mirza, and the khan of the Moghul nation, Sultan-Mahmud Khan, made a pact because they were suffering from Umar-Shaykh Mirza's misconduct. Sultan-Ahmad Mirza married one of his daughters to Sultan-Mahmud Khan, and on the above-mentioned date Sultan-Ahmad Mirza from the south of the Khodzhent River and Sultan-Mahmud Khan from the north led their armies out against Umar-Shaykh Mirza.

At this point a strange event occurred. It has been mentioned that [6b] the Akhsi fortress is situated atop a high ravine, with the buildings at its edge. On Monday, the fourth of Ramadan of this year [June 8, 1494], Umar-Shaykh Mirza toppled into the ravine with his doves and dovecote and gave up the ghost.[22] He was thirty-nine years old.

UMAR-SHAYKH MIRZA

His birth and lineage. He was born in 860 [1456] in Samarkand. He was Sultan-Abusa'id Mirza's fourth son, younger than Sultan-Ahmad Mirza, Sultan-Muhammad Mirza, and Sultan-Mahmud Mirza. Sultan-Abusa'id Mirza was Sultan-Muhammad Mirza's son. Sultan-Muhammad Mirza was the son of Miranshah Mirza, Temür Beg's third son, who was younger than Umar-Shaykh Mirza and Jahangir Mirza, and older than Shahrukh Mirza.

His realm. First Sultan-Abusa'id Mirza gave Kabul to Umar-Shaykh Mirza and sent him off with Baba Kabuli as his *beg atäkä*.[23] He recalled him from Daragaz to Samarkand for the mirzas' circumcision feast. Since Temür Beg had given Fergana to the elder Umar-Shaykh Mirza, he gave him the province of Andizhan and sent him off with Khudab-erdi Tughchï Temürtash as his beg atäkä.

His appearance and habits. He was short in stature, had a round beard and a fleshy face, and was fat. [7] He wore his tunic so tight that to fasten the ties, he had to hold in his stomach; if he let himself go, it often happened that the ties broke. He was unceremonious in both dress and speech. He wore his turban over a *dastarpech*.[24] At that time, all turbans were twisted four times, but he wrapped his without twisting and left the fringe hanging. In the summertime, except when he was holding court, he wore a Mongol cap.[25]

His character. He was a Hanafi[26] by sect and orthodox of belief. He never neglected the five prayer times. Throughout his lifetime he always made up missed prayers and often recited the Koran. He was devoted to Khwaja Ubaydullah[27] and considered it an honor to participate in his gatherings. The khwaja addressed him as "my son." He was well read and literate and had read both *Khamsas*, the volumes of the *Mathnawi*, and histories.[28] He often read the *Shahnama*.[29] He had some poetic talent, but he paid no attention to composing poetry. His sense of justice was great: Once when he learned that a caravan from Cathay with a thousand beasts of burden had been trapped by heavy snow at the foot of the mountains to the east of Andizhan and only two persons had survived, he sent his revenuers to make a record of all the

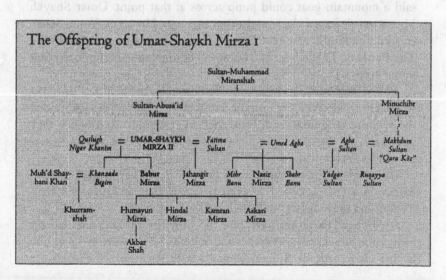

The Offspring of Umar-Shaykh Mirza I

goods in the caravan. [7b] Although he himself was in need, he kept the goods until, a year or two later, the heirs could be brought from Samarkand and Khurasan and the goods could be turned over to them.

He was liberal, and his moral character was equal to his liberality. He was a good-natured, talkative, eloquent, and well-spoken man. He was brave and valiant. Twice he performed more courageously than any of his warriors in wielding the sword. Once was at the gate of Akhsi, and another was at the gate of Shahrukhiyya. He was a middling shot. He packed quite a punch, however, and no one was ever hit by him who did not bite the dust. On account of his urge to expand his territory he turned many a truce into battle and many a friend into a foe.

He used to drink a lot. Later in life he held drinking parties once or twice a week. He was fun to be with in a gathering and was good at reciting poetry for his companions. He grew rather fond of *ma'jun*,[30] and under its influence would lose his head. He was of a scrappy temperament and had many scars and brands to show for it. He played backgammon a lot and occasionally gambled.

His battles and frays. He fought three battles. The first was with Yunus Khan at a place called Täkkä Segritkü[31] on the bank of the Jaxartes to the north of Andizhan. [8] The place was thus named because the river is so narrowed by the skirt of the mountain that it is said a mountain goat could jump across at that point. Umar-Shaykh Mirza was defeated there and taken prisoner. However, Yunus Khan treated him kindly and gave him permission to return to his province. The Battle of Täkkä Segritkü became a chronological reference point in the area.

The second battle took place in Turkistan on the banks of the Arys River. He crossed the river on the ice, beat the Uzbeks who had raided the vicinity of Samarkand, took back the prisoners and booty they were carrying, and returned all to their owners without coveting a single object for himself.

He fought another battle with his eldest brother, Sultan-Ahmad Mirza, in a village called Khavast between Shahrukhiyya and Ura-Tyube, and there he was defeated.

His realms. His father gave him the province of Fergana, and for some time he also held Tashkent and Sayram, which were given to him by his elder brother Sultan-Ahmad Mirza. He took Shahrukhiyya through a ruse, and for some time remained in control of it. Toward the end of his life Tashkent and Shahrukhiyya were lost. There remained the province of Fergana, together with Khodzhent—which some do not count as part of Fergana—and Ura-Tyube, which originally was called Usrushana or Ustrush. [8b] When Sultan-Ahmad Mirza rode to Tashkent against the Moghuls and was defeated on the banks of the Chir River,[32] Hafiz Beg Dulday was in Ura-Tyube, and he gave it to Umar-Shaykh Mirza. From that time on, Usrushana was held by Umar-Shaykh Mirza.

His offspring. Three sons and five daughters survived. The eldest of all the sons was I, Zahiruddin Muhammad Babur. My mother was Qutlugh Nigar Khanïm.

Another son was Jahangir Mirza, who was two years younger than I. His mother was from the *tümän begs*[33] of the Moghuls, Fatima Sultan by name.

The third son was Nasir Mirza. His mother was a concubine named Umed from Andizhan. Nasir Mirza was four years younger than I.

The eldest of the daughters was Khanzada Begim, who was my sibling. She was five years older than I. The second time I took Samarkand, [in 1501], although I had suffered a defeat at Sar-i-Pul, I held the fortress for five months. The padishahs and begs from the surrounding territories gave me no aid or assistance whatsoever. Despondent, I gave up and left. During that interregnum Khanzada Begim fell captive to Muhammad Shaybani Khan. They had one son named Khurramshah, a worthy lad. He was given Balkh, [9] and a year or two after his father died, he too passed away. When Shah Isma'il defeated the Uzbek at Merv, Khanzada Begim was there. For my sake Shah Isma'il treated her well and had her honorably escorted to Konduz, where she joined me. We had been parted for ten years; when Muhammadi Kükäldash and I arrived together, the begim and those with her did not recognize me, even when I told them. A while later they realized who I was.

Another daughter was Mihr Banu Begim. She was a sibling to Nasir Mirza and two years older than I.

Another was Shahr Banu Begim. Eight years younger than I, she too was a sibling to Nasir Mirza.

Another was Yadgar Sultan Begim, whose mother was Agha Sultan, a concubine.

Another was Ruqayya Sultan Begim. Her mother was Makhdum
Sultan Begim, who was called Qara Köz[34] Begim. The latter two were
born after the mirza's death. Yadgar Sultan Begim was brought up by
my grandmother Esän Dawlat Begim. When Shaybani Khan took Andizhan and Akhsi [in 1503], Yadgar Sultan Begim fell to Hamza Sultan's son Abdul-Latif Sultan. She rejoined me in Khuttalan when I
crushed the Uzbek princes led by Hamza Sultan and took Hissar
[1511–12]. During that same interregnum Ruqayya Sultan Begim fell
to Jani Beg Sultan. [9b] They conceived one or two sons who did not
survive. News recently arrived that Ruqayya Sultan Begim had gone to
God's mercy.

His wives and concubines. One wife was Qutlugh Nigar Khanïm,
Yunus Khan's second daughter. She was Sultan-Mahmud Khan's and
Sultan-Ahmad Khan's elder sister. Yunus Khan was from the lineage of
Chaghatay Khan, Genghis Khan's second son. He was Yunus Khan,
son of Ways Khan, son of Sher-Ali Oghlan, son of Muhammad Khan,
son of Khizr Khwaja Khan, son of Tughluq Temür Khan, son of Esän-
Buqa Khan, son of Dua Khan, son of Baraq Khan, son of Yäsüntöä, son
of Möätükän, son of Chaghatay Khan, son of Genghis Khan.

Since we have a chance here, let us give a brief mention of the
khans.

A BRIEF MENTION OF THE
CHAGHATAYID KHANS

Yunus Khan and Esän-Buqa Khan were sons of Ways Khan. Yunus
Khan's mother was the daughter or granddaughter of Shaykh Nuruddin Beg, a Qipchaq beg of Turkistan who was patronized by Temür
Beg. When Ways Khan was killed, the Moghul nation divided into two
factions. One faction took Yunus Khan's part, while the majority was
for Esän-Buqa Khan. Prior to this Ulughbeg Mirza had betrothed
Yunus Khan's elder sister to his son Abdul-Aziz Mirza. On that occasion Erzän, a tümän beg of the Barin tribe, and Mirak the Turcoman,
who was a [10] tümän beg of the Chiras tribe, brought the khan to
Ulughbeg Mirza along with three or four thousand heads of households of the Moghul nation to receive aid in gaining control of its people. Ulughbeg Mirza did not do well by them: some he imprisoned,

The Offspring of Yunus Khan

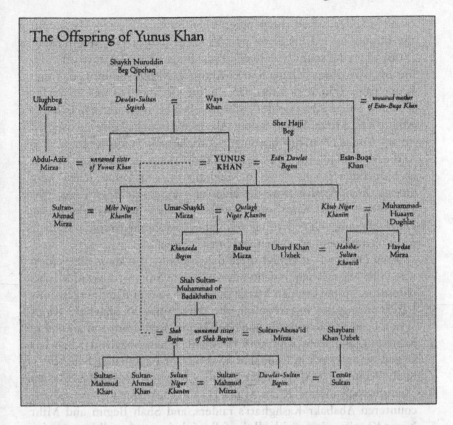

others he dispersed singly throughout the province. The Diaspora of Erzän became a date to remember among the Moghuls.[35]

The khan was sent to Iraq.[36] He stayed more than a year in Tabriz, the padishah of which at that time was Jahanshah the Qaraqoyunlu. From there he went to Shiraz, where Shahrukh Mirza's second son, Ibrahim-Sultan Mirza, was. Five or six months later Ibrahim-Sultan Mirza died, and his son Abdullah Mirza took his place. The khan was a liege man to Abdullah Mirza and paid him homage. For seventeen or eighteen years the khan was in Shiraz and those regions.

During the strife between Ulughbeg Mirza and his sons, Esän-Buqa Khan seized the opportunity to enter Fergana and plunder the province as far as Kanibadam. Continuing on, he took Andizhan and made prisoners of all the people. When Sultan-Abusaʿid Mirza took the throne, he led his army past Yangi to Ashpara in Moghulistan, [10b] where he soundly defeated Esän-Buqa Khan. To stave off trouble by Esän-Buqa Khan, Sultan-Abusaʿid Mirza summoned Yunus Khan from Iraq and Khurasan on the occasion of his marrying Khanïm, Yunus Khan's elder sister who had been formerly married to Abdul-Aziz Mirza. When Sultan-Abusaʿid Mirza had given feasts and he and Yunus Khan had become friends, he sent Yunus Khan as khan to the Moghul nation. The Saghrïchï tümän begs, having taken offense at Esän-Buqa Khan, came to Moghulistan, and Yunus Khan went among them. At that time the chief of the Saghrïchï begs was Sher Hajji Beg.[37] Yunus Khan took to wife Sher Hajji Beg's daughter Esän Dawlat Begim, and according to Moghul custom the couple was made to sit on a piece of white felt and lifted as khan.[38]

Esän Dawlat Begim had three daughters by the khan. The eldest was Mihr Nigar Khanïm, who was married to Sultan-Abusaʿid Mirza's eldest son, Sultan-Ahmad Mirza; she had no sons or daughters by him. Later, during the interregnum, she fell captive to Shaybani Khan. When I came to Kabul, she and Shah Begim went from Samarkand to Khurasan, and from Khurasan to Kabul. When Shaybani Khan besieged Nasir Mirza in Kandahar, I set out for Laghman. Khan Mirza, Shah Begim, and Mihr Nigar Khanïm went to Badakhshan. When Mubarakshah invited Khan Mirza [11] to the Zafar fortress, he encountered Ababakr Kashghari's raiders, and Shah Begim and Mihr Nigar Khanïm, along with all the folk of their people, fell into captivity, whereupon they bade farewell to this mortal world in that evil tyrant's prison.

The second daughter was my mother, Qutlugh Nigar Khanïm. She was with me during most of my guerilla engagements and interregna. She passed away in 911 [1505] five or six months after I took Kabul.

The third daughter was Khub Nigar Khanïm. She was given in marriage to Muhammad-Husayn Küragän Dughlat, by whom she had a daughter and a son. The daughter[39] was married to Ubayd Khan. When I took Bukhara and Samarkand, she was unable to leave and stayed behind. When Sultan-Saʿid Khan's uncle Sayyid-Muhammad Mirza Dughlat came to me in Samarkand as an emissary from Sultan-Saʿid Khan, she joined him and went to Kashghar, where Sultan-Saʿid Khan married her. Khub Nigar's son was named Haydar Mirza. After his father was killed by the Uzbeks, he came and joined my retinue for three or four years. Later he requested permission to go to the khan in Kashghar. "Everything returns to its source—pure gold, silver, or tin." As of this date it is said that he has repented and discovered the right path.[40] Calligraphy, painting, arrows, arrow barbs, string grip—at each of these he has a deft hand. He also has poetic talent. [11b] I have received a petition of his, and his composition is not bad.

Another wife of the khan's was Shah Begim. Although he had other wives, the mothers of the sons and daughters were these two, Esän Dawlat Begim and Shah Begim. Shah Begim was a daughter of Shah Sultan-Muhammad, the shah of Badakhshan. The Badakhshan shahs' lineage goes back to Alexander, son of Philip.[41] Another daughter of this shah, who would be Shah Begim's elder sister, was married to Sultan-Abusa'id Mirza and bore Ababakr Mirza. By Shah Begim the khan had two sons and two daughters. Eldest of the four, but younger than the aforementioned three daughters by Esän Dawlat Begim, was Sultan-Mahmud Khan, whom some in Samarkand and those regions call Khanika Khan. Younger than Sultan-Mahmud Khan was Sultan-Ahmad Khan, who was known as Alacha Khan. They say that in the Qalmaq and Moghul language *alachi* means killer; because Sultan-Ahmad Khan defeated the Qalmaq several times and killed many people, he was called Alachi, which through frequent repetition became Alacha. The khans will be mentioned repeatedly in this history, and their circumstances will be given in the appropriate places.

Younger than these two, and the elder of the two daughters, [12] was Sultan Nigar Khanïm, who was given in marriage to Sultan-Mahmud Mirza, by whom she bore a son, Sultan-Ways by name. He will be mentioned in this history. After Sultan-Mahmud Mirza died, she took her son and, without telling anyone, went to her elder brothers in Tashkent. A few years later they gave her to Adik Sultan, who was one of the Kazakh sultans descended from Jochi, Genghis Khan's eldest son. When Shaybani Khan defeated the khans and took Tashkent and Shahrukhiyya, she fled with ten or twelve of her Moghul retainers to Adik Sultan. By him she had two daughters, one of whom she married to one of the Shaybani princes and the other of whom she gave to Sultan-Sa'id Khan's son, Rashid Sultan. After Adik Sultan's death the khan of the Kazakh nation,[42] Qasim Khan, married her. They say that among the Kazakh khans and sultans no one kept order within the nation like Qasim Khan. His army was counted at close to three hundred thousand. After Qasim Khan's death the lady went to Kashghar to Sultan-Sa'id Khan.

The youngest was Dawlat Sultan Khanïm. During the debacle of Tashkent she fell captive to Shaybani Khan's son Temür Sultan. [12b] By him she had a daughter, and they left Samarkand with me. For three or four years she stayed in Badakhshan, but later she went to Kashghar to Sultan-Sa'id Khan.

RETURN TO UMAR-SHAYKH MIRZA'S WIVES AND CONCUBINES

Another of Umar-Shaykh Mirza's wives was Ulus Agha, a daughter of Khwaja Husayn Beg. Ulus Agha had a daughter who died in infancy; a year to a year-and-a-half later Ulus Agha was sent out of the harem.

Another was Fatima Sultan Agha, who was of the Moghul tümän begs. The mirza married Fatima Sultan Agha before any of the others.

Another was Qara Köz Begim, whom he married much later. She was truly beloved by him. To please the mirza they gave her a lineage to Minuchihr Mirza, the elder brother of Sultan-Abusa'id Mirza. There were many mistresses and concubines too, one of whom was Umed Agha, but she predeceased the mirza. Toward the end of the mirza's life Tun Sultan, who was a Moghul, and Agha Sultan were other mistresses.

His officers. One was Khudaberdi Temürtash, descended from the elder brother of Aq Buqa Beg, the governor of Herat. When Sultan-Abusa'id Mirza besieged Juki Mirza at Shahrukhiyya and gave Fergana Province to Umar-Shaykh Mirza, he assigned this Khudaberdi [13] Temürtash to the office of lord of the gate. At that time Khudaberdi Temürtash was twenty-five years old. Although he was young, his management and administration were excellent. A year or two later when Ibrahim Begchik was raiding the vicinity of Osh, Khudaberdi Temürtash went out in pursuit, fought, and was defeated and killed. At that time Sultan-Ahmad Mirza was in Ura-Tyube at a summer pasture called Aq Qachghay, eighteen leagues east of Samarkand. Sultan-Abusa'id Mirza was at Baba Khaki, which is twelve leagues east of Herat. The news was sent via Abdul-Wahhab Shiqavul and dispatched to the mirza at a gallop: the 126-league road was traveled in four days.

Another was Hafiz Muhammad Beg Dulday, a younger brother of Ahmad Hajji Beg and son of Sultan Malik Kashghari. After Khudaberdi Beg died, Hafiz Muhammad Beg Dulday was sent as lord of the gate. He did not get on well with the begs of Andizhan, and after Sultan-Abusaʻid Mirza's death, he went to Sultan-Ahmad Mirza's service in Samarkand. When Sultan-Ahmad Mirza suffered defeat at the Chir, he was in Ura-Tyube. [13b] Intent upon taking Samarkand, Umar-Shaykh Mirza attacked Ura-Tyube, which he turned over to the mirza's retainers before joining the mirza's retinue. Umar-Shaykh Mirza gave him the governorship of Andizhan. Later he went to Sultan-Mahmud Khan, who entrusted Mirza Khan to him and gave him Dzhizak. Before Kabul was taken he set out for Mecca via Hindustan. Along the way he went to God's mercy. He was an unassuming person of few words.

Another was Khwaja Husayn Beg. He was a good person of dervish temperament. As was the fashion then, he recited verse well at drinking parties.

Another was Shaykh Mazid Beg. He was appointed my first beg atäkä. His management and administration were unquestionable. He had served Abu'l-Qasim Babur Mirza. There was no greater beg in Umar-Shaykh Mirza's service than he, but he was a vicious man who kept catamites.

Another was Ali Mazid Beg. He was a Qauchin.[43] He rebelled twice, once at Akhsi and once at Tashkent. He was hypocritical, debauched, ungrateful, and worthless.

Another was Hasan Yaʻqub Beg. He was unambitious, goodnatured, and nimble. This line is by him:

Come back, O phoenix, for without the parrot of your down the raven is about to carry away my bones.

He was valiant and a good shot. He played polo well. [14] He leapt well at leapfrog. After Umar-Shaykh Mirza's death he became lord of my gate. He was of a dark temperament, impatient, seditious, and suspicious.

Another was Qasim Beg. He was a Qauchin. He was a veteran of the Andizhan Corps. After Hasan Beg he became lord of my gate. Until the end of his life his rank and importance grew, never decreasing. He was a valiant man. Once he pursued the Uzbeks who were raiding the vicinity of Kassan and defeated them soundly. He wielded his sword for Umar-Shaykh Mirza. He also fought well at the Battle of Yassy Kechit [ca. July 1499]. During my guerilla engagements, when I set out to go from the Matcha mountains to Sultan-Mahmud Khan, Qasim Beg detached himself and went to Khusrawshah. In 910 [1504], when I captured Khusrawshah and defeated Muqim in Kabul, Qasim Beg came. I patronized him as I had before. When we raided the Turcoman Hazaras at Khush Valley [in 1505], because Qasim Beg distinguished himself among the warriors, despite his advanced years, I gave him the province of Bangash as a reward. Later [14b] he went to Kabul, where I made him Humayun's beg atäkä. During the time we were taking Zamin Dawar, [in 1522], he died. He was a good Muslim, religious, and pious. He avoided suspect food. His tactics and strategy were excellent. He told good jokes. Although he was illiterate, his humor indicated that he had a poetic nature.

Another was Baba-Qulï, son of Baba-Ali Beg. He was descended from Shaykh Ali Bahadur. After Shaykh Mazid Beg died, they made him lord of my gate. When Sultan-Ahmad Mirza marched against Andizhan, he went over to Sultan-Ahmad Mirza and gave him Ura-Tyube. After Sultan-Mahmud Mirza's death, as he was fleeing from Samarkand, Sultan-Ali Mirza came forth from Ura-Tyube, defeated him in battle, and killed him. His management and equipment were excellent, and he maintained his retainers well. He did not perform his prayers or fast. He was tyrannical and heathenish.

Another was Ali Dost Taghayï, from the tümän begs of the Saghrïchï tribe.[44] He was a relative of my mother's mother, Esän Dawlat Begim. I patronized him more than he had been in Umar-Shaykh Mirza's time. They said he would be useful, but during the years he was with me, nothing worth mentioning ever came from him. [15] He served Sultan-Abusa'id Mirza. He claimed to know how to work the rain stone. He was a falconer. He was a person of worthless morals and manners, stingy, seditious, crude, hypocritical, egotistical, and of harsh words and cold expression.

Another was Ways Laghari. He was of the Tughchï people of

Samarkand. At the end of Umar-Shaykh Mirza's life, Ways Laghari was a great confidant. He was with me during my guerilla encounters. His tactics and strategy were excellent, but he was a bit seditious.

Another was Mir Ghiyas Taghayï, a younger brother of Ali Dost's. Among the Moghul princes no one was farther forward at Sultan-Abusa'id Mirza's gate. Sultan-Abusa'id Mirza's square seal was in his keeping. At the end of Umar-Shaykh Mirza's time he became a close confidant. He was a chum of Ways Laghari's. When Sultan-Mahmud Khan was given Kassan, Mir Ghiyas Taghayï went into the khan's service, where he stayed until the end of his life. The khan patronized him greatly. He was a happy, joking person and flagrant in his debauchery.

Another was Ali Darwesh from Khurasan. He had served Sultan-Abusa'id Mirza in the circle of Khurasan pages. When Sultan-Abusa'id Mirza consolidated the throne of Khurasan and Samarkand [ca. 1459], [15b] he organized the battle-worthy warriors from the two capitals into elite corps and called them the Khurasan Page Corps and the Samarkand Page Corps. For me he performed well at the Samarkand gate. He was a valiant man. He wrote the *nasta'liq*[45] script beautifully. He was a sycophant, and parsimony prevailed in his nature.

Another was Qambar-Ali Moghul. He was from the equerry class. Because his father was a butcher for some time after he entered the province, he was called Qambar-Ali Sallakh.[46] He served Yunus Khan as a ewer bearer and later became a beg. He was promoted to high rank in my service. Up until the time of battle his enthusiasm was superb, but when it came time for action his falseness was apparent. He was a talkative blitherer. It is certain that anyone who talks too much will speak much nonsense. His capacity was limited, and he was addlebrained.

When the accident happened to Umar-Shaykh Mirza, I was in the *charbagh*[47] in Andizhan. On Tuesday the fifth of Ramadan in 899 [June 9, 1494] the news reached Andizhan. I mounted in consternation and set out for the fortress with the retainers and servants who were there with me. When we arrived at the mirza's gate, Sherim Taghayï took my horse's reins and led me toward the *namazgah*.[48] It occurred to him that if Sultan-Ahmad Mirza, a great padishah, [16] were to come with a large army, the begs would turn both me and the province over to him. Sherim Taghayï would therefore take me to Uzgen and the highlands so that if the province were turned over, at least I would not fall captive and could go to one of my uncles, Alacha Khan or Sultan-Mahmud Khan.

Khwaja Mawlana Qazi was the son of Sultan-Ahmad Qazi and of the lineage of Shaykh Burhanuddin Qilich, who traced his descent on his mother's side to Sultan Elig Mazi. His family had provided the province with religious authorities and *shaykhu'l-islams*,[49] and they will be mentioned repeatedly here. When he and the begs inside the fortress heard this news, they dispatched Khwaja Muhammad Darzi, a retainer of Umar-Shaykh Mirza's and atäkä to one of his daughters, to set our minds at ease. Just as we were approaching the namazgah, he came and took me back to the citadel, where I alighted. Khwaja Mawlana Qazi and the begs came to me, and it was decided in council to make fast the tower and rampart of the fortress. Hasan Ya'qub, Qasim Qauchin, and some of the begs who had been sent to reconnoiter in Margilan and those parts came a day or two later and joined my retinue wholeheartedly and set to work with great zeal [16b] to hold the fort.

Sultan-Ahmad Mirza took Ura-Tyube, Khodzhent, and Margilan and camped in Kuva, four leagues from Andizhan. At this juncture Darwesh Gav, a lord of Andizhan, was executed for unseemly speech. After this example all the people came into line.

Khwaja Qazi and Uzun Hasan, brother of Khwaja Husayn, were sent as emissaries with the following message for Sultan-Ahmad Mirza: he would certainly be stationing one of his loyal men in the province. As I was both loyal and like a son, if he entrusted this service to me, it would be executed better and more easily. Sultan-Ahmad Mirza was a man of few words, unassuming and mild, who made no decision on anything without his begs. The begs paid no attention to these words of ours but gave some harsh replies and marched on.

God, who by his perfect power has brought to fruition as desired every labor of mine at every time without obligation to any created being, here too effected a few events that caused them not merely to change their minds about coming but actually to regret having set out. So they returned without achieving their goal.

One reason was that the river at Kuva was a morass and could be crossed only at the bridge. When this vast army approached [17] and amassed at the bridge, many horses and camels fell into the water and perished. Three or four years before, they had been dealt a defeat at the Chir River ford; the experience at Kuva recalled the earlier one, and the army was overcome by terror. Moreover, at the same time, an epidemic broke out among the horses, who fell in droves and began to die. But our army and followers showed such single-mindedness of purpose and dedication that they shirked at no sacrifice so long as their lives and bodies held out. Therefore, when hard pressed, the attackers sent Darwesh Muhammad Tarkhan from a league away from Andizhan. From inside, Hasan Ya'qub went out to the vicinity of the namazgah and met with Darwesh Muhammad. After a truce was arranged, they withdrew.

Meantime, from north of the Khodzhent River, Sultan-Mahmud Khan set forth and laid siege to Akhsi, where Jahangir Mirza was.[50] The following begs were manning Akhsi: Ali Darwesh Beg, Mirza-Qulï Kükältash, Muhammad Baqir Beg, and Shaykh Abdullah Eshikaqa. Ways Laghari and Mir Ghiyas Taghayï had also been there, but fearing the approaching begs, they went to Kassan, which was Ways Laghari's territory. Since Ways Laghari was Nasir Mirza's beg atäkä, Nasir Mirza was in Kassan. When the khan reached the vicinity of Akhsi, these begs went over to the khan [17b] and turned over Kassan. Mir Ghiyas remained in the khan's retinue, but Ways Laghari took Nasir Mirza to Sultan-Ahmad Mirza, who turned him over to Muhammad Mazid Tarkhan. As the khan approached Akhsi, he fought a few battles but was not able to gain any ground because the begs and warriors in Akhsi fought so valiantly. Meanwhile, Sultan-Mahmud Khan fell ill and, weary of battle, returned to his own territory.

AbaBakr Dughlat Kashghari, who bowed his head to no one, had been ruling Kashghar and Khotan for several years. Intent upon expansion, he approached Uzgen, subjected the fortress to bombardment, and began to wreak devastation on the province. Khwaja Qazi and all the begs were assigned to go drive Kashghari off. When they advanced, Kashghari realized that he was not equal to such a force. Leaving Khwaja Qazi to mediate, he escaped through wiles and subterfuge.

During the occurrence of such momentous events, the begs who were left from Umar-Shaykh Mirza's time performed manly feats of valor. The mirza's mother, Shah Sultan Begim, Jahangir Mirza, the women of the harem, and the begs came to Andizhan from Akhsi. There they performed the rites of mourning and distributed food to the poor and unfortunate. [18]

After the completion of these tasks, arrangements for the disposition of the army and province were made. The governorship and lordship of the gate were settled upon Hasan Ya'qub. Osh was assigned to Qasim Qauchin. Uzun Hasan and Ali Dost Taghayï were appointed to Akhsi and Margilan. Umar-Shaykh Mirza's other begs and warriors were each assigned lands, estates, stipends, and maintenance according to their ranks.

When Sultan-Ahmad Mirza was two or three stages into his return march, he fell ill and developed a raging fever. When he reached Aq Su in the vicinity of Ura-Tyube, around the middle of Shawwal 899 [July 1494], he bade farewell to the mortal world at the age of forty-four.

SULTAN-AHMAD MIRZA

His birth and lineage. He was born in 855 [1451], the year Sultan-Abusa'id Mirza took the throne. He was the eldest of all Sultan-Abusa'id Mirza's sons. His mother was Ordu Buqa Tarkhan's daughter, the elder sister of Darwesh Muhammad Tarkhan.[51] She was the mirza's principal wife.

His appearance and habits. He was tall of stature, had a brown beard on his chin and a red face, and was fat. [18b] He was well-spoken. He wrapped his turban, in accordance with the fashion of the time, in four folds and left the fringe forward over his eyebrows.

His character. He was a man of orthodox Hanafi belief.[52] He never missed the five daily prayers, even when he was drinking. He was devoted to Khwaja Ubaydullah, who was his patron and protector. He was polite, and especially respectful in the khwaja's company. It is said that in the khwaja's assembly he never sat shifting from one leg to the other. Only once in the khwaja's presence did he, contrary to his custom, change his position; after the mirza had gone, the khwaja ordered the place where he had been sitting to be searched, and they found a bone there. He never read at all and was unlettered. Although he had grown up in the city, he was rustic and simple. He had not a shred of poetic talent. He was equitable, and, as he followed in the khwaja's footsteps, most of his affairs were decided according to Islamic law. His word was absolutely reliable: never did he break his promise. He was brave, and although he never got a chance really to do battle, they say that in several frays his courage was obvious. [19]

He was an excellent archer, and his arrows and shafts usually hit the bull's-eye. Mostly he could hit the target while charging from one end of the field to the other. Toward the end of his life he got fat and hunted pheasant and quail with a flail, seldom missing. He was a great lover of falconry, and quite good at it too. Aside from Ulughbeg Mirza, no king was so given to it. He was extremely modest. They say that even in privacy with his confidants and *ichkis*[53] he used to keep his feet covered. He was a good drinker. Once he started drinking, he drank continually for twenty or thirty days, but when he stopped he did not drink again for the same amount of time. On the days he was not drinking he would take his meals casually. At an assembly, he could sit all night and through the next day. His temperament was dominated by parsimony. He was a man of few words and humane. His affairs were managed by his begs.

His battles. He fought four battles. He fought Shaykh Jamal Arghun's younger brother Ni'mat Arghun in the vicinity of Zaamin at Aqar Tozï and won. Another time he fought Umar-Shaykh Mirza at Khavast and won. Another time was with Sultan-Mahmud Khan beside the Chir River in the vicinity of Tashkent. Although it was not a real battle, [19b] Moghul raiders came from his rear by ones and twos and got hold of the baggage, and such a huge army fell to pieces without any fighting or endeavor or any encounter at all. Many of the soldiers were drowned in the Chir River. Another time he defeated Haydar Kükäldash near Yar Yaylagh.

His domain. He held Samarkand and Bukhara, which his father had given him. After Abdul-Quddus killed Shaykh Jamal Arghun, he seized Tashkent, Shahrukhiyya, and Sayram, which remained under his control for a while. Later he gave Tashkent and Sayram to his younger brother, Umar-Shaykh Mirza. Khodzhent and Ura-Tyube were held by Sultan-Ahmad Mirza for a time.

His children. He had two sons who died in infancy and five daughters, four of whom were borne by Qataq Begim. The eldest was Rabi'a Sultan Begim, who was called Qara Köz[54] Begim. During the mirza's lifetime she was married to Sultan-Mahmud Khan, by whom she had one son named Baba Khan. He was a nice little boy, but when the Uzbeks martyred the khan at Khodzhent, they killed him and several other children. After Sultan-Mahmud Khan's death Jani Beg [20] Sultan married her.

The second daughter was Saliha Begim, who was called Aq Begim. After Sultan-Ahmad Mirza's death Sultan-Mahmud Mirza arranged wedding feasts and married her to his eldest son, Sultan-Mas'ud Mirza. Later she went to Kashghar with Shah Begim and Mihr Nigar Khanïm.

The third daughter was Ayisha Sultan Begim. When I was five years old and went to Samarkand, we were affianced. Later, during my rencontres,[55] she came to Khodzhent and I married her [in March 1500]. The second time I took Samarkand she had a little girl who died within several days. Shortly before the debacle of Tashkent [in 1503], she left me at her elder sister's instigation.

The fourth daughter was Sultanïm Begim, who became the wife of Sultan-Ali Mirza. After the Mirza's death Temür Sultan married her, and after his death Mahdi Sultan married her.

The youngest daughter was Ma'suma Sultan Begim. Her mother was Habiba Sultan Begim, niece of Sultan-Husayn Arghun of the Arghuns.[56] When I went to Khurasan, I saw her, liked her, and asked for her hand. I had her brought to Kabul and married her. She had one daughter but died in childbirth. The girl was named for her mother.

His wives and concubines. The first was Mihr Nigar Khanïm, whom Sultan-Abusa'id Mirza chose for him. She was Yunus Khan's eldest daughter and my mother's elder sister. [20b]

Another was Tarkhan Begim, who was of the Tarkhans.

Another was Qataq Begim. She was Tarkhan Begim's *kükäldash.*[57] Sultan-Ahmad Mirza married her for love. He adored her passionately, but she was utterly domineering. She also drank wine. During her lifetime Sultan-Ahmad Mirza did not go to any of his other wives. In the end he had her killed and obtained release from disgrace.

Another was Khwanzada Begim. She was of the *khwanzadas*[58] of Termez. Sultan-Ahmad Mirza had just married her when I went to Samarkand at age five. Her face was still covered; they had me remove her veil, as is the Turkish custom.

Another was Ahmad Hajji Beg's granddaughter named Latif Begim. After the mirza died Hamza Sultan married her. By him she had three sons. When I defeated the sultans under Hamza Sultan and Temür Sultan and took Hissar, these and other princes fell into my hands. I freed them all.

Another was Habiba Sultan Begim, a niece of Sultan-Husayn Arghun.

His officers. One was Jani Beg Dulday, Sultan Malik Kashghari's younger brother. Sultan-Abusa'id gave him the governorship of Samarkand and the lordship of Sultan-Ahmad Mirza's gate. [21] He was eccentric, and many unusual stories are told of him. One is that while he was governor of Samarkand, an Uzbek emissary renowned in the Uzbek nation for his strength arrived in Samarkand. (Uzbeks call a strong man *bökä*.) Jani Beg asked, "Are you a bökä? If you are, come on, let's wrestle." The emissary refused as much as he could, but Jani Beg would not desist. They wrestled and Jani Beg threw him. He was a valiant man.

Another was Ahmad Hajji Beg, son of Sultan Malik Kashghari. Sultan-Abusa'id Mirza gave him the governorship of Herat for a time. After the death of his uncle Jani Beg, he was awarded his uncle's rank and sent to Samarkand. He was talented poetically, and valiant. His pen name was Wafa'i, and he compiled a *divan*.[59] His poetry is not bad. This line is by him:

I'm drunk, *muhtasib*.[60] Chastise me on a day you find me sober.

Ahmad Hajji Beg accompanied Mir Ali-Sher Nawa'i from Herat to Samarkand, but after Sultan-Husayn Mirza became padishah Ahmad Hajji Beg went to Herat, where he received a great deal of patronage. There he kept and rode fine horses, [21b] most of which were bred in his own stables. He was brave, but his ability to command was not equal to his valor. He was careless of his affairs, all of which were handled by his servants and retainers. When Baysunghur Mirza did battle and defeated Sultan-Ali Mirza in Bukhara, Ahmad Hajji Beg was taken prisoner and put to death dishonorably, charged with the murder of Darwesh Muhammad Tarkhan.

Another was Darwesh Muhammad Tarkhan, son of Ordu Buqa Tarkhan. He was a maternal uncle to Sultan-Ahmad Mirza and Sultan-Mahmud Mirza. He was the greatest and most important of all the mirza's begs. He was a good Muslim, humane, and unassuming. He always copied Korans.[61] He played chess often and well and was well versed in falconry. In the end, during the troubles between Baysunghur Mirza and Sultan-Ali Mirza, he died in suspicious circumstances at the height of his greatness.

Another was Abdul-Ali Tarkhan, a close relative of Darwesh Muhammad Tarkhan, whose younger sister, the mother of Baqi Tarkhan, was his wife. Although Darwesh Muhammad Tarkhan was higher than Abdul-Ali Tarkhan in rank and position, this mountain of arrogance did not deign to so much as look at Darwesh Muhammad. For some years he held the governorship of Bukhara. [22] His retainers numbered three thousand, and he kept them splendidly. His liberality, concern for his realm, his court and accoutrements, table and assembly were regal, but he was harsh, tyrannical, vicious, and conceited. Although Shaybani Khan was not his overlord, he was with Shaybani Khan for a time, together with the many young and petty princes who served in his retinue. The direct cause for Shaybani Khan's attaining such success and the ruin of such ancient families was this Abdul-Ali Tarkhan.

Another was Sayyid-Yusuf Oghlaqchï. His grandfather must have come from the Moghuls. His father was patronized by Ulughbeg Mirza. His strategy and tactics were excellent, and he possessed valor. He played the *qopuz*[62] well. When I first came to Kabul, he was with me. He was truly worthy of patronage, and I promoted him to high rank. The first year the army marched to Hindustan, I stationed Sayyid-Yusuf Beg in Kabul, where he passed away at that time.

Another was Darwesh Beg, a descendant of the Eygü Temür Beg patronized by Temür Beg. He was a devotee of Khwaja Ubaydullah. He knew something about music and played the *saz*.[63] He had poetic talent. [22b] When Sultan-Ahmad Mirza was defeated on the banks of the Chir, he was drowned in the river.

Another was Muhammad Mazid Tarkhan, Darwesh Muhammad Tarkhan's younger brother. He was the governor of Turkistan City for several years, and it was from him that Shaybani Khan took Turkistan. His tactics and strategy were excellent, but he was flamboyantly vicious. He was with me the second and third times I took Samarkand, and I patronized him well. He died at the Battle of Köl-i-Malik [in 1512].

Another was Baqi Tarkhan, a son of Abdul-Ali Tarkhan and cousin to Sultan-Ahmad Mirza. After his father's death he was given Bukhara. During Sultan-Ali Mirza's time he grew extremely grand, and his retinue reached five or six thousand in number. He was not obedient or submissive to Sultan-Ali Mirza. He fought with Shaybani Khan at the Dabusi fort and lost. In that same defeat Shaybani Khan took Bukhara. Baqi Tarkhan was fond of falcons, of which, they say, he had seven hundred. His character was nothing worth mentioning. He grew up in princeliness and riches. Because his father had done some favors for Shaybani Khan, Baqi Tarkhan went to Shaybani Khan, but that unmanly ingrate gave him no patronage at all in return. [23] Baqi departed this world in misery and wretchedness in the province of Akhsi.

Another was Sultan-Husayn Arghun. Because he held the governorship of Karakul for a while, he became known as Sultan-Husayn of Karakul. His tactics and strategy were excellent. He was in my service.

Another was Qul-Muhammad Baghdadi, a Qauchin. He was valiant.

Another was Abdul-Karim Ashrit, an Uyghur.[64] He was lord of Sultan-Ahmad Mirza's gate. He was generous and valiant.

———

After Sultan-Ahmad Mirza's death [in 1494] the begs agreed to send someone posthaste across the mountains to invite Sultan-Mahmud Mirza to take the throne.

Malik-Muhammad Mirza, son of Sultan-Abusa'id Mirza's elder brother Minuchihr Mirza, aspiring to rule, gathered to himself some hooligans and rabble and left the camp. He went to Samarkand but was unable to do anything. He was the cause of his own death and that of several innocent princes.

SULTAN-MAHMUD MIRZA TAKES THE THRONE OF SAMARKAND

As soon as Sultan-Mahmud Mirza heard of his brother's death, he went to Samarkand and took the throne without opposition. However, highborn and low, military and civilian alike were repelled by several of Sultan-Mahmud Mirza's actions. The first was as follows. [23b] He sent his cousin and son-in-law, the above-mentioned Malik-Muhammad Mirza, to the Kök Saray[65] with four other mirzas. Two of them were released, but Malik-Muhammad Mirza and one other mirza were executed. (Some of these could never have achieved the status of padishah; moreover, they had no such ambitions.) Although Malik-Muhammad Mirza was slightly at fault, the other was totally innocent.

In addition, although his administration and military management were quite excellent and he took pride in attending to his divan and knew accounting, he was by nature inclined to tyranny and viciousness. As soon as he entered Samarkand he began to lay the foundations of a new administration and tax imposts. His soldiers began to be aggressive and to bring force to bear upon Khwaja Ubaydullah's people, by whose protection many poor and unfortunate had escaped tyranny and hostility during former impositions and exactions. The assault even affected the khwaja's own sons. Moreover, Sultan-Mahmud Mirza's begs and retainers were all just as tyrannical and vicious as he. The people of Hissar, particularly Khusrawshah's dependents, were always addicted to wine and fornication. Once one of Khusrawshah's great liege men seized a man's wife. [24] When the husband sought redress from Khusrawshah, he answered, "She's been with you for many years. Let her be with him for a few days."

Moreover, the young sons of civilians, merchants, even the sons of Turks and soldiers, could not leave their houses for fear of being turned into catamites. The people of Samarkand, who had lived in ease and comfort for twenty or twenty-five years under Sultan-Ahmad Mirza, most of whose affairs were conducted, thanks to Khwaja Ubaydullah, with justice and in accordance with the religious law, were scandalized and outraged by such tyranny and vice. Lowborn and noble, poor and unfortunate, all opened their mouths with curses and raised their hands in supplication.

Beware of festering inner wounds, for inner wounds surface in the end.
Distress no one insofar as you are able, for one cry of anguish can upset the whole world.

As a consequence of tyranny and vice, he ruled in Samarkand no more than five months.

EVENTS OF THE YEAR 900
(1494-95)⁶⁶

An emissary named Abdul-Quddus Beg came to me from Sultan-Mahmud Mirza. He brought gifts from the celebration of the marriage of Sultan-Mahmud Mirza's eldest son, Sultan-Mas'ud Mirza, to Sultan-Ahmad Mirza's second daughter, Aq Begim: gold and silver ornaments in the shapes of almonds and pistachios.

The emissary, who was probably related to Hasan Ya'qub, must have been sent to make promises to entice Hasan Ya'qub to look favorably upon Sultan-Mahmud Mirza. [24b] Hasan Ya'qub gave him smooth replies and, making as though he had been won over, gave him leave to withdraw. Five or six months later Hasan Ya'qub's manner changed for the worse, and he began to quarrel with the men around me. His disposition was so altered that he would have dismissed me and installed Jahangir Mirza as padishah. But he was on bad terms with all the officers and military men too, and everyone knew what was on his mind. Khwaja Qazi, Qasim Qauchin, Ali Dost Taghayï, Uzun Hasan, and some of my other supporters met with my grandmother Esän Dawlat Begim and decided to depose Hasan Ya'qub and put down the conspiracy. (For tactics and strategy, there were few women like my grandmother, Esän Dawlat Begim. She was intelligent and a good planner. Most affairs were settled with her counsel.) Hasan Ya'qub was in the citadel. My mother and grandmother were in the gatehouse in the outer fortress. Intent upon deposing Hasan Ya'qub, I mounted and headed toward the citadel. Hasan Ya'qub had ridden out to go hunting, but as soon as he heard of my approach, he left immediately, straight for Samarkand. [25] All the men and begs who were with him were arrested, including Muhammad Baqir Beg, Sultan-Muhammad Dulday's father Sultan-Mahmud Dulday, and some others. Some were given leave to go to Samarkand. The lordship of the gate and the governorship of Andizhan were settled upon Qasim Qauchin.

While on his way to Samarkand, Hasan Ya'qub stopped at Kani-badam and set out a few days later with ill intentions for Akhsi and the Kokand Orchin region. When his route was learned, some begs and warriors were dispatched to attack him, but only after a detachment of warriors was sent as an advance party. Hasan Ya'qub, however, surprised the party in the dark of night and attacked Uy Müngüzi with a barrage of arrows. One of Hasan Ya'qub's own men shot him in the cheek; before he could flee, he fell prey to his own action.

When you have done evil, be not secure from calamity, for retribution is a law of nature.

—

This year I began to abstain from suspect food. I was careful about knives, spoons, and tablecloths. Even the after-midnight prayer was seldom omitted. [25b]

In the month of Rabi' II [December 30, 1494–January 27, 1495], Sultan-Mahmud Mirza was stricken with a severe illness and within six days passed from this world. He was forty-three years old.

SULTAN-MAHMUD MIRZA

His birth and lineage. He was born in 857 [1453], the third son of Sultan-Abusa'id Mirza. He was a full brother to Sultan-Ahmad Mirza.

His features. He was short in stature, had a scanty beard, and was a fat and rather ill-shaped person.

His character and conduct were good. He never missed his prayers. His administration was excellent. He knew accounting well. Not a dirhem or a dinar was spent in his domain without his knowing about it. He never denied his liege men their allowances. His assemblies, table, and divan were very good. Everything was done according to rule and with military precision. Neither military nor civilians were able to go against any arrangement or plan he made. He is said formerly to have ridden hard to falcons, and later he did a lot of battue hunting. He was addicted to vice and debauchery. He drank wine continually. He kept a lot of catamites, and in his realm wherever there was a comely, beardless youth, he did everything he could to turn him into a catamite. He turned his begs' sons and his sons' begs and kükäldashes into catamites—he even demanded this service of his own kükäldashes' sons. [26] During his time this shameful vice was so widespread that there was no one at all who did not have catamites. To keep them was considered a virtue, and not to keep them a fault. His sons all died young of shameful immoderation and debauchery.

Sultan-Mahmud Mirza had poetic ability and made a divan, but his poetry was weak and flat. He composed too much; he probably should have composed less. He was irreligious and made fun of Khwaja Ubaydullah. He was cowardly and had little modesty. Around him he had buffoons and clowns who performed lewd, indecent acts during his divan, right out in front of people. He did not express himself well, and no one could understand immediately what he meant.

His battles. He twice fought battles, both times with Sultan-Husayn Mirza. Once he was defeated at Astarabad, and once at a place near Andkhui called Chakman Saray. Twice he made raids into Kafiristan south of Badakhshan, and for this reason [26b] was styled "Sultan-Mahmud Ghazi" on his seal.[67]

His domain. Sultan-Abusa'id Mirza gave Astarabad to Sultan-Mahmud Mirza, who went to Khurasan during the Iraqi debacle.[68] At that time Qambar-Ali Beg, the governor of Hissar, mobilized the Hindustan army at Sultan Abusa'id Mirza's order and was following the mirza to Iraq. When Qambar-Ali reached Khurasan, he joined Sultan-Mahmud Mirza. As soon as the people there heard of Sultan-Husayn Mirza's approach, they attacked Sultan-Mahmud Mirza and drove him from the province. He then went to Sultan-Ahmad Mirza in Samarkand. A few months later, Sayyid-Badr, Khusrawshah, and some other warriors led by Ahmad Mushtaq took Sultan-Mahmud Mirza and fled with him to Qambar-Ali Beg in Hissar. Thereafter the region to the south of the Iron Gates[69] and the Kohtan Mountains, that is, Termez, Chaghanian, Hissar, Khuttalan, Konduz, and Badakhshan up to the Hindu Kush range, was under Sultan-Mahmud Mirza's control.

After the death of his elder brother, Sultan-Ahmad Mirza's possessions also came under his control.

His children. He had five sons and eleven daughters. The eldest son was Sultan-Mas'ud Mirza, whose mother was [27] the daughter of Mir Buzurg of Termez.

Baysunghur Mirza was another, and his mother was Pasha Begim.

Another son was Sultan-Ali Mirza, whose mother was Zuhra Begi Agha, an Uzbek concubine.

Another son was Sultan-Husayn Mirza. His mother was Khwanzada Begim, a granddaughter of Mir Buzurg. He died during the mirza's lifetime at the age of thirteen.

Another was Sultan-Ways Mirza, whose mother was Yunus Khan's daughter, my mother's younger sister Sultan Nigar Khanïm. Accounts of these four princes will be mentioned in this history under the relevant years.

Of the three daughters who were full sisters to Baysunghur Mirza, the eldest was married to Malik-Muhammad Mirza, the son of Minuchihr Mirza, Sultan-Mahmud Mirza's paternal uncle.

Five daughters were conceived by Khwanzada Begim, Mir Buzurg's granddaughter. The eldest married AbaBakr Kashghari after Sultan-Mahmud Mirza's death. [27b]

The second was Bikä Begim. When Sultan-Husayn Mirza was besieging Hissar, before making peace and withdrawing, he betrothed her to Haydar Mirza, his son by Sultan-Abusa'id Mirza's daughter Payanda Sultan Begim.

The third daughter was Aq Begim.

The fourth was affianced to Jahangir Mirza when, [ca. 1490], Sultan-Husayn Mirza attacked Konduz and Umar-Shaykh Mirza sent his son Jahangir Mirza with the Andizhan regiment as reinforcements. In 910 [1504–05], Baqi Chaghaniani came to me on the banks of the Oxus to pay homage.[70] These ladies were then in Termez with their mothers and came with Baqi Chaghaniani's train and joined me. When we reached Kahmard, Jahangir Mirza married her. He had one daughter by her. At this date she is with her grandmother, Khwanzada Begim, in Badakhshan.

The fifth daughter was Zaynab Sultan Begim. When I took Kabul, I married her through the good offices of my mother, Qutlugh Nigar

Khanïm. She was not congenial, however, and two or three years later she died of smallpox.

Another daughter, Makhduma Sultan Begim, was Sultan-Ali Mirza's elder sister. She is now in Badakhshan.

Two other daughters were conceived by concubines. [28] One was Rajab Sultan, the other Muhibb Sultan.

His wives and concubines. Sultan-Mahmud Mirza's chief wife was Khwanzada Begim, daughter of Mir Buzurg of Termez. She was Sultan-Mas'ud Mirza's mother. The mirza loved her very much and grieved greatly when she died. Later he married Mir Buzurg's grand-daughter, who was Khwanzada Begim's brother's daughter. She too was called Khwanzada Begim. She was the mother of five daughters and one son.

Another was Pasha Begim, the daughter of Ali-Shukr, a Turcoman beg of the Baharlu tribe[71] of the Qaraqoyunlu confederation. She had been married to Jahanshah Mirza Barani Qaraqoyunlu's son Muhammadi Mirza. When Uzun Hasan of the Aqqoyunlu confederation took Azerbaijan and Iraq from Jahanshah's sons, Ali-Shukr Beg's sons entered Sultan-Abusa'id Mirza's service along with four or five thousand households of Qaraqoyunlu Turcomans. When Sultan-Abusa'id Mirza was defeated, they came to Transoxiana and entered Sultan-Mahmud Mirza's service when he went to Hissar from Samarkand. It was then that the mirza married this Pasha Begim, who became the mother of one son and three daughters.

Another was Sultan Nigar Khanïm, whose lineage has already been given with that of the khans. [28b]

Sultan-Mahmud Mirza had many concubines and mistresses. The chief concubine was Zuhra Begi Agha, an Uzbek he took during Sultan-Abusa'id Mirza's lifetime. She had one son and one daughter. He had many mistresses. By two of them he had the two daughters already mentioned.

His officers. One was Khusrawshah, a Qipchaq[72] from Turkistan. In his youth he rendered confidential service to the Tarkhan begs but later became a liege man to Mazid Beg Arghun, who immediately promoted him. During the Iraqi debacle he joined Sultan-Mahmud Mirza and accompanied him, rendering worthy services for which Sultan-Mahmud Mirza patronized him. Later he really grew grand. During

Sultan-Mahmud Mirza's time his retinue numbered five or six thousand. From the Oxus to the Hindu Kush mountains, apart from Badakhshan, all belonged to him, and he devoured the entire revenue from it. His table was excellent, as was his liberality. Despite his rusticity he knew how to acquire, and what he obtained he spent lavishly. After Sultan-Mahmud Mirza's death, during the time of his sons, he grew extremely grand, his retainers numbering close to twenty thousand. Although he performed his prayers and abstained from suspect food, he was mean and vicious. He was also stupid, unintelligent, faithless, and ungrateful. [29] For the sake of this transitory world he had blinded one of his benefactor's sons whom he had looked after himself, and killed another. He was sinful in the sight of God and damnable in the sight of men. He became worthy of being cursed at resurrection. For the sake of this transitory world he did such evil things, but with so much flourishing territory and so many armed retainers he couldn't say boo to a goose. He will be mentioned in this history.

Another was Pir-Muhammad Elchi-Buqa, a Qauchin. During the Hazaraspi battle, he fought with determination for Sultan-Abusa'id Mirza at the gates of Balkh.[73] He was a valiant man. He always served the mirza, and the mirza acted on his opinion. When Sultan-Husayn Mirza was besieging Konduz, Pir-Muhammad, unarmed and without plan, staged an ambush with only a few men, in rivalry to Khusrawshah. He was unable to accomplish anything. What did he think he could gain against such a vast army? While being pursued, he threw himself into the river and was drowned.

Another was Ayyub. He had served Sultan-Abusa'id Mirza in the Khurasan Page Corps. He was valiant. He was Baysunghur Mirza's beg atäkä. He dressed and ate frugally. He liked to joke and was talkative. Sultan-Mahmud Mirza used to address him as "impudent." [29b]

Another was Wali, a full brother to Khusrawshah. He kept his men well. It was he who had Sultan-Mas'ud Mirza blinded and Baysunghur Mirza killed. He found fault with everyone. He was an evil-tongued, foulmouthed, conceited, and dull-witted fellow. He approved of nothing anyone other than himself did. When I went from Konduz and cut off Khusrawshah from his retainers and servants at Kilagai and in the vicinity of Dowshi and dismissed him, he too went to Andarab and Sarab in fear of the Uzbeks. The nomadic clans in those regions defeated and plundered him and then came to Kabul as our supporters.

Wali went to Muhammad Shaybani, who had him beheaded in Samarkand.

Another was Shaykh Abdullah Barlas. He was married to Shah Sultan-Muhammad's daughter, who would be an aunt to AbaBakr Mirza and Sultan-Mahmud Khan. He wore his tunic fashionably tight. He was humane and noble.

Another was Mahmud Barlas, of the Barlases of Nawandak. He was a beg in Sultan-Abusa'id Mirza's service. When the province of Iraq was subjugated by Sultan-Abusa'id Mirza [in 1468], he gave Kerman to Mahmud Barlas. [30] When Mazid Beg Arghun and the Qaraqoyunlu Turcoman begs joined AbaBakr Mirza to attack Sultan-Mahmud Mirza at Hissar, and Sultan-Mahmud Mirza went to his elder brother in Samarkand [in 1469], Mahmud Barlas refused to give up Hissar and guarded it well. He was a poet and put together a divan.

———

Khusrawshah concealed Sultan-Mahmud Mirza's death from the people and plundered the treasury. But how could he keep such a thing hidden? The news immediately spread throughout the city. That day became a great moment of rejoicing for the people of Samarkand. Both soldier and peasant rose up in rebellion against Khusrawshah. Ahmad Hajji Beg and the Tarkhan begs put down the insurrection and sent Khusrawshah to Hissar.

During Sultan-Mahmud Mirza's lifetime he had sent his eldest son, Sultan-Mas'ud Mirza, to rule Hissar, and Baysunghur Mirza to rule Bukhara. When he died, neither was present. After expelling Khusrawshah the begs of Samarkand and Hissar agreed to send someone to Bukhara to bring Baysunghur Mirza to Samarkand, where they enthroned him. When Baysunghur Mirza became padishah, he was eighteen years old.

At that time Sultan-Mahmud Khan, acting upon the advice of Sultan-Junayd [30b] Barlas and some of the notables of Samarkand, gathered his army and went to the Kambay region, intent upon taking Samarkand. Baysunghur Mirza charged out of Samarkand with a large, well-equipped, and well-armed army and engaged in battle in the vicinity of Kambay. Haydar Kükäldash, the commander in chief of the Moghul army, was the vanguard. All dismounted and began to fire, but just then a large mounted division of fanatical fighters from Samarkand and Hissar charged, and the dismounted troops under

Haydar Beg's leadership fell under the horses' hooves. After being put to flight they were unable to fight and were defeated. Many Moghuls were killed, and many lost their heads in Baysunghur Mirza's presence. There were so many corpses that the royal tent had to be moved three times.

At this point Ibrahim Saru (who was from the Manglïgh people and, having served my father from childhood, had been promoted to beg but was later dismissed for some fault) entered the Isfara fortress and announced his rebellion by pronouncing the *khutba*[74] in Baysunghur Mirza's name.

THE SIEGE AND BATTLE OF ISFARA

In the month of Sha'ban [April–May 1495] the army mounted to put down Ibrahim Saru's rebellion. [31] At the end of the month we made camp to lay siege to Isfara. The warriors made light of the situation, and as soon as they reached the outside of the fortress, they took the section where a new roof was being built. That day Sayyid-Qasim Eshik-aqa went forth and distinguished himself in wielding the sword. Sultan-Ahmad Tambal and Muhammad Dost Taghayï also got into the fray with their swords, but the *ülüsh* was taken by Sayyid-Qasim. (The *ülüsh*, the champion's portion, is an old custom among the Moghuls: at every banquet and feast, whoever has distinguished himself with the sword receives the *ülüsh*.) When I went to Shahrukhiyya to see my uncle Sultan-Mahmud Khan, Sayyid-Qasim took the ülüsh. On the first day of battle my atäkä Khudaberdi was hit by an arrow from a crossbow. Since combat had been enjoined without armor, several unprotected warriors were lost and many were injured. Ibrahim Saru had a crossbowman who shot better than had ever been seen before and who was responsible for most of the wounded. After the fortress was taken he joined me.

The siege continued. It was ordered that siege machines be erected in two or three places, mines run, [31b] and the implements of siege be brought in, in earnest. The siege lasted forty days. Finally Ibrahim Saru, helpless, chose to submit through the mediation of Khwaja Mawlana Qazi, and in the month of Shawwal [June 1495] he hung his sword and bowcase around his neck and came out to yield the fortress.

Khodzhent had long belonged to Umar-Shaykh Mirza's adminis-

Assault of the Fortress of the Knights of St. John at Smyrna, from a *Zafarnama* (Book of Triumph) of Sharafuddin Ali Yazdi. Herat (?), dated A.H. 872 (A.D. 1467–68). Opaque watercolor, ink, and gold on paper. John Work Garrett Library, The Johns Hopkins University, Baltimore.

tration. However, because the rule in that administrative area had become slack during this interregnum, the people had begun to look to Sultan-Ahmad Mirza. With such an opportunity at hand, a move was made against it. Mir Moghul's father, Abdul-Wahhab Shiqavul, was in Khodzhent, but as soon as the army arrived he gave up the fortress without a fight.

At that point Sultan-Mahmud Khan came to Shahrukhiyya. Prior to this, when Sultan-Ahmad Mirza went to the vicinity of Andizhan, the khan too had gone and laid siege to Akhsi, as has been mentioned. It crossed my mind that since the distance was slight and the khan was like my father and elder brother, if I were to patch up our past differences, it would have excellent propagandistic value. So saying, I went to pay homage to the khan in the garden built by Haydar Beg outside of Shahrukhiyya.

The khan was seated in a large pavilion set up in the middle of the garden. [32] Immediately upon entering the tent, I knelt thrice. The khan rose to honor me. After our interview I backed off and knelt, and then he invited me to his side and showed me much kindness. One or two days later I set out for Akhsi and Andizhan via the Kindirlig Pass. Upon reaching Akhsi I paid my respects at my father's tomb. I left at noon on Friday and reached Andizhan late in the evening via the Band-i-Salar road, a distance of nine leagues. Among the inhabitants of the wilderness in Andizhan are the Chakrak people. A numerous folk, numbering five to six thousand households, they live in the mountains between Fergana and Kashghar. They have many horses and sheep, as well as yaks instead of cattle. Since the mountains are inaccessible and located on the borderlands, the people are unaccustomed to paying tribute—which Qasim Beg was dispatched with an army to obtain from them. He went there and took close to twenty thousand sheep and a thousand or fifteen hundred horses to be distributed among his men.

After the army returned from the Chakrak, they rode against Ura-Tyube, [32b] which had long been under Umar-Shaykh Mirza's control but was lost the year he died and was being held for Baysunghur Mirza by his younger brother, Sultan-Ali Mirza. When Sultan-Ali Mirza was apprised of the situation, he himself went out to the mountains of Palghar and Matcha, leaving his atäkä, Shaykh Zu'n-Nun, in Ura-Tyube. From halfway between Khodzhent and Ura-Tyube, Khalifa was sent with a message to Shaykh Zu'n-Nun, but that senseless fellow, instead of giving a satisfactory answer, had Khalifa seized and ordered him executed. Since it was not God's will that it happen, Khalifa escaped and with much difficulty returned barefoot and naked two or three days later. We went to the vicinity of Ura-Tyube. Since winter was approaching, the people had taken in all their supplies and

An encampment of nomadic people. Detail from a *Gulistan* (Rose Garden) of Sa'di, dated A.H. 891 (A.D. 1486), fol. 31v. Herat (?), opaque watercolor, ink, and gold on paper. Art and History Trust Collection.

grain. For these reasons we withdrew several days later in the direction of Andizhan. After we moved out, the khan's men attacked Ura-Tyube, where the troops, unable to withstand the assault, gave up and left. The khan gave Ura-Tyube to Muhammad-Husayn Kürägän, and it remained in his hands until 908 [1503].

EVENTS OF THE YEAR 901
(1495-96)[75]

Sultan-Husayn Mirza led his army from Khurasan against Hissar [33] and reached the other side of the river from Termez during the winter. Sultan-Mas'ud Mirza also gathered an army, and camped in Termez, facing him. For his part, Khusrawshah fortified Konduz and sent his younger brother Wali to Sultan-Mas'ud Mirza's army. All the forces spent most of the season on the riverbank, unable to cross.

Sultan-Husayn Mirza was an experienced ruler who knew what he was doing: He moved farther up the river toward Konduz, and dispatched five or six hundred warriors under Abdul-Latif Bakhshï to the Kelif crossing. By the time the army opposite him had become aware of his presence, he had crossed with his men and secured the riverbank. As soon as this news reached Sultan-Mas'ud Mirza, Khusrawshah's brother Wali did his utmost to launch an assault on those who had crossed, but, due either to Sultan-Mas'ud Mirza's timidity or to the efforts of Baqi Chaghaniani, who was hostile to Wali, no offensive was made, and Sultan-Mas'ud's army retired in confusion to Hissar.

Just before Sultan-Husayn Mirza crossed the river to Termez, he sent Badi'uzzaman Mirza, Ibrahim-Husayn Mirza, Muhammad Wali Beg, and Zu'n-Nun Arghun to attack Khusrawshah, and Muzaffar Mirza [33b] and Muhammad Burunduq Barlas to Khuttalan. He himself went against Hissar, but the Hissar people learned of his approach as he drew near. Sultan-Mas'ud Mirza did not consider it prudent to stay there, so he went to his brother Baysunghur Mirza in Samarkand farther up the Kumrud River via the Sary-Tag road.[76] Wali withdrew toward Khuttalan. Baqi Chaghaniani, Mahmud Barlas, and Qoch Beg's father Sultan-Ahmad made fast the Hissar fortress. Several years before, Hamza Sultan and Mahdi Sultan had left Shaybani Khan and joined Sultan-Mahmud Mirza's retinue. Now, with all their Uzbeks, and Muhammad Dughlat and Sultan-Husayn Dughlat with all the Moghuls living in the Hissar province, they retired in the confusion toward Karategin.

Learning of these events, Sultan-Husayn Mirza sent Abu'l-Muhsin Mirza and some warriors farther up the Kumrud valley in pursuit of Sultan-Mas'ud Mirza. Although the pursuers reached the defile, they were unable to make their offensive. Mirza Beg Firangibaz wielded his sword there. Sultan-Husayn Mirza sent Ibrahim Tarkhan, Ya'qub Ayyub, and some other soldiers to attack Hamza Sultan and the Moghuls in Karategin. There they caught up with them, and a battle was enjoined. Although they defeated Sultan-Husayn Mirza's detachment [34] and unhorsed most of the begs, they let them go.

With this exodus Hamza Sultan, Mahdi Sultan, Hamza Sultan's son Mamaq Sultan, Muhammad Dughlat, who later became known as Muhammad of Hissar, Sultan-Husayn Dughlat, the Uzbeks who belonged to these princes, and Sultan-Mahmud Mirza's liege Moghuls who were living in Hissar province all opted for us and came to Andizhan in Ramadan [May–June 1496]. At that time, in accordance with the practice of Timurid rulers, I used to sit on a raised cushion. When Hamza Sultan, Mahdi Sultan, and Mamaq Sultan arrived, I rose to honor the princes, descended from the cushion platform, and held an interview with them, for which I seated them in the place of respect, to my right. All the Moghuls led by Muhammad of Hissar came and elected to pay homage.

Sultan-Husayn Mirza arrived and camped, besieging the Hissar fortress. There was no rest night or day: tunnels were dug in four or five places, the fortress was bombarded, rocks were hurled, and mortars were cast. The tunnel being dug toward the city gate had progressed far when the defenders, digging their own tunnel, discovered it. From above, the defenders [34b] forced down smoke on the attackers, who closed the opening, thus driving the fumes back up onto the defenders, who fled from the jaws of death. Finally, by bringing bucket after bucket of water and pouring it down, they drove the attackers from the tunnel.

Another time a group of nimble warriors sallied forth and drove away the warriors who were on top of the tunnel. Yet another time, from north of the mirza's camp, they installed a mortar, hurled many stones, and weakened a tower, which collapsed late that night. Some of the warriors importuned for permission to fight, but the mirza refused, saying, "It is nighttime." By daybreak the defenders had completely rebuilt the tower. That morning no battle was fought. For two or two-and-a-half months, there was no real battle, only punitive sallies, mining, the building of siege engines, and the catapulting of stones.

When Badi'uzzaman Mirza and as many of the group as he had sent against Khusrawshah camped three or four leagues below Konduz, Khusrawshah arrayed the men he had, set out from Konduz, stopped for one night, then attacked Badi'uzzaman Mirza and his army. All the mirzas and begs [35]—if they weren't double the number Khusrawshah had, they were easily one-and-a-half times that—nonetheless opted for safety and did not emerge from their trenches. Khusrawshah's men, good and bad, great and small, must have been four or five thousand men. For the sake of this ephemeral world and of faithless followers ready to flee at a moment's notice, Khusrawshah elected this evil and ill repute. A man who made his watchwords tyranny and injustice, and who seized so many lands and maintained so many liege men and retainers that toward the end of his time his servants numbered upward of twenty to thirty thousand, whose realm dwarfed that of his own padishah and mirzas—in his entire lifetime this was his one engagement! For such a deed as this, Khusrawshah and his followers became known as great and bold commanders, while those who did not leave the trenches gained a reputation for cowardice and became synonymous with timidity.

Badi'uzzaman Mirza marched away and came in a few marches to camp at Alghu Tagh at Taligan. Khusrawshah was in the Konduz fortress. His brother Wali he sent with a troop of warriors to Ishkamish, Falul, and those foothills to give additional harassment to the mirza from outside. Muhibb-Ali Qorchï also took a troop of warriors and grappled with some of them on the bank of the Khuttalan River, [35b] defeated them, unhorsed a few, and brought back some heads. The next time, trying to outdo this, Sayyidim Ali Darban and his younger brother Qulï Beg, Bahlul Ayyub, and a party of warriors encountered the Khurasan troops on their march in the vicinity of Khwaja Changal on the slopes of Anabar Koh. However, as very many reached the fray, Sayyidim Ali, Qul Baba, and several warriors were completely unhorsed.

SULTAN-HUSAYN MIRZA
WITHDRAWS FROM HISSAR

This news reached Sultan-Husayn Mirza. Moreover, the army was distressed by the spring rains in Hissar. A truce was proposed, and Mahmud Barlas on behalf of the defenders and Hajji Pir Bökäül on behalf of the attackers went out to make arrangements. The great ladies came with whatever musicians and singers there were, and Sultan-Mahmud Mirza's eldest daughter by Khwanzada Begim was taken for Haydar Mirza, whose mother was Payanda Sultan Begim and who was thus Sultan-Abusa'id Mirza's grandson. Leaving Hissar, the mirza headed toward Konduz.

Upon reaching Konduz, Sultan-Husayn Mirza made some punitive raids and laid siege. Finally Badi'uzzaman Mirza intervened, peace was made, prisoners were exchanged, [36] and the Khurasanis withdrew. Sultan-Husayn Mirza's coming twice and withdrawing without being able to seize Khusrawshah were the cause for Khusrawshah's aggrandizement to such an extent and his undertaking things beyond his capacity.

When Sultan-Husayn Mirza reached Balkh, he gave it to Badi'uzzaman Mirza in the interests of Transoxiana, and he gave Badi'uzzaman Mirza's province of Astarabad to Muzaffar-Husayn Mirza. The two princes were made to kneel in homage for Balkh and Astarabad at the same assembly. That was why Badi'uzzaman was offended, and that was the cause for the rebellions and revolts that lasted so many years.[77]

THE TARKHAN REVOLT

This same Ramadan there occurred in Samarkand the Tarkhans' revolt. It came about as follows. Baysunghur Mirza was not on such friendly terms with the begs and soldiers of Samarkand as he was with those of Hissar. His favorite beg was Shaykh Abdullah Barlas, and his sons were such confidants and ichkis that they were as close as lovers and beloveds. The Tarkhan begs and some of the Samarkand begs were offended by this, and Darwesh Muhammad Tarkhan came from

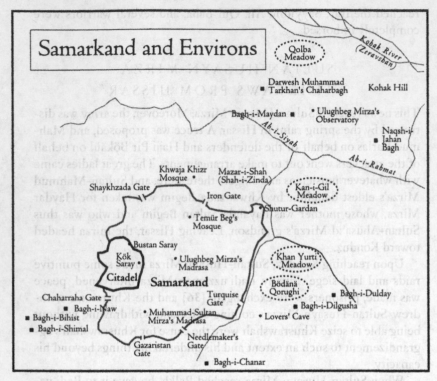

Samarkand and environs, after Golombek and Wilber 1988, and Pougatchenkova 1981.

Bukhara, had Sultan-Ali Mirza brought from Karshi, made him padishah, and went with him to the Bagh-i-Naw,[78] where Baysunghur Mirza was. Making Baysunghur Mirza a sort of captive, [36b] they separated him from his liege men and servants and took him to the citadel. There both mirzas were made to stay in one place. They thought of taking Baysunghur Mirza to the Kök Saray late that afternoon. On the pretext of making his ablutions, Baysunghur Mirza entered a room in one of the buildings on the northeast side of the Bustan Saray.[79] The Tarkhans were standing at the door. Muhammad-Quli Qauchin and Hasan Sharbatchï entered along with the mirza. By chance, in the back of the room, where the mirza came in to make his ablutions, there was another door leading to the outside that had been bricked up. They immediately destroyed the blockage, got out through the aqueduct leading from the citadel rampart on the Ghatfar side, jumped from the water-course rampart, and went to Khwajaka Khwaja's house in the Khwaja Kafshir quarter. Those who were standing at the door to the water closet looked in after a while and saw that the mirza had escaped. The next morning the Tarkhans gathered and went to Khwajaka Khwaja's gate. The khwaja refused to hand him over. The Tarkhans for their part were unable to use force, for the khwajas were of too exalted a station for them to be able to do so. A day or two later Khwaja Abu'l-Makarim, Ahmad Hajji Beg, and some other begs and soldiers, along with the people of the city, launched a massive attack, [37] brought the mirza out of the khwaja's house, and laid siege to Sultan-Ali Mirza and the Tarkhans in the citadel. They were not able to hold the citadel for even a day. Muhammad Mazid Tarkhan departed by the Charraha Gate for Bukhara. Sultan-Ali Mirza and Darwesh Muhammad Tarkhan were taken prisoner.

Baysunghur Mirza was in Ahmad Hajji Beg's house when Darwesh Muhammad Tarkhan was brought in. Baysunghur Mirza asked him one or two questions, but Darwesh Muhammad was unable to give a satisfactory answer; in view of what he had done, he was sentenced to death. In his helplessness, he clung to a column. Did he think they would let him go if he just held on? They took him to his execution. Baysunghur Mirza ordered Sultan-Ali Mirza taken to the Kök Saray to be blinded.

One of the magnificent structures Temür Beg had built was the Kök Saray, located in the Samarkand citadel. It is a building with amazing properties. All of Temür Beg's offspring who raised their heads and sat on the throne sat there. All who lost their heads in quest of the throne lost it there. To say, "They've taken the prince to the Kök Saray," meant that they had killed him.

Sultan-Ali Mirza was taken to the Kök Saray and a needle was drawn across his eyes. But, whether intentionally or unintentionally on the part of the surgeon, [37b] no permanent damage was done. Without revealing this immediately, he went to Khwaja Yahya's house and escaped two or three days later to the Tarkhans in Bukhara.

Consequently a rivalry sprang up between Khwaja Ubaydullah's sons—the elder son supporting the elder prince, and the younger taking the part of the younger.[80] A few days later Khwaja Yahya also went to Bukhara.

Baysunghur Mirza gathered his army and went out against Sultan-Ali Mirza in Bukhara. When they were near Bukhara, Sultan-Ali Mirza and the Tarkhan begs arrayed their army and sallied forth. There was a little skirmish. Victory went to Sultan-Ali Mirza, and Baysunghur Mirza suffered defeat. Ahmad Hajji Beg and a few warriors were taken prisoner, and most of them were put to death. Ahmad Hajji Beg, charged with the murder of Darwesh Muhammad Tarkhan, was dishonorably put to death by Ahmad Hajji Beg's servants. Sultan-Ali Mirza rode straight to Samarkand in pursuit of Baysunghur Mirza.

BABUR LAYS SIEGE TO SAMARKAND

We received news of this in the month of Shawwal [June–July 1496] in Andizhan. That same month, our army mounted in pursuit of our desire for Samarkand. Sultan-Husayn Mirza had withdrawn from Hissar and Konduz. Sultan-Mas'ud Mirza and Khusrawshah's minds were at ease. [38] With a like desire for Samarkand, Sultan-Mas'ud Mirza had come to Shahrisabz. Khusrawshah had sent his brother Wali to join the mirza. For three or four months we besieged Samarkand from three directions. Khwaja Yahya came on behalf of Sultan-Ali Mirza and delivered a message of solidarity. We decided to meet, and so I took my army from Samarkand two or three leagues down from Sughd. Sultan-Ali came from that direction with his army. From the other side Sultan-Ali Mirza with four or five of his men, and from this side I with four or five of my men crossed to an island in the middle of the Kohak River, held an interview on horseback, and asked after each other. Then they withdrew in their direction and I in mine.

While there I saw Mulla Banna'i and Muhammad Salih in the khwaja's service. I glimpsed Muhammad Salih only that one time, but Mulla Bannai was long in my service later on. After my interview with Sultan-Ali Mirza, since winter was approaching and the people of Samarkand were not in dire straits, I returned to Andizhan, and Sultan-Ali Mirza to Bukhara. Sultan-Mas'ud Mirza was quite desirous of marrying Shaykh Abdullah Barlas's daughter. He married her, gave up his desire for territory, and withdrew to Hissar. [38b] Indeed, she was the only reason for his coming. Mahdi Sultan fled from Shiraz and Kambay to Samarkand, and Hamza Sultan left Zaamin with permission to go to Samarkand.

EVENTS OF THE YEAR 902
(1496-97)[81]

This winter things were looking up for Baysunghur Mirza. When Abdul-Karim Ashrit came to the vicinity of Kufin on behalf of Sultan-Ali Mirza, Mahdi Sultan came against him from Samarkand, leading Baysunghur Mirza's force. Abdul-Karim Ashrit and Mahdi Sultan met face-to-face. Mahdi Sultan stabbed Abdul-Karim's horse with his Circassian sword,[82] and the horse dropped. As he was picking himself up, Mahdi Sultan lobbed off his hand at the wrist. Having seized him, they gave his troops a sound defeat.

When the sultans saw Samarkand's affairs and the mirza's gate about to topple, they foresightedly went to Shaybani Khan.

The Samarkandis pulled themselves together enough to assemble their army to face Sultan-Ali Mirza. Baysunghur Mirza went to Sar-i-Pul. Sultan-Ali Mirza went to Khwaja Kardzan. At this point Khwaja Abu'l-Makarim and the Andizhan begs [39] Ways Laghari and Muhammad Baqir, as well as Qasim Dulday and a troop of Baysunghur Mirza's ichkis, were instigated by Khwaja Munir of Osh to attack Bukhara. As they approached, the people in Bukhara learned of them. Their attempt failed and they withdrew.

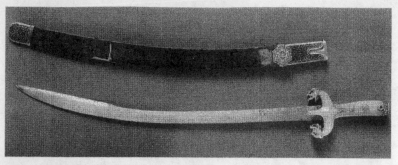

Saber with dragon-headed hilt and scabbard, Iran or Central Asia, fifteenth century. Watered steel, white jade (nephrite), and gold. Topkapi Palace Armory, Istanbul, 1/220.

SECOND SIEGE OF SAMARKAND

When I held my interview with Sultan-Ali Mirza, it was decided that during the summer he from Bukhara and I from Andizhan would go lay siege to Samarkand. Accordingly, in Ramadan [May 1497], we rode from Andizhan. When we reached the vicinity of Yar Yaylagh and learned that the mirzas were camped opposite, we sent Tolun Khwaja forward with two or three hundred scouts. Baysunghur Mirza got wind of our approach, broke ranks, and retreated. Our scouts caught up with their rear during the night, shot and captured many men, and brought back much booty.

Two or three days later we arrived at the Shiraz fortress, which was Qasim Dulday's. His prefect was unable to hold Shiraz and surrendered the fort, which then became Ibrahim Saru's responsibility. The next morning we performed the prayer for the Fitr holiday[83] there and, setting out against Samarkand, reached Abyar field. That very day, Qasim Dulday, Ways Laghari, Hasan Nabira, Sultan-Muhammad Sayghal, [39b] and Sultan-Muhammad Ways came with three or four hundred men and paid homage. They said, "As soon as Baysunghur Mirza moved back we separated ourselves and came in fealty to the padishah." In the end it became apparent that these men must have left at Baysunghur Mirza's behest and come in order to hold the Shiraz fort. Since the fate of Shiraz had turned out thus, there was nothing they could do but come to us.

When camp was made in Qara Bulaq, the Moghuls who had run

amok over some of the villages and hamlets that had surrendered were seized and brought in. Qasim Beg ordered two or three of them cut to pieces as exemplary punishment. Four or five years later during our guerilla rencontres as we were headed through here from Matcha to the khan, because he feared retaliation for this order Qasim Beg left us and went to Hissar.

We moved out of Qara Bulaq, crossed the river, and camped opposite Yam. That very day some of the ichki begs got into a fracas with Baysunghur Mirza's men right on the Khiaban. Sultan-Ahmad Tambal's throat was pierced with a lance, but he was not unhorsed. Khwajagi Mulla Sadr, Khwaja Kalan's eldest brother, was shot in the neck and died instantly. He was a good warrior my father had promoted and made his seal keeper. He was also a scholar [40] and knew many words. His composition was not bad either. He was an expert falconer and could work the rain stone.

While we were in the vicinity of Yam a lot of merchants and other people came out of the town and set up a market in the camp. One afternoon a general riot broke out, and all these good Muslims were pillaged. Discipline in the army was so dependable, however, that when an order was issued for the return of all the items, before the end of the first watch of the following day not so much as a strand of thread or broken needle was left in the soldiers' hands. Everything was returned to its owner.

We left there and camped at Khan Yurtï, three *kos*[84] to the east of Samarkand. For forty or fifty days we sat there, while several times the hotheaded warriors from our side and theirs hacked away at each other on the Khiaban. Once Ibrahim Begchik got into the fray on the avenue and was hit in the face with a sword. Thereafter he was called Ibrahim Chaplïq.[85] Another time, on the avenue at the Mughak Bridge, Abu'l-Qasim Kohbur wielded the flail. Another time on the avenue in the vicinity of Tarnaw, a fracas broke out. [40b] Mir Shah Qauchin wielded the flail, but he was so cut up that his neck was severed through halfway—at least his artery was not cut.

One day the defenders sent someone to us in Khan Yurtï with a deceitful message: "Come by night to Lovers' Cave and we'll turn over the fort." To this end we mounted and rode to the Mughak Bridge with a contingent of warriors and foot soldiers. The defenders had taken out four or five of our nimblest men before the rest realized what was happening. One named Hajji had served me from my childhood. Another was called Mahmud Kundarsangak. They were all killed.

While settled there, so many townspeople and merchants came out of Samarkand that the camp had become a regular town. Everything that one might want in a city was to be found there. During that time, with the one exception of Samarkand, all the fortresses and highlands and lowlands—except a fort called Urgut in the foothills of the Shavdar mountains—had come over to us. By necessity we left the camp and rode against Urgut. Unable to resist, they surrendered through Khwaja Qazi's mediation. [41] We pardoned their offenses and returned once again to the siege of Samarkand.

SULTAN·HUSAYN MIRZA
AND BADI'UZZAMAN MIRZA
COME TO BLOWS

During this year the feud between Sultan-Husayn Mirza and Badi'uzzaman Mirza turned into open hostilities. The details are as follows. The year before, Balkh was given to Badi'uzzaman Mirza, and Astarabad to Muzaffar-Husayn Mirza, and the two princes were made to kneel in acceptance, as has already been related. From that time until now many emissaries went back and forth. Finally Ali-Sher Beg came as emissary, but, try as he may, Badi'uzzaman Mirza refused to turn over Astarabad to his younger brother, saying, "At my son Muhammad-Mu'min Mirza's circumcision feast Sultan-Husayn Mirza awarded it to him."

One day an exchange took place between Ali-Sher Beg and the mirza that is indicative of the mirza's quick understanding and the softness of Ali-Sher Beg's heart. Ali-Sher Beg had spoken many things in confidence to the mirza and then said, "You had best forget my words." The mirza immediately replied, "What words?" Ali-Sher Beg was moved to tears.

In the end the contention between fathers and sons resulted in father leading army against father and son against son in Balkh and Astarabad.[86] [41b]

Into the Belcheragh meadow at the foot of Gurzuwan came Sultan-Husayn Mirza from below and Badi'uzzaman Mirza from above. On Wednesday, the first of Ramadan [May 3, 1497], Abu'l-Muhsin Mirza advanced with a few of Sultan-Husayn Mirza's officers and light troops. There was not much of a battle, and Badi'uzzaman's troops were defeated. Many of his warriors were taken prisoner, and Sultan-Husayn Mirza had them all beheaded. It was not just here that he did this: every time his sons rebelled and he defeated them in battle, he had all their fallen followers beheaded. What was he to do? He was right to do so. The princes were so besotted with their debauchery and pleasure that when an experienced ruler like their father was within a half-day's journey and only one night was left before a blessed and holy month like Ramadan, without notice of their father and without fear of God they went right on with their drinking and carousing. It is certain that such a person will be defeated and anyone will gain the upper hand over one who passes his time thus. In the several years during which the governorship of Astarabad was in Badi'uzzaman Mirza's hands his retinue and entourage were splendidly bedecked and arrayed. Gold and silver vessels and utensils were many, and his brocaded youths and [42] fine horses were without number. There he lost everything. In his flight he was faced with a mountain road on which he encountered a precipice, down which he descended himself with difficulty, losing many of his men over the cliff.

After Sultan-Husayn Mirza's defeat of his son he went to Balkh, where Badi'uzzaman Mirza had stationed Shaykh Ali Taghayï, who, unable to resist, surrendered. Sultan-Husayn Mirza gave Balkh to Ibrahim-Husayn Mirza, and with him he stationed Muhammad-Wali Beg and Shah Husayn Chuhra. Sultan-Husayn Mirza himself then withdrew to Khurasan.

After his defeat, Badi'uzzaman Mirza dragged himself, along with what was left of his destitute horsemen and foot soldiers, to Khusrawshah in Konduz. Khusrawshah received him hospitably and presented so many horses, camels, tents, and military arms and armor of all sorts to the mirza and those who were with him that those who saw it said that the only difference between his former and his new arms was the difference between gold and silver.

SULTAN-MAS'UD MIRZA AND
KHUSRAWSHAH HAVE A FALLING-OUT

Given the inordinate behavior of the one and the self-aggrandizement of the other, disputes and quarrels broke out between Sultan-Mas'ud Mirza and Khusrawshah. Therefore Khusrawshah attached Wali and Baqi [42b] to Badi'uzzaman Mirza and sent them against Sultan-Mas'ud Mirza in Hissar, but they were unable to get near the fort. Once or twice they engaged in skirmishes in the outlying areas, and once at Qushkhana, to the north of Hissar, Muhibb-Ali Qorchï separated himself from the main body and came forward to fight valiantly. He was unhorsed, but just as he was about to be taken captive, his men drove in and rescued him. After a few days a truce was made and they retired.

A few days later Badi'uzzaman Mirza got himself across the mountain roads to Kandahar and Zamin Dawar to Zu'n-Nun Arghun and his son, Shah-Shuja' Arghun.[87] Despite his stinginess and miserliness Zu'n-Nun Arghun served him well. In one presentation he gave him forty thousand sheep.

It is a strange coincidence that on the very Wednesday on which Sultan-Husayn Mirza defeated Badi'uzzaman Mirza, Muzaffar-Husayn Mirza defeated Muhammad-Mu'min Mirza in Astarabad. It is even stranger that a man named Charshamba ("Wednesday") unhorsed Muhammad-Mu'min Mirza and brought him in.

EVENTS OF THE YEAR 903
(1497-98)[88]

Camp was made in the Qolba Meadow behind the Bagh-i-Maydan.[89] The inhabitants of Samarkand, civilian and military alike, came out in droves to the vicinity of the Muhammad Chap Bridge. Since our people were not ready, **[43]** by the time the warriors were prepared Sultan-Qulï and Baba-Qulï had been unhorsed and taken to the fortress. A few days later we moved out and camped at the head of Qolba behind the Kohak. That day Sayyid-Yusuf Beg was expelled from Samarkand. He came to us and rendered homage.

The people in Samarkand, civilian and military alike, imagining that our move from one camp to another meant that we had withdrawn, came out as reinforcements as far as the Mirza Bridge and through the Shaykhzada Gate as far as the Muhammad Chap Bridge. We ordered the warriors there to arm themselves and get to horse. From both sides, from the Mirza and the Muhammad Chap bridges, they brought force to bear. By God's grace the enemy was defeated. They unhorsed some very great warriors and officers, among them Muhammad Miskin. Hafiz Dulday's index finger was cut off and brought in. Another was Muhammad Qasim Nabira, who was unhorsed by his younger brother Hasan Nabira and brought in. Many such warriors were well known to the soldiers and folk. From the city rabble they brought in Dewana Jamabaf and Kal Qashuq, who were outstanding in pitching rocks and scrapping. **[43b]** In revenge for the foot soldiers killed at the Lovers' Cave it was ordered that those two be tortured to death. This was a big defeat for the people of Samarkand. After this they ceased to sally forth from the fortress. The situation went so far that our men could go right up to the edge of the trench and capture slaveboys and girls.

The sun entered Libra. It began to turn cold. The begs who participated in council were summoned, and it was decided as follows: "The people of the city are worn down. Perhaps even today, by God's favor, we will take the city. If not, probably tomorrow. Instead of suffering in the cold outside, we should remove ourselves from near the city and establish winter quarters in some fort. If one had then to move, one could do so without much hesitation." The Khwaja Didar fort was considered suitable for winter quarters, so we moved off and camped in the meadow facing it. Upon entering the fortress, we assigned places for living and storage, stationed overseers and commissars, and settled into camp. We stayed in the meadow for a few days while the winter rooms were being made ready.

During this time Baysunghur Mirza sent a stream of people to Shaybani Khan in Turkistan to request assistance. [44] Shaybani Khan hastened from Turkistan and, reaching our camp the very Wednesday morning our winter quarters were ready and as we were entering the fortress, stood poised for attack. Our army was not together: some had gone to Rabat-i-Khwaja for winter supplies, some to Kabud, some to Shiraz. Nonetheless, we arrayed what army we had and made a sortie. Shaybani Khan was unable to make a stand and withdrew toward Samarkand, where he eventually went. Since Shaybani Khan did not share Baysunghur Mirza's ambitions, they did not hit it off. A few days later Shaybani Khan returned to Turkistan, disappointed at not being able to effect any action.

Baysunghur Mirza, by holding out against the siege for seven months, fulfilled his one hope. However, eventually he gave up and got himself, along with two or three hundred hungry dependents, to Khusrawshah in Konduz.

When Baysunghur was crossing the Oxus River in the vicinity of Termez, the governor there, Sayyid-Husayn Akbar, a relative of Sultan-Mas'ud Mirza's and person of importance in his service, learned of his approach and attacked. The mirza made it across, but Mirim Tarkhan was drowned. The personnel, camp followers, and baggage that were left behind were seized. Baysunghur Mirza's page, Tahir-Muhammad, was also taken prisoner. Khusrawshah welcomed Baysunghur Mirza. [44b][90]

We received news as soon as Baysunghur Mirza departed, and so we mounted and set out from Khwaja Didar for Samarkand. The notables, begs, and warriors came out one after the other to greet us along the way. We camped in the Bustan Saray in the citadel. In Rabi' I [October–November 1497] the city of Samarkand and the surrounding province were taken and occupied.

A DESCRIPTION OF SAMARKAND

Few cities in the civilized world are as pleasant as Samarkand. It is in the fifth clime, 99° 56' longitude, 40° 40' latitude.[91] Samarkand is the seat of the province, which is Transoxiana. Because it has not been stormed and seized by enemies, Samarkand is called *balda-i-mahfuza*.[92] Samarkand became Muslim during the time of the caliph Uthman.[93] One of the Companions,[94] Qutham son of Abbas, went there, and his tomb outside the Iron Gate is now called Mazar-i-Shah.[95] Samarkand is supposed to have been built by Alexander. The Moghuls and Turks call it "Semizkand" (Fat City).[96] Temür Beg was the first to make it his capital.

I ordered that the fortress be paced off atop the wall; the count came to 10,700 paces.

The people are all Sunnis and orthodox followers of the religious law. Ever since the time of the Prophet, no province has been known to have produced so many leaders of Islam as Transoxiana. [45] Shaykh Abu-Mansur, who is one of the great exponents of dialectic theology, was from a suburb of Samarkand called Maturid. Theologians are divided into two groups, the Maturidites and the Ash'arites. The attribution of the Maturidites is to this Shaykh Abu-Mansur.[97] Another, the author of the *Sahih of Bukhari*, Khwaja Isma'il,[98] was also from Transoxiana. The author of the *Hidaya*, a book of jurisprudence that holds a high place of distinction in the sect of Abu-Hanifa,[99] was from the Margilan area of Fergana, which is within Transoxiana.

Samarkand lies on the edge of the civilized world. To the east are Fergana and Kashghar, to the west Bukhara and Khwarazm, to the north Tashkent and Shahrukhiyya, which are also called Shash and Banakath, respectively, and to the south Balkh and Termez.

Detail of the facade of the large Friday mosque, or *masjid-i-jami'*, built by Temür in Samarkand around 1398–1405 and known today as the Bibi Khanïm Mosque. From the Turkestanskii Al'bom, 1872, made for K. P. von Kaufman; vol. 1, no. 73. Library of Congress.

Two kos north of Samarkand flows the Kohak River. Between this river and Samarkand is located a hill called Kohak.[100] Because the river flows at the foot of this hill, it is called the Kohak River. From it branches off a large waterway—indeed, it is a small river—called the Dargham. It is one league south of Samarkand, and from it are irrigated the orchards and exurbs of Samarkand as well as some of the subdistricts. As far as Bukhara and Karakul, nearly thirty or forty leagues away, the land is irrigated and cultivated from the Kohak. [45b] Such a large river, however, receives no increase from the cultivation and habitation for which it supplies water, and indeed, for three or four months during the summer no water reaches Bukhara. The grapes, melons, apples, and pomegranates—indeed all fruits—in Samarkand are excellent, but two types of Samarkand fruit are renowned: the apples and *sahibi*[101] grapes of Samarkand. The winter is terribly cold, although the snowfall is not so great as in Kabul. The air is good in the summer but not so good as in Kabul.

In Samarkand and its suburbs are many of Temür Beg's and Ulughbeg Mirza's buildings and gardens. In the Samarkand citadel, Temür Beg had constructed a large four-story pavilion known as the Kök Saray. It is a superb building. Near the Iron Gate, inside the walls, he had a Friday mosque built of stone. Most of the stonemasons sent from Hindustan worked there. The inscription on the mosque, the Koranic verse, "And Abraham and Ishmael raised the foundations of the house" etc.,[102] is written in script so large that it can be read from nearly a league away. This too is a superb building. To the east of Samarkand he had two gardens constructed. The farther of the two is called Bagh-i-Dulday and the nearer Bagh-i-Dilgusha.[103] An avenue was made from the Dilgusha garden to the Turquoise Gate, and on both sides poplar trees were planted. In the Dilgusha a large pavilion was constructed and in it [46] Temür Beg's India campaign[104] was depicted. At the foot of Kohak Hill, above the still river at Kan-i-Gil, which is known as the Ab-i-Rahmat River, a garden called Naqsh-i-Jahan was constructed. When I saw it the garden was in ruins, nothing more than

Detail of the facade of the Friday mosque of Temür.

a name remained. To the south of Samarkand near the fortress is the Bagh-i-Chanar; on the lower side of Samarkand are the Bagh-i-Shimal and the Bagh-i-Bihisht.[105] Temür Beg's grandson, Jahangir Mirza's son Muhammad-Sultan Mirza, had a *madrasa*[106] constructed in the gateway to the outer wall of Samarkand. The tombs of Temür Beg and all of his descendants who ruled Samarkand are there.

Of Ulughbeg Mirza's buildings inside the walls of Samarkand are a madrasa and a *khanaqah*.[107] The dome over the khanaqah is huge—few domes in the world are so large. Near the madrasa and khanaqah is a beautiful bathhouse known as the Mirza's Bath. It is paved in all sorts of stone. In all of Khurasan and Samarkand no such bath is known to exist. [46b] To the south of the madrasa was constructed a mosque called the Muqatta' Mosque, because many little pieces of wood are carved in floral and geometric patterns.[108] All the walls and ceiling are in this style. The kiblah of this mosque differs greatly from that of the madrasa, probably because the kiblah of Muqatta' was determined astronomically.[109]

Another superb building on Kohak Hill is the observatory, which is an instrument for compiling astronomical tables. It is three stories tall. Ulughbeg Mirza used this observatory to compile the *Zij-i-Gurkani*, which is the table used throughout the world now, others being little used.[110] Prior to it the *Zij-i-Ilkhani*, which was done by Khwaja Nasir Tusi in Maragha in the time of Hülägü Khan, was current.[111] It was Hülägü Khan who was called the Ilkhan.

Probably not more than seven or eight observatories have been constructed in the whole world. One was made for the Caliph Ma'mun, for whom the *Zij-i-Ma'muni* was compiled. Another was made by Ptolemy.[112] Another, currently in use by the Hindus, was compiled in India in the time of Raja Vikramaditya the Hindu in Ujjain and Dhar, which is the kingdom of Malwa, now known as Mandu. Compiled [47] 1,584 years ago, it is the least complete of all these catalogues.[113]

On the western side of Kohak Hill was constructed a garden called Bagh-i-Maydan, in the middle of which was built a superb building called Chil Sutun,[114] two stories high with columns of stone. On its four towers are raised four towers, like minarets, through which are the passageways to the top. In all other places there are columns of stone, some fluted in spirals, and on the four sides of the upper story are porticos with columns of stone. In the middle is a *chardara*.[115] The building's plinth is paved in stone. Going from this building toward Kohak Hill is another small garden where yet another portico was built. Inside the portico was placed a large stone slab—approximately fourteen or fifteen yards long, seven or eight yards wide, and a yard thick—brought from a great distance. In the middle is a crack that people say developed after the stone was brought here. In this same small garden is a chardara, called the Chinikhana, [47b] with porcelain all around the dado. Someone was sent to Cathay to bring the porcelain. Inside the Samarkand city wall is yet another ancient building called the Laqlaqa Mosque.[116] If one stamps in a certain place under the middle of the dome, the whole dome reverberates with a clacking sound. No one knows the secret behind this strange phenomenon.

During the time of Sultan-Ahmad Mirza, men of high rank and low constructed many gardens, large and small. For pleasure, good air, and superb vista, few are like Darwesh Muhammad Tarkhan's charbagh. It is situated below the Bagh-i-Maydan on a rise overlooking the Qolba Meadow, so that the entire meadow lies stretched out below it. Planted in straight lines in the charbagh are beautiful ornamental trees, cypresses, and poplars. It is a truly magnificent spot, the only flaw being the lack of a great stream.

The city of Samarkand is an amazingly ornamented city. One peculiarity here is found in few other cities: every trade has a separate market, and they are not commingled. This is a wonderful custom. There are excellent bakeries and cook shops. The best paper in the world comes from Samarkand. The water for the paper factories comes from the beautiful Kan-i-Gil Meadow, beside which is a still water, [48] the Qara Su, which is also called Ab-i-Rahmat. Another product of Samarkand is red velvet, which is exported everywhere.

All around the city are exquisite meadows, including the famous Kan-i-Gil, one league to the east and slightly to the north of the city. The Qara Su, a seven- or eight-mill stream, which is also called Ab-i-Rahmat, flows through it. Beside the river are reservoirs.[117] Some say that the original name of this meadow was Kan-i-Abgir, but in histories it is always called Kan-i-Gil. The rulers of Samarkand have always made this meadow a protected reserve and come out every year to stay for a month or two.

Higher up, to the southeast, is another meadow, the Khan Yurtï, which is one league to the east of Samarkand. The still river that flows through it before reaching Kan-i-Gil makes such a twisting course that there is sufficient room for an army to camp. The exit is extremely narrow. Seeing the advantage of this place, we camped here for a time while besieging Samarkand.

Another meadow is [48b] the Bödänä Qorughï, between the Dilgusha garden and Samarkand. Another, fabulous meadow is the Lake Mughak meadow, nearly two leagues to the west and slightly to the north of Samarkand. On one side is a lake, for which reason it is called the Lake Mughak meadow. During the siege of Samarkand, while I stayed in Khan Yurtï, Sultan-Ali Mirza stayed there.

Another, fairly small one is the Qolba Meadow. North of it is Qolba village and the Kohak River, to the south is the Bagh-i-Maydan and Darwesh Muhammad Tarkhan's charbagh, and to the east is Kohak Hill.

The province of Samarkand, Transoxiana, has excellent districts and subdistricts. The largest district comparable to the city of Samarkand is Bukhara, twenty-five leagues to the west of Samarkand, which also has subdistricts. It is a fantastic city with abundant and good fruit. In all Transoxiana no melons are so abundant and good as those of Bukhara. Although a melon called *mirtimuri* comes from Akhsi in Fergana province that is sweeter and has thinner rind than the Bukhara melon, nonetheless all sorts of excellent melons are to be found in Bukhara.[118] Bukhara plums are famous and without equal. Dried plums with the skins removed are taken from province to province as presents. [49] Medicinally they are effective laxatives. There are many domestic fowl and geese there. Throughout Transoxiana no wine is stronger than Bukhara wines. When I first drank in Samarkand, I drank Bukhara wines.

Another is the district of Kish, which is nine leagues to the south of Samarkand. Between Samarkand and Kish is Itmäk Dabanï, a mountain that is the source of all the stone used by stone carvers in the area. Since the countryside, city, roofs, and walls all turn beautifully green in the spring, the town is also called Shahrisabz.[119] Temür Beg, who was born and raised in Kish, endeavored to make it his capital and had superb buildings constructed there. For his own use as court he built a large *peshtaq*[120] with two smaller peshtaqs on either side for the divan begs and *tovachi*[121] begs to hold court in. On every wall of this *divankhana*[122] he made many little arches for plaintiffs at court to sit in.

Few such superb arches can be pointed out in the world. They say that it is more splendid than Chosroës' Arch.[123] Temür Beg also built a madrasa and tomb in Kish. Jahangir Mirza and some of his other descendants are buried there. [49b] Since Kish did not have the capacity to become the city that Samarkand did, in the end Temür Beg chose Samarkand as his capital.

Another is the district of Karshi, which is also called Nasaf and Nakhshab. Karshi is the Mongolian term for tomb. This name probably came about after Genghis Khan's domination. It is a place with little water, but the spring is nice. The sown crops and the melons are good. It is eighteen leagues south of Samarkand and slightly to the west. A little bird there rather like the sand grouse is called *qil quyruq*. Because there is no end to these birds in Karshi, in that region they call it a Karshi bird.

Others are the district of Khuzar and the district of Karminiyya, which is between Samarkand and Bukhara. Another is the district of Karakul, the farthest downstream of all, seven leagues northwest of Bukhara.

Samarkand has excellent subdistricts. Among them are Sughd and its adjacent subdistricts. From Yar Yaylagh all the way to Bukhara there is not a league in which there is not a village or cultivated land. It is well known that Temür Beg said, "I have a garden thirty leagues long"—by which he meant these subdistricts.

Another is the subdistrict of Shavdar, adjacent to the city and suburbs of Samarkand. It is a really excellent subdistrict. It is bounded on one side by a mountain situated between Samarkand and Shahrisabz. [50] The villages are mostly on the slopes of this mountain. On the other side it is bounded by the Kohak River. It is a beautiful subdistrict with a pleasing climate and abundant water and inexpensive produce. Travelers who have seen Egypt and Syria cannot point to its equal. Although Transoxiana has other subdistricts, they are not like the ones mentioned, so these will suffice.

Temür Beg gave the governorship of Samarkand to Jahangir Mirza. After Jahangir Mirza's death he assigned it to Jahangir's eldest son, Muhammad-Sultan. Shahrukh Mirza bestowed the whole province of Transoxiana upon his eldest son, Ulughbeg Mirza. Ulughbeg Mirza's son Abdul-Latif Mirza seized it from him, and for the sake of this transitory world he martyred his own learned and aged father. The chronogram for Ulughbeg Mirza's death has been excellently found in the following:

> Ulughbeg, ocean of knowledge and wisdom, by whom the world and religion were supported, quaffed the draught of martyrdom from Abbas, and his chronogram became "Killed by Abbas."[124]

Abdul-Latif Mirza ruled no more than five or six months, as the famous line says,

> A patricide is unworthy of kingship, and even if he be worthy he will not last six months.

Abdul-Latif too has an excellent chronogram:

> Abdul-Latif, a Chosroës as splendid as Jamshed, [50b] among whose slaves were numbered Faridun and Zoroaster, was shot by Baba Husayn on Friday. Write this as his chronogram: "Baba Husayn killed him."[125]

After Abdul-Latif Mirza, Abdullah Mirza, who was Shahrukh Mirza's grandson, Ibrahim-Sultan Mirza's son, and Ulughbeg's son-in-law, took the throne. He ruled for a year-and-a-half, or nearly two years. After him Sultan-Abusa'id Mirza took Samarkand. During his lifetime he gave it to his eldest son, Sultan-Ahmad Mirza, who ruled as padishah after Sultan-Abusa'id Mirza's death. When Sultan-Ahmad Mirza died, Sultan-Mahmud Mirza took the throne of Samarkand, and after him, Baysunghur Mirza was made padishah. During the Tarkhan revolt[126] Baysunghur Mirza was seized and his younger brother, Sultan-Ali Mirza, was enthroned for a day or two, but Baysunghur Mirza regained it, as has been mentioned in this history. From Baysunghur Mirza, I took Samarkand. Other information will be given for subsequent events.

As soon as I took the throne of Samarkand, I reconfirmed the begs of Samarkand in the favor and estates they had formerly enjoyed. I also promoted and awarded the begs who had been with us according to their status. [51] Of them all, Sultan-Ahmad Tambal was shown the greatest favor. He had been in the circle of ichkis but was promoted to the circle of great lords.

Upon taking Samarkand with great difficulty after seven months of siege, when we first entered the city some booty had fallen to the people of the army. With the one exception of Samarkand, all the province had joined either me or Sultan-Ali Mirza. It was not possible to attack the areas that had already joined. How too was it possible to take anything from the districts that had already suffered such pillage and plunder? The booty the army had taken came to an end. When I took Samarkand, the city was in such distress that it needed assistance, seed, and monetary advances. What then was anyone to take from it? For these reasons the army suffered penury. We were in no position to give them anything. Thinking of their homes, they began to desert one by one and two by two. The first to desert was Khan-Quli Buyan-Quli, and then Ibrahim Begchik. The Moghuls all deserted. Later even Sultan-Ahmad Tambal deserted.

To quell this mutiny, we sent Khwaja Qazi, of whom Uzun Hasan considered himself a great devotee, [51b] to come to an agreement with Uzun Hasan to punish some of the deserters and send others back to us. After all, it was the ingrate Uzun Hasan who had stirred up the revolt and instigated the deserters to act so foully. They all took up an openly bad attitude after Sultan-Ahmad Tambal left.

During these several years while we had been leading the army in all earnestness to conquer Samarkand, no substantive assistance was forthcoming from Sultan-Mahmud Khan. But after Samarkand was taken he began to have designs on Andizhan. At that point, when most of the army and Moghuls had deserted and gone to Andizhan and Akhsi, Uzun Hasan and Tambal had designs on that province for Jahangir Mirza. It was impossible for several reasons that they be given it. One was that even if the province had not actually been promised to the khan, he still claimed it; it would be necessary to come to an agreement with him if it were to be given to Jahangir Mirza. With the people deserting and going to that province, he was also claiming it out of arrogance. If this subject had been broached before, [52] there would have been a good reason for it. But who could tolerate his impertinence? What Moghuls there were, the Andizhan regiment, and some of the begs and ichkis too had gone to Andizhan. In Samarkand around a thousand men all told were left with me.

Since circumstances did not turn out the way Uzun Hasan and Sultan-Ahmad Tambal had thought they would, they summoned the people who had deserted and attached them to themselves. This was what the cowards in their fear had been hoping for. They led the army from Akhsi to Andizhan and openly asserted their rebellion and hostility.

Tolun Khwaja was one of the valiant fighting men of the Barin tribe. My father, Umar-Shaykh Mirza, had favored him, and he was still very much in favor. I had promoted him to beg status. He was a phenomenally valiant and bold warrior and deserved commendation. Because Tolun Khwaja was our most reliable man among the Moghuls, when the Moghul people began to desert from Samarkand he was sent to advise them and calm their apprehension lest they do something foolish out of fear. [52b] These ingrates and sowers of strife had put the Moghuls in such a state that no amount of promises, advice, or threats was of any avail. Tolun Khwaja's march lay through Iki Su Arasï, which is also known as Rabatak Orchin. Uzun Hasan and Sultan-Ahmad Tambal sent a detachment to attack Tolun Khwaja. They took him by surprise, seized him, and killed him. Uzun Hasan and Tambal then took Jahangir and laid siege to Andizhan.

THE SIEGE OF ANDIZHAN

When the army rode out for Samarkand, Ali-Dost Taghayï had been stationed in Andizhan, and Uzun Hasan in Akhsi. Later Khwaja Qazi had gone too. Many warriors had left Samarkand. At the beginning of the siege Khwaja Qazi, in a show of support for me, distributed eighteen thousand sheep to the warriors in the fortress and to the families of the warriors who were with us. Letters arrived constantly from my mother and her people and Khwaja Qazi saying, "They have us under siege. If you do not come help us, it will be all over. Samarkand was taken through the strength of Andizhan. [53] If Andizhan is held, and God wills, Samarkand can be taken." Letters of this import came one after another.

Just then I fell ill. I recovered, but I was unable to take proper care of myself during convalescence and had a relapse. This time I was so critically ill that I could not speak for four days and they had to dribble water into my mouth from a piece of cotton. The brave warriors remaining with me despaired of my life and began to make their own plans. At this juncture the begs showed bad judgment and, before giving him leave to depart, showed me to Uzun Hasan's liege man, who had come as emissary with absurd proposals. Four or five days later my condition was a bit better, but I still had difficulty in speaking. Several days after that I was back to my old self.

With such letters coming from my mother and her mother, Esän Dawlat Begim, and also from my master and guide, Khwaja Mawlana Qazi, making such earnest pleas, how could one have the heart to stand idle?

On a Saturday in the month of Rajab [March 1498] we left Samarkand for Andizhan. This time [53b] I had ruled as padishah in Samarkand for one hundred days. It was the next Saturday by the time we reached Khodzhent. That same day someone brought news from Andizhan that seven days before, that is, the day we left Samarkand, Ali-Dost Taghayï had turned the Andizhan fortress over to the enemy. The details are as follows:

When the enemy laid siege to the Andizhan fortress, Uzun Hasan's liege man, who had been shown me in my illness before being given permission to withdraw, went and said to them, "The padishah is unable to speak and water is being dribbled into his mouth with a piece of cotton." He went to Ali-Dost at the Khakan Gate and swore that the report was true. Hearing this news, he lost his nerve, summoned the enemy, came to terms with them, and turned over the fortress. Of supplies and fighting men there was no lack in the fortress. It was a result of that hypocritical turncoat's unmanliness, but he used the report just mentioned as an excuse for what he did.

After Andizhan was taken and they heard that I had come to Khodzhent, they disgracefully martyred Khwaja Mawlana Qazi at the citadel gate. [54] Khwaja Qazi's name was Abdullah, but he had become known as Mawlana Qazi. On his father's side he was descended from Shaykh Burhanuddin Qilich, and on his mother's from Sultan Elig Mazi. The family had become religious leaders, shaykhu'l-islams, and cadis in Fergana. Khwaja Qazi was a disciple of Khwaja Ubaydullah's and had been trained by him. Of Khwaja Qazi's being a saint I have no doubt. What better proves his sainthood than that within a short time there was no trace left of those who had him killed? Khwaja Qazi was remarkable, he knew no fear. No one so bold has ever been seen. His bravery, too, indicates his sainthood, for no matter how valiant other people may be, they still have a touch of apprehension and fear. The Khwaja, however, had absolutely none. After his death the people who were attached to him—liege men, servants, tribes, and clans—were all seized and plundered.

We had lost Samarkand for the sake of Andizhan, and now Andizhan too was lost. Taken unawares, we were, as the saying goes, "driven from pillar to post." It was hard to deal with because as long as I had been padishah I had not been separated in such a way from my subjects and realm. [54b] I had never known such pain or distress.

No sooner had we come to Khodzhent than some hypocrites who could not endure seeing Khalifa at my gate had prevailed upon Muhammad-Husayn Mirza and some others to have Khalifa dismissed to Tashkent. Qasim Beg had already been sent to the khan in Tashkent to ask for help in attacking Andizhan. The khan had led his army out through the Ahangaran valley and was camped at the base of the Kindirlig Pass when I went out from Khodzhent to see my uncle the khan. We went through the pass and camped on the Akhsi side. From there the enemy gathered what forces they had and came to Akhsi.

At that time the Pap fortress opted for me and made fast the fort, but because of something amiss in the khan's advance, the enemy stormed the fortress and took it. The khan was a man of moral character, but when it came to soldiering and commanding he had little merit. It was so close that if he had made one more march the province would almost certainly have been taken without a fight, but at such a point he chose to listen to the wily words of the enemy and initiate peace talks [55] by sending Khwaja Abu'l-Makarim and Tambal's elder brother Beg Telbä, who was then lord of the khan's gate, as emissaries. To save themselves, Tambal and Hasan mingled truth and falsehood in what they said and agreed to pay bribes to the khan or the intermediaries. With this the khan pulled back.

The families of most of the begs, ichkis, and warriors who remained with me were in Andizhan. Having despaired of taking Andizhan, begs and warriors all, some seven or eight hundred of them, deserted me. Among those who deserted were Ali Darwesh Beg, Ali Mazid Qauchin, Muhammad Baqir Beg, Shaykh Abdullah Eshik-aqa, and Mirim Laghari. Those who remained with me, opting for exile and deprivation, were something more than two hundred but less than three hundred all told. Among the begs were Qasim Qauchin Beg, Ways Laghari Beg, Ibrahim Saru Mïnglïgh Beg, Sherim Taghayï, and Sidi Qara Beg. Among the ichkis were Mir Shah Qauchin, Sayyid Qasim Eshik-aqa Jalayir, Qasim Ajab, Ali-Dost Taghayï's Muhammad-Dost, Muhammad Ali Mubashshir, Khudaberdi Tughchï Moghul, Yarak Taghayï, Baba-Qulï's Sultan-Qulï, Pir Ways, Shaykh Ways, [55b] Yar-Ali Bilal, Qasim Mirakhur, and Haydar Rikabdar.

It was difficult for me. I wept involuntarily. From there I went to Khodzhent, where my mother and grandmother were sent to me with the families of those who remained with me.

That Ramadan [April–May 1498] was spent in Khodzhent. I sent someone to Sultan-Mahmud Khan to ask for help and then mounted to attack Samarkand. Assigning his son Sultan-Muhammad Khanika and Ahmad Beg along with four or five thousand soldiers to go against Samarkand, the khan himself rode as far as Ura-Tyube. I saw the khan there and then set out against Samarkand via Yar Yaylagh. Sultan-Muhammad and Ahmad Beg had already reached Yar Yaylagh by a different route. I came to Börkä Yaylagh and Sanzar, which is the prefecture fortress of Yar Yaylagh. However, when Sultan-Muhammad Sultan and Ahmad Beg learned that Shaybani Khan was raiding Shiraz and that area, they turned back. I too was forced to return to Khodzhent.

When one has pretensions to rule and a desire for conquest, one cannot sit back and just watch if events don't go right once or twice. Thinking of advancing upon Andizhan, I went to Tashkent to ask the khan for assistance. [56] I had not seen Shah Begim or the family for seven or eight years. Upon this pretext I went to see them. Several days later they assigned Sayyid Muhammad Mirza Dughlat, Ayyub Begchik, and Jan Hasan Barin with a force of seven or eight hundred to help us. Taking this assistance and without stopping in Khodzhent, we rode straight through, putting Kanibadam to our left, set up our ladders by night, and took by stealth the Nasukh fortress, which is ten leagues from Khodzhent and three leagues from Kanibadam.

It was melon season. In Nasukh is a kind of melon called Isma'il-Shaykhi. It has a yellow skin as soft as glove leather, seeds like an apple's, and flesh four fingers thick: it is amazingly delicious. There are no other melons like it in those parts.

The next morning the Moghul begs said, "Our men are few. What's to be gained by taking this one fort?" In truth it was so. Finding that it was not in our interests to stay there or to hold the fort, we withdrew to Khodzhent.

KHUSRAWSHAH AND BAYSUNGHUR MIRZA TAKE HISSAR FROM SULTAN-MAS'UD MIRZA

That same year, Khusrawshah and Baysunghur Mirza led their forces to Chaghanian and deceitfully and treacherously sent an emissary to Sultan-Mas'ud Mirza to say, [56b] "Come, advance upon Samarkand. If Samarkand is conquered, one mirza will rule in Samarkand and another in Hissar." Sultan-Mas'ud Mirza's begs, ichkis, and warriors had been offended by him because Shaykh Abdullah Barlas, being the mirza's father-in-law, had been disproportionately favored when he left Baysunghur Mirza for Sultan-Mas'ud Mirza. Although Hissar is a poor and small province, his allowance was set at ten million *fulus*[127] and he was given outright the province of Khuttalan, in which were the fiefs of many of Sultan-Mas'ud Mirza's begs and ichkis. Shaykh Abdullah took control of the whole, and he and his sons also managed the office of the gate in all matters large and small. Those who were thus angered began to desert to Baysunghur Mirza.

Since Sultan-Mas'ud Mirza was caught off guard by Khusrawshah and Baysunghur's deceptive message, they galloped out of Chaghanian and took the Hissar fortress at dawn. At the time, Sultan-Mas'ud Mirza was outside the fortress in the suburbs in a building his father had built called the Dawlatsara. Unable to get into the fortress, he fled with Shaykh Abdullah Barlas for Khuttalan. He parted from Shaykh Abdullah Barlas along the way, crossed the Oxus at the Aivadzh ford, and went to Sultan-Husayn Mirza. [57] As soon as Hissar was taken, Khusrawshah enthroned Baysunghur Mirza in Hissar, gave Khuttalan to his brother Wali, and a few days later rode out with the intention of attacking Balkh. He sent ahead his great liege man Nazar Bahadur with three or four thousand men to the vicinity of Balkh, and three or four days later took Baysunghur Mirza and laid siege to Balkh, where Ibrahim-Husayn Mirza and many of Sultan-Husayn Mirza's begs were. Khusrawshah attached a large force to his brother Wali and dispatched him to assail Sheberghan and plunder those regions. Wali went but was unable to fulfill his mission, so he sent the forces he had to raid the people and tribes in Zardak Chöl. There he attacked, bringing back more than one hundred thousand sheep and nearly three thousand camels. Wali then raided and plundered the San-u-Charyak province, took prisoner some of the people holed up in the mountain, and joined his brother in Balkh.

One day while Khusrawshah was besieging Balkh, he sent Nazar Bahadur, his liege man, who has already been mentioned, to destroy the Balkh water channels. One of the defenders, Tengriberdi [57b] Samanchï, Sultan-Husayn Mirza's greatly favored beg, sallied forth with seventy or eighty warriors, faced Nazar Bahadur, struck him down, cut off his head, and went back into the fortress. He performed valiantly and did an outstanding deed.

REBELLIONS AGAINST SULTAN·HUSAYN MIRZA

In this same year Sultan-Husayn Mirza led his forces to Bust to repel Zu'n-Nun Arghun and his son Shah-Shuja'. These two had become retainers of Badi'uzzaman Mirza, given him a daughter in marriage, and taken up a position hostile to Sultan-Husayn. Camped in Bust, the army was receiving no grain from any direction and was close to giving up from hunger when the prefect of Bust surrendered the fort. With the help of the supplies in Bust, Sultan-Husayn returned to Khurasan.

When a great padishah like Sultan-Husayn Mirza, with so much equipment and paraphernalia, led his army several times against Konduz, Hissar, and Kandahar and was unable to take them, his sons and officers were emboldened to rebel and sow strife. In the spring Sultan-Husayn Mirza dispatched a large force of begs led by Muhammad Wali Beg to put down his son Muzaffar-Husayn Mirza, who had taken control of Astarabad and was in rebellion. He himself was camped in Nishin Meadow when Badi'uzzaman Mirza and Zu'n-Nun's son Shah Beg [58] took him by surprise. Fortuitously Sultan-Mas'ud Mirza, who had lost Hissar and was coming to Sultan-Husayn Mirza, arrived that very day. The army on its way to Astarabad also arrived that day and joined him. As soon as the armies faced each other, Badi'uzzaman Mirza and Shah Beg realized that they were not up to battle and fled.

Sultan-Husayn Mirza received Sultan-Mas'ud Mirza well, had him kneel before him as son-in-law, and was showing him every favor when Sultan-Mas'ud Mirza was instigated by Khusrawshah's younger brother Baqi Chaghaniani, who had joined Sultan-Husayn Mirza's retinue before this, to make some pretext about not being able to stay in Khurasan and left without Sultan-Husayn Mirza's permission to go to Khusrawshah.

Khusrawshah summoned Baysunghur Mirza from Hissar. At the same time, Miranshah Mirza rebelled against his father, Ulughbeg Mirza, and joined the Hazaras. Because of some indiscretion he was unable to remain among the Hazaras, so he too went to Khusrawshah. Some shortsighted people were of the opinion that all three princes should be killed and the khutba read in Khusrawshah's name. He did not deem it wise to go that far, but this treacherous little man did seize Sultan-Mas'ud Mirza, [58b] whom he had taken care of and raised from childhood, whose beg atäkä he was, and, for the sake of this transitory world, which not only proved faithless to him but will also prove faithless to everyone, had him blinded with the needle.

Some of his own kükäldashes, personal servants, and retainers went with Sultan-Mas'ud Mirza to Kish, thinking they would take him to Sultan-Ali Mirza in Samarkand. However, Sultan-Ali Mirza's party also had evil intentions, so they fled from Kish, crossed the Oxus at the Chardzhu ford, and went to Sultan-Husayn Mirza.

A hundred thousand curses upon anyone who performs or has performed such a despicable act! Until the dawn of doomsday let anyone who hears of the deeds of Khusrawshah curse him! Anyone who hears of this and does not curse him deserves to be cursed himself!

After this detestable act, Khusrawshah made Baysunghur Mirza padishah and gave him leave to go to Hissar. He assigned Sayyid Kamil to help Miranshah Mirza and sent them off to Bamian.

EVENTS OF THE YEAR 904
(1498-99)[128]

We had repeatedly gone out of Khodzhent to Samarkand and Andizhan and returned without accomplishing anything. Khodzhent is a miserable place. A man with a couple of hundred liege men would have a hard time there. [59] How could someone with greater ambitions sit around as a spectator?

BABUR LEAVES KHODZHENT
FOR PISHAGAR

In furtherance of our ambition to wage another Samarkand campaign, we sent men to talk with Muhammad-Husayn Kürägän Dughlat in Ura-Tyube. We requested him to lend us Pishagar to stay in over the winter so that we might return to Samarkand when the opportunity presented itself. (Pishagar is a village in Yar Yaylagh that had belonged to Khwaja Ahrar, but during the recent periods of instability it had come into Muhammad-Husayn Kürägän's possession.) Muhammad-Husayn Mirza agreed, and we set out from Khodzhent for Pishagar.

When we reached Zaamin, I came down with a fever. Despite my illness, we galloped from Zaamin across the mountain road to Rabat-i-Khwaja, the prefecture of Shavdar district, to take the fortress by surprise. We arrived at dawn, but the people had already learned of our approach, so we withdrew and went back to Pishagar without stopping. Without respite from my fever, I had traversed a difficult, laborious road of thirteen or fourteen leagues.

Several days later we assigned Ibrahim Saru, Ways Laghari, and Sherim Taghayï, with some ichki begs and warriors, to capture the fortresses of Yar Yaylagh by either parlay or force. [59b] Sayyid Yusuf Beg was then in Yar Yaylagh. He had remained behind when I left Samarkand and had been patronized by Sultan-Ali Mirza. To manage the forts of Yar Yaylagh, Sayyid Yusuf Beg had sent his younger brother and his son. Ahmad Yusuf, who at present holds the governorship of Sialkot, was in the forts. Our begs and warriors spent the entire winter winning control of them—some forts they acquired by treaty, some by battle and force, and some by stealth and subterfuge. Because of the Moghuls and Uzbeks, not a single village in that region is without a fort. During that time, Sultan-Ali Mirza became suspicious of Sayyid Yusuf, his brother, and his son's dealings with us and dismissed them to Khurasan.

That winter passed in such a tug-o'-war. When summer came Khwaja Yahya was sent to sue for peace. Sultan-Ali Mirza himself went, at the army's urging, to Shiraz and Kabud. The soldiers we had with us were between two and three hundred, and had powerful enemies on every side. When we roamed around Andizhan, the stars gave no assistance. When we raised our hand against Samarkand, nothing was accomplished. Of necessity we made a truce and returned to Pishagar. [60]

Khodzhent is a miserable place—even a beg would have a hard time there. We were there for nearly half a year with all our families and dependents. The good people, during that time, insofar as they were able, spared no expense and shirked no duty. With what honor could I go back to Khodzhent? And if we did go to Khodzhent, what were we to do? "No home to go to, no safe place to stay."

In the end we left with great trepidation for the summer pastures south of Ura-Tyube. For some time we wandered perplexed, not knowing where to go or where to stay. One day, Khwaja Abu'l-Makarim, an exile like ourselves, came to see me; he sought to ascertain from us where we would go, where we would stay, and what we intended to do. He became quite touched and, feeling sorry for us, recited the Fatiha and left. I too was touched and pitied him.

MARGILAN RECOVERED

In the late afternoon of that very day a rider appeared at the foot of the valley. It was Ali-Dost Taghayï's liege man, Yolchuq. He had been sent to deliver this message: "If grave faults have been committed by me, I am yet hopeful that you will show favor and forgive my shortcomings. [60b] If you will come hither I will turn over Margilan and serve you humbly. My sin will be washed clean and I will be delivered of my shame."

When this news arrived in the midst of such perplexity and indecision, I set out immediately, without thought or hesitation, just as the sun was setting, and galloped to Margilan, which was approximately twenty-four or twenty-five leagues from the place we were. I rode, without stopping, all night and through the morning until noon the next day, when I stopped at Tang Ab, a village in Khodzhent. We let our horses cool down and gave them some food, then rode out of Tang Ab at midnight at the time of the drums. All that night, all the next day, and all the following night we rode until, coming within a league of Margilan just before dawn, Ways Beg and some others hesitated and said, "Do you realize what an untrustworthy person Ali-Dost is? With what assurance are we to proceed, seeing that no intermediaries have come or gone, no deliberations held, no pacts made?" In truth their hesitation was not out of place. We halted and held council. Finally it was decided that although their hesitation was for good reason, [61] it should have been thought about before. We had now traveled twenty-four or twenty-five leagues in three days and nights without rest. Neither the horses nor the men could go any farther. How could we turn back from here? If we did, where were we to go? Having come this far, we might as well continue. Nothing happens without God's will. Deciding thus, we put our trust in God and moved out.

The sun was high when I came to the gate of the Margilan fortress. Ali-Dost Taghayï stood behind the unopened gate and asked for terms. These granted, he opened the gate and made obeisance. After I held an interview with Ali-Dost we were shown to quarters in a suitable place inside the walled town. I had with me 240 men, all told.

Uzun Hasan and Sultan-Ahmad Tambal had perpetrated much injustice on the people of the province and been harsh, so the people were desirous of me. Two or three days after entering Margilan, we attached to Qasim Beg more than one hundred of the Pishagaris, those who had newly joined our retinue, and Ali-Dost Beg's men and sent them to the mountain folk to the south of Andizhan, [61b] such as Ashparian, Turuq Sharan, Chakrak, and those regions, to recruit them either with enticements or by force. Ibrahim Saru, Ways Laghari, and Sidi Qara were sent with nearly one hundred men toward Akhsi to cross the river at Khodzhent and win over, by whatever means, the mountain people and fortresses on that side of the river.

A few days later Uzun Hasan and Sultan-Ahmad Tambal took Jahangir Mirza, gathered what forces and Moghuls they had, mustered as many troops as possible from Andizhan and Akhsi, and, intent upon laying siege to Margilan, came to Supan, a village one league to the east of Margilan. A day or two later they arrived, armed and in battle array, on the outskirts of Margilan. Since Qasim Beg and the troops under Ibrahim Saru and Ways Laghari had been sent out in two directions, only a few men remained with me. What warriors there were set forth in array and kept the enemy from proceeding past the outlying districts. That day Khalil Chuhra Dastarpech went out and did valiant combat. The enemy came on but was unable to accomplish anything. They did not get close to the fortress again. [62]

Thanks to Qasim Beg, who had gone to the mountains to the south of Andizhan, the peasants and tribesmen in the hills and lowlands of Ashparian, Turuq Sharan, Chakrak, and those regions joined us. Soldiers from the enemy camp also began to desert and come over to us one by one and two by two. The Pap fortress and two others joined the troops under Ibrahim Saru and Ways Laghari that had gone to the Akhsi side of the river.

Uzun Hasan and Tambal were tyrannical, debauched, and heathenish men. The peasantry and people of the province had been reduced to misery by them. A group under Hasan Degcha, a notable of Akhsi, and a band of ruffians and rabble had taken clubs and driven into the citadel those who were in the outer fortress of Akhsi. They then summoned the troops led by Ibrahim Saru, Ways Laghari, and Sidi Qara and let them into the Akhsi outer fort.

Sultan-Mahmud Khan had assigned to us as auxiliaries Haydar Kükäldash's son Banda-Ali, Hajji Ghazi Manghït, who had recently deserted Shaybani Khan and joined the khan, and the Barin tümän and its begs. They arrived just then.

When Uzun Hasan learned this news he went to pieces and assigned his favorite liege men [62b] and bold warriors to help the Akhsi citadel. They arrived at the riverbank at dawn. When our and the Moghul forces learned of their approach, they had a contingent of men strip their horses and cross the river. In confusion the troops who had come to help began to shoot arrows from the place they had crossed without pulling their boat farther upstream. Unable to traverse to the fort, they floated downstream. Our troops and the Moghul forces, who had stripped their horses, began to pour down from all sides. Those in the boat could not fight at all. Qarlughach Bakhshï called out one of Moghul Beg's sons, grabbed his hand, and killed him with a blow. What was the use? It was too late for such deeds. This action caused most of those in the boat to go to their deaths. Instantly they made a clean sweep of those who were in the river and put them to death. Among Uzun Hasan's highest-ranking men were Qarlughach Bakhshï, Khalil Dewana, and the slave Qazi: of these only Qazi escaped on the excuse of being a slave. Also among his high-ranking warriors were Sayyid Ali, who is now of importance in my service, Haydar-Qulï, and Qulka Kashghari. Of seventy or eighty valiant warriors only these five or six escaped. [63]

Unable to remain in the Margilan region after hearing of this debacle, the men decamped in disarray in the direction of Andizhan. There they left Nasir Beg, Uzun Hasan's sister's husband. If he was not Uzun Hasan's second, there is no question that he was his third. He was an experienced man of valor. When he learned the particulars and realized that they had no ground upon which to stand, he made fast the Andizhan fortress and sent someone to me.

When Uzun and Tambal reached Andizhan and discovered that the fortress was shut tight against them, they could come to no agreement, so Uzun Hasan took himself off in disarray to his family in Akhsi. Sultan-Ahmad Tambal went to his own province of Osh. A few ichkis and warriors took Jahangir Mirza from Uzun Hasan and fled to join Tambal, who had not yet reached Osh.

ANDIZHAN RECOVERED

I received news that Andizhan had been made fast. I left Margilan as the sun was rising and rode without stopping to Andizhan, arriving at noon. I saw Nasir Beg and his sons Dost Beg and Mirim Beg and gave them reason to be hopeful of my favor. In Dhu'l-Qaʻda of the year 904 [June–July 1499] my father's province, [63b] which had been lost for nearly two years, was once more conquered and subdued.

Sultan-Ahmad Tambal had gone off with Jahangir Mirza to Osh, but as soon as he entered the town, the rabble took up clubs and cudgels and drove him out. Then they sent someone to inform us that they were holding the fortress in our name. Jahangir Mirza, Tambal, and a few others went off in total confusion to Uzgen.

Intelligence was received that Uzun Hasan, unable to enter Andizhan, had gone to Akhsi and entered the citadel there. Since he was the leader of the rebellion, we set out for Akhsi as soon as we heard, stopping not more than four or five days in Andizhan. When we reached Akhsi, he could do nothing but sue for quarter and turn over the fortress.

We stayed in Akhsi a few days to arrange affairs in Akhsi, Kassan, and that side of the river and dismissed the Moghul begs who had come to help. Uzun Hasan and his family and dependents were taken to Andizhan, and Qasim Ajab, a member of the ichki circle who had been promoted to beg in my service, was left in temporary command in Akhsi.

Since a promise had been made to Uzun Hasan that no harm would be done to him or his property, he was given leave to go by the Karategin road. [64] He went with a few people to Hissar. All his other liege men left him and stayed behind. These were the very ones who had seized and plundered the people who belonged to us and to Khwaja Qazi during the interregnum. I agreed with some of the begs, who said, "It was this group who wrought such havoc and destruction and seized and plundered the good believers who were dependent upon us. Have they been so faithful to their own lords that they would be faithful to us? What harm would there be in our seizing them? Especially since we saw them with our own eyes mounting our own horses, putting on our own clothes, and eating our own sheep. Who could endure such a thing? If you have compassion on them and do not allow them to be seized or plundered, at least let there be an order that the goods recognizably belonging to those who were with us during the rencontres and troubles be returned. If they are let go with just this much, they will have reason to be grateful."

That certainly seemed reasonable. It was ordered that those who had been with us should take what possessions they could identify. Although this action was justified, it was a bit hasty. There was no sense in frightening these people away while a pest like Jahangir Mirza was sitting next door. [64b] In taking realms and administering kingdoms, although some things appear rational on the surface, one has to consider a hundred thousand things behind every act. From our issuing this order without reflection, how much contention and strife arose! In the end this one ill-considered command resulted in our having to leave Andizhan a second time, and for that reason the Moghuls allowed themselves to act out of fear and apprehension to move through Rabatak Orchin (also called Iki Su Arasï) toward Uzgen and send someone to Tambal.

My mother had fifteen hundred to two thousand of the Moghul nation with her. An equal number of Moghuls had come from Hissar with Hamza Sultan, Mahdi Sultan, and Muhammad Dughlat. (Havoc and destruction have always emanated from the Moghul nation. Up to the present date they have rebelled against me five times—not from any particular impropriety on my part, for they have often done the same with their own khans.) Sultan-Qulï Chanaq, whose late father, Khudaberdi Buqaq, [65] I had favored among the Moghuls, was with the Moghuls and did well to bring me the news. (However, later he did such a heinous act, as will be related, that it could not be made up for by a hundred such good deeds, and that deed was the direct result of his being a Moghul.) As soon as the information arrived, I gathered the begs and held deliberations. The begs said, "This is insignificant. What necessity is there for the padishah to ride out? Let Qasim Beg lead the begs and army." That is how it was decided. It was taken too lightly, and this tactic was wrong. That very day Qasim Beg rode out leading his begs and troops. By the time they bivouacked, Tambal had come and joined the Moghuls. Early the next morning our men crossed the Ilamish River at a crossing called Yassy Kechit and faced the enemy. They clashed mightily. Qasim Beg himself faced Sultan-Muhammad Arghun, took two or three swings at him with his sword, and kept him from raising his head. Many of our warriors got into the fray, but in the end they were defeated. [65b] Qasim Beg, Ali-Dost Taghayï, Ibrahim Saru, Ways Laghari, Sidi Qara, and another three or four begs and ichkis got away. Most of the other begs and ichkis were taken captive, among them Ali Darwesh Beg, Mirim Laghari, Toqa Beg, Taghayï Beg Muhammad-Dost, Ali-Dost, Mir Shah Qauchin, and Mirim Diwan.

In this battle two warriors fought outstandingly: for our side one of Ibrahim Saru's younger brothers, Samad by name, and for the other side a Moghul of Hissar, Shahsuwar by name, faced each other. Shahsuwar gave such a blow that it passed right through Samad's helmet and sank well into his head. Despite his wound Samad struck so hard

Portrait of a standing warrior. Iran or Turkey, late sixteenth century. Album leaf; opaque color on paper. Harvard University Art Museums, Arthur M. Sackler Museum, Collection of Edwin Binney 3rd, 1985.224.

that his sword broke off a piece of bone the size of the palm of the hand from Shahsuwar's skull. Shahsuwar had no helmet. They trepanned his head wound, and he recovered. There was no one to trepan Samad's head, so he died three or four days later.

As we had just been delivered of our misfortune and the necessity for guerilla fighting, and just as we had regained our province, this was a singularly untimely defeat. Qambar-Ali Moghul, one of our principal supporters, had gone to his territory when we took Andizhan and so was not there. [66]

Having accomplished this much, Tambal took Jahangir and camped a league away from Andizhan in a meadow in front of the Aysh Hill. Once or twice he advanced in battle array past Childukhtaran to the slope of Aysh Hill, but when our warriors came out in battle array from the suburbs and orchards, he withdrew, unable to advance, to the other side of the hill. When he came to this vicinity, he killed our fallen begs Mirim Laghari and Toqa. He stayed in the area for nearly a month unable to accomplish anything and then withdrew in the direction of Osh. Osh had been given to Ibrahim Saru, and his man there made fast the city.

EVENTS OF THE YEAR 905
(1499–1500)[129]

Commissars were sent off urgently to get Qambar-Ali and all who had gone to their districts to muster cavalry and foot soldiers, and energetic ordnance officers were assigned to get shields, picks, axes, and other implements of war.

Liege men and commanders who had gone off in all directions to tend to their own affairs drove their horsemen and foot soldiers from the provinces and gathered at the camp. Trusting in God, I set forth on the eighteenth of Muharram [August 25, 1499] to Hafiz Beg's garden. [66b] We stayed there for a day or two, and when the remaining implements and equipment were ready, we set out for Osh in full battle array—right wing, left wing, center, vanguard, cavalry, and infantry—to face the enemy.

When we approached Osh, we learned that the enemy had not been able to make a stand in the vicinity of Osh and had gone toward Rabat-i-Sarhang Orchin, north of Osh. That night we camped in Latkand Village. The next morning we formed battle array and were passing through Osh when news came that the enemy had gone toward Andizhan, so we headed for Uzgen. A strike force was sent forward to attack the outskirts of Uzgen. The enemy went to Andizhan, but when they stole into the ditch by night and got their ladders up against the rampart, they were discovered by the defenders and had to withdraw without accomplishing anything.

MADY FORTRESS IS TAKEN

Tambal put his younger brother Khalil with two hundred, 250 men in the Mady fortress, one of the fortresses of Osh renowned for its impregnability, [67] and made fast the fort. We turned back to the fortress and enjoined battle with force.

The northern face of the fortress, which is on a riverbed, is exceedingly high; an arrow shot from the river might reach the rampart. The water channel is on this side. Something like a lane with a rampart has been built on either side of the fortress to reach the water. At the sides toward the high ground is a ditch. Huge river rocks like the ones used for mortars had been brought up to the fortress. In our experience of battle no fortress has had such large rocks thrown as those that were hurled from Mady fort.

Abdul-Quddus Kohbur, Kätä Beg's elder brother, made it to the bottom of the rampart; they dropped so many rocks from the rampart that, from such a high place, he turned a flip without touching the ground and then rolled to the base of the glacis of the fort. Uninjured, he immediately mounted his horse and rode off.

At the double water channel they hit Yar-Ali Bilal in the head with a rock. In the end his head had to be trepanned. Many were killed by the rocks. [67b] The assault was waged at dawn; a little before breakfast time the water channel was taken, and the fighting continued until evening. Since the water channel had been taken, they were unable to hold out and the next morning they sued for quarter and emerged. Seventy, eighty, or a hundred men under Tambal's brother Khalil were put into chains and sent to Andizhan to be kept under guard. Some of our begs, ichkis, and valiant warriors had been taken prisoner by them, but the affair turned out very well.

Having taken Mady, we went to Ünchü Topa, a village in Osh, and camped. From the other side Tambal withdrew from Andizhan and camped in Ab-i-Khan, a village in Rabat-i-Sarhang Orchin. About a league separated the two armies. Just then Qambar-Ali went to Osh on account of illness.

We sat there for a month or forty days. There was no battle, but every day our foragers and theirs got into a fracas. The camp perimeter was closely guarded at night. A trench was dug, and where there were no trenches, stakes were set up. The soldiers went out fully armed to the edge of the trenches. [68] Despite such precautions, every three or four nights an uproar or alarm was sounded in the camp. One day Sidi Beg Taghayï went out in front of the foragers, and the enemy came in great strength and in one fell swoop took him right in the middle of the fight.

BAYSUNGHUR MIRZA MURDERED BY KHUSRAWSHAH

That same year Khusrawshah, contemplating leading his army against Balkh, summoned Baysunghur Mirza to Konduz and rode off to Balkh. When they reached Aivadzh, Khusrawshah, this wretched traitor aspiring to rule—as though such a virtueless nobody, with no origins, no lineage, no virtue, no worth, no organization, no courage, no equity, no justice, could ever attain sovereignty—seized Baysunghur Mirza and his begs, strung his bow and, on the tenth of Muharram [August 17, 1499], martyred this prince who was so full of poetic talent, so learned, and of such good lineage and personal worth. Of his begs and ichkis too he killed a few.

BAYSUNGHUR MIRZA

His birth and lineage. He was born in 882 [1477–78] in the province of Hissar. He was Sultan-Mahmud Mirza's second son, younger than Sultan-Mas'ud Mirza, and older than Sultan-Ali Mirza, Sultan-Husayn, and Sultan-Ways Mirza, who was known as Khan Mirza. His mother was Pasha Begim.

His features. [68b] He had big eyes, a full face, a medium build, and Turcoman features—altogether a good-looking young man.

His character. He was a just and humane, poetically inclined, and learned prince. His teacher, Sayyid Mahmud, is said to have been a Shiite, and for this reason Baysunghur Mirza was similarly tainted. They say that later in Samarkand he renounced this vile doctrine and became orthodox. He was too fond of the wine cup, but when he was not drinking he performed his prayers. He was moderate in his liberality and generosity. He wrote the nasta'liq script very well,[130] and his hand was not bad at painting either. He composed some marvelous poetry. His pen name was Adili, but he did not compose enough poetry to make a divan. This is one of his verses:

> Like a shadow I stumble and fall from weakness. If I don't lean against
> a wall I fall down.

Baysunghur Mirza's poetry was so popular in Samarkand that there were few houses in which you would not find some of his poems.

His battles. He fought two battles. Once he fought with Sultan-Mahmud Khan. When he first came to the throne, Sultan-Mahmud Khan was enticed by Sultan-Junayd Barlas and some others to take Samarkand. [69] He led his army through Aq Kotal to the vicinity of Rabat-i-Sughd and Kambay. Baysunghur Mirza came forth from Samarkand and defeated Sultan-Mahmud Khan at Kambay. He had three or four thousand Moghuls beheaded. Haydar Kükäldash, who was the khan's factotum, died in this battle.

Another time at Bukhara he fought Sultan-Ali Mirza and was defeated.

His realm. His father Sultan-Mahmud Mirza gave him Bukhara. After his father died, his father's begs agreed to make him padishah in Samarkand. Bukhara was also within his jurisdiction for a while, but he lost it after the Tarkhans' revolt. When I took Samarkand he went to Khusrawshah, who took Hissar and gave it to him.

He had no children. When he went to Khusrawshah, he married his uncle Sultan-Khalil Mirza's daughter. He had no other wife or concubine. He never ruled so autonomously as to have elevated anyone or made anyone a high-ranking beg. His begs were those of his father and uncle. [69b]

After the death of Baysunghur Mirza, Qoch Beg's father, Sultan-Ahmad Qaravul, left Karategin with his brothers, family, and dependents and came to join us. Qambar-Ali, who was ill in Osh, got off his sickbed and came too. At such a juncture I took Sultan-Ahmad Qaravul's providential arrival with his people as a good omen, and the next morning we formed our ranks and rode against the enemy, who made no stand at Ab-i-Khan and decamped, leaving some tents, rugs, and baggage to fall into our army's hands. We then camped where they had been.

That evening Tambal took Jahangir and, circling around to our right, entered a village called Khunan, about three leagues away from us on the Andizhan side. The next morning we arrayed the right and left wings, the center, and the vanguard, armed ourselves in mail, formed our ranks, put the foot soldiers holding shields before us, and marched against the enemy. In our right wing were Ali-Dost Taghayï and his men; in the left were Ibrahim Saru, Ways Laghari, Sidi Qara, Muhammad Ali Mubashshir, [70] Khwaja Kalan Beg's elder brother Kichik Beg, and some ichkis. Sultan-Ahmad Qaravul and Qoch Beg and his brothers were assigned to the left wing. Qasim Beg was with me in the center. The vanguard was Qambar-Ali and some other ichkis. We had reached a village called Saqa, a league to the southeast of Khunan, when the enemy emerged from Khunan in battle array. We moved on a bit faster. When the encounter was made the shielded foot soldiers who had been arranged with such caution and care fell behind. Thank God there was no need for them. When they met, the men of our left wing grappled with their right wing. Khwaja Kalan's brother Kichik Beg really got into the fray, and after him was Muhammad Ali Mubashshir. Unable to withstand such fighting, the enemy fled. The battle never even reached the right wing or the vanguard. Many warriors were brought in, and we ordered them beheaded. Our begs Qasim Beg and Ali-Dost Beg—and mostly Ali-Dost—maintaining caution and good generalship, did not think it advisable to send anyone far in pursuit. [70b] For that reason not many more were taken prisoner. We camped at Khunan. This was the first real battle I had fought in. God, by his great generosity, granted me victory and triumph. We took it as a good omen.

The next day my father's mother, my grandmother Shah Sultan Begim, came from Andizhan, thinking that if Jahangir had been taken captive she would ask for his release.

WINTER QUARTERS SET UP
IN IKI SU ARASÏ

Since winter was approaching and grain supplies were exhausted, and it was not thought wise to move against Uzgen, we returned to Andizhan. Several days later we held council and decided that the enemy would suffer nothing by our wintering there, whereas it was probable they would gain strength through hit-and-run strikes. It was necessary to winter some place where the army would not be helpless for lack of grain and the enemy might be driven to desperation by something like a siege. To accomplish this we moved out of Andizhan with a mind to winter in the vicinity of Armian and Noshab in Rabatak Orchin, which is also called Iki Su Arasï. [71] Arriving in those villages, we set up winter quarters.

All around the vicinity are good hunting grounds. In the thick forests on the Ilamish riverbanks mountain goat, deer, and boar abound. In the small woods are many pheasants and hares, and many foxes of all sorts in the hills. The foxes there run faster than foxes in other locales. I went hunting every two or three days. We set fire to the large forests to trap goat and deer, and made a circle around the small woods to hunt pheasant with falcons and darts. The pheasants were incredibly fat, and plentiful as long as we were there.

Khudaberdi Tughchï, whom I had recently promoted to beg, went down two or three times, defeated Tambal's raiders, and brought in their heads. From Andizhan and Osh our own raiding warriors went out incessantly and drove our opponents' herds away, thus enfeebling them considerably. If we had been able to stay the entire winter in those quarters, it is quite likely that [71b] by spring they would have been overcome without fighting.

As we were thus wearing down our enemy, Qambar-Ali requested permission to go home. The more I tried to keep him from going by reminding him of these considerations, the more stupidly he acted. What an amazingly unreliable and indecisive fellow he was! There was nothing to be done: he was given permission to go home. His territory had first been Khodzhent, but when we took Andizhan this time he was given Isfara and Kanibadam too. Among all our begs the one with the most territory and the most retainers was Qambar-Ali. No one had men and lands as he did.

We had been in those winter quarters for forty or fifty days. At Qambar-Ali's recommendation leave was also given to some of the army, and we ourselves went to Andizhan.

SULTAN-MAHMUD KHAN SENDS REINFORCEMENTS TO TAMBAL

During the time we were in winter quarters and Andizhan, Tambal's man was constantly coming and going to and from the khan in

Tashkent. Ahmad Beg, who was was beg atäkä to the khan's son Sultan-Muhammad Sultan, and was the khan's favorite beg, was Tambal's paternal uncle. Beg Telbä, lord of the khan's gate, was Tambal's elder brother. With all this coming and going they persuaded the khan to send help to Tambal. Before doing so, Beg Telbä, [72] who had been in Moghulistan all his life and grown up among Moghuls, had never entered a civilized country, had never served the padishah of a civilized country, and had only served khans. He put his retinue, domestics, and family in Tashkent and came to join his brother Tambal.

Just then a strange thing happened. Qasim Ajab, who had been temporarily stationed in Akhsi, went out in pursuit of a few brigands and, crossing the Khodzhent River at Bikhrata, ran into a large contingent of Tambal's men and followers.

When Tambal learned that our soldiers had gone away and that his brother Telbä had talked the khan into letting him come, he rode out of Uzgen, assured that help was on the way, and went to Iki Su Arasï. At the same time, the news from Kassan was confirmed that the khan had assigned his son Sultan-Muhammad Khanika (known as Sultanïm) and Ahmad Beg to join Tambal with an army of five or six thousand. Taking the road through Archakent, they laid siege to Kassan. Not even thinking of those of our men who were far away, we took the men we had, put our trust in God, and in the dead of winter took the Band-i-Salar road from Andizhan, riding without halt against Sultanïm and Ahmad Beg. [72b] Without stopping that night, we dismounted in Akhsi the next morning. That evening it had been so cold that some got frostbite on their hands and feet, and many men's ears got blistered like apples. Resting only momentarily in Akhsi, we put Yarak Taghayï temporarily in Qasim Ajab's place and proceeded against Kassan. When we were within a league of Kassan, news came that Ahmad Beg had learned of our approach and turned back with Sultanïm in haste and disarray.

Tambal must have learned of our riding out, for he came hurriedly to help his elder brother. It was late afternoon when the outline of Tambal's troops could be seen in the direction of Naukent. Astonished and confused by his brother's quick retreat and our rapid approach, he stopped where he was.

"God has brought him in this fashion," we said. "He has come at full gallop. If we strike, and if God wills, not one of them will escape."

"It is late in the day," Ways Laghari and some others said. "If nothing happens today, [73] where can he go tomorrow morning? At dawn we will meet him wherever he may be." That is, they did not think it wise to make a strike immediately, and so a foe who had come thus to the gate got off scot-free. A proverb says, "If you don't seize what is at hand you will rue it until old age."

One must act in a timely fashion, for untimely acts are ineffective.

By the next morning the enemy had taken advantage of the opportunity and had gone by night without halt and entered the Arkhian fortress. The next morning we rode against them; they were not to be found, so we went out in pursuit. We did not deem it wise, however, to lay close siege to the fortress, where Tambal was, so we camped a league away in Ghazna Namangan, where we stayed for thirty to forty days. A few men at a time would go out from our side and a few would come from theirs; they would charge each other, then turn around. One night they staged a surprise attack. They shot a few volleys of arrows from outside our camp, but since the camp had been defensively surrounded with trenches and pylons, they were unable to accomplish anything and withdrew.

While we were in camp Qambar-Ali got angry two or three times [73b] and threatened to leave for home. Once he actually got on his horse and was riding off, but we sent some begs after him and managed with great difficulty to get him to return.

Meanwhile Sayyid-Yusuf Mujum sent a man to Sultan-Ahmad Tambal to say that Sayyid-Yusuf was relying upon Tambal. (The Uyghurs in the foothills of Andizhan are called Mujum.) There are two foothill areas, and Sayyid-Yusuf Mujum was the chief of one of them. He later became a well-known personage at my gate. Having surpassed the status of chief, he gave himself airs of being a beg, although no one ever made him one. He was an astonishingly hypocritical and inconstant little man. From my taking of Andizhan the last time until that date he must have rebelled against Tambal and joined me two or three times and rebelled against me and joined Tambal two or three times. This was to be the last time he would rebel. We rode out to cut him off from Tambal. He had many tribes and clans with him. In one night's halt we came to the Pishkaran region. Tambal's men had come earlier and entered the Pishkaran fortress. A detachment of our begs with Ali Darwesh Beg, Qoch Beg, and his brothers got up to the Pishkaran Gate and engaged in a good imbroglio. Qoch Beg and his brothers performed well. [74] We camped on a rise a league from Pishkaran. Tambal took Jahangir and camped with the fortress at his back.

Three or four days later the begs who disagreed with us, Ali-Dost and Qambar-Ali Sallakh's followers, began to propose a truce. I and my supporters had no knowledge whatsoever of this truce and would never have agreed to it. However, since these two fellows were great begs, if we did not listen to them and make overtures of peace, they were likely to make trouble. Our hand was forced. A truce was arranged whereby the territory on the Akhsi side of the Khodzhent River would be Jahangir's and the Andizhan side would be mine. They would leave Uzgen in our jurisdiction after they got their families out. When affairs in the two territories were settled, Jahangir Mirza and I would join forces and proceed together against Samarkand. As soon as the Samarkand throne was secure, Andizhan would be given to Jahangir Mirza. [74b] This is how things were left. The next morning, toward the end of the month of Rajab [February 1500], Jahangir Mirza and Tambal came and rendered homage, and pledges and promises were made. Jahangir Mirza was given leave to go to Akhsi, and I myself returned to Andizhan.

With my arrival in Andizhan, Tambal's brother Khalil and the men in chains were set free, presented with robes of honor, and given leave to depart. Our begs and ichkis held by them, that is, those under the command of Taghayï Beg Muhammad-Dost, Mir Shah Qauchin, Sidi Beg, Qasim Ajab, Pir Ways, and Mirim Diwan, were released and sent to us.

After coming to Andizhan, Ali-Dost underwent a radical change and began to quarrel with those who had been with me during our rencontres and times of trouble. First he dismissed Khalifa. Next, for no ostensible fault he had Ibrahim Saru and Ways Laghari seized, plundered, stripped of their territories, and dismissed. He constantly clashed with Qasim Beg. He openly claimed that Khalifa and Ibrahim had been supporters of Khwaja Qazi and were going to take revenge on him. His son Muhammad-Dost took on regal airs [75] and began hosting receptions and dinners and holding court like a sultan. This father-son pair initiated such actions because they had Tambal's backing. I no longer had enough power to forbid such unreasonable behaviors, and so, with a foe like Tambal backing and protecting them, they did as they pleased. It was a highly delicate situation and impossible for me to say anything. Much humiliation was suffered at the hands of this father and son during that period.

MARRIAGE AND FIRST LOVE

Sultan-Ahmad Mirza's daughter Ayisha Sultan Begim, who had been affianced to me while my father and uncle were still alive, came to Khodzhent, and we were married in the month of Shaʻban [March 1500]. In the early days after the wedding, although my affection for her was not lacking, since it was my first marriage and I was bashful, I went to her only once every ten, fifteen, or twenty days. Later on I lost my fondness for her altogether, and I was still shy. Once every month or forty days my mother the khanïm drove me to her with all the severity of a quartermaster.

During this time [75b] there was a boy from the camp market named Baburi. Even his name was amazingly appropriate.[131]

I developed a strange inclination for him—rather I made myself miserable over him.

Before this experience I had never felt a desire for anyone, nor did I listen to talk of love and affection or speak of such things. At that time I used to compose single lines and couplets in Persian. I composed the following lines there:

May no one be so distraught and devastated by love as I; May no beloved be so pitiless and careless as you.

Occasionally Baburi came to me, but I was so bashful that I could not look him in the face, much less converse freely with him. In my excitement and agitation I could not thank him for coming, much less complain of his leaving. Who could bear to demand the ceremonies of fealty? One day, during this time of infatuation, a group was accompanying me down a lane, and all at once I found myself face-to-face with the boy. I was so ashamed I almost went to pieces. There was no possibility of looking straight at him or of speaking coherently. [76] With a hundred embarrassments and difficulties I got past him. These lines by Muhammad Salih came to my mind:

> I am embarrassed every time I see my beloved. My companions are looking at me, but my gaze is elsewhere.[132]

It is amazing how appropriate this verse was. In the throes of love, in the foment of youth and madness, I wandered bareheaded and barefoot around the lanes and streets and through the gardens and orchards, paying no attention to acquaintances or strangers, oblivious to self and others.

> When I fell in love I became mad and crazed. I knew not this to be part of loving beauties.

Sometimes I went out alone like a madman to the hills and wilderness, sometimes I roamed through the orchards and lanes of town, neither walking nor sitting within my own volition, restless in going and staying.

> I have no strength to go, no power to stay. You have snared us in this state, my heart.

SULTAN-ALI MIRZA QUARRELS WITH THE TARKHANS

This same year a disagreement broke out between Sultan-Ali Mirza and Muhammad Mazid Tarkhan. The reason was as follows. The Tarkhans had risen to the pinnacle of power and prestige. They had taken Bukhara as their exclusive property [76b] and gave not a penny of the revenue to anyone else. In Samarkand, Muhammad Mazid Tarkhan was in power and had taken the whole province for his sons and followers. Except for the little salary they had fixed, not a penny from the city reached Sultan-Ali Mirza through any channel. Sultan-Ali Mirza was a young man of great stature—how was he to tolerate such treatment? He and a few of his ichkis plotted an attempt on

Muhammad Mazid Tarkhan's life. Muhammad Mazid Tarkhan got wind of the affair and fled the city with his servants, followers, and what begs were there, such as Sultan-Husayn Arghun, Pir-Ahmad, Uzun Hasan's brother Khwaja Husayn, Qara Barlas, Salih Muhammad, and some other begs and warriors.

At that time the khan had attached Muhammad-Husayn Dughlat, Ahmad Beg, and a large contingent of Moghul begs to Mirza Khan and assigned them to take Samarkand. Mirza Khan's beg atäkäs were Hafiz Beg Dulday and his son Tahir Beg. Hasan Nabira, Hindu Beg, and some warriors deserted Sultan-Ali Mirza because they were related to Hafiz Beg and Tahir Beg [77] and went over to Mirza Khan. Muhammad Mazid Tarkhan sent some men to invite Mirza Khan and the Moghul army. They went to the Shavdar region, where he had an interview with Mirza Khan and met with the Moghul begs. The Moghul begs and Muhammad Mazid Beg did not hit it off well—in fact they thought of taking him prisoner. His begs understood this and separated themselves on some pretext from the Moghul army. With them gone the Moghul forces could not make a stand, so they withdrew, but while they were camped in Yar Yaylagh, Sultan-Ali Mirza rode out from Samarkand with a few men and attacked Mirza Khan and the Moghul forces, who, unable to fight, were routed. This, done toward the end of his life, was the one fairly good action taken by Sultan-Ali Mirza.

Despairing of these princes, Muhammad Mazid Tarkhan and his men sent Mir Moghul, the son of the Abdul-Wahhab who had formerly been with me and served valiantly and faithfully with Khwaja Qazi during the siege of Andizhan, to invite me to come.

We had been devastated by all this business. It was to settle all that that we had made a truce with Jahangir and resolved to move against Samarkand. We immediately sent Mir Moghul by post horse to Jahangir Mirza. [77b] In the month of Dhu'l-Qa'da [May–June 1500] the army mounted for Samarkand and, stopping twice along the way, we camped in Kuva. That afternoon news came that Sultan-Ahmad Tambal's brother Khalil had taken the Osh fortress by stealth. The details are as follows. When the truce was made, the prisoners under Khalil's command were released, as has been mentioned. Tambal sent Khalil to get their kith and kin out of Uzgen. Under the pretext of getting his family out, he entered Uzgen and kept saying he would leave that day or the next, but he never did. When our army mounted, he seized the opportunity of finding Osh empty and stole it by night. When we received this news, we thought for several reasons that it was unwise either to remain or to antagonize these people and so set out toward Samarkand. One reason was that our soldiers had gone off in all directions, wherever any had homes, to get military equipment. Relying on the truce, we were unaware of the treachery and deceit of these people. Another reason was that several times actions had been manifested by our great commanders Ali-Dost [78] and Qambar-Ali that precluded any reliance upon them, as has been mentioned. A third reason was that all the Samarkand begs under Muhammad Mazid Tarkhan had sent Mir Moghul to fetch me. With a capital like Samarkand there for the taking, who would be inclined to waste his time in a place like Andizhan?

We went from Kuva to Margilan, which had been given to Qoch Beg's father, Sultan-Ahmad Beg. He had other commitments and involvements, however, and was unable to join me. His son Qoch Beg and one or two of his brothers accompanied me instead.

We were on the road to Isfara. We camped in a village of Isfara called Mihan. By happy coincidence Qasim Beg and Ali-Dost with troops and Sayyid-Qasim with another large contingent of warriors all arrived as though by prearrangement and joined us that night in Mihan. We rode out of there through the Khuspan plain, crossed the Chupan Bridge, and arrived in Ura-Tyube.

Qambar-Ali, trusting in Tambal, went from his own territory of Khodzhent to Akhsi to discuss army matters. No sooner did he arrive than Tambal had him taken prisoner [78b] and attacked his territory. There is a Turkish proverb: "Trust not your friend: he will stuff your hide with straw." Along the way Qambar-Ali managed to escape on foot and make his way with great difficulty to Ura-Tyube.

While in Ura-Tyube news came that Shaybani Khan had defeated Baqi Tarkhan at the Dabusi fort and was marching against Bukhara. We went from Ura-Tyube to Sanzar via the Börkä Yaylagh road. The prefect of Sanzar yielded the fortress. Since Qambar-Ali had allowed himself to be made prisoner and had been brought along, we placed him in Sanzar and proceeded.

While we were camped at Khan Yurtï, the Samarkand begs under Muhammad Mazid Tarkhan's command came and paid homage. With them we discussed how to subdue Samarkand. They said, "Even Khwaja Yahya supports the padishah. And if the khwaja agrees, Samarkand can easily be taken without fighting or battle." Based on that counsel, we sent people to hold discussions with Khwaja Yahya several times. Khwaja Yahya did not send word absolutely that he would admit us into Samarkand, but neither did he speak discouragingly.

We left Khan Yurtï and went to the banks of the Dargham. From there we sent Khwaja Muhammad-Ali Kitabdar to Khwaja Yahya, and he returned with the message: [79] "Come. We will give you the city." It was nearly night when we mounted by the Dargham and set out. Sultan-Mahmud Dulday, Sultan-Muhammad Dulday's father, fled from the camp and took word of this agreement to the foe. Once they had learned of it, it was not possible to carry out our plan. We returned and camped on the banks of the Dargham.

Ibrahim Saru Mïnglïgh, one of my favorite begs, had been seized and plundered by Ali-Dost. When I came to Yar Yaylagh, he came with Sayyid-Yusuf Beg's eldest son, Muhammad Yusuf, and paid homage. Ali-Dost had chased away some of our liege begs and ichkis who were opposed to him, had plundered others and held others prisoner. One by one they banded together and came. Ali-Dost had grown weak because he had had Tambal's backing in tormenting me and my supporters. Even my nature was repulsed by this fellow. No longer able to stay on account of shame and fear, he requested leave. I did him a favor and let him go. As soon as they were given leave, Ali-Dost and Muhammad-Dost went to Tambal. [79b] As they became intimates of Tambal, much sedition and evil issued from this father-son pair. A year or two later Ali-Dost died from an abscess on his hand. Muhammad-Dost went to the Uzbeks and did not do altogether badly, but he fled from them after some act of ingratitude and went to the foothills of Andizhan, where he fomented rebellion and strife. Finally, when he fell into the Uzbeks' hands, they had him blinded. As the saying goes, "Salt took his eyes."[133]

After I gave Ali-Dost and Muhammad-Dost leave to depart, Ghuri Barlas and a few warriors were sent to Bukhara to reconnoiter. Word was sent that Shaybani Khan had taken Bukhara and was headed for Samarkand. Not considering it wise to be in those parts, we set out for Kish, where most of the Samarkand begs' families were.

SHAYBANI KHAN TAKES POSSESSION
OF SAMARKAND

A week or two after coming to Kish news came that Sultan-Ali Mirza had yielded Samarkand to Shaybani Khan. The details are as follows. Sultan-Ali Mirza's mother, Zuhra Begi Agha, had stupidly and irrationally sent a secret message to Shaybani Khan saying that if Shaybani Khan [80] would marry her, her son would give Samarkand to Shaybani Khan. When Shaybani Khan had taken Sultan-Ali's father's territory, he could give it to Sultan-Ali Mirza. Sayyid-Yusuf Arghun must have known of this plan; indeed, that traitor probably coached her in it.

EVENTS OF THE YEAR 906
(1500-1501)[134]

Shaybani Khan responded to that woman's promise and camped in the Bagh-i-Maydan. At noon Sultan-Ali Mirza, without informing any of his begs or warriors, and without consulting anyone, went out through the Charraha Gate with an insignificant few of his immediate retinue, headed for Shaybani Khan in the Bagh-i-Maydan. He was not well received by Shaybani Khan, who seated him in a less honorable place than himself after the interview. When Khwaja Yahya learned that the prince had gone out, he was upset. There was nothing he could do but go out too. Shaybani Khan received him without rising and spoke somewhat reproachfully. However, when Khwaja Yahya rose to leave, Shaybani Khan rose respectfully.

Jan-Ali, Khwaja Ali Bay's son, was in Rabat-i-Khwaja. When he learned that his prince had gone out to Shaybani Khan, he went too. In her lust to get a husband, that wretched, feebleminded woman brought destruction on her son. [80b] Shaybani Khan paid her not the slightest attention and regarded her as less than a concubine.

Sultan-Ali Mirza was at a loss and regretted having gone out. Some of his retinue understood what was up and thought they could get the prince out. Sultan-Ali Mirza refused to consent. Since his time had come, nothing could save him. He stayed with Temür Sultan, and four or five days later they executed him in the Qolba Meadow. For the sake of this transitory life he departed with a bad name. By listening to the words of women, he removed himself from the circle of those of good repute. Of such a person no more can be written; of such horrible acts no more need be heard.

After Sultan-Ali Mirza was killed Jan-Ali too was dispatched after his prince. Since Shaybani Khan was in some fear of Khwaja Yahya, he dismissed him and his two sons, Khwaja Muhammad Zakariya and Khwaja Baqi, to Khurasan. A few Uzbeks followed behind them, and in the vicinity of Khwaja Kardzan they martyred the khwaja and the two young boys. Even worse, Shaybani Khan claimed that the affair of the khwaja was not his doing, [81] that it had been done by Qambar Bey and Köpäk Bey. As the saying goes, "The excuse is worse than the crime." If begs have free rein to engage in such acts without the knowledge of their khan or padishah, what is the use of khanate or kingship?

We set out from Kish for Hissar as soon as the Uzbeks took Samarkand. The Samarkand begs under Muhammad Mazid Tarkhan moved out with their kith and kin along with us. While camped at Chaltu Meadow in Chaghanian, the Samarkand begs under Muhammad Mazid Tarkhan left and joined Khusrawshah's retinue.

There we were, deprived of city and province, not knowing where to go or where to stay. Although Khusrawshah had inflicted untold misery upon our dynasty, we had no choice but to pass through his territory.

I had had one thought, and that was to go through the Karategin and Alay mountains to my uncle Alacha Khan. Since that was not possible, we proceeded instead up the Kumrud and went through the Sary-Tag pass. When we reached the vicinity of Nawandak, Khusrawshah's servant brought a *toquz*[135] of horses and fabric. While camped at the mouth of the Kumrud, Sher-Ali [81b] Chuhra deserted and went to Wali, Khusrawshah's brother. The next morning Qoch Beg deserted and went to Hissar.

We entered the Kumrud valley and headed up. In the narrows, precipitous roads, and treacherous defiles many horses and camels were lost. After stopping to camp three or four times we reached the Sary-Tag defile. A defile, and what a defile! Never had such a high and narrow defile been seen. Never had such narrow and precipitous roads been met with. With much difficulty and hardship we got through the dangerous narrows and cliffs, passing through the mortal danger of the high and narrow defiles, and came to the Fan region. In the midst of the Fan Mountains is a large lake, approximately a league in circumference. It is a fabulous place and not a little strange.

Word was received that Ibrahim Tarkhan had made fast the Shiraz fortress and was sitting tight. In the fortresses of Yar Yaylagh were holed up Qambar-Ali and Abu'l-Qasim Kohbur, who had been in Khwaja Didar but, unable to remain there when the Uzbeks took Samarkand, had gone to the lower fortresses of Yar Yaylagh and made them fast.

We put Fan to our right and proceeded toward Kishtud. The headman of Fan was renowned far and wide for his generosity and hospitality. [82] When Sultan-Husayn Mirza attacked Hissar, Sultan-Mas'ud Mirza took this way to go to his brother Baysunghur Mirza in Samarkand, and the headman of Fan presented him with seventy or eighty horses and performed other services of equal value. To me he sent a second-rate horse without even coming himself. When it came to us, these people so renowned for their generosity had turned stingy, a folk so known for their cooperativeness had forgotten how to be so. It has been mentioned what services Khusrawshah, also known for his beneficence and graciousness, performed for Badi'uzzaman Mirza. Baqi Tarkhan and other begs too he received with the greatest of kindness. However, the two times we passed through his territory, despite the reception he gave our peers, he did not show us the consideration one would show to the least of our servants. Indeed he treated us less well than he did them.

> Who has seen, O heart, good of the people of the world? Expect no good of him in whom there is no good.

After passing through Fan we hurried to Kishtud, thinking that the Uzbeks were in the fortress there. We found the Kishtud fort was in ruins, however, and with no signs that anyone had been there recently. On leaving, [82b] we camped on the banks of the Kohak River, which we then crossed by the bridge opposite Yori. The begs under Qasim Beg were sent to take the Rabat-i-Khwaja fortress by stealth. We went through Yori, down Shunqarkhana Mountain, and reached Yar Yaylagh. When the begs who had gone to Rabat-i-Khwaja put up their ladders, the defenders either discovered them or had been tipped off in advance. Unable to take the fortress, they withdrew.

BABUR RENEWS HIS ATTACK
ON SAMARKAND

Qambar-Ali was in Sanzar. He came and had an interview with me. Abu'l-Qasim Kohbur and Ibrahim Tarkhan sent their brave warriors to pay homage and show their servitude and obeisance. We went to Isfedak Fort, a village in Yar Yaylagh. Shaybani Khan was then in the vicinity of Khwaja Didar with three or four thousand Uzbeks. That many more too had gathered from other places. The prefecture of Samarkand had been given to Jan-Wafa Mirza, who was inside the Samarkand fortress with five or six hundred men. Hamza Sultan and Mahdi Sultan were camped with their followers in Bödänä field near Samarkand. Our men, all told, were 240 in number. [83]

In consultation with all the begs and warriors, we decided that since Shaybani Khan had only recently taken Samarkand, neither were the people yet attached to him nor was he to them. If we could take action now we would accomplish something. If we could get ladders up against the Samarkand walls and take them by stealth, the people of Samarkand would be with us. What choice did they have? Even if they did not assist us, they would not fight for the Uzbeks. After we got hold of Samarkand, what would be would be.

Having made this decision, we rode out of Yar Yaylagh in the afternoon and continued all through the evening, reaching Khan Yurtï at midnight. Thinking that the people had been warned of our approach, we returned to Khan Yurtï without coming nearer the fortress. It was morning when we crossed the Kohak below Rabat-i-Khwaja and came again to Yar Yaylagh.

One day a group of ichkis—Dost Nasir, Noyan Kükäldash, Qasim Kükäldash, Khan-Qulï, Karimdad, Shaykh Darwesh, Khusraw Kükäkdash, and Mirim Nasir—were present and sitting with me in Isfedak Fort. On all sides everyone was asking when, God willing, [83b] we would take Samarkand. Some said by summer (it was then late autumn), some said a month, some said forty days, some said twenty days. Noyan Kükäldash said, "We'll take it in fourteen days." Through the grace of God, in exactly fourteen days we took Samarkand.

About that time I had a strange dream. I dreamed that Khwaja Ubaydullah had arrived and I had gone out to greet him. He came and sat down. The tablecloth must have been laid somewhat unceremoniously before him, for it seemed that he was offended. Mulla Baba looked at me and motioned. I motioned back as if to say, "It's not my fault. The steward is to blame." The khwaja understood and accepted this apology. Then he rose, and I rose to escort him. In the entryway he took me by the arm, the right or the left, I don't remember which, and lifted me so that one of my feet was off the ground. In Turkish he said, "*Shaykh Maslahat berdi.*"[136] A few days later I took Samarkand.

SAMARKAND IS TAKEN BY SURPRISE

A day or two later we moved from Isfedak Fort to Wasmand Fort. Although we had already been to Samarkand, let ourselves be discovered, and returned, [84] once again we put our trust in God and, with that same plan in mind, charged from Wasmand after noon. Khwaja Abu'l-Makarim was along too. At midnight, when we reached the Mughak Bridge on the Khiaban, we sent ahead a detachment of seventy or eighty brave warriors to put ladders opposite Lovers' Cave, attack and take control of the Turquoise Gate, and send someone to inform us. The warriors went, set their ladders opposite the cave, and got up. No one was aware. From there they made it to the gate and attacked Fazil Tarkhan, who was not one of those other Tarkhans but a Turkistani merchant Tarkhan who had served Shaybani Khan in Turkistan and been promoted.[137] They fought with Fazil Tarkhan and a few of his men, killed them, broke the lock with an ax, and opened the gate. I arrived just at that time and entered through the Turquoise Gate.

Abu'l-Qasim Kohbur did not come himself but sent his younger brother Ahmad Qasim with thirty or forty servants. None of Ibrahim Tarkhan's men was there. After I entered the city and took up my station in the khanaqah, his younger brother Ahmad Tarkhan [84b] came with a few liege men.

The people of the city were still asleep. Shopkeepers looked out of their shops, recognized us, and called down blessings upon us. A little while later the people got wind, and a strange joy and jubilation came over our people and the people of the city. Like mad dogs they stoned and clubbed the Uzbeks to death in the gutters. Somewhere between forty and a hundred Uzbeks were killed in this fashion. The city prefect Jan-Wafa was in Khwaja Yahya's quarters. He got out and fled to Wormwood Khan.

Entering through the gate, I proceeded straight to the madrasa and khanaqah and sat down under the khanaqah arch. Dawn broke to alarms and chaos on all sides. Some of the lords and shopkeepers came as soon as they received word, joyfully bringing us what food they had on hand and pouring blessings upon our head. After dawn word came that the Uzbeks had fortified themselves between the outer and inner gates at the Iron Gate and were putting up a fight. I immediately got to horse and set out for the Iron Gate. With me were ten, fifteen, twenty men. The wretches were ransacking the new city, everyone occupied in some spot out of curiosity. [85] By the time I arrived they had driven the Uzbeks out of the Iron Gate. When Wormwood Khan learned of this he came in alarm, reaching the Iron Gate with a hundred, 150 men just as the sun was rising. He arrived at an odd moment, and I had only a few men with me, as has been mentioned. Wormwood Khan saw that he could do nothing, so he turned and got out fast. I went to the Bustan Saray in the citadel. The lords, notables, and headmen of the city came to see me and offer congratulations.

For nearly 140 years the capital Samarkand had been in our family. Then came the Uzbeks, the foreign foe from God knows where, and took over. Now the property that had slipped from our hands had been restored by God. The plundered and pillaged kingdom once again entered our domain.

SULTAN·HUSAYN'S SEIZURE OF
HERAT COMPARED TO BABUR'S
SEIZURE OF SAMARKAND

Sultan-Husayn Mirza also took Herat by surprise. However, it is obvious to knowledgeable persons and clear to people of discernment that between his seizure of Herat and my seizure of Samarkand lies a vast difference. First, Sultan-Husayn Mirza was a padishah who had seen and experienced much, and was great in years. Second, his opponent was Yadgar-Muhammad Nasir Mirza, a youth seventeen or eighteen years old with no experience. [85b] Third, someone with inside knowledge of the foe, Mir-Ali Mirakhur, sent people to the prince and let them take their opponent by surprise. Fourth, his opponent was not in the fortress but was in the Bagh-i-Zaghan.[138] The night Sultan-Husayn

Mirza took Herat, Yadgar-Muhammad Mirza and his retainers were so besotted with drink that they stationed only three men at the gate, and they were drunk too. Fifth, he came and took Herat by surprise.

When I took Samarkand, I was nineteen years old. Neither had I seen many things nor experienced much. Second, my opponent was a seasoned and elderly person like Wormwood Khan. Third, no one let us into Samarkand. Although the people of the city were for us in heart, they were unable to think of actually doing anything out of fear of Wormwood. Fourth, my opponent was in the fortress: the fortress was taken and the opponent was driven out. Fifth, we had gone once to attack Samarkand but were discovered by the enemy and had to come a second time, when God brought it about and Samarkand was conquered.

I do not say this to denigrate anyone else. [86] What I have said is all fact. I do not intend to aggrandize myself with what I have written. What I have written is the truth.

For this conquest the poets composed chronograms. Among them this line sticks in my mind:

Wisdom spake and said, "Know that the chronogram is 'the conquest of Babur Bahadur.' "

After the conquest of Samarkand the fortresses in the nearby districts of Shavdar and Sughd began to come over to me one by one. In terror the Uzbek prefects threw up some of the fortresses and left. The men in some of them chased the Uzbeks out and opted for us. Others imprisoned the prefects and made fast the fortresses.

That time Wormwood Khan and his Uzbeks' kith and kin had come from Turkistan. Wormwood was in Khwaja Didar and Aliabad. When he saw the fortresses coming over to us and the people returning to us like that, he left the place he was staying and decamped toward Bukhara. Through God's favor most of the Sughd and Mian Kal fortresses returned to us in three or four months. Baqi Tarkhan took the opportunity to enter the Karshi fortress. Both Khuzar and Karshi slipped from the Uzbeks' control. Abu'l-Muhsin Mirza's man [86b] came from Merv and took Karakul. Things were looking up for us.

After I had left Andizhan, my mother and her people had gone with great difficulty to Ura-Tyube. Someone was sent to bring them to

Samarkand. Within a few days a daughter was born to Sultan-Ahmad Mirza's daughter Ayisha Sultan Begim, the first to enter marriage with me. The girl was named Fakhrunnisa. She was my firstborn, and I was then nineteen years old, but within a month to forty days she died.

After the conquest of Samarkand, emissaries and commissars were constantly sent to request aid from the rulers and princes of the surrounding areas and the borders. Some, prior experience notwithstanding, took it lightly. Others, who had suffered insults and unpleasantness from these people, hid their heads in the sand in fear. Others who did send assistance sent nothing of substance, as each will be recorded in its proper place.

The second time I took Samarkand, Ali-Sher Beg [87] was still alive. This time he sent me a letter. I sent him a letter too. On the back I wrote a line of poetry in Turkish, but before the reply could come chaos had broken out. When Wormwood Khan took Samarkand, Mulla Banna'i joined his service and was still with him. A few days after our conquest he came to Samarkand. Qasim Beg was suspicious of him and dismissed him to Shahrisabz. But a few days after that, since he was a learned man and had committed no fault, we had him brought to Samarkand. He always composed *qasidas* and *ghazals*.[139] He made a musical composition in the *nawa*[140] mode dedicated to me. At the same time, he composed this quatrain:

> I have neither grain on which to be nourished / Nor grain sack with which to be clothed. / How can he who has neither food nor clothing / Devote himself to learning and art?

At that time I composed lines of poetry in ones and twos, but I had not yet completed a whole ghazal. I wrote a little quatrain in Turkish and sent it to him:

> All things will be as your heart desires. / Stipend and position will both be commanded. / That grain and sack of which you spoke—I know / You will fill a garment, and grain will fill your house.

Mulla Banna'i took this quatrain of mine, [87b] turned it into another quatrain by making the rhyme of my first hemistich a refrain and adding another rhyme, and sent it to me.[141]

My prince, who will be shah of land and sea, / Will be legend throughout the world for virtue. / He has shown such favor in rewarding nonsense: / Were my words reasonable, what all would there be?

Just then Khwaja Abu'l-Baraka Firaqi came to Samarkand from Shahrisabz. He said that it was necessary to reply in the first rhyme. He composed this quatrain:

Fate will be called to account for the cruelty it has perpetrated, / And the sultan of grace will accept your plight. / If what has been poured out is not filled, O cupbearer, / Our empty cups shall be filled in this age.

In these winter quarters things were looking up for us, while Wormwood Khan's fortune was on the wane. One or two untoward affairs, however, took place during that time. The men who had come from Merv and overcome Karakul were unable to hold it, and Karakul reverted to the Uzbeks. Then Ibrahim Tarkhan's brother, Ahmad Tarkhan, who was in Dabusi fort, was besieged by Wormwood. By the time we gathered our forces and were prepared, he had taken it by force and massacred the people.

When I took Samarkand, I had 240 men. [88] Within five or six months, thanks to God's great favor, there were enough to engage in battle someone like Wormwood Khan at Sar-i-Pul, as will be mentioned. From the surrounding areas and from the khan, Ayyub Begchik, Qashqa Mahmud, and the Barins four or five hundred men came to help. From Jahangir Mirza came Tambal's brother Khalil with a hundred or two. From an experienced padishah like Sultan-Husayn Mirza, who knew Wormwood's ways better than anyone, came no assistance. No one came from Badi'uzzaman Mirza either. In his fear Khusrawshah sent no one; since our family had suffered untold evil at his hands, as has been mentioned, his fear of us was rather great.

THE BATTLE OF SAR-I-PUL

In the month of Shawwal [April–May 1501], I moved out for the Baghi-Naw, intent upon fighting Wormwood Khan. We stayed in the Baghi-Naw for five or six days to gather our forces and make ready. Riding from there we proceeded, march by march, and camped past Sar-i-

Pul. We fortified the perimeter of the camp with pylons and trenches.
[88b] From the other side Wormwood Khan approached and camped
in the vicinity of Khwaja Kardzan, with about a league between us. For
four or five days we sat where we were. During the day our men and
his would ride from their respective sides against each other and do
combat. One day rather many of the enemy came forward, and there
was a large battle, but neither side gained a great advantage. Somebody
from our side bearing a standard made a hasty retreat and entered the
trenches. Some said, "That was Sidi Qara Beg's standard." Sidi Qara
was a man of strong bark, but his sword lacked bite. One night Wormwood Khan staged a surprise attack, but the perimeter of the camp was
well fortified with pylons and trenches and he was unable to do anything. They shouted from outside the trenches, shot a few arrows, and
retreated.

I exerted myself for the coming battle. So did Qambar-Ali. Baqi
Tarkhan was camped in Kish with one or two thousand men and
would join us in two days. Sayyid-Muhammad Mirza Dughlat came as
reinforcement from my uncle the khan with a thousand or fifteen hundred men [89] and camped in Diyul, four leagues away. They would
join us the next morning. At such a time we hastened the battle.

Who reaches hastily for the sword will bite the back of his hand in regret.

The reason for my anxiousness was so that on the day of battle the
Pleiades would be between the two armies. If the day had passed, the
Pleiades would have been behind the enemy for thirteen or fourteen
days.[142] Such considerations were futile, and I hastened the battle for
naught.

That morning we put on our mail for battle, armored the horses,
and set forth with right and left wings, center and vanguard arrayed. In
the right wing were Ibrahim Saru, Ibrahim Jani, Abu'l-Qasim Kohbur,
and some other begs. The left wing was Muhammad Mazid Tarkhan,
Ibrahim Tarkhan, and the Samarkand begs Sultan-Husayn Arghun,
Qara Barlas, Pir-Ahmad, and Khwaja Husayn. The center was Qasim
Beg and some other close ichkis. The vanguard was Qambar-Ali Sallakh, Banda-Ali Khwaja Ali, Mir Shah Qauchin, Sayyid-Qasim Eshik-

aqa, Banda-Ali's brother Khaldar, Haydar Qasim Beg's son Qoch. All
the great warriors and ichkis were assigned to the vanguard.

As we set out in battle formation, the enemy appeared arrayed for
battle directly opposite. [89b] In the right wing were Mahmud Sultan,
Jani-Beg Sultan, and Temür Sultan. In the left wing were Hamza Sultan, Mahdi Sultan, and some other princes. As the formations drew
near each other, the point of the foe's right wing advanced toward our
rear. I turned to face them. Our vanguard, to which had been assigned
all the warriors we had who were experienced in wielding the sword,
was left to my right. No one was left in our fore; nonetheless, we fought
those who advanced and drove them back to their center. Things had
gone this far when some of Wormwood Khan's aged chiefs said, "We
must move. The battle is past making a stand." However, he maintained
his stand. The foe's right wing broke our left wing and went on toward
our rear. Since our vanguard was left to our right, our front was exposed. From front and rear the enemy attacked and began to shoot. The
Moghul troops who had come as reinforcements had no endurance for
battle. They left the battle and began to unhorse and plunder our own
men. It was not just here they did this: these wretched Moghuls [90] always do this. If they win they take booty; if they lose they unhorse their
own people and plunder them for booty. A few times we pressed hard
on those who were in front of us and fought them back. Those who
were forward did the same. But the enemy who had circled around behind came up and rained arrows down on our standard. They pressed
from front and rear, causing our men to move off.

One great merit of the Uzbeks in battle is the flank assault. They
never do battle without using it. Another is that they all, officers and
ordinary soldiers alike, from front to rear, charge at a gallop shooting
arrows. In retreat they do not go off pell-mell but withdraw orderly.

Ten or twelve men were left with me. The Kohak River was near.
The tip of my right wing was pressed against the river. We went
straight for the river. It was the time of the river's flood. Reaching the
river, we plunged right in with mail and horse armor. A bit more than
halfway across, the horses could reach the bottom, but after that it was
too deep, and for an arrow shot we in full mail had to make the armored horses swim. Once across we cut off the horses' armor and
ditched it. Having crossed to the north of the river, [90b] we were free

of the enemy, but these damn Moghuls were all over unhorsing my friends one by one and stripping them bare. Ibrahim Tarkhan and many other great warriors were unhorsed, plundered, and killed. Moving along the north shore of the Kohak, we then recrossed the water in the vicinity of Qolba. It was afternoon when we entered by the Shaykhzada Gate and went to the citadel.

Some great begs and superb warriors, such as Ibrahim Tarkhan, Ibrahim Saru, and Ibrahim Jani, were lost in this battle. It is strange that in one battle three great begs named Ibrahim were lost. Also lost in this battle were Haydar Qasim Beg's eldest son, Abu'l-Qasim Kohbur, Khudaberdi Tughchï, and Sultan-Ahmad Tambal's brother Khalil, who has been mentioned several times.[143] Others scattered in all directions. Among them was Muhammad Mazid Tarkhan, who went to Khusraw-shah in Hissar and Konduz. Another was Qambar-Ali Sallakh Moghul, who was our greatly favored beg and had received such patronage but who at such a time refused to cooperate and took his family out of Samarkand and went to Khusrawshah. [91] Other ichkis and warriors like Karimdad Khudadad the Turcoman, Janka Kükäldash, and Mulla Baba of Pishagar went to Ura-Tyube. Mulla Baba was not then a liege man but rode as a guest. Others were like Sherim Taghayï and his band: although he had entered Samarkand at my side and had been at the consultations when we decided to make the Samarkand fortress fast and defend it to the last, when my mother and sisters stayed in the fortress, he sent his family and retainers out to Ura-Tyube and stayed by himself with a few of his people in the fortress. This was not the only time he did this. Every time circumstances got rough he displayed just such unreliability and uncooperativeness.

BABUR IS BESIEGED IN SAMARKAND

The next morning Khwaja Abu'l-Makarim, Qasim Beg, and all the begs, ichkis, and warriors who were admitted to council were convoked. In deliberation we decided to make fast the fortress and get ready to defend it to the teeth. Qasim Beg, my immediate ichkis and warriors, and I were to be reserves. To facilitate this, I had a tent set up on the roof of Ulughbeg Mirza's madrasa in the middle of the city, and there I stayed. [91b] Positions were distributed among the other begs and warriors at the gates and along the ramparts encircling the city.

Two or three days later Wormwood Khan camped close to the city wall. The rabble of Samarkand, district by district and lane by lane, gathered in throngs and came to the madrasa gate shouting prayers before going out to fight. When Wormwood Khan mounted for battle, he was unable to get near the walls. Several days passed in this fashion. The rabble, who had not experienced sword and arrow wounds and had not seen battle in the field, grew bold from the encounters and began to sortie farther. If warriors who had seen action tried to prevent these worthless sorties, they were reviled.

One day Wormwood Khan directed his attack at the Iron Gate. The mob, having grown bold, went far out as usual in their daring way. Some cavalrymen were sent out behind them. Some of our kükäldashes and close ichkis, such as Noyan Kükäldash, Qul-Nazar, Taghayï Mazid, and some others, went out toward Shutur-Gardan. Two or three Uzbeks charged them. [92] They exchanged sword blows with Qul-Nazar. The Uzbeks dismounted and pressed hard, making the city mob move back and jamming them against the Iron Gate. Qoch Beg and Mir Shah Qauchin dismounted and stood beside the Khwaja Khizr Mosque. As the people on foot were moved back, the forward horsemen were pressed toward the mosque. Qoch Beg moved out and fought well with the advancing Uzbeks. He really did an outstanding job. All the people stood and watched. Those escaping below were occupied with making their escape. The affair was beyond shooting arrows and standing to fight. I was shooting with a slur bow from atop the gate. Some others near me were shooting too. The enemy retreated, unable to advance past the mosque because of our fire from above.

Every night during the siege we made the rounds of the top of the fortress rampart. Sometimes I, sometimes Qasim Beg, sometimes other begs and ichkis made the rounds. From the Turquoise Gate to the Shaykhzada Gate it was possible to go on horseback atop the ramparts. In other places we had to go on foot. [92b] By the time one made an entire round on foot, dawn would be breaking.

One day Wormwood Khan directed his attack between the Iron Gate and the Shaykhzada Gate. I, who was reserve, went there as soon as the fighting broke out, unconcerned about the side between the Gazaristan Gate and the Needlemakers' Gate.[144] That day I made a good shot with my slur bow from atop the Shaykhzada Gate at a horseman's gray horse. It died instantly. Just then they mounted such an attack that they made it to the bottom of the rampart in the vicinity of Shutur-Gardan. While we were thus occupied with the battle and completely heedless of the other side, they had made ready twenty-five or twenty-six ladders wide enough for two or three men to go up side by side. Seven or eight hundred brave warriors with their ladders ambushed the area between the Gazaristan and the Needlemakers' gates and began to do battle from that side. When all our men were occupied with the battle and their posts vacated, they emerged from their ambush [93] and quickly set up their ladders against the ramparts between the two gates opposite Muhammad Mazid Tarkhan's quarters. That was the post of Qoch Beg and Muhammad-Qulï Qauchin and another band of warriors who were staying in Muhammad Mazid Tarkhan's quarters. The Needlemakers' Gate was Qara Barlas's post. The Gazaristan Gate was the post of Sherim Taghayï and his brothers, Qïlsaq and Qutlugh Khwaja Kükäldash. Since the fighting had broken out on the other side, the men at this post were unaware and they and their servants had gone off to their houses or the market on business. The begs of the post were left with one or two tough civilians. Qoch Beg, Muhammad-Qulï Qauchin, Shah Sufi, and another warrior fought bravely and valiantly. Some of the enemy made it to the top of the rampart. Others were getting up. These four men ran and fought hard and, chopping away with their swords, fought them back and put them to flight. Qoch Beg made the best showing. This was certainly one of his outstanding shows. He got into the fray twice during this siege. Qara Barlas was also left alone at his post, [93b] and he too held out well. Qutlugh Khwaja Kükäldash and Qul-Nazar Mirza were at their posts at the Gazaristan Gate. They too held out well with few men and made good attacks on the enemy's rear.

Another time, Qasim Beg led his warriors out of the Needlemakers' Gate in pursuit of the Uzbeks as far as Khwaja Kafshir, unhorsed a few, and brought back their severed heads.

The grain was now ripe, but no one was bringing any new grain into town. The days of siege wore on. The people were in want. The situation got so bad that the poor and unfortunate began to eat dogs and donkeys. Feed for horses was in such short supply that they fed them leaves. Experience taught that mulberry and elm leaves agreed with horses the best. Some shredded dry wood, wet the chips, and fed that to the horses.

For three or four months Wormwood Khan kept moving around the city walls from fairly far out without ever coming close in. Once around midnight, while the people were off guard, they came to the Turquoise Gate side and beat drums and let out whoops. I was in the madrasa. [94] There was much apprehension and trepidation. After that they came every night beating drums and shouting to create confusion.

No matter how many emissaries and envoys were sent in every direction, aid and assistance came from no one. They had not sent help or assistance when we were strong and had not experienced defeat or need. In a situation such as this with what expectation should they send assistance? It was useless to remain besieged in hopes of help from anyone. Our predecessors have said that to hold a fortress under siege, a head, two arms, and two legs are necessary. The head is the commander, the two arms are reinforcements coming from two directions, and the two legs are the water and provisions of the fortress. We were looking for help from those around us, while they were each and all of a different opinion. A brave and experienced padishah like Sultan-Husayn Mirza not only gave us no assistance and sent no envoy with a word of encouragement but also actually dispatched Kamaluddin Husayn of Gazargah on an embassy to Wormwood Khan during the siege.

Tambal went from Andizhan to the vicinity of Beshkent. The khan, Ahmad Beg, and a party went out to face him. In the vicinity of Laklakan [94b] and Turak Charbagh they faced each other but parted without fighting. Sultan-Mahmud Khan was not a fighting man and was devoid of any ability to command. When he faced Tambal, cowardly words and actions were manifested by the khan. Ahmad Beg was a simple, rustic man, but he was brave and a good supporter. In his coarse way he said, "How much of a man is this Tambal for you to be so scared? If your eyes are afraid, shut them and let's go face him."

EVENTS OF THE YEAR 907
(1501-2)[145]

The siege dragged on for a long time. No supplies or provisions were coming from any direction. No help or reinforcement arrived from any side. Soldier and civilian alike left the fortress in desperation one by one and two by two. Wormwood Khan, realizing that the people inside the walls were distressed, camped in the vicinity of Lovers' Cave. I moved directly opposite him in Malik Muhammad Mirza's quarters in the Kuy-i-Payan. Just about that time Khwaja Husayn's brother Uzun Hasan, who had caused Jahangir Mirza's rebellion and forced us to quit Samarkand before, as has been mentioned,[146] [95] entered the fortress with ten or fifteen liege men. To make such an entrance was a brave thing to do.

Want and deprivation became grave for soldier and civilian. Members of my immediate circle and important people began to desert over the walls. Begs of renown like Ways Shaykh and old retainers like Ways Laghari escaped and fled. We gave up all hope from any quarter. No hope was left from anywhere. Provisions and supplies had been scant to begin with, and no more came from any direction. What there was came to an end. At just this point Wormwood Khan initiated truce talks. Had there been any hope or supplies, who would have listened to an offer of terms? There was nothing to be done. We made peace, and around the second watch of the night we left through the Shaykhzada Gate.

BABUR LEAVES SAMARKAND

I took my mother the khanïm with me. Two other women came out too. One was Khalifa's Bichka and the other was Menglig Kükäldash. My elder sister Khanzada Begim fell into Wormwood Khan's hands while we were leaving. In the dark of night we lost our way among the great canals in Sughd and with great difficulty passed Khwaja Didar as the sun was coming up. Early that morning [95b] we scrambled up Qarbugh Hill. By noon we were at the foot of Judak Village to the north of the hill headed for Ilan Otï and still moving. Along the way Qambar-Ali, Qasim Beg, and I were racing. My horse pulled ahead, and I turned to see how far behind they were. My girth strap must have snapped, for the saddle slipped over and I fell on my head. Although I stood up immediately and got back on, my brain did not return to normal until that evening. Events happening in the world were like dreams and phantoms were passing before my eyes and through my mind. Late that afternoon we stopped in Ilan Otï, killed a horse, and cooked the meat on skewers. After giving the horses a moment's rest we remounted. A little before dawn we stopped in the village of Khaliliyya. From there we went to Dzhizak.

Hafiz Muhammad Beg Dulday's son Tahir Dulday was then in Dzhizak. Fat meat, abundant bread made of fine flour, sweet melons, good grapes—from such hardship we had come to such plenty, from such catastrophe to such safety.

From fear and hardship we found release—new life, a new world we found.

The fear of death was driven from our minds, [96] and the pangs of hunger were alleviated. Never in our lives had we been so relieved. Never had we appreciated safety and comfort so much. Ease and relief seem all the more pleasurable after hardship and distress. Four or five times in our life we went from such distress to ease and from such difficulty to relief. This was the first time. We had escaped the clutches of an enemy and the affliction of hunger and reached the ease of safety and the relief of plenty.

We rested in Dzhizak for three or four days. Then we set out for Ura-Tyube. Pishagar was a little way off the road. Since I had been there before,[147] I made an excursion to see it as we passed by. In the Pishagar fort I chanced to meet Atun, who had long been in my lady mother's service but had been left behind in Samarkand due to lack of mounts. I greeted her and asked how she was. She had walked all the way here from Samarkand.

My mother's younger sister, Khub Nigar Khanïm, had passed away. At Ura-Tyube they told my mother and me the news. My father's mother had also passed away at Andizhan. [96b] This too they told us here. My mother had not seen her stepmother, Shah Begim, or her younger brother and sisters, Sultan-Mahmud Khan, Sultan Nigar Khanïm, and Dawlat Sultan Khanïm, since my grandfather the khan had died. Their separation had lasted for thirteen or fourteen years. She set out for Tashkent to see her family.

I spoke with Muhammad-Husayn Mirza and decided to winter in a place called Dakhkat, a mountainside village near Ura-Tyube. I left my family in Dakhkat and set out a few days later for Tashkent to see Shah Begim, my uncle the khan, and my kinsmen. I paid homage to Shah Begim and my uncle the khan and stayed there a few days. My mother's full sister Mihr Nigar Khanïm also came from Samarkand. My mother the khanïm fell ill. It was very serious and she was critically ill.

Khwajaka Khwaja had left Samarkand and was living in Farkat. I went to Farkat to see him. I was hopeful that my uncle the khan would show favor and give me some territory or a province. He had promised Ura-Tyube, but Muhammad-Husayn Mirza [97] would not give it up. I don't know whether he refused on his own accord or whether he was acting on orders from above. Some days later I came back to Dakhkat, which is situated at the base of a large mountain. The other side of the mountain is Matcha. Although the villagers here were Sarts, they kept herds and flocks like Turks. The sheep of Dakhkat were numbered at forty thousand. We settled in the peasants' houses in the village.

I stayed in the house of a headman. He was aged, seventy or eighty years old, but his mother was still alive—she was 111 years old. When Temür Beg invaded Hindustan, one of this woman's kinsmen went to the army, and she remembered it and talked about it. In Dakhkat alone there were ninety-six of this woman's own children, grandchildren, great-grandchildren, and great-great-grandchildren. Counting those who had died, there were two hundred. One of her great-great-grandchildren was a young man of twenty-five or twenty-six with a jet-black beard.

While in Dakhkat I used often to go for walks in the surrounding mountains. Mostly I walked barefooted. [97b] My feet got so that mountains and stones made no difference. One day on one of those walks in the late afternoon or early evening we saw a cow going down a narrow, scarcely distinguishable path. I said, "I wonder where this path leads to. Keep your eyes on the cow. Don't lose it so we can find out where the path goes." Khwaja Asadullah made a joke and said, "What should we do if the cow gets lost?"

This same winter some of the soldiers, unable to go with us on our raids, requested permission to go to Andizhan. With much insistence Qasim Beg said to me, "Since these men are going, send something special you have worn to Jahangir Mirza." I sent a sable hat. Qasim Beg insisted even more, saying, "Why not send something to Tambal?" I was not disposed to do it, but because Qasim Beg insisted I sent Tambal the big broad sword that Noyan Kükäldash had had made for himself in Samarkand. This was the sword that later came crashing down on my head, as will be reported in the events of the coming year.[148]

Some days after that my grandmother, Esän Dawlat Begim, [98] who had remained behind when I left Samarkand, arrived with the hungry and lean family members who had stayed in Samarkand.

In the middle of the winter Wormwood Khan crossed the Khodzhent River on the ice and raided the vicinity of Shahrukhiyya and Pskent. As soon as we received word we mounted, without regard for how few our men were, and set out for opposite Hasht Yak, a village downriver. There was a terrible cold snap. In this region the wind from Ha Darwesh never ceases and always blows hard. It was so bad then that within two or three days two or three men died. I needed to make my ablutions. I went to do so at a canal. Its edges were completely frozen, but in the middle the water ran fast, and there I made my ablutions. I went under sixteen times. The cold water had a great effect. The next morning we crossed on the ice opposite Khasslar and arrived in Pskent. Wormwood Khan had raided the vicinity of Shahrukhiyya and withdrawn.

Pskent was then in the hands of Mulla Haydar's son Abdul-Mannan. He also had another son younger than Abdul-Mannan, a worthless scatterbrain named Mu'min. He had come to me while I was in Samarkand, and I had shown him great favor. I don't know what he and Noyan Kükäldash had quarreled over in Samarkand, [98b] but this sodomite nurtured a hatred of Noyan. When we had news that the Uzbek raiders had withdrawn, we decamped from Pskent and stopped for three or four days in some villages of Ahangaran. Because they were acquainted in Samarkand, Mu'min invited to a banquet Noyan Kükäldash, Ahmad Qasim, and some others who had stayed in Pskent when I left. He set up a party for the group on the edge of a cliff. We went on to a village called Samsarek in Ahangaran. The next morning, news came that Noyan Kükäldash had died from falling off the cliff while drunk. Noyan's uncle Haqqnazar and a party were sent. They searched the area where Noyan had fallen, buried him in Pskent, and came back. They had found Noyan's body at the foot of the high cliff an arrow shot away from the place where the party was held. Some suspected that Mu'min, nurturing a grudge from Samarkand, had murdered Noyan. No one ever discovered the truth. I was singularly affected. Rarely have I been so moved by anyone's death. I wept for a week or ten days. [99] His chronogram was found thus: "Noyan passed away."[149]

Several days later I went back to Dakhkat. News came that when spring arrived Wormwood Khan was going to move against Ura-Tyube. Because Dakhkat was flat, we went through the Oburdan pass up to the Matcha hills. Oburdan is the lowest village in Matcha. A bit down from Oburdan is a spring, next to which is a shrine. What is above this spring is inside Matcha. Below belongs to Palghar. I had this poetry carved in a rock next to the spring:

I have heard that glorious Jamshed[150] wrote on a stone at a spring, / "Like us many have spoken over this spring, but they were gone in the twinkling of an eye. / We conquered the world with bravery and might, but we did not take it with us to the grave."

In those mountains it is customary to carve poetry and other sayings on the rocks.

While we were there in Matcha, Mulla Hajri the poet came from

Hissar and paid homage to me. Around that same time I composed this opening line:

> With whatever artifice your portrait is made, you are still more. / They call you "soul," but without artifice you are more than a soul.

Wormwood Khan came to the outskirts of Ura-Tyube and wrought a bit of havoc before withdrawing. While he was there, [99b] without regard for the fact that our men were few and without arms, we left the family in Matcha and went down the Oburdan pass to the vicinity of Dakhkat so that just before dawn we could sneak up to the gate and not miss the opportunity. Wormwood, however, pulled out quickly, and we returned to Matcha through the pass.

"To wander aimlessly from mountain to mountain," I thought, "with no realm and no place to stay is useless. Let's go to the khan in Tashkent." Qasim Beg was not happy with such a move because previously he had had three or four Moghuls executed as examples in Qara Bulaq, as has been mentioned.[151] It was probably for that reason that he was afraid to go there. Insist as we might, he wouldn't go, and so took his brothers and followers to Hissar. We took the Oburdan pass and set off to see the khan in Tashkent.

About the same time, Tambal led his army to the Ahangaran valley. Men at the head of his army, such as Muhammad Dughlat, known as Muhammad Hisari, conspired with his brother Sultan-Husayn Dughlat and Qambar-Ali Sallakh to assassinate Tambal. Tambal learned of the plot, however, so they could remain no longer and fled to the khan.

The Feast of the Sacrifice[152] found us in Shahrukhiyya, and I proceeded without halt to Tashkent.

POETICAL COMPOSITION

I had composed the following quatrain, but I had some hesitation about the rhyme because at that time I had not yet made a study of the technique of poetry. [100] The khan had a poetic nature and composed poetry, although his successful ghazals were rather few. I presented my quatrain to him and told him of my doubts, but I did not receive a satisfactory answer. Probably he had not studied the technicalities of poetry much either. The quatrain is this:

No one remembers anyone in tribulation. / No one gladdens anyone in exile. / In this exile my heart has not been gladdened. / No one can be comforted at all in exile.

Afterward I found out that for purposes of rhyme, *t* and *d* are interchangeable, as are *gh* and *q* and *k* and *g*.[153]

THE MOGHUL YAK-TAIL STANDARD CEREMONY

A few days later Tambal moved against Ura-Tyube. As soon as the news was received, the khan rode out of Tashkent with his army. The right and left wings were arrayed between Pskent and Samsarek, and a count was taken. According to Moghul custom the yak-tail standards were acclaimed. The khan dismounted, whereupon nine standards were set up before him. A Moghul tied a long piece of white cloth to a cow's shank and held the other end in his hand. Another three long pieces of cloth were tied to the standards below the yak tails and wrapped down to the bottom of the standard poles. The end of one piece of cloth was brought for the khan to stand on. I stood on the end of another, and Sultan-Mahmud Khanika stood on the third. [100b] The Moghul took hold of the cow's shank to which the cloth was tied, said something in Mongolian, and, facing at the standards, made a sign. The khan and all those standing by threw their koumiss[154] toward the standards. All at once the clarions and drums were sounded, and the army standing in ranks let out whoops and shouts. Three times they did this. After that the army got on their horses, shouted, and galloped around.

Among the Moghuls the arrangement of the army is exactly as Genghis Khan left it. Right wing, left wing, center—from father to son they remain where they were assigned. In the right and left wings the higher a man's rank, the closer to the edge he stands. In the right wing the Chiras and Begchik clans have always quarreled over the edge. At that time the tümän beg of the Chiras was Qashqa Mahmud, who was a brave man. The tümän beg of the Begchik tümän, which is known simply as "the tümän," was Ayyub Ya'qub. They fought over who was to be at the edge. They had even drawn swords at each other. Finally it must have been decided that in the *jergä*[155] one would stand in a more honorable position and in the array the other would be at the edge.

The next morning they formed a circle in Samsarek and held a hunt. Camp was made in Turak Charbagh. [101]

The first ghazal I ever completed I finished that day in that place. It begins:

Other than my own soul I never found a faithful friend. / Other than my own heart I never found a confidant.

It consisted of six lines.[156] Thereafter, every ghazal that was completed was written down in that same arrangement.

From there they went march by march to the banks of the Jaxartes. One day we crossed the river on an excursion, cooked some food, and made merry with the warriors and pages. That day my gold belt clasp was stolen. By the next morning Khan-Qulï Buyan-Qulï and Sultan-Muhammad Ways had deserted to Tambal. Everyone suspected them of the deed, although it was never proven. Ahmad Qasim Kohbur also requested leave to go to Ura-Tyube. He never came back but went instead to Tambal.

EVENTS OF THE YEAR 908
(1502–3)[157]

This expedition of the khan's turned out to be fairly useless. He went and returned without taking any forts or defeating any enemies.

During this period in Tashkent I endured much hardship and misery. I had no realm—and no hope of any realm—to rule. Most of my liege men had departed. The few who were left were too wretched to move about with me. If I went to my uncle the khan's gate, I went sometimes with one other person and sometimes with two—at least the khan was a relative and not a stranger. [101b] After meeting with him, I used to go to see Shah Begim, as though I were entering my own house, bareheaded and barefoot.

Finally I had had all I could take of homelessness and alienation. "With such difficulties," I said to myself, "it would be better to go off on my own so long as I am alive, and with such deprivation and wretchedness it would be better for me to go off to wherever my feet will carry me, even to the ends of the earth." I decided to go to Cathay on my own. From my childhood I had had a desire to go to Cathay, but because of having to rule and other obstacles, it had never been possible. Now there was nothing for me to rule. My mother had rejoined her brothers and kinfolk. Impediments to my travel had disappeared, as had my former ambitions. Through the intermediary of Khwaja Abu'l-Makarim, I stated the following case to the khan: An enemy like Wormwood Khan had appeared on the scene, and he posed a threat to

Turk and Moghul alike. He should be dealt with now while he had not yet totally defeated the nation or grown too strong, as has been said:

> Put out a fire today while you can, for when it blazes high it will burn the world. / Do not allow the enemy to string his bow while you are able to pierce him with an arrow.

My mother's people had not met with my uncle Kichik Khan for twenty or twenty-five years, and I had never seen him. Would it be possible for me to go and both meet my uncle Kichik Khan and be instrumental in creating a meeting? It was my aim to leave here on this pretext [102] and go to Moghulistan and Turfan, since there was no longer any impediment and my reins were in my own hands. No one knew of this plan of mine. It was not possible either to let anyone know because it was out of the question to broach the subject with my mother. Also, the people around me, great and small, followed me and endured deprivation in other hopes. There was no delight to be derived in speaking of such things to these people.

As soon as Khwaja Abu'l-Makarim spoke to Shah Begim and my uncle the khan, he perceived that they would be agreeable. It then crossed their minds, however, that I might be requesting permission to leave because I had not been shown favor. Since this touched upon their honor, they hesitated somewhat in granting their permission.

KICHIK KHAN COMES TO TASHKENT

At this juncture someone came from my uncle Kichik Khan with news that he was actually on his way. So my scheme came to naught. As soon as another person reported that Kichik Khan was near, Shah Begim and my uncle Kichik Khan's sisters, Sultan Nigar Khanim and Dawlat Sultan Khanim, all went out with Sultan-Muhammad Khanika, Mirza Khan, and myself to meet my uncle Kichik Khan.

Between Tashkent and Sayram there are several hamlets and a village called Yaghma, the location of Ata Ibrahim's and Ata Ishaq's tombs.[158] We went as far as these villages. Since we did not know for certain when my uncle Kichik Khan would be coming, [102b] I had ridden out without a care. All of a sudden the khan loomed before us. I rode forward. As I dismounted, my uncle Kichik Khan became aware of me and was very upset. He had probably planned to dismount somewhere, seat himself, and meet me ceremoniously, but I was quite near when I dismounted, and there was no time for that. He did not even have a chance to dismount.[159] I knelt and went forward to meet him. Flustered and agitated, he immediately ordered Sultan Sa'id Khan and Baba Khan Sultan to dismount, kneel, and meet me. Of the khan's sons, only these two had come. They were thirteen or fourteen years old. Having met with them, we mounted and went to Shah Begim. They sat around talking about old times until midnight.

The next morning my uncle Kichik Khan, in accordance with Moghul custom, presented me with a robe, a quiver, his own horse and saddle, a Moghul hat, an embroidered Chinese brocade tunic, and a Chinese quiver with its stone and satchel in the old fashion. On the left side of the satchel were hung three or four items such as ladies hang on their collars, like an ambergris bottle and its reticule. On the right side too were hung three or four objects.[160]

From there they set out in the direction of Tashkent. [103] My uncle Ulugh Khan had also come out three or four leagues from Tashkent in greeting. Canopies were set up, and Ulugh Khan sat there. As Kichik Khan approached he circled around behind the khan's left and stopped in front of him. When he reached the place for the meeting, he knelt nine times, as for the encounter. Ulugh Khan rose as Kichik Khan approached, and they met. They stood embracing each other for a long time. As he withdrew, Kichik Khan knelt nine times, as many times as the gifts were presented. After that he came forward, and they sat down.

All Kichik Khan's men were outfitted in the Mongolian manner—Mongolian hats, embroidered Chinese brocade tunics, green leather Mongolian bowcases and saddles, Mongolian horses, and fantastic finery. Kichik Khan had come with rather few men—more than a thousand but fewer than two thousand. My uncle Kichik Khan was a peculiar man. He was manly and brave but held tight to his sword. Of all his weapons, he trusted most in his sword. "Six-flanged mace, flail, hatchet, and battle ax work in one place when they strike," he would say, "but when a sword hits the mark it works from head to foot." He was never separated from his sharp sword—it was either at his side [103b] or in his hand. Because he had grown up in a remote place he was somewhat rustic and coarse of speech.

Wearing the Mongolian finery I have mentioned, I accompanied my uncle Kichik Khan. Khwaja Abu'l-Makarim was with my uncle Ulugh Khan, and they did not recognize me. "What Moghul prince is this?" they asked, although they knew me after I spoke.

Immediately upon reaching Tashkent, they led the army to Andizhan against Sultan-Ahmad Tambal, setting out via the Kindirlig Pass road. When we reached the Ahangaran valley, Kichik Khan and I were dispatched ahead.

After going through the pass, a troop review was held one day in Zabarqan in the vicinity of Karnon. The soldiers numbered thirty thousand. From ahead, news began to come that Tambal had gathered his forces and was moving toward Akhsi. The khans consulted and decided to assign me a contingent. I would cross the Jaxartes, go toward Osh and Uzgen, and circle around behind him. Having decided this, Ayyub Begchik with his battalion, Jan Hasan Barin with the Barins, and Muhammad Hisari Dughlat, Sultan-Husayn Dughlat, and Sultan-Ahmad Mirza Dughlat by themselves—the Dughlat battalions were not there—and Qambar-Ali Sarïghbash Mirza of the Itarji were put in charge of the forces and assigned to me.

We left the khans at Karnon, crossed the Jaxartes by raft in the vicinity of Sakan, passed through the Kokand [104] district, attacked Kuva, and rode against the Alayluq district and Osh.

At dawn we took the Osh citadel by surprise. Those of Osh were unable to do anything but surrender. Those of the province were naturally inclined toward us, but out of fear of Tambal and because we had been far away they had not been able to do anything about it. As soon as we entered Osh, the people of highland and lowland to the east and south of Andizhan all joined us. (Uzgen, which was formerly the capital of Fergana, has a good citadel and is located on the border.) They accepted fealty to us, sent emissaries, and came over to me.

A few days later the people of Margilan beat up their prefect, chased him away, and joined me. With the exception of Andizhan itself, all the citadels on the Andizhan side of the Jaxartes were with me. During these days, although there was much unrest and strife, Tambal had still not come to his senses and so, faced with the khans and their cavalry and infantry between Akhsi and Karnon, he fortified himself with pilings and trenches and sat there. A few skirmishes took place, but there was no clear victory or defeat for either side.

When the tribes, clans, fortresses, and countryside on the Andizhan side [104b] joined me, the townspeople of Andizhan were naturally desirous of me, but there was nothing they could do about it.

A SKIRMISH AT CHILDUKHTARAN

It occurred to me that if someone could get near Andizhan by night and slip inside, and if we could confer with the khwaja and the lords, it was probable that they would get us in somehow. With this plan in mind we rode from Osh and came opposite Childukhtaran, a league from Andizhan. At midnight Qambar-Ali Beg and some other begs were sent forward to get someone inside the citadel by stealth and confer with the khwaja and lords. We remained on horseback waiting for the begs who had gone—some apprehensive, others dozing. It must have been the third watch of the night when all at once the sound of drums and war cries were heard. Not knowing how many or how few they were, these surprised and drowsy people, without looking at each other, turned around and fled. I had no chance to reach them. I raced toward the enemy. Mir Shah Qauchin, Baba Sherzad, and Dost Nasir moved out with me. Aside from us four, everyone started to flee. I had withdrawn a bit when the warriors reached me, firing arrows and giving war cries. One man on a horse with a blaze on its forehead snuck up close to me. I shot his horse. It turned a flip. They made as though to retreat a bit. [105]

The three men with me said, "In the pitch black of night we don't know how many or how few the enemy are. The forces we had have all gone away. How much harm can we four inflict? We should go reach our men and fight." We went off in pursuit and caught up with the men, but no matter how hard we whipped them, they would not assemble. We four returned and shot arrows, holding them off for a little while. When they looked a time or two and saw that we were no more than three or four, they busied themselves pursuing and unhorsing men. I went three or four times in a similar manner and tried to hold them off. When they could no longer be held off, I pulled back with my three men, let a few arrows fly, and forced the enemy to withdraw. They pursued us two or three leagues to the hill opposite Kharabek and Pishamun. Upon reaching the hill, Muhammad Ali Mubashshir appeared. "These are but a few men," I said. "Let's stand

and charge." We stood and charged. When we reached them, they just stood there.

The men who had scattered in all directions gathered. Some very great warriors had gone straight to Osh in this fray.

Such were the circumstances when some Moghuls from Ayyub Begchik's battalion separated from us at Osh and went as brigands to the outskirts of Andizhan. Having heard of the chaos in our army, they snuck up and exchanged passwords. (Passwords are of two sorts, [105b] and every group has its own. Some use the word "*durdana*" as a password, others use "*tuqpay*," some use "*lulu*."[161] When an entire army is engaged in an action, two words are used as sign and countersign so that when they encounter each other during an action they exchange passwords, one saying the sign and the other the countersign, and by this means friend can be distinguished from foe.) During this campaign the passwords were "Tashkent" and "Sayram." If one said "Tashkent" or "Sayram," the other would reply "Sayram" or "Tashkent." During the exchange Khwaja Muhammad Ali was rather far forward. The Moghuls came saying "Tashkent Tashkent." Khwaja Muhammad Ali, a Sart fellow, was flustered and kept saying "Tashkent Tashkent" too. The Moghuls, thinking he was one of the enemy, let out a war cry, beat the drums, and fired arrows. By this mistake chaos broke out, and we were scattered. The plan I had envisioned failed. In retreat we went to Osh.

ANOTHER ATTEMPT ON ANDIZHAN

Five or six days later Tambal and his followers were demoralized when highland, lowland, fortress, and citadel rejoined me, and his forces and people began to flee in threes and fours into the hills and plain. Some of those who had come from inside Andizhan said, "Tambal's strategy is crumbling. Within three or four days it will be all over and he will withdraw." As soon as this news was received, we mounted to go to Andizhan. In the Andizhan citadel was Tambal's youngest brother, Sultan-Muhammad Kalpuk. Coming by the Tutluq road, a midday raid was made on Khakan to the south of Andizhan. [106] I myself rode behind the raiders and came to the foot of Aysh Hill on the Khakan side. News came from the scouts that Sultan-Muhammad Kalpuk had gone out with his men to the foot of Aysh Hill outside the city quarters and orchards. The raiders had still not assembled. Without looking to see if the scouts were gathering, I moved quickly, without stopping, toward the enemy. Kalpuk's men were more than five hundred. Although our men were more numerous, our forces had dispersed for the strike. As we came face-to-face we were just about equal in number. Without regard to array and arrangement, we set off at full gallop toward the enemy. As we approached, the enemy could not maintain their position. They could not even strike a blow of the sword but instead turned and fled. Up to near the Khakan Gate, Tambal's men were pursued and felled.

By the time the enemy was defeated and we reached Khwaja Kata at the edge of the suburbs, it was evening. It was my plan to reach the gate quickly. The aged and experienced Dost Beg's father, Nasir Beg, and Qambar-Ali Beg said, "It's late. It would be ill-advised to sneak up on the citadel at night. Let's pull back and camp. At dawn what can they do but hand over the citadel?" Acting upon these experienced begs' advice, we retreated to the edge of the suburbs. [106b] If we had gone on to the citadel gateway, doubtless the citadel would have fallen into our hands.

It was nighttime. We crossed the Khakan irrigation canal and camped beside the village of Rabat-i-Zaurak. Since news had been received that Tambal was as good as beaten and would retreat to Andizhan, from inexperience I made a mistake. Instead of camping in a fortifiable place alongside a canal such as the Khakan, we crossed and camped in the flat open ground beside Rabat-i-Zaurak village. No scouts, no rear guard—we lay down open to attack.

At dawn's first light everyone was dozing peacefully when Qambar-Ali Beg rushed in shouting, "The enemy is upon us! Get up!" Having said this, he paused not an instant and ran straight through without returning. Even in times of security I never took off my tunic or quiver but simply lay back as I was. I jumped up, fastened my sword and quiver, and immediately got to horse. With no time for the *tughchi*[162] to secure the yak tail, he mounted with it in his hand. We set off in the direction from which the enemy was coming. As I rode out I had with me ten or fifteen men. We had gone about an arrow shot when we encountered about as many enemy raiders as there were of us. Proceeding quickly, we shot and moved up, taking the foremost men. We had pursued them the distance of another arrow shot when we encountered their center. Sultan-Ahmad Tambal was standing, maintaining his position with around a hundred men. [107] Tambal himself was standing with one other man a bit forward of his battle array, shouting, "Strike! Strike!" However, most of his men had turned aside, wondering whether or not to flee. At that point three men were left with me, Dost Nasir, Mirza-Qulï Kükäldash, and Karimdad Khudadad the Turcoman. I shot an arrow I had in my thumb ring at Tambal's helmet. Then I reached into my quiver. My uncle the khan had given me a fresh *goshagir,*[163] and that is what came to hand. It would have been a shame to throw it away, but by the time I reached back into the quiver I could have shot two more arrows. When I had another arrow on the string, I went forward. The other three remained behind.

Of the two men who were before me, one was Tambal, and he too came forward. There was a highway between us, I on one side and he on the other. We both entered the road and came face-to-face, I with my right arm toward the enemy and Tambal with his right arm toward us. Tambal had on all his armor except for the horse mail. I had none save my quiver and sword. I took aim at his mailed head with the arrow I had in my hand and shot. Just then an arrow struck me in the thigh, piercing straight through. I had an underhelmet cap on my head. Tambal landed such a blow on my head that my head went numb. [107b] Although not a thread of the cap was cut, my head was badly wounded. I had not unsheathed my sword: it was still in the scabbard. There was no time to draw my sword. There I remained, alone in the midst of the numerous enemy, but it was no place to stand still. As I turned my reins, another sword blow landed on my arrows. I had retreated about seven or eight paces when the three on foot joined me. After wielding his sword against me, Tambal was aiming blows at Dost Nasir. They came after us, about an arrow shot away.

The Khakan canal is a large irrigation main, and it runs too deep to be crossed everywhere. Thank God, we came directly opposite a ford in the canal. As soon as we were across, Dost Nasir's horse weakened and collapsed. We stopped long enough to get him rehorsed and went toward Osh by way of the rise between Kharabek and Qaraghina. When we got up on the rise, Mazid Taghayï joined us. He too had been struck by an arrow below the right knee. The arrow had not gone all the way through, and he reached Osh only with great difficulty. My brave warriors had been felled. Nasir Beg, Muhammad Ali Mubashshir, Khwaja

Muhammad Ali, Khusraw Kükäldash, and Nu'man Chuhra all fell there, as did many other brave young men.

The khans went straight out after Tambal and camped in the vicinity of Andizhan. Ulugh Khan camped beside the meadow [108] in my grandmother Esän Dawlat Begim's garden called Qush Tegirmän. Kichik Khan camped near the Baba Tükäl Langar. Two days later I came to Osh. I saw Ulugh Khan at Qush Tegirmän. When I came to see the khan, the towns that had joined me were given to Kichik Khan. By way of justification to me they said that since an enemy like Wormwood Khan had taken a city like Samarkand and was constantly growing stronger, they had brought Kichik Khan from Lord knows where. Here he had neither place to stay nor realm to rule. It was necessary to give Kichik Khan the area to the south of the Jaxartes to Andizhan to make his home. I was promised the area to the north of the Jaxartes with Akhsi at its head. They said that after they had consolidated this area they would take the province of Samarkand and give it to me. Thereafter the whole of Fergana would be Kichik Khan's. They were probably deceiving me with these words. It was uncertain whether it would actually come to pass, even if it were possible. I could do nothing about it, however, so like it or not, I gave my consent.

In Ulugh Khan's presence we mounted to go see Kichik Khan. Along the way Qambar-Ali Beg, known as Sallakh, rode up beside me and said, "You see? They have taken away the regions you had in the bag. Nothing's going to come your way from these people. [108b] Now that you've got Osh, Margilan, Uzgen, and the provinces and people who have joined you in your pocket, you should go to Osh and reinforce those who are there. Then send somebody to make peace with Sultan-Ahmad Tambal, strike the Moghuls, drive them out, and divide up the area between you like brothers."

"Would such a thing be possible?" I replied. "It is more important for me to serve my kinsmen the khans than to rule over Tambal as king." He saw that his words had made no impact on me and regretted having spoken.

A VISIT TO KICHIK KHAN

I went to see my uncle Kichik Khan. The last time, I had come upon him unprepared. There had been no chance for him to dismount, and hence we met without ceremony, as has been mentioned.[164] This time, as I drew near, he came running out to the end of the tent ropes. Because of the arrow wound in my leg I was holding a staff and walking with difficulty. When we met, he took my arm and led me into the tent, saying, "You must be my little brother the hero." A smallish tent had been pitched. He had grown up in a remote place, and kept his tent and dwelling unadorned. It looked like a robber's den—melons and grapes and horse trappings strewn all over. I left Kichik Khan and went to my own camp.

A Moghul surgeon named Atika Bakhshi was sent to tend to my wound. The Moghul people call a surgeon *bakhshi*.[165] He was quite an expert at surgery. If somebody's brains had spilled out, [109] he gave him some medicine. He could easily treat any sort of wound from his herb bag. For some wounds he prescribed a salvelike medicine; for others he dispensed medicine to be swallowed. For the wound on my thigh he ordered an animal's foot to be rubbed on it, and he did not apply a dressing. Once he had me swallow something herbal. He used to say, "A fellow broke his leg. It was shattered for a span. I hollowed out the flesh, took out all the bone splinters, made a paste, and put it in place of the bone. The medicine healed just like bone where the bone had been." He told me all sorts of strange and remarkable maladies the surgeons in our country were incapable of treating.

Three or four days later Qambar-Ali grew apprehensive over what he had said to me and fled to Andizhan. A few days later the khans came to an agreement and put Ayyub Begchik and his battalion, Jan-Hasan and the Barin battalion, and Sarïghbash Mirza in charge of the troops, assigned about two thousand men to me, and sent us to Akhsi.

Tambal's brother Shaykh-Bayazid was at Akhsi. Shahbaz Qarlïgh was at Kasoan. At that time Shahbaz came, took Naukent citadel, and sat there. We crossed the Jaxartes at Bikhrata and rode against Shahbaz at Naukent. When we reached the vicinity of Naukent shortly before dawn, [109b] the begs said, "This person has learned of our plan. It would be appropriate for us to get closer in without breaking formation." We proceeded slowly. Shahbaz was unprepared. As we approached Naukent, however, he learned of our advance and fled inside. Thus it often happens. You don't take an enemy seriously when you think he has discovered you, and the chance for action is lost. Experience is made of such wisdom. It is important, when opportunity knocks, not to waver in determination. Regrets later on are useless.

At dawn there were a few skirmishes around the citadel, but we did not enjoin serious battle.

To make a raid, we left Naukent for the mountain in the direction of Pishkaran. Shahbaz Qarlïgh used the occasion to flee to Kassan. We returned and set ourselves up in Naukent. During those days the forces made a few forays on the outlying areas. Once they raided the villages of Akhsi. Another time they invaded Kassan. Shahbaz and Uzun Hasan's stepson Mirim came out to do battle, but they were pushed back. Mirim died there.

One of the strongest fortresses around Akhsi is the one at Pap. The people of Pap made fast the fortress and dispatched someone to us. Sayyid-Qasim was sent with a few warriors. [110] They crossed the river opposite the villages above Akhsi and entered the Pap fortress. A few days later a strange thing happened. Ibrahim Chapïq, Taghayï Ahmad, Qasim Kohbur, Qasim Khanika Arghun, and Shaykh-Bayazid were then in Akhsi. One night Tambal banded together these and another two hundred warriors and sent them to make a surprise attack on the fortress. Sayyid-Qasim had not taken adequate precautions and laid himself open to attack. The fortress was reached, ladders were put in place, the gate was taken, a rolling bridge was moved up, and seventy or eighty armed warriors were inside before Sayyid-Qasim was aware of what was happening. Half-asleep and in his nightshirt, Sayyid-Qasim and five or six of his men shot arrows and fought them off. A few heads were cut off and sent. Although it was unmilitary to lay oneself open to a surprise assault like that, it was still heroic to drive off so many armed warriors with blows of the sword and with so few men.

At this time the khans were busy besieging the Andizhan fortress. Those inside would not let anyone get near the citadel. Warriors came outside on horseback to fight.

Shaykh-Bayazid started making overtures of fealty by sending people from Akhsi and issuing us a serious invitation. His object was to separate me from the khans by whatever ruse he could. [110b] If I were parted from them, the khans would not be able to maintain their stand. Apparently Shaykh-Bayazid's solicitation of me was made with the connivance of his elder brother, Tambal. Without the khans, I would have been unable to make an agreement with Shaykh-

Bayazid and Tambal. We indicated to the khans that a summons had been issued.

"Let him go," the khans said of me. "Let him get hold of Shaykh-Bayazid by any means at all." Such a deceitful trick was not in our way of conduct, especially with a pact in effect. How could I break my word? It occurred to me that if we got ourselves to Akhsi somehow or other, either Shaykh-Bayazid would break with Tambal and come over to our side, or something would happen that would be to our advantage. We also sent an envoy. Pacts and promises were made, and he invited us to Akhsi. We went. He came out to greet me with my brother Nasir Mirza and took us into the Akhsi citadel. He assigned me to quarters in the buildings my father had built in the outer fortress. I went and camped there.

Tambal sent his elder brother, Beg Telbä, to Wormwood Khan to make overtures of submission and invite him. Missives came from Wormwood Khan saying that he was coming. As soon as the khans heard this, they went to pieces and, unable to stay where they were, left Andizhan.

Kichik Khan had a reputation for justice and for being a good Muslim. Contrary to expectations, however, the Moghuls he had stationed in the fortresses at Osh, Margilan, and the other places that had come over to us began to inflict overbearing tyranny. [111] As soon as the khans left Andizhan, the people of Osh and Margilan attacked, seized, and plundered the Moghuls who were in the citadels and chased them out.

Without crossing the Jaxartes, the khans withdrew to Margilan and Kanibadam and forded there. Tambal pursued the khans as far as Margilan. Here we hesitated. I did not feel confident that they would make a stand, but it did not seem well to strike out without good reason.

AN ATTEMPT TO DEFEND AKHSI

Jahangir Mirza escaped from Tambal and arrived one morning from Margilan. I was in the bath when he came, and there I received him. At that time Shaykh-Bayazid also came in a totally confused state. The mirza and Ibrahim Beg said, "We should seize Shaykh-Bayazid. We must get hold of the citadel." In fact, that is precisely what we should have done, but I said, "A pact has been made. How can we break our word?" Shaykh-Bayazid went to the citadel. Someone should have been stationed at the bridge, but we had not done it. All these things happened through inexperience. At dawn Tambal came with two to three hundred men, crossed the bridge, and entered the citadel. My men, to begin with, were few. As soon as he infiltrated Akhsi, some were sent in all directions to the citadels, some to the prefecture and the tax office. I had more than a hundred men in Akhsi. [111b] We were about to mount with the men we had stationed at the head of every lane and arm ourselves for battle when Shaykh-Bayazid, Qambar-Ali, and Muhammad Dost came galloping from Tambal to discuss a truce.

I stationed in their places those who were assigned to fight, went to my father's tomb for consultation, and summoned Jahangir Mirza. Muhammad Dost returned. Shaykh-Bayazid and Qambar-Ali Beg came. We were seated in the portico to the south of the tomb ready for dialogue when Jahangir Mirza and Ibrahim Chapïq decided that those men should be apprehended. Jahangir Mirza whispered into my ear, "They should be seized."

"Don't make a ruckus," I said. "Things are past seizure. Let's see— perhaps with a truce the situation will get better. Not only are they many and we few, but they are strong in the citadel while we are weak in the outer fortress." Shaykh-Bayazid and Qambar-Ali were present at this consultation. Jahangir Mirza signaled to Ibrahim Beg not to do it. I do not know whether he really misunderstood or whether he only pretended to misunderstand: anyway, he immediately captured Shaykh-Bayazid. The warriors standing by rushed in from all directions [112] and roughed them up. That put an end to thoughts of peace and truce. We handed over the two men and mounted for battle.

Jahangir Mirza was given responsibility for one side of the city. Since he had only a few men, I posted a detachment of my own men as reinforcements. Upon first arriving there I assigned the men to fight everywhere, and then I went to one side. In the middle of the city was a fairly open space. I dispatched a troop of warriors there. A large number of cavalry and infantry came and forced them up from there into a lane. At just that moment I arrived and raced in. Unable to make a stand, they wheeled around and fled. Having driven them out of the lane into the open space, they shot arrows at my horse's feet just as I was brandishing my sword. My horse reared and threw me to the ground in the midst of the enemy. I jumped up and shot an arrow. Sahib-Qadam Kahil had a wretched little horse. He got off and gave it to me. I stationed some men here and headed for the head of the lane. Sultan-Muhammad Ways saw how wretched my horse was, dismounted and offered me his, which I mounted.

Just then Qambar-Ali Beg, Qasim Beg's son, came wounded from Jahangir Mirza. He said that a short while ago Jahangir Mirza had been pressed and forced to move off. [112b] We were perplexed. Just then Sayyid-Qasim, who had been in the Pap fortress, appeared. What an extraordinarily untimely arrival! At such a time it would have been wonderful to have such a strong fortress in hand. I asked Ibrahim Beg what was to be done. He was slightly wounded. I don't know if it was because of that or because he was confused, but he was unable to give a considered opinion. My plan was to cross the bridge, destroy it, and head for Andizhan. Baba Sherzad made an excellent suggestion. "We'll force our way through the gate and get out," he said. Acting upon Baba Sherzad's advice, we headed toward the gate. At that point Khwaja Mirmiran also spoke bravely. As we were coming down the lane, Sayyid-Qasim, Dost Nasir, and Baqi the Catamite were hacking away. Ibrahim Beg, Mirza-Qulï Kükäldash, and I were ahead. Just as we reached the gate I saw Shaykh-Bayazid wearing nothing but a fur vest over his shirt, coming through the gate with three or four horsemen. I drew the arrow I had in my thumb ring and shot. It grazed his neck, but it was an able shot. Just as he came with trepidation through the gate he took off down a lane to the right. We lit out after him. That morning, when we had seized Shaykh-Bayazid and his companions against our will, they were left with Jahangir Mirza's men. When they left they took Shaykh-Bayazid along, planning to kill him. It was good they did not kill him and let him escape, for just as he was going out the gate I chanced upon him. Mirza-Qulï Kükäldash took down a foot soldier with his flail. [113] After Mirza-Qulï crossed, another foot soldier took aim at Ibrahim Beg, but just as Ibrahim Beg crossed yelling "hey, hey," the soldier shot me in the side from a short distance away. Two plates of my Qalmaqi armor[166] were pierced and broken. I shot at his back as he fled.

Just then a foot soldier was escaping across the top of the rampart. I took aim at his cap through the crenellations of the fortification and shot. The arrow pinned his cap to the crenellation, and his turban tumbled into his hands in tatters. Another horseman was escaping past me toward the lane down which Shaykh-Bayazid had fled. With the tip of my sword I pierced the tuft on his cap. He almost fell off his horse, but he righted himself against a wall in the lane and kept himself from collapsing. With great difficulty he escaped and was saved. We drove the remaining horsemen and foot soldiers from the gate and took it. It was too late for tactics: two to three thousand armed men were in the citadel, and we were a hundred or two in the outer fortress. They had chased Jahangir Mirza out a little while before. Half of our men had left with him. Nonetheless, out of inexperience, we stood at the gate and sent someone to Jahangir Mirza to tell him to come if he was nearby and we would press on together. It was too late for that, however. Either because his horse was weak or because he was wounded, Ibrahim Beg said to me, "My horse is finished." Muhammad Ali Mubashshir had a servant named Sulayman. [113b] In a situation like that, with no one telling him to, he got down and gave his horse to Ibrahim Beg. It was a manly thing to do. Kichik Ali, now the governor of Koil, made a brave showing there at the gate. At that time he was Sultan-Muhammad Ways's servant and had made two able demonstrations at Osh. We paused at the gate until the man who had gone to Jahangir Mirza came back. When he arrived he said that Jahangir Mirza had fled some time ago. It was too late to make a stand, so we moved off too. It had been a mistake to stay as long as we had. Twenty to thirty men were left with us. As soon as we began to move, many mailclad men came. We were across the rolling bridge when the enemy arrived on the city side of the bridge. Banda-Ali Beg, the maternal grandfather of Qasim Beg's son Hamza, shouted to Ibrahim Beg, "You have always boasted of your zeal. Stand and let's exchange blows!" Ibrahim Beg was beside me. "Come on," he shouted, "what's keeping you?" This senseless man was for making a show of zeal in the midst of such defeat—a most untimely ardor. It was no time to make a stand. We raced on with the enemy hard at our heels and felling our men.

BABUR FLEES AKHSI

When we had passed the Baz Gumbadh meadow a league out of Akhsi, Ibrahim Beg called out to me. I looked back and saw [114] that one of Shaykh-Bayazid's pages was catching up with him. I turned my

reins. Khan-Qulï Buyan-Qulï was at my side. He said it would be ill
timed to turn back. He took my reins and moved on. By the time we
reached Sang, which is two leagues from Akhsi, most of our men had
been felled. When we passed Sang, neither our men nor the enemy was
visible, so we went up river at Sang. Only eight of us were left: Dost
Nasir, Qasim Beg's Qambar-Ali, Khan-Qulï Buyan-Qulï, Mirza-Qulï
Kükäldash, Shahïm Nasir, Sidi Qara's Abdul-Quddus, and Khwaja
Husayni. I was the eighth.

Above the river we came across a pretty good little road. We started
up the valley on this deserted passageway, off from the beaten track,
keeping the water on our right, and entered a protected valley. It was
noon the next day when we emerged from the hills onto an open plain.
On the plain, off in the distance, a mass of people could be seen. I had
my men stay in a safe place and had gone out myself on foot to a
hillock to scout when, from behind us, many horsemen came galloping
over the crest of the hill. We had no time to ascertain how many or
how few they were. We jumped on our horses and took off. They were
twenty to twenty-five in pursuit; we were eight, as has been mentioned. If we had known then for certain how few they were, we would
have fought hard. However, I thought more pursuers would be following these, [114b] so we took off. Be a fleeing enemy however many, he
cannot turn to face even a few pursuers, as is said: "For ranks already
on the run it is sufficient to say 'boo.' "

"This is no good," Khan-Qulï said. "They'll take us all. You take two
good horses and ride at full gallop with Mirza-Qulï Kükäldash. Maybe
you can get away." This was not bad advice. Since it was impossible to
fight, if this worked there was a possibility of escape; however, I did
not like the idea of leaving anybody without a horse in the midst of the
enemy. Finally, one by one, they fell behind.

The horse I was on was fairly weak, so Khan-Qulï got off of his and
we traded. Just then Shahïm Nasir and Sidi Qara's Abdul-Quddus,
both of whom had lagged behind, were felled. Khan-Qulï too lagged.
It was no time to give protection and assistance. One had to judge the
strength of one's horse and proceed accordingly. When one's horse
was unable to go on, one trailed. Dost Beg's horse wearied and faltered.
The horse I was on was also beginning to tire, so this time Qambar-Ali
traded horses with me. When he mounted mine, he lost ground.
Khwaja Husayni was lame, but he managed to make it to the hills. I was

left with Mirza-Qulï Kükäldash. It was no longer possible to gallop, [115] but we trotted on. Mirza-Qulï's horse started weakening. I said, "If I leave you, where shall I go? Ride on! Life and death are all the same to me." I rode toward Mirza-Qulï a few times, but finally he said, "My horse is worn out. It can't go any farther. Don't let yourself get caught on my account. Go on! Maybe you can get away." I had an odd feeling. Mirza-Qulï fell behind, and I was left alone.

Two of the enemy appeared. One was named Baba Sayrami, the other Banda-Ali. They were closing in on me. My horse was tired, and the mountain was a league away. An outcropping of rock loomed ahead. I had a vision of my horse collapsing while the mountain was still far off. Where was I to go? I had about twenty arrows in my quiver. I would dismount and fight to my last arrow at the outcropping. Then it occurred to me that I might be able to make it to my destination: I would put a few arrows into my belt and scramble up the mountain. I had confidence in my footing. With this plan in mind I proceeded. My horse was no longer able to canter. My pursuers had come within arrow range but to save my arrows, I did not shoot. [115b] They came closer cautiously, closing in on me. The sun was setting as I reached the mountain. They cupped their hands to their mouths and shouted, "You've come this far, but where are you going? We already have Jahangir Mirza, and Nasir Mirza is in our hands." I was really frightened by these words, for if we all fell into their hands the probability of danger was great. I did not answer but continued toward the mountain. We had covered a lot of ground before they began to speak again, this time more politely than before. I got off my horse, without paying attention to what they were saying. I traveled through the valley until nightfall. Finally I reached a rock the size of a house. I circled round it. The drop-offs there were too steep for a horse to go there. They too dismounted. They were still speaking respectfully and deferentially.

"Lost like this in the black of night and no road, where are you going to go?" they said. Then they swore oaths and said, "Sultan-Ahmad Beg will make you padishah."

"I don't believe it," I said. "It is out of the question to go there. If you have any intention of doing a service, then it would be a greater service than you could render in years of waiting at the gate [116] to show me a road that will take me to the khans. I will reward you with more than your hearts could desire. If you won't do this, then go back the way you came. That too would be a great service to me."

"Would that we had never come," they said. "Now that we are here, how can we let you go and return? Since you won't go there, we'll serve you wherever you go."

"Swear that you're telling the truth," I said. They swore a solemn oath on the Koran. I felt a great relief.

"Near this valley the road to Keng Qul was pointed out to me," I said. "Guide me there." Although they had sworn, I still did not feel totally at ease, so I had them ride ahead with me behind. We had gone two leagues when we reached a stream.

"This is not the way to Keng Qul," I said.

They acted surprised and said, "The road is way ahead." It probably was the Keng Qul road, but they were acting deceitfully to keep it from me. Around midnight we reached another stream. This time they said, "We were caught off guard. The Keng Qul road lies behind."

"Then what are we to do?" I asked.

"Nearby ahead of us is the road to Gava," they replied. "It leads to Farkat." [116b] They led me to that road.

By the third watch we came to the road. We reached the Karnon stream, which branches off and flows this way from Gava.

"You stay here," said Baba Sayrami. "I'll go check out the Gava road and come back." Some time later he returned and said, "A few men led by a man in a Mongol hat are on the road. We can't go that way."

I was stunned to hear this—in the midst of the province, dawn near, and our goal yet distant.

"Lead us to a place where we can rest during the day," I said. "When night falls we can get hold of some horses, cross the river, and go down the other side toward Khodzhent."

"There's a hill over there," they said. "You can rest there."

Banda-Ali was the prefect of Karnon. He said, "We have to get food for ourselves and our horses. I'll go to Karnon and bring back what I can." We doubled back in the direction of Karnon. We stopped a league from Karnon. Banda-Ali proceeded. He was gone a long time. It was morning when he returned at last, bringing nothing. He was quite upset. When Banda-Ali came galloping in at dawn, he had brought no feed for the horses, but he did bring three loaves of bread. Distressed, each of us put a loaf into his bosom and went back up the hill. Having tied our horses in the valley, each of us went off in a different direction onto a promontory to keep watch.

It was nearly noon [117] when Ahmad Qushchï and four horsemen came from Gava headed in the direction of Akhsi. I thought of calling out to him and persuading him to give us his horses, for ours had been through hell for a day and a night. Having had nothing to eat, they were finished. However, something told me not to trust them. It was decided among us that the two with me would go that evening to Karnon, which they would enter by stealth, and we would obtain horses that would enable us to get ourselves somewhere. It was noon when, in the far distance, something on horseback could be seen reflecting the light. We had no idea what it was. It turned out to be Muhammad Baqir Beg, who had been with us at Akhsi. When we got out of Akhsi everyone had taken off in all directions. Muhammad Baqir Beg had come this way and was traveling clandestinely.

Banda-Ali and Baba Sayrami said, "The horses have had nothing to eat for two days. Let's stop in the dale and let them graze." We mounted and rode to the dale, were the horses grazed. It was evening when a rider came up the hill. I recognized him as Qadirberdi, the headman of Gava. I said, "Let's call out to Qadirberdi." We called and he came. When I saw him, I asked how he was and spoke kindly and favorably. Giving him assurances of safety, I sent him to bring some rope, a sickle, an ax, paraphernalia for crossing water, feed for the horses, food for us, [117b] and, if possible, horses. We made a rendezvous for that night at that same spot.

It was late in the evening when a horseman could be seen going from the direction of Karnon toward Gava. We asked him who he was but he would not say. It must have been Muhammad Baqir Beg going to hide himself again in a different place from the one we had seen him in around noon the previous day. He had so disguised his voice that, although he had been with me for years, I did not recognize him at all. If we had recognized him and let him join us, it would have been good. There was much trepidation over his passing. We could not stay to meet Qadirberdi at Gava.

"There are some abandoned gardens in the outskirts of Karnon where no one will suspect us," said Banda-Ali. "Let's send word to

Qadirberdi to meet us there." With this plan in mind I mounted and went to the outskirts of Karnon. It was winter and very cold. Someone brought me an old sheepskin coat, which I put on. A cup of millet-flour soup was next, I drank it. God it felt good!

"Did you send someone to Qadirberdi?" I asked Banda-Ali.

"I did," he said, but in fact those wretched village fellows had conspired with Qadirberdi to send word to Tambal in Akhsi.

I went up on a roof, lit a fire, and closed my eyes to sleep. The fellows busied themselves and then said, "We can't move from here until we get word from Qadirberdi. This place is in the middle of the residential area. There are empty orchards nearby. [118] If we go there, no one will suspect."

At midnight I mounted and went to one of the orchards. Baba Sayrami was on the roof keeping watch in all directions. Near noon he jumped down and came to me saying, "Yusuf the prefect is coming." I was oddly apprehensive.

"Find out if he knows I'm here," I said.

Baba Sayrami went out, talked with Yusuf the prefect, and returned. "Yusuf says that a foot soldier appeared at the Akhsi gate," he reported. "The soldier said that the padishah was in such and such a place in Karnon. Without informing anyone, he hid the soldier with Wali Khizanachï, who had fallen prisoner to him in the battle, and came to you as fast as he could. The begs know nothing of this."

"What do you think?" I asked.

"We are all your servants," he said. "What's to be done? We must go. They'll make you padishah."

"With all this chaos and fighting, with what assurance can I go?" I asked.

We were speaking thus when Yusuf fell to his knees before me and said, "Why hide it? Sultan-Ahmad knows nothing of this. Shaykh-Bayazid Beg found out where you were and sent me." Suddenly I felt odd. There is nothing worse in the world than fear for one's life.

"Speak the truth!" I said. "If it is otherwise I will prepare for my death."

Yusuf swore, but who could believe him? [118b] I felt that I could endure no more. I rose and went to a corner of the orchard. I thought to myself that whether one lived to a hundred or a thousand, in the end one had to die.

Be it a hundred years[167] or one day, in the end one must depart from this noxious palace.

I readied myself for death. There was running water in the orchard. I made my ablutions and performed two cycles of prayer. I put my head down for intimate conversation with God and was making my requests when I dozed off. I dreamed that Khwaja Ya'qub, son of Khwaja Yahya and grandson of Khwaja Ubaydullah, was coming straight toward me on a dappled horse, surrounded by a group also mounted on dappled horses. "Grieve not," he said. "Khwaja Ahrar has sent me to you. He has said that we were to assist you and seat you on the royal throne. Whenever you are in difficult straits, think of us and speak. We will be there. Now victory and triumph are coming to you. Raise your head and awake!"

I awoke happy just as Yusuf the prefect and his comrades were conspiring together, saying, "We must seize him and tie him up."

When I heard this I said, "This is how you speak? I'd like to see which of you will come and take me!" No sooner had I spoken than from outside the orchard wall came the sound of many riders. [119] Yusuf the prefect said, "If we had seized you and taken you to Tambal, it would have been better for us. Now he has sent many men. It is certain that it is to take you, for this is the sound of the horses of the men Tambal has sent."

When I heard this, my trepidation increased and I did not know what to do. At that very instant the horsemen, without waiting to break down the gate, crashed through a hole they made in a crumbling place in the wall. I saw that they were Qutlugh Muhammad Barlas and Baba Parghari, who had been my faithful servants for ten to fifteen years. They paused in their approach to get down from their horses, kneel from afar, and fall respectfully at my feet. I felt as though God had granted me a new lease on life.

"First seize Yusuf the prefect and his mercenary henchmen standing here, and tie them up," I said. The villains had fled, but one was caught, tied up, and brought back.

"Where did you come from?" I asked. "And how did you find out where I was?"

Qutlugh Muhammad Barlas answered, "When we fled from Akhsi and got separated, I came to Andizhan because the khans had gone there. In a dream I saw Khwaja Ubaydullah saying, 'Babur Padishah is in a village called Karnon. [119b] Go, get him and come, for the royal throne belongs to him.' When I had this dream I rejoiced and told it to Ulugh Khan and Kichik Khan. I said to them, 'I have five or six brothers and sons. I'll take a few warriors of your platoon to Karnon and bring news.' The khans said, 'It seems to us that what has happened will happen again.' They assigned ten men and said, 'Go there, investigate thoroughly, and report all that you find.' While we were speaking, Baba Parghari said, 'I too want to help.' He joined with two brave brothers of his, and we rode out. We have been on the road for three days. Thank God we have found you."

Then they said, "Come, get to horse. Take these men who are tied up and get going. It would be better not to stay here. Tambal knows that you have come here. Let's join the khans however we may."

Immediately we mounted and set out for Andizhan. I had not eaten anything for two days. It was afternoon when we found some victuals, stopped in a spot, and roasted some meat, of which I ate my fill. Then we remounted, traversed at a gallop a five-day distance in two days and nights, and came to Andizhan. There I had an audience with my uncles Ulugh Khan and Kichik Khan and told them all about the past days.

I remained with the khans for four months. More than three hundred of my liege men gathered from wherever they had fled to. [120] I wondered how long I would have to wander about Fergana Province, but in Muharram [June–July 1504], I rode out of Fergana for Khurasan in search of a quest wherever the opportunity might present itself.

PART TWO

KABUL

The kingdom of Kabul and Zabulistan had formed part of Sultan-Abusa'id Mirza's empire, and he gave the kingdom to his son Ulughbeg Mirza II, who ruled there until his death in 907 (1501–02). Ulughbeg Mirza was succeeded by his son, Abdul-Razzaq Mirza, who was too young to rule, and, as usual, strife broke out among the officers attendant upon the young prince. The amir who took over the regency for Abdul-Razzaq Mirza, Sherim Zäkä, was assassinated by his fellow officers, and Kabul was thrown into chaos. Into the void stepped Zu'n-Nun Beg's son, Muhammad-Muqim Arghun, who led his Hazara and Negüdäri forces into Kabul, drove out Abdul-Razzaq Mirza, seized power, and married Ulughbeg Mirza's daughter. At this point Babur, who has set out from Tashkent for exploits in Khurasan, is advised by Baqi Beg Chaghaniani, Khusrawshah's younger brother and governor of Termez, to go to Kabul to distance himself as far as possible from the Uzbeks—and get hold of a kingdom to rule as well.*

WMT

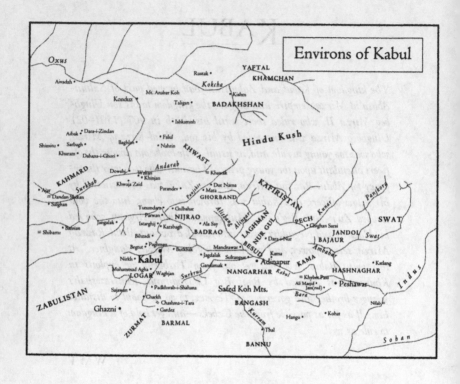

Environs of Kabul

In the month of Muharram (June–July 1504), I left Fergana for Khurasan, stopping at Ilak Yaylagh, one of the summer pastures of Hissar Province. Here, at the beginning of my twenty-third year, I first put a razor to my face. Great and small alike were rushing to join me with great expectations. There must have been between two and three hundred men, mostly on foot, with clubs in their hands, rough boots on their feet, and shepherd's cloaks on their backs. Hardship had reached such proportions that among all of us there were only two tents. My own tent was pitched for my mother, and I stayed in a rude hut made for me at each campsite.

Although we had set out for Khurasan, hope issued from this province and from Khusrawshah's liege men. Every few days someone came to give encouraging reports of the tribes and folk of the region. At this juncture Mulla Baba Pishaghari, who had been sent as a messenger to Khusrawshah, brought no pleasing words from Khusrawshah but did convey promises from the tribes. [120b]

In two or three marches we went from Ilak to a place called Khwaja Imad. Muhibb-Ali Qorchï came to the camp as emissary from Khusrawshah who, though known for his generosity and liberality, had not offered us the courtesy one would show to the least of people during the two times we had passed through his domain.

We tarried at each halting place. Sherim Taghayï, who was then the greatest of my men, could not bear to go to Khurasan and thought of leaving on his own. When we were defeated at Sar-i-Pul,[2] he had sent his family off and stayed by himself to command the fort. He was rather unmanly. He acted in such a fashion several times.

When we reached Kabadian, Khusrawshah's younger brother Baqi Chaghaniani, who held Chaghanian, Shahrisafa, and Termez, sent Khatib Qarshi to make offers of fealty and say that he stood ready to join us. After we crossed the Oxus at Aivadzh, he came to pay homage. At Baqi's own behest he went opposite Termez, sent his family across, and joined us. We headed toward Kahmard and Bamian, places then belonging to Ahmad Qasim, Khusrawshah's nephew, to fortify the women and household at the Kahmard fortress in the Ajar valley and take the necessary action should anything turn up. [121] As we reached Aibak, Yar-Ali Bilal, who had formerly been with me and wielded a good sword but had left me during the interregnum, reported that Khusrawshah's Moghuls were supporting me. When we reached Dara-i-Zindan, Qambar-Ali Beg, who was also called Sallakh, deserted and came to me.

In three or four marches we came to Kahmard and left the women at the Ajar fortress. While we were there, Sultan-Mahmud Mirza and Khwanzada Begim's daughter, who had been affianced to Jahangir Mirza while the mirzas were still alive, became espoused to Jahangir Mirza.

At this same time Baqi Beg said to me time and again,

Two padishahs in one province and two generals in one army cause strife and tribulation, as has been said: "Ten poor men can sleep on one rug, but two kings cannot fit into one clime. / If a man of God eats half a loaf of bread, he gives the other half to the poor: / A king may take possession of an entire clime, but he will still hunger for another."[3]

He continued: "There is hope that today or tomorrow all of Khusraw-shah's liege men will come and accept to serve you as padishah. How-ever, some mischievous men there, like Ayyub's sons, [121b] and others have constantly fomented strife and dissent among our princes. If Jahangir Mirza is permitted now to go freely into Khurasan, will you not regret it tomorrow morning?"

Since it was not in me to allow my brothers or relatives to suffer from me on account of some breach of etiquette, although Jahangir Mirza and I had formerly had many fallings-out over territory and liege men, this time he had come along with me from our homeland and had taken up the proper stance of brother and servant. Until now he had done nothing to provoke a quarrel. Let Baqi Beg repeat his words as much as he wanted, I refused to accept; but, in the end, exactly as he said, those sowers of strife, Yusuf Ayyub and Bahlul Ayyub, deserted me, went to Jahangir Mirza, and worked their sedition by separating him from me and taking him to Khurasan.

LETTERS FROM SULTAN-HUSAYN MIRZA

During this same time long drawn-out letters with similar contents came from Sultan-Husayn Mirza to Badi'uzzaman Mirza, me, Khusrawshah, and Zu'n-Nun. [122] (I still, as of this date, have in my possession one or two of those letters.) The contents were as follows:

> When Sultan-Ahmad Mirza, Sultan-Mahmud Mirza, Ulughbeg Mirza, and those brothers conspired and set forth, I had the banks of the Murghab River fortified. When the princes approached, they withdrew, unable to take any action. Even now, should the Uzbeks approach, I shall fortify the banks of the Murghab. Let Badi'uzzaman Mirza station armed men at the fortresses in Balkh, Sheberghan, and Andkhui, and let him fortify Gurzuwan, Dara-i-Zang, and those highlands.

When I reached these regions, news of me had already gone forth. He wrote to me, saying,

> You fortify the mountain spur at Kahmard and Ajar. Let Khusrawshah place trusty men in the fortresses at Hissar and Konduz, and let him and his younger brother Wali reinforce the mountains of Badakhshan and Khuttalan. The Uzbeks, unable to take action, will withdraw.

These letters of Sultan-Husayn Mirza caused despair. At that date no padishah within Temür Beg's domain was greater in age, estate, or army than he. It would have been expected that emissaries and commissars would be coming hard on each other's heels in all seriousness and urgency bearing orders, for example, to build boats at the Termez,

Kelif, and Kerki crossings, [122b] gather material for bridges, and keep a close watch on the Toquz Ölüm fords above. In this manner the people who had been disheartened by years of Uzbek disruption would take heart and become hopeful. If a great padishah like Sultan-Husayn, sitting in Temür Beg's stead, said merely to fortify localities rather than to attack the enemy, what hope was left to the people?

We left in Ajar all the hungry relatives and hangers-on who had come with us, as well as Baqi Chaghaniani's family and belongings and his son Ahmad Qasim's soldiers and tribes, and led the army forth.

Men began to come continually from Khusrawshah's Moghuls, saying, "From Taykhan to Taligan we have accepted fealty to the illustrious padishah, and we have led the Moghul people who were there to Ishkamish and Falul. Let the padishah exert all effort and come, for most of Khusrawshah's men are in disarray and will come to serve the padishah." At that time news was delivered that Wormwood Khan had taken Andizhan and had mounted his army against Hissar and Konduz. When he heard the account, Khusrawshah, unable to hold Konduz, moved out the men he had and set forth for Kabul. [123] As soon as Khusrawshah left Konduz, his old liege man and warrior, Mulla Muhammad Turkistani, fortified Konduz for Wormwood Khan.

While we were proceeding along the Shimitu road toward the Red River,[4] three to four thousand householders that had belonged to Khusrawshah in Hissar and Konduz came and joined the train of the Moghul nation.

The oft-mentioned Qambar-Ali Moghul was a blitherer, and Baqi Beg did not like him. On Baqi Beg's account he was given leave to withdraw. His son Abdul-Shakur became attached to Jahangir Mirza's retinue from that time on.

KHUSRAWSHAH OFFERS
TO JOIN BABUR

When Khusrawshah heard that the Moghul nation had joined us, he lost his nerve and, unable to do anything about it, sent his son-in-law Ya'qub Ayyub as emissary to make a show of fealty and offer his servitude if a pact was made. Since Baqi Chaghaniani was powerful, no matter how much he wished us well, he was not going to relinquish his elder brother's part. He insisted that a pact be made to the effect that his life would be spared and that he would not be prevented from taking as many of his possessions as he chose. After Ya'qub was permitted to leave, we moved down the Red River and camped near the confluence with the Andarab. [123b]

The next morning, the middle of Rabi' I [end of August], I crossed the Andarab without a large retinue and sat down beneath a large plane tree in the Dowshi region. Khusrawshah came from the other side with many of his retinue and much panoply. According to protocol he dismounted from afar and approached. When we met he knelt thrice and when he withdrew he knelt thrice; he knelt once both when he asked my condition and when he presented his gifts. He did the same with Jahangir Mirza and Mirza Khan. This fat old man, who had conducted himself as he wished for many years and stopped short only of having the khutba read in his name, genuflected twenty-five or twenty-six times coming and going. He got so confused he almost fell down. After the ritual of interview and presentation of gifts I ordered him to be seated. He sat down for a *ghari*[5] or two, rambling on about this and that. His cowardice and ingratitude were apparent in his meaningless and tasteless words. In such a situation, with his trusted and important liege men flocking before his very eyes to become mine, this twerp who had ridden out acting like a padishah was reduced to a sorry state and, like it or not, had had to come for this interview. [124]

Khusrawshah made two strange comments. One was when he was being consoled for his liege men's departure. In reply he said, "These liege men have left me like this four times, but they've always come back." Another was when I asked him when his younger brother Wali would come and where he would cross the Oxus. He said, "If he finds a crossing he will come speedily, but when the water rises the crossings change, as the saying goes, 'The water carried off the crossing.'" God put these words in his mouth when his fortune and liege men departed. A ghari or two later I mounted and went to my camp, and he went to where he was staying.

From noon the next day until the late afternoon, all his officers and liege men, great and small alike, left him in droves with their families and possessions and began to join us until no one was left with him.

Say, O God, thou givest kingdom to whomsoever thou willest, and thou takest away kingdom from whomsoever thou willest. Thou ennoblest whomsoever thou willest, and thou humblest whomsoever thou willest. In thy hand is goodness. Thou art omnipotent above all things.

What a fantastically omnipotent God! A man who had twenty to thirty thousand liege men and who controlled Sultan-Mahmud Mirza's territory from Qahalgha—which is also called the Iron Gates—to the Hindu Kush mountains, [124b] one of whose tax collectors, an old villain called Hasan Barlas, extracted harsh tribute from Ilak to Aivadzh and made us move out and camp elsewhere, without battle, without raid, had been so humiliated and disgraced in half a day in front of two hundred, 250 wretched, ragtag men like us that he retained no power over his servants, his possessions, or his life.

The evening after I saw Khusrawshah and returned, Mirza Khan came to me and declared blood revenge for his elder brothers. Some of those among us were supportive of his claim. Actually, according to both religious and customary law, it would have been proper for such persons to be punished. However, since a pact was in effect, Khusrawshah was freed and an edict was issued that he should appropriate his possessions as stipulated. He took jewels, gold, silver, and precious objects loaded on three or four trains of mules and camels. I sent Sherim Taghayï along and said that he should escort Khusrawshah in the direction of Khurasan via Ghori and Dahana and then go himself to Kahmard and bring our family after us to Kabul.

Setting out from camp and moving for Kabul, we came to Khwaja Zaid. That very day an Uzbek strike force led by Hamza Bey Manghït raided Dowshi. Sayyid-Qasim Eshik-aqa and Ahmad Qasim Kohbur [125] were dispatched with some of our warriors. They went, dealt the raiders a decisive defeat, and brought back to our new camp a few severed heads.

At this same campsite the arms in Khusrawshah's storehouse were distributed. These seven or eight hundred breastplates and helmets were just part of the loot Khusrawshah left behind. A great deal of china also fell to us, but otherwise nothing worth looking at.

From Khwaja Zaid we marched in four or five bivouacs to Ghorband. As we camped at Ushturshahr we learned that Sherka Arghun, Muqim's chief officer, had mustered an army and was sitting on the banks of the Baran, unaware of us, and not allowing people who crossed on the Panjshir road to go to Abdul-Razzaq Mirza, who at that time had fled from Kabul and was in the Laghman region among the Tarklani Afghans.[6] As soon as we heard this news we set out in the afternoon and rode hard for several days, passing through the Hupian Pass at dawn.

I had never seen the star Canopus.[7] As we went through the pass we noticed a brilliant star low on the southern horizon. "Is this not Canopus?" I asked. They replied that it was. Baqi Chaghaniani recited this line:

Canopus, how far do you shine and when do you rise? / You are a sign of fortune to all upon whom your eye lights.

The sun had risen a spear length when we stopped at the foot of Sinjit valley.[8] The scouts who had gone ahead of us [125b] joined hands with some other warriors in the Egri Yar region below Karabagh when they reached Sherka Arghun. They got embroiled in a minor skirmish, but moved off when arrows were fired. They nevertheless unhorsed Sherka and seventy or eighty valiant warriors and took them prisoner. I spared Sherka's life and attached him to my retinue.

Khusrawshah left Konduz for Kabul without a thought for his people, who were made up of five or six groups. In Badakhshan one group of Sayyidim Ali Darban's, who was in the Rusta Hazara, crossed the Panjshir and made obeisance to us at our camp. Another party, of Yusuf Ayyub and Bahlul Ayyub's, also gathered to make obeisance. Another, from Khuttalan and belonging to Khusrawshah's brother Wali, and another of Yilanchuq, Negüdäri, Qaqshal, and aymaqs dwelling in Konduz province—one or two of these groups came to Andarab and Sarab imagining they would also cross the Panjshir. The aymaqs were ahead at Sarab when Wali approached from behind. The aymaq blocked his way and defeated him in a fight. He himself fled to the Uzbek. Wormwood Khan had him decapitated at the marketplace in Samarkand. His retainers, plundered and taken prisoner, joined the aymaqs at the camp in servitude. Sayyid-Yusuf Beg Oghlaqchï also arrived with them. [126]

BABUR TAKES KABUL

We left that camp and stopped at Aq Saray Meadow beside Karabagh. Khusrawshah's men, who had learned how to tyrannize, had begun to oppress the people. Finally I had one of Sayyidim Ali Darban's warriors clubbed at the gate for having stolen a pot of oil. He died under the blows. The people were cowed by this punishment.

We held deliberations at the camp about whether to move immediately against Kabul. Sayyid Yusuf and some others were of the opinion that since winter was fast approaching we should go immediately to Laghman and then do what was appropriate for whatever should happen. Baqi Chaghaniani and some of the others who were decided to move against Kabul—myself among them—left the Aq Saray Meadow and camped at the Aba field.

While there, my lady mother and the *uruq*[9] that had remained at Kahmard passed through great danger and came to join me. The details are as follows. Sherim Taghayï, attached to Khusrawshah, was assigned to escort Khusrawshah to Khurasan and then bring the uruq. When he reached Dahana, Sherim had no choice, and Khusrawshah went right along with him to Kahmard, where Khusrawshah's nephew Ahmad Qasim was. Khusrawshah [126b] convinced him to attack the uruq, who were assembled with many of Baqi Chaghaniani's Moghul liege men. Secretly, however, these men conspired with Sherim to seize Khusrawshah and Ahmad Qasim. But Khusrawshah and Ahmad Qasim escaped by the road beside the Ajar valley and fled to Khurasan. The Moghuls cooperated in order to separate themselves from Khusrawshah. When the uruq and the people were freed from fear of him, they left Ajar for Kahmard but were blocked by the Asiqanchi tribe, who were in revolt. The Asiqanchi seized and plundered most of the uruq and the people belonging to Baqi Beg. Qul-Bayazid's small son Tezak fell prisoner there; three or four years later he came to Kabul. The uruq, having suffered plunder and seizure, escaped via the Qipchaq road, by which we had gone, and joined us at the Aba field.

Leaving there, we made one overnight stop and held deliberations at Chalak Meadow.[10] We decided to lay siege. I left and, with a few men from the center, settled between Haydar Taqi's garden and Qul-Bayazid Bökäül's tomb.[11] Jahangir Mirza and the men from the left flank camped in our large charbagh; Nasir Mirza and the men of the right flank camped in the meadow behind Qutlugh-Qadam's tomb. [127] Our men were constantly coming and going to hold deliberations with Muqim. Sometimes they brought his excuses, sometimes he spoke mildly. The reason for his subterfuge was that when we captured

Sherka he immediately sent someone to his father and elder brother, and he was delaying because he was still hoping to see them.

One day it was ordered that the center and right and left flanks should all arm themselves and their horses and ride close to the fortress to let their arms be seen as an admonition to the people inside. Jahangir Mirza and the right flank advanced directly ahead on the Kucha-i-Bagh.[12] Since the river was ahead of the center, I went with the center toward Qutlugh-Qadam's tomb and emerged on the hill in front of the rise. The vanguard gathered where the Qutlugh-Qadam bridge is now, though at that time there was no bridge. The warriors, making light of the situation, galloped as far as the Charmgaran Gate. The few people who had come out fled back to the fortress without standing to fight. Many citizens of Kabul had come out on the rise of the citadel glacis to watch, but with the retreat and rising dust many fell down. Pits had been dug in the middle of the road on top of the high rise between the bridge and the gate and covered over with straw. [127b] Sultan-Qulï Chanaq and some warriors fell in as they rode forward. From the right flank one or two warriors were wielding their swords against those who had emerged in the Kucha-i-Bagh. Since there was no command for battle they withdrew as they were.

The people of the fortress were in a dither. Muqim decided to commit his officers to my service and turn over Kabul. Through the offices of Baqi Chaghaniani he joined my retinue. We treated him with compassion and favor and calmed his apprehension. It was settled that the next morning he would leave with his liege men, servants, possessions, and property and turn over the fortress. Khusrawshah's people had forgotten their discipline and learned to be aggressive. We appointed Jahangir Mirza, Nasir Mirza, and our great begs and ichkis to escort Muqim and his people, money, and property out of Kabul. We assigned Yurt Hill to Muqim.[13] The next morning the mirzas and begs went to the gates, but seeing the chaos and riotousness of the populace, they sent someone to me to say, "Unless you come yourself no one will be able to control these people." In the end I rode there and had four or five people shot and one or two dismembered. [128] The riot ceased. Muqim went safe and sound with his retinue and camped on the hill.

Toward the end of Rabi' I [September], through God's grace and favor, I regained once more the kingdom of Kabul and Ghazni without bloodshed.

A DESCRIPTION OF KABUL

The province of Kabul is in the fourth clime in the middle of the civilized region. To the east are the Laghman region and Peshawar, in which highlands are Karnu[14] and Ghor. As of this date those mountains are the strongholds of the Hazara and Negüdäri peoples.[15] To the north of Kabul are the provinces of Konduz and Andarab, separated from Kabul by the Hindu Kush mountains. To the south are Barmal, Naghar, Bannu, and Afghanistan.

It is a petty little province, rectangular in shape stretching from east to west and completely surrounded by mountains. The fortress is adjacent to the mountains. Because a shah of Kabul once built an edifice at the summit of the fortress, the mountain itself is called Shah Kabul. The mountain begins at Diurin defile and ends at Ya'qub Deh defile.[16] The perimeter must be two leagues. On the slopes are orchards. During my uncle Ulughbeg Mirza's time, Ways Atäkä, the mirza's tutor, had an irrigation canal run out to the slopes to water the orchards there. At the end of the canal is an area called Gulkana, a secluded, cozy spot where much debauchery is indulged in. Sometimes as a pleasantry [128b] this verse, a parody on a line by Khwaja Hafiz,[17] is recited:

> How happy that time when, unbridled and unconstrained, / we spent a few days in Gulkana with persons of ill repute.

To the south of the fortress, to the east of Shah Kabul, is a large lake nearly a league in circumference. Headed toward the city of Kabul from Shah Kabul Mountain are three small springs. Of the two in the Gulkana area, one is next to the Khwaja Shamu shrine[18] and the other is at Khwaja Khizr's footprint.[19] These two places are promenades for the inhabitants of Kabul. The third spring is opposite Khwaja Abdul-Samad and called Khwaja Rawshanai.

From the Shah Kabul Mountain a spur called Uqabayn juts off. Separate from Uqabayn is another little patch of mountain upon which the Kabul fortress citadel is located, north of the great city wall. The citadel is situated in an exceptionally elevated place with wonderfully good air. It overlooks the large lake and three meadows, Siyah Sang, Song Qorghan, and Chalak, which when green make a beautiful sight. In the spring and summer in Kabul the north wind, which they call the Parwan wind, never dies down. Within the citadel the rooms with apertures facing the north are well ventilated. Mulla Muhammad Talib Mu'amma'i versified a description of the Kabul citadel [129] in this line dedicated to Badi'uzzaman Mirza:

> Drink wine in Kabul citadel, send round the cup again and again, / for there is both mountain and water, both city and countryside.

Hindustanis call everything outside of Hindustan "Khurasan," just as the Arabs call everything not Arab "Ajam." On the land route between Hindustan and Khurasan are two trading depots, Kabul and Kandahar. Caravans come to Kabul from Fergana, Turkistan, Samarkand, Bukhara, Balkh, Hissar, and Badakhshan. From Khurasan, they go to Kandahar. As the entrepôt between Hindustan and Khurasan, this province is an excellent mercantile center. Merchants who go to Cathay and Anatolia do no greater business. Every year seven, eight, or ten thousand horses come to Kabul. From Hindustan, caravans of ten, fifteen, twenty thousand pack animals bring slaves, textiles, rock sugar, refined sugar, and spices. Many Kabul merchants would not be satisfied with a 300 to 400 percent profit. Goods from Khurasan, Iraq, Anatolia, and China can be found in Kabul, which is the principal depot for Hindustan.

Nearby are regions with both warm and cold climates. Within a day's ride from Kabul it is possible to reach a place where snow never falls. But within two hours one can go where the snows never melt— except in the rare summer so severe that all snow disappears. [129b] Both tropical and cold-weather fruits are abundant in Kabul's dependencies, and they are nearby. Among the cold-weather fruits of Kabul and its villages are abundant grapes, pomegranates, apricots, apples, quinces, pears, peaches, plums, jujubes, almonds, and nuts. I had a sour cherry sapling brought and planted. It took well and keeps getting better all the time. Tropical fruits, such as oranges, citrus, *amluk*,[20] and sugarcane are brought in from the Laghman region. I had some sugarcane brought and planted. *Jalghozas*[21] are brought from Nijrao. Much honey comes from the mountains around Kabul, where beehives are kept. Only from the mountains on the western side does honey not come.

Kabul's rhubarb is excellent. The quinces and plums are also good, as are the citrus fruits. One variety of grape called *ab-angur*, is superb. Kabul wine is intoxicating. The wine from the slopes of Khwaja Khawand Sa'id mountain is known for being strong, although at present it can only be praised secondhand.[22]

Only the drinker knows the pleasure of wine. / What enjoyment thereof can the sober have?

Sown crops are not good. A four- or fivefold return on agriculture is considered good. The melons are not good, but if seeds from Khurasan are used the results are not bad. The climate is excellent. In fact, no place in the world is known to have such a pleasing climate as Kabul. In spring and summer one cannot sleep at night without a fur blanket. Although there is usually a heavy snowfall in the winter, the cold is not excessive. Samarkand and Tabriz are also known for their good climates, but the cold there is extreme. [130]

Around Kabul are located four good meadows. Two leagues to the northeast of Kabul is Song Qorghan, an excellent meadow. The grass agrees with horses, and there are few flies. One league to the northwest of Kabul is the Chalak Meadow. It is a broad meadow, but in the spring and summer the flies there trouble the horses. To the west is the Diurin Meadow, which is really two meadows, Teba and Qush Nawar (by which reckoning there are five meadows altogether). The latter two are each a league out of Kabul. Both are rather small, but the grass is good and there are no flies. None among Kabul's meadows are like these. To the east is the Siyah Sang Meadow, and halfway between Charmgaran Gate and this meadow is Qutlugh-Qadam's tomb. It is not much maintained because it attracts so many flies in the summer. Adjacent to this meadow is the Kamari meadow. By this reckoning there are six meadows around Kabul, but they are generally known as four.

Kabul Province is well fortified and difficult for foreign enemies to invade. The Hindu Kush mountains separate Kabul from Balkh, Konduz, and Badakhshan. There are seven roads by which one may traverse the mountains. Three are in Panjshir.[23] The highest is the Khawak Pass.[24] Farther down is Tul, and farther down from that Bazarak.[25] [130b] The best of these passes is Tul, but the road is a bit longer. It is probably for this reason that it is called Tul.[26] The most direct route is Bazarak. Both Tul and Bazarak lead to Sarab. The people of Sarab use the Bazarak pass to descend to a village called Parandev, so they call it the Parandev pass. Another is the Parwan road.[27] Because seven passes fall between the great pass and Parwan, they call it Haft Bachcha.[28] In the direction of the Andarab are two roads that join at the great pass and lead to Haft Bachcha and Parwan. This is a difficult road. There are also three roads in Ghorband. The road nearest Parwan is the Yangï Yol pass. It descends to Walian and Khinjan. The second, also a good road, is the Qipchaq Pass, which descends to the confluence of the Andarab and the Red rivers. The third is through the Shibartu Pass.[29] When the water rises in spring and summer one goes through the Shibartu Pass and proceeds to Bamian and Saighan. In the winter one goes via Ao Dara.[30] For four to five months during the winter all roads are closed, with the one exception of the Shibartu road. Through this pass one gets to the Ao Dara. When the waters rise in spring causing the rivers swell in the hollows, the roads are as bad as they are in the winter because they are impossible to pass. Since one cannot go through the hollows, it is possible to make the crossing only during the three or four months when there is little snow and the streams are low. [131] Kafir highway robbers come down out of the mountains and defiles and hold up travelers.

The road coming from Khurasan goes via Kandahar. It is flat as can be and has no passes.

Four roads lead from Hindustan. One goes via the Laghman region. It has a few passes in the Khyber mountains. The second goes via Bangash, the third via Naghar, and the fourth via Barmal. On all of these roads, which are used when crossing the Indus River at any of its three crossings, are a few passes. Those who cross at the Nilab crossing come via the Laghman region. In winter the Indus and Kabul rivers can be crossed above their confluence. On most of my Hindustan campaigns I traversed at those fords. This last time I conquered Hindustan by defeating Sultan Ibrahim, I crossed at Nilab by boat. Other than that, there is no place the Indus can be crossed other than by boat. Those who cross at Dinkot go to Bangash. Those who cross at Chaupara,[31] if they go via Barmal, come to Ghazni. If they go via Dasht they come to Kandahar.

Various peoples live in Kabul Province. In the glens and plains are

Turks, Aymaqs, and Arabs.[32] The people in the towns and in some villages are Sarts. In some other villages [131b] and throughout the countryside are Pashais, Parachis, Tajiks, Barakis, and Afghans.[33] In the mountains of Ghazni are Hazaras and Negüdäris, among some of whom Mongolian is spoken. In the mountains to the northeast is Kafiristan, such as the Kator and the Gabarik.[34] To the south is Afghanistan.

Eleven or twelve dialects are spoken in Kabul Province: Arabic, Persian, Turkish, Mongolian, Hindi, Afghani, Pashai, Parachi, Gabari, Baraki, and Lamghani. It is not known if there are so many different peoples and languages in any other province.

The province consists of fourteen districts. In Samarkand and Bukhara and those regions, a subprovince under a greater province is called a *tümän*.[35] In Andizhan and Kashghar it is called an *orchin*, and in Hindustan a *pargana*. Although formerly Bajaur, Swat, Peshawar, and Hashnaghar were dependencies of Kabul, as of this date some have been devastated by the Afghan tribes and others have entered the Afghan realm, so the status of province no longer applies to them.

To the east is the Laghman region. This province consists of five districts and two subdistricts. The largest of the districts is Nangarhar, which is called Nagarhar in some histories. Its seat is Adinapur. It is thirteen leagues east of Kabul. The road between Nangarhar and Kabul is tortuous and bad: there are three or four places with very, very narrow passes, [132] and two or three areas with defiles. The Khirilji and Afghans, all of whom are highway robbers, made the road unsafe. Until recently there had not been any cultivation, but I improved the village of Quratu at the foot of the Quruq Say, and then the road became secure.

The dividing line between the warm and cold regions is the Badam Chashma pass. On the Kabul side of the pass snow falls, but on the Laghman side of the Quruq Say it does not. As one comes down from the pass one sees a different world: different trees, grass, animals, manners, and customs. There are nine rivers in Nangarhar. The rice and wheat are good, and so are the plentiful oranges, citron, and pomegranates.

In 914 [1508–9], I had constructed a charbagh garden called Baghi-Wafa[36] on a rise to the south of the Adinapur fortress. It overlooks the river, which flows between the fortress and the garden. It yields many

Literally a "four-garden," Babur's *charbagh*, or *chaharbagh*, is probably a garden constructed with a number (not necessarily four, despite the name) of rising parterres with a central watercourse, the type generally constructed later in Mughal India; the charbagh that became popular in Iran proper has four *charchamans*, herbaceous plots divided by walkways surrounding a central pool.

oranges, citrons, and pomegranates. [In 1524], the year I defeated Pahar Khan and conquered Lahore and Dipalpur, I had a banana tree brought and planted. It thrived. The year before that, sugarcane had been planted, some of which was being sent to Badakhshan and Bukhara. The ground is high, with constant running water, and the weather is mild in winter. In the middle of the garden is a small hill [132b] from which a one-mill stream[37] always flows through the garden. The *charchaman*[38] in the middle of the garden is situated atop the hill. In the southwest portion of the garden is a ten-by-ten pool surrounded by orange trees and some pomegranate trees. All around the pool is a clover meadow. The best place in the garden is there. When the oranges turn yellow it is a beautiful sight—really handsomely laid out.

The Safed Koh Mountains, located to the south of Nangarhar, separate Bangash from Nangarhar. There is no road for a mounted rider. Nine rivers emerge from the range, and the snows there never melt, which is probably the reason it is called Safed Koh.[39] But below, a half-day's journey away in the glens, it never snows. The slopes of the range have excellent climate. The waters are cold, and there is no need for ice.

The Adinapur fortress is situated on a promontory a sheer drop of forty to fifty yards down on either side. To the south of the fortress is the Surkhrud River, and to the north a mountain outcropping. It is a strong fortress. The Safed Koh is between Nangarhar and the Laghman region. Whenever it snows in Kabul, it also snows on the peak of the mountain, so the people in Laghman [133] know that snow has fallen in Kabul.

If one goes from Kabul to the Laghman region via the Quruq Say, one takes the road down through the Diri Pass, crosses the Baran River at Bolan, and proceeds toward Laghman. Another road farther down the Quruq Say crosses at Quratu, crosses the Nurab tributary of the Baran at Uluq, and leads to Laghman through the Badpakh Pass. If one goes via Nijrao, one crosses the Badrao then the Qarangriq and enters the Badpakh Pass.[40]

Although Nangarhar is one of the five districts of Laghman, when speaking of the Laghman region one usually means only three districts. One of the three is Alishang. In the north it consists of huge, impregnable snow-covered mountains adjoining the Hindu Kush. This mountainous region is all Kafiristan. The closest place in Kafiristan to Alishang is Mil, from which the Alishang River flows. The tomb of Noah's father, Mehter Lam, is in the Alishang district. In one history Mehter Lam is called both Lamak and Lamkan. Those people sometimes pronounce *k* as *gh;* that is probably why the province is called Lamghan.[41]

Another district is Alingar. The closest place in Kafiristan to Alingar is Kawar, from which the Alingar River flows. These two rivers join after traversing the Alishang and Alingar districts. The resulting stream joins the Baran River below the Mandrawar district. [133b]

One of the other two districts is Dara-i-Nur. It is situated in an extraordinary place. The fortress is located on a mountain spur at the entrance to the valley with rivers on either side and many rice fields. One can go only where there is a road. The area has oranges and citrons and warm-weather fruits and a few date trees. The banks of the rivers around the fortress are completely covered with trees, most of which are *amluks.* Its fruit, which Turks call *qara yemish,*[42] is plentiful in Dara-i-Nur, although it is not to be seen anywhere else. Dara-i-Nur also has grapes, with vines growing over the trees. Dara-i-Nur wine is famous in the Laghman region. There are two sorts, called *arratashi* and *sawhantashi*. The arratashi is yellowish, while the other is a beautiful bright red. The arratashi is more enjoyable, although neither is equal to its reputation. At a higher elevation, monkeys are found in some of the valleys; higher than this they are not found, though they live in lower elevations, in the direction of Hindustan. The people there used to keep pigs, but they have abandoned the practice in our time.

Kunar and Nur Gul. Another district is Kunar and Nur Gul, located apart from the Laghman region. It is actually inside Kafiristan and forms the border of the province. Although it is about as large as the Laghman districts, the revenue is small because the area is remote [134] and the people do not pay. The Chighan Sarai River enters Kafiristan from the northeastern side, passes through this district, joins the Baran River in the Kama subdistrict, and flows on to the east. Nur Gul is on the western bank of the river, and Kunar is to the east.

Mir Sayyid-Ali Hamadani[43] came here on his travels and passed away a league above Kunar. His disciples carried his body to Khuttalan. There is now a shrine in the spot where he died, which, in 920 [1514–15], when I took Chighan Sarai, I circumambulated.

Oranges, citrons, and rice are abundant, and heady wines are brought from Kafiristan. The people there tell strange stories that seem impossible but are heard over and over. For example: The lower part of the Kunar and Nur Gul district is called Lamata Kandi; below it belongs to Dara-i-Nur and Atar. Throughout the mountains above Lamata Kandi—in Kunar, Nur Gul, Bajaur, Swat, and those regions—it is well known that when a woman dies they put her on a cot and lift it at the four corners. If she has not done an evil deed, she causes the men who are carrying her to shake involuntarily in so violent a manner that if they try to stop themselves from shaking, the corpse falls from the cot. If she has done an evil deed, she causes no movement. Not only has this been heard from these people, but the mountain people from Bajaur and Swat are also unanimous in relating the tale. [134b] Haydar Ali, the sultan of Bajaur, kept an iron control over Bajaur. When his mother died, he did not weep, he did not mourn, and he did not put on black, but he said, "Go put her on the cot. If there is no movement I'll burn her." They put her on the cot and the desired motion caused by the corpse occurred. Only when he heard this did he put on black and begin to mourn.

Chighan Sarai. Another subdistrict is Chighan Sarai, which is only one village, and a wretched place at that. It is at the mouth of Kafiristan. Because the people, though Muslim, have mingled with the Kafirs, they have taken on infidel customs. A large torrent known as the Chighan Sarai River flows from the northeast of Chighan Sarai and comes out behind Bajaur. To the west it is joined by another little river called Pech that comes from Kafiristan. Chighan Sarai produces heavy yellowish wines that are no in way comparable to the wine of Dara-i-Nur. The village has no grapes or orchards of its own, and water has to be brought down from Kafiristan and the Pech. When I took Chighan Sarai, [in 1514–15], the Pech Kafirs came to help these people. Wine is so prevalent there that around the neck of every Kafir hangs a wine skein. Instead of drinking water on the march they drink wine.

Kama. Although Kama is not an independent place and belongs to Nangarhar, it is also called a subdistrict.

Nijrao. Another district is Nijrao. [135] It is located in the mountains to the northeast of Kabul. Beyond it the mountains are all Kafiristan. It is a remarkably inaccessible place with abundant grapes and fruit and much wine—although it is boiled. In the winter they get their chickens very fat. The people drink wine, do not pray, are fearless, and act like infidels.

The mountains have many pine, oak, and wormwood trees. The pines and oaks are found at lower altitudes but not at all above Nijrao—they are really subcontinental trees. The people of the mountains make their torches from jalghoza branches,[44] which burn like candles—very strange. In the Nijrao mountains are flying foxes, animals a bit larger than squirrels, with membranes between their arms and legs, like a bat's wing. They used to bring them to me all the time. It is said that these animals can fly down from tree to tree as far as an arrow shot. I myself did not see one fly, but one was put on a tree, and it scrambled right up. Then they goaded it, and it spread its wings and sailed down as easily as though flying.

The *lucha* bird, which is called *buqalamun,* is also found in these mountains.[45] From head to tail it has five or six different colors as brilliant as a pigeon's throat. It is about as large as a partridge, and probably is the Hindustani partridge. The people there say something amazing about it: As soon as winter sets in, the birds descend to the foothills. If they are put to flight [135b] over a grape orchard they absolutely cannot fly any longer, and can therefore be caught. Another type of rodent called a muskrat is said to be found in Nijrao, but I did not see it myself. The scent of musk is said to be emitted from it.

Panjshir. Another district, Panjshir, is located on the road quite near Kafiristan. The route of the Kafir highway robbers is through Panjshir. Due to its proximity to the Kafirs, the revenue intake is small. This last time I went to conquer Hindustan, [in 1526], the Kafirs came, killed many people from Panjshir, and wrought much havoc.

Ghorband. Another is the district of Ghorband. It is probably called Ghorband because one goes to Ghor through a pass there, and in that region a pass is called *band.* The Hazaras have occupied the entrances to the valleys. A few villages have meager sources of revenue. They say that silver and lapis lazuli mines can be found in the Ghorband mountains.

Altogether there are some twelve or thirteen villages in the mountains, with Mata, Kaja, and Parwan at the top and Dur Nama at the bottom. They produce fruit, and in these parts the wines of Khwaja Khawand Sa'id are the strongest of all. Since the villages are isolated on mountain skirts and summits, the people are not accustomed to paying taxes, although they do give some tribute.

In the foothills below the villages, between the mountain and the Baran River, are two tracts of flatland, one called Kurra Taziyan and the other Dasht-i-Shaykh. In the summer the *chikin tala* grass[46] [136] is very good. Aymaqs and Turks come here in the summer.

Tulips of many varieties cover the foothills. Once, when I had them counted, there turned out to be thirty-two or thirty-three unique varieties. One sort, which gives off a bit of the scent of red roses, for which reason it is called a *gulboy*[47] tulip, is found in Dasht-i-Shaykh and nowhere else. In these same foothills, below Parwan, in a patch of ground at the mouth of the Ghorband defile, the centifoil tulip grows. Between these two flatlands is a smallish mountain on which is a spot of sand extending all the way down the mountain called Khwaja Reg-i-Rawan. They say that in the summer the sound of drums comes from the sand.

Kabul dependencies. Then there are the village dependencies of Kabul. Three leagues southwest of Kabul is a large mountain usually covered year-round with snow. If the Kabul icehouses run short, ice is brought from the mountain to make cold drinking water. The Bamian mountains and this one form part of a single chain, and the Helmand, the Sind,[48] the Dughaba of Konduz, and the Balkhab rivers all have their sources in this range. In a single day it is possible to drink from the waters of all four rivers.

Most of the Kabul dependencies are located on the slopes of the mountain. All sorts of fruit, especially many grapes, are abundant in the orchards. Among the villages, none are like Istalif and Istarghij, which Ulughbeg Mirza used to call [136b] Khurasan and Samarkand.[49]

The village of Paghman is within an arrow shot of the villages. Although its grapes and fruit are not so good as those of the other villages, the climate is incomparable, and the mountain there is snow covered.

There are few places known to equal Istalif. A large torrent that runs through the middle of the village has orchards on both sides. Verdant, pleasant small garden plots abound, and the water is so pure and cold, there is no need for iced water. Ulughbeg Mirza confiscated one of the gardens called Bagh-i-Kalan,[50] for which I then paid the owners. Outside the garden are large plane trees, with pleasant, shady green spots at their bases. A one-mill stream flows constantly from the middle of the garden. On the banks of the stream are plane and other trees. The stream used to run higgledy-piggledy until I ordered it to be straightened. Now it is a beautiful place.

Below the villages and a league or a league-and-a-half above the flatland in a hollow in the foothills is a spring called Khwaja Seyaran that is surrounded by three types of trees.[51] Huge plane trees that give magnificent shade, and to either side of the spring, on the hills at the base of the mountain, are many oak trees—these two oak groves [137] are home to the only oaks in the mountains to the west of Kabul. In front of the spring, in the direction of the flatland, is a large grove of Judas trees—the only ones in the province. They say that these three sorts of trees—plane, oak, and Judas—are miracles of the three saints for whom the spring is named. I had the spring surrounded with stonework plastered and mortared into a ten-by-ten pool,[52] such that the four sides would form straight, symmetrical benches overlooking the entire grove of Judas trees. When the trees blossom, no place in the world equals it. In the foothills, yellow Judas trees bloom together with the red ones.

Southwest of the spring is a constantly flowing stream, a half-mill in force, that comes from a valley. I had a channel dug for it and had it brought to the hillock to the southwest of Seyaran. Atop the hillock I had a large round platform installed, around which were planted willow trees. It turned out to be a beautiful spot. A little higher up on the side of the hillock I had a grape garden constructed. The date of the channel was found in the chronogram *juy-i-khosh.*[53]

Logar. Another district is Logar, in which the largest village is Charkh. Mulla Ya'qub was from Charkh, as was Mullazada Mulla Usman. [137b] Sajawan is among the villages of Logar. Khwaja Ahmad and Khwaja Yunus were from Sajawan. Charkh has many orchards, but the other Logar villages have none. In Kabul the people are called Awghan Shal, which is probably a corruption of Afghan-shu'ar.[54]

Ghazni. Another is the province of Ghazni, which some call a district. It was the capital of Sabuktekin, Sultan Mahmud, and his descendants. Sometimes it is written "Ghaznin." It was also the capital of Sultan Shihabuddin Ghori, who is called Mu'izzuddin in the *Tabaqat-i-Nasiri*[55] and another history of India. Ghazni, in the third clime, is also known as Zabul. Zabulistan consists of this province, and some consider Kandahar to be in Zabulistan. Ghazni is fourteen leagues southwest of Kabul. Those who take this road leave Ghazni at daybreak and arrive in Kabul in the afternoon, whereas the thirteen-league road between Kabul and Adinapur is so poor that no one can do it in a day. It is a miserable province. The river is a four- or five-mill stream. The city of Ghazni and another four or five villages are watered by it, while another three or four others are irrigated by subterranean aquaducts. The grapes and melons of Ghazni are better than those of Kabul; the apples are also good [138] and are taken to Hindustan. The agriculture is laborious because new soil must be brought in every year for whatever amount of land is planted. The yield, however, is better than that of Kabul. They plant madder, the best crop, all of which is taken to Hindustan. Hazaras and Afghans live in the Ghazni countryside, where prices are always better relative to Kabul. The inhabitants are Hanafi by sect, good, orthodox Muslims. Many observe the three-month fast.[56] Their wives and families are kept well secluded.

Mulla Abdul-Rahman, a learned scholar, was one of the eminent men of Ghazni. He taught and was religiously observant and pious. He passed away the same year Nasir Mirza died [in 1515]. Sultan Mahmud's tomb is in one of the suburbs of Ghazni, which is called Rawza[57]—home to the best grapes in the region—because the sultan's tomb, in addition to many other important shrines, is there. Sultan Mahmud's sons Sultan Mas'ud and Sultan Ibrahim are also buried in Ghazni. The year I took Kabul and Ghazni, [in 1505], when I overran Kohat, Bannu, Dasht, and Afghanistan, I passed by Duki and the Ab-i-Istada[58] on my way to Ghazni. I was told that there was a shrine in a village where the tomb moved when prayers were spoken. When I went to inspect it, I could feel the tomb move. [138b] Then it was discovered that it was a trick on the part of the attendants: They had put a screen over the tomb, which, when they made it move, made it seem as though the tomb was moving, just as it seems to people riding in a boat for the first time that the shore is moving. I ordered the attendants to stand away from the screen: then, no matter how many times they spoke prayers, no motion appeared in the tomb. I ordered the screen demolished and a dome built over the grave. The attendants were forbidden on pain of punishment ever to play that trick again.

Ghazni is a truly miserable place. Why kings who hold Hindustan and Khurasan would ever make such a wretched place their capital has always been a source of amazement to me. In Sultan Mahmud's time,[59] there were three or four dams. A large one—forty or fifty yards high and approximately three hundred yards long—was constructed by him on the Ghazni River three leagues upriver to the north of Ghazni. A reservoir was created behind it, and the waterways to the fields were opened according to need. When Ala'uddin Jahansoz Ghuri[60] gained control of this province, he wrecked the dam, torched the tomb of Sultan Mahmud and those of many of his sons, and destroyed and burned the city of Ghazni. The people were pillaged and killed. In massacre and devastation he left no stone unturned. [139] From that time forth the large dam has lain in ruins. But the year I conquered Hindustan, [in 1526], I sent money with Khwaja Kalan to repair it. By the grace of God there is hope that it will flourish once more.

Another dam is the Sakhan dam, two or three leagues to the east of Ghazni. It too has lain in ruins for a long time and is beyond repair. Another is the Sardeh, which is in good condition.

It is recorded in books that if any filth or dirt is thrown into a certain spring in Ghazni, a violent hailstorm breaks out at once. It was seen in a history book that when the Ray of Hind[61] laid siege to Ghazni, Sabuktekin ordered filth and dirt thrown into the spring. A violent hailstorm followed, and the enemy was repelled. No matter how much I searched for the spring in Ghazni, no sign of it could be found.

In these parts Ghazni and Khwarazm are as well known for being as cold as Sultaniyya and Tabriz are in the two Iraqs[62] and Azerbaijan.

Zurmat. Another district is Zurmat, twelve or thirteen leagues south of Kabul, and seven or eight leagues southeast of Ghazni. It consists of seven villages of which Gardez is the seat. Inside the Gardez city wall most of the buildings are three and four stories. [139b] Gardez is a fairly strong place. When they rebelled against Nasir Mirza, they gave him a lot of trouble. The people of Zurmat are Awghan Shal.[63] They sow and harvest crops and have no orchards or gardens. To the south of the district is a mountain called Barakistan. In a high place on the mountain slopes is a spring where Shaykh Muhammad Musalman's tomb is located.[64]

Barmal.[65] Another is the district of Barmal, a wretched place, though its apples are not bad and are taken to Multan and Hindustan. The *shaykhzadas,* the offspring of Shaykh Muhammad Musalman who were patronized in Hindustan during the Afghan period, were from Barmal.

Bangash. Another is the district of Bangash. Since it is completely surrounded by Afghan highway robbers, like the Khugiani, Khirilji, Turi, and Landar, they do not pay the desired amount of tribute. Because I was absorbed in other affairs, such as the conquests of Kandahar, Balkh, Badakhshan, and Hindustan, I did not have a chance to get Bangash under control. If God allows, when I have an opportunity, I will certainly deal with the Bangash bandits.[66]

Ala Say. One of the Kabul subdistricts is Ala Say, which is two or three leagues to the east of Nijrao. Going east from Nijrao one traverses a flat plain and reaches a place called Kura. Right there is a little pass to Ala Say. The Kura Pass is the dividing line between warm and cold climates. It is also the route taken by birds in the autumn. The Pachaghan people, dependents of Nijrao, catch many birds in the pass. [140] In every spot at the mouth of the pass they have built stone blinds. Men sitting in the blinds secure one edge of a net five or six yards away and weight it down with stones. To the middle of the other side they fasten a stick three or four yards long. One end of the stick is held by the man who waits and watches through holes in the blind. As soon as birds approach he raises the net, and the birds enter. By this machination they catch birds faster than they can decapitate them.

In those regions the pomegranates of Ala Say are famous. Although they are not the best kind, they are exported to Hindustan. The grapes are not bad either. Among the wines of Nijrao the Ala Say wines are the strongest and have the best color.

Badrao. Another is the Badrao district, next to Ala Say. There is no fruit there, but the area is cultivated by Kafirs, who harvest grain.

Just as in Khurasan and Samarkand, where Turks and Aymaqs dwell in the countryside, in Kabul live Hazaras and Afghans. Chief among the Hazaras are the Sultan-Mas'udi Hazaras, and among the Afghans, the Mohmand Afghans.

The total revenue of Kabul Province, customs, and countryside was eight lacs.[67] [140b]

The mountains on both the eastern and western sides of Kabul Province are of two sorts. The mountains of Andarab, Khwast, and the Badakhshan region are covered with juniper, have many springs, and are soft, rolling, and hilly. The grass there and in the glens is uniformly good, with most of the grass growing in clumps. In Andizhan they call this kind "clump grass." I never understood why it was so called, but in this region it became obvious: it comes out in clumps.[68] The summer pastures of Hissar, Khuttalan, Samarkand, Fergana, and Moghulistan are all like the summer pastures here, and although they can scarcely be compared to those of Fergana and Moghulistan, the mountains and pastures are similar.

On the other hand the mountains of Nijrao, Laghman, Bajaur, and Swat have many jalghoza, oak, olive, and wormwood trees. The grass also differs from that of those other mountains. It is plentiful and grows high but useless for horses or sheep. Although the mountains are not so high as the former and appear small, they are nonetheless quite impregnable. They seem to be very low and level, but all the hills and peaks are strong and rocky. Many places are impossible to reach on horseback. The mountains are home to many Indian birds and other animals, [141] such as parrots, mynahs, peacocks, luchas, monkeys, nilgais, and *kutahpays*,[69] in addition to many and various types of birds and animals that have not been heard of in India.

The mountains to the west, Dara-i-Zindan, Dara-i-Suf, Gurzuwan, and Gharjistan, are also similar to one another. The grasslands are mostly in the glens, but, unlike that on the other mountains, the grass is a single type—suitable for horses and sheep. There are not many trees or much juniper covering, but there is a lot of game. The mountaintops, where planting is done, are flat enough that one can run a horse on them. The ravines are valley strongholds, most precipitous and inaccessible from above. It is odd that mountain strongholds are generally located in high places, but in these mountains they are in the low-lying areas.

The mountains of Ghor, Karnu, and Hazara are similar to the western mountains just described: the grasslands are in the glens, there are few trees and no juniper, the grass is suitable for horses and sheep, and the game is plentiful. Whereas the strongholds of the aforementioned mountains are in the low places, it is not so in these mountains.

The Khwaja Isma'il, Dasht, Duki, and Afghanistan mountains are also of one sort. They are very low, with little grass and scanty water—treeless and ugly. [141b] They are worthy of their inhabitants, as the proverb says, "There is no noon without a dawn." There are few such worthless mountains in the world.

Although Kabul has a heavy snowfall in the winter, it has good, readily available firewood that one can gather and bring in within a day. The firewoods are wormwood, oak, small almond, and *qarqand*.[70] The best of these is wormwood, which burns bright and green and gives a good odor, with its embers lasting a long time. Oak is also a good firewood: although its flame is less bright, it burns hot and the embers last. It has a curious characteristic: when lit an oak branch with green leaves will kindle and burn up immediately from one end to the other with sparks and crackling. It is quite a sight to see it burn. The small almond is the most abundant and most used, but its embers do not last long. Qarqand is a low-growing, thorny wood that burns equally well either green or cured. All the people of Ghazni burn it.

The province of Kabul lies in the midst of mountains that look like rows of clover. Throughout the mountains are flat valleys and glens in which are scattered inhabited settlements. There is little game or fowl. In the autumn and spring, when the wild mountain sheep are migrating between winter and summer pasture, there are certain hunting grounds kept by eager youths who go out with dogs and hunt. [142] In the direction of Khurd Kabul and the Surkhab[71] there is abundant wild ass but absolutely no small game. Ghazni has both, there being few places that have such fat game as Ghazni.

Kabul has many fowling grounds in the spring. The route of migratory birds is generally along the banks of the Baran River, since mountains are to the east and west and the only great pass through the Hindu Kush is in a direct line with the river. All the birds must therefore go through here. If the pass is hit with wind or covered with even a few clouds, the birds cannot go through and so descend to the Baran plain, at which point the people of the region catch them. Toward the end of winter many ducks come to the banks of the Baran, and they are very fat. After them cranes, herons, and other large birds arrive in large numbers.

On the banks of the Baran, people capture many cranes by the singular method of catching birds with shooting ropes. Gray herons, herons, and pelicans are caught in large numbers in the same fashion. This is how it is done: The hunter twists about an arrow-shot length of thin rope, ties one end to an arrow shaft, and fastens the other end to a *bildürgä*[72] made of a piece of wood as thick as a man's forearm [142b] and a span long. He coils the rope from the shaft end all the way to the piece of wood and then makes fast the bildürgä. He then pulls the piece of wood out from the coiled rope, leaving its place empty inside the coil. Holding the bildürgä, he shoots the shaft into the approaching flocks. It gets tangled around a bird's wings or neck, and the bird falls. All the Baran people catch birds this way, but the method is highly laborious. It is necessary to have a dark, rainy night, when the birds fly low until dawn in fear of wild beasts. On such nights, flying up and down the river they appear white, and the people can then shoot them with the ropes. One night I shot a rope, but it broke and the bird could not be found until the next morning. In this manner the Baran people catch a lot of herons, from which turban plumes, a product exported from Kabul to Iraq and Khurasan, are made.

A group of professional hunter bondsmen, some two to three hundred households of them originally brought by one of Temür Beg's descendants from the Multan region, [143] make their livelihood by catching migratory birds. They dig tanks, stick branches and set traps in the middle of the tanks, and catch all sorts of birds. Not only professional hunters catch birds—all the people living in the Baran cast ropes, set traps, and catch many birds of all sorts by every conceivable method.

During the same season fish migrate in the Baran River and are caught with nets and wattles. In the autumn, when the plant known as *qulan quyruqi*[73] has matured, flowered, and set seed, they break ten to twelve heaps of qulan quyruqï and twenty to thirty heaps of green wormwood into little pieces and throw them in the water. The fishers immediately begin to pick up the drugged fish from the wattles they have set in an appropriate place downstream. Wattles, made of loosely woven willow branches as big around as a finger, are placed in the river in a spot where the water pours down. Stones are piled up so that the water trickles through. As the water goes downstream, the drugged fish remain on top of the wattle, from which they can be picked up. This method is also used on the streams at Gulbahar, Parwan, and Istalif.

In the winter in Laghman the people have an unusual technique of fishing that has not been observed elsewhere. [143b] In a place where water pours down, holes about the size of a tent are dug out and stones are piled up, like stones for a campfire, until they cover the hole, except for one opening underwater. The stones are arranged in such a way that the fish, once having entered, cannot get out except through the one opening. The water runs through the stones, creating a fish tank. In the winter, whenever fish are wanted a person opens one of the holes and takes out anywhere from forty to fifty fish. The opening is in a particular, marked place; the other sides are covered with straw and stones. The opening is made from something like a wattle with its two edges securely fastened together to make a cage.

Inside this contraption is another wattlelike cage, only half as long as the outer cage and one end of which is the size of the opening in the outer cage. Its other end is narrow, so when a fish goes through the inner end of the inner cage, it is inside the big one. The lower end of the big cage is made so that the fish cannot get out. The inner, lower end of the inner cage is also made so that when fish enter the upper end, [144] they can only go one by one through the inner end. They fasten sticks at the inner end, so when the fish passes through this end it enters the large cage and is held fast, unable to get out. If the fish tries to get out the way it entered it is prevented by the sharp sticks at the mouth of the inner cage. Having fastened this cage to the opening, they open the top of the fish tank, which is is made secure all around by straw. Whatever they catch they catch in such tanks. Any fish that escape through the one and only opening fall into the cage and are trapped there.[74]

MUQIM DEPARTS AND LANDS ARE ASSIGNED

A few days after Kabul was taken, Muqim requested leave to go to Kandahar. Since he had come to us under a pact, he and all his men with their belongings were allowed to proceed in safety to his father and brother. After Muqim was given consent to depart, the areas outside of Kabul were divided among the princes and all the guest begs. Ghazni was given to Jahangir Mirza and his followers. Nasir Mirza was awarded the Nangarhar district, Mandrawar, Dara-i-Nur, Kunar, Nur Gul, and Chighan Sarai. Villages and fiefs were turned over to some of the begs and warriors who had been with me during our rencontres. [144b] Of Kabul Province itself nothing was allotted. This was not the only time I treated guests and foreign begs and warriors with more favor than I did my old retainers and the Andizhanis. Indeed, every time God granted a boon I did so. My actions not withstanding, it was an odd reproach that they always gossiped that I did not favor anyone except Andizhanis and old retainers! There is a proverb that says, "What will your enemy not say? What will not enter his dream?"

City gates can be closed but never the mouths of opponents.

Many tribes and clans had come to Kabul from Samarkand, Hissar, and Konduz. Kabul—a military rather than a civilian city—is poor and could not supply money to all the incoming people. We deemed it wise, however, to give some grain to the families of each of the tribes and clans and then ride out on forays. It was decided to levy thirty thousand loads of grain on the provinces of Kabul and Ghazni. We did not know the income or harvest of Kabul, and the province suffered heavily under such an enormous impost.

Around that time I invented the Baburi script.[75] A large tribute of sheep and horses had been imposed on the Sultan-Mas'udi Hazaras. Collectors were sent. Several days later, word was received that the Hazaras refused to pay [145] and were being refractory. Because they had previously held up people on the Gardez and Ghazni roads, we rode out to attack them. We traveled by the flat road, advanced through the Nirkh pass by night, and charged them early in the morning in the vicinity of Chitu.[76] The attack was less than satisfactory. Afterward we returned by the Sang-i-Surakh road and gave Jahangir Mirza leave to go to Ghazni. Soon after our arrival back in Kabul, Darya Khan's son Yar-Husayn came from Bhera to pay homage.

Several days later the army was mustered, and persons who knew the lay of the land were summoned to scout out the surrounding areas. Some said that Dasht was good, others said Bangash was suitable, others thought Hindustan best. In consultation we decided on a campaign to Hindustan.

FIRST INCURSION INTO HINDUSTAN

In the month of Sha'ban [January 1505] when the sun was in the sign of Aquarius we rode out of Kabul for Hindustan. Stopping six times overnight on the Badam Chashma and Jagdalak road, we came to Adinapur. I had never seen a hot climate or any of Hindustan before. When we reached Nangarhar, a new world came into view—different plants, different trees, different animals and birds, different tribes and people, [145b] different manners and customs. It was astonishing, truly astonishing.

Nasir Mirza had come ahead to his province and paid homage at Adinapur. The tribes and clans who had come from the other side had all migrated into the Laghman region for the winter. We stopped there for a day or two to allow those soldiers and those who had remained behind to join us. Then we crossed the Juy-i-Shahi and camped in Khush Gumbaz, where Nasir Mirza requested leave to stay behind to get something from the province for his servants and retainers, and said he would follow us in two or three days. When we marched out of Khush Gumbaz and camped in Garm Chashma, Pikhi, one of the headmen of the Gagiani who had been with a caravan, was brought in. Pikhi was taken along to find roads. In two or three marches we went through the Khyber and camped in Jam.[77]

I had heard tell of the cave called Gurh Kattri. It was a holy place for yogis and Hindus, who came from faraway places to cut their hair and beards there. While camped at Jam, I rode out to see Bigram, where I observed the great banyan tree and explored the vicinity. I asked Malik Bu-Sa'id Kamari, who was my guide, something about Gurh Kattri, but he did not answer. When we got back to the camp, [146] he said to Khwaja Muhammad Amin, "Gurh Kattri was right next to Bigram, but since it is narrow and dangerous I didn't say anything." The khwaja immediately reviled him and told me what he had said. It was too late in the day and too far for us to go back.

A FORAY TO KOHAT

While in this camp we deliberated crossing the Indus and where to go. Baqi Chaghaniani contended that without crossing the river it was possible to go with one night's halt to a place called Kohat, where there would be many tribes with ample herds. He produced a couple of Kabulis who verified what he said. We had never heard of this place, but since my man of great authority thought it wise to go to Kohat and had produced several witnesses to back his claim, we canceled our plan to cross the river toward Hindustan. Instead we marched out of Jam, crossed the Bara, and camped near the Muhammad Pikh Pass.

The Gagiani Afghans were then in Peshawar, but in dread of our army they had withdrawn into the foothills. When the headman of the Gagiani, Khusraw Gagiani, came to our camp to render homage, he was taken along with Pikhi to guide us. [146b] We marched out at midnight, traversed the Muhammad Pikh as day was breaking, and raided Kohat at breakfast time. We took many cows and oxen and many Afghan prisoners too, but released them all. There was no end to the grain in their houses. The raiding party sent off to the banks of the Indus returned after a night and joined us. The army had not acquired anything like what Baqi Chaghaniani had claimed, and he was rather embarrassed by this effort.

Stopping two nights in Kohat, we assembled the raiding forces and discussed where to go. It was decided to raid the Afghans in the vicinity of Bangash and Bannu and then return by either the Naghar or the Barmal road.

Yar-Husayn, Darya Khan's son who had come to pay homage in Kabul, made the following request: "If orders are issued to the Dilazak, Yusufzai, and Gagiani tribes not to transgress my command, I will wield the padishah's sword on the other side of the Indus." Decrees were given according to his request, and he was given leave to depart Kohat.

Marching out of Kohat, we headed up the Hangu road in the direction of Bangash. Between Kohat and [147] Hangu is a valley with a road running through it and mountains on either side. While we were marching through the valley, the Afghans from Kohat and vicinity massed on both sides of the valley, shouting and creating confusion. Malik Bu-Sa'id Kamari, who knew all of Afghanistan well and was our guide on this campaign, said, "Up ahead, on the right side of the road, is a patch of isolated mountain. If these Afghans cross from this mountain to that one, we can circle around and take them." Thank God, the Afghans moved exactly as Malik Bu-Sa'id Kamari has wished. A troop of warriors was sent immediately to take the narrows between the two peaks. The rest of the army was ordered to come in from all directions and give the Afghans their due. When the assault was made from all sides, the Afghans were not able to put up a fight. In a flash a hundred, 150 embattled Afghans were seized. Some were captured alive, but mostly only heads were brought. If Afghans are unable to fight they come before their enemies with grass in their teeth, as if to say, "I am your cow." We witnessed that custom there: [147b] the defeated Afghans held grass in their teeth. Those who were brought in alive were ordered beheaded, after which a tower of skulls was erected in the camp.

The next morning we marched out of there and dismounted in Hangu. The Afghans in that region had turned an isolated mountain into a *sangar*, a word we had heard when we came to Kabul that refers to a fortified mountain.[78] As soon as the army reached it, they smashed the fortifications and cut off the heads of a hundred or so rebellious Afghans, which they brought back to Hangu. Another tower of skulls was erected.

After marching from Hangu we stopped for a night, then camped below Bangash in a place called Thal. Here too the army made raids on the Afghans in the area. One of the raiding parties returned from a sangar rather lightly laden.

When we marched from Thal toward Bannu, without a road to follow, we spent one night along the way before heading down a steep descent and through a long, narrow defile. The soldiers, camels, and horses had had a rough time. We had to leave behind most of the cattle taken as booty. The frequented road lay a league or two to our right; the one we were on was not for horses. It was said to be called Gosfand Lyar because occasionally shepherds and herdsmen brought their flocks and herds down this pass through the defile. [148] (*Lyar* means road in the Afghan language.[79]) Our guide was Malik Bu-Sa'id Kamari. Most of the soldiers blamed him for the difficulty we faced.

Immediately after the Bangash and Naghar mountains, Bannu lies on an open plain as flat as a board. The Bangash river runs through Bannu and provides irrigation. To the north are the mountains of Bangash and Naghar. To the south are Chaupara and the Indus River. To the east is Dinkot, and to the west Dasht, which is also called Bazar and Tank.[80] The Afghan tribes Kurani, Givi, Sur, Isa Khel, and Niazi cultivate this province.

As soon as we stopped in Bannu, we received word that the tribes of the plain had made a sangar in the mountains to the north. The army was dispatched under the command of Jahangir Mirza. Apparently it was the Givis' sangar. In no time at all it was taken, a massacre ensued, and many heads were cut off and brought back. Many fine textiles fell into the soldiers' hands. A tower of skulls was erected. After the sangar was taken, Shadi Khan, one of the Givi chiefs, came with grass between his teeth to pay homage. We pardoned the captives.

When we had raided Kohat, we had decided to raid the Afghans in the vicinity of Bangash and Bannu and then return by the Naghar or Barmal roads. [148b] After raiding Bannu, those who knew the lay of the land said that Dasht was nearby and the people were numerous. Furthermore, the road was good and led to Barmal.

A FORAY TO DASHT

Having decided to raid Dasht and leave by that road, we marched out the next morning and stopped on the banks of the river in a village of the Isa Khel. But the people there had learned of our approach and had taken refuge in the Chaupara mountains. We then headed to the slopes of the mountains, where a raiding party destroyed an Isa Khel sangar and sacked sheep, cattle, and textiles.

That very evening the Isa Khel Afghans staged an ambush on us. We had taken special precautions on that campaign, however, and they were unable to effect their offense. Our defensive measures were to station the right and left wings, center, and vanguard just as they dismounted, and each section went out armed and on foot and stayed all night an arrow shot away from the tents. Every night the entire army was arrayed in this manner, and three or four ichkis took turns patrolling the camp with torches. I also took a turn. [149] Anyone who did not go out had his nose slit and was paraded around the camp. In the right wing were Jahangir Mirza, Baqi Chaghaniani, Sherim Taghayï, Sayyid-Husayn Akbar, and some other begs. In the left wing were Mirza Khan, Abdul-Razzaq Mirza, Qasim Beg, and some other begs. There were no great begs in the center: they were all ichki begs. In the vanguard were Sayyid-Qasim Eshik-aqa, Baba-oghlï, Allah-Qulï Paran, and some other begs. The army was divided into six divisions, each of which was assigned a twenty-four-hour watch.

Headed west from the slopes, we stopped in a waterless depression between Dasht and Bannu. The soldiers dug in the dry riverbed and got water for themselves and their animals. One had to shovel down only a yard or so to find water. It was not only in this dry riverbed that water came forth like that; indeed all the riverbeds of Hindustan are the same. Dig a yard or a yard-and-a-half down and water will gush forth. What a marvelous provision God has made, so that for Hindustan, where no water flows other than in great rivers, water should lie so close.

After marching at dawn from the riverbed, the soldiers who were riding unencumbered reached the vicinity of Dasht in the afternoon. The raiding party attacked a few villages and brought back flocks, textiles, and trade ponies. Through the evening until the next morning till noon the laden trains and camels and people on foot who had lagged behind [149b] kept on coming. That day, a raiding party went and sacked a lot of cattle and sheep and, having encountered some Afghan merchants, brought back a lot of fine textiles, aromatic roots, refined and raw sugar, thoroughbred horses, and trade ponies. Khwaja Khizr Nohani, a well-known and important Afghan merchant, was felled and decapitated by Hindi Moghul. Sherim Taghayï went out after the raiding party, but an Afghan on foot faced him and lopped off his index finger.

RETURN TO KABUL

The next morning we marched and stopped closer to the Dasht villages. Leaving there, we rested on the banks of the Gumal River. From Dasht there were said to be two roads to Ghazni. One was the Sang-i-Surakh, which passes through Barak and leads to Barmal. The other follows the Gumal River to Barmal without going to Barak. Some preferred the Gumal road. While we were in Dasht it rained constantly for two or three days. The Gumal River got so high that it was only with difficulty that we crossed. Moreover, those who knew the way said that it would be necessary to cross several times if we took the Gumal road. There was always uncertainty on that road.

We still had not reached a decision when the marching drums were sounded the next morning. [150] I planned to hold deliberations on horseback about which road to take. It was the Fitr holiday [March 7, 1505].[81] While I was busy performing my ablutions for the holiday, Jahangir Mirza and the begs were talking together. Some said that if we went around the spur of the mountains to the west of Dasht, which are called the Mehter Sulaiman Mountains and lie between Dasht and Duki, the road would be flat. Although that route would require an extra march or two, they decided on that course. By the time I had finished my ablutions the army had taken the flat spur road and most of them were already across the Gumal River. Since we had not seen these roads, we were proceeding according to hearsay without knowing how long they were.

We performed the holiday prayers on the banks of the Gumal. That year Nawroz[82] was close to the holiday, two or three days apart. On that occasion I had composed the following poem:

Happy is the festival for those who see the new moon and the beloved's face together. / For me, separated from your face and brow, there is sadness in the festival moon. / Seize the Nawroz of his face and the festival of union, Babur, / For in a hundred Nawroz festivals there will be nothing better than this.

We crossed the Gumal River and headed south along the mountain slopes. We had gone a league or two [150b] when a few Afghans, intent upon revenge, appeared in the foothills. When they saw us heading for them at a gallop, most of them ran away, but some bravados for-tified themselves in the jagged peaks and cliffs. One Afghan was stand-ing on an isolated mountain. There must have been a cliff on the other side, for he had no way to get away. Sultan-Qulï Chanaq went out armed and fought with him; his outstanding feat in my presence was the reason for his promotion. On another cliff Qutlugh-Qadam ex-changed blows and grappled with an Afghan, and they fell ten or twelve yards straight down. Qutlugh-Qadam cut off the Afghan's head and brought it in. On another mountain, Käpä tangled with an Afghan, and they rolled halfway down it. Käpä brought in that head too. Many of the Afghans were taken prisoner but were later set free.

Umar-Shaykh b. Temür Outwits Ankatura in a Night Encounter, from a *Zafar-nama* (Book of Triumph) of Sharafuddin Ali Yazdi. Iran, Herat (?), dated A.H. 872 (A.D. 1467–68). Opaque watercolor, ink, and gold on paper. John Work Garrett Library, The Johns Hopkins University, Baltimore.

Marching out of Dasht and hugging the skirts of Mehter Sulaiman Mountains, we proceeded in a southerly direction, camping overnight three times, until we reached a small town belonging to Multan called Bila on the banks of the Indus. Some of the inhabitants jumped into boats and crossed the river; others threw themselves into the water. Opposite this village was an island, [151] where the people who had been left behind could be seen. Most of the soldiers, together with their horses and armor, plunged into the water to reach the island. A few—among them one of my servants, Qul Aruq, Jahangir Mirza's servant Mihtar Farrash, and Qaytmas the Turcoman—were swept away. On the island some textiles and articles of baggage fell into the soldiers' hands. The people remaining there were able to get to the other side of the Indus in boats. A few of those who did so, trusting in the breadth of the river, began to brandish their swords. Qul-Bayazid Bökäül, who had reached to the island, stripped himself and his horse and hurled himself into the water opposite these people. The river on the other side of the island was twice as broad as on this side. The horse swam across and, an arrow shot from the people on the other side, found its footing and began to wade, with water up to its girth strap. Qul-Bayazid paused an instant, probably to adjust his arms. With no reinforcement from behind, and no possibility of it, he charged from where he was. They returned an arrow or two, but then turned and fled, unable to maintain their position. All alone with an unsaddled horse and without support, Qul-Bayazid swam across the Indus, put the enemy to flight, and took their position. What bravery! Afterward [151b] the soldiers followed him and brought back textiles and animals as booty. Although Qul-Bayazid had already been in my favor for his previous service and several acts of valor, I bestowed on him great honor and promoted him from the rank of cook to that of royal taster, as will be mentioned.[83] In truth he was worthy of commendation and promotion.

Two marches were made farther down the banks of the Indus. The soldiers ruined their horses galloping off on raids, and the booty they got—nothing but cattle—was not worth the effort. We had taken sheep in Dasht and textiles in other places, but after Dasht there was nothing for us but cattle. A household servant could bring in three or four hundred head of cattle during the marches down the banks of the Indus. In fact, they rounded up so many that many had to be left behind.

We proceeded three marches down the bank, after which we left the Indus opposite Pir Kanu and stopped at Pir Kanu's shrine.[84] I had one of the soldiers hacked to pieces for bothering some of the residents there. This important shrine in Hindustan [152] is located on the slopes of the mountains adjoining the Mehter Sulaiman Mountains.

Our first stop after we left the shrine was at the top of a pass and the second by a river belonging to Duki. While we marched from that camp, some twenty scouts of Shah Beg's liege man Fazil Kükäldash, the prefect of Sibi, were captured and brought in. Since at that time we had no quarrel with him, we let them go with their horses and arms. After stopping overnight we camped near a village in Duki called Chotiali.

Although we made constant raids on our way to the Indus, and continued them along the Indus riverbank, plenty of fodder and green grain had been available for the horses. Once we left the banks at Pir Kanu, there was no more green grain. Every two or three marches we would find a grain field, but without fodder. The soldiers' horses began to lag. After Chotiali my tent had to be left behind for lack of pack animals. At that camp it rained so hard one evening that the water was up to our shins inside the tents. I piled rugs up in one spot and sat on them the whole miserable night through.

A PLOT IS DISCOVERED

Two marches later Jahangir Mirza came and whispered to me, "I need a word with you in private." When we were alone he told me, "Baqi Chaghaniani came to me and said, 'Let's dismiss the padishah with eight to ten men, send him across the Indus, and make you padishah.'"

"Who else was in on this plot?" I asked.

"Baqi Beg spoke to me just now," he said. "I don't know who else is involved."

"Find out who the others are," I said. "Sayyid-Husayn Akbar, Sultan-Ali Chuhra, and some of Khusrawshah's other begs and warriors are probably in on it."

This was truly an excellent deed by Jahangir Mirza, a brotherly act in return for what I did for him at Kahmard, when that same wretched Baqi Beg tried to tempt me and lead me astray with regard to Jahangir Mirza.[85]

After moving out of that camp and stopping in another, those whose horses were able were put under Jahangir Mirza's charge and sent to raid the Afghans living in the area.

Many of the soldiers' horses began to be left behind—some two hundred, three hundred horses were abandoned. Great warriors went on foot. Shah-Mahmud Oghlaqchï, one of my great ichkis, was among them, having lost all his horses. This happened all the way to Ghazni.

Three or four marches later Jahangir Mirza [153] raided a band of Afghans and brought back some sheep. Two or three marches after that we reached the Ab-i-Istada. A strange, large body of water came into view, and the plateaus on the other side could not be seen at all. The water seemed to be joined to the sky, and the mountains and hills on the other side seemed to hang between the earth and the sky, like a mirage. All this water had collected from the Katawaz riverbed, the Zurmat glen, the springtime rain runoff from the Karabagh meadow of the Ghazni River, and the overflow from the spring floods.

As we approached within a kos of the Ab-i-Istada, we noticed something strange. Between the water and the sky a reddish glow like dawn could be seen flashing on and off. It continued the same as we approached. When we were quite near, we discovered that this spectacle was made of flocks of geese—not ten or twenty thousand but so many geese innumerable in flight that when they beat their wings sometimes their red feathers showed on and off. Not only these birds but birds of every sort beyond number also came to the edges of the water to lay eggs. [153b]

Two Afghans who had come to gather eggs threw themselves into the water when they saw us. A few men went out nearly half a kos and brought them back. For as far as they went the water was the same depth, up to a horse's underbelly. Since the land was so flat the water was not deep.

We went along the bank of the riverbed coming to the Ab-i-Istada from the Katawaz plateau and camped. The few times we had passed here before, the riverbed had been dry. This time, however, because of the spring rains, there was so much water, we could find no place to cross; although it was not wide, it was extremely deep. The horses and camels were made to swim across, and some of the baggage was tied to ropes and hauled over. After reaching the other side we went through

Old Nani and past the Sardeh Dam to Ghazni. Jahangir Mirza hosted us for a day or two, giving banquets and presents.

Most rivers were so swollen that year that no ford could be found in the Ya'qub Deh river.[86] A boat I had made at the lake was put in the water opposite Kamari, and our crossing was made by boat.

Proceeding straight through the Sajawan pass and forging the river at Kamari by boat, [154] we arrived in Kabul in the month of Dhu'l-Hijja [May 1505]. Sayyid-Yusuf Beg had died of colic a few days before.

NASIR MIRZA'S MISCONDUCT

Nasir Mirza, who had been granted leave at Khush Gumbaz to gather some articles from his territory for his servants, said he would follow us two or three days later. Once parted from us, he sent a party against Dara-i-Nur to deal with some disobedience among the Dara-i-Nur people. It has been mentioned before that Dara-i-Nur is difficult of access because its fortress is so well shielded on a mountain outcropping and because the surrounding lands are rice fields. The commander of Nasir Mirza's force, Fazli, failed to take the necessary precautions and let his raiders scatter over ground so rough and with a road that could only be traversed single file. When the Dara-i-Nur people pressed the scattered raiders back, the soldiers were unable to maintain their position and fled. A few were killed and many horses and arms were seized. This is bound to happen under the command of someone like Fazli! Either for this reason or because Nasir Mirza's heart was crooked, Nasir did not follow us and stayed where he was.

In addition to him, none were more evil, seditious, wrongheaded, or puffed up with pride than Ayyub's sons, Yusuf and Bahlul. Yusuf was given Alingar, and Bahlul was given Alishang. [154b] The two were supposed to get items from their territories and then join Nasir Mirza. When Nasir did not come, they did not either. That winter they were Nasir Mirza's drinking partners and comrades. Once they raided the Tarklani Afghans. When spring came they drove away all the outland tribes and clans' families and herds that had come to Nangarhar and Laghman. They themselves went to the banks of the Baran River.

While Nasir Mirza was in Baran and that region, he had received news that the Badakhshanis had united against the Uzbeks and killed some of them. The details are as follows. Shaybani Khan gave Konduz to Qambar Bey and withdrew to Khwarazm. To mollify the people of Badakhshan, Qambar sent Muhammad Makhdumi's son, Mahmud by name, to Badakhshan. Mubarakshah, whose forefathers had been begs to the kings of Badakhshan, raised his own head in rebellion, cut off the heads of Makhdumi's son and a few other Uzbeks, and made fast the Shaf Tannur fort, which he renamed Fort Zafar. Muhammad Qorchï, one of Khusrawshah's qorchïs,[87] was then holding Khamlangan. Muhammad killed Shaybani Khan's finance minister in Rustak and a few other Uzbeks and fortified Khamlangan. Zubayr of Ragh, [155] whose forefathers were begs to the kings of Badakhshan, rebelled in Ragh. Jahangir the Turcoman, a liege man to Khusrawshah's brother Wali, withdrew from his beg during these troubles, gathered a few deserters and clans left behind by Wali, and holed up in the mountains.

When Nasir Mirza learned all this, at the instigation of a few silly, shortsighted men who coveted Badakhshan, he caused the families and herds of the outland tribes that had come from the Transoxus to move and drove them down the Shibartu and Ao Dara roads.

THE FATE OF KHUSRAWSHAH

When Khusrawshah and Ahmad Qasim had fled from Ajar and headed toward Khurasan, they met Badi'uzzaman Mirza and Zu'n-Nun Beg along the way. Together they all went to pay homage to Sultan-Husayn Mirza in Herat. These were the very men who had rebelled against the mirza for so many years and who by their many breaches of etiquette had left not a few scars on the mirza's heart. They had all left my presence in disgrace and misery and sought the mirza. Had I not reduced Khusrawshah to such a state by separating him from his servants and liege men, and had I not taken Kabul from Zu'n-Nun Beg's son Muqim, it would not have been possible for them to go to the mirza. Badi'uzzaman Mirza, putty in their hands, [155b] was incapable of protesting against anything they said. Sultan-Husayn Mirza received them well without reproaching them for their past offenses and even rewarded them.

After some time Khusrawshah asked to return to his territories, saying, "If I am permitted to go I will take all those provinces." Since he had come without arms or retinue, they delayed in granting him leave.

The more they delayed the more he repeated his request. When he became excessively importunate, Muhammad Burunduq gave him a superb answer: "When you had thirty thousand liege men and all your territory, what did you accomplish? Now that you have five hundred men and your territory is in the hands of the Uzbeks, what do you propose to do?" They gave him good advice and spoke reasonably, but since his fate was sealed, it had no effect. He persisted so much that in the end they granted him his wish. With three or four hundred men he went straight to the border at Dahana. Khusrawshah got to Dahana just as Nasir Mirza was crossing to that side.

The Badakhshan commanders had invited Nasir Mirza alone, not Khusrawshah. No matter how Nasir Mirza tried, Khusrawshah, well understanding what was happening, refused to go into the mountains. His plan was to trick the mirza [156] and get hold of the territory himself. Finally, unable to agree, they drew up their battle ranks, dressed their horses in armor, and got ready for combat near Ishkamish and retreated. Nasir Mirza withdrew toward Badakhshan. Khusrawshah, who had gathered a troop of ragtags and ruffians, set out intending to lay siege to Konduz with about a thousand men altogether. He proceeded a league or so and camped at Khwaja Chartaq.

Muhammad Shaybani Khan, who had taken Sultan-Ahmad Tambal in Andizhan, moved against Hissar and left the province without a battle or engagement. Sherim Chuhra was in Hissar with a troop of brave warriors. Although their begs had left the province and fled, the men holed up in the Hissar fortress, refusing to yield. Shaybani Khan put Hamza Sultan and Mahdi Sultan in charge of the siege and went himself to Konduz, which he gave to his younger brother, Mahmud Sultan. Shaybani Khan himself then headed directly to Khwarazm to engage Chïn Sufi. No sooner had he reached Samarkand than his brother Mahmud Sultan died in Konduz, which was then given to Qambar Bey of Merv.

When Khusrawshah arrived, Qambar Bey was in Konduz. Qambar Bey sent messenger after messenger to Hamza Sultan and the other Uzbek princes to request reinforcements. [156b] Hamza Sultan, having come as far as Sarai on the banks of the Oxus, put his sons and begs in charge of the army and sent them to Konduz. When they appeared, Khusrawshah could not fight. That fat little man could not even flee. Just then Hamza Sultan's men unhorsed him and killed his nephew

Ahmad Qasim, Sherim Chuhra, and some other brave warriors. Khus-rawshah was brought to Konduz and beheaded, and his head was sent to Shaybani Khan in Khwarazm.

Just as he had said they would do, Khusrawshah's men changed their demeanor toward me when Khusrawshah reached Konduz. Most of them betook themselves to Khwaja Rawash and those parts. Most of the men with me had been his men. The Moghuls reacted well and remained loyal. The news of Khusrawshah's death quenched his men's unruliness like water on fire.

EVENTS OF THE YEAR 911
(1505-6)[88]

In the month of Muharram (June 1505) my mother, Qutlugn Nigar Khanïm, fell ill with spotted fever. She was bled without effect. A Khurasani physician named Sayyid Tabib prescribed watermelon in accordance with the treatment in Khurasan. As her time must have come, she passed away six days later, on Saturday. [157]

Ulughbeg Mirza had constructed a garden called Bagh-i-Nawrozi[89] on the mountain slope. With the permission of the heirs, Qasim Kükäldash and I bore her to the garden on Sunday and entrusted her to the earth. While I was in mourning they told me of the deaths of my younger uncle Alacha Khan and of my grandmother Esän Dawlat Begim. It was almost the fortieth day of my lady mother's death when the khans' mother Shah Begim and my aunt Mihr Nigar Khanïm, who had been the wife of Sultan-Ahmad Mirza, came from Khurasan with Muhammad-Husayn Kürägän Dughlat. Grieving was renewed; the pain of separation was unbearable. After performing the rites of mourning, distributing food to the poor and unfortunate, and praying for the souls of the departed, we pulled ourselves together and took off our black mourning. After completing those tasks we got an army mounted at Baqi Chaghaniani's insistence to strike Kandahar.

We had set out and were stopped in Qush Nawar when I fell ill with a really strange malady. No matter how often they woke me, I would immediately fall back asleep. After four or five days I was much better.

Just then there occurred such an earthquake that most of the ramparts of forts and walls of gardens collapsed, leaving houses in towns and villages in rubble. Many died trapped beneath falling houses and walls. [157b] All the residences in the village of Paghman collapsed. Seventy or eighty strong villagers died when a wall fell. Between Laghman and Begtut a section of ground a good stone's-throw wide slid down the distance of an arrow shot and caused springs to open up. From Istarghij to Maydan, a span of approximately six or seven leagues, the earth was so split open that in some places it rose up an elephant's height, and in others it sank as deep. In some places a person could enter the cracks. When the earthquake struck, dust rose from the summits of all the mountains. Nurullah Tamburachï was playing the saz for me and had another beside him. He had just picked them both up when he was so shaken that they crashed together. Jahangir Mirza was in the *ayvan*[90] of an upper apartment in one of Ulughbeg Mirza's buildings in Teba. When the earthquake struck, he got out without injury, but one of his comrades was in the upper apartment, and the roof fell on him. It was through God's protection that he suffered no injury. Most of the houses in Teba were flattened. The earth shook thirty-three times that day. For a month at least the earth shook once a day. The begs and soldiers were ordered to repair the cracks and breaches in the towers and ramparts. [158] In twenty days to a month the cracks and breaks in the fortress were fixed thanks to their energetic action.

The former start we had made for Kandahar was delayed by my illness and the earthquake. When I had recovered and the fortress had been fixed, our former campaign was resumed, but we still had not decided whether to go via Kandahar or to scout the highlands and lowlands for raiding possibilities. While camped at the foot of the Sh'niz, I gathered Jahangir Mirza and the begs for consultation, during which it was decided to go against Qalat. Jahangir Mirza and Baqi Chaghaniani lobbied hard for this campaign.

When we reached Tazi, we received word that Sher-Ali Chuhra, Kichik Baqi Dewana, and another few men were planning to desert. They were seized, and Sher-Ali Chuhra, who had caused all sorts of strife and evil for me and others too both in Transoxiana and here, was executed. The others were stripped of their horses and arms and let go.

Immediately upon reaching Qalat we attacked from all sides without our arms and implements. It was a great battle. Khwaja Kalan's elder brother, Kichik Beg, was a valiant warrior who wielded his sword well in my presence several times, as will be recorded in this history.[91] He got himself up to the tower on the western side of Qalat [158b] and just as he was about to go up, a spear hit him in the eye. He died of this wound a day or two after taking Qalat. Kichik Baqi Dewana, who had been seized when he and Sher-Ali were about to desert, in expiation for that baseness died here of an injury inflicted on him by a rock when he went under the rampart at the gateway. Another one or two died too. The fighting continued in this manner until after noon. Just as our warriors were worn out from the battle, the defenders sought quarter and yielded the fortress. Zu'n-Nun Arghun had given Qalat to Muqim. His liege men Farrukh Arghun and Qara Bulut hung their bow cases and swords around their necks and came out. We pardoned their offenses. It was not my intent to alienate these people, for if we did so with a foe like the Uzbek menacing us, what would they say who heard of it from far and near?

Inasmuch as this campaign had been made at the insistence of Jahangir Mirza and Baqi Beg, we put Qalat into the mirza's charge. However, he refused to accept. Baqi was similarly unable to make a suitable response in this regard. To have taken Qalat with so much effort and battle was in vain.

We raided the Afghans to the south of Qalat in Sawa Sang, Ala Tagh, [159] and those areas and returned to Kabul.

The evening we dismounted in Kabul, I went to the fortress, but my tent and stable were in the Charbagh. A Khirilji thief came and made off from the Charbagh with a bay horse of mine and its armor and my personal mule.

THE FATE OF BAQI CHAGHANIANI

Ever since Baqi Chaghaniani had come and joined us on the banks of the Oxus, no one had held such authority. Whatever was said, whatever was done, it was his word and his deed, notwithstanding the fact that no service worthy of mention or civility one might expect had ever been seen of him. Indeed I had received from him all sorts of discourtesies and ill treatment, and he was a niggardly, coarse, envious, spiteful, and ill-natured bully. His miserliness was of such a degree that after he gave up Termez and joined us with his family and possessions, at every campsite his own huge personal flocks—which may have numbered some thirty or forty thousand head—passed before our eyes. To our warriors and braves tormented by hunger he gave not a single one. Finally in Kahmard he gave fifty sheep. Although he acknowledged me as his padishah, he had the *naqara*[92] beat at his gate. He was on good terms with no one and was jealous of everyone. What revenue there is from Kabul comes from the *tamgha*,[93] which he held autonomously, as well as the office of prefect of Kabul, [159b] Panjshir, Gadi Hazara, and Kushkak and the office of lord of the gate. Despite all this favor and promotion he was neither satisfied nor grateful. No matter how many ill-conceived plans he laid—as have been mentioned—we neither showed our displeasure nor threw them in his face. He was always whining asking for leave. We suffered his behavior and apologized for not granting him leave. This would put him off for a day or two, but then he would be back asking for leave again. He had gone too far with his complaints and absences. Sick to death of his manners and his deeds, we dismissed him, after which he changed his mind and began to agitate. It was no use. He had a letter written and delivered to me, saying, "You stipulated that I would not be called to account until I had committed nine offenses."[94] I had Mulla Baba write a memorandum enumerating eleven offenses one by one and sent it to him. That got him. He asked for leave to take his family and possessions to Hindustan. A few of his retainers took him through the Khyber Pass, then he joined Baqi Gagiani's caravan and crossed the Indus at Nilab.

At that time Darya Khan's son Yar-Husayn was in Kachakot. He had taken the decrees he had received at Kohat and used them to form an alliance with a band of Dilazak and Yusufzai Afghans and another band of Jats and Gujars[95] and then set about waylaying and plundering. When he got word of Baqi, [160] he blocked the way and made off with Baqi and everybody with him. He killed Baqi and took his wife. We had let Baqi go without doing him any ill, but his own misdeeds caught up with him and he fell prey to his own evil.

Entrust to fate him who does you evil, for fate is an avenging servant for you.

A RAID ON THE TURCOMAN HAZARAS

That winter we stayed put in the Charbagh until it had snowed once or twice. Ever since we had come to Kabul, the Turcoman Hazaras had committed all sorts of breaches of etiquette and highway banditry. Planning to attack them, we went to town to the Bustan Sara, the building Ulughbeg Mirza had built, and in the month of Sha'ban rode out to attack the Turcoman Hazaras. We made a raid at Jangalak at the mouth of Khush Valley and defeated a few Hazaras. A band of Hazaras was said to be hiding in a cave near Khush Valley. Shaykh Darwesh Kükäldash, who had been with me during most of my rencontres and held the post of *qor begi*,[96] could draw a strong bow and was a good shot. He went incautiously right up to the mouth of the cave, and a Hazara shot him in the chest. He died that day. Most of the Turcoman Hazaras were wintering in Khush Valley. We set out for them. Khush Valley is superbly located. A defile nearly half a kos long is situated at its entrance, and the road [160b] is along the face of the mountain with a drop-off of fifty to sixty yards straight down. Above the road is sheer. Horsemen have to go single file. We got through the defile and kept on going until midafternoon that day without meeting anyone, so we stopped for the night. A fat camel belonging to the Hazaras was brought in for slaughter. We roasted some of the meat and cooked some in a ewer. I had never eaten such delicious camel meat, which some could not distinguish from mutton.

Early the next day we marched off toward the Hazara winter campsite. It was the first *pahar*[97] when a man came from ahead saying that the Hazaras had blocked a ford in a defile with branches, had stopped our men, and were fighting. As soon as we heard this we charged forward. We had not gone far before we reached the area. That winter a lot of snow had fallen, and the water at the edge of the gully was completely frozen. On account of the ice and snow it was not possible to cross the river except at the road. Many boughs the Hazaras had cut were piled where the road crossed the river. They themselves, mounted and on foot in the gully and sides, were shooting and fighting. [161]

Muhammad Ali Mubashshir was one of my newly favored begs. He was brave and worthy of favor. Without armor he advanced to where the limbs were stacked on the road. They shot him from all sides and he died instantly. We had come forward in haste, mostly without armor. An arrow or two whizzed by and fell to the ground. Ahmad Yusuf Beg grew agitated and kept saying, "Are you going in unarmed? I saw a couple of arrows go right by your head."

"Be brave," I said. "Many like this have gone past my head." This was the state of affairs when Qasim Beg in his chain mail managed to cross the river to my right. The Hazaras were unable to maintain their position in the face of the charge and fled. Those who remained to engage in hand-to-hand combat were felled and driven back.

For this action Qasim Beg was given Bangash as a reward. Hatim Qorbegi did not do badly in this action either, and for that reason he was given Shaykh Darwesh Kükäldash's post as qor begi. Keyik Qul Baba also made a good showing for which he was rewarded with a village.

Sultan-Qulï Chanaq was in pursuit of the Hazaras, but because of the heavy and deep-packed snow he could not get off the road. I went along with the warriors. [161b] Near the Hazaras' winter quarters we came across their flocks and herds. I myself rounded up four or five hundred sheep and twenty-five horses. Sultan-Qulï and another two or three men were near....[98] Twice I participated in a raid. This was the first time; the second was when we were coming from Khurasan and raided these same Turcoman Hazaras, bringing in a lot of sheep and horses. The Hazara women and children ran off on foot to the snow-covered hills and stayed there. We hung around idly for a while, but it was getting late in the day so we went back and camped in the Hazaras' tents. That winter the snow was extremely heavy. When we got off the road in that area it was right up to a horse's girth strap. Because it was so deep, those who went out on patrol at night stayed in the saddle all night long.

The next morning we headed back, stayed the night in the Hazaras' winter camp in Khush Valley, and then went on and stopped in Jangalak. Yarak Taghayï and some other latecomers were ordered to take the Hazaras who had shot Shaykh Darwesh. Those wretches on whom vengeance was to be wrought were still in the cave. They smoked out seventy or eighty Hazaras and put most of them to the sword.

As we were returning from our Hazara campaign we went to the vicinity of Ay Tughdï at the foot of the Baran to collect tribute from

Nijrao. Jahangir Mirza [162] came from Ghazni to pay homage while we were in the Ay Tughdï area. Around this same time, on the thirteenth of Ramadan [February 7, 1506], I was afflicted with terrible sciatic pain. It was so bad that for forty days someone had to turn me from one side to the other.

Known for insolence and fearlessness throughout the Nijrao valleys, and in particular the Pachaghan valley, were the headman of the village of Ghain, Husayn Ghaini, and his brothers. Jahangir Mirza was put in charge of the army and dispatched to deal with them. Qasim Beg was along too. The army went, took by storm the place that had been fortified, and put a number to death.

Because I had sciatica, I had a contraption like a litter built to take me to town from the banks of the Baran. They put me in the Bustan Sara, where I stayed for a few days that winter. No sooner had I recovered from that illness than I got a boil on my right cheek. It was lanced, and I took a purge too. When I was well, I went out to the Charbagh.

JAHANGIR MIRZA'S MISCONDUCT

Jahangir Mirza came to pay homage. Ayyub's sons Yusuf and Bahlul had been misbehaving and stirring up strife ever since they joined Jahangir Mirza, and this time Jahangir Mirza was not as he had been before. A few days later he marched from Teba, armed himself, and rode at a gallop to Ghazni. He took the Nani fortress, killed a few men, and plundered all the people. Then, marching off with what men he had, [162b] he went toward Bamian among the Hazaras. God knows that neither myself nor my people had said any word or done anything to cause such ill feeling. Later I heard that he went off because of the following exchange: When Jahangir Mirza came from Ghazni, Qasim Beg and some other begs went out to meet him. Jahangir sent a falcon off after a quail. When the falcon reached the quail and was about to dig its talons in, the quail hurled itself to the ground. "Did it take it?" all shouted. Qasim Beg said, "How could it let a foe escape that makes itself so vile? Of course it took it." His remark was taken as an insult and was one reason they went off. In addition, they used as excuses a few other old-womanish peevishnesses even sillier and more baseless than this. After leaving Ghazni in that state, they went off through the

Hazaras to the Aymaqs. The Aymaqs had just withdrawn from Nasir Mirza but had not yet joined the Uzbeks. They were in the summer pastures of Yay, Astarob, and those regions.

About that time Sultan-Husayn Mirza resolved to repel Shaybani Khan and summoned all his sons. He sent Sayyid Sultan-Ali Khwab-bin's son, Sayyid Afzal, to invite me too. We felt it necessary to go to Khurasan for several reasons. One was that when a great padishah like Sultan-Husayn Mirza, who sat on Temür Beg's throne, [163] sent out a summons to all parts to his sons and begs and was mounting a campaign against a foe like Shaybani Khan, if others were going on foot, we would go on our heads, and if others were going armed with clubs, we would go armed with rocks. Another reason was that, given the bad feeling with which Jahangir Mirza had gone off, either I would have to resolve the dispute or I would have to ward off an attack by him.

That very year Shaybani Khan had besieged Chïn Sufi in Khwarazm for ten months. There had been a lot of fighting and the Khwarazm warriors had performed bravely with no shortcoming. They had shot so well that arrows had pierced shields and armor, sometimes even two layers thick. They had held out under siege for ten months without reinforcement from any quarter. Finally, some of Chïn Sufi's men despaired and opened negotiations with the Uzbeks. As he was firing trying to unhorse the Uzbeks who were being let into the fortress, he was hit by an arrow shot from behind by his own page and died. No one was left to fight, so they yielded the fortress. God have mercy on Chïn Sufi—he did all he could to fight valiantly. [163b]

Shaybani Khan gave Khwarazm to Köpäk Bey and went to Samarkand.

In the latter part of the year, in Dhu'l-Hijja [May 1506], having led his army against Shaybani Khan as far as Baba Ilahi, Sultan-Husayn Mirza died.

SULTAN-HUSAYN MIRZA

Birth and lineage. He was born at Herat in 842 [1438] during Shahrukh's reign [1405–47]. He was Sultan-Husayn Mirza son of Mansur son of Bayqara son of Umar-Shaykh son of Amir Temür. Mansur Mirza and Bayqara Mirza did not rule.

Detail, *Portrait of Sultan-Husayn Mirza* (1438–1506), attributed to Bihzad (d. ca. 1535), Iran or Central Asia, ca. 1500–1525. Ink and gold on paper. Harvard University Art Museums, Arthur M. Sackler Museum; Gift of John Goelet, 1958.59.

His mother was Firoza Begim. Through her he was a grandson both of Temür Beg's grandson Sultan-Husayn[99] and of Miranshah Mirza, and thus noble on both sides—a king born. Mansur Mirza and Firoza Begim had two sons, Bayqara Mirza and Sultan-Husayn Mirza, and two daughters, Äkä Begim and Badka Begim,[100] whom Ahmad Khan married.

Although Bayqara Mirza was older than Sultan-Husayn Mirza, Sultan-Husayn was still his liege lord. Bayqara Mirza was not always present at court, although at other than divan court they sat on the same cushion. The younger brother gave the elder brother the province of Balkh, where he ruled for a few years. Bayqara Mirza had three sons, Sultan-Muhammad Mirza, Sultan-Ways Mirza, and Sultan-Iskandar Mirza.

Äkä Begim **[164]** was the prince's elder sister. She was married to

Sultan-Ahmad Mirza, Miranshah Mirza's grandson,[101] and had one son named Kichik Mirza. At first he was in his maternal uncle's service, but later he left the military and took up study. It is said that he became a scholar. He had a talent for poetry. This quatrain is his:

My whole life I took great pains to acquire piety; / In asceticism I showed myself to be outstanding. / When love arrived, where did my asceticism and piety go? / Thank God I tested myself.

It is very similar to a quatrain by Mulla Jami.[102] In the end he went on the pilgrimage.

Badka Begim was also older than the mirza. During his rencontres she was married to Ahmad Khan, the khan of Astrakhan. There were two sons by this marriage, both of whom went to Herat and were long in the mirza's service.

His appearance. His eyes were slanted and he had the build of a lion, slender from the waist down. Even when he was old and had a white beard he favored clothes of beautiful red and green silk. He wore either a karakul cap or a *qalpaq*.[103] Occasionally on feast days he would put on a flat, badly wrapped little trifold turban, stick a heron feather in it, and go to the prayer.

His character. When he first took the throne, he thought to have the Twelve Imams' names read in the khutba;[104] [164b] however, Ali-Sher Beg and others kept him from doing so. Later all of his acts were in accordance with the Sunni sect. His arthritis kept him from performing prayers; he did not fast either. He was talkative and good-humored. His character was a bit sharp, as were his words. In some of his dealings he maintained the religious law scrupulously. Once, he turned over his son, who had killed a man, to the dead man's heirs and sent him to the tribunal.

He was abstinent for six or seven years when he first came to the throne, but he later took to drink. For the nearly forty years that he was king in Khurasan not a day passed that he did not imbibe after the midday prayer, though he never had a morning draught. His sons and all his military and civilian men were addicted to drink and lived with inordinate revelry and debauchery.

He was brave and courageous. Many times he took to the sword himself, and he often brandished it in battle. Of Temür Beg's progeny no one is known to have wielded the sword as Sultan-Husayn Mirza did. He had poetic talent and composed a divan (see illus. below). He composed in Turkish too, with the pen name of Husayni. Some of his lines are not bad, but his divan is all in one meter. Although he was a great king in terms of both longevity and rule, [165] he kept rams and doves like a little child and also indulged in gamecocks.

His battles. During his rencontres he once caused his horse to swim across the Gurgan River and soundly defeated a band of Uzbeks.

Folio of poetry from a partially dispersed *Divan* of Sultan-Husayn Mirza (1438–1506). Herat, ca. 1490. Collage. Freer Gallery of Art, Smithsonian Institution, F1929.66.

Another time, Sultan-Abusa'id Mirza sent three thousand troops into battle under Muhammad-Ali Bakhshï. Sultan-Husayn Mirza enjoined battle with only sixty warriors and beat them hands down. This was one of Sultan-Husayn Mirza's outstanding feats.

At Astarabad he fought with and beat Sultan-Mahmud Mirza.

Another time at Astarabad he defeated Sa'dlïq Sa'd, son of Husayn the Turcoman.

After taking the throne, he defeated Yadgar-Muhammad Mirza at Chanaran.

He attacked from Sar-i-Pul on the Murghab River and surprised Yadgar-Muhammad Mirza, who was prone from drink in the Bagh-i-Zaghan. With that capture he secured Khurasan.

Again he fought with Sultan-Mahmud Mirza at Chakman Saray in the vicinity of Andkhui and Sheberghan and beat him.

By defeating Ababakr Mirza, who had joined with the Qaraqoyunlu Turcomans[105] who had come from Iraq and beaten Ulughbeg Mirza at Takana and Khimar, Sultan-Husayn Mirza took Kabul. Because of the turmoil in Iraq he left Kabul, went through the Khyber Pass, crossed the Khushab[106] near Multan, and reached Sibi. Leaving there, he took Kirman; unable to hold it, however, [165b] he attacked and seized the province of Khurasan.

At Belcheragh he once defeated his son Badi'uzzaman Mirza. Once again at Halwa Chashma he defeated two of his sons, Abu'l-Muhsin Mirza and Kipik Mirza.

Once he led his army to assault Konduz but, unable to take it, withdrew. Another time he attacked Hissar, which he was also unable to take. Yet another time he moved against Zu'n-Nun's province. The prefect of Bust turned over Bust, but nothing else was accomplished. He even left Bust and withdrew. In these two or three campaigns a brave and great king like Sultan-Husayn Mirza failed to show royal resolve and retired without accomplishing anything.

At Nishin Meadow he defeated his son Badi'uzzaman Mirza, who had come with Zu'n-Nun's son Shah Beg. Here a strange coincidence of events occurred. The army with Sultan-Husayn Mirza was small, most of his troops having been sent to Astarabad. The very day of the encounter the troops who had gone to Astarabad arrived and joined him. From the other side Sultan-Mas'ud Mirza, who had let Baysunghur Mirza take Hissar, was coming to Sultan-Husayn Mirza. He too arrived that very day, and so did Haydar Mirza, who had gone to attack Badi'uzzaman Mirza in Sabzawar.

His realm. His realm was Khurasan, Balkh in the east, Bistam [166] and Damghan in the west, Khwarazm in the north, and Kandahar and Seistan in the south. When a city like Herat fell to his possession, he did nothing night and day but revel and carouse. Among his followers and retainers there was no one who did not indulge in revelry and carousal. He abandoned the toil and trouble of conquest and military leadership. Consequently, as time passed, his retainers and realm dwindled instead of increasing.

His children. Fourteen sons and eleven daughters survived infancy. The eldest son was Badi'uzzaman Mirza, whose mother was Bikä Sultan, the daughter of Sanjar Mirza of Merv.

Next was Shah-Gharib Mirza. He was lame and, although deformed, his nature was good. Despite the weakness of his body, his words were pleasing. His pen name was Ghurbati, and he made a divan and composed in both Turkish and Persian. This line is his:

I spied a beauty in the lane and became mad for her. / What is her name? Where does she live? I do not know her house.

For some time Shah-Gharib Mirza was given the governorship of Herat by Sultan-Husayn Mirza. He died during his father's lifetime, leaving no offspring.

Another was Muzaffar Mirza. He was Sultan-Husayn Mirza's favorite son, although his character and actions were not so lovable. Because the other sons saw him so much more favored, most of them rebelled. The mother of these two sons, Muzaffar and Shah-Gharib, was Khadija Begim, who had been a concubine of Sultan-Abusa'id Mirza, [166b] by whom she had a daughter named Aq Begim.

Another was Abu'l-Muhsin Mirza; and another was Kipik Mirza, whose name was Muhammad-Muhsin. The mother of these two was Latif Sultan Aghacha.

Another was Abu-Turab Mirza. Formerly he was much spoken of as a prodigy. When his father's illness was growing worse, he received news to the contrary and fled with his younger brother Muhammad-Husayn Mirza to Iraq, where he abandoned the military and became a dervish. Thereafter nothing was heard of him. He left one son, Suhrab

Mirza, who was with me [in 1511] when I defeated the Uzbek princes led by Hamza Sultan and Mahdi Sultan and took Hissar. He was blind in one eye and exceptionally ill-featured, and his character was equal to his looks. For committing an act of immoderation he could not stay with me and fled, but he was painfully put to death for that intemperateness by Najm II in the vicinity of Astarabad.

Another was Muhammad-Husayn Mirza. He and Shah Isma'il were confined together in Iraq, and it must have been then that he became a devotee of Shah Isma'il. Later he became a dyed-in-the-wool Shiite. Although his father and brothers were all Sunni, he died astray in that heresy in Astarabad. He is said to have been brave and heroic, but no deed of his is so outstanding as to be worthy of writing about. He had some poetic talent. This line is by him:

> Covered with dust, whom are you hunting down? / Drenched in sweat, into whose warm heart have you penetrated?

Another was Faridun-Husayn Mirza. [167] He pulled a hard bow and was an excellent shot. His crossbow is said to have weighed forty *batmans*.[107] He was exceptionally courageous, but he was not victorious in battle. Every time he fought he was defeated. At Robat-i Dudar, Faridun-Husayn Mirza and his younger brother Ibn-i Husayn Mirza fought Wormwood Khan's attack under Temür Sultan and Ubayd Sultan; they were defeated, although Faridun-Husayn Mirza made several good showings. At Damghan, Faridun-Husayn Mirza and Muhammad-Zaman Mirza were taken prisoner by Shaybani Khan. Instead of executing them, he let them both go. Later, when Shah-Muhammad Dewana fortified Kalat, he went there. When the Uzbek took Kalat, he was taken prisoner and killed. All three of these princes were sons of Mengli Bey Aghacha, an Uzbek concubine.

Another was Haydar Mirza. His mother was Payanda Sultan Begim, Sultan-Abusa'id Mirza's daughter. During his father's lifetime he governed Mashhad and Balkh for a time. When Sultan-Husayn Mirza attacked Hissar, Sultan-Mahmud Mirza's daughter by Khwanzada Begim was affianced to him, after which he left Hissar. One little daughter survived infancy. Shad Begim by name, she later came to Kabul and was given in marriage to Adil Sultan. Haydar Mirza departed this world during his father's lifetime. [167b]

Another was Muhammad-Ma'sum Mirza. He was given Kandahar, upon which occasion Ulughbeg Mirza's daughter was affianced to him. She was brought to Herat and a large banquet was given for which a beautiful pavilion was set up. Although he was given Kandahar, no matter what he did it was really Shah Beg Arghun who handled everything. This prince had no say of importance in any matter. For this reason he left Kandahar and went to Khurasan. He passed away during his father's lifetime.

Another, Farrukh-Husayn Mirza, also predeceased his father.

Another was Ibrahim-Husayn Mirza. His temperament was not bad, but by overindulging in Herat wine he drank himself to death during his father's lifetime.

Another two were Ibn-i-Husayn Mirza and Muhammad-Qasim Mirza. They will be mentioned later. The mother of the latter five mirzas was Papa Aghacha, a concubine.

The eldest daughter was Sultanïm Begim. She was without siblings, and her mother was Chöli Begim, of the Adaq begs. She had a large vocabulary but not much zest in her words. She was married to her cousin, Bayqara Mirza's middle son, Sultan-Ways Mirza, and had by him a daughter and a son. The daughter was given in marriage to Esänqulï Sultan, younger brother of Yili Bars Sultan of the Shaban sultans. The son is Muhammad-Sultan Mirza, to whom at this date I have given the governorship of the province of Kannauj. [168] Sultanïm Begim died at Nilab as she was bringing her grandson from Kabul to Hindustan. Her people took her remains and returned to Kabul. Her grandson came on to Hindustan.

By Payanda Sultan Begim there were four daughters. The eldest was Aq Begim, who was married to Muhammad-Qasim Arlat, a grandson of Abu'l-Qasim Babur Mirza's sister Bikä Begim. By him she had a little girl named Qara Köz Begim. Nasir Mirza married her.[108] Payanda's second daughter was Kichik Begim. Sultan-Mas'ud Mirza was fond of her, but no matter how he tried, Payanda Sultan Begim viewed him askance and would not give her to him. Later she was married to Mulla Khwaja, a descendant of Sayyid Ata.[109] She married her third daughter, Bikä Begim, and her fourth daughter, Agha Begim, to her younger sister Rabi'a Sultan Begim's sons Babur Mirza and Sultan-Murad Mirza.

By Mengli Bey Aghacha he had two daughters. The elder was named Maryam Sultan, and she was married to Sayyid Abdullah

Mirza of the Andkhui sayyids, a grandson of Bayqara Mirza by one of his daughters. They had one son, Sayyid Baraka. When I took Samarkand, he entered my service. Later he went to Urgench and made a claim for the throne, but the Qïzïlbash killed him at Astarabad. Another girl was named Fatima Sultan. She was married to Yadgar Mirza, who was of Timurid descent.[110]

There were three daughters by Papa Aghacha. The eldest was Sultan-Nizhad Begim. She was married to Sultan-Husayn Mirza's brother's youngest son, Iskandar Mirza. The middle girl was Begim Sultan, who was given in marriage to Sultan-Mas'ud Mirza after his eyesight was damaged. [168b] They had a daughter and a son. The daughter was raised by Sultan-Husayn Mirza's wife Apaq Begim. She left Herat, came to Kabul, and was married to Sayyid Mirza Apaq. After Sultan-Mas'ud Mirza was killed by the Uzbeks, Begim Sultan took her son on the pilgrimage. Lately it has been heard that both she and her son are in Mecca and that he has become rather grand. The third daughter was married to one of the Andkhui sayyids who is usually styled Sayyid-Mirza.

There was another daughter by another concubine, and she was called Ayisha Sultan. Her mother was Zubayda Agha, and she was a granddaughter of Hasan Shaykh-Temür. She was married to Qasim Sultan, one of the Shaban sultans. By him she had a son named Qasim Husayn Sultan. He joined my service in Hindustan, was present during the campaign against Rana Sanga, and has been given Budaun. After Qasim Sultan she married a relative of her first husband, Puran Sultan, by whom she had a son named Abdullah Sultan. As of this date he is in my service, and although he is young his service is not bad.

His wives and concubines. His first wife was Bikä Sultan Begim, daughter of Sanjar Mirza of Merv. Badi'uzzaman Mirza was born of her. Bikä Sultan Begin was ill-tempered, and Sultan-Husayn Mirza, who suffered greatly from her, came to such grief that in the end he put her away and was delivered. What was he to do? [169] He had every right.

An evil woman in a good man's house is hell on earth.[111]

May God not afflict any Muslim with this catastrophe. O God, may there be no more ill-tempered, irascible women in the world.

Another was Chöli Begim of the Adaq begs,[112] the mother of Sultaním Begim.

Another was Shahrbanu Begim, daughter of Sultan-Abusa'id Mirza. Sultan-Husayn Mirza married her after ascending the throne. At the Battle of Chakman the mirza's ladies got out of their litters and mounted horses—all except this one, who, relying upon her younger brother,[113] did not get out of hers. When the incident was reported to the mirza, he divorced her and married her younger sister, Payanda Sultan Begim. After the Uzbeks took Khurasan, Payanda Sultan Begim went to Iraq, where she died in a foreign land.

Khadija Begim[114] had been Sultan-Abusa'id Mirza's concubine, and by him she had one daughter, Aq Begim by name. After Sultan-Abusa'id Mirza's defeat in Iraq she came to Herat, where Sultan-Husayn fell in love with and married her. From the rank of concubine she advanced to the status of begim, after which she became completely dominant. Muhammad-Mu'min Mirza was killed through her machinations. It was mostly her doings that caused Sultan-Husayn Mirza's sons to rebel. She thought herself clever, but she was a brainless chatterbox female. She was also a Shiite. Shah-Gharib Mirza and Muzaffar-Husayn Mirza [169b] were born of her.

Apaq Begim had no children.[115] Papa Aghacha, who was so dear to the mirza, was her kükäldash. Having no offspring, she cared for Papa Aghacha's as her own. During the mirza's illnesses she nursed him beautifully; none of his women could care for him as she did. The year I came to Hindustan, she came from Herat, and I did her as much honor and paid her as much respect as I possibly could. During the siege of Chanderi, I heard the news of her death in Kabul.

Latif Sultan Aghacha was a concubine.[116] She was from Charshamba and was the mother of Abu'l-Muhsin Mirza and Kipik Mirza.

Mengli Bey Aghacha was an Uzbek. She was one of Shahrbanu Begim's retinue and the mother of Abu-Turab Mirza, Muhammad-Husayn Mirza, and Faridun-Husayn Mirza. There were also two daughters.

Papa Aghacha was Apaq Begim's kükäldash. The mirza saw her, fell in love with her, and took her as a concubine. She was the mother of five sons and four daughters, as has been mentioned.

Begi Sultan Aghacha had no children.

There were many other concubines and mistresses of no consequence. The important wives and concubines are those who have been mentioned.

It is strange that of the fourteen sons of a great king like Sultan-Husayn Mirza, the ruler of an Islamic city like Herat, only three were legitimate. In the mirza himself, [170] in his sons, his people, and his nation, vice and debauchery were rife and rampant. It was due to their shamefulness that, of such a great house, within seven or eight years the only remaining trace of them was Muhammad-Zaman Mirza.

HIS AMIRS

Muhammad Burunduq Barlas. He was descended from Chäkü Barlas: Muhammad Burunduq, son of Ali, son of Burunduq, son of Jahanshah, son of Chäkü Barlas. He was a beg under Abu'l-Qasim Babur Mirza. Afterward he was also patronized by Sultan-Abusa'id Mirza, who gave Kabul jointly to him and Jahangir Barlas and made him beg atäkä to Ulughbeg Mirza. After Sultan-Abusa'id Mirza's death, Ulughbeg Mirza rose up in rebellion against the Barlas tribe, but they learned of it, kidnapped the prince, and moved the tribe toward Konduz. From atop the Hindu Kush they graciously sent the prince back to Kabul and then went themselves to Khurasan to Sultan-Husayn Mirza, who patronized them well. Muhammad Burunduq was extremely intelligent and a great military leader. He was so inordinately fond of hawking that when a falcon died or was lost, he would call his sons' names and say, "If so-and-so were to die or break his neck, what would it be compared to the death or loss of this bird?"

Muzaffar Barlas. He was present during the mirza's rencontres. I do not know what it was in him that pleased the mirza so, but he certainly patronized him greatly. He was of such importance that Sultan-Husayn Mirza guaranteed him that of whatever realms were conquered two-thirds would be the mirza's [170b] and one-third would be his. This was a strange promise. When one is king, how can it be right to make a subject a co-ruler? One does not make such a commitment to one's own brother or son, much less to a beg. After ascending the throne he regretted having made such an oath, but it was too late. The dull-witted jerk had received such patronage that he had visions of grandeur even though the mirza never took his advisement. In the end they say he was poisoned, but God only knows the truth of the matter.

Ali-Sher Beg Nawa'i. He was not a beg but a companion. He and Sultan-Husayn were schoolmates in their youth and were close friends. I do not know for what offense Sultan-Abusa'id Mirza expelled him from Herat, but he went to Samarkand and stayed there a few years under Ahmad Hajji Beg's patronage and protection. Ali-Sher Beg is well known for his temperamental delicacy. People imagined that it was due to pride in his wealth, but it probably was not so: this characteristic was simply innate in him. While he was in Samarkand he was just as finicky. Ali-Sher Beg had no equal. No one composed so much or so well in the Turkish language as he did.

He composed six mathnawis, five in imitation of the *Khamsa* and one called *Lisan al-tayr,* in the meter of *Mantiq al-tayr.*[117] He completed four divans of ghazals titled *Gharayib al-sighar, Nawadir al-shabab, Badi' al-wasat,* and *Fawayid al-kibar.*[118] He has some good quatrains also. Some compositions by him, in comparison with the ones mentioned, [171] are inferior and weak. Among these are his epistolary compositions, which he gathered in imitation of Mawlana Abdul-Rahman Jami.[119] In short, he collected every letter he ever wrote to anybody for anything. Another of his works is the *Mizan al-awzan* on metrics.[120] It is full of mistakes. Of the twenty-four quatrain meters he has made errors in four, and has done the same in the scansion of some of the meters. This will be obvious to anybody who knows metrics. He also made a Persian divan in which he uses Fani as his pen name. Some of his lines are not bad but most are flat and of low quality. He also composed excellent melodies in music. He has some good *naqsh*[121] and preludes.

No one is known ever to have been such a patron and encourager of artists as was Ali-Sher Beg. Master Qul-Muhammad, Shaykhi the flutist, and Husayn the lutanist, who are tops on their instruments, gained advancement and reputation through the beg's patronage and encouragement. It was through the beg's good offices that master Bihzad (see illus. p. 193) and Shah-Muzaffar became so famous for painting.

Few have built as many charitable edifices as Ali-Sher Beg Nawa'i did. He had no children or family and lived exceptionally single and unencumbered. At first he was a seal keeper; later he became a beg and governed Astarabad for a time. In the end he gave up the military. He took nothing from the mirza but rather made gifts to him every year of substantial sums. [171b]

Page from the Turkish *Divan* of Ali-Sher Nawa'i (1441–1501). Probably Tabriz, ca. 1530. Calligraphy by Abdul-Rahim Khwarazmi. Opaque watercolor, ink, and gold on paper. Art and History Trust Collection.

When Sultan-Husayn Mirza was returning from the Astarabad campaign, Ali-Sher Beg Nawa'i went out to greet him. As he was standing up after his interview with the mirza, he had a seizure and could not rise. They got him up, but the physicians were incapable of making a diagnosis. The next morning he passed away. One of his lines of poetry is appropriate:

Since no disease is apparent in this pain of which I am dying, / What can physicians do for this calamity?

Ahmad Tükäl Barlas. For a time he held the governorship of Kandahar.

Wali Beg. A descendant of Hajji Sayfuddin Beg and a Nüküz, he was one of the mirza's great begs. He did not live long after Sultan-Husayn Mirza ascended the throne. He was observant of the prayers and was coarse but sincere.

Hasan Shaykh-Temür. He was promoted by Abu'l-Qasim Babur Mirza to the rank of beg.

Noyan Beg. His father was of the Termez sayyids; on his mother's side he was kin to both Sultan-Abusa'id Mirza and Sultan-Husayn Mirza. He was patronized by Sultan-Abusa'id Mirza and was an important beg in Sultan-Ahmad Mirza's service. He also served Sultan-Husayn Mirza and was well rewarded. He was an adventurer, a roué, and a heavy drinker who loved to have a good time. Hasan Ya'qub became known as Noyan's Hasan because he was in Noyan's service.

Jahangir Barlas. For a while he ruled Kabul jointly with Muhammad Burunduq. [172] Later he joined Sultan-Husayn Mirza's service and was well compensated. He was elegant and refined in his manners. He knew how to have fun. Because he was skilled in the methods of hunting and falconry Sultan-Husayn Mirza left most of these things to him. He was a companion to Badi'uzzaman Mirza and used to reminisce about being with him.

Mirza Ahmad Ali Farsi Barlas. Although he did not compose poetry, he had talent and understood poetry. He was elegant and a scoundrel.

Abdul-Khaliq Beg. Firozshah Beg, whom Shahrukh Mirza patronized so greatly, was his grandfather, for which reason he was known as Abdul-Khaliq Firozshah. He held Khwarazm for a while.

Ibrahim Dulday. He knew finance and administration very well. He was Muhammad Burunduq's right-hand man.

Zu'n-Nun Arghun. He was courageous and wielded the sword well in Sultan-Abusa'id Mirza's service in his man-to-man combats. Afterward he joined the fray whenever he could. There was no disputing his bravery, but he was rather crazy. He left the service of our Miranshahid mirzas[122] and entered that of Sultan-Husayn Mirza, who gave him Ghur and the Negüdäri. With seventy or eighty men [172b] he

won many battles in those regions. With very, very few men he subdued many, many Hazaras and Negüdäri; no one else has ever maintained order among them as he did. For some time after, he was given
Zamin Dawar. His son Shah-Shuja' Arghun, even in his childhood,
did battle alongside his father. Against Zu'n-Nun's wishes, Sultan-
Husayn Mirza promoted Shah-Shuja' and made him co-ruler with his
father in Kandahar. Later this father and son caused rebellion and
stirred up strife between the father and son Sultan-Husayn and
Badi'uzzaman Mirza. When I captured Khusrawshah, separated him
from his retainers, and took Kabul from Zu'n-Nun's youngest son,
Muqim, Zu'n-Nun and Khusrawshah, unable to counter me, went to
see Sultan-Husayn Mirza. He grew even greater after Sultan-Husayn
Mirza died, when he was given the piedmont region around Herat,
such as Obeh and Chaghcharan. When Badi'uzzaman Mirza and
Muzaffar Mirza became co-rulers, he was Badi'uzzaman Mirza's
steward, while Muhammad Burunduq Barlas was Muzaffar Mirza's
steward.

Although he was brave, he was a bit of a fool. If he were not, would
he have been so susceptible to flattery and disgraced himself? The details are as follows. He held such a position of authority and importance in Herat that several shaykhs and mullas went to him and said,
"We are in touch with the Qutb. He has named you 'Lion of God,' and
you will conquer the Uzbeks." He swallowed this praise and, throwing
a shawl around his neck, said prayers of gratitude. [173] When Shaybani Khan had defeated the mirzas one by one at Badghis, Zu'n-Nun,
believing those words to be true, faced Shaybani Khan at Kara Robat
with a hundred or 150 men. A large contingent came forth, seized
them, and took them away. Zu'n-Nun was executed.

He was quite orthodox and never missed his prayers. He often performed supererogatory prayers too. He adored chess and put his whole
heart and soul into playing however he wanted. Avarice and stinginess
were dominant in his character.

Darwesh Ali Beg. He was Ali-Sher Beg's younger brother. For a time
he governed Balkh, where he commanded well. He was dull-witted
and devoid of talent. When Sultan-Husayn Mirza first attacked Konduz, he was taken captive due to his own stupidity and relieved of the
governorship of Balkh. When I went to Konduz in 916 [1510–11], he
came to me. He was vacant and babbling, not worthy to be a beg, and

with no aptitude for companionship. It must have been through Ali-Sher Beg's influence that he was ever promoted.

Moghul Beg. For a time he held the governorship of Herat. Later he was given Astarabad. From Astarabad he fled to Ya'qub Beg in Iraq. He was a scoundrel and an inveterate gambler.

Sayyid Badr. He was strong, extremely graceful, and [173b] amazingly well mannered. He was a fantastic dancer and performed inimitable dances that must have been his own invention. He was in the mirza's service for a long time and always invited to drinking parties.

Islim Barlas. He was a coarse individual but certainly knew falconry well. He could draw a thirty- or forty-batman bow and send a reed straight through the target. In the *qabaq*[123] field he could charge from one end of the field, unstring his bow, string it again, shoot, and hit the target. He could tie his string grip to one end of a string a yard or a yard-and-a-half long and then tie the other end to a tree, pull it, and fire an arrow through the string grip. He could do a lot of such amazing feats. He was always in the mirza's service and attended every party.

Sultan-Junayd Barlas. In his old age he joined Sultan-Ahmad Mirza. He is the father of the Sultan-Junayd Barlas who is now the co-governor of Jaunpur.

Shaykh Abu-Sa'id Khan "Dar miyan." I do not know whether it is because he brought a horse to the mirza during a battle or because he repelled an assailant that he gained his nickname.[124]

Bihbud Beg. Early he served in the circle of pages. During the mirza's rencontres [174] he favored Bihbud Beg to such an extent that his name appeared on customs stamps and coinage.

Shaykhïm Beg. Because his pen name was Suhayli, he was called Shaykhïm Suhayli. He composed some fantastic poetry in which he used ferocious words. One of his compositions is the following:

> On the night of grief the whirlpool of my cries swept the celestial spheres away: / The dragon of my torrential tears carried off the inhabited quarter of the world.

It is well known that once when he recited these words to Mawlana Abdul-Rahman Jami, the Mawlana quipped, "Mirza, are you out to compose poetry or to frighten people?" He has put together a divan and has written mathnawis also.

Muhammad-Wali Beg. The Wali Beg who has been mentioned[125] was his son. In the end he became a high-ranking officer in the mirza's service but, although he was a great beg, he never abandoned his station. Day and night he leaned against the gate, and even his meals were brought to him right there. A person who serves thus will of course get promoted. What a ghastly time this is that a beg who sees five or six bald and blind people behind him has trouble getting to the gate. Where is that old type of service? Well, it's their own wretchedness. Muhammad-Wali's victuals were good, and his servants were kept in smart livery. [174b] He usually dispensed charity to the poor with his own hand. He was a foulmouthed swearer. When I took Samarkand in 917 [1511], Muhammad-Wali Beg and Darwesh Ali Kitabdar were with me. At that time he was paralyzed, his words were without flair, and he wasn't worthy of promotion. Probably all that service got him to the rank he attained.

Baba Ali the Gatekeeper. He was first patronized by Ali-Sher Beg and raised to the rank of beg. Yunus Ali, who at this date is one of my begs, courtiers, and intimates and will be mentioned often, is his son.

Badruddin. Formerly he was with Mirak Abdul-Rahim, Sultan-Abusa'id's finance minister. He was nimble and quick. They say he could jump over seven horses. He and Baba Ali were chums.

Hasan-i Ali Jalayir. His name was originally Husayn Jalayir, but he became known as Hasan-i Ali. His father, Ali Jalayir, was patronized by Babur Mirza and made a beg. Later when Yadgar-Muhammad Mirza came to power, there was no one greater than Ali Jalayir. Hasan-i Ali Jalayir was a falconer for Sultan-Husayn Mirza. He was a poet with the pen name Tufayli. He wrote good qasidas for me and was the premier qasida writer of his time. In 917 [1511–12], when I took Samarkand, he joined me and remained with me for five or six years. He was an insouciant and extravagant individual. [175] He kept catamites. He always played backgammon and was an inveterate gambler.

Khwaja Abdullah Murvari[d]. He was a finance minister before he became an ichki, a courtier, and a beg. He was a highly learned man. No one could play the dulcimer the way he did: the *girift* style in dulcimer playing is his invention. He was also good at calligraphy, especially the *ta'liq* script. His epistolary style was noteworthy, he was a good conversationalist, and he composed poetry, in which his pen name was Bayani. It was quite inferior to his other accomplishments, but he knew poetry well. He was a libertine and a rake. Due to his shameful debauchery he was afflicted by the pox and lost the use of his hands and feet. For many years he suffered various and sundry pains and hardships, and in the end he passed from this world with this affliction.

Muhammad son of Sayyid Urus. Urus Arghun, who was a great and powerful beg when Sultan-Abusaʿid took the throne, was his father. In those days there were youths who were expert archers, and he was one of the best. His bow was strong, his arrow long, and he was an expert shot. He held the governorship of Andkhui for a while.

Mir Ali the Stablemaster. It was he who sent somebody to lead Sultan-Husayn Mirza to take Yadgar-Muhammad Mirza by surprise.

Sayyid Hasan Oghlaqchï. He was the younger brother of Sayyid Yusuf Beg and son of Sayyid Oghlaqchï. He also had an accomplished and talented son named Mirza Farrukh. [175b] In 917 [1511], when I took Samarkand, he came to me. Although he composed but little poetry, it was pretty respectable. He knew all about astrolabes and astronomy. His conversation was good and he mixed well with everyone. He was fairly bad when in his cups. He died at the Battle of Gizhduvan.[126]

Calligraphy by Khwaja Abdullah Murwardid Bayani (1460–1525). Herat (?), dated A.H. 921 (A.D. 1515). Album page; ink on paper. Art and History Trust Collection.

Tengriberdi Samanchï. He was a coarse but brave, sword-wielding beg. At the gates of Balkh he battled beautifully with Nazar Bahadur, Khusrawshah's great liege man, as has been mentioned.[127]

Several other Turcoman begs came to the mirza's service and found favor. One of the first was Ali Khan Bayïndïr. Others were the brothers Asad Beg and Tahamtan Beg. Tahamtan Beg's daughter was married to Badi'uzzaman Mirza, and she was the mother of Muhammad-Zaman Mirza. Another was Ibrahim Chaghatay. Another was Amir-Umar Beg, who was later with Badi'uzzaman Mirza and was brave, a real Turk, and a good person. One of his sons, Abu'l-Fath by name, came to me from Iraq. At this date he is still with me, but he is a weak, timorous, and unreliable coward. Such a son from such a father!

Abdul-Baqi Mirza, a descendant of Temür Beg's through Miran-shah,[128] was one of those who came to Khurasan later, after Shah Isma'il had taken control of Iraq and Azerbaijan. Formerly Miran-shah's descendants went to that territory and, having gotten their pre-tense to the throne out of their heads, [176] entered the service of the kings there and attained honor. This Abdul-Baqi Mirza's paternal uncle Temür Usman was a great and respected beg in Ya'qub Beg Aqqoyunlu's service. Once he planned to send a large force against Khurasan, but when Abdul-Baqi Mirza arrived, Sultan-Husayn Mirza showed him great favor by making him his son-in-law, giving him Sul-tanïm Begim, the mother of Muhammad-Sultan Mirza.

Another of those who came later was Murad Beg Bayïndïr.

FINANCE MINISTERS

Mir Sarbirahna.[129] He is from a village in Andizhan and pretends to be a sayyid. He is an able conversationalist and speaker and has poetic tal-ent. Among the learned men and poets of Khurasan his word carries great weight. He has wasted his life, however, on an imitation of the story of Amir Hamza and has produced a lengthy, overlong pack of lies contrary to good taste and sound reason.

Kamaluddin Husayn of Gazargah. Although he was no Sufi, he pre-tended to be one. A lot of pseudo-Sufis who indulged in ecstatics and music hung around Ali-Sher Beg, but Kamaluddin's manners were better than most of theirs—he was probably patronized for his deport-ment, for otherwise he had no particular accomplishment. He has one

work called *Majlis al-ushshaq*,[130] in which he attributed what he wrote
to Sultan-Husayn Mirza, but it is weak and mostly false [176b]—he
writes tasteless and impious words, so much so that sometimes it is
near blasphemy, for he ascribes carnal love to many of the prophets
and saints and invents a paramour for each of them. Another piece of
folly is that in the introduction, Sultan-Husayn Mirza writes that it is
"my own composition." But at the head of each of the poems by Kamaluddin Husayn included in the book is written "by the writer." It
was due to this very Kamaluddin Husayn's sycophancy that Zu'n-Nun
Arghun was dubbed "Lion of God."

VIZIERS

Pir Majduddin Muhammad. He was the son of Shahrukh Mirza's divan
plenipotentiary, Khwaja Pir-Ahmad of Khwaf. Early on there was no
order in Sultan-Husayn Mirza's divan, and extravagance and squander
were rife—neither was the peasantry well maintained nor did the sol-
diery have any reason to be grateful. At that time Majduddin Muhammad was a clerk and was called Mirak. Once when the mirza needed a
little money and asked the divanis, they answered, "There is none,
there is no income." Majduddin Muhammad was present and smiled.
When the mirza asked why he had smiled, he withdrew in private and
told him what was in his heart, saying, "If the mirza should stipulate
that my hand be strengthened and that my word not be crossed, in a
little while I shall make it so that the realm will flourish, [177] the
peasantry will be grateful, the treasury full, and the army numerous."
The mirza granted his request and put him in charge of all of
Khurasan and turned over all tax collection to his care. He in turn endeavored to the best of his ability, and in a short while the army and
peasantry were satisfied and grateful: he caused plenty of money to
pour into the treasury and made the realm flourish. But he was at odds
with all the begs and officeholders, with Ali-Sher Beg at their head.
For this reason they became upset with him and intrigued to have him
deposed from office. Nizamulmulk became divan in his stead. After
some time they put a stop to Nizamulmulk too and had him killed.
After him Khwaja Afzal was brought from Iraq and made divan. When
I came to Kabul, they had made Khwaja Afzal a beg, and he affixed the
seal in the divan.

Khwaja Ata. Although he did not hold such an office as others did and was not a divan, in all parts of Khurasan no decision was made without consulting Khwaja Ata. He was pious, observant of his prayers, and religious. He is still active.[131]

LEARNED MEN

Sultan-Husayn Mirza's followers and retainers are those who have been mentioned. Sultan-Husayn [177b] Mirza's time was marvelous. Khurasan, especially the city of Herat, was filled with people of talent and extraordinary persons. Everyone who had an occupation was determined to execute his job to perfection. Among them was *Mawlana Abdul-Rahman Jami.*[132] In esoteric and exoteric knowledge there was no one like him at that time. His fame is such that it is beyond need of description. It occurs to me, however, that, by way of good omen, at least a mention of him should be made in these miserable pages.

Shaykhu'l-Islam Sayfuddin Ahmad. He was a descendant of Mawlana Sa'duddin Taftazani, of whose family there have been many shaykhu'l-islams in Herat and Khurasan. He was a scholarly person and knew the Arabic sciences and the traditional disciplines well. He was pious and religious. Although he was Shafiite by sect, he honored all the sects. They say that for seventy years he never missed a congregational prayer. When Shah Isma'il took Herat [in 1510], he martyred him. No one remains of his line.

Mulla Shaykh Husayn. Although his career took place during the time of Sultan-Abusa'id, since he lived into Sultan-Husayn's time, he is mentioned here. [178] He knew well the philosophical and rational sciences and dialectic theology. He could express much in a few words, and to speak with precision was his invention. In Sultan-Abusa'id's time he was close to the royal personage and powerful. He had a hand in all dealings in the realm. No one managed the office of enforcer of public morals better than he. Because he was of Sultan-Abusa'id's elite, during Sultan-Husayn Mirza's time such a peerless person was subjected to insults.

Mulla Usman's Mullazada. He was from a village called Charkh in the Logar district, one of the districts of Kabul. In Ulughbeg Mirza's time, at the age of fourteen, because he studied so much they called him Mulla Madarzad.[133] As he was on his way back to Samarkand from the pilgrimage to Mecca, Sultan-Husayn Mirza prevented him and kept him in Herat. He was a scholarly man; at that time no one was more learned than he. They say that he reached the level of a *mujtahid*,[134] but he did not practice. It is told of him that he used to say, "How can one forget something one has heard?" He had quite a prodigious memory.

Mir Murtaz. He knew well the philosophical and rational sciences. He earned his nickname by fasting so much.[135] [178b] He was so addicted to chess that while playing with one person he would grab another person's skirt to keep him from getting away.

Mulla Mas'ud Shirwani was another.

Mulla Abdul-Ghafur of Lar. He was Mawlana Abdul-Rahman Jami's disciple and student. Most of Jami's works were turned over to him. He has written something like a commentary on the *Nafahat*.[136] He was adept at the exoteric sciences and was not unadept at the esoteric sciences. He was remarkably unaffected and unceremonious. He had no objection to letting anyone who called himself mulla copy his notes. Whenever he heard of a dervish, he did not rest until he had gone to see him. When I went to Khurasan, Mulla Abdul-Ghafur was ill, and when I visited Jami's tomb I paid a call on him in Jami's madrasa. A few days later he died of that same illness.

Mir Jamaluddin Muhaddith. No one in Khurasan knew hadith as he did. Extremely aged, he is, as of this date, still alive.

Mir Ata'ullah of Mashhad. He knows the Arabic sciences well. He has written a treatise in Persian on rhyme. Its only fault is that he uses only his own poetry as examples [179] and deems it necessary to preface every line with the words "as in this line of mine." Some critics have made justifiable criticisms of it. Another of his treatises on rhetorical devices, called *Badayi' al-sanayi'*[137] is very good. There is said to be some deviation in his religion.

Qazi Ikhtiyar. He executed the office of cadi with distinction. He wrote a superb treatise in Persian on jurisprudence. He also made a selection of Koranic verses that have similar meanings. Qazi Ikhtiyar and Muhammad Mir Yusuf joined the princes at the Murghab River to come see me. A question was asked about my Baburi script. He requested the individual letters, which I wrote down for him. During that very session, he learned the letters, mastered the principles, and wrote something in it.

Mir Muhammad Yusuf. He was the Shaykhu'l-Islam's pupil. Later he was appointed to the Shaykhu'l-Islam's place. In some assemblies the Shaykhu'l-Islam sits above Qazi Ikhtiyar; in others it is vice versa. Later he became so infatuated with military science and military command that he talked of nothing else, although he did not have the slightest talent for either. In the end he ruined himself and all he had on account of his obsession. He is said to have been a Shiite.

POETS

Of this group the most outstanding [179b] was Mawlana Abdul-Rahman "Jami." Two others were Shaykhïm "Suhayli" and Husayn Ali "Tufayli" Jalayir, whose names and descriptions have already been given under Sultan-Husayn's circle of begs and ichkis.[138]

"Asafi." Because he was the son of a vizier he adopted "Asafi" as his pen name.[139] His poetry is not devoid of verve and benefit, although he does not exhibit any trace of love or ecstasy. His own claim was that he had never made effort to collect his own ghazals, but this was an affectation on his part, because he left it to a brother or some other relative to do it. Aside from ghazals he composed little poetry. When I went to Khurasan, he paid homage to me.

"Banna'i."[140] He was from Herat. His father, Ustad Muhammad, was a master builder and for this reason adopted the pen name Banna'i. His ghazals exhibit verve and ecstasy. He has made a divan and has composed mathnawis. He has one mathnawi in the *mutaqarib*[141] meter about fruit, but it is not a polished piece and he wasted his time on it. Another is a short mathnawi in the *khafif* meter[142] and another is a rather long one also in the khafif meter, which he finished later.

Early in his career he knew nothing of music, for which he was taunted by Ali-Sher Beg. One year when the mirza went to Merv for the winter Ali-Sher Beg went too. Banna'i stayed in Herat and studied music, and by summer had progressed to the point of composing. That summer when the mirza returned to Herat, [180] Banna'i presented a vocal and instrumental composition. Ali-Sher Beg was astonished but complimented him nonetheless. Banna'i had some really fine musical compositions. One of them is a naqsh called Nuh Rang,[143] in which there is a nine-fold theme and variation on a naqsh in the rast mode.[144] Banna'i was a great rival of Ali-Sher Beg and suffered much ill treatment in that regard. Finally he could take no more and went to Ya'qub Beg in Iraq and Azerbaijan. He did not do badly at Ya'qub Beg's court and became a fixture at parties. After Ya'qub Beg's death he left that country and returned to Herat, still with his witticisms and ready retorts. One day at a chess party Ali-Sher Beg stretched out his leg and touched Banna'i's backside.

"What a sad state this is," Ali-Sher Beg said in jest, "that in Herat one cannot stretch out a leg without poking a poet in the ass."

"Yes," Banna'i retorted, "and if you pull your leg back in, you'll poke another." In the end he left Herat for Samarkand because of such witticisms.

Many items were designed for Ali-Sher Beg, and anyone who devised something of any sort and wanted it to sell called it "Alisheri." Many elegant articles were thus named for him. For example, just because Ali-Sher Beg had tied his head up in a handkerchief when he had an earache, the triangular blue kerchief ladies used was dubbed an "Alisheri comforter." When Banna'i decided to leave Herat, [180b] he commissioned an outrageous saddle cloth for his donkey, and it became known as an Alisheri.

"Sayfi" of Bukhara. He had reached the pinnacle of mullahood. To prove that he was a mulla he would show a list of all the books he had read. He composed a divan, and did another one for tradesmen and craftsmen. He wrote many proverbs. He has written no mathnawis, as he himself said in this piece:

> Although the mathnawi is the stock in trade of poets, I consider the ghazal obligatory upon myself. If there are five lines that are pleasing, they are better than the two *Khamsa*s.

He has a Persian treatise on metrics in which he says too much and too little: the necessary words are not written and the obvious ones are dotted and pointed. He is said to have been bad at drinking and a reprobate. He was a powerful boxer too.

Abdullah Mathnawi-guy. He is from Jam and is a nephew of Mulla Jami. His pen name was Hatifi. He has composed mathnawis in imitation of the *Khamsa*.[145] The mathnawi he wrote in imitation of the *Haft paykar* he called *Haft manzar*, and his imitation of the *Sikandarnama* is

Temürnama.[146] Of these mathnawis his *Layli u Majnun* is the most famous, although it is not so nice as it is reputed to be.

Mir Husayn "Mu'amma'i." Probably no one has composed so many riddles. He spent all his time thinking them up. He was an amazingly unambitious and inoffensive person. **[181]**

Mulla Muhammad "Badakhshi." He was from Ishkamish, but since Ishkamish is not in Badakhshan it is strange that he took the pen name Badakhshi. His poetry is not equal to that of the poets already mentioned. He wrote a treatise on the riddle, but his riddles are not very good. He was also an able conversationalist. He paid me homage in Samarkand.

Yusuf "Badi'i." He was from the province of Fergana and composed fairly good qasidas.

"Ahi." He composed really good ghazals. Toward the end of his career he joined Ibn-i Husayn Mirza's retinue. He also has written a divan.

Muhammad "Salih." He has delightful ghazals, although they are not so uniform as they are delightful. He composed Turkish poetry too, which is not bad. Later he joined Shaybani Khan and was well patronized. He wrote a mathnawi in Turkish in the meter *ramal* hexameter, which is to say the meter of the *Subhat* and dedicated it to Shaybani Khan.[147] It is weak and of poor quality. Anyone who reads it will lose faith in Muhammad Salih's poetry. The one good line from it is this:

A fat man settled in Fergana: he turned Fergana into Tambalkhana.[148]

(Andizhan Province is called Tambalkhana.) Not another such line is known to exist in that mathnawi. He was an evil, iniquitous, and pitiless man.

Shah-Husayn "Kami." His poetry is not bad. He composed ghazals and is said to have written a divan.

"Hilali." As of this date he is still alive. His ghazals are uniformly delightful but shallow. He has written a divan and a mathnawi in the khafif meter called **[181b]** *The Shah and the Dervish*. Although some lines are wonderful, the content is hollow and the premise terrible. When poets of mathnawis in former times wrote on love, they gave the attributes of the lover to a man and those of the beloved to a woman. Hilali, on the other hand, has made a dervish the lover and a king the beloved, a shameless strumpet in fact. It is really an affront that, in the

interests of his poem, he describes a young man—and a king at that—as a brazen woman or prostitute. He is supposed to have prodigious recall and to have memorized thirty or forty thousand lines of poetry. It is said that he has committed most of the two *Khamsa*s to memory. He has a good recollection of the sciences of metrics, rhyme, and poetics.

"*Ahli.*" He is a commoner, but his poetry is not bad and he has composed a divan.

ARTISTS

Among the many calligraphers in Sultan-Husayn Mirza's time, the most outstanding of all in *naskh-ta'liq* was Sultan-Ali of Mashhad.[149] He copied a great deal both for the mirza and for Ali-Sher Beg. Every

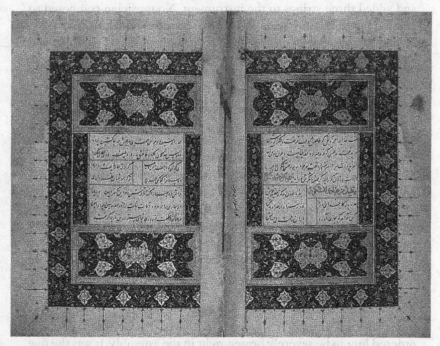

Calligraphy by Sultan-Ali Mashhad (fl. 1453–1519). From the *Gulistan* (Rose Garden) of Sa'di, Herat (?), dated A.H. 891 (A.D. 1486), fols. 2v, 3r. Double-page frontispiece; opaque watercolor, ink, and gold on paper. Art and History Trust Collection.

day he copied thirty lines for the mirza and twenty lines for Ali-Sher Beg.

Bihzad was one of the painters. He painted extremely delicately, but he made the faces of beardless people badly by drawing the double chin too big. He drew the faces of bearded people quite well.[150]

Shah-Muzaffar also painted delicately, [182] and did swift and delicate floral work. He did not live long, however, passing away just as he was gaining advancement.[151]

MUSICIANS

Among musicians no one could play the dulcimer the way Abdullah Murwari did, as has been mentioned.

Qul-Muhammad was a lutanist. He played the *ghichak* beautifully and added three strings to the instrument. No musician composed so many fine preludes as he did. There are no others like him.

Shaykhi the flutist played the lute and the ghichak superbly, and from the age of twelve or thirteen also performed well with the reed. Once at a gathering at Badi'uzzaman Mirza's he produced an exquisite melody on the reed. Qul-Muhammad, who was unable to reproduce it on the ghichak, claimed that the ghichak was a limited instrument. Shaykhi immediately took the ghichak from Qul-Muhammad's hand and played it without flaw. Other such stories are also told about Shaykhi. He had such a recall of melodies that he could identify any melody he heard and say whose it was and in what mode, but he did not do much composition, only one or two naqsh.

Shah-Qulï the guitarist was from Iraq. He came to Khurasan and learned the instrument, attaining great heights. He composed many naqsh, *peshraw*, and *ish*.[152]

Husayn the lutanist composed tasteful tunes on the lute. He could make all its strings play as one. His flaw lay in that he performed too coquettishly. [182b] He once made a big fuss when Shaybani Khan ordered him to play, and not only played badly but also did so on an inferior instrument instead of his own. Shaybani Khan caught on and ordered him to be severely beaten right in the assembly. It was the one good deed Shaybani Khan did in this world. Temperamental fellows deserve such punishment.

Another musician was Ghulam Shadi, the son of Shadi the singer. Although he could play, he did not play so well as the others. He had a pleasant voice and created some beautiful naqsh. At that time there was no one equal to him in voice composition. In the end Shaybani Khan sent him to the Khan of Kazan, Muhammad Amin Khan. He was never heard from again.

Mir Izzu did not play but he did compose. Although he wrote only a few works, they were nice.

Banna'i the poet[153] was also a musician and has some good vocal and instrumental compositions.

Another incomparable was Pahlawan Muhammad Bu-Sa'id, an outstanding wrestler who also composed poetry and wrote vocal and instrumental music. He has a beautiful naqsh in the *chargah* mode.[154] To have such accomplishments and be a wrestler too is a marvel. He was good company.

When Sultan-Husayn Mirza died, only the princes Badi'uzzaman and Muzaffar-Husayn were present. Muzaffar-Husayn was the favorite son, and Muhammad Burunduq Barlas, his atäkä, was the chief beg. Muzaffar-Husayn's mother was Khadija Begim, [183] the mirza's principal wife. The mirza's people also often referred to Muzaffar Mirza. For these reasons Badi'uzzaman Mirza was apprehensive and thought of not coming. Muzaffar Mirza and Muhammad Beg got on their horses and went to him to allay his fears and get him to come.

Sultan-Husayn Mirza was brought to Herat with all royal honors and ceremony and buried in his madrasa.

At this time Zu'n-Nun Beg was also present. Muhammad Burunduq Beg and the begs who remained met with the princes and agreed that Badi'uzzaman Mirza and Muzaffar-Husayn Mirza should be made kings jointly on the throne of Herat. Badi'uzzaman Mirza's steward was Zu'n-Nun Beg, and Muzaffar-Husayn Mirza's was Muhammad Burunduq Beg. On Badi'uzzaman Mirza's behalf the civil prefect was Shaykh-Ali Taghayï, and on Muzaffar Mirza's behalf was Yusuf Ali Kükäldash. It was a strange arrangement: never has a joint kingship been heard of. It is against the purport of Shaykh Sa'di's words in the *Gulistan:* "Ten poor men can sleep under one blanket, but two kings cannot fit into one clime."[155]

EVENTS OF THE YEAR 912
(1506-7)[156]

In the month of Muharram (May–June 1506) we took the Ghorband and Shibartu roads to Khurasan to repel the Uzbeks. [183b]

Jahangir Mirza had left the province in a huff. If he gathered the tribesmen around him, I wondered what mischief some of those evil and seditious people would stir up. I remarked, "Let's leave our baggage train at Ushturshahr in the custody of Wali the treasurer and Dawlat-Qadam Qaravul and get hold of the tribes as fast as possible." So saying, we set out unencumbered and reached Fort Zahhak that day. Thence we came by way of the Gumbazak Pass, took Saighan, went through the Dandan Shikan Pass, and stopped at Kahmard meadow. Sultan-Muhammad Dulday was attached to Sayyid-Afzal Khwabbin, and a report that we had set out from Kabul was sent to Sultan-Husayn Mirza.

Jahangir Mirza had lingered a bit behind. As we approached Bamian twenty or thirty men were coming from the opposite direction also toward Bamian. As they got nearer they could see the tents of our camp followers who had stayed behind. Thinking they were we, they quickly retreated. As soon as they reached their own camp they decamped without care for anything, and without so much as a backward look they withdrew to Yakawlang.

Shaybani Khan had laid siege to Balkh, where Sultan Qulanchaq was. He had sent two or three princes with three or four thousand troops to attack Badakhshan. At that time Mubarakshah and Zubayr had joined Nasir Mirza. [184] Although previously there had been quarrels and bad blood, they had assembled their forces and camped at the eastern side of the Kishm River in Shakhdan below the Kishm when, at dawn, the Uzbeks made a surprise attack, crossing the river and assailing Nasir Mirza, who immediately withdrew to the hills. He gathered his troops from the hillsides and, sounding the charge, advanced and took the Uzbeks. The Kishm River was swollen, and as they crossed it many were shot or fell to the sword, and many more were taken prisoner or died in the water. Mubarakshah and Zubayr were farther up the Kishm than the mirza. As the Uzbeks came down upon them they forced them to flee to the hills. When Nasir Mirza had routed his foes and learned that the enemy had put Mubarakshah and Zubayr to flight, he advanced upon that group. From above, the begs of Kohistan regrouped their cavalry and infantry and charged, and the Uzbeks, unable to make a stand, were routed. Of this group too, many were taken prisoner, and others were hit, run through, or drowned in the river. Perhaps a thousand or fifteen hundred Uzbeks died. This was one good victory of Nasir Mirza's. News of this was brought to us by one of his men while we were in the Kahmard plain.

BABUR PROCEEDS TOWARD KHURASAN

While we were in this region our army obtained grain from Ghori and Dahana. [184b] Here we received letters from Sayyid-Afzal and Sultan-Muhammad Dulday, who had been sent to Khurasan, with the news of Sultan-Husayn Mirza's death. Nonetheless, out of concern for the good name of this dynasty, we set out for Khurasan, although we also had other reasons for going. We went through the Ajar valley, Top, and Mundagan, crossed the Balkh River, and emerged at Koh-i-Saf. When we received news of the Uzbek's raid on San-u-Charyak, we sent troops with Qasim Beg against the raiders. He met them, defeated them soundly, and brought back many severed heads.

We sent men to Jahangir Mirza and the Aymaqs and camped for several days in the Koh-i-Saf summer pasture until they could bring back news. This region has an awful lot of deer.[157] We went hunting once. After a day or two all the Aymaqs came and swore fealty to me. Several times Jahangir Mirza had directed people to the Aymaqs, once sending Imaduddin Mas'ud. But they did not go to him—they came to me instead. Finally there was nothing the mirza could do, so he came to see me when I went down from Koh-i-Saf and camped in Dara-i-Bai. As we were anxious over Khurasan, with no attention to him and no concern for the tribes, we advanced through Gurzuwan, Almar, Qaisar, and Chechaktu, passed through Fakhruddin Ölümi, and arrived at a place called Dara-i-Bam, a dependency of Badghis. [185]

As this was a world in strife, anyone who stretched forth his hand could usurp the province and people. We, too, for our part, imposed a tribute on the Aymaqs and Turks of those regions and began to take something. Within a month or two we had received perhaps three hundred Kepeki tümäns.[158]

A few days before us the Khurasan troops and Zu'n-Nun's forces had soundly defeated the Uzbek raiders at Pand Deh and Maruchak and killed many of the enemy.

Badi'uzzaman Mirza, Muzaffar Mirza, Muhammad Burunduq Barlas, and Zu'n-Nun Arghun's son Shah Beg had decided to move against Shaybani Khan, who was besieging Sultan Qulanchaq at Balkh. To this end people were sent from Herat to summon all of Sultan-Husayn Mirza's sons. As they reached Badghis, Abu'l-Muhsin Mirza came from Merv and joined them at Chehil Dukhtaran. Later Ibn-i-Husayn Mirza came from Tun and Qayin. Kipik Mirza was in Mashhad. Many people were sent, but he behaved in an unreasonable and unmanly fashion and refused to come because of his jealousy of Muzaffar Mirza, of whom, when he became king, he said, "How can *I* go before *him*?" At such a juncture, when all the brothers were gathering in one place and [185b] agreeing to move against an enemy like Shaybani Khan, he indulged in petty rivalry and refused to come. His behavior is now attributed to resentment but everybody will eventually call it cowardice. In the end, only qualities survive a person in this world. Anyone who has a modicum of intelligence will take steps so that he will not be ill spoken of afterward. Why should someone who has a trace of awareness not take pains that his actions be approved? The wise have said that a good memory is a second life.

Emissaries came to me too. Later, even Muhammad Burunduq Barlas came. Why should I not go? I had already traversed a road of one or two hundred stages for this purpose. I set out at once with Muhammad Beg. By that time the mirzas had come to the Murghab River.

BABUR MEETS HIS COUSINS
AND VISITS HERAT

On Monday the eighth of Jumada II [October 26, 1506], I met with the mirzas. Abu'l-Muhsin Mirza came out half a kos to greet me. As we approached each other, I dismounted on one side and he on the other. We walked forward, met, and then remounted. Farther on, near the camp, Muzaffar Mirza and Ibn-i-Husayn Mirza appeared. They were both younger than Abu'l-Muhsin Mirza and should have come farther out to welcome me. Their delay was probably due to a hangover, after having indulged in revelry and pleasure, [186] not to arrogance or a desire to offend. Muzaffar Mirza apologized profusely, and we met on horseback. A similar meeting was held with Ibn-i-Husayn Mirza. We dismounted at Badi'uzzaman Mirza's gate. What an awful crowd there was. It was so congested that during the gathering some were lifted up off the ground and carried three or four paces. Others who thought they would get out for some reason were picked up and carried backward four or five paces.

We reached Badi'uzzaman Mirza's court tent. It had been settled that I would kneel as soon as I entered. Badi'uzzaman Mirza would rise and come forward, and there we would meet each other. As I entered the tent I knelt once and started forward without delay. Badi'uzzaman rose quite sluggishly and came slowly forward. Qasim Beg, a partisan whose honor was dependent upon my own, gave a tug on my belt. I realized what was going on. Moving more slowly I advanced to my appointed spot.

Four cushions had been placed in this huge shelter. Badi'uzzaman Mirza's tents were always provided with a doorway on one side, and he always sat on the doorway side. One of the cushions had been placed there for him and [186b] Muzaffar Mirza. Another was positioned on the right-hand place of honor; Abu'l-Muhsin Mirza and I sat there. To the left of Badi'uzzaman Mirza, to my right, sat Qasim Sultan the Uzbek and Ibn-i-Husayn Mirza. (Qasim Sultan of the Shaban Sultans was the mirza's son-in-law and father of Qasim Husayn Sultan.) One more cushion was for Jahangir Mirza and Abdul-Razzaq Mirza. Muhammad Burunduq and Zu'n-Nun Beg were seated to the right with Qasim Beg, in a position much inferior to that of Qasim Sultan and Ibn-i-Husayn Mirza.

Food was served, although the gathering was not convivial. Trays were set with gold and silver vessels. In former times our fathers and forefathers meticulously observed the Genghisid Code.[159] In assemblies and court, at banquets and dinners, in sitting and serving, nothing was allowed to go counter to the code. However, Genghis Khan's code is not a binding text according to which a person must act absolutely. Rather, it is necessary to act in accordance with a good rule when someone leaves one behind; if an ancestor has set a bad precedent, however, it should be replaced by a good one.

After dining we mounted our horses and returned to where we were staying, a league from the mirzas' camp [187].

When we returned for a second visit, Badi'uzzaman Mirza did not do me the courtesy he had before. I said to Muhammad Burunduq Beg and Zu'n-Nun Beg that although I was young in years, my rank was nonetheless high. Twice by dint of the sword I had recaptured and sat on my ancestral throne in Samarkand. Who had fought with foreigners and rebels for the sake of this dynasty as I had done? To delay in honoring me was inexcusable. As soon as this was mentioned to him—since it was reasonable, after all—he apologized and showed me the appropriate courtesy.

Another time when I went before Badi'uzzaman Mirza in the afternoon, there was a drinking party. At that time I did not drink. It was a really elaborate gathering. On the tables were foodstuffs of every description: roast fowl, goose, and much more. It was truly a quietly elegant gathering that lacked nothing. Badi'uzzaman Mirza's parties were much talked about. Two or three times I attended his drinking parties on the banks of the Murghab. Since they knew I did not drink, they did not offer me any.

Once I went to a party at Muzaffar Mirza's. Hasan-i Ali Jalayir and Mir Badr were in attendance. [187b] The people were friendly, and when everyone was feeling good, Mir Badr danced. He danced well, of a type probably of his own devising.

It took three or four months for the mirzas to get out of Herat, come to an agreement, gather themselves, and get to the Murghab. Sultan Qulanchaq was forced to turn over the Balkh fort to the Uzbeks. After taking Balkh the Uzbeks learned of the mirzas' gathering and so returned to Samarkand. Although these mirzas were outstanding in the social graces, they were strangers to the reality of military command and the rough and tumble of battle.

While we were camped at the Murghab, news arrived that Haqq-nazar Chapan had overrun the Chechaktu region with four or five hundred men. All the mirzas were present, but no matter what they did they could not manage to send a force against this raider. Between the Murghab and Chechaktu was ten stages. I volunteered for this mission, but as it touched upon their honor they did not let me go.

Since Wormwood Khan had withdrawn, and it was getting late in the year, it was decided that the mirzas should winter over wherever it was convenient and then move together against the enemy next spring.

They insisted that I winter over in Khurasan. Kabul and Ghazni were evil places filled with strife, and Turks, Moghuls, tribesmen and nomads, Afghans and Hazaras were lurking there. [188] By the shortest route, which was through the mountains, it would take a month to get from Khurasan to Kabul—provided there was no snow or other impediment. By the low country it was a forty- to fifty-day journey. The country was also not fully devoted to me.

Not one of our well-wishers thought it wise for us to winter there. We made our apologies to the mirzas, but they would not accept. They insisted. The more excuses we made, the more they pressed their invitation. Finally Badi'uzzaman Mirza, Abu'l-Muhsin Mirza, and Muzaffar Mirza rode over to my tent to urge me to stay the winter. We could not say no to the mirzas' faces, when such royalty had come themselves. Besides, I really wanted to see Herat, which had no equal in all the world and which during Sultan-Husayn Mirza's reign had been adorned and decorated ten, nay twenty times over. For these reasons we decided to remain.

Abu'l-Muhsin Mirza went to his province of Merv. Ibn-i-Husayn Mirza went to Tun and Qayin. Badi'uzzaman Mirza and Muzaffar Mirza set out for Herat. Two or three days later I also started for Herat via the Chehil Dukhtaran and Tash Robat roads.

All the ladies, my aunt Payanda Sultan Begim, Khadija Begim, and some of my other aunts, Sultan-Abusa'id Mirza's daughters, were gathered at the Sultan-Husayn Mirza Madrasa. All the women [188b] were at the mirza's tomb when I went to see them. First I knelt to Payanda Sultan Begim and had an interview. Then, without kneeling to Apaq Begim, I had a meeting with her. After that I knelt to Khadija Begim and did the same. We stayed for a while and, after some recitation from the Koran, went to the south madrasa, where Khadija Begim's tent had been set up. Khadija Begim's food was served. After dining I went to Payanda Sultan Begim's tent and stayed that night with her.

A campsite was first assigned to me in the Bagh-i-Naw, where I came at dawn. I spent one night there, but since I found it unsuitable I was assigned Ali-Sher Beg's quarters, where I remained until I left Herat. Every two or three days I went to the Bagh-i-Jahanara[160] and paid court to Badi'uzzaman Mirza.

A PARTY AT MUZAFFAR MIRZA'S

Several days later Muzaffar Mirza sent me an invitation to his quarters in the Bagh-i-Safed.[161] Khadija Begim was there too. Jahangir Mirza went along with me. After dinner was served in Khadija Begim's presence, Muzaffar Mirza took us to an edifice built by Babur Mirza called the Tarabkhana,[162] where a drinking party was held. The Tarabkhana was situated in the middle of a small garden. It was a modest building of two stories and rather pleasant. The upper level had been elaborately constructed. Each of the four corners had an alcove, but otherwise the space in the middle and between the alcoves was like one room. [189] Between the alcoves were things like *shahnishins* (see illus. p. 227). Every side of the room was painted; the work had been commissioned by Sultan-Abusa'id Mirza to depict his battles and encounters.

On the shahnishin on the north side two cushions were facing each other, with their sides toward the north. Muzaffar Mirza and I sat down on one of those; Sultan-Mas'ud Mirza and Jahangir Mirza sat on the other. Since we were guests in Muzaffar Mirza's quarters, he had me seated in a place of greater honor. The pleasure cups were filled and the cupbearers began to circulate and offer them to the guests, who started gulping down the clear wine as though it was the water of life. The party grew heated as the wine went to people's heads.

They thought they could make me drink and draw me into the circle. Although at that time I had not committed the sin of drinking to tipsiness, had not experienced drunkenness, and did not know the delight and pleasure of being drunk as it should be known, not only was

Bahram Gur Wins the Crown, from a *Shahnama* of Firdawsi, copied by Na'imuddin Ahmad b. Mun'imuddin Muhammad al-Awhadi al-Husayni, Iran (Shiraz), January 1518, fol. 502a. Opaque watercolor, ink, and gold on paper. Arthur M. Sackler Gallery, Smithsonian Institution; Purchase—Smithsonian Unrestricted Trust Funds, Smithsonian Collections Acquisition Program, and Dr. Arthur M. Sackler, S1986.58.1. A *shahnishin*, a dais or bench, often with three raised sides, is shown.

I inclined to have a drink of wine but my heart was also urging me to cross that valley. In my childhood I had no desire for wine, for I was unaware of the enjoyment of it. Occasionally my father had offered me some, but I had made excuses. [189b] After my father's death I was abstinent and followed piously in Khwaja Qazi's blessed footsteps. How could I, who avoided suspect food, have committed the sin of drinking wine? Later, with the desires of young manhood and the promptings of the carnal soul, when I had an inclination for wine, nobody offered— no one even knew that I was interested. So, although I was willing, it was difficult to do all by oneself. It crossed my mind that since they were making such proposals, and here we had come to a fabulous city like Herat, where all the implements of pleasure and revelry were ready and present, and all the devices of entertainment and enjoyment were close at hand, if I didn't drink now, when would I? Deliberating thus with myself, I resolved to make the leap. It then occurred to me, however, that since I had not accepted a drink from Badi'uzzaman Mirza, who was the elder brother, if I took a drink in his younger brother's house, it might constitute an affront. I voiced my hesitation. Agreeing that my excuse was reasonable, they did not proffer any wine at this gathering. It was decided that Badi'uzzaman Mirza and Muzaffar Mirza should assemble in one place and that I should drink at the invitation of both mirzas together.

The entertainers at this party [190] were Hafiz Hajji, Jalaluddin Mahmud the flutist, and Ghulam Shadi's brother Shadi Bachcha, who played the harp. Hafiz Hajji, like all Heratis, recited beautifully—low, delicately, and evenly. Jahangir Mirza had one of his singers along, a Samarkandi named Mir Jan. He sang in high voice, coarsely and unevenly. In the heat of pleasure Jahangir Mirza ordered him to sing, and it was terrible. Khurasanis all lead a life of elegance. One of them blocked up his ears at this fellow's singing while another made a face. But because Jahangir was a prince, no one could tell him to stop.

Late in the evening we left the Tarabkhana and went to Muzaffar Mirza's newly established winter quarters. There Yusuf Ali Kükäldash, high as a kite, got up and danced, which he did well and with much elegance. In those quarters the conviviality really waxed warm. Muzaffar Mirza gave me a sword belt, a lambskin jacket, and a gray thoroughbred horse. Janak recited in Turkish. Muzaffar Mirza's slaves Kätä Mah and Kichik Mah were also there, and in the midst of the drunkenness they did some obscene impertinences. The party went on quite animated until late, when the gathering broke up. That night I stayed over.

When Qasim Beg heard that the mirzas were going to offer me wine, he sent somebody to Zu'n-Nun Beg, who gave the mirzas some pretty strong admonition. Thereafter all suggestions of wine ceased. [190b]

A PARTY AT BADI'UZZAMAN MIRZA'S

When Badi'uzzaman Mirza heard of Muzaffar Mirza's entertainment, he arranged an assembly in the Bagh-i-Jahanara in the Muqawwakhana and sent me an invitation. Some of our ichkis and warriors were also summoned. They could not drink in my presence out of respect for me, and when they did drink, maybe once every thirty to forty days, they would do it with the door bolted fast and with a hundred trepidations. Invited, they went, but it was difficult for them to drink. Sometimes they tried to distract me, and sometimes they held up their hands to conceal what they were doing, although all those in attendance had blanket permission from me because the party was given by someone who was like my father or elder brother. They brought in willows. Among the branches—whether they were real or artificial I don't know—were hung strips of gilded leather cut very thin the length of the branches. They looked fantastic.[163]

At this gathering they placed a roast goose before me. Since I had never carved or disjointed a fowl, I did not touch it. Badi'uzzaman Mirza asked, "Do you not care for it?" I said that I did not know how to do it. Immediately Badi'uzzaman Mirza carved and disjointed it and set it before me. [191] In such things Badi'uzzaman Mirza was without equal. At the end of the entertainment he gave me a jewel-studded belt, a dagger, a *charqab*,[164] and a thoroughbred horse.

SIGHTSEEING IN HERAT

On each of the twenty days I was in Herat I went out on horseback to tour the places I had not seen. My guide on these excursions was Yusuf Ali Kükältash. At every place we stopped, he had me served something to eat. During these twenty days, with the exception of Sultan-Husayn Mirza's khanaqah, there was no place we did not see.

I saw Gazargah, Ali-Sher Beg's garden, Juwaz-i-Kaghidh, Takht-i-Asitana, Puligah, Kahdistan, the Bagh-i-Nazargah,[165] Ni'matabad, the Gazargah Avenue, Sultan-Ahmad Mirza's burial enclosure, the Takht-i-Safar, the Takht-i-Nawa'i, the Takht-i-Barkir, Takht-i-Hajji Beg,

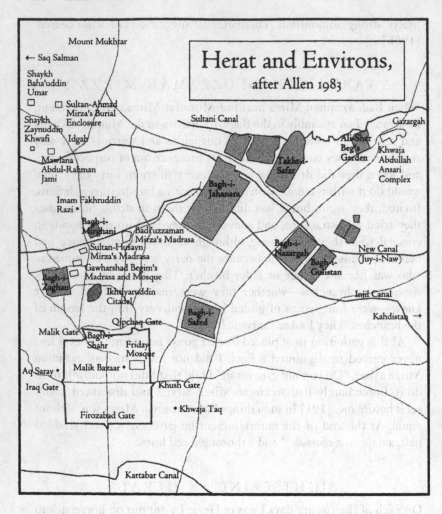

Map labels:
Mount Mukhtar
← Saq Salman
Shaykh Baha'uddin Umar
Sultan-Ahmad Mirza's Burial Enclosure
Shaykh Zaynuddin Khwafi
Idgah
Mawlana Abdul-Rahman Jami
Imam Fakhruddin Razi
Bagh-i-Mirghani
Bad'uzzaman Mirza's Madrasa
Sultan-Husayn Mirza's Madrasa
Gawharshad Begim's Madrasa and Mosque
Bagh-i-Zaghan
Ikhtiyaruddin Citadel
Qipchaq Gate
Malik Gate
Bagh-i-Shahr
Friday Mosque
Malik Bazaar
Aq Saray
Iraq Gate
Khush Gate
Firozabad Gate
Khwaja Taq
Kartabar Canal
Sultani Canal
Gazargah
Ali-Sher Beg's Garden
Khwaja Abdullah Ansari Complex
Takht-i-Safar
Bagh-i-Jahanara
Bagh-i-Nazargah
Bagh-i-Gulistan
New Canal (Juy-i-Naw)
Injil Canal
Bagh-i-Safed
Kahdistan →

Herat and Environs, after Allen 1983

Shaykh Baha'uddin Umar, Shaykh Zaynuddin's and Mawlana Abdul-Rahman Jami's shrines and tombs, the Mukhtar namazgah, the Hawz-i-Mahian, Saq Salman and Bulwari, which was originally the shrine of Abu'l-Walid, Imam Fakhr, the Bagh-i-Khiaban,[166] the mirza's madrasas and tombs, Gawharshad Begim's madrasa, tomb, and Friday mosque, the Bagh-i-Zaghan, the Bagh-i-Naw, the Bagh-i-Zubayda,[167] the Aq Saray built by Sultan-Abusa'id Mirza outside the Iraq Gate, [191b] Puran, the Suffa-i-Tirandazan, Cheragh Meadow, Amir Wahid, the

Malan Bridge, Khwaja Taq, the Bagh-i-Safed, the Tarabkhana, the Bagh-i-Jahanara, Kushk, the Muqawwakhana, the Susanikhana, the Duwazdah Burj, the great pool on the northern side of Jahanara and the four structures along its four sides, the five gates to the fort, the Malik Gate, the Iraq Gate, the Firozabad Gate, the Khush Gate, the Qipchaq Gate, the Malik Bazaar, the marketplace, Shaykhu'l-Islam's madrasa, the Maliks' Friday mosque, the Bagh-i-Shahr,[168] Badi'uzzaman Mirza's madrasa on the banks of the Injil Canal, Ali-Sher Beg's quarters, which were called Unsiyya, his tomb and Friday mosque, which were called Qudsiyya, his madrasa and khanaqah called Khalasiyya and Ikhlasiyya, and his bath and hospital, which were called Safa'iyya and Shifa'iyya. All these I saw in a short period of time.[169]

Before the time of instability, Ma'suma Sultan Begim, Sultan-Ahmad Mirza's youngest daughter, had been brought to Khurasan by her mother, Habiba Sultan Begim. One day when I went to see my *äkä*,[170] she came with her mother and saw me. Upon first laying eyes on me she felt a great inclination toward me. By secret messenger my äkä and *yengä*,[171] [192] as I called Payanda Sultan Begim and Habiba Sultan Begim, discussed the matter and decided that after I left, yengä would take her daughter to Kabul.

Muhammad Burunduq Beg and Zu'n-Nun Beg tried hard to get me to stay for the winter but were not forthcoming with good arrangements for either a place or provisions. It was now winter, and snow had fallen in the mountains between Herat and Kabul. I was getting ever more apprehensive over Kabul. In the end there was nothing else to do, although we could not say so frankly.

BABUR LEAVES HERAT FOR KABUL

On the pretext of finding winter quarters, we left Herat on the seventh of Sha'ban [December 23, 1506]. We marched, stopping a day or two at a time in the Badghis region, so that those who had gone to their estates to collect revenue and on business could join us. We halted and delayed so much that two or three days out of Langar-i-Mir Ghiyas we saw the Ramadan moon. Some of the warriors who had gone to their estates rejoined us; others came to Kabul twenty days to a month later than we, while still others stayed and joined the mirzas' service. One of these was Sayyidim Ali Darban. He remained and became an attendant to Badi'uzzaman Mirza. I had promoted none of Khusraw-shah's attendants more than him. When Jahangir Mirza left Ghazni, he turned it over to Sayyidim, and when he in turn had come away with the army, he had stationed his brother-in-law, Dost [192b] Eygü Shaykh, in Ghazni. Truly among Khusrawshah's retainers none was better than Sayyidim Ali Darban and Muhibb-Ali Qorchï.

Sayyidim was a man of good character and disposition. He was courageous with the sword. His quarters were never without a convivial gathering and hearty conversation. He was generous and amazingly organized and competent. His elegance and grace were superb, his company and conversation sweet. He was jovial, talkative, and witty. His only fault was that he practiced vice and pederasty, and also deviated somewhat in his religion. He was slightly hypocritical, a characteristic some attributed to his wit, but there was more to it than that. When Badi'uzzaman Mirza let Wormwood take Herat and went to Shah Beg, because Sayyidim Ali was duplicitous with the mirza and Shah Beg, the mirza killed him and had him thrown into the Helmand River. Muhibb-Ali's story will come in its proper place in the history.[172]

Leaving Langar-i-Mir Ghiyas, we skirted the villages of Gharjistan and came to Chaghcharan. There was snow all the way from Langar to Gharjistan. The farther we went the deeper it was. Chaghcharan belonged to Zu'n-Nun Beg and was under the charge of his servant Mirak Jan Apardi. We purchased all of Zu'n-Nun Beg's grain. Two or three marches out of Chaghcharan the snow was so deep it came above the horses' stirrups, [193] and in most places the horses' hooves did not reach the ground. Still it kept on snowing.

Out of Cheraghdan the road was completely obscured. In the Langar-i-Mir Ghiyas region we deliberated over which road we should take to Kabul. I and most of the others were of the opinion that since it was winter, the mountain road would be fraught with danger. The Kandahar road, although slightly longer, would be safer. Qasim Beg said that the latter road was too long and we should go by the former. In so saying he made a great mistake, but by that road we went.

Our guide was a Pashai named Sultan. Whether he was too old or fainthearted, or whether because of the depth of the snow, in any case he lost the road and could not guide us. Since it was at Qasim Beg's insistence that we had come by this road, and it reflected upon his honor, he and his sons trampled down the snow, found the road again, and went on ahead. One day the snow was so deep and the road so obscured that no matter what we did we could not go on. There was nothing for us to do but turn back and camp in a place with firewood. I appointed seventy or eighty warriors to retrace our steps to find and bring to guide us any Hazaras who were wintering in the valley. We did not move from this camp for three or four days until those who had gone out returned. When they did return, they did not bring with them anyone who could show us the way. [193b] Trusting in God, we sent Sultan Pashai ahead and set out back down the very road where we had gotten lost. During those few days we endured much hardship and misery, more than I had experienced in my whole life. At that time I composed this line:

> Is there any cruelty or misery the spheres can inflict I have not suffered? / Is there any pain or torment my wounded heart has not suffered?

For nearly a week we proceeded, unable to cover more than a league or a league-and-a-half a day. I became a snow trampler with ten or fifteen of my ichkis, Qasim Beg, his sons Tengriberdi and Qambar-Ali, and another two or three of their servants. We progressed on foot. One person would advance for eight to ten yards, trampling down the snow. Every time we put our foot down we would sink in to the waist or chest and pack down the snow. After going however many paces, the lead man would stop, exhausted. Then another would move to the front. Together these ten, fifteen, or twenty people could pack down enough snow for an unmounted horse to be led through. Sinking down to the stirrups or girth strap, the horse could be pulled forward for ten or fifteen paces before it gave out. It was drawn aside and another unmounted horse could be led forward. In this manner we ten to twenty persons [194] trampled down the snow, and our horses were dragged through. Then all the rest of those who enjoyed the titles of fearless warriors and begs entered the prepared, packed-down road without dismounting and proceeded with their heads hung low. It was no time to compel or insist. Anyone with stamina and fortitude will join in such a labor without waiting for an invitation. By compressing the snow and creating a road, we made it in three or four days from that horrible place to a cave known as Khawal Qutï, below what is called the Zirrin Pass.

That day there was an amazing snowstorm. It was so terrible we all thought we were going to die. The people there call the caves and hollows in the mountains *khawals*. As we arrived the storm was unbelievably fierce. We dismounted right in front of the khawal. The snow was so deep that the horses had difficulty coming across a road that had been trampled and packed down. The days were at their shortest, and it was still light when the first people reached the cave. By the prayer and nighttime they were still coming. Thereafter they dismounted where they stood. Many spent the night on horseback.

The cave seemed to be rather small. I took a shovel and cleared away enough snow at the mouth of the cave to make myself a place to sit. I dug down chest deep, and still I did not reach the ground, [194b] but it was a bit of shelter from the wind. There I sat down. Several people asked me to come inside, but I refused. I figured that to leave my people out in the snow and the storm, with me comfortable in a warm place, or to abandon all the people to hardship and misery, with me here asleep without a care, was neither manly nor comradely. Whatever hardship and difficulty there was, I would suffer it too. Whatever the people could endure, I could too. There is a Persian proverb: "Death with friends is a feast." In the midst of such a storm there I sat in a dug-out hole. By the time of the night prayer the snowstorm was still raging so much that I sat all huddled up. Four spans of snow were on my back and covering my head and ears. My ears got frostbite. At the night prayer those who had made a thorough inspection of the cave called out, "The cave is really big. There's enough room for everybody." When I heard this, I shook the snow off myself and, calling the warriors who were nearby to come in, went into the cave. There was enough room for forty or fifty people comfortably. Everyone brought out their provisions, hardtack, parched grain, and whatever they had. In the midst of such cold and such a storm, what a marvelously warm, safe, and secure place we had!

At dawn the storm stopped. We set out early and, by trampling down the snow again, made it to the top of the pass. [195] The road itself seemed to take a turn and go higher up to the Zirrin Pass. We did not follow it higher but went right down the valley bottom. It was late in the day before we reached the other side of the pass. We spent the night at the mouth of the valley: it was bitterly cold, and spent in utter misery and hardship. Many people got frostbitten: Käpä's feet, Sevindük the Turcoman's hands, and Akhi's feet. Early the next day we proceeded straight down the valley. Although we could see this was not the road, we put our trust in God and marched through the valley bottom. In places with treacherous slopes and precipices we had to dismount. It was evening when we emerged through the mouth of the valley. Not even the oldest men with the longest memory could remember this pass having been crossed with the snow so deep; it was not even known whether it had ever occurred to anyone to attempt a crossing at this time of year. Although for a few days we had experienced a great deal of difficulty, in the end it was due to the depth of the snow that we were able to get ourselves to our destination. If it had not been so deep, how could those trackless slopes and falls have been crossed? [195b] Had it not been so deep, the horses and beasts of burden would all have been stuck on the first slope.

> Whatever happens, good or bad, when you look closely, you'll find that it is all for the best.

Night had fallen by the time we reached Yakawlang. The Yakawlang people had heard of our arrival and we were greeted with warm houses, fat sheep, hay and fodder for the horses, abundant water, and plenty of kindling and dung for fires. To be delivered from such cold and snow and to find such a village and warm houses, to be saved from hardship and misery and to discover bread and fat sheep—this is a comfort that only those who have endured hardships can know, a relief that only those who have undergone travails can comprehend. Easy of mind and heart we stayed in Yakawlang for one day. From there we proceeded one stage. The next day was the Ramadan feast.[173] Passing through Bamian and crossing the Shibartu Pass, we stopped before reaching Jangalak.

A RAID ON THE TURCOMAN HAZARAS

The Turcoman Hazaras were camped for the winter with their people and animals right along our path, utterly unaware of our approach. While on the march that morning, we stopped among their corrals and tents. We plundered two or three corrals; the Hazaras themselves abandoned their possessions, grabbed their infants and children, [196] and fled to the hills. Word was received from ahead that a few Hazaras had blocked the army's way and were shooting arrows to prevent the soldiers from proceeding. As soon as I heard this, I set out in haste. When I reached the spot, I saw that instead of finding a defile, I saw only a few Hazaras shooting from a mountain spur. Like intrepid warriors my men had piled up their baggage and were gathered there:

Seeing the mass of the enemy, they stood perplexed and idle. / I hastened in their direction as I arrived, galloping forward and yelling, "Stand and fight!" / It was my intent to hurry my men, to make them fight the enemy. / I pulled myself forward, but no one heard my words. / Without armor, horse, armor or arms, I had only good arrows and quiver. / If I stopped they would all halt too, as though slain by the enemy. / When you make someone a servant it is so that he may save your life someday, / Not in order that the servant may stand idle while his lord is abandoned in the fray. / Of what use is such a servant? Neither is he fit for your service nor is he worth his keep. / Finally I spurred my horse forward and drove it to the mountain. [196b] / Seeing me, the men rode forward, leaving their fear behind. / We reached the mountain and clambered up, disregarding the shower of arrows. / Some dismounted, some on horseback, the men raced fearlessly forward. / The foe was raining down arrows from the mountain, but took to flight when they saw our strength. / We emerged onto the hill in pursuit of the Hazaras, tracking them down like deer, across hill and dale. / We shot them down and divided the plundered herds and flocks. / We made captive the people of the defeated Turcoman Hazaras. / The menfolk we captured and their women and children we took prisoner.

I too rounded up a few of the Hazaras' sheep, which I turned over to Yarak Taghayï before I proceeded to the front. Across peaks and valleys we drove the Hazaras' horses and sheep to Temür Beg's Langar[174] where we camped. Fourteen or fifteen of the Turcoman Hazara renegades and bandit chiefs had been captured, and it was my plan, when we had camped, to execute them with various tortures to serve as examples to all bandits and renegades. Along the way, however, they encountered Qasim Beg, [197] who, with misplaced clemency, freed them.

Brackish earth does not yield hyacinths, so waste not seeds of hope therein. / Doing good to the evil is as bad as doing evil to the good.[175]

Nonetheless, he had compassion and the prisoners were set free.

While raiding these very Turcoman Hazaras it was heard that Muhammad-Husayn Mirza Dughlat, Sultan-Sanjar Barlas, and a band of men had won over the Moghuls who had stayed in Kabul, set up Mirza Khan as padishah, and laid siege to Kabul. They had also spread a rumor among the people that Badi'uzzaman Mirza and Muzaffar Mirza were holding me, the padishah, prisoner and had sent me to Herat's Ikhtiyaruddin Fortress, which is now known as Ala Qorghan.[176] In command of the Kabul fortress were Mulla Baba of Pishagar, Khalifa, Muhibb-Ali Qorchï, Ahmad Yusuf, and Ahmad Qasim. They did a good job of making fast and defending the fortress.

BABUR PROCEEDS TO KABUL

From Temür Beg's Langar we wrote to the begs in Kabul a description of how we had come to this place and sent the letter from Toqpay with Qasim Beg's servant, Muhammad of Andizhan. It was then decided that we would go through the Ghorband defile and attack. The sign would be that we would light a fire as soon as we had crossed Manar Mountain. "You too light a large fire on top of the old pavilion in the citadel (which is now the treasury) so that we may know that you know we are coming. [197b] As we come from this direction, you emerge from inside and make no mistake about it." After ensuring that Muhammad of Andizhan understood these words, I sent him off.

The next morning we mounted at the Langar and rode to opposite Ushturshahr. From there we got an early start and around midday reached the Ghorband defile, where we dismounted at the bridge. After watering the horses and letting them rest, we rode around noon. We saw no snow as far as Tutqavul, but the farther we got from Tutqavul the deeper the snow was. Rarely in our lives had we experienced such cold as we did between Zamma Yakhshï and Manar.

Ahmad Yasavul and Qara Ahmad Yurtchï were also sent to the begs in Kabul with the following message: "We are coming as planned. Be aware and be brave." After crossing Manar Mountain and dismounting in the foothills, we could not stand the cold any longer and had to light a fire. Although it was no time to be doing so, the cold was unbearable without it. Just before the break of dawn we rode from the foothills. Between Manar and Kabul the snow was up to the horses' knees and had become hard. Anyone who left the path had rough going. We had to advance the whole distance single file, and for this reason we made it to Kabul undiscovered just after sunup. [198] A little before we reached Bibi Mahruy we knew from a large fire in the citadel that they were aware of our presence.

THE REBELS ARE ATTACKED IN KABUL

When we approached the Sayyid Qasim bridge, the men of the right wing were sent with Sherim Taghayï to the Mulla Baba Bridge. We took the Baba Luli road with the left wing and center. At that time there was a small garden where Khalifa's garden stands today, rather like a *langar*, that had been made by Ulughbeg Mirza. Although it no longer had trees and shrubs, the surrounding wall still stood. Mirza Khan was stopping there. Muhammad-Husayn Mirza was in the Bagh-i-Bihisht, also made by Ulughbeg Mirza. I had reached the cemetery on the side of the Mulla Baba garden lane when those who had gone raced forward and were forced back to join us. Four men had gone ahead and entered Mirza Khan's quarters: Sayyid Qasim Eshik-aqa, Qambar-Ali son of Qasim Beg, the Moghul Sher-Qulï Qaravul, and Sultan-Ahmad Moghul from Sher-Qulï's group. They had marched fearlessly right into Mirza Khan's quarters and created an uproar, causing Mirza Khan to jump on a horse and flee. Abu'l-Hasan Qorchï's brother Muhammad Husayn had become a servant of Mirza Khan. [198b] He had slashed at Sher-Qulï, had him down, and was about to cut his head off when Sher-Qulï escaped. The four men, with sword and arrow wounds, rejoined us in the above-mentioned place.

In the narrow lane the horsemen crowded together, unable to go forward or backward. I said to the warriors near me, "Dismount and fight!" Dost Nasir, Khwaja Muhammad-Ali Kitabdar, Baba Sherzad, Shah Mahmud, and a few others dismounted and started shooting to force the enemy to flee.

We were waiting for the men from the fortress, but in the midst of battle they could not get to us; after forcing the enemy back, however, they managed to cut their way through, one by one and two by two. I was on the verge of entering the garden where Mirza Khan was staying when one of the men from the fortress, Ahmad Yusuf the son of Sayyid Yusuf, came. Together we entered the garden. I saw that Mirza Khan was not there—he had flown the coop. I ran back with Ahmad Yusuf on my heels. Dost Sarpuli, a foot soldier who had been promoted for bravery to the rank of castellan and stationed in Kabul, came through the garden gate with a naked sword in his hand, headed straight for me. I was wearing my armor, but I had not fastened the plates. [199] I did not have my helmet on either. I kept calling out, "Hey, Dost! Hey, Dost!" Ahmad Yusuf was also shouting. He did not recognize me—either because my face had been burned by the cold and snow, or because the battle caused so much confusion—in any case he made a fearless swipe at my unprotected arm with his sword. Thank God it did not cut me at all.

If the sword of the world moves from its place, it will sever no vein unless God wills.

I had recited the following prayer, and it was through its efficacy that God warded off this harm and averted the catastrophe that was headed straight for me. The prayer is this:

In the name of God, the compassionate, the merciful. O God, thou art my lord. There is no god but thou. In thee, lord of the great throne, have I put my trust. What God wills comes to be, and what God wills not is not. There is no might or strength save through God the exalted, the mighty. I know that God is of all things capable, that he has encompassed everything with his knowledge, and that he has reckoned the number of everything. O God, I take refuge with thee from the evil of mine own soul and from the evil of others and from the evil of every evil thing and from the evil of every beast, which thou holdest by the forelock. Thou art the lord of the great throne.

I emerged from there and went to the Bagh-i-Bihisht, where Muhammad-Husayn Mirza was staying. He had fled and gone into hiding. In the breach of the garden wall of Muhammad-Husayn Mirza's quarters stood seven or eight men armed with bows and arrows. I spurred my horse toward them. [199b] Unable to make a stand, they escaped. As I came upon them I swiped one of them with my sword. The way he went rolling made me think his head had been knocked off. I passed on. The person I had lobbed with my sword turned out to be Mirza Khan's kükäldash, Tüläk Kükäldash. The blow must have landed on his back.

When I reached the gateway to the quarters inhabited by Muhammad-Husayn Mirza, on the roof was a Moghul I recognized, for he had been my servant. He had an arrow drawn in his bow aimed at me. From all directions men came running and shouting, "Hey! It's the padishah!" He turned his arrow away, let it go, and ran. It was too late to be shooting arrows anyway: the mirza's officers had fled, the mirza had been captured. On whose behalf was he going to shoot?

To that very place Sultan-Sanjar Barlas was brought, bound at the neck. (This Sultan-Sanjar Barlas had been patronized and favored with the Nangarhar district, but during this disturbance he had joined those others.) Greatly agitated, he shouted, "Hey! What have I done wrong?"

"Can there be any greater wrong than your being one of the ringleaders in cahoots with these people?" I replied. However, since he was the nephew of Shah Begim, my uncle the khan's mother, I gave the order, "Do not place him so dishonorably on the ground. There is no death sentence."

Upon leaving there I sent Ahmad Qasim Kohbur, one of the begs from the fortress, [200] with a contingent of warriors in pursuit of Mirza Khan.

Shah Begim and Mihr Nigar Khanïm had had their tents pitched and were staying beside the Bagh-i-Bihisht, where I went to see them. The inhabitants and rabble of the city had taken clubs and were attacking, holding up people in corners and crannies and plundering their belongings. I stationed men to beat off all these people and drive them away. Shah Begim and Khanïm were sitting together in a tent. I dismounted at the usual distance and came forward, as politely as ever, to have an interview with them. Shah Begim and Khanïm were agitated, upset, and embarrassed in the extreme. Neither could they make reasonable excuses nor were they able to get through the pleasantries of affectionate conversation. I would not have expected it of them. However impolite this group may have been, it was not as though they were people who would not listen to a begim or a khanïm. Mirza Khan was Shah Begim's own grandson and was with her day and night. If she had not become a party to these people, she would not have had to give Mirza Khan up and could have kept him with her. The few times I had been separated from my throne, kingdom, liege men, and servants by the adverse vicissitudes of fortune and fate [200b] and had taken refuge with them—and my mother too—we had not seen the least favor or affection from them. My "little brother" Mirza Khan and his mother Sultan Nigar Khanïm had rich, cultivated lands. My mother and I—not to speak of lands—were unable to possess a single village or a few pair of oxen. Was my mother not the daughter of Yunus Khan, and was I not his grandson?

Whenever any of this clan came to me when I was enjoying good fortune, insofar as I could I recognized the obligation of kinship and did well by them. For example, when Shah Begim came, I assigned her Paghman, one of the best places in Kabul. I failed in no way in filial duty and service to her. Sultan Sa'id Khan, the khan of Kashghar, came to me with five or six naked foot soldiers. I regarded him as one of my own younger brothers and gave him the district of Mandrawar in Laghman. When Shah Isma'il captured Shaybani Khan in Merv, when I crossed the Oxus to Konduz, and the people of Andizhan, looking toward me, chased out some of their prefects, made fast some localities, and sent a messenger to me, I turned over all my retainers to Sultan Sa'id Khan, gave him reinforcements, granted him the living from the province of Andizhan, and sent him forth as khan. Up to this very date none of that clan who has come to me has been treated with anything but what is due a kinsman—witness Chïn Temür Sultan, Esän Temür Sultan, Tokhta Sultan, [201] and Baba Sultan,[177] who are with me at this date. I have treated them all better and shown them more favor than my own flesh and blood.

I have not written all this to complain: I have simply written the truth. I do not intend by what I have written to compliment myself: I have simply set down exactly what happened. Since I have made it a point in this history to write the truth of every matter and to set down no more than the reality of every event, as a consequence I have reported every good and evil I have seen of father and brother and set down the actuality of every fault and virtue of relative and stranger. May the reader excuse me; may the listener take me not to task.

I left that place and went to the garden where Mirza Khan had been staying. Notices of victory were sent to the various provinces and to the tribes and clans. After that I rode to the citadel.

THE REBELS ARE ARRESTED

Muhammad-Husayn Mirza had run away in fear to Khanïm's *töshäkkhana*[178] and wrapped himself up in a mattress sack. We assigned Mirim Diwan and some others from the fortress to search the tents, find Muhammad-Husayn Mirza, and bring him in. When Mirim Diwan reached Khanïm's gate, he spoke rather rudely [201b] but in any case found Muhammad-Husayn Mirza in the töshäkkhana and brought him to me in the citadel. I rose in his honor, as I always had in the past, and did not take him to task very harshly. But if I had had him ripped to pieces for undertaking such heinous and shameful actions and for initiating and engaging in such mutiny and treason, it would have been proper. He deserved to die under torture. However, since we had family connections, his sons and daughters being my own aunt Khub Nigar Khanïm's children, I kept these claims in mind and let him go free. He was given leave to go to Khurasan. This cowardly ingrate completely forgot all my goodness toward him in sparing his life and instead spread gossip and complaints of me to Wormwood Khan. Well, it wasn't long before Wormwood put him to death and gave him his just deserts.

> Entrust to fate him who does you ill, for fate is a vengeful servant of yours.

Ahmad Qasim Kohbur and the few other warriors who had been sent in pursuit of Mirza Khan caught up with him in the hills of Qargha Yaylagh. He was unable to flee; indeed, he did not have the strength or the audacity to wave his hand. They seized him and brought him in [202] to me while I was seated in the portico on the northeastern side of the old divankhana. "Come," I said, "let us see each other." In his confusion he stumbled twice by the time he knelt and came forward. After our interview I had him sit beside me to give him courage. I had sherbet brought; to lessen his fear I tasted the sherbet first, then offered it to him.

Since the soldiers, civilians, Moghuls, and Chaghatays who had joined Mirza Khan were fearful and anxious, as a precaution we ordered him to stay in his elder sister's house for a few days. Since these people and tribes were still hesitant, however, I saw that it was not politic for Mirza Khan to remain in Kabul and gave him leave a few days later to go to Khurasan.

EXCURSION TO KOH DAMAN

After dismissing them we went to the Baran, Chash Töpä, and the Gulbahar hills. In the spring the plains of the Baran, the plateau of Chash Töpä, and the hills of Gulbahar are extremely beautiful. Compared to other places in the province of Kabul the greenery there is luxurious. All sorts of tulips blossom. Once I had the types of tulip counted, and there turned out to be thirty or forty varieties. As a line of poetry describing these places says:

With its greenery and flowers, Kabul is paradise in the spring, / Especially the Baran plain and Gulbahar at this season.

While on this excursion I completed this ghazal:

My heart is steeped in blood like a rosebud—[202b] / Even if there were a hundred thousand springs, what possibility would there be of its opening?

Truly there are few places equal to these for springtime excursions, hawking, and shooting birds, as was mentioned briefly in the descriptions of Kabul and Ghazni.[179]

NASIR MIRZA IS DRIVEN
FROM BADAKHSHAN

This same year, the Badakhshan begs Muhammad Qorchï, Mubarakshah, Zubayr, and Jahangir were not merely angered by the treatment they received from Nasir Mirza and his henchmen but were actually forced into rebellion. They joined forces, gathered and arrayed their foot soldiers and horsemen on the Kokcha River plain near Yaftal and Ragh, and proceeded through the hills to the vicinity of Khamchan.

The mirza and his inexperienced begs met them unstrategically and incautiously and enjoined battle in the hills. The battleground was uneven and the Badakhshani foot soldiers were many. When they charged on horseback once or twice, the Badakhshanis held their ground and then counterattacked to drive back their opponents, who were unable to resist and ran away. The Badakhshanis, having defeated Nasir Mirza, pillaged and plundered his followers and dependents who were there.

Nasir Mirza and his comrades, beaten and plundered, went through Ishkamish and Nahrin to Kilagay, then up the Red River to the Ao Dara road and through the Shibartu Pass. Finally he and seventy or eighty retainers and servants, beaten and stripped bare, hungry and naked, arrived in Kabul.

What an amazingly omnipotent God he is! Two or three years previously Nasir Mirza had driven out all the tribes and clans and left Kabul in rebellion [203] for Badakhshan, where he had gone about fortifying valleys and fortresses, who knows with what all in mind. Now he was humbled by his past deeds, ashamed of the way he had gone off, and distraught. I, for my part, did not berate him in the slightest but received him warmly and soothed his distress.

EVENTS OF THE YEAR 913
(1507-8)[180]

We rode out of Kabul intending to raid the Ghilzai, but when we stopped at Sardeh, word was received that some Mohmands[181] were camped open to attack at Mest and Sehgana, about a league away from Sardeh. The begs and warriors were of the opinion that we should raid them. I said, "Is this right? With what intention should we ride? Should we raid our own subjects and return without reaching our goal? This is impossible!"

From Sardeh we rode through the Katawaz plain in the dark of night. Pitch black, across absolutely flat ground, neither mountain or hill nor road or track visible—no one could guide us. Finally I took the lead. Once or twice I had been through this region, and based on that I led my men, keeping the North Star to my right. Thank God, we came to the Ulabatu and Qayaqtu rivers to the place where the Ghilzai were camped, where Khwaja Isma'il's tomb is,[182] where the road crosses the river. Stopping along the bank, [203b] we slept a bit and the horses rested before setting out at dawn. The sun was up when we emerged from the hills and valleys into the plain. It was a good league away from the place where the Ghilzai were camped. From there we could see something, either the outline of the Ghilzai themselves or the smoke of their campfires. The soldiers galloped off impetuously.[183] Riding for a league or two, I managed to stop them by shooting arrows at men and horses, but it is very difficult to contain an army of five or six thousand galloping raiders. Thank God they stopped. Proceeding along the road about a league more we could see the amassed Afghans, and the raid was on. Many sheep were taken, more so, in fact, than in any other assault. After bringing the animals back with us and camping, bands of Afghans streamed into the plain from all directions to provoke a fight. Some of the begs and ichkis went against one of the bands and made a clean sweep, killing every one of them. Nasir Mirza rode against another band and killed them all. A tower of dead Afghan skulls was erected. The infantryman Dost the Castellan, whose name has been mentioned,[184] was shot in the foot and died after returning to Kabul.

Marching from Khwaja Isma'il we stopped again at the Ulabatu. Some of the begs and ichkis were ordered to tend to the taking of the fifth of the booty. As a favor to Qasim Beg and some others we did not take all our share. [204] The fifth that was recorded amounted to sixteen thousand sheep, from a total of eighty thousand. Taking into consideration those that were lost and those given as favors, the whole amount must have been at least a lac of sheep.[185]

A HUNT

Riding out early one day from that camp we made a hunting circle in the Katawaz plain around many wild asses and deer. There are always many fat wild asses and deer there. I galloped off after a wild ass and shot an arrow at it as I got near. I shot another arrow too, but the wounds were not enough to fell the animal although they did slow it down. I spurred my horse on. As I got closer I drew my sword and slashed the deer just behind its ears. The blade cut through down to its windpipe, whereupon the animal flipped over and its hind legs hit my stirrup. My aim was superb. The ass was incredibly fat, with the thickness on its ribs only a bit less than a span. Sherim Taghayï and those who had seen game in Moghulistan were amazed and said, "We have seldom seen such fat animals even in Moghulistan." That day I shot another wild ass too. Most of the wild asses and deer felled in that hunt were the same but none was as plump as the one I killed. After the hunt we rode back to Kabul.

SHAYBANI KHAN MOVES
AGAINST KHURASAN

At the end of the previous year Wormwood Khan had set out from Samarkand with his army to take Khurasan. [204b] That vile ingrate Shah Mansur Bakhshï, that pederast's whore who was in Andkhui, sent messengers to Wormwood Khan to hasten his march. When Wormwood arrived in Andkhui this catamite, relying on the fact that it was he who had sent word to the Uzbek, stuck a plume in his turban and went out with gifts and presents. The unruly Uzbeks swarmed over him from all directions and ripped this catamite, his retinue, and his gifts and presents to shreds.

Badiʿuzzaman Mirza, Muzaffar Mirza, Muhammad Burunduq Barlas, and Zu'n-Nun Arghun were all camped with their forces in Baba Khaki, neither intent upon battle nor decided upon fortifying the fortress in Herat. Unclear about what action to take, they sat in confusion. Muhammad Burunduq Beg was a man who knew the score. He said, "Let Muzaffar Mirza and me go to the Herat fortress. Let Badiʿuzzaman Mirza and Zu'n-Nun Beg go to the mountains around Herat, and let them attach to themselves Sultan-Ali Arghun from Seistan, and Shah Beg and Muqim and their forces from Zamin Dawar. Then let them collect what Hazara and Negüdäri forces there are and ride out ready for battle. The enemy will find it difficult to reach the mountain and will not be able to attack the fortress for fear of the forces outside." He spoke well, and his plan was well thought out. [205]

Although Zu'n-Nun Arghun was brave, he was stingy and avaricious in addition to being impractical and rather stupid and crazy. At that time, when the two brothers were ruling jointly in Herat, he was the lord of Badiʿuzzaman Mirza's gate, as has been mentioned.[186] He was so avaricious that he could not abide to have Muhammad Burunduq stay in the city, for he himself had plans to stay there, but in no way could he make himself Muhammad Burunduq's equal. Nothing is more indicative of his stupidity and craziness than that he degraded himself by swallowing the flattery of deceitful and ambitious men. The details are as follows. While he was in power in Herat, a few shaykhs and mullas came to him and said, "We are in touch with the Qutb.[187] You have been named Lion of God and you will conquer the

Uzbek." He believed it and, putting his shawl around his neck, made declarations of thanks. For the same reasons Muhammad Burunduq's good advice was not followed, and the fortress was not made fast, battle weapons were not made ready, reconnoiterers and scouts were not sent to give information on the enemy's advance, and the army was not adequately prepared for battle should the enemy have approached.

SHAYBANI KHAN TAKES HERAT

Wormwood Khan had crossed the Murghab in the month of Muharram [May–June 1507] and approached the vicinity of Sirkay. [205b] When the Heratis learned of it, they went to pieces and were unable to do anything—they could not gather their men or array their forces. Instead each set out on his own. Zu'n-Nun Arghun, taken in by the above-mentioned flattery, took up a stand with some hundred, 150 men at Kara Robat in the face of forty to fifty thousand Uzbeks. When this massive force moved in they swept Zu'n-Nun's men aside, captured him, and cut off his head.

The princes' mothers, sisters, wives, and treasuries were in the Ikhtiyaruddin Fortress, or Ala Qorghan. The princes reached the city late at night, and by midnight they had put their horses to rest and gone to sleep. At dawn they moved out. They could give no thought to fortifying the fortress. At such a juncture they left their mothers, sisters, wives, and children to be taken prisoner by the Uzbeks and fled.

Sultan-Husayn Mirza's wives, with Payanda Sultan Begim and Khadija Begim at the head, as well as Badi'uzzaman Mirza and Muzaffar Mirza's wives and small children and the princes' treasuries and workshops were all inside the Ala Qorghan. They had not fortified the fortress adequately, nor had the reinforcements for the fortress arrived. Mazid Beg's brother Ashiq-Muhammad Arghun escaped from the army on foot and entered the fortress. [206] Amir Umar's son Ali-Khan, Shaykh-Muhammad Abdullah Bökäül, Mirza Beg Kaykhusrawi, and Miraki Kor Diwan were also there.

Two or three days after Wormwood Khan arrived, the shaykhu'l-islam and the elders of the city made terms and went out with the keys to the fortress. Ashiq-Muhammad held the fort for sixteen or seventeen days. A mine was laid from outside near the horse market and lit, and a tower was blown up. Thereupon the people inside the fort lost heart and, unable to hold it any longer, gave themselves up.

When Wormwood Khan took Herat, he maltreated the princes' wives and children. Not only with them but also with all the people, even rustics and insignificant little people, he left behind a bad name for his love of this fleeting world. First among his improper deeds in Herat was that for the sake of this filthy world he turned over Khadija Begim to Shah Mansur Bakhshi's wife for safekeeping and let her be tormented in all sorts of ways. He had the Moghul Abdul-Wahhab hold a saintly person like Shaykh Puran prisoner, and each of Shaykh Puran's sons was handed to a different person. All the poets and literati were put in Mulla Banna'i's charge.[188] In this connection the following occasional piece became famous among the wits of Khurasan:

> Except for Abdullah the donkey's prick no poet today has seen the face of gold. / Banna'i craves gold from poets: perhaps he will get the donkey's prick. [206b]

As soon as Wormwood Khan seized Herat he married Muzaffar Mirza's wife, Khanzada Khanïm, without waiting for the prescribed interval to elapse.[189] His illiteracy notwithstanding, he presumed to give lessons in Koranic interpretation to Qazi Ikhtiyar and Muhammad Mir Yusuf, who were among Herat's renowned and talented mullas. To the calligraphy of Sultan-Ali Mashhadi and the painting of Bihzad he took his pen and made corrections.[190] Moreover, every few days he would compose insipid poetry and have it recited from the pulpit and hung in the marketplace to receive accolades from the populace. He rose with the dawn and never neglected the five daily prayers, and he knew how to recite the Koran well, but he nonetheless did and said a multitude of stupid, imbecilic, audacious, and heathenish things.

Ten or fifteen days after taking Herat, Wormwood Khan left the Kahdistan meadow for Pul-i-Salar, put his nephews Temür Sultan and Ubayd Sultan in charge of the army, and sent them against Abu'l-Muhsin Mirza and Kipik Mirza, who were sitting vulnerable in Mashhad. Once they thought of fortifying Kalat; another time they heard that the Uzbek army was approaching and were going to set out against Wormwood Khan by a different route. These were excellent plans, but while they were sitting there unable to agree on any concerted action, Temür Sultan and Ubayd Sultan's army poured down on them. The princes arrayed their forces and went out to battle. Abu'l-Muhsin [207] Mirza was soon overcome and routed. Kipik Mirza attacked his elder brother's foe with a few men: he too was carried off, and so both brothers were felled. When the two brothers were brought together, they embraced, kissed each other, and made their farewells. Abu'l-Muhsin Mirza showed a lack of courage, but Kipik Mirza was not affected in the slightest. Both princes' heads were sent to Wormwood Khan in Pul-i-Salar.

At this time Shah Beg and his brother Muhammad Muqim, in trepidation over Wormwood Khan, were constantly sending emissaries and letters to make a display of their amity and friendship. Muqim himself explicitly invited me in one of his letters. Certainly it was not seemly for us to stand by and look on while the Uzbeks were completely overrunning the province. With such emissaries and letters being sent inviting us, there remained little doubt that they would come to pay homage to me. Upon consultation with all the begs and counselors it was decided to mount the army and, after joining these Arghun begs,[191] to reach a decision to proceed against Khurasan as they saw fit. With this intention we set out for Kandahar.

As had been mentioned,[192] Habiba Sultan Begim, whom I called Yengä, had brought her daughter, Ma'suma Sultan Begim, as had been decided in Herat. [207b] We met in Ghazni. With them came Khusraw Kükäldash, Sultan-Qulï Chanaq, and Gadai Bilal, who had escaped from Herat and been with Ibn-i-Husayn Mirza. From there they went to Abu'l-Muhsin Mirza. Unable to remain with him, they escorted the ladies to us.

When we reached Qalat, we discovered a lot of Indian merchants who must have come to Qalat to trade and were unable to escape. When the army came upon them, most were of the opinion that in time of rebellion those who came to outlaw areas should be plundered. I refused to give my sanction, saying, "What fault is it of the merchants? If we see God's pleasure in forgoing such meager profits, in return God will grant us great benefits, just as only a few days ago while we were riding to storm the Ghilzai, most of you were of the opinion that we should attack the Mohmand Afghans who were a league away with their flocks, herds, and kinfolk. For this same reason I withheld my consent, and the next morning God granted the soldiers more of the rebel Afghans', that is, the Ghilzais', sheep than had ever fallen their lot before in any raid." As we camped on the other side of Qalat, we took something from each of the merchants as a "gift."

After we passed through Qalat, Mirza Khan, who had been dismissed to Khurasan after I took Kabul, and Abdul-Razzaq Mirza, who had remained behind when I left Khurasan, [208] fled from Kandahar and came to me. With these mirzas came the mother of Pir-Muhammad Mirza, son of Jahangir Mirza and grandson of Bahar Mirza, to pay homage to me.

Men and letters were sent to Shah Beg and Muqim to say, "We have come as you requested. A foreign invader like the Uzbek has taken Khurasan. Come, let us agree on a plan in our best interests." They sent back impertinent, impolite replies, denying that they had invited us. One of their rude acts was that on the back of the letter Shah Beg wrote to me, he put his seal in the middle of the page, the spot where begs normally place their seal when writing to other begs, or when superior begs write to inferior ones. If he had not been so imprudent, the conflict would not have gone so far, as the line says:

A mere word can stir up strife that will bring down an ancient line.

It was through such spite and rudeness that they ruined many families and destroyed thirty to forty years of accumulated wealth.

One day while in the vicinity of Shahr-i-Safa a false alarm broke out in camp. All the men armed themselves and got to horse. I was taking a bath at the time. [208b] The begs were upset, and when I was finished I got on my horse. Since it was only a false alarm things quieted down after a time.

We proceeded march by march until we camped at the mouth of a valley. Here too we made an attempt to hold discussions with the Arghuns, but they paid no attention and kept up their obstinate, haughty stance. Our friends who knew the lay of the land reported that since the source of the waterways that flow to Kandahar was in the direction of Baba Husayn Abdal and Khalishak, we should head to that area and destroy[193] the waterways. With this decided, the next morning we armed ourselves, arrayed the right and left wings, and marched to Khalishak.

THE BATTLE OF KANDAHAR

Shah Beg and Muqim had set up an awning in front of the mountain outcropping where I later had a building carved from the rock, and there they sat. Muqim's men hastened to come rather near among the trees. All by himself Tufan Arghun, who had run away and come to us while we were in Shahr-i-Safa, sneaked up near the Arghuns' battle lines. A man named Ishqullah was coming toward him with a detachment of seven or eight men. Ishqullah was somewhat ahead of the others. Alone Tufan Arghun faced him, they exchanged sword blows, and Tufan unhorsed his opponent, cut off his head, and brought it while I was passing Sang-i-Lakhshak. We took it as a good omen. Since this place was in the midst of the suburbs and orchards, we did not think it wise to fight here and so were skirting the hills. We had chosen a place in a meadow on the Kandahar side of the waterway in front of Khalishak [209] and were dismounting when Sher-Qulï Qaravul rushed in to report that the foe was upon us in full battle array.

On our march from Qalat the soldiers had suffered greatly from hunger. As soon as we reached the vicinity of Khalishak most of the men had dispersed up and down to look for sheep and cattle and grain and fodder. We jumped on our horses to attack without a thought for gathering the army. In toto the men we had at the time were nearly two thousand, but, as I have just said, when we made camp, many had gone hither and yon. When the battle broke out they were unable to rejoin us, so our men who participated in the battle were around a thousand in number. Although our men were few, I had arranged them in an excellent formation. Never before had I made such a good battle array. Under my immediate command I had a select band of warriors upon whom I knew I could depend, and I had posted them in groups of ten and fifty under commanders of ten and fifty. Each group had its place to stand in the right and left wings and knew what they were to do during battle. As soon as the right wing, left wing, right flank, left flank, right side and left side, right and left, were mounted for battle, the army moved out, each in its proper place, without the trouble of arraying them and without the necessity of tovachïs. [209b]

BATTLE ARRAY

Although "right wing," "right arm," "right flank," and "right" all basically mean the same, I use them to distinguish different facets. For example, in the array the right and left wings, which are called *baranghar* and *javanghar,* are not included in the center, which we call *qol.* Here, therefore, those separate units are called "right wing" and "left wing" exclusively. Then, the center, which is a unit all by itself, has its own right and left, which will be called "right arm" and "left arm" to distinguish them. Also within the center, the right and left of the royal contingent are called "right flank" and "left flank." Then, within the royal contingent are the warriors who form the *boy*—in Turkish a solitary unit is called boy, but that is not the meaning I am using here. I use it to mean "close." Their right and left are called simply "right" and "left."

Vanguard. Nasir Mirza, Sayyid Qasim Eshik-aqa, Muhibb-Ali Qorchï, Baba-oghlï, Allahverän the Turcoman, Sher-Qulï Qaravul Moghul and his brothers, and Muhammad-Ali.

Right wing. Mirza Khan, Sherim Taghayï, Yarak Taghayï and his brothers, Chalma Moghul, Ayyub Beg, Muhammad Beg, Ibrahim Beg, Ali Sayyid Moghul with his Moghuls, Sultan-Ali Chuhra, Khudabakhsh, and Abu'l-Muhsin and his brothers.

Left wing. Abdul-Razzaq Mirza, Qasim Beg, Tengriberdi, Qambar-Ali, Ahmad Elchi Buqa, Ghuri Barlas, Sayyid-Husayn Akbar, and Mir Shah Qauchin.

Center to my right. Qasim Kükäldash, Khusraw Kükäldash, Sultan-Muhammad Dulday, Shah-Mahmud Parvanachï, Qul-Bayazid Bökäül, [210] and Kamal Sharbatchï.

Center to my left. Khwaja Muhammad-Ali, Dost Nasir, Mirim Nasir, Baba Sherzad, Khan-Qulï, Wali Khizanachï, Qutlugh-Qadam Qaravul, Maqsud Suchï, and Baba Shaykh. All in the center were ichkis, with no great begs. None of those mentioned had yet been promoted to the rank of beg.

Boy. Sher Beg, Hatim Qorbegi, Keyik Qul Baba, Abu'l-Hasan Qorchï, and of the Moghuls Urus Ali, Sayyid Darwesh Ali, Sayyid Khoshkeldi, Chalma Dostkeldi, Chalma Yaghchï, Damachï Hindi, and the Turcomans Mansur, Rustam-Ali and his brothers, Shahnazar and Sevindük.

The enemy was divided into two contingents, one under Shah-Shuja' Arghun, who will be called Shah Beg from now on, and the other under his younger brother, Muqim. The Arghun masses were estimated at six to seven thousand. That they were at least four to five thousand armed men there was no doubt.

Center and right wing faced each other. Muqim faced the left wing. His forces may have been somewhat fewer than those of his elder brother, and he launched a hard attack on our left wing, which was under Qasim Beg. Before the fighting began two or three men came from Qasim Beg to request reinforcements. Since our own foe was pressing down on us, we could not spare anyone. Without hesitation we charged the enemy. When the arrows started flying, [210b] our vanguard was forced back upon the center. When we advanced with a volley of arrows, they wasted no time in returning the round as though to make a stand. Someone in front of me called out to his men as he dismounted, planning to shoot, but he was unable to resist our rapid charge and jumped back on his horse and rode away. This man who had dismounted turned out to be none other than Shah Beg himself. During the battle Piri Beg the Turcoman and his four or five brothers took their turbans in their hands, abandoned the rebels, and joined us. (This Piri Beg is one of those Turcomans who had come under Abdul-Baqi Mirza and Murad Beg Bayïndïr when Shah Isma'il conquered the Bayïndïr sultans and gained control of Iraq.)[194]

Our right wing had already overrun the enemy: those at the tip speared their way as far as the place where I have since had a garden made. Our left wing went cascading into the great watercourse far, far downriver from Baba Hasan Abdal. Muqim was directly opposite the men of the left wing who, all told, were many fewer than their opponent Muqim. Thank God that between the foe and the left wing three or four main irrigation canals were directed toward Kandahar and the villages. They held the ford and kept the enemy from crossing. The men of the left wing, despite their small number, held their ground well.[211] Qambar-Ali and Tengriberdi exchanged sword blows right in the water with Halvachï Tarkhan from the Arghun side. Qambar-Ali was wounded. Qasim Beg was struck in the forehead by an arrow. Ghuri Barlas was struck above the eyebrow with an arrow, which came out above his cheek.

At this point, having forced our opponents to take flight, we went from the irrigation canals toward an outcropping of Murghan Mountain. While we were crossing the canals a man on a gray horse at the base of the mountain seemed to be hesitating whether to come our way or go the other way. Finally he went off in one direction. I thought it looked like Shah Beg, and it probably was.

Having routed their foes, all the soldiers went off in pursuit. Eleven men, of whom Abdullah Kitabdar was one, remained with me. Muqim was still holding his ground and fighting. Disregarding how few our men were, and relying upon God, we had the drums sounded and headed toward the foe.

God grants victory both to the many and to the few: no one has might in the divine court.

"Many a small band has defeated a large one with God's permission."[195] Hearing the sound of our drums and realizing that we were charging in his direction, the enemy abandoned his ground and took flight, thank God. After defeating our foe we went to Kandahar and camped in Farrukhzad's garden, no trace of which now remains. [211b]

BABUR ENTERS KANDAHAR

When Shah Beg and Muqim fled, they were unable to enter the Kandahar fortress. Shah Beg went to Shal and Mastung, and Muqim toward Zamin Dawar. No one was left to man the fortress. Ahmad Ali Tarkhan, one of Qulï Beg Arghun's brothers, was inside, together with some others whose loyalty to me was known. During deliberations they pleaded for their brothers' lives, and as a favor to them their request was granted. They opened the Mashur Gate but, seeing the unruliness of the soldiers, would not open the other fortress gates. Sherim Beg and Yarim Beg were stationed at the one opened gate. I myself entered with the ichkis I had with me and ordered one or two of the unruly ones executed to set an example.

First I came upon Muqim's treasury in the outer fortress. Abdul-Razzaq Mirza got there before me. He was granted a few items from the treasury as a favor, and then Dost Nasir Beg, Qul-Bayazid Beg Bökäül, and Muhammad Bakhshï, one of the bakhshïs, were assigned to the treasury. From there I went to the citadel. Khwaja Muhammad Ali, Shah Mahmud, and Taghayï Shah Bakhshï from the bakhshïs were assigned to Shah Beg's treasury. Mirim Nasir and Maqsud Suchï were sent to the house of Zu'n-Nun's divan Mir Jan, and he was put in Nasir Mirza's custody. Shaykh Abu-Sa'id Tarkhan was turned over to Mirza Khan's custody. [...][196] was put into Abdul-Razzaq's custody. [212]

Never had so much silver coin been seen in those countries. In fact, nobody had heard of anyone who had seen so much. I spent that night in the citadel. Shah Beg's slave Sambhal was captured and brought in. Although he was then an intimate, he had not yet received much regard. I had him put into custody, but he was not well guarded and was allowed to escape. The next morning I went to Farrukhzad's garden, where the army camp was.

I gave the province of Kandahar to Nasir Mirza. When the treasury was inventoried and loaded to go, Nasir Mirza took a camel train of silver *tankas*[197] from the citadel treasury and kept them. I did not ask for them back but simply gave them to him as a favor.

Leaving there, camp was made in Qushkhana Meadow. While the army was sent on the march, I made an excursion and returned rather late. It was not the same old camp! What had happened to the place I knew? There were beautiful, fine horses, strings and strings of camels and mules with fine textile trappings, brocade and velvet tents and canopies. In every tent there were piles of chests. These two brothers' possessions had been kept in separate treasuries. From each had come chest after chest and bale after bale of textiles and bag after bag and sack after sack of tankas. In every man's tent were spoils of every description. There were many sheep too, but the men paid little attention to them. [212b]

To Qasim Beg, I gave Muqim's retainers in Qalat under Qoch Arghun and Tajuddin Mahmud along with their possessions. Since Qasim Beg was savvy, he did not consider it wise for us to remain in the Kandahar region, and by telling me this over and over and worrying and fretting he got us to move off. As has been mentioned,[198] Kandahar was given to Nasir Mirza, and he was given leave to depart. We set out for Kabul.

There had been no opportunity to distribute the treasury while we were in Kandahar, but we stopped in Karabagh for four or five days and divided it there. It was so difficult to count it had to be weighed in scales and apportioned. All the begs, retainers, and the *tabin*[199] packed up and took away load after load and sack after sack of silver coins for their own pay and the subsistence of the soldiers. With much spoil and booty we returned to Kabul with great honor.

When I arrived in Kabul, I was married to Sultan-Ahmad Mirza's daughter, Ma'suma Sultan Begim, whom I had invited and had brought from Khurasan.

SHAYBANI KHAN LAYS SIEGE
TO KANDAHAR

Six or seven days later one of Nasir Mirza's retainers brought the news that Wormwood Khan had laid siege to Kandahar. It has already been mentioned[200] that Muqim fled to Zamin Dawar. When he got there he went to see Wormwood Khan. Messengers constantly went from Shah Beg too. Instigated by them, [213] Wormwood Khan rode from Herat across the mountain road to attack Kandahar, thinking he would find me there. It was as a precaution against this very eventuality that the experienced Qasim Beg had insisted we move out of Kandahar.

That which a youth sees in the mirror an old man sees in a baked brick. Wormwood arrived and laid siege to Nasir Mirza in Kandahar.

As soon as I heard of this I summoned the begs for consultation. The following topics were discussed. A foreign people like the Uzbeks and an old enemy like Wormwood Khan had overrun the territory held by Temür Beg's descendants. Turk and Chaghatay, in every nook and cranny where they were left, had joined the Uzbeks, some willingly and others unwillingly. Only I was left in Kabul. The foe was powerful, and we were weak. There was neither any possibility for coming to terms nor any scope for resisting. Such potency and strength did not allow us to think of any territory for ourselves, and at this juncture there was no way we could get far enough away from such a mighty foe. We would have to go either to Badakhshan or to Hindustan. It was necessary to decide on a direction.

Qasim Beg and Sherim Beg and their followers were of the opinion that we should go to Badakhshan, where just then the most prominent men were the Badakhshanis Mubarakshah and Zubayr. There were also Jahangir the Turcoman and Muhammad Qorchï, who had driven Nasir Mirza out but had not joined the Uzbeks. [213b] I and some of the ichki begs preferred Hindustan, and so we set out for Laghman.

After the conquest of Kandahar, I had bestowed upon Abdul-Razzaq Mirza the territories of Qalat and Tarnak and stationed him in Qalat. When the Uzbeks laid siege to Kandahar, Abdul-Razzaq Mirza could not remain there, so he abandoned Qalat and came to us just as we were marching out of Kabul. He was stationed there in Kabul.

Since no kings or princes were left in Badakhshan, Mirza Khan was inclined to go there—either because Shah Begim was connected to the ancient kings of Badakhshan or because she approved. He was given leave to go there, and Shah Begim set out with him.[201] My aunt Mihr Nigar Khanïm was also going to go to Badakhshan, although it would have been more proper for her to be with me since we were blood relatives. No matter how I tried to dissuade her, however, she refused to be deterred and went off with the others.

A SECOND HINDUSTAN CAMPAIGN
IS LAUNCHED

In the month of Jumada I [September–October 1507] we set out for Hindustan. Proceeding through Khurd Kabul, we traveled via Robat-i-Surkh and descended into the Quruq Say.

The Afghans between Kabul and Laghman, even in times of peace, are robbers and bandits. For just such an event as this they had been praying but so far had not obtained. Now that they knew I was leaving Kabul for Hindustan, their evil increased tenfold, and even the good ones turned foul. [214] Things got so bad that on the morning we were marching out of Jagdalak, the Afghans between there and Laghman, the Khizr Khel, Shimu Khel, Ghilzai, and Khugiani, took up positions on the northern mountain to block the Jagdalak pass and began to beat their drums and brandish their swords. I mounted and ordered the army to proceed to the mountain from all directions. The men set out at a gallop from every valley and side. The Afghans were not able to hold their stance for even a moment or to fire so much as an arrow before taking flight. I went up the mountain in pursuit of them. An Afghan was running below me. I shot him in the arm. Both he and a few other Afghans were caught and brought in, and several of them were impaled to set an example.

We dismounted before the Adinapur fortress in Nangarhar district. Before that we had given no thought to a place to camp, and neither had we established anywhere to go nor had we assigned any site to stay. Four detachments were sent up and down to bring fresh news. It was late in the autumn, and in the flatlands the rice had mostly been harvested. Those who knew the land reported that the Mil Kafirs upriver in the Alishang district grew much rice, and there was some likelihood that winter supplies of grain for the army could be had there. We rode fast from the Nangarhar glen, crossed at Saygal, and went as far as the Parayin Valley. [214b] The soldiers took a lot of rice from the rice fields at the foot of the mountain. The people ran away, and some Kafirs were killed. A few warriors had been sent to a lookout on a spur of the valley. While they were returning, the Kafirs charged the mountain and began to shoot. They reached Qasim Beg's son-in-law Puran and were hacking at him with an ax and about to take him when some other warriors turned back and, forcing the Kafirs to flee, got him out. We spent one night in the Kafirs' rice fields and then returned to the camp with much grain.

Around this same time, Muqim's daughter Mah Chüchük, who is now married to Shah-Hasan, was affianced to Qasim Kükäldash in Mandrawar district.

Since it was not considered advantageous to go to Hindustan, Mulla Baba Pishaghari and some warriors were dispatched to Kabul. We left the Madrawar area and went to Atar and Siwa, where we stayed a few days. From Atar, I went on an excursion to Kunar and Nur Gul. From Kunar, I rode a raft back to camp. I had not ridden a raft before then, but afterward they became common.

SHAYBANI KHAN WITHDRAWS FROM KANDAHAR

Around that same time, Mulla Mirak Farkati came from Nasir Mirza with the news that Wormwood Khan had taken the Kandahar fortress but withdrew without being able to take the citadel. After Wormwood's retreat Nasir Mirza had, for several reasons, abandoned Kandahar [215] and gone to Ghazni.

A few days later Wormwood Khan returned and took Kandahar by surprise. Unable to hold the outer fortress, the defenders had given it up. Wormwood Khan's men ran mines in several places around the citadel, and several battles were fought. Nasir Mirza was struck in the neck by an arrow. The attackers were close to taking the citadel. In such a precarious situation Khwaja Muhammad Amin, Khwaja Dost Khawand, Muhammad-Ali Piyada, and Shami left the fortress. The defenders had lost hope and were ready to give up when Wormwood Khan initiated a truce and again withdrew. He did this because he sent his womenfolk to Niratu, where it was learned someone had rebelled and taken over the fortress.

Although it was the middle of winter, we took the Badpakh road to Kabul. I ordered the date of this crossing to be carved in a rock at the top of Badpakh. Hafiz Mirak wrote it and Ustad Shah-Muhammad did the carving, but since we were in a hurry it was not done well.

I gave Ghazni to Nasir Mirza. To Abdul-Razzaq Mirza were given the districts of Nangarhar, Mandrawar, Dara-i-Nur, Kunar, and Nur Gul.

Up to this time the descendants of Temür Beg had been called mirza, even when they were ruling. At this time I ordered that they call me padishah.

THE BIRTH OF HUMAYUN, BABUR'S FIRST SON

At the end of this year, on Tuesday evening the fourth of Dhu'l-Qa'da [March 6, 1508], [215b] when the sun was in Pisces, Humayun was born in the Kabul citadel. Mawlana Masnadi the poet composed the chronogram for his birth, *Sultan Humayun Khan*. Another minor poet of Kabul found the chronogram *shah-i firoz-qadr*.[202] Three or four days later he was named Humayun. Five or six days after his birth I went out to the Charbagh and gave a feast in celebration. All the begs, great and small, brought offerings. More silver coins were piled up than had ever been seen before in one place. It was an excellent feast.

EVENTS OF THE YEAR 914

(1508-9)[203]

This spring a band of Mohmand Afghans was raided in the vicinity of
Mukur.

A MOGHUL REBELLION

A few days after returning to camp from the raid, Qoch Beg, Faqir Ali
Karimdad, and Baba Chuhra planned to desert, but their scheme was
discovered and someone was sent to seize them below Istarghij. Bad
reports had been had of them even while Jahangir Mirza was alive. I
ordered them executed in the marketplace. They were taken to the
gate and ropes were put around their necks, but Qasim Beg sent Khalifa to beg for clemency for them. For Qasim Beg's sake I spared their
lives and ordered them thrown in prison instead.

During this period those who were left of Khusrawshah's chief
liege Moghuls from Hissar and Konduz, [216] Chalma Ali, Sayyid
Samka, Sher-Quli, and Eygü Salim, along with the Chaghatay liege
men patronized by Khusrawshah with Sultan-Ali Chuhra and Khudabakhsh at their head, and two or three thousand Turcoman warriors
led by Sevindük and Shahnazar, connived and decided to rebel. They
situated themselves from the Song Qorghan Meadow in front of
Khwaja Rawash to the Chalak Meadow. Abdul-Razzaq Mirza came
from Nangarhar and stationed himself in Deh-i-Afghan.

Muhibb-Ali Qorchï told Khalifa and Mulla Baba once or twice that these men were plotting, and they had indicated it to me; it was too incredible to believe, however, so I paid no attention. Quite late that evening I was seated in the divankhana in the Charbagh when Musa Khwaja and another man rushed up to my side and whispered to me, "It is certain that the Moghuls are going to revolt, but we have not ascertained whether Abdul-Razzaq Mirza will join them or not. They are not decided on rebelling this very night." I pretended to take no notice and went a moment later toward the harem. At that time the ladies were in the private garden and the Bagh-i-Yorunchqa.[204] When I approached, the pages and other menials and night watchmen withdrew. After the people went back [216b] Sarwar the slave and I set off for the city. I had gone as far as the trench and the Iron Gate when Khwaja Muhammad-Ali, coming the opposite way down the market road, met me....[205]

EVENTS OF THE YEAR 925
(1519)[206]

On Monday the first of Muharram [January 3, 1519] a violent earthquake lasting nearly half an hour struck the foot of the Jandol glen.

BAJAUR FORTRESS IS TAKEN

The next morning, while marching from that camp to attack the Bajaur fortress, we dismounted our destination and sent an important man to Bajaur to the Dilazak Afghans to advise the sultan and people of Bajaur to pay homage to us and turn over the fortress. Those ignorant, wretched people refused to accept this advice and sent back ridiculous replies. The army was then ordered to make ready shields and ladders and implements of siege. To accomplish this, we stayed in that camp for a day.

On Thursday the fourth of Muharram [January 6] the soldiers were ordered to arm themselves and get to horse. The left wing was commanded to charge forward, cross the river above the Bajaur fortress where the water entered, and stop on its northern side. The center was not to cross the river but was to stop on the rough, uneven ground to the northwest of the fortress. [217] The right wing was to stop to the west of the lower gate. When the begs of the right wing under Dost Beg's leadership forded the river and stopped, a hundred to 150 foot soldiers charged out of the fortress shooting arrows. The begs, brandishing swords, rushed in, pressed the foot soldiers back against the fortress, and got the bottom of the ramparts. Mulla Abdul-Malik of Khwast, acting like a madman, charged his horse up to the rampart. If the shields and ladders had been ready and it had not been late in the day, that very hour the fortress would have been taken. Mulla Turk Ali and Tengriberdi's liege man crossed swords with the enemy and brought back some heads. To each of them a reward was promised.

Although the Bajauris had never seen firearms, they showed no fear of the sound of matchlocks, and even made fun of the noise with obscene gestures when they heard it. Ustad Ali-Quli shot five men with his that day; Wali Khazin shot two men with his. Other men showed great prowess in firing their guns and performed well, shooting through shield, mail, and *gavsaru*.[207] By evening, perhaps seven, eight, or ten Bajauris had been shot down. [217b] Thereafter it got so that no one could put his head up because there was so much matchlock fire. The order was given: "It is night. Let the army make ready its implements and swarm over the fortress at dawn."

At dawn on Friday the fifth of Muharram [January 7] it was ordered that the battle drums be beaten and every man should charge the fortress from his appointed place. The left wing and center advanced with their shields in place, fixed their ladders, and swarmed up the fortress. The entire left arm of the center, led by Khalifa, Shah-Hasan Arghun, and Ahmad Yusuf, was commanded to reinforce the left wing. Dost Beg's men went to the base of the northeastern tower of the fortress and began undermining and toppling it. Ustad Ali-Quli was there too. That day he fired his matchlock skillfully many times. Twice he fired his ballista. Wali Khazin also brought down a man with his matchlock. From the left arm of the center Malik Ali Qutbi was the first to climb the ladder, and he fought hard for a long time. From the post of the center Muhammad-Ali Jang-Jang and his brother Nawroz each went up a ladder and fought with spear and sword. Baba Yasavul scaled another one and got to work hacking through the roof with an ax. Most of the warriors performed well there, shooting volleys of arrows [218] and preventing the enemy from putting their heads out. Some others, paying no attention to the enemy's battling and not regarding the arrows and stones in the slightest, busied themselves with determination to breach the fort. By breakfast time the northeastern tower, which Dost Beg's men had been undermining, was breached, and the men got up into the tower and drove the enemy out. At that same time the men of the center were the first to get up their ladders and into the fortress. Through God's grace and favor a strong and well-fortified fortress was conquered in two or three hours. Our valiant warriors distinguished themselves heroically and earned great name and fame.

Since the people of Bajaur were rebels, and infidel customs had spread among them, and the religion of Islam had been lost, they were put to massacre and their women and children were taken captive. As there had been no battle on the eastern side, a few men managed to escape from that direction but more than three thousand were put to death.

I entered the conquered fortress to make an inspection. On the walls and in the rooms, streets, and lanes lay corpses in untold numbers. Those who were coming and going had to step over the dead bodies. Upon returning from the investigation we sat in the sultans' house [218b] and gave the province of Bajaur to Khwaja Kalan. Then,

Umar-Shaykh b. Temür Commands the Attack on Urgench from a *Zafarnama* (Book of Triumph) of Sharafuddin Ali Yazdi, Herat (?), dated A.H. 872 (A.D. 1467–68); fol. 116b. Opaque watercolor, ink, and gold on paper. John Work Garrett Library, The Johns Hopkins University, Baltimore.

after assigning many great warriors as reinforcements, we returned to camp in the evening.

The next morning we marched out and stopped at the Baba Kara spring in the Bajaur glen. At Khwaja Kalan's intercession we pardoned all the remaining prisoners, rejoined them to their wives and children, and dismissed them. Some of the sultans and rebels who had been taken prisoner were executed. Their heads were sent to Kabul with news of the victory. Notices and heads were also sent to Badakhshan, Konduz, and Balkh.

Shah Mansur of the Yusufzai was there at the conquest and massacre. He was clad in a robe and given leave to depart after orders and threats were written for the Yusufzai.

Our minds at ease concerning the Bajaur fortress, we marched out on Tuesday the ninth of the month [January 11]. A league farther down the Bajaur glen we stopped and ordered a tower of skulls erected on a rise.

On Wednesday the tenth of Muharram [January 12] we mounted for an excursion to the Bajaur fortress, and a drinking session was held in Khwaja Kalan's quarters. The Kafirs from the Bajaur vicinity brought a few jugs of wine. The wine and fruit of Bajaur all come from neighboring regions of Kafiristan. [219]

I spent the night there, and the next morning inspected the tower and ramparts of the fortress and returned to camp. We set out the following morning and dismounted on the banks of the river at Khwaja Khizr.

Marching from there, we camped on the banks of the Jandol. It was ordered that those who had been assigned as reinforcements should go to Bajaur by themselves. On Sunday the fourteenth of the month Khwaja Kalan was granted a yak-tail standard and given leave to go to Bajaur. A day or two after he was dismissed, this little verse came to my mind. I wrote it down and sent it to him:

My pact and covenant with my beloved was not thus; he chose separation and left me distraught. / What can one do with the whims of fate, which has separated friend from friend by force.[208]

On Wednesday the seventeenth of Muharram [January 19], Sultan Alauddin of Swat, the rival of Sultan-Ways of Swat, came and paid homage.

On Thursday the eighteenth we hunted the mountain between Bajaur and Jandol. The deer there are jet black, except for their tails; probably farther down the deer of Hindustan are also jet black. On the same day a yellow bird was felled; it too was black,[209] even its eyes. The same day, Bürküt took a deer.[210]

The soldiers had rather little grain, so we went to the Kahraj Valley [219b] and took some. Then, with the intention of going to Swat to raid the Yusufzai Afghans, we marched out on Friday and camped between the Panjkora River and the joined Jandol and Bajaur rivers. Shah Mansur Yusufzai brought some delicious and intoxicating *kamali*.[211] We divided one into three pieces, and I had one, Gadai Taghayï had one, and Abdullah Kitabdar had one. It was fantastic. That evening, when the begs gathered for council, I was unable to come out. These days, if I were to eat a whole kamali, I don't know if it would produce half the high.

Marching on from there we stopped in front of Panjkora near the mouth of the Kahraj and Peshgram valleys. While in that camp a lot of snow fell. Since in those parts it snows only occasionally, the people were surprised. In agreement with Sultan-Ways of Swat a levy of four thousand loads of grain for the army was imposed on the people of Kahraj, and Sultan-Ways was dispatched to collect it. The mountain villagers, who had never borne such an imposition, were unable to give it and were ruined.

On Tuesday the twenty-third of the month Hindu Beg was put in charge of a detachment and sent to raid Panjkora. [220] Panjkora lies more than halfway up the mountain, and to reach its villages one has to go through a pass nearly a kos long. The people had fled, but some flocks, herds, and cattle and a lot of grain were brought back. The next morning Qoch Beg was put in charge of a detachment and sent on a raid.

On Wednesday the twenty-fifth we stopped in the Mandesh villages in the Kahraj valley to get grain for the army.

After Humayun several infants were born to Humayun's mother, but none survived. Hindal had not been born yet.[212] While in this region a letter came from Mahïm in which she wrote, "Whether it be a boy or a girl, I will take my chances. Give the child to me and I will raise it as my own."[213] On Friday the twenty-sixth, at this same camp, I gave the as-yet-unborn Hindal to Mahïm and wrote letters for Yusuf Ali Rikabdar to take to Kabul.

While at this same camp, I had a platform built on a hill in the middle of the Mandesh district large enough for the *peshkhana*[214] of a felt tent. The stones for the platform were carried by all the ichkis and soldiers.

One of the Yusufzai chieftains, Malik Shah Mansur, son of Malik Sulayman Shah, had come and become one of my supporters. [220b] To confirm my ties to the Yusufzai I had asked for his daughter in marriage.[215] While we were at this camp word came that Shah Mansur's daughter was coming with the Yusufzai tribute. That night there was a wine party to which Sultan Alauddin was invited, seated, and granted a royal robe. On Sunday the twenty-eighth we left the Kahraj valley and camped. Taus Khan Yusufzai, Shah Mansur's younger brother, brought his niece to this camp.

Because the people of Besud had a connection to the Bajaur fortress, Yusuf Ali Bökäül was sent to march them to it. Written orders were sent for the soldiers who had remained in Kabul to come.

On Friday the third of Safar [February 4] camp was made at the confluence of the Panjkora and Bajaur rivers.

On Sunday the fifth we left that camp for Bajaur, and Khwaja Kalan held a wine party in his quarters.

On Tuesday the seventh, I summoned the begs and the Dilazak Afghans to council, where the following topics were discussed. It was the end of the year, only a day or two left in Pisces. The lowland grain had all been taken in, and if we went now to Swat the soldiers would not find any grain and would suffer. [221] We should take the Ambahar—Paniyali road, cross the Swat River above Hashnaghar, and ride against the Yusufzai and Muhammadzai Afghans who were in the lowlands in front of the Yusufzais' Mahura aerie. Next year we should come earlier, at harvest time, and make these Afghans our primary concern. Things were left at this, and the next morning, Wednesday, Sultan-Ways and Sultan Alauddin were presented with horses and robes of honor and given safe pass. We marched off and stopped opposite Bajaur. Shah Mansur's daughter was placed in the Bajaur fortress until the army should return.

The next morning we passed Khwaja Khizr and camped. Khwaja Kalan was given leave to depart. The *uruq*, the grain, and most of the army's equipment and heavy baggage were sent to Laghman by the Kunar road. The next morning we marched off, and the heavy baggage and camels were put under Khwaja Mirmiran's charge and dispatched by the Churghatu and Darwaza roads through the Qara Köbä defile, while we ourselves rode unencumbered through the Ambahar defile and stopped at Paniyali in the early afternoon. Ughanberdi was sent forward with a band to reconnoitre. Since the Afghans were not far from us we did not move early. It was midmorning when Ughanberdi returned. He had taken an Afghan and cut off his head, [221b] which he dropped on his way back. He did not bring any satisfactory information, and it was around noon when we started off. We crossed the Swat River and stopped in the late afternoon. That night we mounted and rode fast. The sun was up a spear length when Rustam the Turcoman, who had been sent forward as a scout, brought word that the Afghans had learned of our approach and were agitated. One group of Afghans was going up the mountain road. As soon as we heard this, we galloped off and sent a detachment ahead to raid. They killed a few Afghans, cut off their heads, and brought back a few captives and cattle and flocks. The Dilazak Afghans also cut off some heads and brought them in. We went on, stopping in the vicinity of Katlang. A guide was sent to bring the uruq, which Khwaja Mirmiran was leading, to join us in Maqam. The next morning we marched and camped between Katlang and Maqam. Shah Mansur's man came. Khusraw Kükäldash and Ahmadi Parwanachï were sent with a party to meet the uruq.

On Tuesday the fourteenth [February 15], while camped at Maqam, the uruq joined us. Some thirty or forty years ago a wandering dervish named Shahbaz Qalandar had led a part of the Yusufzai and Dilazak into heresy. On a spur of the Maqam mountains is a rather low mountain [222] that overlooks the whole plain; there, on an airy hill that commands superb vistas, was Shahbaz Qalandar's tomb. I went on an excursion to examine it. It occurred to me that a heretic wandering dervish had no business having a tomb in such a pleasant spot, so I ordered it reduced to rubble. Since it was an agreeable place and the air was so good, I had some ma'jun and sat there for a while.

FIRST ENTRY INTO HINDUSTAN

We turned away from Bajaur with Bhera on our minds. Ever since coming to Kabul we had been thinking about a Hindustan campaign, but for one reason or another it had not been possible. The Bajaur campaign had taken three or four months, and nothing of any consequence had fallen to the soldiers. Since Bhera, the border of Hindustan, was nearby, it occurred to me that if we crossed the Indus immediately, unencumbered, the soldiers might get something. After turning away with this thought in mind, raiding the Afghans, and camping in Maqam, some of my supporters said, "If we are going to enter Hindustan, we should enter prepared. Some of the army have stayed in Kabul. Some of our warriors have been stationed in Bajaur. Many of the soldiers have gone back to Laghman because their horses were so lean. The horses of those who have come this far are so worn out that they no longer have the strength for one day's hard ride." Although these words were reasonable, since a determination had been made we marched off early the next morning, disregarding these considerations, and set out for the Indus crossing. [222b] A detail was assigned to Mir Muhammad Jalaban and his brothers and sent up and down the river to inspect the crossings.

Having gotten the camp marching toward the river, I myself went toward Swati, which is also called Kargkhana, to hunt rhinoceros. Several were found, but they did not come out of the thick forest. One with a calf ventured into the open and began to run away. Many arrows were shot at it, but it managed to get itself back into the thicket. Even when fire was set to the forest, it could not be caught. A calf was burned, however, and lay there writhing. It was slaughtered and everybody took a trophy share.

Coming back from Swati, I wandered around a good bit before returning to camp late that night. Those who had gone to inspect the crossings had come back. The next morning, Wednesday the sixteenth, the horses and camels were sent across at the ford with the baggage. The camp market, foot soldiers, and donkeys were taken across by raft. That same day, while at the ford, the people of Nilab came and presented me with a mail-clad horse and three hundred *shahrukhis*. By noon everybody had crossed and we marched until the first watch of the night, camping near the Kachakot river. The next morning we made it across the river, went through the Sangdaki defile around noon, and stopped. [223] Sayyid-Qasim Eshik-aqa was in command of the rear guard. He caught some Gujars coming up on our rear, cut off their heads, and brought them in. At dawn we marched out of Sangdaki, crossed the Sohan River a little before noon, and stopped. The camp followers kept on coming until midnight. It was a long march, especially difficult because the horses were so worn out and thin. Many horses were left behind.

Seven kos to the north of Bhera is a mountain called Koh-i-Jud in the *Zafarnama*[216] and other books. I had not known why it was so named but I later found out that there are two clans on this mountain descended from a single ancestor, and one is called Jud and the other Janjua. The members of the clans have become the traditional rulers of the mountaineers and of the people and tribes between Nilab and Bhera. Their rule, however, is benevolent and brotherly: they do not take whatever they want, but the people give no more and no less than the rates that were fixed long ago, that is, one shahrukhi per yoke of oxen and seven shahrukhis per household. The people also serve in the army. Both Jud and Janjua consist of several branches. The mountains, which are seven kos from Bhera, break off from the Kashmir Mountains, which are connected to the Hindu Kush, [223b] and go southwest until they end at the foot of Dinkot on the Indus.[217] Half of the mountains are Jud, and half are Janjua. By attribution to the Jud, the mountains are called Koh-i-Jud. Among them the great chieftain is given the title *ray*, and his younger brothers and sons are called *malik*.[218] The Janjua are maternal uncles to Langar Khan.

The ruler of the tribes and clans in the Sohan River area is Malik Hast. Originally his name was Asad, but the Hindustanis often drop such vowels. For instance, they pronounce *khabar*[219] as *khab'r* and the name Asad as As'd, which over time became Hast. As soon as we stopped in Janjua, Langar Khan was sent to Malik Hast. He hastened there, convinced him of our good intentions and favor and brought him back that night. He presented a mail-clad horse and paid homage. He must have been twenty-two or twenty-three years old. There were many of these people's flocks and herds all around the camp.

Since we had always had in mind to take Hindustan, we regarded as our own territory the several areas of Bhera, Khushab, Chenab, and Chiniot, which had long been in the hands of the Turk. We were determined to gain control ourselves—be it by force or peaceful means—and therefore it behooved us to treat the mountain people well. [224] It was ordered that no one was to harm their flocks or herds in any way whatsoever.

Early the next morning we marched out, reached Kalda Kahar at midday, and stopped. All around were fields of grain. Kalda Kahar is a remarkable place. It is located on flat ground ten kos from Bhera in the midst of the Jud Mountains, and in the middle of the plain is a large lake created by rainwater from the surrounding mountains. The perimeter of the lake must be nearly three kos. To the north is a beautiful meadow. To the west, at the base of the mountains, is a spring, the water of which stays in the hills overlooking the lake. Since it was a worthy spot, I had a garden called Bagh-i-Safa[220] laid out. It was a pleasant place with good air, as will be presently described.[221] At dawn we rode out of Kalda Kahar. At the head of the Hamtatu defile a few local people came bearing some paltry tribute and paid homage. We attached those who had come to Abdul-Rahim Shiqavul and sent them to Bhera to gain the trust of the Bhera people. "These districts have long belonged to the Turk," we said. "Beware lest the men give them cause for fear or bring ruin upon them, for our regard is upon this district and its people. There will be no pillage or plunder."

At midmorning we stopped at the bottom of the defile [224b] and sent ahead seven or eight men under Qurban Charkhi and Abdul-Malik Masti to bring news. One of those sent ahead, Mahdi Khwaja's Mir Muhammad, brought in a man. Meanwhile the chieftains of the Afghans came with a few presents and paid homage. We attached them to Langar Khan and sent them to allay the fears of the Bhera people. When we were through the defile and out of the forest, we marched for Bhera with the right and left wings and center in formation. When we approached Bhera, Deva Hindu, one of the servants of Dawlat Khan Yusuf-Khel's son Ali Khan, and Siktu's son came with the notables of Bhera to present a horse and pay homage. At midday, camp was made in a field beside the Bahat River[222] so that we would not harm or harass the people of Bhera.

RECENT HISTORY OF BHERA

Ever since Temür Beg entered Hindustan,[223] the several districts of Bhera, Khushab, Chenab, and Chiniot had been under the control of his sons and their followers and dependents. At one time Sultan-Mas'ud Mirza, grandson of Shahrukh Mirza and son of Soyurghat-mïsh Mirza, held the governorship of Kabul and Zabul (for which reason he was called Sultan-Mas'ud Kabuli). One of his protégés, Mir

Ali Beg, had three sons, Baba Kabuli, Darya Khan, [225] and Apaq Khan, who was later called Ghazi Khan. After the deaths of Sultan-Mas'ud Mirza and his son Ali-Asghar Mirza, the three gained such dominance that they took over control of Kabul and Zabul and the above-mentioned districts and parganas in Hindustan. During Sultan-Abusa'id Mirza's time Kabul and Ghazni slipped from their grasp, but the Hindustan districts remained in their control.

In 910 [1504–05], the year I first came to Kabul, I went through the Khyber to Peshawar intent upon entering Hindustan, but through the machinations of Baqi Chaghaniani we marched farther down to Bangash, that is, Kohat, raided much of Afghanistan, plundered Bannu and Dasht, and came out via Duki. At that time the rule of Bhera, Khushab, and Chenab was in the hands of Mir Ali's grandson, Sayyid-Ali Khan, Ghazi Khan's son. He had the khutba read in the name of Sikandar Bahlul, to whom he owed allegiance. Terrified of our army's approach, he abandoned Bhera, crossed the Jhelum, and made himself a seat in Sherkot, one of the villages of Bhera. A year or two later the Afghans became suspicious of Sayyid-Ali Khan's intentions toward us, and once again he allowed himself to give way to fear and turned over the districts to Dawlat Khan, the son of Tatar Khan Yusuf-Khel, who was then the governor of Lahore. [225b] Dawlat Khan gave Bhera to his eldest son, Ali Khan. Bhera was then under Ali Khan's control. Dawlat Khan's father Tatar Khan was one of the seven or eight commanders who had rebelled, taken over Hindustan, and set up Bahlul as padishah. All the areas to the north of Sirhind and the Sutlej River belonged to Tatar Khan, and these districts had a revenue of more than three crores.[224] After Tatar Khan's death, Sultan Sikandar in his capacity as padishah seized the territory from Tatar Khan's sons. A year or two before I came to Kabul he gave Lahore only to Dawlat Khan.[225]

————

The next morning raiding parties were sent to some likely places. That same day I toured Bhera, and Sankar[226] Khan Janjua came, presented a horse, and paid homage.

On Wednesday the twenty-second [February 23], I summoned the chieftains and *chaudharis*[227] of Bhera, fixed an amnesty of four hundred thousand shahrukhis, and appointed collectors. I mounted, toured around, got on a boat, and had some ma'jun. Haydar Alamdar was sent to the Baloches[228] living in Bhera and Khushab. Thursday morning they brought a horse the color of almond blossoms and paid homage. It was reported that the soldiers were acting unruly and harassing the people of Bhera. [226] Some men were sent to execute the unruly ones, and others had their noses slit and were paraded around camp.

On Friday a petition came from the people of Khushab. Shah-Shuja' Arghun's son Shah-Hasan was assigned to go to Khushab. On Saturday the twenty-fifth he was dispatched. On Sunday it rained so hard that the whole plain was flooded. Between Bhera and the mountains where we were camped was a stream, which by midday was as broad as a lake. There was no crossing within more than an arrow shot near Bhera. The men had to make their horses swim across. In midafternoon I mounted to inspect the rushing waters. The rain and storm were so bad that on the way back we wondered if we would reach the camp. I had to make my horse swim across the rushing water. The soldiers were scared too. Most of them left their tents and heavy baggage behind, shouldered their mail, armor, and weapons, stripped their horses bare, and made them swim across. The flatlands were completely covered by water. The next morning boats were brought in, and most of the soldiers used them to get their tents and baggage across. Around noon Qoch Beg's men went a league upriver to find a ford, where those who were left crossed. We stayed one day in the Bhera fortress, which is called Jahannuma, [226b] and Tuesday morning we marched out and, fearful of flooding, camped on some hills north of Bhera. There had been some negligence in collecting the agreed-upon money, so the area was divided into four districts and begs were ordered to take care of the affair. Khalifa was assigned to one district, Qoch Beg to another, Dost Nasir to another, and Sayyid-Qasim and Muhibb-Ali to another. Since we regarded the territories occupied by the Turk as ours, there was no pillage or plunder.

The people were always saying, "If envoys are sent to negotiate a peace treaty, they will not cause any interference in the territories that belong to the Turk." Therefore, on Thursday the first of Rabi' I [March 3], Mulla Murshid was sent on such a mission to Sultan Ibrahim, who had then attained the rulership of India, his father Sultan Sikandar having died five or six months before. We sent him a hawk and laid claim to the territories that had belonged to the Turk. We handed Mulla Murshid letters we had written to Dawlat Khan and

Sultan Ibrahim, imparted some important oral instructions, and gave him leave to depart. These Hindustan people, especially the Afghans, are amazingly devoid of sense and wisdom and far off the path of tactics and strategy. Neither were they able to come out and make a stand like an enemy [227] nor did they know how to adhere to the path of amity. Dawlat Khan kept our man in Lahore for a few days without seeing him or sending him to Ibrahim. A few months later he went back to Kabul without having received a reply.

On Friday the second, Shïbaq Piyada and Darwesh-Ali Piyada, who is now a matchlockman, brought reports from Kabul with news of Hindal's birth. Since this news came while India was being subjugated, I took it as a good omen and named the child Hindal.[229] Qambar Beg also brought letters from Muhammad-Zaman Mirza in Balkh.

The next morning after leaving the divan, we mounted for an excursion, got on a boat, and drank spirits. The members of the party were Khwaja Dost Khawand, Khusraw, Mirim, Mirza-Qulï, Muhammadi, Ahmadi, Gadai, Nu'man, Langar Khan, Ruhdam, Qasim Ali Tiryaki, Yusuf Ali, and Tengri-Qulï. At the front of the boat was a platform with a flat top. I and some others sat there while still others sat under the platform. At the back of the boat was also room to sit, and Muhammadi, Gadai, and Nu'man settled there. We drank until the late afternoon, and then, disgusted by the bad taste of the spirits, agreed to switch to ma'jun. Those at the other end of the boat did not know we were doing so, [227b] and kept on drinking spirits. Late that night we got off the boat, mounted our horses, and rode back to camp. Muhammadi and Gadai, thinking I was drinking spirits and imagining they were doing me a service, took turns carrying the jug on their horses. They arrived in high spirits, saying, "On such a dark night we took turns carrying the jug." Later, when they realized the intoxication was of another sort—some high on ma'jun and others drunk—they got angry since ma'jun parties and wine parties never mix.

"Don't spoil the party," I said. "Let those who want to drink drink, and let those who want to have ma'jun have it. Let no one speak in reproach to anyone else." Some had spirits, and others had ma'jun. For a time the party continued in strained politeness. When we got to the tent, we invited Baba Jan the qopuz player, who had not been part of the party. He chose to drink. We also invited Turdï-Muhammad Qipchaq and put him with the drinkers. It was no time before the drunks began to talk all sorts of nonsense, mostly barbs aimed at ma'jun and ma'jun eaters. Baba Jan got drunk and talked a lot of nonsense. The drunks kept filling goblet after goblet and giving them to Turdï-Muhammad, and in a little while they got him roaring drunk. No matter how we tried to get the party under control, [228] nothing worked. It turned into an uproar. It became unenjoyable, and everybody went his own way.

On Monday the fifth [March 7], Bhera was presented to Hindu Beg. On Tuesday, Chenab was granted to Husayn Ekräk, and he and the Chenab people were given leave to depart. Meanwhile Sayyid-Ali Khan's son Minuchihr Khan, having opted for us, had run into Tatar Gakhar while coming along the upper road from Hindustan. Tatar Gakhar had detained him and married him to his daughter. After staying with him for a while, he finally came and paid us homage.

Aside from the people of Jud and Janjua there were Jats, Gujars, and many other peoples living in villages in every valley and hill in the mountains between Nilab and Bhera, which are connected to the mountains of Kashmir. Their rulers and chieftains belong to the Gakhar clan, whose chieftainship is like that of Jud and Janjua.[230] At that time, the chieftains of the peoples on the mountainsides were two cousins, Tatar Gakhar and Hati Gakhar. Their strongholds were the ravines and cliffs. Tatar's seat was Pharhali, which is way below the snow-covered mountains. Hati, whose territory was adjacent to the mountains, had gained dominance over Kalinjar, which belonged to Babu Khan of Bisut. [228b] Tatar Gakhar had seen Dawlat Khan and owed him total allegiance; Hati, however, had not seen him and maintained a rebellious attitude toward him. With the advice and agreement of the Hindustan begs, Tatar had gone and camped at a distance as though to lay siege to Hati. While we were in Bhera, Hati seized upon some pretext to make a surprise attack on Tatar, kill him, and lay hands on his territory, his wives, and everything he had.

At midday we rode off on an excursion, got on a boat, and drank spirits. The members of the party were Dost Beg, Mirza-Qulï, Ahmadi, Gadai, Muhammad-Ali Jang-Jang, Asas, and Ughanberdi Moghul. The entertainers were Ruhdam, Baba Jan, Qasim Ali, Yusuf Ali, Tengri-Qulï, Abu'l-Qasim, Ramazan, and Luli. We drank on the boat until late that night, left the boat roaring drunk, and got on our horses. I took a torch in my hand and, reeling to one side and then the other, let the horse gallop free-reined along the riverbank all the way

Detail, *A Drunken Babur Returns to Camp at Night*, inscribed to Farrukh Beg. From a manuscript of the *Baburnama* of Zahiruddin Muhammad Babur, Lahore, Mughal period, dated 1589. Opaque watercolor, ink, and gold on paper. Arthur M. Sackler Gallery, Smithsonian Institution; Purchase—Smithsonian Unrestricted Trust Funds, Smithsonian Collections Acquisition Program, and Dr. Arthur M. Sackler, S1986.231

to camp. I must have been really drunk. The next morning they told me that I had come galloping into camp holding a torch. I didn't remember a thing, except that when I got to my tent I vomited a lot.

On Friday, I rode out and crossed the river by boat. While looking at the orchards, blossoms, and land planted in sugarcane, we saw a bucket and wheels and not only asked how they drew water with them [229] but also had them draw water repeatedly. During this excursion we were eating ma'jun. We returned and got back on the boat. Minuchihr Khan was also given some ma'jun, and he got so high that it took two men to hoist him up. Anchor was dropped in the middle of the river and we stayed there for a while. Eventually we went way downstream, but after some time had the boat hauled back upstream. That night we slept right on the boat and returned to camp at dawn.

On Saturday the tenth of Rabi' I [March 12] the sun entered Aries. At midday we rode out for an excursion, got on a boat, and started drinking spirits. The members of the party were Khwaja Dost Khawand, Dost Beg, Mirim, Mirza-Qulï, Muhammadi, Ahmadi, Yunus Ali, Muhammad-Ali Jang-Jang, Gadai Taghayï, Mir Khurd, and Asas. The entertainers were Ruhdam, Baba Jan, Qasim Ali, Yusuf Ali, Tengri-Qulï, and Ramazan. We went up a tributary, then we went downstream for a while and got back to camp late. That same day Shah-Hasan came from Khushab, where he had been sent as an envoy to lay claim to the territories that belonged to the Turk, negotiate peace terms, and get some of the stipulated amount of money.

The hot season was approaching. Shah-Muhammad Muhrdar, his brother Dost Muhrdar, and some other suitable warriors were assigned as reinforcements to Hindu Beg. Each one was allocated a stipend appropriate to his rank. [229b] I gave Khushab to Langar Khan, who had been the motivating factor in these campaigns, awarded him a yak-tail standard, and assigned him as reinforcement to Hindu Beg. We increased the stipends and maintenance of the Turks and local soldiers who were in Bhera and stationed them as reinforcements to Hindu Beg. One of these was Minuchihr Khan, whose name has been mentioned.[231] Another was Nazar-Ali Türk, who was related to Minuchihr Khan. Two others were Sankar Khan Janjua and Malik Hast Janjua.

Having somehow consolidated the territory with hopes of peace, we moved out of Bhera on Sunday the eleventh of Rabi' I [March 13] to return to Kabul. We made it to Kalda Kahar and camped. That day there was an unbelievable rainstorm. With cloaks or without, it made no difference. The tail end of the camp kept coming until late that night.

Those who knew the lay of the land hereabouts, especially the Janjua, who were old enemies of the Gakhar, reported that Hati Gakhar had recently turned outlaw. He was engaging in highway robbery and bringing ruination upon the people. It was necessary to do something to drive him from the area or else to teach him a good lesson. In agreement with them, the next morning we assigned Khwaja Mirmiran and Mirim Nasir to the camp and left the camp at midmorning to ride to Pharhali against Hati Gakhar, who had killed Tatar a few days before and taken over Pharhali, [230] as has been mentioned.[232] We stopped in the late afternoon, fed the horses, and rode off by night. Our guide was a servant of Malik Hast's, Surpa by name. We cleared the road and stopped near dawn. Beg Muhammad Moghul was sent back to camp. As it was becoming light we mounted, and at midmorning we put on our armor and charged. With one league left to go we could see the outline of Pharhali. Off we galloped. The right wing went to the east of Pharhali. Qoch Beg, who was with the right wing, was sent to reinforce its rear. The men of the left wing and center were pouring down on Pharhali. Dost Beg was directed to support the rear of the left wing, which was also attacking.

Pharhali, situated among ravines, has two roads. The one to the southeast—the road by which we were traveling—is atop the ravines and is surrounded by ravines and gullies on both sides. Half a kos from Pharhali the road becomes such that in four or five places before reaching the gate the ravines are so precipitous that it is necessary to ride single file the distance of an arrow shot. The other road to Pharhali is to the northwest and leads through a wide valley. It too is precarious, and there is no other road on any side. Although it has no ramparts or battlements, there is no place to bring force to bear either. All around are ravines seven, eight, or ten yards straight down. [230b]

The men farthest forward in the left wing passed through the narrows and gathered at the gate. Hati drove back the attackers with thirty to forty armed horsemen and many foot soldiers. When Dost Beg, who was reinforcing the rear of the attackers, arrived, he brought a lot of force to bear, unhorsed many men, and defeated the foe. Hati Gakhar was renowned in those parts for his valor, but regardless of how well he fought he could not maintain his stand and was forced to retreat. He was unable to hold the narrows, and when he made it to the fortress he could not make it fast either. The attackers poured into the fortress behind him and ran through it to the narrow ravine on the northwest, but Hati got out and fled unencumbered. Here Dost Beg performed a good action and received the *jüldü*.[233] Meanwhile I entered the fortress and dismounted at Tatar's quarters. Some of those who had been assigned to stay with me while the attack was launched had nevertheless gone on to join the fray. Among them were Amin-Muhammad Tarkhan Arghun and Qaracha, who for their disobedience were attached to the Gujar guide Surpa and sent into the wilderness without their cloaks to meet the camp. The next morning we got across the northwest ravine and camped in a grain field. Wali Khizanachï was assigned a few valiant warriors and sent to meet the camp.

On Thursday the fifteenth [March 17] we marched out and stopped at Anderana on the banks of the Sohan. [231] Long ago the Anderana fortress had belonged to Malik Hast's father, but after Hati Gakhar killed Hast's father it fell to ruins, which was its condition when we found it. That night the part of the camp that had been detached at Kalda Kahar arrived and joined us.

After Hati took Tatar he sent his relative Parbat to me with a mail-clad horse and gifts. Before catching up with me Parbart encountered the men of the camp who had stayed behind and came along with the uruq to present his gifts and pay homage. Langar Khan also came with the uruq on several matters of business, and when finished, he and some local people were given leave to depart for Bhera. Marching on and crossing the Sohan, we stopped on a hill. Parbat was given a robe of honor, and Muhammad-Ali Jang-Jang's servant was sent to Hati with letters of appeasement.

Several of Humayun's servants under the leadership of Baba Dost and Halahil had been summoned to receive the prefecture of Nilab and the Qarluq Hazara, which had been given to Humayun. Thirty to forty men under the leadership of Sankar Qarluq and Mirza Malwi Qarluq arrived with chieftains of the Qarluq. They presented a mail-clad horse and paid homage. The Dilazak Afghan army also came. Early the next morning we marched out for two leagues and stopped. Going up on a rise and looking around, we ordered [231b] that the camp camels be counted. There turned out to be 570 of them.

We had heard of the qualities of the spikenard, and at this camp we saw some. On the slopes of the mountain a few of the plants were scattered here and there. Farther down, the spikenard is abundant and grows large. It will be mentioned when we describe the flora and fauna of Hindustan.[234]

At the time of the naqara we marched out of that camp, stopped at midmorning at the bottom of the Sangdaki defile, continued on at noon through the defile and across the river, and camped on a rise. At midnight we left to inspect the crossing we had used on our way to Bhera and found that a large grain raft was stuck in the mud. The owners had tried everything but were unable to get it moving. The grain was seized and distributed among those with us, and it came in handy. Around noon we stopped between the rivers above Old Nilab and down from the confluence of the Kabul and Indus rivers. Six boats were brought from Nilab and divided among the right wing, left wing, and center, and the men busied themselves with the crossing. They kept on crossing the Monday we arrived, that evening, all Tuesday, and Wednesday. On Thursday a few were still coming over. Parbat, who had been attached to Muhammad-Ali [232] Jang-Jang's servant at Anderana and sent to Hati, came to the riverbank bringing a mail-clad horse from Hati. The people of Nilab also brought a mail-clad horse and paid homage. Muhammad-Ali Jang-Jang was anxious to stay in Bhera, but since that region had been given to Hindu Beg, he was awarded the territories between Bhera and the Indus, such as the Qarluq Hazara, Hati, Ghiyaswal, and Kitib. Let him who bows his head in submission act like a subject, but any place and any territory that does not bow its head—

> Whoever does not bow his head, strike him, strip him, and make him obey.

In addition I gave Muhammad-Ali Jang-Jang a royal black velvet headgear and royal Qalmaqi armor.[235] He was also rewarded with a yak-tail standard. Hati's relative was given leave to depart and take Hati a sword, a robe of honor, and letters of good will.

On Thursday we went out to the riverbank as the sun was coming up. That day we ate ma'jun. How strange the fields of flowers appeared under its influence. Nothing but purple flowers were blooming in some places, and only yellow ones in other areas. Sometimes the yellow and the purple blossomed together like gold fleck. We sat on a rise near the camp and just looked at the fields. [232b] Like a painting, on all sides of the hill yellow and purple flowers in regular clumps were arranged in a hexagon shape. On two sides there were somewhat fewer numbers, but as far as the eye could see were fields of blossoms. In the spring there are beautiful flowers in the vicinity of Peshawar.

We marched out of that camp at dawn. As we approached, a tiger emerged from the riverbank, growling. As soon as the horses heard its sound they took their riders off in all directions and hurled themselves into the gullies and pits. The tiger turned around and went back into the thicket. We ordered an ox put into the bushes to flush the tiger out. It worked: the animal again came out growling, and the men shot at it from all sides. I too shot an arrow. Khalu Piyada stabbed it, whereupon the tiger bit off the end of the lance. Having endured so many arrow wounds, the tiger slunk back into the underbrush. But Baba Yasavul drew his sword and approached the tiger, giving it a blow on the head. When Ali of Seistan struck at its waist, the tiger threw itself into the river, where the men were finally able to kill it. When it was brought out of the water, we ordered it skinned.

Early the next day we marched off and, reaching Bigram, went to see Gurh Kattri. We entered a small, dark chamber like a monk's cell, and after passing through the door and down two or three steps, we had to lie down to get in. It was impossible to see without a candle. All around was an unending pile of hair and beard that had been clipped there. [233] Many chambers like the ones in madrasas and caravansaries surround Gurh Kattri. The first year I came to Kabul, [in 1504], when we raided Kohat, Bannu, and Dasht, I went to the great banyan tree in Bigram[236] and was sorry not to have seen Gurh Kattri, but it turned out not to be much to be sorry for.

That same day an excellent hawk of mine that Shaykhïm Mirshikar had taken care of got lost. It had moulted two or three times and had caught so many cranes and herons and other things that it had made a hawker out of a person as disinterested as I.

Of the spoils of Hindustan, to each of six chieftains of the Dilazak Afghans under Malik Nohan and Malik Musa were given a hundred mithcals of silver, a robe, three oxen, and a buffalo, and to others were awarded, according to their rank, coins, textiles, cattle, and buffalo. When we stopped at Ali Masjid, a Dilazak of the Ya'qub-Khel named Ma'ruf presented ten sheep, two loads of rice, and eight large pieces of cheese.

From Ali Masjid we went to Yada Bir. From there we reached Juy-i-Shahi at midday and dismounted. That same day Dost Beg got a raging fever. We marched out of Juy-i-Shahi at dawn, stopped at Bagh-i-Wafa, and moved out again at midday. We crossed the still water at Gandamak, let our horses graze in the evening in a grain field, and mounted again a ghari or two later. After we crossed the Surkhab,[237] [233b] we dismounted at Garg and went to sleep. Before sunup we rode out, and I went off on the Quratu road with five or six men to see the garden I had had made there. Khalifa, Shah-Hasan Beg, and a few others were sent along the main road to wait for us in Quruq Say. When I reached Quratu, Shah Beg Arghun's tovachï named Qïzïl brought the news that Shah Beg had attacked and plundered Kahan and withdrawn.

It was ordered that no one was to carry ahead news of us. It was midday when we reached Kabul. We got as far as the Qutlugh-Qadam bridge before anyone learned of our approach. Thereafter Humayun and Kamran were apprised and did not even have time to get on their horses. They had their pages carry them to a spot between the city gate and the citadel gate, where they paid homage.

Late that afternoon Qasim Beg, the city cadi, the members of the retinue who had stayed in Kabul, and the notables made their obeisance. Late afternoon on Saturday the first of Rabiʿ II [April 2] there was a wine party at which I awarded Shah-Hasan a royal robe of honor. At dawn the next day we got on a boat and had a morning draught, during which Nur Beg played the lute. Just then he was not abstaining. At midday we left the boat, toured the garden between Gulkana and the mountain, and late that afternoon went to the Bagh-i-Banafsha,[238] where we drank. That evening I got over the rampart by Gulkana and went to the citadel.

THE DEATH OF DOST BEG

On Tuesday evening, the fifth of the month [April 6], Dost Beg, who had come down with a raging fever en route, [234] passed away. We were terribly shocked and saddened. His body was taken to Ghazni and placed at the gate to Sultan Mahmud's tomb. Dost Beg was a valiant warrior and still advancing in rank. Before being a beg, while he was an ichki, he performed several outstanding feats. One of them was a league away from Andizhan at Rabat-i-Zaurak where Sultan-Ahmad Tambal made a surprise attack.[239] I charged with ten or fifteen men, struck the approaching force, and drove them back. When we reached his center, he made a stand with around a hundred men. Three of my men were left, and I made the fourth. One of them was Dost Nasir, and the others were Mirza-Qulï Kükäldash, and Karimdad. I had only put on my vest. Tambal and one other were standing somewhat forward of his troop array. Squaring off with Tambal, I let an arrow fly at his helmet, then shot another that pierced his shield and armor plates. I got shot in the thigh; Tambal struck a blow at my head. What was amazing was that I had a helmet cap on, and not a thread was broken, although my head was badly wounded. No reinforcements were arriving, and no one was left with me. I could do nothing but turn my reins and get out of there. Dost Beg was right behind me. Tambal turned his attention from me and struck a blow at him.

Another of Dost Beg's feats of valor was when, coming out of Akhsi,[240] [234b] he exchanged sword blows with Baqi the Catamite, who, although he was called a catamite, was powerful and manly with the sword. When we got out of Akhsi, I had eight men left with me. Dost Beg was the third to be unhorsed.

After he became a beg, when Sevinchäk Khan came with the Uzbek princes and laid siege to Ahmad Qasim in Tashkent, Dost Beg drove a wedge through them and entered the city. During the siege he risked his life many times. Without informing him Ahmad Qasim gave up and fled. Then too Dost Beg rode right over the khans and Uzbek princes and made a valiant exit from Tashkent.

Later, when Sherim Taghayï, Mazid, and their henchmen rebelled, Dost Beg charged up from Ghazni with two or three hundred men, and the Moghuls sent three or four hundred brave warriors to oppose him. In the vicinity of Shirukan he defeated those who had been sent against him, unhorsed many men, and cut off a lot of heads. At the Bajaur fortress too, Dost Beg's men were up and over the ramparts before any others. At Pharhali, Dost Beg charged, beat Hati into flight, and conquered Pharhali. After Dost Beg's victory I awarded the territory to his younger brother Mirim Nasir.

On Friday the eighth of Rabi' II [April 9], I left the fortress for the charbagh. On Tuesday the twelfth, Sultanïm Begim, Sultan-Husayn Mirza's eldest daughter and the mother of Muhammad-Sultan Mirza, arrived in Kabul. She had settled in Khwarazm during the times of turmoil, and Yïlï Bars Sultan's younger brother, Esän-Qulï Sultan, had married her daughter. [235] She was assigned a private garden to live in. After she had settled in, I went to see her. As she was an elder female relative, I knelt to show respect. She too knelt and then stood up, and we had an interview. Later, the same rituals were always observed.

On Sunday the seventeenth, I pardoned the traitor Baba Shaykh, released him from the chains in which he had long been held, and awarded him a robe of honor.

On Tuesday the nineteenth at midday we rode out toward Khwaja Seyaran. I was fasting that day. Yunus Ali and the others were surprised and said, "You fasting on Tuesday? This is strange." When we got to Bihzadi we dismounted at the cadi's house. That evening there was a call for a party, but the cadi said, "I don't have such goings-on in my house, but Your Highness is the ruler." Although everything was ready for the party, to please the cadi the booze was put aside.

On Wednesday we went to Khwaja Seyaran.

On Thursday the twenty-first we had a large, round platform made on the outcropping of the mountain where a garden had been laid out.

On Friday we got on a raft at the bridge. When we were opposite the fowlers' houses, they brought a bird called a *dhek*[241] they had caught. I had never seen one before. [235b] It is a strange-looking bird that will be described in the section on the animals of Hindustan.[242]

On Saturday the twenty-third, saplings of plane trees and willows were planted together above the round platform. At midday there was a wine party. At dawn the next day we had a morning draught on the new platform. After noon we mounted and headed back to Kabul. Dead drunk when we got as far as Khwaja Hasan, we dozed off for a moment. Riding off from Khwaja Hasan, we reached the charbagh at midnight. While drunk at Khwaja Hasan, Abdullah threw himself fully clothed into the water. It was fairly late when we got on our horses, and he was too chilled to come, so he stayed the night at Qutlugh Khwaja's estate. The next morning, chastened by his excesses of the previous day, he arrived sworn off drink. I said, "Is such an oath possible? Swear instead that you won't drink anywhere except at my parties." He agreed and kept his word for a few months, but then he couldn't keep it any longer.

On Monday the twenty-fifth, Hindu Beg came. He had been stationed in Bhera and that region, and since there had been hopes of peace he had been left understaffed. As soon as we had departed, many Afghans and Hindustanis, paying no attention to their pledges of peace and in total disregard for us and our promises, had gathered and attacked Hindu Beg in Bhera. The local landholders also went over to the Afghans. Hindu Beg was unable to make a stand in Bhera, so he went to Khushab and came to Kabul through the Dinkot area and Nilab. [236] Deva Hindu, Siktu's son, and every other Hindu that was brought from Bhera in chains were ransomed and released. These Hindus were awarded horses and robes of honor and given leave to depart.

On Friday the twenty-ninth a fever appeared in my body. I had myself bled, but the fever returned every two or three days. Once it struck it did not abate until I was drenched in sweat. Ten or twelve days later Mulla Khwajaka gave me some wine mixed with narcissus. I drank it once or twice, but it did no good.

On Sunday the fifteenth of Jumada I [May 15], Khwaja Muhammad-Ali came from Khwast bringing a saddled horse as a present and also alms money. Muhammad Sharif the astrologer and the Mirzadas of Khwast also came with Khwaja Muhammad-Ali to pay homage. The next morning, Monday, Mulla Kabir came from Kashghar. He had come to Kabul from Andizhan by way of Kashghar.

On Monday the twenty-third, Malik Shah-Mansur Yusufzai came from Swat with six or seven Yusufzai chieftains to pay homage.

On Monday the first of Jumada II [May 31] the Afghan chieftains with Shah-Mansur were awarded robes of honor. Shah-Mansur was given a brocaded underrobe with buttons, another was given a brocaded robe with fringe, and six others were clad in brocaded robes and given leave. It was stipulated that they were not to interfere in the territory of Swat above Abuha and they should release all the peasants belonging to that territory. [236b] Furthermore, the Afghans who cultivated Bajaur and Swat should remit to the divan six thousand loads of grain.

On Wednesday the third, I drank some julep. Two days later I drank some more. On Saturday the sixth, I took a purgative. On Monday the eighth the wedding offering of Qasim Beg's youngest son Hamza and Khalifa's daughter arrived. It was a thousand shahrukhis. They also presented a saddled horse.

On Tuesday, Shah-Hasan son of Shah Beg requested permission to give a wine party and took some begs and ichkis under Khwaja Muhammad-Ali to his house. Yunus Ali and Gadai Taghayï were with me. I was still sworn off wine. "It has never happened," I said, "that I sit sober while everybody else drinks wine, or that I stand by stone sober while everybody else gets drunk. Come on, drink in my presence. I'll watch for a while and find out how drunks and sober people get along." A little tent had been erected on the southeastern side of the picture gallery I had built at the Bagh-i-Chanar Gate and occasionally I sat there. That is where the party took place. Later Ghiyas the buffoon came too. As a joke, several times orders were given to oust him from the party. Finally he created a ruckus and gained admittance through his antics. We invited Turdï-Muhammad Qipchaq and Mulla Kitabdar to the gathering. Mulla Kitabdar composed the following impromptu quatrain and sent it to Shah-Hasan [237] and the members of the party who were at his house.

We have no invitation into the assembly of those beloved ones at whose banquet a rose garden is but chaff. / If there are ease and comfort in that gathering, a hundred thanks that this gathering is not indisposed.

It was sent with the page Ibrahim. That afternoon the members of the party got drunk and departed.

During this illness I was carried about on a litter. A few days before I had drunk mixed wine, but since it did not help I did not drink any more, although I did drink some at a party given under an apple tree on the southwestern side of the Talar lawn toward the end of my con-valescence.

On Friday the twelfth, Ahmad Beg and Sultan-Muhammad Dulday came. They had been stationed as auxiliaries in Bajaur.

On Wednesday the seventeenth, Tengriberdi gave a party in Hay-dar Taqi's garden for some of the begs and warriors. I too went to this party and drank. We left there late that night, and there was more drinking in the large white tent.

On Thursday the twenty-fifth it was fixed that lessons in jurispru-dence would be read with Mulla Mahmud.

On Tuesday the last day of the month Abu-Muslim Kükäldash came as an envoy from Shah-Shuja' Arghun, bringing a thoroughbred horse as a present. This same day, Yusuf Ali Rikabdar swam around the pool in the Bagh-i-Chanar a hundred times. He was awarded a robe of honor, a horse and saddle, and some money.

On Wednesday the eighth of Rajab [July 6], I went to Shah-Hasan's house and drank. [237b] Most of the begs and ichkis were there.

On Saturday the eleventh there was a gathering. Late that afternoon we went up on the roof of the large pigeon house to drink. It was rather late when several horsemen could be seen approaching the city from the direction of Deh-i-Afghan. We realized it must be Darwesh-Muhammad Sarban coming as an envoy from Mirza Khan. We called to him from the roof, saying, "Take off your emissary's badge and buckle. Come on up and be informal." Darwesh-Muhammad came, presented his gifts, and joined the party, but since he was then sworn off wine he did not drink. The rest of us drank there until we were dead drunk. In the divan the next morning, he came with all ritual and ceremony and presented the gifts Mirza Khan had sent.

The year before, with great difficulty and by means of promises and enticements, we had forced the Aymaqs to migrate and come to Kabul from the other side of the Hindu Kush. However, Kabul is a confined territory and does not provide adequate summer and winter pasture for the flocks and herds of the Aymaqs and Turks. If left to their own devices nomadic people would never have any desire for Kabul. They waited on Qasim Beg and suggested that he mediate permission for them to cross back to the other side. Qasim Beg made an eloquent speech. Finally he got permission for the Aymaqs to cross over to Konduz and Baghlan.

Hafiz Mir Katib's elder brother had come from Samarkand. At this time he was given leave to return to Samarkand, and I sent my divan with him to Pulad Sultan. On the back of the divan I wrote the following little occasional piece: [238]

If you reach the sanctuary of that cypress, O zephyr, / make mention to his heart of this one wounded by separation. / May God have mercy on him, he has not thought of Babur. / Is there hope that God may cast compassion into his steely[243] heart?

On Friday the seventeenth, Shah-Mazid Kükäldash brought alms tribute and a horse from Muhammad-Zaman Mirza and paid homage. This same day, Shah Beg's envoy, Abu-Muslim Kükäldash, was given a robe of honor, granted favors, and allowed to depart. Khwaja Muhammad-Ali and Tengriberdi were also given leave to go to their lands, Khwast and Andarab.

On Thursday the twenty-third, Muhammad-Ali Jang-Jang, who had been stationed in Kachakot and the Qarluq region and was responsible for those territories, came with Mirza Malwi Qarluq's son Shah-Hasan, and Hati's man. This same day, Mulla Ali-Khan, who had gone to Samarkand to get his wife, came and paid homage.

The Abdurrahmani Afghans were living on the border of Gardez, but they were not satisfactory in their tribute or their dealings. They harassed caravans passing through. On Wednesday the twenty-ninth of Rajab we rode out to attack them. We stopped at the Waghjan Pass and ate, remounting after midday and riding off. That night we lost the road and wandered a good deal among the hills and dales to the southeast of Padkhwab-i-Shahana. [238b] Sometime later we got back on the road. Passing through the Chashma-i-Tara defile, we emerged onto level ground on the Gardez side from the Baqishliq Valley at sunup and the attack force was sent out. One detachment galloped toward Karmash Mountain, which is southeast of Gardez. To their rear was dispatched the right flank of the center under Khusraw, Mirza-Qulï, and Sayyid-Ali. Most of the army galloped up the glen to the east of Gardez, with Sayyid-Qasim Eshik-aqa, Mir Shah Qauchin, Qiyam, Hindu Beg, Qutlugh-Qadam, and Husayn's men at their rear.

Since most of the soldiers had gone up the glen, after having sent these off I rode after them. Up the glen were some men far away. The horses of the soldiers who went up the glen were worn out, and nothing much fell into their hands. Forty or fifty Afghans on foot could be seen on the flat ground, and those who had gone to the rear of the army set out toward them and sent a messenger to me. I too rode as fast as I could. As I arrived, Husayn Hasan, alone and unarmed, charged his horse. As he reached the midst of the Afghans and started swinging his sword, they shot his horse and brought it down. No sooner was he on his feet than they slashed at his legs with their swords and felled him. From all sides they struck him with their knives and cut him to pieces, while our warriors stood by watching and offering no assistance. As soon as I heard this, I sent ichkis and warriors at a gallop under Gadai Taghayï, Payanda-Muhammad [239] Qaplan, Abu'l-Hasan Qorchï, and Mu'min Atäkä and set out myself as fast as I could. Before anyone else Mu'min Atäkä felled an Afghan with his spear and cut off his head. Abu'l-Hasan Qorchï also went bravely forward without protective armor, cut off the Afghans' way, charged his horse, took a swipe at an Afghan, knocked him down, and cut off his head. He himself received three wounds, and his horse also received a wound. Payanda-Muhammad Qaplan also went forward bravely, took a swipe at an Afghan, and brought in his head. Although Abu'l-Hasan and Payanda-Muhammad Qaplan's bravery was known before now, they showed their mettle even more in this campaign. The forty or fifty Afghans were all shot or cut to ribbons. After these Afghans were killed we dismounted in a field, and I ordered the Afghans' heads piled into a tower.

Along the way the begs who had been with Husayn came. I said in admonition and anger, "So many men stand by and watch while a bunch of Afghans on foot overpower such a warrior on terrain as flat as a board! You should be stripped of your rank and station, driven from your lands and estates, and paraded around town with your beards cut so that anyone who lets such an enemy defeat such a warrior and stands by watching on such flat ground without lifting a finger may get his just deserts!" [239b]

The soldiers who had gone to Karmash captured sheep and booty and brought them back. Baba Qashqa Moghul had gone along. An Afghan had attacked him with his sword, but Baba Qashqa had stood his ground valiantly, fixed an arrow, and shot the Afghan dead.

The next morning we headed back to Kabul. Muhammad Bakhshï, Abdul-Aziz Mirakhur, and Mir Khurd Bökäül were ordered to stop at Chashma-i-Tara and get some pheasants from the people. I and several others went by the road to the Rustam Plain, which I had not seen before. It is situated in the midst of the mountains. Near the top of the mountain is not a pleasant place. Between two mountains is a broad glen. On the southern side, on the skirt of a hill, is a rather small spring with large poplar trees. Along the road on the Gardez side of the Rustam plain are springs. There are many trees but they are small. Although the glen is rather narrow, at the base of these small trees is a beautiful, very green meadow. The glen is not without charm. We went up the mountain on the southern side of the Rustam plain. Below we could see the Karmash and Bangash mountains. On the other side of the Karmash Mountains the monsoon clouds could be seen piled up one on top of the other. [240] On the side where there is no monsoon there were no clouds to be seen.

We reached Huni at midday and camped. The next morning we stopped in the vicinity of the village of Muhammad Agha and had some ma'jun. We also threw some fish drug into the water and caught a number of fish.

On Sunday the third of Sha'ban [July 31] we reached Kabul.

On Tuesday the fifth [August 2] we summoned Darwesh-Muhammad Fazli and Khusraw's servant, held an enquiry into those who had failed when Husayn was taken, and stripped them of their rank and station. At midday there was a wine party under a plane tree. Baba Qashqa Moghul was awarded a robe of honor.

On Friday the eighth came Käpä, who had gone to Mirza Khan.

Thursday afternoon I rode out on an excursion to Khwaja Seyaran, Baran, and Koh Daman. Late that night we camped at Mama Khatun. The next morning we stopped at Istalif. That day we had some ma'jun.

On Saturday there was a wine party at Istalif. The next morning we rode out of Istalif and passed through the Sinjit valley. When we were near Khwaja Seyaran, a huge snake as big around as a man's forearm and a fathom long was killed. From inside the snake came a smaller snake that must have just been swallowed: it was completely whole. The smaller snake was only a bit shorter than the big one. [240b] Then, from inside the smaller snake came a big rat. It too was whole, and none of it had been digested.

Having reached Khwaja Seyaran, we had a wine party. This same day, Kichikkinä the night watchman was sent with orders and a rendezvous for the begs on the other side to say that the army was being mounted and that they should take care to reach the rendezvous as appointed.

The next morning we rode out and ate some ma'jun. At the confluence of the Parwan River we threw some fish drug into the water, as the people there do, and caught a lot of fish. Mir Shah Beg brought food and horses. We rode from here and went to Gulbahar. That evening there was a wine party. Darwesh-Muhammad Sarban was there. Although he was a warrior and a soldier, he was abstinent and did not drink wine. Qutlugh Khwaja Kükäldash had long since given up soldiering and become a dervish. He was fairly old too and had a white beard. He was always a good drinker at these parties. I said to Darwesh-Muhammad, "Qutlugh Khwaja's beard shames you! He's a dervish and an old man with a snow-white beard, but he always drinks wine. You are a soldier and a warrior with a black beard, but you never drink. What's wrong?" Since it was not my way to offer wine to someone who did not drink, this was just a joke. He was not offered any wine. The next morning we had a morning draught.

On Wednesday [241] we rode out of Gulbahar and stopped in Atun's village, where we ate and then rode on to Baghat-i-Jam. After midday there was a wine party. The next morning we rode from there, circumambulated Khwaja Khawand Sa'id's tomb, and then got on a raft

Tankard, China, Ming dynasty, fifteenth century. Porcelain with transparent glaze over cobalt underglaze. Freer Gallery of Art, Smithsonian Institution, F1951.15. Babur's china "cup" may have been similar to this one.

at the China fortress. At the confluence of the Panjshir River the raft struck a rocky outcropping of the mountain and started to sink. Ruhdam, Tengri-Qulï, and Mir Muhammad the raftsman were thrown into the water when it struck. Ruhdam and Tengri-Qulï were pulled back onto the raft only with difficulty. My china cup, a spoon, and a tambourine fell into the river. Farther down, opposite Sang Burida, the raft struck either a limb or a piling for a dam. Shah-Hasan son of Shah Beg was thrown backward and, clutching at Mirza-Qulï Kükäldash, pulled him over too. Darwesh-Muhammad Sarban also went overboard. Mirza-Qulï's fall was remarkable. He had been cutting a melon just before he fell, and he stuck the knife into the mat on the raft as he went over. He swam in all his clothes and got out of the water without coming onto the raft. When we got off the raft, we were put up for the night in the raftsmen's houses. Darwesh-Muhammad presented me with a porcelain cup exactly like the one that had disappeared into the water.

On Friday we rode up the riverbank. Headed down through a narrow mountain pass, we stopped on the slopes of Koh-i-Bachcha, where we gathered toothpicks with our own hands.[244] **[241b]** Passing on from there we ate with the people of Khwaja Khizr and rode on. At midday we stopped in Qutlugh Khwaja's estate in the village of Lamghani, where he presented a meal of what was on hand. We partook, mounted, and rode back to Kabul.

On Monday the twenty-fifth [August 22], Darwesh-Muhammad Sarban was awarded a royal robe and a horse with saddle and made to kneel in fealty.

I had not had my hair cut for four or five months. On Wednesday the twenty-seventh, I finally did. There was a wine party that day.

On Friday the twenty-ninth, Mir Khurd was made to kneel as tutor to Hindal and had a thousand shahrukhis brought in as a gift.

On Wednesday the fifth of Ramadan [August 31] a retainer of Tüläk Kükäldash, Barlas Chäkäni by name, brought a letter from Tüläk. Uzbek raiders had encroached on that area, and Tüläk had gone out against them. One Uzbek was brought in alive and another's head was brought back.

Friday evening the eighth [September 3] we went to Qasim Beg's quarters and broke our fast. A horse with saddle was presented to me.

On Saturday evening the fast was broken at Khalifa's quarters. A horse and saddle were offered. The next morning Khwaja Muhammad-Ali and Jan Nasir,[245] who had been summoned to the army, came from their territories.

On Wednesday the twelfth came Kamran's uncle Sultan-Ali, [242] who, as has been mentioned, went to Kashghar the year I went from Khwast to Kabul.[246]

On Thursday the thirteenth, I mounted, fully determined to repulse the Yusufzai, and camped in the meadow on the Kabul side of Deh-i-Ya'qub. As we were mounting, Baba Jan the equerry brought me my horse in a rather sloppy manner. I was so angry I hit him in the face and dislocated my thumb. It did not hurt much then, but by the time we reached the campsite it was giving me a lot of trouble. I suffered for a long time and could not write, but it finally healed. While in this same campaign camp my aunt Dawlat Sultan Khanïm's kükäldash, Qutlugh Muhammad,[247] brought letters and gifts from my lady in Kashghar. The same day Nohan and Musa, chieftains of the Dilazak, came with presents and paid homage.

On Sunday the sixteenth, Qoch Beg came.

On Wednesday the nineteenth we marched out past Butkhak and camped where we always did on the banks of the Butkhak river. Because Qoch Beg's territories of Bamian, Kahmard, and Ghori were near the Uzbeks, he was excused from this campaign, awarded a turban I had used myself and a robe of honor, and given leave to depart for his territory.

On Friday the twenty-first we camped at Badam Chashma. [242b] The next morning we stopped at the Barikao. I myself went to inspect Quratu. At this same site honey was found in a tree. We set out, march by march.

On Wednesday the twenty-sixth we stopped at the Bagh-i-Wafa. On Thursday, I just stayed in the garden.

On Friday we marched, passed Sultanpur, and stopped. This day Shah Mir Husayn came from his territory. The chieftains of the Dilazak under Nohan and Musa also arrived today. I had determined to repulse the Yusufzai in Swat, but the Dilazak maliks said that there were many tribes in Hashnaghar, where much grain was to be found. They lobbied for Hashnaghar. After consultation it was decided that the Afghans in Hashnaghar should be raided, the fortress of Hashnaghar or Peshawar put in order, part of the grain stored, and a detachment of warriors stationed there under Shah Mir Husayn. To this end Shah Mir Husayn was given a fifteen-day leave to go to his territory and get his arms ready.

The next morning we marched to Juy-i-Shahi and camped. Tengriberdi and Sultan-Muhammad Dulday caught up and joined us there. Hamza also came from Konduz.

On Sunday the last of the month [September 25] we marched out of Juy-i-Shahi and stopped at Qïrq Arïq. [243] I got on a raft with a few of my special retinue. While at this camp, we saw the festival moon. A few mule-loads of wine had been brought from Dara-i-Nur, so after the evening prayer there was a wine party. The members of the party included Muhibb-Ali Qorchï, Khwaja Muhammad-Ali Kitabdar, Shah-Hasan son of Shah Beg, Sultan-Muhammad Dulday, and Darwesh-Muhammad Sarban. Darwesh-Muhammad was abstaining. From my childhood it had been my rule not to force drink on anyone who did not drink. Darwesh-Muhammad was always at these parties, and no coercion was ever exerted. However, Khwaja Muhammad-Ali would not leave him alone and kept trying to compel him to drink.

On Monday morning, the feast day, we marched off. Along the way we ate some ma'jun to get rid of our hangover. While we were high on the ma'jun someone brought a colocynth.[248] Darwesh-Muhammad had never seen one before. I said, "It is the watermelon of Hindustan." I cut a slice and gave it to him. He bit into it with great relish. It took him until that evening to get the bitterness out of his mouth.

We camped on a hill at Garm Chashma. Stew was being dished out when Langar Khan, who had been on his lands for some time, showed up and presented a horse and some ma'jun.

Next we camped at Yada Bir. That afternoon I and several of my retinue sailed down the river about a kos. The next morning we marched, stopping at the bottom of the Khyber pass. [243b] The same day, Sultan-Bayazid came from Nilab by the Bara road, and after hearing of us followed and caught up with us. He reported that the Afridi Afghans were camped with their families and animals in Bara. They had planted a lot of rice, which was ripe and still standing. Since we had planned to raid the Yusufzai Afghans in Hashnaghar, we paid no attention.

At midday there was a drinking party in Khwaja Muhammad-Ali's tent. During the party an account of how we had come this far was written and sent with Sultan Tirahi to Khwaja Kalan in Bajaur. On the margin of the document, I wrote this line:

Zephyr, say softly to that lovely fawn, "You have driven us to the mountains and wilderness."

The next morning we moved out, descended through the Khyber pass, and dismounted at Ali Masjid. At midday we remounted and separated ourselves from the baggage. It was the second watch when we reached the bank of the Kabul River and slept a bit. At dawn we found a crossing and forded it. Word came from the scouts that the Afghans had learned of us and fled. We rode forward, crossed the Swat River, and dismounted in the midst of the Afghans' fields. We did not find a half, not even a fourth, of what had been described. Now the plan for fortifying Hashnaghar with the hoped-for grain had to be changed. [244] On this account the Dilazak maliks, at whose urging this campaign had been launched, were ashamed.

That afternoon we recrossed over to the Kabul side of the Swat River and dismounted. The next morning we moved out, crossed the Kabul River, and stopped. The begs who attended council were summoned and it was decided that we should raid the Afridi Afghans whom Sultan-Bayazid had spoken of and that someone should be stationed at the Peshawar fortress, which could be provisioned with the Afridis' animals and grain. Hindu Beg Qauchin and the Mirzadas of Khwast caught up with us at this station. Today some ma'jun was eaten. Darwesh-Muhammad Sarban, Muhammadi Kükäldash, Gadai Taghayï, and Asas were there. Later we invited Shah-Hasan too. Late in the afternoon, after the meal was served, we got on a raft and called out to Langar Khan Niazi to join us on it. That evening we got off the raft and went back to camp.

As had been decided, we moved at dawn from the riverbank, passed Jam, and stopped where the Ali Masjid river gushes out. Sultan-Ali's Abu'l-Hashim, who had caught up with us, said, "On Arafa night[249] at Juy-i-Shahi, I crossed the Jamrud with someone who had come from Badakhshan. He said that Sultan-Sa'id Khan had attacked Badakhshan. I have come to warn the padishah." I called the begs for consultation, and in view of the news it was decided to return and head for Badakhshan without tending to the matter of the fortress. [244b] Langar Khan was presented with a robe of honor, assigned to reinforce Muhammad-Ali Jang-Jang, and given leave to depart. That evening there was a wine party in Khwaja Muhammad-Ali's tent. Early the next morning we marched through the Khyber pass and dismounted at the bottom of the defile.

Many improper acts had been committed by the Khizr-Khel.[250] The soldiers who had stayed behind on the riverbank while the army went on were shot at and their horses were carried off. It seemed imperative to teach them a lesson. With this in mind we set out at dawn from the bottom of the defile, spent midday in Deh-i-Ghulaman feeding the horses, and then rode off. Muhammad-Husayn Qorchï was sent posthaste to Kabul with orders to imprison all the Khizr-Khelis in Kabul and to make a detailed report of their possessions. Whatever news came from Badakhshan was to be written in detail and sent to me as fast as possible. That night we rode until the second watch, and a little past Sultanpur stopped and slept a bit. The Khizr-Khel inhabited the region from Bahar and Panjgram to Kira Su. We arrived just at dawn and started the raid. Most of their animals and small children fell prey to the soldiers. A few of them withdrew in safety to the nearby mountains.

The next morning we dismounted in Qelaghu. [245] Here pheasants were caught. The uruq, which had remained behind, joined us here. The Waziri Afghans had never given tribute that was satisfactory in the slightest, but after this punitive raid on them they brought in three hundred sheep.

I had not written anything since my thumb got dislocated,[251] but at this camp on Sunday the fourteenth [October 9], I wrote a little. The next morning the Afghan chieftains under the Ghilzai and Samu-Khel came. The chieftains of the Dilazak begged me to pardon their offenses, so I set them free. Their tribute was set at four thousand sheep, the chieftains were given robes of honor, and collectors were assigned and sent out.

Having settled these matters, we moved out on Thursday the eighteenth and stopped in Bahar and Panjgram, reaching the Bagh-i-Wafa the next morning. It was a time of beauty in the Bagh-i-Wafa. The open spaces were full of clover, and the pomegranate trees had turned a beautiful autumnal bright yellow. The fruit on the trees was bright red, and the orange trees were green and fresh, filled with innumerable oranges, although they were less yellow than one might wish. The pomegranates were quite good, but not so good as the best ones of our country. This was one time we really enjoyed the Bagh-i-Wafa. The three or four days we were in the garden [245b] the soldiers ate pomegranates to excess.

On Monday we left the garden. I stayed until the first watch and had some oranges gathered. Shah-Hasan was given the oranges of two trees. Some begs were given the oranges of one tree each, and others were given a half-share. Since I planned to tour Laghman that winter, I ordered about twenty orange trees around the pool kept in reserve. That day we stopped at Gandamak and dismounted the next morning at Jagdalak. Around supper time most of the ichkis attended a wine party. Toward the end Qasim Beg's nephew Gadai Bahjat created an uproar. He fell back drunk on the cushion beside me. Gadai Taghayï picked him up and took him out.

Early the next morning we moved on. I went on an excursion up and down the Barikao on the Quruq Say side. A few poplar trees had taken on beautiful autumnal foliage. We stopped there and were served stew. Autumn was the cause. Wine was drunk. A sheep was brought and I ordered it roasted. We set fire to holm oak branches and enjoyed watching them burn. Mulla Abdul-Malik Dewana begged to take the news of my coming to Kabul, so he was dispatched to do so. Hasan Nabira had opted for me and come from Mirza Khan to pay homage. [246] We drank until sunset, then got on our horses. The members of the party had gotten pretty drunk. Sayyid Qasim was so inebriated that his two servants had trouble getting him on his horse and bringing him back to camp. Dost-Muhammad Baqir was so drunk that no matter how Amin-Muhammad Tarkhan and Masti Chuhra's people tried they could not get him on his horse. They splashed water on his head, but that didn't do any good either. Just then a band of Afghans appeared. Amin-Muhammad Tarkhan was so drunk he thought that rather than leaving Dost-Muhammad to be taken by the Afghans we should cut off his head and take it with us. With great difficulty they threw him up on his horse and took off. We got back to Kabul at midnight.

The next morning in the divan Qulï Beg, who had gone as envoy to Sultan Sa'id Khan in Kashghar, came and paid homage. Bishka Mirza Itarji[252] had been sent back as envoy with Qulï Beg. He brought some items from that country as presents.

On Wednesday the first of Dhu'l-Qa'da [October 25], I went out by myself to Cain's tomb and had a morning draught. Later the members of the party straggled in by ones and twos. When the sun was well up, we went to the Bagh-i-Banafsha and drank by the side of the pool. At midday we had a nap and then started drinking again in the afternoon. During this gathering, I gave wine to Tengri-Qulï and Beg Hindi, who had not previously been given any. [246b] That evening I stayed the night at the bath.

On Thursday, Yahya Nohani's party of Hindustan merchants were given robes of honor and dismissed.

On Saturday the fourth Bishka Mirza was given a robe of honor and granted leave to depart.

On Sunday a party was held in the little picture gallery over the gate. Although it was a small chamber, sixteen people attended.

A TOUR OF THE AUTUMN HARVEST

On Monday we went to Istalif to tour the autumn harvest. We ate ma'jun, and that night it rained a lot. Most of the begs and ichkis came with me into my tent, which had been set up in the Bagh-i-Kalan. The next morning, at a wine party in this same garden, we drank until night, then had a morning draught the next morning. We got drunk and went to sleep. At midday we rode out of Istalif, having some ma'jun along the way. In the late afternoon we came to Bihzadi. The autumn was beautiful. While touring the harvest my companions who were inclined to wine began to agitate for some. Although we had had some ma'jun, since the autumn colors were so beautiful, we sat down under the colorful trees and drank. The party continued there until late that night. When Khalifa's Mulla Mahmud came, we invited him to join the party. Abdullah, who was extremely drunk, let slip a word against Khalifa. [247] Unaware of Mulla Mahmud, he recited this line:

All upon whom you gaze are afflicted with the same brand.

Mulla Mahmud was sober and objected to Abdullah's having recited this line in jest. When Abdullah realized what he had done, he spoke nicely.

On Thursday, I went out to tour the autumn harvests and returned late that evening to the Charbagh.

On Friday the sixteenth [November 9],[253] I ate some ma'jun in the Bagh-i-Banafsha and got on a boat with some of my retinue. Humayun and Kamran came later. Humayun made a good shot at a duck.

A PRIVATE PARTY

On Saturday the eighteenth, I rode out of the charbagh at midnight. I sent the night watchman and the equerry back. I crossed the Mulla Baba Bridge, went out through the Diurin narrows, circled around Qush Nawar behind the Bazaris' *karez*[254] and Khirskhana, and reached Turdï Beg Khaksar's karez just before dawn the next day. When Turdï Beg learned that I was there, he came running in agitation. Turdï Beg's financial straits were well known. I had brought a hundred shahrukhis with me when I left, and I gave them to him. "Make ready wine and implements," I said. "I feel like having a very private bash." Turdï Beg went off toward Bihzadi to get wine. I sent my horse off to a valley with one of Turdï Beg's slaves and went myself and sat down on a hill behind the karez. It was the first watch [247b] when Turdï Beg brought a jug of wine. We started drinking, just the two of us. While Turdï Beg was bringing the wine, Muhammad Qasim Barlas and Shahzada got wine and followed him on foot, unaware of my presence. We invited them to the party. Turdï Beg said, "Hulhul Anikä wants to drink wine with you."

"I've never seen a woman drink," I said. "Invite her to the party." We also invited a wandering dervish named Shahi and a couple of karez men who played the *rubab*. We sat drinking on the hill behind the karez drinking until nightfall. Then we went to Turdï Beg's house and continued by candlelight until late at night. It was a really relaxed party. I lay back, and the others went off to another house and drank until the naqara was beat. Hulhul Anikä came and talked a blue streak until finally I got rid of her by pretending to be drunk.

I thought I would surprise the people by riding back by myself to Istarghij, but they found out and spoiled my plan. At the sound of the drum I got on my horse. I told Turdï Beg and Shahzada, and together the three of us rode to Istarghij. At dawn we reached Khwaja Hasan, at the foot of Istalif. We rested for a while, had some ma'jun, and toured the harvest. The sun was up when we stopped at the Istalif garden, [248] where we ate some grapes. Then we mounted again and rode to Khwaja Shihab, one of the village dependencies of Istarghij, where we took a nap. Ata Mirakhur's house must have been around there, for he had cooked some food and brought a jug of wine by the time we woke up. It was an excellent vintage. We had a few goblets and got on our horses. At midday we stopped in a beautiful autumnal garden in Istarghij and held a party. A little later Khwaja Muhammad-Amin came. We drank until late that night. That day and night Abdullah, Asas, Nur Beg, and Yusuf Ali all arrived. The next morning we had some food, got on our horses, and toured the Padishahi Bagh[255] below Istarghij. We saw an apple sapling with beautiful autumnal foliage that had five or six leaves arranged regularly on each branch—if painters had exerted every effort they wouldn't have been able to depict such a thing.

We rode out of Istarghij, had a meal at Khwaja Hasan, and reached Bihzadi that evening. We drank in the house of Khwaja Muhammad-Amin's servant, Imam-Muhammad. The next morning, Tuesday, we went to the Charbagh in Kabul.

On Thursday the twenty-third we entered the fortress.

On Friday, Muhammad-Ali Haydar Rikabdar caught a falcon, brought it in, and presented it to me.

On Saturday the twenty-fifth there was a party in the Bagh-i-Chanar. Late that night we got on our horses. Sayyid-Qasim was embarrassed by past events. We stopped at his house and drank a few cups.

On Thursday the first of Dhu'l-Hijja [November 24], [248b] Tajuddin Mahmud came from Kandahar and paid homage.

On Monday the nineteenth [December 12], Muhammad-Ali Jang-Jang came from Nilab.

On Tuesday, Sankar Khan Janjua came from Bhera and paid homage.

On Friday the twenty-third, I finished arranging by meter a selection I had made of Ali-Sher Beg's four divans.[256]

On Tuesday the twenty-seventh there was a party in the citadel. It was ordered that anybody who got drunk was to be put out and not invited back.

On Friday the last of Dhu'l-Hijja we rode out on an excursion to Laghman.

EVENTS OF THE YEAR 926
(1519-20)[257]

On Saturday the first of Muharram [December 23, 1519] we went to Khwaja Seyaran. A wine party was held beside the new irrigation canal that had been made on the hill. The next morning we rode out to see Reg-i-Rawan, and went to Sayyid-Qasim's "nightingale house," where we had a party. The next morning we mounted and ate some ma'jun on our way to Malgar. The following day we had a morning draught without having drunk anything the night before. At midday we went to Dur Nama, where we had a drinking party. Early the next day we had a morning draught. Haqqdad, the headman of Dur Nama, presented me with his garden.

On Thursday we rode out to Nijrao and the village of the Tadzhiks.

On Friday we hunted in Ghar Mountain between Chihil Qolba and the Baran River. A lot of game was bagged. [249] I had not shot an arrow since my hand had been injured, but now I shot a deer in the leg with an easy bow. The arrow went in halfway up the feathers. Late that afternoon, when we returned from hunting, we went to Nijrao. The next morning the tribute of the people of Nijrao was fixed at sixty gold pieces.

AN EXCURSION TO LAGHMAN

On Monday we mounted intending to make an excursion to Laghman. It was planned that Humayun too should be with us on this excursion, but he was inclined to stay and was given leave to depart at the Kura Pass. We stopped in Badrao. Riding on from there, we stopped in....²⁵⁸ The fishermen at the Baran River caught some fish. Late that afternoon we got on a raft and drank, and that evening when we got off the raft we kept on drinking in a felt tent. Haydar Alamdar had been sent to the Dawartin Kafirs. At the foot of Badpakh the Kafir chieftains brought a few skins of wine and paid homage. As we were descending from the *kotal*,²⁵⁹ we saw an incredible number of locusts.²⁶⁰ The next morning, with two rafts, we ate some ma'jun, got off below Bulan, and went to the camp.

On Friday we moved out and stopped on the slopes below Mandrawar. That night there was a drinking party.

On Saturday we got on a raft, went through the Darunta narrows, and disembarked above Jahannumay. We went to the Bagh-i-Wafa opposite Adinapur. Qiyam Ordu Shah, the governor of Nangarhar district, came to pay homage as we were getting off the raft. [249b] Langar Khan Niazi had been in Nilab for some time. He came to pay homage to us while we were on the road. We stopped in the Bagh-i-Wafa. The oranges had turned a beautiful yellow, and the greenery was full. It was very pleasant. We stayed in the Bagh-i-Wafa for five or six days. Having vowed to give up drinking at age forty, with only one year left to my fortieth year I was drinking to excess out of anxiety.

On Sunday the sixteenth [January 7, 1520], I had a morning draught, got sober, and had some ma'jun. Mulla Yarak played a tune he had composed in the *panjgah* mode on a *mukhammas*.²⁶¹ He had composed quite nicely. I had not indulged in such diversions for a long time, and I too was tempted to create something. Shortly thereafter I wrote an air in the chargah mode, as will be mentioned in its place.

On Wednesday, after my morning draught, I said in jest that anyone who sang a song in Persian would be allowed to drink a cup of wine. Lots of people drank on that account. Early that morning we sat under some willow trees in the middle of the meadow. Then it was proposed that anyone who sang a song in Turkish would be allowed to drink a cup. Many also drank on that account. When the sun was well up, we went to the edge of the pool under the orange trees and drank.

The next morning we got on a raft at Darunta and went through the Juy-i-Shahi to Atar. From there we got on horses and made a tour of Dara-i-Nur. When we got to the village of Susan, we turned back and stopped at Amla. [250] Khwaja Kalan had inventoried Bajaur well, but since he was a companion of mine I summoned him and put Shah Mir Husayn in his place in Bajaur.

On Saturday the twenty-second [January 13], Shah Mir Husayn was given leave to depart. This day we drank in Amla. The next morning it rained, and we went to Kulahgram in Kunar, where Malik-Quli's house was. We stopped at his middle son's house, which overlooked an orange grove. Since it was raining we stayed there and drank rather than going to the grove. The rain was inordinately hard. I knew a charm and taught it to Mulla Ali-Khan. He wrote it on four pieces of paper and hung them on four sides. As soon as he did this the rain stopped and the weather began to clear. We got on a raft for a morning draught. Some other warriors got on another raft.

In Bajaur, Swat, Kunar, and those regions they make a type of beer, something called *kim*, made from herbal roots and spices. They shape it into a round like a loaf of bread and dry it out to keep, then use it as the fermenting agent for the beer. Some beers are extremely intoxicating, but they are also bitter and evil tasting. We thought we would drink some of it, but it was so distasteful we could not drink it and had some ma'jun instead. Asas, Hasan Ekräk, and Masti, who were on another raft, were ordered to drink some. They got drunk. Hasan Ekräk began to create a ruckus. [250b] Asas got roaring drunk and kept doing such unseemly stunts that we all got sick of him. I thought I would have him put off the raft on the other side, but some others begged me not to do it.

At this time we had given Bajaur to Shah Mir Husayn and summoned Khwaja Kalan, who was a companion and had been in Bajaur for a long time. I also imagined the administration of Bajaur was rather easy. Shah Mir Husayn ran into me at the Kunar River crossing on his way to Bajaur. I summoned him, gave him some oral instructions, presented him with my own quiver, and granted him leave.

When we reached opposite Nur Gul, an old man was there begging. Everyone on the raft gave him something, such as robes, turbans, and shawls. He got quite a lot. At a bad place in midstream the raft struck something with a shock, and everyone was alarmed. Mir-Muhammad the raftsman fell into the water. That night we were near Atar.

On Tuesday we went to Mandrawar. Qutlugh-Qadam and his father, Dawlat-Qadam, gave a party in the fortress. Although it was an unpleasant place, we drank a few cups for their sake and returned to the camp in the late afternoon.

On Wednesday we made an excursion to the spring at Kandagar, a village in the Mandrawar district. In all of the Laghman area it is the only village that has dates. Kandagar is situated above the mountain slopes, [251] with the date grove on the eastern side and the spring, next to the grove, in an out-of-the-way spot. Six or seven yards below the spring, stones have arranged to form a sheltered area for bathing. The spring water, which is quite moderate in temperature, pours down on the bather's head. Even on winter days one can bathe in it. At first it seems a bit chilly, but the longer one stays in it the better it feels.

On Thursday, Sher-Khan[262] Tarklani had us stop at his house, where he gave a banquet. At midday we mounted and went to the fish tanks and caught some fish. A description of these small fish tanks has already been given.[263]

On Friday we stopped near Khwaja Mirmiran's village. That evening there was a gathering.

On Saturday a hunt was held on a mountain between Alishang and Alingar. The Alingaris on one side and the Alishangis on the other formed a circle and drove the game down from the mountain. Much game was killed. On our way back from the hunt we stopped in Alingar in the maliks' garden and had a party.

Half of one of my front teeth had broken off. On this day the other half broke while I was eating.

The next morning we mounted and had nets cast to catch fish. It was noon when we went to Alishang and drank in a garden. The next morning Hamza Khan, the malik of Alishang who had performed evil deeds and shed innocent blood, was turned over to the families of those he had killed, and they had him executed.

On Tuesday, [251b] I recited a litany and took the Yan Bulaq road back to Kabul. Late that afternoon we crossed the river at Ulughtu, and that evening arrived at Quratu, where we fed the horses and some ready food was brought. When the horses finished their barley, we remounted....[264]

PART THREE

HINDUSTAN

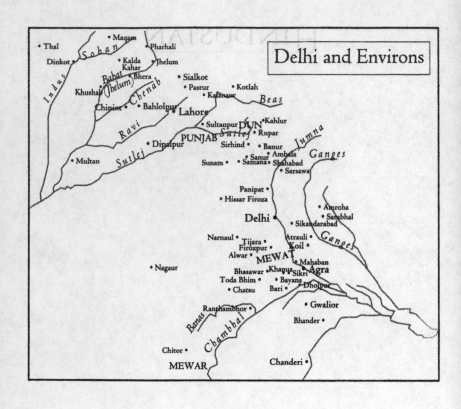

Delhi and Environs

Thal · Maqam · Pharhali
Dinkot · Sohan
Kalda
Kahar · Jhelum
Khushab Bahat (Jhelum) Bhera · Sialkot
Chiniot · Pasrur · Kotlah
Bahlolpur Kalanaur
Lahore Beas
Sultanpur DUN Kahlur
PUNJAB Sutlej Rupar
Dipalpur Sirhind · Banur
Multan Sutlej Sunam Sanur Ambala
Samana Shahabad
Sarsawa

Panipat ·
· Hissar Firoza

Delhi ·
Amroha
Sambhal
Sikandarabad
Narnaul · Tijara Atrauli Ganges
Firozpur · Koil
Alwar · MEWAT Mahaban
· Nagaur Bhasawar · Khanua Sikri Agra
Toda Bhim Bayana Dholpur
· Chatsu Bari ·

Ranthambhor · · Gwalior
Banas Bhander ·
Chambhal

Chitor ·
MEWAR Chanderi ·

EVENTS OF THE YEAR 932
(1525-26)[1]

On Friday the first of Safar 932 [November 17, 1525], with the sun in Sagittarius, we set out on an expedition to Hindustan, passed the Yak Langa hill, and camped in the meadow to the west of the river at Deh-i-Ya'qub.

Abdul-Malik Qorchï, who had been gone for seven or eight months on a mission to Sultan Sa'id Khan, came to the camp with the khan's man Yangï Beg Kükäldash. He brought letters and paltry presents and gifts from the khanïms and the khan. We stayed at the site for two days seeing to the army and then set out, spending one night on the road and the next at Badam Chashma. We had some ma'jun there.

On Wednesday, at Barikao, one of Nur Beg's younger brothers brought twenty thousand shahrukhis worth of gold, *ashrafis,*[2] and tankas, which Khwaja Husayn the divan had forwarded from the Lahore revenues. Most of it was sent for the benefit of Balkh by Mulla Ahmad, one of the lords of Balkh.

On Friday the eighth, [252] while stopped at Gandamak, I got a violent cold. Thank God it went away without complication.

On Saturday we reached the Bagh-i-Wafa, where we waited for a few days for Humayun Mirza and the army from the other side of the Hindu Kush. The Bagh-i-Wafa has been mentioned several times in this history for its extent, pleasure, and delight.[3] It is really charmingly situated. Anyone who looks at it with a buyer's eye will realize what sort of place it is. During the few days we were there we mostly drank and had morning draughts on drinking days; on nondrinking days we held ma'jun parties. Since Humayun was long overdue I sent him some harshly worded letters.

On Sunday the seventeenth of Safar we were having our morning draught when Humayun finally appeared. I rebuked him quite a lot for being so late. Khwaja Kalan also arrived from Ghazni. That evening we marched out and camped in the new garden I had made between Sultanpur and Khwaja Rustam.

On Wednesday we got on a raft and drank wine all the way to Khush Gumbaz, where we disembarked and camped. The next morning we set the camp to march, returned to the raft, and had some ma'jun. The site we always camped in was Qïrq Arïq, but when we reached the opposite bank we looked and found no trace of the camp. [252b] Not even the horses were there. It occurred to me that Garm Chashma was nearby and shady, and that the camp may have been moved there. It was quite late by the time we got to Garm Chashma, whence we proceeded all night, although we did stop the raft and sleep a bit. At dawn we got out at Yada Bir. As the sun was coming up the soldiers began to arrive. The army had camped in the Qïrq Arïq region, but we had not seen them.

There were many people on the raft who could compose poetry, such as Shaykh Abu'l-Wajd, Shaykh Zayn, Mulla Ali-Khan, Turdï Beg Khaksar, and some others. During the party this line of Muhammad Salih's was quoted:

> What is one to do with the loveliness of every coquette? / There where you are, what is one to do with others?[4]

"Let's compose another like it," they said. Those who had poetic talent were in a composing mood. Since there had been much joking with Mulla Ali-Khan, the following funny line came spontaneously to mind:

> What is one to do with a dope like you? / What is one to do with every female ass with a hole as big as a cow's?

Before this, whatever came to mind, good and bad, serious and humorous, was often put into poetry as a joke. No matter how obscene or improper, it got written down. While I was versifying the *Mubin,*[5] however, it occurred to my weak mind and saddened heart that [253] it was a pity for obscene words to emerge from a tongue engaged with lofty expressions, and for improper images to occur to a mind manifesting pious thoughts. From then on I eschewed satirical and humorous poetry. At the time I made up that line, however, no such thing had ever occurred to me.

A day or two later, while camped at Bigram, I had an attack of the rhume, which led to a fever and a cough. Every time I coughed I hemorrhaged. I realized where the admonition was from and what I had done to deserve this suffering.

> Whoever shall violate his oath, will violate the same to the hurt only of his own soul: but whoever shall perform that which he hath covenanted with God, he will surely give him a great reward.

> What am I to do with you, O tongue? On your account my innards are bloody. / No matter how gracefully you compose humorous poetry, part of it is obscene and part is false. / If you wish not to burn for this crime, turn your reins from this field.

> O Lord, we have dealt unjustly with out own souls; and if thou forgive us not, and be not merciful unto us, we shall surely be of those who perish.[6]

Once again I sought forgiveness and apologized anew, and I freed my mind from and broke my pen to these sorts of vain thoughts and improper activities. Such a counsel from the divine court is an immense source of wealth for a disobedient human. Anyone who is thus admonished has attained great felicity.

Marching from there, we camped at Ali Masjid. [253b] Because the site is narrow, I always camped on a hill there, which overlooked the valley where the soldiers camped. By night the soldiers' campfires glowed beautifully. This time, and every time we camped there, we had a party and drank. Before morning I had some ma'jun and then mounted. I was fasting that day. We dismounted near Bigram.

The next morning, at the Bigram campsite, we mounted for a rhinoceros hunt. We crossed the dark water opposite Bigram and formed the battue downriver. After walking for a while, a man came from behind to say that a rhinoceros had entered a small patch of forest. The men encircled it, and we rode there as fast as we could. With the battue advancing into the forest and making a lot of noise, the rhinoceros emerged onto the open land and started to run away. Humayun and the men who had come from the other side of the Hindu Kush had never seen a rhinoceros before and stood watching with delight. We pursued it for nearly a kos, shot a lot of arrows, and brought it down. The rhinoceros had not made a good charge at either man or horse. Two more rhinoceroses were killed. I always used to wonder how a rhinoceros and an elephant would act if they were brought face-to-face. This time the elephant keepers were just bringing forward the elephants when a rhinoceros emerged. [254] When the keepers drove the elephants forward, the rhinoceros ran off in another direction.

The day we were stopped at Bigram, some begs and ichkis were divided into six or seven administrative units with the bakhshis and divans and assigned to the boats at Nilab crossing to write down all the soldiers' names one by one and make a head count.

That evening I had a recurrence of fever from the rhume, which resulted in a cough. Every time I coughed I spat blood. I was really scared. Thank God it went away after two or three days.

We marched from Bigram and camped beside the Kabul River in the rain. News came from Hindustan that Dawlat Khan and Ghazi Khan had amassed twenty to thirty thousand troops and brought them to Kalanaur, intent upon attacking Lahore. Mu'min Ali Tovachï was sent at a gallop with this urgent message: "We are coming as fast as we can. Do not engage in battle until we arrive." After two bivouacs we camped on the banks of the Indus on Wednesday the twenty-eighth of the month [December 14].

On Saturday the first of Rabi' I [December 16], we crossed the Indus and the Kachakot river and camped. The begs, bakhshis, and divans who had been stationed on the boats brought me the count of the men who had come on this campaign. All told—great and small, good and bad, liege and other—twelve thousand men had been counted.

This year the monsoon rainfall had been small on the flatlands but good in the mountainside areas. [254b] We therefore set out by the

Sialkot road for the mountain slopes to get grain. Opposite Hati Gakhar's region there was standing river water everywhere, all of it frozen, but not too thick—about a span at most. Such ice is rare in Hindustan. For the several years that we had been in Hindustan, we had seen no trace of ice or snow except for this.

Five marches away from the Indus we came on the sixth march to the river that was the Bakyals' campsite, at the base of Balinath Mountain, which is connected to Mount Jud. The next morning we stayed in that camp so the men could obtain grain. That day spirits were drunk. Mulla Muhammad Parghari talked a lot—rarely had he talked so much. It was Mulla Shams who was an old chatterbox: once he started talking he never stopped. The slaves, servants, and everybody who had gone for grain went on past the fields and scattered in the forests, mountains, and places of difficult access. Having gone out unarmed, some of them were taken prisoner. Kichikkinä the night watchman died there.

Marching from there, we forded the Bahat River below Jhelum and camped. Wali Qïzïl, whose district was in Bimrugiri and Akriyawa[7] and who had been assigned as reinforcement to Sialkot, came to see me. We were chastising him severely for not keeping Sialkot [255] when he said, "I left to go to my district. When Khusraw Kükäldash left Sialkot, he did not even inform me." I listened to his excuse and then said, "Since you did not keep the fort, why didn't you go join the begs in Lahore?" That shut him up. Since battle was fast approaching, I overlooked his offense.

Sayyid Tufan and Sayyid Lachin were sent from camp with spare horses to the men in Lahore to say, "Do not engage in battle. Come to our camp at Sialkot and Pasrur." Everybody was saying that Ghazi Khan had gathered thirty to forty thousand troops and that Dawlat Khan, despite his advanced age, had strapped two swords to his waist, and they were intent upon enjoining battle. The proverb that says, "Ten friends are better than nine" occurred to me. Since he was not going to go away, we would join the Lahore people to ourselves and then fight. While men were sent to the begs, we bivouacked and then camped beside the Chenab River. Along the way we toured Bahlolpur, which is royal land. The fortress stands on a tall cliff beside the river. I liked it a lot. We had the idea of bringing the Sialkot men here. God willing, when I had the chance I would do it. From Bahlolpur we came back to camp by boat [255b] and had a party. Some drank spirits, others drank beer, while some had ma'jun. We left the boat late that night and continued drinking a while in the tent. We gave the horses a day's rest there beside the river.

On Friday the fourteenth of Rabi' I [December 29] we camped at Sialkot. Every time we went to Hindustan, innumerable Jats and Gujars from the mountains and plains came to plunder our cattle and oxen. Those wretches acted so intractably and tyrannically. Before, when these regions had been the enemy, they were ill administered. This time, even though the people had become our subjects, they started their act again. No sooner had the poor, miserable men of Sialkot entered the camp than an uproar started and plunder began. The instigators were located, and I had two or three of them hacked to pieces. Shahim and Nur Beg were dispatched from Sialkot to the Lahore begs to find out where the rebels were, to learn from someone who knew the area where they could join us, and to send the news.

ALAM KHAN'S DEFEAT
BY SULTAN IBRAHIM

While at this campsite, a merchant came and reported that Alam Khan had been defeated by Sultan Ibrahim. The details are as follows: After Alam Khan was dismissed he made double time to Lahore in the hot weather without regard for his companions. When he was given leave to depart for Hindustan, [256] all the Uzbek khans and princes came and laid siege to Balkh. We too mounted to ride against Balkh. From Lahore, Alam Khan tried to muster the begs in Hindustan, saying, "The padishah has assigned you as reinforcements to me. Join me and set forth. We will get Ghazi Khan to march with us on Delhi and Agra."

"With what assurance should we ride with Ghazi Khan?" the begs replied. "Our orders are to assemble with Ghazi Khan when and if he sends his brother Hajji Khan and his son to court or else to Lahore as hostages. Otherwise we are not to join him. Yesterday you fought and lost. Are you sure you want to go with him? It is not politic for you to ride with him."

No matter how they attempted to dissuade him, Alam Khan refused to listen. He sent his son Sher Khan to enter into deliberations with

Dawlat Khan and Ghazi Khan. With him he took Dilawar Khan, who had been held prisoner for a time and had gone to Lahore after escaping two or three months before. Mahmud Khan the son of Khanjahan, who had been given a district in Lahore, also went along. They agreed that Dawlat Khan and Ghazi Khan would take responsibility not only for the begs stationed in Hindustan but also for the whole region, and that Dilawar Khan and Hajji Khan would be enlisted to Alam Khan. [256b] These latter would take the Delhi and Agra region. Isma'il Jilwani and some other amirs came and joined Alam Khan, then they all set out for Delhi, marching as fast as possible. When they reached Inderi, Salman Shaykhzada also came and joined them. Their numbers now amounted to thirty or forty thousand, and with these they laid siege to Delhi. But they were unable either to provoke a battle or to cause serious concern to the defenders in the fortress.

When Sultan Ibrahim learned of the assembled force, he mounted his army to ride against them. But the troops discovered his approach and, withdrawing from the fortress, regrouped to face him. "If we fight during the day," they thought, "the Afghans will make it a point of honor for each other not to desert. If we attack in the dark of night, no one will be able to see anyone else and the commanders will go off in various directions." So thinking, they made a night raid from six kos away. Twice they mounted at noon to prepare a surprise attack by night; they remained in their saddles until the second or third watch, unable either to turn back or to go forward, and unable to come to an agreement. On the third try, with one night watch remaining, they made their attack, during which they were to set fire to tents and huts. They came during the last watch, set fires, and created confusion. Jalal Khan Jighat, with some other amirs joined Alam Khan. Sultan Ibrahim, with a few of his elite cavalry, did not budge from his pavilion. He remained there until dawn, while Alam Khan's men had were busy pillaging and plundering. [257] Sultan Ibrahim's forces saw that their opponents were few, so they set out in their direction with a small detachment and an elephant. When the animal advanced, the opponents were unable to stand their ground and fled. Alam Khan retreated toward the Doab and through the Panipat region to Panipat. When they reached Inderi, they took three or four lacs from Mian Sulayman on some pretext and deposited it. Isma'il Jilwani, Biban, and Alam Khan's eldest son, Jalal Khan, separated themselves from him and got themselves to the Doab. A portion of the troops Alam Khan had gathered, such as Sayf Khan, Darya Khan, Mahmud Khan Khanjahan, and Shaykh Jamal Farmuli as well as some others, had deserted before the battle and gone over to Ibrahim. Alam Khan, Dilawar Khan, and Hajji Khan received news of our taking Malot as they were crossing Sirhind. Since Dilawar Khan had always been one of our supporters and had suffered three or four months of prison for our sake, he separated himself, joined his family at Sultanpur,[8] and came to pay homage to us at Malot three or four days after we had taken it. Alam Khan and Hajji Khan crossed the Sutlej River and holed up in a fastness called Gangota in the mountains between Dun and the plain. Our strike force left the Afghans and Hazaras [257b] and laid siege to them. They were near to taking such a strong fortress when it got too late in the day. Alam Khan and Hajji Khan planned to retreat but were blocked by the horses that had fallen at the gateway. They had elephants too. When they drove the elephants forward, they crushed most of the horses to death. Nonetheless, they were still unable to escape over the horses. Only in the dark of night and on foot did they, with great difficulty, get out and join Ghazi Khan who, unable to enter Malot, had fled to the mountains. As Ghazi Khan did not give them a warm welcome, Alam Khan could do nothing but come to the Phillaur region below Dun and make obeisance to me. In Sialkot someone came from the people in Lahore to say that the next morning all would come and pay homage. The next morning we marched and camped at Pasrur. Muhammad-Ali Jang-Jang, Khwaja Husayn, and some other warriors came and paid homage.

The enemy's camp was on the Lahore side of the Ravi River. We sent troops under Böchkä to gather information. It was near the third watch of the night when the news was brought that the enemy had abandoned each other and fled as soon as they got wind of us. Early the next morning we moved forward fast, while Shah Mir Husayn and Jan Beg were left in charge of the uruq and camp followers. At midafternoon we arrived and camped in Kalanaur. Muhammad-Sultan Mirza, Adil Sultan, and other begs came there to pay homage. [258]

As we marched early out of Kalanaur, news of Ghazi Khan and those who had fled was obtained from nearby. Muhammadi, Ahmadi, Qutlugh-Qadam, Wali Khazin, and most of the begs who had knelt this time for the office of beg in Kabul were sent in pursuit of the fugitives. It was decided that if they could catch them, well and good; if not, they should set up a close guard on the environs of Malot fortress to prevent the men there from escaping. The object of the guard was Ghazi Khan. Having sent these begs forward, we crossed the Beas River and camped opposite Kanwahin. Stopping twice for the night, we then camped at the mouth of the Malot fortress valley. The begs who had come before and the begs in Hindustan were ordered to lay close siege to the fortress. Dawlat Khan's grandson, Isma'il Khan, Ali Khan's eldest son, came here. He was sent back to the fortress with some enticing promises and threats.

On Friday the army was marched forward, and we camped close to half a kos from the fortress. I myself went to see the fortress, then assigned the right and left flanks and the center and went back to camp. Dawlat Khan sent a man to say, [258b] "Ghazi Khan has fled to the hills. If you will pardon my offense, I will submit and turn over the fortress." Khwaja Mirmiran was sent to allay Dawlat Khan's fear and bring him back. Dawlat Khan and his son Ali Khan came together. I ordered him to hang around his neck the very same two swords he had strapped to his waist to fight us. Was he such a stupid bumpkin of a fellow that when his affairs had come to this pass he was still making excuses? He was brought forward, and I had the swords taken from his neck. When it was time for the interview, he was slow to kneel, so I ordered his leg pulled to make him kneel. When I had him seated before me, I said to someone who knew Hindustani, "Tell him these words one by one and make him understand. Say, 'I called you father. I honored and respected you more than you could have wanted. I saved you and your sons from wandering like the Baluch.[9] I rescued your clan and women from Ibrahim's sequestration. I awarded you with Tatar Khan's three-crore estates. Did I do you ill that you strapped two swords to your waist and led your army against our domains and caused such strife and turmoil?' "

The confused old man mumbled a word or two in the back of his throat [259] but said nothing in response. What could he say to such unanswerable words? It was decided that their clan and womenfolk would be turned over to them but that the rest of their possessions would be confiscated. He was ordered to lodge with Khwaja Mirmiran.

On Saturday the twenty-second of Rabi' I [January 6, 1526], in order to send out their clan and women safe and sound, I went myself and camped on a rise facing the gate to the Malot fortress. Ali Khan came out and presented a few ashrafis. In the afternoon they began to take their clan and women out. Although some said that Ghazi Khan had already left, others said they had seen him inside the fortress; some ichkis and pages were stationed at the gate to search suspicious persons lest Ghazi Khan, the principal object of this search, slip by. Also, if jewels and gems were being smuggled out, they should be confiscated too. I had a tent pitched on the rise before the gate and stayed there that night. The next morning Muhammadi, Ahmadi, Sultan-Junayd, Abdul-Aziz, Muhammad-Ali Jang-Jang, Qutlugh-Qadam, and a few ichki begs were ordered to go inside and confiscate the treasuries and possessions. [259b] The troops were raising a ruckus at the gate: as peremptory punishment I shot a few of them. All at once a fateful arrow hit Humayun's storyteller, and he died on the spot.

After spending two nights on this hill, on Monday I entered the fortress for an inspection and went into Ghazi Khan's library, which held a few valuable books. I gave some of them to Humayun and sent others to Kamran. Although there were many learned books, there were not so many valuable ones as I expected. That night, I stayed at the fortress, returning to camp the next morning. We thought that Ghazi Khan stayed in the fortress too, but in fact that dastardly coward had abandoned his brothers, mother, and sisters in Malot and fled to the hills with a few men.

See that vile one who will never see the face of good fortune: he chooses ease for himself and abandons his wife and child to hardship.

On Wednesday we moved from camp and headed toward the mountain to which Ghazi Khan had fled. We traveled a kos from the camp at the mouth of Malot and stopped in a valley. Dilawar Khan came to pay homage. We had Dawlat Khan, Ali Khan, Isma'il Khan, and a few of their grandees put in chains and turned over to Kätä to be taken to the Malot fort in Bhera[10] and held under guard. [260] For the others, who had been given to various persons, ransoms were set with the agreement of Dilawar Khan. Some were released, and others kept in chains.

Kätä took the prisoners away. Dawlat Khan died upon reaching Sultanpur. We made the Malot fortress Muhammad-Ali Jang-Jang's responsibility. Thereupon he stationed his elder brother Arghun there with a troop of warriors, and assigned some 250 Hazaras and Afghans as reinforcements.

Khwaja Kalan had brought several camels loaded with Ghazni wine. Khwaja Kalan's campsite was on a hill overlooking the fortress and army camp. There a fabulous party was held in which some drank wine and others drank spirits.

Marching from there and passing by the low, ragged hills of Malot, we came to Dun. In the language of Hindustan, *dun* means a glen. One flowing river in Hindustan[11] is in this dun, around which are many villages that form the estate of the Jaswal, Dilawar Khan's maternal uncles. Dun is a fantastic glen. Meadows flank the banks of the swift-flowing river, and rice is planted in some places. The current in the middle of the river is of a three- or four-mill force. The glen is a kos or two wide, and in some places [260b] three. The mountains are extremely small and hill-like, with villages situated on the slopes. Where there are no villages there are many peacocks and monkeys. There is also a plentiful fowl like the domestic chicken except that they are of one color.

Since there was no confirmed news of Ghazi Khan's being in any one place, we assigned Turdika and Prem Dev Malihas to go to wherever Ghazi Khan was and get hold of him however they could.

In the small hills around Dun are magnificent, impregnable fortresses. On the northeastern side is one called Kotla. All around it are sheer ravines seventy to eighty yards deep, except on the side of the main gateway, where it is only seven to eight yards deep. The area where one would launch a rolling bridge is ten to twelve yards wide; two large poles had been placed there to form a bridge over which horses and flocks were made to pass. This was one of the fortresses Ghazi Khan had fortified. His men were inside. When the strike force arrived, a battle ensued. The impregnable fortress was finally taken when, late that night, the defenders abandoned it and fled. Another strong fortress in the vicinity of Dun is Gangota. It too is surrounded by ravines, but it is not so secure as Kotla. Alam Khan had entered this Gangota fortress, as has been mentioned.[12] [261]

BABUR SETS OUT AGAINST
SULTAN IBRAHIM

After sending a party out in pursuit of Ghazi Khan, we placed our feet
in the stirrup of resolve, grabbed the reins of trust in God, and directed ourselves against Sultan Ibrahim, son of Sultan Sikandar son of
Bahlul Lodi the Afghan, who controlled the capital Delhi and the
realm of Hindustan at that time. He was said to have a standing army
of one hundred thousand, and he and his begs had nearly a thousand
elephants. After one march Baqi Shiqavul was given Dipalpur and dispatched as reinforcement to Balkh. Much money was sent to the aid of
Balkh, and presents of the booty that fell to us during the conquest of
Malot were sent to the families and children in Kabul.

After a march or two down from Dun, Shah Imad Shirazi brought
letters from Arayish Khan and Mulla Muhammad Muzahhib exhibit-
ing some show of support and concern for this campaign. We sent back
with a foot soldier decrees of favor, then marched on. The raiding party
that had gone to Malot took Harwar, Kahlur, and all the mountain
fortresses in that region (which for a long time no one had gone against
because they were known to be impregnable), pillaged the inhabitants,
and returned to us. Alam Khan had also been ravaged and came naked
and on foot. We sent begs and ichkis out to meet him with horses. While
we were in that region he came [261b] and paid homage.

Raiding parties also went into the mountains and valleys of the region and returned after a night or two with nothing substantial having
been gained. Shah Mir Husayn, Jan Beg, and some warriors requested
permission to go on a raid. While we were in Dun, petitions had come
two or three times from Isma'il Jilwani and Biban. From here decrees
were dispatched as they had desired.

Marching from Dun we came to Rupar. While we were there, it
rained a lot of rain and was extremely cold, and many hungry, naked
Hindustanis perished. From Rupar we marched to Karal[13] opposite
Sirhind, where a Hindustani came to our camp saying that he was Sultan Ibrahim's envoy. Although he had no letter or credentials, he asked
us to send an emissary. We sent back with him a night watchman from
Swat. No sooner had the poor fellows arrived than Ibrahim threw them
both into chains. A few months later, the very day we defeated
Ibrahim,[14] the Swati escaped and returned to us.

Bivouacking once, we camped beside the torrent at Banur and Sanur, which is one of the few flowing streams in Hindustan aside from the great rivers. It is called the Ghaggar River. We rode out for an expedition upstream. Three or four kos above Chitar,[15] which is also on the banks of this river, the torrent emerges from a bubbling spring. We toured the area above the torrent and found a four- or five-mill-force river emerging from a wide valley. [262] Farther up are pleasant, charming places with good air. I commanded a garden to be made at the spot where the river emerges from the valley. As the water comes into the plain, it goes for a kos or two and then spills into the torrent. The Ghaggar River is three or four kos downstream from the place where the water flowing from the spring spills. During the monsoon season the water in the torrent swells, joins the Ghaggar River, and goes on to Samana and Sunam.

At camp we received news that Sultan Ibrahim, who was on this side of Delhi, was on the move in this direction. The provost of Hissar Firoza, Hamid Khan Khassa-Khel, had come out ten to fifteen kos near us with the royal cavalry and the troops of Hissar Firoza and that region. Kätä Beg was sent to Ibrahim's camp to gather information, and Mu'min Atäkä went to the Hissar Firoza army to do the same.

On Sunday the thirteenth of Jumada I [February 25] we marched from Ambala and camped on the shore of a lake. Mu'min Atäkä and Kätä Beg met us there. To attack Hamid Khan we assigned Humayun with all the men of the right wing under Khwaja Kalan, Sultan-Muhammad Dulday, and Wali Khazin, as well as Khusraw, Hindu Beg, Abdul-Aziz, and Muhammad-Ali Jang-Jang of the begs who had remained in Hindustan, and Shah-Mansur Barlas, Kätä Beg, Muhibb-Ali, and a contingent of ichkis and warriors from the center. [262b] Bihan also came and paid homage. These Afghans are quite rustic and insensitive. Although Dilawar Khan was greater than he was in terms of liege men and rank, he would not sit in my presence. Alam Khan's sons, who were his princes, would not either. Yet this fellow asked if he could be seated. Who could listen to such nonsense?

On Monday morning, the fourteenth of the month, Humayun set out against Hamid Khan after dispatching a hundred or 150 warriors as scouts. As his men drew near and started to clash with the enemy, the enemy soldiers scattered amidst Humayun's main body of troops who appeared from behind. A couple of hundred men were unhorsed.

Half were decapitated and half were brought in alive with seven or eight elephants. On Friday the eighteenth, Beg Mirak Moghul brought to camp the news of Humayun's victory. Humayun was immediately awarded a royal robe and a horse from the royal stables and assigned a prize.

On Monday the twenty-first [March 5], at the same camp, Humayun brought in around a hundred prisoners and seven or eight elephants and paid homage. [263] Master Ali-Quli and his matchlockmen were ordered to shoot all the captives. This expedition was the first time Humayun saw action, and it was taken as a good portent. The pursuit party chased the enemy soldiers to Hissar Firoza, where they caught them and pillaged the area before returning. Humayun was awarded the one-crore district of Hissar Firoza and its dependencies and a crore of cash.

We marched from there to Shahabad, where we remained while someone was sent to Sultan Ibrahim's camp to gather information. Rahmat Piada was dispatched to Kabul with proclamations of victory. In this camp, on that same day, Humayun first put the razor and scissors to his face.[16]

On Monday the twenty-eighth of Jumada I [March 12], while in that same camp, the sun entered Aries. News began to pour in continually from Ibrahim's forces to the effect that they were marching a kos or two and bivouacking for two or three days at each camp. We too set out, bivouacked for two nights at Shahabad, and proceeded down the bank of the Jumna to opposite Sarsawa, where we camped. Khwaja Kalan's liege man Haydar-Quli was sent to gather intelligence. I forded the Jumna and made a tour of Sarsawa. We had some ma'jun that day. In Sarsawa is a spring from which a little water flows. It is not a bad place. Turdï Beg Khaksar praised it. [263b] "It's yours," I said, and thus Turdï Beg was given Sarsawa.

I had a cabin constructed on a boat, and used it sometimes for touring and sometimes during marches. We had proceeded two marches downstream of camp when Haydar-Quli brought news that Daud Khan and Haysam Khan had been ordered to cross into the Doab with five or six thousand men. They had formed a camp and were staying three or four kos this side of Ibrahim's site. On Sunday the eighteenth of Jumada II [April 1], we dispatched Chïn Temür, Muhammad-Sultan Mirza, Mahdi Khwaja, and Adil Sultan and the whole left wing under Sultan-Junayd, Shah Mir Husayn, and Qutlugh-Qadam, and from the center Yunus Ali, Abdullah, Ahmadi, and Kätä Beg. At noon they started crossing the river and moved out from the other side between midafternoon and evening. Biban used the fording expedition as an excuse to desert. They reached the enemy a little after dawn, finding that they had made some attempt to form a battle array and made as though to come out. When our men arrived, they moved on until they stopped opposite Ibrahim's camp. They unhorsed Haysam Khan, Daud Khan's elder brother, and one of his commanders and brought in to me seventy to eighty prisoners and six or seven elephants. [264] Most of the prisoners were executed as retributive justice.

PREPARATION FOR BATTLE

We marched from there, arrayed the right and left wings and center, and had a *dim*.[17] We had fewer men than we had estimated. I ordered the whole army, in accordance with rank, to bring carts, which numbered about seven hundred altogether. Master Ali-Qulï was told to tie them together with ox-harness ropes instead of chains, after the Anatolian manner,[18] keeping a distance of six to seven large shields between every two carts. The matchlockmen could then stand behind the fortification to fire their guns. Five or six days were spent arranging it, and when it was ready I summoned to general council all the begs and great warriors who knew what they were talking about. We discussed the following: Panipat was a town with lots of suburbs and houses. The suburbs and houses would protect one side, but it was necessary to fortify our other sides with the carts and shields and to station matchlockmen and foot soldiers behind them. This having been decided, we marched, bivouacked, and then came to Panipat on Wednesday the last day of Jumada II [April 12].

To our right were the town and suburbs. Directly before us were the arranged shields. To the left [264b] and elsewhere were trenches and pylons. At every distance of an arrow shot, space was left for one hundred to 150 cavalrymen to emerge. Some of the soldiers were hesitant, but their trepidation was baseless, for only what God has decreed from all eternity will happen. They cannot be blamed, however, for being afraid, even if God was on their side. They had traveled for two or three months from their homeland, and had had to deal with an unfamiliar people whose language we did not know and who did not know ours.

A group confused, peace of mind shattered. A people preoccupied, a very strange people.

Sultan Ibrahim's army was estimated at one hundred thousand. He and his commanders were said to have nearly a thousand elephants. Moreover, he possessed the treasury left over from two generations of his fathers. The custom in Hindustan is to hire liege men for money before major battles. Such people are called *badhandi*.[19] If Sultan Ibrahim had had a mind to, he could have hired one hundred thousand to two hundred thousand troops. Thank God he was able neither to satisfy his warriors nor to part with his treasury. How was he to please his men when his nature was so overwhelmingly dominated by miserliness? He himself was an inexperienced young man who craved beyond all things the acquisition of money—neither his oncoming nor his stand was calculated to have a good end, [265] and neither his march nor his fighting was energetic.

When the edges of the army had been arranged and stationed in Panipat with carts, pylons, and trenches, Darwesh Muhammad Sarban said, "With so much precaution what possibility is there that he will come?"

"Are you comparing them to the Uzbek khans and princes?" I asked. "The year we left Samarkand and went to Hissar, all the khans and princes of the Uzbeks gathered and came against us in unison from the Iron Gates. We got all our soldiers and the Moghuls' camp followers and possessions into the suburbs and blockaded the lanes. Since the khans and princes knew all about battle tactics, they realized that we had fortified Hissar to within an inch of its life. Calculating that it was not worth their while to attack Hissar province, they withdrew through Nawandak to Chaghanian. Don't think that these people are like the Uzbeks! How would they know how to evaluate the odds of a battle?"

Thank God it happened as I said. During the seven or eight days we were in Panipat, our men went out in small parties as far as the enemy camp and shot many of them, cut off their heads, and brought them back. The enemy made no move and undertook no action. [265b] Finally, acting upon some supportive Hindustani begs' opinion, we sent four or five thousand men on a sneak attack led by Mahdi Khwaja, Muhammad-Sultan Mirza, Adil Sultan, Khusraw, Shah Mir Husayn, Sultan-Junayd Barlas, Abdul-Aziz Mirakhur, Muhammad-Ali Jang-Jang, Qutlugh-Qadam, Wali Khazin, Khalifa's Muhibb-Ali, Muhammad Bakhshï, Jan Beg, and Qaraquzi. Unable to act in unison by night, they got scattered and achieved nothing. Just before dawn they were near the enemy's camp. The enemy's men were having the drums beat and were going out in battle array with their elephants. Although they were not able to accomplish any action, they contended with many men and got out safe and sound without anyone's being taken prisoner. Muhammad-Ali Jang-Jang was hit by an arrow in the foot. Although it was not fatal, he was not fit for battle afterward. When I learned of this, I sent Humayun with his army a kos-and-a-half opposite them while I myself arrayed the remaining soldiers and set out. Those who had gone on the sneak attack went to Humayun. When the enemy did not come farther forward, we also withdrew. That night in camp we heard war cries for nearly a ghari. The noise caused trepidation among those who had never witnessed such pandemonium, but the confusion was only a false alarm, and after a while it died down. [266]

THE BATTLE OF PANIPAT

On Friday the eighth of Rajab [April 20] news came at dawn from the scouts that the enemy was coming in battle array. We put on our armor, armed ourselves, and got to horse. The right wing consisted of Humayun, Khwaja Kalan, Sultan-Muhammad Dulday, Hindu Beg, Wali Khazin, and Pir-Qulï Sistani. The left wing consisted of Muhammad-Sultan Mirza, Mahdi Khwaja, Adil Sultan, Shah Mir Husayn, Sultan-Junayd Barlas, Qutlugh-Qadam, Jan Beg, Muhammad Bakhshï, and Shah Husayn Yaraki Moghul Ghanchi. The right flank of the center was Chïn Temür Sultan, Sulayman Mirza, Muhammadi Kükäldash, Shah-Mansur Barlas, Yunus Ali, Darwesh Muhammad Sarban, and Abdullah Kitabdar. The left flank of the center was Khalifa, Khwaja Mirmiran, Ahmadi Parwanachï, Qoch Beg's Turdï Beg, Khalifa's Muhibb-Ali, and Mirza Beg Tarkhan. The vanguard was Khusraw Kükäldash and Muhammad-Ali Jang-Jang. Abdul-Aziz Mirakhur was assigned to the reserve. At the tip of the right wing Wali Qïzïl and

Baba Qashqa's Malik Qasim and his Moghuls were assigned for the flank assault. At the tip of the left wing we arrayed Qaraquzi, Abu'l-Muhammad Nayzabaz, Shaykh Ali, Shaykh Jamal Barin, Hindi, and Tengri-Qulï Moghul for the flank assault so that when the enemy got near, these two troops could circle around to the enemy's rear from the right and left. **[266b]**

The enemy's troops appeared, headed toward the left wing. For this reason Abdul-Aziz, who had been assigned to the reserve, was dispatched as reinforcement to the left wing. Sultan Ibrahim's army could be seen nearby, coming quickly without stopping. However, as they came farther forward and our troops became visible to them, they broke the ranks they had maintained and, as though undecided whether to stand or proceed, were able to do neither.

The order was given for the men who had been assigned to the flank assault to circle around to the enemy's rear from left and right, shoot their arrows, and begin to fight, and for the right and left wings to advance and engage the enemy. The flank assaulters circled around and began to shoot. From the left wing Mahdi Khwaja had already reached the enemy; advancing upon him was a contingent with an elephant, but by shooting many arrows he drove them back. Ahmadi Parwanachï, Qoch Beg's Turdï Beg, and Khalifa's Muhibb-Ali were sent from the center to help the left wing. Fighting was going on in the right wing too. Muhammadi Kükäldash, Shah-Mansur Barlas, Yunus Ali, and Abdullah were ordered to advance to directly opposite the center and fight. Master Ali-Qulï got off a few good gunshots from in front of the center. Mustafa the artilleryman also fired some good shots from the mortars mounted on carts to the left of the center. **[267]** Right wing, left wing, center, and flank assault shot arrows into the enemy from all sides and fought in all seriousness. Once or twice the enemy tried halfhearted assaults in the direction of our right and left wings, but our men pushed them into their own center by shooting. The enemy's right and left flanks were so crowded into one spot that they were not able to go forward or to find a way to escape.

The sun was one lance high when battle was enjoined. The fighting continued until midday. At noon the enemy was overcome and vanquished to the delight of our friends. By God's grace and generosity such a difficult action was made easy for us, and such a numerous army was ground into the dust in half a day. Five or six thousand men were killed in one place near Ibrahim. All told, the dead of this battle were estimated at between fifteen and sixteen thousand. Later, when we came to Agra, we learned from reports by the people of Hindustan that forty to fifty thousand men had died in the battle. With the enemy defeated and felled, we proceeded. Along the way the men began to capture the fallen commanders and Afghans and bring them in. Droves of elephants were caught and presented by the elephant keepers. [267b] Thinking that Ibrahim may have escaped, we assigned Qïsïmtay Mirza, Baba Chuhra, and Böchkä's troops from the royal tabin to pursue him behind the enemy lines and move with all speed to Agra. Crossing through the midst of Ibrahim's camp, we inspected the tents and pavilions and then camped beside a still river. It was midafternoon when Tahir the Axman, Khalifa's brother-in-law, discovered Sultan Ibrahim's body amidst many corpses and brought in his head.

That very day we assigned Humayun Mirza, Khwaja Kalan, Muhammadi, Shah-Mansur Barlas, Yunus Ali, Abdullah, and Wali Khazin to proceed swiftly and unencumbered, get hold of Agra, and confiscate the treasury. We appointed Mahdi Khwaja, Muhammad-Sultan Mirza, Adil Sultan, Sultan-Junayd Barlas, and Qutlugh-Qadam to separate themselves from the baggage and ride fast, enter the Delhi fortress, and guard the treasuries. The next morning we proceeded for a league and then, for the sake of the horses, camped beside the Jumna.

BABUR ENTERS DELHI

On Tuesday, after two bivouacs, I circumambulated Shaykh Nizam Awliya's tomb and camped beside the Jumna directly opposite Delhi. That evening I toured the Delhi fortress, where I spent the night; the next morning, Wednesday, I circumambulated Khwaja Qutbuddin's tomb and toured Sultan Ghiyasuddin Balban's and Sultan Alauddin Khalji's tombs, buildings, [268] and minaret, the Shamsi pool, the Khass pool, and Sultan Bahlul's and Sultan Iskandar's tombs and gardens.[20] After the tour I returned to the camp, got on a boat, and drank spirits.

I made Wali Qïzïl the provost of Delhi; I made Dost the divan of the province of Delhi; and I had the treasuries there sealed and turned over to them for safekeeping.

On Thursday we marched out and camped beside the Jumna directly opposite Tughluqabad.

On Friday we stayed in camp. Mawlana Mahmud, Shaykh Zayn, and some others went to perform the Friday prayer in Delhi and read the proclamation in my name. Having distributed some money to the poor and unfortunate, they returned to camp.

On Saturday the army proceeded by forced march toward Agra. I went for a tour of Tughluqabad and returned to camp.

On Friday the twenty-second of Rajab [May 4] we stopped in Sulayman Farmuli's quarters in the suburbs of Agra. Since this site was far from the fortress, we moved the next morning to Jalal Khan Jighat's palace. Humayun had gone on ahead, but the men inside the fortress made excuses to keep him out. When they noticed how unruly the people were, they maintained watch over the exit, afraid someone might pilfer the treasury, until we should get there.

The ancestors of Bikramajit the Hindu, the rajah of Gwalior, had been ruling Gwalior for more than a hundred years. [268b] Iskandar stayed in Agra for several years planning the taking of Gwalior. Afterward, during Ibrahim's time, A'zam-Humayun Sarwani had kept up serious fighting for a period of time. Finally [in 1518] Gwalior was taken by truce, and the rajah was given Shamsabad. Bikramajit died and went to hell when Sultan Ibrahim was defeated. His sons and clan were in Agra.[21] When Humayun got to Agra, the people of Bikramajit's clan were thinking of fleeing, but the men Humayun had stationed there seized them and held them under guard. Humayun did not let them be plundered, and by their own agreement they presented Humayun with many jewels and gems, among which was a famous diamond Sultan Alauddin had acquired. It is well known that a gem merchant once assessed its worth at the whole world's expenditure for half a day. It must weigh eight mithcals. When I came, Humayun presented it to me, but I gave it right back to him.

One of the knowledgeable people from among the soldiers in the fortress was Malikdad of Kara. Another was Malli Surduk, and another Firoz Khan of Mewat. They had engaged in some dishonesty and were sent to be executed. When Malikdad of Kara was taken out for execution, some people pleaded on his behalf. With the coming and going it was four or five days before a decision could be made. We showed him great favor and granted his wishes, exempting all his possessions. Ibrahim's mother and her retinue were granted a one-crore estate in cash, and she was taken out of Agra with her baggage and settled a league downstream. **[269]**

On Wednesday afternoon the twenty-eighth of Rajab [May 10], I entered Agra and camped in Sultan Ibrahim's quarters.

From the year 910 [1504–5], when Kabul was conquered, until this date I had craved Hindustan. Sometimes because my begs had poor opinions, and sometimes because my brothers lacked cooperation, the Hindustan campaign had not been possible and the realm had not been conquered. Finally all such impediments had been removed. None of my little begs and officers was able any longer to speak out in opposition to my purpose. In 925 [1519] we led the army and took Bajaur by force in two or three gharis, massacred the people, and came to Bhera. The people of Bhera paid ransom to keep their property from being plundered and pillaged, and we took four hundred thousand shahrukhis worth of cash and goods, distributed it to the army according to the number of liege men, and returned to Kabul.[22]

From that date until 932 [1525–26], we led the army to Hindustan five times within seven or eight years. The fifth time, God through his great grace vanquished and reduced a foe like Sultan Ibrahim and made possible for us a realm like Hindustan. From the time of the Apostle until this date only three padishahs gained dominion over and ruled the realm of Hindustan. The first was Sultan Mahmud Ghazi, who, with his sons, occupied the throne of Hindustan for a long time.[23] **[269b]** The second was Sultan Shihabuddin Ghuri and his slaves and followers, who ruled this kingdom for many years.[24] I am the third. My accomplishment, however, is beyond comparison with theirs, for when Sultan Mahmud subdued Hindustan, the throne of Khurasan was under his control, the rules of Khwarazm and the marches were obedient to him, and the padishah of Samarkand was his underling. If his army was not two hundred thousand strong, it must have been at least one hundred thousand. Moreover, his opponents were rajahs. There was not a single padishah in all of Hindustan. Every rajah ruled independently in a different region.

After Sultan Mahmud was Sultan Shihabuddin Ghuri. Although he did not possess Khurasan, his elder brother Sultan Ghiyasuddin Ghuri did. In the *Tabaqat-i-Nasiri*[25] it is recorded that once he led an army of

120,000 armored warriors into Hindustan. His opponents too were rays and rajahs. Not all of Hindustan belonged to one person.

When we went to Bhera we were fifteen hundred—two thousand at most—strong. The fifth time, I came, defeated Sultan Ibrahim, and conquered the realm of Hindustan. Never before had I had such an army on a Hindustan campaign. What with liege men, merchants, servants, and all those with the army, twelve thousand persons were registered. [270] The provinces that belonged to me were Badakhshan, Konduz, Kabul, and Kandahar, but no substantial assistance was forthcoming from them—in fact, since some of them were so close to the enemy, it was necessary to send much assistance there. Moreover, the whole of Transoxiana was in the hands of an old enemy, the Uzbek khans and princes, who had nearly one hundred thousand soldiers. The kingdom of Hindustan, from Bhera to Bihar, was under the control of Afghans, whose padishah was Sultan Ibrahim. By land calculation he should have had an army of five hundred thousand. However, just then the amirs of Purab were in rebellion, and his standing army was estimated at one hundred thousand. He and his commanders were said to have one thousand elephants. In such a state of affairs and with such strength, we put our trust in God, turned our backs on one hundred thousand old Uzbek enemies, and faced a ruler with a huge army and vast realm like Sultan Ibrahim. In recognition of our trust, God did not let our pains and difficulties go for naught and defeated such a powerful opponent and conquered a vast kingdom like Hindustan. We do not consider this good fortune to have emanated from our own strength and force but from God's pure loving-kindness; we do not think that this felicity is from our own endeavor but from God's generosity and favor.

DESCRIPTION OF HINDUSTAN

Hindustan is a vast and populous kingdom and a productive realm. [270b] To the east and south, in fact to the west too, it ends at the ocean. To the north is a mountain range that connects the mountains of the Hindu Kush, Kafiristan, and Kashmir. To the northwest are Kabul, Ghazni, and Kandahar. The capital of all Hindustan is Delhi. After Sultan Shihabuddin Ghuri's reign until the end of Sultan Firozshah's, most of Hindustan was under the control of the Delhi sultans. Up to the time that I conquered Hindustan, five Muslim padishahs and two infidels had ruled there. Although the mountains and jungles are held by many petty rays and rajahs, the important and independent rulers were the following five.

One was the Afghans, who took the capital Delhi and held in their grasp from Bhera to Bihar. Before the Afghans, Jaunpur was held by Sultan Husayn Sharqi,[26] and the dynasty was called Purabi. The Purabi ancestors were cupbearers for Sultan Firozshah and those sultans; after Firozshah, they gained control over the kingdom of Jaunpur. Delhi was in Sultan Alauddin's hands, and the dynasty was the Sayyids.[27] When Temür Beg took Delhi, he gave the governorship of Delhi to their ancestors and left. Sultan Bahlul Lodi the Afghan and his son Sultan Iskandar seized Delhi and Jaunpur, and the two capitals formed one kingdom.[28]

The second was Sultan Muzaffar in Gujarat,[29] who passed away several days before the defeat of Sultan Ibrahim. [271] He was a religiously observant ruler and a student of the religious sciences, he read hadith, and he always copied Korans. His dynasty was called the Tang. Their fathers also were cupbearers for Sultan Firozshah and those sultans. After Firozshah, they gained control of the province of Gujarat.

Third were the Bahmanids in the Deccan,[30] but as of this date the sultans of the Deccan have no power of their own left—the great begs have gained control of all the provinces. If the sultan needs anything, he has to ask the begs for it.

Fourth was Sultan Mahmud in the province of Malwa, which is also called Mandu. The dynasty was called the Khalji.[31] Rana Sanga the Infidel defeated him and seized most of the province, but he had grown weak. The ancestors of this dynasty were patronized by Firozshah. Afterward they seized the province of Malwa.

Fifth was Nusrat Shah in Bengal.[32] His father became padishah in Bengal and was a sayyid known as Sultan Alauddin.[33]

Nusrat Shah ruled by hereditary succession. There is an amazing custom in Bengal: rule is seldom achieved by hereditary succession. Instead, there is a specific royal throne, and each of the amirs, viziers, or officeholders has an established place. It is that throne that is of importance to the people of Bengal. For every place, a group of obedient servants is established. [271b] When the ruler desires to dismiss anyone, all the obedient servants then belong to whomever he puts in that person's place. The royal throne, however, has a peculiarity: anyone who succeeds in killing the king and sitting on the throne becomes king. Amirs, viziers, soldiers, and civilians all submit to him, and he becomes the padishah and ruler like the former ruler. The people of Bengal say, "We are the legal property of the throne, and we obey anyone who is on it." For instance, before Nusrat Shah's father, Sultan Alauddin, an Abyssinian killed the king, took the throne, and reigned for a time.[34] The Abyssinian was killed by Sultan Alauddin, who then became king. Sultan Alauddin's son has now become king by hereditary succession. Another custom in Bengal is that it is considered disgraceful for anyone who becomes king to spend the treasuries of former kings. Whoever becomes king must accumulate a new treasury, which is a source of pride for the people. In addition, the salaries and stipends of all the institutions of the rulers, treasury, military, and civilian are absolutely fixed from long ago and cannot be spent anywhere else.

The five great Muslim padishahs with vast realms and huge armies are the five who have been mentioned.

Of the infidels, the greater in domain and army [272] is the rajah of Vijayanagar.[35] The other is Rana Sanga,[36] who had recently grown so great by his audacity and sword. His original province was Chitor. When the sultans of Mandu grew weak, he seized many provinces belonging to Mandu, such as Ranthambhor, Sarangpur, Bhilsan, and Chanderi. Chanderi had been in the *daru'l-harb*[37] for some years and held by Sanga's highest-ranking officer, Medini Rao, with four or five thousand infidels, but in 934 [1528], through the grace of God, I took it by force within a ghari or two, massacred the infidels, and brought it into the bosom of Islam, as will be mentioned.[38]

All around Hindustan are many rays and rajahs. Some are obedient to Islam, while others, because they are so far away and their places impregnable, do not render obedience to Muslim rulers.

Hindustan lies in the first, second, and third climes, with none of it in the fourth clime. It is a strange country. Compared to ours, it is another world. Its mountains, rivers, forests, and wildernesses, its villages and provinces, animals and plants, peoples and languages, even its rain and winds are altogether different. Even if the Kabul dependencies that have warm climates bear a resemblance to Hindustan in some aspects, in others they do not. Once you cross the Indus, the land, water, trees, stones, people, tribes, manners, and customs [272b] are all of the Hindustani fashion. The mountain range in the north that has been mentioned—as soon as the Indus is crossed these mountains are dependent provinces to Kashmir. Although as of this date the provinces in this range, like Pakhli and Shahmang, mostly are not obedient to Kashmir, nonetheless they used to be inside Kashmir. Once past Kashmir, there are innumerable peoples, tribes, districts, and provinces in this range. There are people continuously in these mountains all the way to Bengal, even to the ocean. This much has been ascertained and confirmed by the people of Hindustan, but of these groups no one can give any real information. All they say is that the people of the mountains are called Khas. It has occurred to me that since Hindustanis pronounce the sound *sh* as *s*, since the principal city in the mountains is Kashmir, which means "mountain of the Khasis," since *mir* means mountain and the people of this mountain are called Khasia, and since aside from Kashmir no other city has ever been heard of in these mountains, this may be why they call it Kashmir. The products of the people of the mountains are musk, yak tails, saffron, lead, and copper. The people of India call the range Sivalik Parbat. In the language of India *sava* means a quarter, *lak* means a hundred thousand, and *parbat* means mountain—therefore Siwalik Parbat means "a quarter lac plus a hundred thousand mountains," that is, 125,000 mountains. The snow never melts on these mountains, and the snow-covered caps can be seen from some of the provinces of Hindustan, such as Lahore, Sirhind, and Sambhal. In Kabul this mountain range is called the Hindu Kush. From Kabul the range runs to the east and slightly to the south. South of it is all Hindustan. [273] To the north of the range and the unknown tribes who are called Khas is the province of Tibet. Many large rivers rise in this range and flow through Hindustan. Six large rivers to the north of Sirhind—the Indus, the Bahat,[39] the Chenab, the Ravi, the Beas, and the Sutlej—all join at one place in the vicinity of Multan. After they all join it is called the Indus. It flows to the west, passes through the province of Tatta, and joins the Indian Ocean. Aside from these six, there are other great rivers like the Jumna, the Ganges, the Rapti, the Gomati, the Gogra, the Sarju, the Gandak, as well as many other large ones, all of which join the Ganges. Flowing to the east, the Ganges passes through Bengal and spills into the ocean. The source of all of these is the Sivalik Range.

There are still other large rivers that rise in the mountains of Hindustan, like the Chambhal, Banas, and Betwa, but there is never any snow on these mountains. These rivers also join the Ganges.

Hindustan has other mountain ranges too. Among them is a range that runs from north to south beginning in the province of Delhi at a building made by Firozshah called the Jahannuma, which is situated on a rocky little mountain. Running from there are patches of rocky little mountains in the vicinity of Delhi. When they reach the province of Mewat, the mountains become larger. Passing through Mewat [273b] they go to the province of Bayana. The mountains of Sikri, Bari, and Dholpur are of this same range. Although it is not contiguous, Gwalior, which is also called Galior, is a spur of the range. The mountains of Ranthambhor, Chitor, Mandu, and Chanderi are also of this range. In some places there are breaks of seven or eight leagues. They are low, rugged, rocky, and forested and never have any snow on them. Some rivers in Hindustan have their sources in these mountains.

Most of the provinces of Hindustan are located on flat terrain. So many cities and so many provinces—yet there is no running water anywhere. The only running water is in the large rivers. There are still waters in some places, and even in cities that have the capability of digging channels for running water they do not do so. This may be for any one of several reasons. One is that the agriculture and orchards have absolutely no need for water. Fall crops are watered by the monsoon rains, and strangely the spring crops come even if there is no rain. For a year or two sapling trees are watered either by waterwheel or by bucket, but after that they have no need of irrigation. Some vegetables are watered. In Lahore, Dipalpur, Sirhind, and those regions a waterwheel is used. Two long pieces of rope are looped the size of the well. Wooden stakes are fastened across the two pieces of rope, and jars are fastened to the wooden stakes. [274] The ropes to which the jars are fastened are thrown around a wheel that is over the well. Another wheel is put on the other end of the axle of this wheel. Next to this wheel yet another wheel like the first one is put. As an ox turns this wheel, the spokes enter the spokes of the second wheel and turn the wheel with the jars. A trough is put at the place where the water spills out, and by means of the trough the water is taken wherever it is needed.

In Agra, Chandwar, Bayana, and those regions they irrigate by means of the bucket. This is a laborious and filthy method. A forked stick is raised next to a well, and across the fork a pulley is fastened. A large bucket is fastened to a long rope, which is thrown over the pulley. One end of the rope is tied to an ox. It takes one person to lead the ox and another to empty the water from the bucket. Every time the ox is led out to pull up the bucket and then led back, the rope is dragged through the ox's path, which is sullied with ox urine and dung, as it falls back into the well. For some types of agriculture that need irrigation, water is carried in jars by men and women.

The cities and provinces of Hindustan are all unpleasant. All cities, all locales are alike. The gardens have no walls, and most places are flat as boards.

On the banks of some large rivers and riverbeds, due to the monsoon rains, are gullies [274b] that prevent passage. In some places in the plains are forests of thorny trees in which the people of those districts hole up and obstinately refuse to pay tribute. In Hindustan there is little running water aside from the great rivers. Occasionally in some places there are still waters. All the cities and provinces live from well or pond water, which is collected from the monsoon rains. In Hindustan the destruction and building of villages and hamlets, even of cities, can be accomplished in an instant. Such large cities in which people have lived for years, if they are going to be abandoned, can be left in a day, even half a day, so that no sign or trace remains. If they have a mind to build a city, there is no necessity for digging irrigation canals or building dams. Their crops are all unirrigated. There is no limit to the people. A group gets together, makes a pond, or digs a well. There is no making of houses or raising of walls. They simply make huts from the plentiful straw and innumerable trees, and instantly a village or city is born.

ANIMALS THAT ARE PECULIAR TO HINDUSTAN: BEASTS

Elephant. One of the beasts is the elephant, which the Hindustanis call *hathi.* They are found up to the borderlands of Kalpi. The farther east one goes from there, the more wild elephants there are. Elephants are captured and brought from those regions. In Kara and Manikpur thirty to forty villages gain their livelihood by capturing elephants. [275]

They are responsible directly to the divan for elephants. The elephant is a huge and intelligent animal. It understands what it is told and does what it is ordered to do. The price depends upon the size, and they are sold by the measure. The larger the animal, the higher the price. It is said that on some islands there are elephants ten yards tall, but recently none larger than four to five yards tall has been seen. Elephants eat and drink with their trunks. If they did not have trunks they could not live. On either side of the trunk, on the upper jaw, it has a large tusk. An elephant can put these tusks against a wall or tree and push it down. Likewise it can perform any sort of hard labor with its tusks. The tusks are called ivory, and are valuable. The elephant has no hair as other animals do. This animal is of great importance to the people of Hindustan. Indian armies have several elephants in every unit as a matter of course. Elephants have several good qualities: they can easily carry heavy loads across large and swift-running rivers. Three or four elephants can haul mortar carts that would take four or five hundred men to pull. They eat a lot, however: an elephant eats as much as two strings of camels.

Rhinoceros. The rhinoceros is also a large animal, [275b] the size of three oxen. The statement that is well known in our country,[40] that is, that a rhinoceros can lift an elephant on its horn, is certainly false. It has one horn in the middle of its snout. The horn is longer than a span, and none longer than two spans has been seen. From one large horn a drinking vessel and a set of backgammon pieces were made, and maybe three or four fingers of horn were left over. Its hide is thick. Even if you draw way back with a stiff bow and the arrow hits it right, the arrow will penetrate only four fingers deep. It is said that an arrow will easily pierce some places in its hide. Around its forelegs and hind legs the skin is loose. From a distance it looks like it is wearing a veil. It resembles a horse more than it does any other animal. As a horse does not have a large belly, neither does the rhinoceros; as a horse has solid bone in its pastern, so does the rhinoceros; as a horse has a hoof, so does the rhinoceros. It is more rapacious than an elephant and, unlike an elephant, cannot be tamed. There are many of them in the forests around Peshawar and Hashnaghar and in the forests between the Indus River and Bhera. In Hindustan many of them are found along the banks of the Gogra River. Rhinoceroses were killed during the Hindustan campaigns [276] in the forests of Peshawar and Hashnaghar. They wield their horns in an amazing way. During hunts they gored a lot of men and horses. During one hunt a page named Maqsud had his horse thrown a spear length by one. Thereafter he was nicknamed Rhinoceros Maqsud.

Another is the wild buffalo, which is much larger than our oxen. Like ours, however, its horns curve backward without touching the back. It is a dangerous, ferocious animal.

Nilgai. The nilgai is as tall as but more slender than a horse. The male is blue, which is probably why it is called *nilgau*.[41] It has two smallish horns. On its throat it has hair longer than a span that resembles a yak tail. Its hooves are like those of a cow. The female's color is like that of a doe, and it has no horns or hair on its throat. The female is also plumper than the male.

Hog deer. The hog deer is as large as a white deer, but its fore- and hind legs are shorter, for which reason it is called *kutahpay*.[42] Its horns are branched like a stag's but smaller. Like the stag it sheds its horns annually. It is a poor runner, and for that reason it never leaves the forest.[43]

Another deer is like a male gazelle. Its back is black and its underbelly white.[44] [276b] Its antlers are longer than a stag's and more twisted. The Hindustanis call it *kalhara*. Originally it was *kala haran*, "black deer," but they shortened it to *kalhara*. The female is white. People use the kalhara to catch deer. They fasten a trap ring to the kalhara's antlers, then tie a large stone to its leg at the ankle, which prevents it from going far after it has snared a stag. When they have spotted a stag to be caught, they put the kalhara opposite it. The stag, being quite pugnacious, immediately begins to do battle. The animals clash, lock antlers, and go back and forth, during which the stag's antlers become snared in the ring tied to the antlers of the bait stag. If the wild stag wants to escape, the tame one cannot go far because the stone is tied to its leg. In this way many stags are caught and then tamed to catch still more deer. Traps are also used to catch deer, and tame deer are made to fight in houses, which they do well.

In the foothills of the mountains of Hindustan there is a small deer, about as large as a one-year-old wild mountain lamb.[45]

Another is the gynee, a small cow[46] the size of a large ram in our country. Its meat is tender and delicious.

Monkeys. Then there are monkeys, which Hindustanis call *bandar*, of which there are many varieties. One is the kind that is taken to our country and the gypsies teach to do tricks. [277] This kind occurs in the Dara-i-Nur mountains and in the foothills of Safed Koh in the Khyber region and lower, as well as throughout Hindustan. Higher than that it does not occur. Its fur is yellow, its nose white, and its tail short.

Another sort of monkey not seen natively in Bajaur, Swat, and those regions is taken to our country. It is much larger than other monkeys. Its tail is also long. Its fur is whitish, but its face is jet black. This sort of monkey is called *langur* and is found in the mountains and forests of Hindustan. There are none in our country. Still another sort of monkey has a black face, black fur, and all its limbs are black. It is brought from some islands in the ocean. Another kind, brought from the Nicobar Islands, has a bluish yellow color. An amazing thing about this monkey is that its penis is always erect and never limp.

Another is the *nawal*,[47] which is slightly smaller than a weasel. It climbs trees. Some call it a palm rat, and it is considered to be a lucky.

Another sort of rodent is called *gilahri*.[48] It is always in the trees, running up and down in an amazingly quick and agile fashion.

BIRDS[49]

Peacock. The peacock is a colorful and ornamental animal, although its body, like that of a crane but not so tall, is not equal to its color and beauty. On both the male's and female's head are twenty to thirty feathers two to three fingers long. The female has no other colorful plumage. The male's head has an iridescent collar, and its neck is a beautiful blue. [277b] Below the neck its back is painted yellow, green, blue, and violet. The eyes on its back are very, very small. From its back down to the tip of the tail are much larger eyes in these same colors. The tails of some peacocks are as long as a human being. Under the eye feathers are shortish feathers like those of other birds. Its true tail and wing feathers are red. The peacock occurs in Bajaur and Swat and lower; farther up, in Kunar and Laghman, it occurs nowhere. It is less capable of flight than even the pheasant and cannot do more than one or two short flutters. Because it is all but flightless it sticks to mountains and forests. It is strange that in the forests where peacocks are, there are also many jackals. With a tail a fathom long, how can it run from forest to forest and not fall prey to the jackals? Hindustanis call the peacock *mor.* In the sect of Imam Abu-Hanifa[50] it is licit to eat it. Its meat is not without flavor, rather like the partridge, but one eats it, like the camel, only with reluctance.

Parrot. Parrots occur in Bajaur and lower. In the summer only, when berries are ripe, they come to Nangarhar and Laghman. Parrots are of many varieties. One is the sort that is taken to our country and taught to talk. Another sort is smaller [278] than that parrot, and it too can be taught to talk. This sort is called "jungle parrot," and there are many of them in Bajaur, Swat, and that region. When they fly in flocks of five or six thousand, a difference in the size of the bodies of these two variations is evident, although their coloration is the same.

Another sort is even smaller than the jungle parrot. Its head is red, and the tops of its wings are also red. An area of two fingers at the tip of its tail is white. Some of this kind have iridescent heads. This kind cannot be taught to speak. They call it a Kashmir parrot. Yet another sort is like the jungle parrot but smaller. Its beak is black and it has a wide black ring around its neck. Beneath its wings is red. It learns to speak well. We used to think that parrots and myna birds said whatever they were taught, not that they could think on their own. Recently, however, Abu'l-Qasim Jalayir, a member of my close retinue, told me something strange. He had covered the cage of a parrot of this kind, and the bird said, "Uncover me. I'm stifling." Another time the porters who were carrying it sat down to rest as passersby were coming and going. The parrot said, "The people have gone. Aren't you going?" The responsibility for the veracity of this report lies with the one who told it. Without hearing it with one's own ears it is difficult to believe.

Another kind of parrot is a beautiful bright red. There are other colors too. [278b] Since I do not remember exactly what they are, I haven't written them in detail. The red one is nicely shaped. It can be taught to talk, but unfortunately its voice is as unpleasant and shrill as a piece of broken china dragged across a brass tray.[51]

Starlings. There are many of them in Laghman. Farther down in Hindustan they are quite numerous and occur in many varieties. One kind is the one found so often in Laghman. Its head is black, its wings are spotted, its body is a bit larger and rounder than a lark.[52] It can be taught to talk. Another kind brought from Bengal is called *baindawali.* It is solid black, and its body is much bigger than the former starling. Its beak and feet are yellow, and on each ear is a yellow skin that hangs down and looks ugly. It is called a myna, and it too can be taught to speak both well and eloquently.[53] Another kind of starling is more slender and has red around its eyes. This kind cannot be taught to speak. It is called a "wood starling."[54] When I made a bridge across the Ganges and crossed to rout my enemies, in the vicinity of Lucknow and Oudh a kind of starling was seen that had a white breast, spotted head, and black back. It had never been seen before. This kind probably cannot learn to speak.[55]

Lucha.[56] This bird is also called *buqalamun.*[57] From head to tail it has five or six different colors that shimmer like a pigeon's throat. [279] It is about the size of a snow cock. It most likely is the Indian snow cock, for it runs about mountaintops like a snow cock. It occurs in the Nijrao mountains of Kabul Province and in mountains farther down, but not higher than that. The people there tell an amazing story about it: in winter it descends to the mountain foothills, and if it is made to fly over a vineyard, it cannot fly any more and can be caught.[58] It is edible and has quite delicious flesh.

Partridge. The partridge is not peculiar to Hindustan but is found in warm climates. However, because certain kinds are not found anywhere except in Hindustan, I mention it here. The black partridge's body is the size of a snow cock. The male's back is the color of a female pheasant. Its throat and breast are black, and it has bright white spots. Red lines come down either side of its eyes. It has an fantastic cry. *Sher daram shakarak*[59] can be heard from its cry. It says *sher* like *qit,* but it pronounces *daram shakarak* quite correctly. The partridges in Astarabad say *qat meni tuttilar,*[60] and those in Arabia and thereabouts say *bi'sh-shukri tadumu 'n-ni'am.*[61] The female's coloration is like that of a young pheasant. They occur below Nijrao.

Another kind of partridge is the gray partridge, which has a body the size of a black partridge. Its cry greatly resembles that of the partridge, but its sound [279b] is much shriller. The male and female have only a slight difference in coloration. It occurs in the Peshawar and Hashnaghar regions and farther down, but not higher up.

Phul-paykar.[62] It is as long as a Himalayan snow cock. Its body is the size of the domestic chicken. Its color is that of a hen. From its gullet down to its breast it is a beautiful red. The phul-paykar is found in the mountains of Hindustan.

Wild fowl. The difference between this fowl and a domestic one is that the wild fowl flies like a pheasant and, unlike the domestic fowl, does not occur in all colors. It is found in the Bajaur mountains and lower but not farther up than that.[63]

Chälsi.[64] Its body is like that of the phul-paykar, which has, however, a more beautiful color. It occurs in the Bajaur mountains.

Sham.[65] It is as long as a domestic fowl but has unique colors. It too occurs in the Bajaur mountains.

Quail. Although the quail is not limited to Hindustan, four or five kinds are peculiar to Hindustan. One is the quail that goes to our country.[66] Another quail, somewhat smaller than the one that goes to our country,[67] has wings and tail of a reddish color. This kind of quail flies in flocks like the sparrow. Another kind, smaller than the one that goes to our country, has much black on its throat and breast.[68] [280] Another, which very seldom goes to Kabul, is a tiny quail, a bit longer than a swallow.[69] In Kabul it is called a *quratu.*

Kharchal. It is as long as a bustard and probably is the bustard of Hindustan. Its flesh is delicious. In some birds the thigh is good, and in others the breast is good. All the kharchal's meat is delicious and good.

Charz.[70] It is a little smaller than the bustard in body. The male's back is like the bustard's, but its breast is black. The female is one color. The meat of the charz is also quite delicious. As the kharchal resembles the great bustard, the charz resembles the lesser bustard.

Indian sand grouse. It is smaller and slenderer than other sand grouses. The black of its tail is less, and its cry is less shrill.

BIRDS THAT LIVE IN
AND BESIDE WATER

Among the birds that live in water and on the banks of rivers is the *adjutant.* It has a huge body, and each of its wings spans a fathom. There are no feathers on its head or neck. From its throat hangs something like a pouch. Its back is black, and its breast white. Occasionally it goes to Kabul. One year an adjutant was caught in Kabul and brought to me. It became nicely tame and ate meat that was tossed to it, never missing as it caught the meat in its bill. Once it swallowed a shoe, another time a whole chicken—wings and feathers and all. [280b]

Saras. The Turks in Hindustan call it a "camel crane." It is smaller than an adjutant, but its neck is longer. Its head is brilliant red. It is kept in houses and becomes quite tame.

White-necked stork. Its neck is almost as long as that of the saras, but its body is smaller. It is much larger than a white stork, which it resembles, and its black bill is correspondingly longer. Its head is iridescent, its neck is white, and its wings are variegated: the tips and edges are white and the midsection black.

Stork. Its neck is white, but its head and all its limbs are black. It is smaller than the storks that go to our country. Hindustanis call it *bag dhek*. Another kind of stork has a color and body exactly like those of the ones that go to our country except that its bill is rather dark and it is much smaller.

Another bird resembles the gray heron and the stork. Its bill is bigger and longer than the heron's, and its body is smaller than the stork's.

The great black ibis is as large as a buzzard. The back of its wings is black, and it has a loud cry. Another is the white ibis, whose head and bill are black. It is much larger than the ibises that go to our country but smaller than the Hindustan ibis. [281]

Ducks. One kind of duck is called the spotted-billed. It is larger than common ducks. Both male and female are of one color. There are always some in Hashnaghar. Occasionally they go to Laghman too. Its meat is quite delicious.

Another kind of duck is called the comb duck. It is slightly smaller than a goose. On top of its bill is a hump. Its breast is white, its back black. Its flesh is good to eat.

Another is the black hawk-eagle. It is as long as an eagle, and black. Another is the *sar*. Its back and tail are red.[71]

Pied crow. The pied crow of Hindustan is somewhat smaller and slenderer than the crows of our country. It has a bit of white on its throat.

There is another bird that resembles the crow and the magpie. In Laghman they call it "forest bird." Its head and breast are black, its wings and tail reddish, and its eyes deep red. Since it has difficulty flying, it does not emerge from the forest, for which reason they call it a "forest bird."[72]

Another is the great bat called *chamgiddar*. It is as large as an owl. Its head resembles a puppy's. When it is going to hang on to a tree, it grabs a branch and hangs upside down. It is strange.

Indian magpie. The Hindustan magpie is called *mata* and is slightly smaller than a common magpie. The magpie is mottled black and white; the mata is pale mottled.

There is another little bird the size of a nightingale. [281b] It is a nice red color and has small black markings on its wings.

Swift. It is like a swallow but much larger. It is solid jet black.

Cuckoo. It is as long as but much slenderer than a crow. It sings beautifully. It is the nightingale of Hindustan. The people of Hindustan have great respect for the nightingale. It inhabits gardens with many trees.

Another bird is like the green magpie. It clings to trees. It is as large as a green magpie and is green in color like a parrot.[73]

AQUATIC ANIMALS

One is the alligator,[74] which lives in still waters and resembles a lizard. They say it carries off not only men but also oxen.

Another is the crocodile. This too is like a lizard. It is in all the rivers of Hindustan. One was captured and brought to me. It was nearly four or five yards long and as big around as a sheep. They are said to get even bigger. Its snout was longer than half a yard. The upper and lower jaws contain narrow rows of little teeth. It comes out and lies on the banks of rivers.

Another is the dolphin. It too is found in all the rivers of Hindustan. It pops up all at once out of the water. Its head appears and disappears, and then it dives into the water and its tail can still be seen. Its snout is long [282] like a crocodile's, and it has rows of little teeth. Otherwise its head and body are like a fish. When it frolics in the water it looks like a water bag. When the dolphins play in the Gogra River, they leap right out of the water. Like fish, these animals never leave the water.

Another is the alligator.[75] It is said to grow large, and the soldiers saw many of them in the Gogra. They are also said to carry off people. While we were on the banks of the Gogra they carried off an old slave-woman or two. Between Ghazipur and Benares they carried off three or four soldiers. In that same region I too saw a crocodile from rather far away, but I did not see it distinctly.

There is the *kaka* fish. It has two bones three fingers long sticking out in front of its ears. When it is caught it moves these bones and makes a strange noise. It is probably on account of that noise that it is called kaka.

The fish of Hindustan are delicious. They have neither odor nor spiny bones. They are amazingly agile. Once a net had been thrown from either side of a river and was being drawn up, and both ends of the net were more than half a yard above the water. Many fish got by by jumping a yard higher than the net.

In some of the rivers of Hindustan are little fish [282b] that jump up from half a yard to a yard out of the water if there is a loud noise or footsteps.

Although the frogs of Hindustan are like frogs elsewhere, they can run seven or eight yards across the surface of the water.

FLORA PECULIAR TO HINDUSTAN

Mango. Most people in Hindustan pronounce the *b* in this word without a vowel, and since such a pronunciation is ugly[76] some call the mango *naghzak*, as Khwaja Khusraw says:[77]

Our naghzak, beautifier of the garden, most beautiful fruit of Hindustan.

When the mango is good it is really good. As many as are eaten, the really good ones are scarce. Mostly they are picked unripe and allowed to ripen at home. The unripe mango serves as a condiment for meals, and preserves made from it are also excellent. In fact, the mango is the best fruit of Hindustan. The tree is elegantly tall, but the trunk of the tree is ugly and ill shaped. Some people praise the mango to such an extent that they prefer it to all fruit except the melon, but it is not so good as to warrant such praise. The mango resembles the *kardi* peach, and ripens during the monsoon. There are two ways to eat it. One is to mash it to a pulp, make a hole in it, and suck the juice. The other is to peel it like a peach and eat it. Its leaf somewhat resembles a peach leaf. Good mangoes are found in Bengal and Gujarat.

Plantain. The Arabs call it *mawz*. The tree is not very tall. [283] In fact, it cannot really be called a tree—something between a tree and a shrub. The leaf resembles that of the *aman qara*,[78] but a plantain leaf can get up to two yards long and nearly a yard wide. From the middle of the leaf emerges a branch, which is the bud, which is as large as and shaped like a sheep's heart. As each leaf of the bud opens, a row of six or seven flowers is seen at the base of the leaf. The flowers become the plantains. As the heart-shaped branch lengthens, the leaves of the large bud open and the row of plantain flowers becomes more apparent. Each plantain tree bears fruit only once. The plantain has two nice features. One is that it can be easily peeled, and the other that it has no seeds or fiber. It is longer and slenderer than an eggplant. It is not too sweet, although the plantains of Bengal are said to be very sweet. It is a good-looking tree with its broad, flat, beautiful green leaves.

Tamarind is what they call the date of India. It has tiny leaves that mostly resemble bay leaves but are finer. It is an attractive tree and offers much shade. The tree is quite tall, and many tamarinds grow wild.

Mahua is also called *gul-i-chakan*.[79] The tree is quite tall. The houses of the people of Hindustan are mostly made of mahua wood. [283b] Liquor is distilled from the flowers, which are also dried and eaten. The dried flower mostly resembles the raisin but has a bad taste. The fresh flower is not bad and is edible. This also grows wild. The fruit is tasteless, the seed rather large, and the skin thin. Oil is extracted from the pulp of the seeds.

Although the mimusops tree is not tall, it is not short either. The fruit is yellow in color and more slender than the jujube. The taste resembles grapes but leaves a slight aftertaste that is not too bad. It is edible. The seed has a thin husk.

The leaf of the eugenia looks a lot like a willow leaf, but it is rounder and greener. The tree is not bad looking. The fruit resembles black grapes. It has a rather tart taste and is not terribly good.

Kamrak[80] is five sided and about as large as a *ghinyalu*[81] and four fingers long. It is ripe when it is yellow. It too has no seeds. When picked unripe it is very bitter. When allowed to ripen well, it has a pleasant tartness that is not bad and not unattractive.

The jackfruit is unbelievably ugly and bad tasting. It looks exactly like [284] sheep intestines turned inside out like stuffed tripe. It has a cloyingly sweet taste. Inside it has seeds like hazelnuts that mostly resemble dates, but these seeds are round, not long. The flesh of these seeds, which is what is eaten, is softer than dates. It is sticky, and for that reason some people grease their hands and mouths before eating it. The fruit is said to grow on the branches, the trunk, and the roots of the tree and looks like stuffed tripe hung all over the tree.

Monkey jack is the size of an apple. It doesn't have a bad odor. When unripe it is singularly insipid and tasteless. When ripe it is soft and can be skinned with the hands and eaten anywhere. It is not bad. Its taste bears a great resemblance to overripe quince. It has a nice but very tart taste.

The lote fruit is called *kunar* in Persian. There are many varieties. It is somewhat larger than the plum. Another variety is the size of the Husayni grape.[82] Mostly they are not very good. We saw a lote fruit in Bhander that was tasty. The tree sheds its leaves in Taurus and Gemini and puts out leaves in Cancer and Leo, which is the true monsoon, and becomes fresh and verdant. The fruit ripens in Aquarius and Pisces.

Corinda grows on bushes, like the *chäkä*[83] in our country. [284b] Chäkä grows in the mountains, but this grows on the plains. In taste it resembles rhubarb, but it is sweeter and less juicy than rhubarb.

Paniyala[84] is larger than the plum and resembles an unripe red apple. It has a slight tart flavor but is pretty good. The tree is larger than a pomegranate tree, and the leaves resemble the leaves of the almond but are slightly smaller.

The fruit of the clustered fig resembles the common fig when it emerges from the trunk of the tree. It is an oddly insipid fruit.

The myrobalan is also five sided and resembles an unopened cotton boll. It is coarse and tasteless, but preserves made from it are not bad. It is a quite beneficial fruit, and the tree has a nice shape. The leaves are tiny.

The chironjia nut tree is said to grow in the mountains. Later I realized that there were three or four roots of it in our gardens. It looks a lot like the mahua.[85] The nut is not bad—something between a walnut and an almond. It is smaller than a pistachio, and round. It is put into custards and confections.

The date is not peculiar to Hindustan, but since there were none in our country it is mentioned here. There are date trees in Laghman. The branches are in only one place at the top of the tree. The leaves grow from the base of the branch out to the end along both sides. The trunk is rough and an ugly color. The fruit is like a bunch of grapes [285] but much bigger. They say that among plants the date tree resembles animals in two ways. One is that just as animals' lives are ended if their heads are cut off, the date tree too will dry up if its head is cut off. The other is that just as animals cannot propagate without the male, the date tree too will not bear fruit unless a branch of a male date is brought into contact with the female. The truth of this statement is not known. The head of the date tree mentioned above is spoken of as its "cheese." Date "cheese" refers to the area where the branches and leaves emerge, where it is as white as cheese. As the branches and leaves lengthen they turn green. The "cheese" of the date is not bad at all. It closely resembles the walnut. A score is made in the place where the cheese is, and into the wound a date leaf is inserted so that whatever liquid comes from the wound flows across the top of the leaf. The leaf is positioned over the mouth of a jar, and the jar is tied to the tree. Whatever liquid is produced from the wound is collected in the jar. If drunk immediately the liquid is rather sweet. If drunk three or four days later they say it has a really intoxicating effect. Once when I went to Bari,[86] [285b] I made an excursion through the villages along the bank of the Chambhal River. Along the way we came upon some people in a valley who were making this sort of date liquor, and we drank a good deal of it. Its intoxicating effect was not obvious. Probably one has to drink a lot for a little effect to be felt.

The coconut is Arabicized by the Arabs into *narjil*. The people of Hindustan call it *naliyar*,[87] probably a popular error. The fruit of the coconut is the *jawz-i-hindi*[88] from which ladles are made. The larger ones are made into ghichak bowls. The tree looks exactly like the date palm, but the coconut branch has more leaves, and the leaves are shinier. Just as there is a green husk on top of the walnut, there is a green husk on top of the coconut, but the coconut's husk is quite fibrous. Ropes for all boats and ships are made from this coconut fiber, as is cord for seaming boats. When the coconut fiber is stripped, there are revealed three holes arranged in a triangle on the nut, two hard and one soft. The soft one is easily pierced with pressure. Before the kernel sets there is liquid inside. One can pierce the hole and drink the liquid, which does not have a bad taste—rather like liquified date cheese.

The branches of the palmyra also grow at the top. [286] Like the date, a jar can be tied to the palmyra and the liquid caught and drunk. This liquid is called "toddy,"[89] and its intoxicating effect is said to be stronger than that of date liquor. There are no leaves on the palmyra branch for half a yard to a yard. After that, thirty to forty leaves spread out in one place at the end of the branch. The leaves are nearly a yard long. People often write Hindi script on them as they do on account books. If the people of Hindustan are not wearing rings in the large holes in their ears, they put rolls of palmyra leaves in them instead. They make such things in the markets. The trunk of the palmyra is more beautiful and more even than the trunk of the date palm.

The orange and fruits that resemble it in shape. In Laghman, Bajaur, and Swat, oranges are abundant and good. Those of Laghman are smaller and are navel oranges. They are nice, delicate, and juicy beyond comparison with the oranges of the Khurasan region. They are so fragile that by the time they are brought from Laghman to Kabul, a distance of thirteen or fourteen leagues, some of them are spoiled. The Astarabad orange can be transported to Samarkand, a distance of 270 or 280 leagues, and does not spoil because its skin is thick and it has little juice. [286b] Bajaur oranges are as large as quinces. They have a lot of juice, which is more sour than the juice of other oranges. Khwaja Kalan said, "We counted the oranges of this sort taken from just one tree in Bajaur, and there were seven thousand." I had always thought that the word for orange, *naranj,* seemed Arabicized. It turned out to be so, for the people of Bajaur and Swat call the orange *narang.*[90]

Another is the lime. It is abundant. In size it is as big as an egg. It is said that if the fibers are boiled and drunk by someone who has been poisoned, it will avert the danger.

Another fruit that resembles the orange is the citron. The people of Bajaur and Swat call it *balang,* for which reason the marmalade is called balang marmalade. In Hindustan the citron is called *bajauri.* There are two kinds of citron. One is sweet and insipid—sickeningly sweet and unsuitable for eating—although the peel is good for marmalade. The Laghman citron is just as sweet. The other is the Bajaur and Hindustan citron, which is nicely sour. Sherbet made from it is really delicious. The citron is as large as a Khusravi melon. Its rind is wrinkled and uneven. The end is tapered like a nose. The citron is more yellow than an orange. The tree has no trunk but is smallish and shrublike. [287] The leaf is longer than the leaf of the orange.

Another fruit that resembles the orange is the *sangtara.* In color and shape it is like the citron, but its skin is smooth, not rough. It is slightly smaller than the citron. The tree grows large, like the apricot tree, and its leaf resembles that of the orange. It has a nice tartness, and its sherbet is tasty. Like the lime, it has a strengthening effect on the stomach, not a debilitating one like the orange.

Another fruit like the orange is the large lime they call the galle-galle[91] lime in Hindustan. In shape it resembles a goose egg, but the ends are not tapered like an egg. The skin is even like a sangtara. It is unbelievably juicy.

The *jambhiri* lime is also like an orange. It is shaped like an orange but its color is yellow, not orange. It smells like a citron and has a nice tartness too.

Another is the *sadaphal*, which is shaped like a pear. In color it is like a quince. It is sweet, but not sickly sweet like the orange. Another is the *amrit phal*. Still another is the *karna* citron, which is the size of a galle-galle lime and is sour.

Another fruit that resembles the orange is the *amal bed*, which has just now been seen after three years in Hindustan.[92] They say that a needle put in it will dissolve, [287b] either because it has acidity or some other property. It is as tart as an orange and a lime.

FLOWERS OF HINDUSTAN

There are some marvelous flowers in Hindustan. One is the hibiscus, which some Hindustanis call *gudhal*. It is not a shrub but a tree with stems. It is somewhat taller than the red rose, and its color is deeper than the pomegranate flower. It is as large as a red rose. The red rose blossoms all at once after budding, but when the hibiscus blossoms, from the middle of the petals yet another slender stalk is formed, as long as a finger, from which still more hibiscus petals open. The result is a double, fairly amazing flower. The flowers look beautiful in color on the tree but do not last long. They blossom and fade within a day. They bloom well and plentifully during the four months of monsoon and often throughout most of the year. Despite their profusion they have no odor.

Another flower is the oleander, which occurs in both white and red. It has five petals like the peach blossom. The red oleander bears a resemblance to the peach blossom, but the oleander blooms with fourteen or fifteen flowers in one place, so that from a distance it looks like one big flower. The bush is larger than the red rose. The red oleander has a faint but agreeable smell. It too blooms beautifully and abundantly during the monsoon and can be found throughout most of the year. [288]

The screw pine is another. It has a delicate scent. Whereas musk has the disadvantage of being dry, this could be called "wet musk." In addition to the plant's having a strange appearance, the flowers can be from one-and-a-half to two spans long. The long leaves are like those of the reed and have spines. When compressed like a bud, the outer leaves are spiny and greenish and the inner leaves soft and white. Nestled among the inner leaves are things like in the middle of a flower, and the good scent comes from there. When it first comes up, before it develops a stalk, it resembles the male reed bush. The leaves are flattish and spiny. The stalk is extremely unharmonious. The roots are always exposed.

Then there is the jasmine. The white variety is called champa. It is larger and has a more pronounced fragrance than the jasmine in our country.

DIVISIONS OF TIME

In our country there are four seasons, but in Hindustan there are three: four months of summer, four of monsoon, and four of winter. The months begin with the crescent moon in opposition. Every three years one month is added to the monsoon months, then three years later a month is added to the winter months, then three years later a month is added to the summer months. This is their intercalation. [288b]

The summer months are Chait, Baisakh, Jeth, and Asarh, corresponding to Pisces, Aries, Taurus, and Gemini. Those of the monsoon are Sanwan, Bhadon, Kuar, and Katik, corresponding to Cancer, Leo, Virgo, and Libra. The winter months are Aghan, Pus, Magh, and Phagun, corresponding to Scorpio, Sagittarius, Capricorn, and Aquarius.

Having assigned four months each to the seasons, they take two months of each season to be the hottest, the rainiest, or the coldest. Of the summer months the last two, Jeth and Asarh, are the ones of extreme heat. Of the monsoon months the first two, Sanwan and Bhadon, are the height of the rains. Of the winter months the middle two, Pus and Magh, are the months of extreme cold. By this reckoning they have six seasons.

They also have names for the days of the week: Sanichar, Etwar, Somwar, Mangal, Budh, Brihaspati, Sukrawar.[93]

In our country a day and night is conventionally divided into twenty-four parts, each of which is called an hour, and every hour is divided into sixty parts, each of which is called a minute, so there are 1,440 minutes in a day and night. The duration of a minute is about what it takes to say the Fatiha with the Basmala six times,[94] [289] so that during a day and night the Fatiha and the Basmala could be recited 8,640 times.

The people of India divide the day and night into sixty parts, each of which is called a ghari.[95] Moreover, the night and the day are each divided into four parts, each of which is called a *pahar,* or what in Persian is called a *pas.* In Transoxiana, I had heard the expressions *pas* and *pasban,*[96] but I did not know what they denoted. For keeping time, in all the important towns of Hindustan a group of men called *ghariyalis* is appointed and assigned. They cast a disc of brass as large as a tray and two fingers thick. This brass object, called a *ghariyal* is hung in a high place. Another vessel has a hole in the bottom, like an hourglass, that fills up once every ghari. The ghariyalis take turns putting the vessel in water and waiting for it to fill up. For example, when the vessel that they put in water at daybreak fills up once, they strike the ghariyal with a mallet. When it fills up twice, they strike it twice, and so on until a watch is completed. The close of each watch is announced by the striking of the ghariyal many times in rapid succession. When the first watch of the day is finished, after repeated striking, [289b] the ghariyalis pause and strike once. When the second watch is finished, they strike many times and then strike twice. For the third, thrice; for the fourth, four times. When the four watches of the day have ended and the night watches have begun, the night watches are introduced in the same way. They used to announce the new watches by striking only when the previous ones were finished, but people who woke up during the night and heard the sound of three or four gharis being struck did not know whether it was for the second or the third watch. I therefore ordered them to herald the watches of the night and cloudy days by striking only after they had struck the ghari first. For example, after striking the third ghari of the first watch of the night, they would pause and announce the watch by striking once more, so it was obvious that it was the third ghari of the first watch. After striking the fourth ghari of the third watch of the night, they would pause before striking three times. It was a great idea. Whenever people woke up at night and heard the sound of the ghariyal, they knew which watch and which ghari it was.

Every ghari is divided into sixty parts, each of which is called a *pal*, [290] so that a day and night contain 3,600 pals. They say that a pal lasts the time it takes to shut and open the eyes sixty times, so during a day and a night you could shut your eyes and open them 216,000 times. By experiment it has been determined that a pal is approximately the length of time it takes to say *qul huwa'llah* and *bismillah* eight times,[97] so during a day and night you could say *qul huwa'llah* and *bismillah* 28,800 times.

WEIGHTS AND MEASURES

The people of India also have wonderful weights and measures. Eight *rattis* equal 1 *masha*; 4 *mashas* equal 1 *tank*, or 32 *rattis*; 5 *mashas* equal 1 *mithcal* or 40 *rattis*; 12 *mashas* equal 1 *tola*, or 96 *rattis*; 14 *tolas* equal 1 *seer*. It is set everywhere that 40 *seers* equal 1 *maund*. Twelve *maunds* equal 1 *mani*; 100 *manis* is called a *manyasa*.[98] Jewels and pearls are weighed by the tank.

The people of India have also an excellent system of numbering. One hundred thousand equal 1 lac; 100 lacs equal 1 crore; 100 crores equal 1 *arb*; 100 *arbs* equal 1 *kharb*; 100 *kharbs* equal 1 *nil*; 100 *nils* equal 1 *padam*; 100 *padams* equal 1 *sankya*. The creation of these numbers indicates the vast wealth of Hindustan.

Most of the people of Hindustan are infidels, whom the people of India call Hindu. Most Hindus believe in reincarnation. Tax collectors, artisans, and craftsmen are all Hindus. In our country the people who move about the countryside have clan names, but in India even those who dwell in towns and villages [290b] have clan names. Every craft and trade is passed down from father to son.

Hindustan is a place of little charm. There is no beauty in its people, no graceful social intercourse, no poetic talent or understanding, no etiquette, nobility, or manliness. The arts and crafts have no harmony or symmetry. There are no good horses, meat, grapes, melons, or other fruit. There is no ice, cold water, good food or bread in the markets. There are no baths and no madrasas. There are no candles, torches, or candlesticks.

Instead of candles and torches they have a numerous group of filthy people called *deotis* who carry the lamps. In their left hands the deotis hold a small wooden tripod; on the end of one of its legs an iron piece like the top of a candlestick is fastened to the wood of the tripod. Next to it they fasten a wick as thick as a thumb. In their right hands the deotis carry a gourd with a narrow slit from which oil can be trickled. Whenever the wick needs oil, they pour it from the gourd. Great men keep deotis by the hundred and use them in place of candles or torches. When kings and noblemen have business at night that requires lighting, the filthy deotis [291] bring this sort of lamp and hold it nearby.

Aside from the streams and still waters that flow in ravines and hollows, there is no running water in their gardens or palaces, and in their buildings no pleasing harmony or regularity.

The peasantry and common people parade around stark naked with something like a loincloth tied around themselves and hanging down two spans below their navels. Under this rag is another piece of cloth, which they pass between their legs and fasten to the loincloth string. Women fasten around themselves one long piece of cloth, half of which they tie to their waists and the other half of which they throw over their heads.

The one nice aspect of Hindustan is that it is a large country with lots of gold and money. The weather turns very nice during the monsoon. Sometimes it rains ten, fifteen, or twenty times a day; torrents are formed in an instant, and water flows in places that normally have no water. During the rainy season, the weather is unusually good when the rain ceases, so good in fact that it could not be more temperate or pleasant. The one drawback is that the air is too humid. During the monsoon, bows from that country cannot be used to shoot or they are ruined. [291b] Armor, books, bedding, and textiles are also affected. Buildings do not last long either. Aside from the monsoon, there are periods of good weather during both winter and summer, but the constant north wind always stirs up a lot of dust. Near the monsoon it gets so strong at least four or five times and creates so much dust that people cannot see each other. The wind is called *andhi*. In the summer during Taurus and Gemini it gets hot, but the heat is not so intense, nothing like the heat of Balkh and Kandahar, and it lasts only half as long.

Another nice thing is the unlimited numbers of craftsmen and practitioners of every trade. For every labor and every product there is an established group who have been practicing that craft or professing that

Construction of the Masjid-i Jami' in Samarkand, from a *Zafarnama* (Book of Triumph) of Sharafuddin Ali Yazdi. Herat (?), dated A.H. 872 (A.D. 1467–68). Opaque watercolor, ink, and gold on paper. John Work Garrett Library, The Johns Hopkins University, Baltimore, fol. 360a.

trade for generations. For instance, in the *Zafarnama,* Mulla Sharaf writes eloquently that during Temür Beg's building of the stone mosque two hundred stonemasons from Azerbaijan, Fars, Hindustan, and other places were employed on it daily. In Agra alone there were 680 Agra stonemasons at work on my building every day.[99] Aside from that, in Agra, Sikri, Bayana, Dholpur, Gwalior, and Koil, 1,491 stonemasons were laboring on my buildings. [292] There are similar vast numbers of every type of craftsman and laborers of every description in Hindustan.

The regions from Bhera to Bihar that are currently under my control are worth 52 crores, as can be seen in the following table. Of these, eight to nine crores' worth are districts of rays and rajahs who are in obedience and have been awarded these districts for their maintenance as of old.

Estimate of the total revenue of as much of Hindustan as has presently come under conquest:[100]

Trans-Sutlej, Bhera, Lahore, Sialkot, Dipalpur, etc. 33,315,989 tankas	Kalpi and Seondha 42,855,950 tankas	Saran 11,018,373 tankas
Sirhind 12,931,985 tankas	Kannauj 13,663,358 tankas	Champaran 19,086,060 tankas
Hissar Firoza 13,075,174 tankas	Sambhal 13,844,000 tankas	Kandhla 4,330,300 tankas
The capital Delhi and the Doab 36,950,254 tankas	Laknaur and Buxar 13,982,433 tankas	Tirhut (tribute from Rajah Rup Narayan) 255,000 silver tankas
Mewat (not inside the realm at the time of Sikandar[101]) 16,981,000 tankas	Khairabad 1,265,000 tankas	2,750,000 black tankas
	Oudh and Bahraich 11,701,369 tankas [293a]	Ranthambhor, including Buli, Chatsu, and Malana 2,000,000
Bayana 14,414,930 tankas	Jaunpur 40,088,333 tankas	Nagaur
Agra 2,976,919 tankas	Kara and Manikpur 16,327,282 tankas	Rajah Bikramajit of Ranthambhor
		Kalinjar
Central provinces 29,100,019 tankas	Bihar 40,560,000 tankas	Rajah Singh Deo
Gwalior 22,357,450 tankas	Sarwar 15,517,506.5 tankas	Rajah Bikam Deo Rajah Bikam Chand

[293b] As much of the characteristics and peculiarities of the peoples and places of Hindustan as has been ascertained has been written. Hereafter, whenever anything worth writing about is noticed or anything worth telling is heard I will write it down.

DISTRIBUTION OF THE TREASURY IN AGRA

On Saturday the twenty-ninth of Rajab [May 12] examination and distribution of the treasury began. Humayun was given twenty lacs. I gave him outright another room of the treasury, which had not been inventoried or counted. Some of the begs were given ten lacs, some eight, seven, or six. All the Afghan Hazaras, Arabs, and Baluch[102] in the army and every other group were given cash from the treasury in accordance with their station. Every merchant and student, indeed every person who was along with the army, took away a large share. Large portions of the treasury went even to those who were not in the army: seventeen lacs went to Kamran and fifteen to Muhammad-Zaman Mirza, and to Askari and Hindal and to all relatives and kinsfolk, large and small alike, went much gold and silver stuff, textiles, jewels, and slaves. Many gifts went to the begs and soldiers who were on the other side. To Samarkand, Khurasan, [294] Kashghar, and Iraq went gifts for relatives and kinfolk. Offerings went to the shaykhs in Samarkand and Khurasan; one was even sent to Mecca and Medina. There was a shahrukhi of largesse for every living soul, male and female, bondsman and free, adult and child alike, in the province of Kabul and the district of Wersek.

When we first came to Agra, a strange antagonism and hatred was felt between our soldiers and the natives. The native soldiers and peasants ran away as far as they could from our people. With the sole exceptions of Delhi and Agra, all the places that had fortresses made them fast and refused obedience. In Sambhal was Qasim of Sambhal; in Bayana was Nizam Khan; in Mewat was Hasan Khan of Mewat himself, that little heretic who was the instigator of all this trouble. In Dholpur was Muhammad Zaytun; in Gwalior was Tatar Khan Sarangkhani; in Rapri was Husayn Khan son of Nohani Khan; in Etawah was Qutb Khan; in Kalpi was Alam Khan; Kannauj and that side of the Ganges were full of Afghans in opposition, like Nasir Khan Nohani, Ma'ruf Farmuli, and many other amirs who had rebelled two or three years before Ibrahim's death [in 1526]. When I conquered Ibrahim [on April 20, 1526], they seized Kannauj and all the districts on that side and camped a march or two this side of Kannauj. Darya Khan's son Pahar Khan [294b] they made king and named Sultan Muhammad. His slave Marghub was in Mahaban. Having come this near, he went no farther for some time.

DISAFFECTION IN THE ARMY

When we came to Agra it was the hot season, and the people all fled in fear. Neither grain for ourselves nor straw for the horses was to be found. The villages had been so plundered and pillaged that the people had turned to brigandage and thievery. The roads could not be traveled. We had not yet had a chance to divide the treasury or assign able men to every district and locality. Also, that year was extremely hot. Many began to sicken and die as though under the influence of a pestilent wind. For these reasons most of the begs and great warriors lost heart. They were unwilling to stay in Hindustan and began to leave. Now if aged and experienced begs say such things, it is no fault, for once having spoken, such men have enough sense and intelligence to distinguish between prudence and imprudence and to discern good from evil after a decision has been made. Such a person considers everything for himself and knows that when something has been decided there is no sense in endlessly repeating words that have already been spoken. Among the lesser types what is the value of such words and such [295] insipid ideas? It is strange that among the lesser officers a few had been newly appointed to the rank of beg when we mounted in Kabul this time. I expected that if I went into fire or water and emerged, they would come in with me and emerge along with me and be at my side wherever I went—not that they would speak out in opposition to my purpose. No matter what task or action we decided with the counsel and agreement of all, they would disagree with it before they ever left the assembly. If they acted badly, Ahmadi Parwanachï and Wali Khazin acted even worse. No sooner had we left Kabul, defeated Ibrahim, and taken Agra than Khwaja Kalan acted well several times. He spoke courageously and gave high-minded opinions, but several days after taking Agra his thoughts changed radically. One who was serious about leaving was Khwaja Kalan.

Realizing this trepidation in the men, we summoned all the begs for council. I said, "Rule and conquest do not come about without tools and implements. Kingship and princehood are not possible without liege men and domains. For some years we have struggled, experienced difficulties, traversed long distances, led the army, and cast ourselves and our soldiers into the dangers of war and battle; [295b] through God's grace we have defeated such numerous enemies and taken such vast realms. What now compels us to throw away for no reason at all the realms we have taken at such cost? Shall we go back to Kabul and remain poverty-stricken? Let no one who supports me say such things henceforth. Let no one who cannot endure and is bound to leave be dissuaded from leaving." By addressing the men with such reasonable and justified words, we alleviated their fears.

KHWAJA KALAN LEAVES HINDUSTAN

Since Khwaja Kalan did not have the heart to stay, it was decided that he, who had many retainers, would take the gifts and go. There were a few men in Kabul and Ghazni, and he would take charge of them. I awarded Khwaja Kalan with Ghazni, Gardez, and the Sultan-Mas'udi Hazaras. He was also given the three- or four-lac pargana of Ghuram in Hindustan. It was also decided that Khwaja Mirmiran would go to Kabul and be in charge of the gifts. As pursers Mulla Hasan the money changer and Tuka Hindu were appointed. Since Khwaja Kalan hated Hindustan, he wrote the following line of poetry on the wall of his quarters in Delhi when he left: [296]

If I cross the Indus in safety, may my face turn black if I ever desire to see Hindustan again.

To compose such a facetious line and write it was inexcusable. That he left was one reason to be cross with him; such nastiness gave me another reason. I too composed an extemporaneous quatrain, and sent it to him:

Give a hundred thanks, Babur, that the generous Pardoner of all has given you Sind and Hind and a vast kingdom. / If you cannot endure the heat and say, "I would see the face of cold," there is Ghazni.

At this time Mulla Apaq, whose rank had formerly been very low, but who had gathered his brethren two or three years previously and made a splendid troop, was given the Urukzai and some of the Afghans on the banks of the Indus. He was sent to Koil, and letters of conciliation were dispatched to the yeomen and soldiers who were in that region. Shaykh Ghuran came and paid sincere homage. Two or three thousand of the yeomen of the Doab came and paid homage too.

When Yunus Ali had lost his way and gotten separated from Humayun, he encountered Ali Khan Farmuli's sons and relatives on the road between Delhi and Agra. There was a skirmish, and he defeated Ali Khan's sons and brought them in in chains. About this time, one of Ali Khan's captured sons was attached to Dawlat-Qadam Türk's son Mirza Moghul [296b] and sent with letters of conciliation to Ali Khan, who had gone to Mewat during the turmoil. To favor Ali Khan he was awarded a splendid twenty-five-lac pargana.

Sultan Ibrahim had sent few officers under the leadership of Mustafa Farmuli and Firoz Khan Sarangkhani to attack the rebel officers in Purab. Mustafa waged war well against these officers and dealt them several defeats, but he died before Ibrahim was overthrown. Since Ibrahim was on campaign, Mustafa's younger brother Shaykh Bayazid sent his elder brother's people away. Firoz Khan, Shaykh Bayazid, Mahmud Khan Nohani, and Qazi Jia entered my service. They were favored and rewarded with more than they had expected: Firoz Khan was given Jaunpur and 14,605,000 tankas; Shaykh Bayazid was given Oudh and 14,850,000 tankas; Mahmud Khan was given Ghazipur and 9,035,000 tankas; Qazi Jia was given 2,000,000 tankas from Jaunpur.

AWARDS CEREMONY

Several days after the Shawwal festival[103] a great party was held in the domed portico with stone columns in the middle of Sultan Ibrahim's harem. Humayun was given a charqab, a girth sword, and a horse with a gold saddle. Chïn Temür Sultan, Mahdi Khwaja, [297] and Muhammad-Sultan Mirza were also given charqabs, girth swords, and girth daggers. The other begs and warriors were given girth swords, and girth daggers and robes of honor according to their rank, as is shown in the following table:

Fine horses with saddles	Knife with golden hilt
2	1
Jewel-studded daggers	Jewel-studded *jamdhars*
25	(illus. p. 361)
	2
Jewel-studded girth swords	Charqabs
2	4
Scarlet robes	Fine woolens
28	51 lengths
Jewel-studded etc. *kattars* (illus. p. 361)	
16	

On the day of the party there was an incredible lot of rain. It rained thirteen times. Those who had to stand outside got drenched. Muhammadi Kükäldash was rewarded with Samana and assigned to raid Sambhal. Hissar Firoza had been given as a reward to Humayun; now Sambhal was also given him. Hindu Beg was assigned to Humayun, and thereupon the following were sent on an expedition to Sambhal in Muhammadi's stead: Hindu Beg, Kätä Beg, Baba Qashqa's Malik Qasim with his brothers, Mulla Apaq, and Shaykh Ghuran with his Doab yeomen. Three or four times a man had come from Qasim of Sambhal to say, [297b] "Biban the ingrate has laid siege to Sambhal and reduced the defenders to dire straits. Send an expeditionary force." When Biban had fled from us as he had, he had skirted the mountain and gathered the dispersed Afghans and Hindustanis. Finding the place open to attack during the turmoil, he had laid siege to Sambhal. Hindu Beg, Kätä Beg, and the expeditionary force reached the Ahar ford and were busy making the crossing. Baba Qashqa's Malik Qasim was sent forward with his brothers. When Malik Qasim crossed the river, a hundred to 150 of his brethren galloped to the attack and reached Sambhal around noon. Biban came forth from camp with his troops arrayed. Malik Qasim and his men rushed in, put the fortress to their backs, and began hand-to-hand battle. Biban was unable to maintain his stand and retreated. A few heads were severed, and several elephants and a lot of horses and plunder were taken. The next morning the begs of the expeditionary force arrived. Qasim of Sambhal came for an interview, but he did not want to turn over the fortress to them and used a subterfuge. One day Shaykh Ghuran was talking to Hindu Beg and the others and managed somehow to bring Qasim of Sambhal into the presence of our begs and to get our men into the Sambhal fortress. They sent Qasim of Sambhal's womenfolk and retainers out safe and sound.

Qalandar Piada was dispatched to Bayana with enticements and threats for Nizam Khan. [298] This little poem was composed extemporaneously and sent along:

> Trifle not with the Turk, O Mir of Bayana, / For the agility and bravery of the Turk are obvious. / If you do not come soon and listen to reason, / What need is there for clarification[104] of the obvious?

The fortress at Bayana is one of the most famous in Hindustan. This ridiculous fellow relied on the impregnability of his fortress and sent back claims far beyond his capacity. Instead of giving a satisfactory answer to his envoy, we made ready to lay siege.

Detail, *Zardhank Khatni Brings the Key to Maltas, the Prison Keeper,* from the *Hamzanama.* India, ca. 1562–77. Opaque watercolor and gold on cloth. Freer Gallery of Art, F1949.18. The daggers thrust into the center warriors' sashes are either *kattar*s or *jamdhar*s. The distinction is lost to time.

Baba-Qulï Beg was dispatched to Muhammad Zaytun with threatening decrees. He too excused himself and took to subterfuge.

Although an envoy had come to us from Rana Sanga the Infidel while we were in Kabul and offered his support, saying, "If the padishah comes from that direction to the environs of Delhi, I will attack Agra from this direction," I had defeated Ibrahim and taken Delhi and Agra. Up till then this infidel had done nothing. Some time later he did lay siege to the fortress known as Kandar, in which was Makkan's son Hasan. Several times men came from Hasan Makkan, but Makkan himself had not yet come to see me. [298b] The fortresses in the area, like Etawah, Dholpur, Gwalior, and Bayana, had not yet entered my domain. To the east the Afghans were acting obstinate and rebellious and had moved their army two or three marches from Kannauj in the direction of Agra. I was not yet completely sure even of the nearby environs. For this reason I could not send Hasan Makkan any reinforcements. Two or three months later Hasan, reduced to extremities, was forced to make a truce and hand over Kandar.

Husayn Khan, who was in Rapri, panicked and left, and Rapri was given to Muhammad-Ali Jang-Jang.

Qutb Khan, who was in Etawah, was sent several times both threats and enticements, but he neither came to see us nor gave over Etawah. Mahdi Khwaja was awarded Etawah, and Muhammad-Sultan Mirza was sent to attack Etawah with a large contingent of begs and ichkis under Sultan-Muhammad Dulday, Muhammad-Ali Jang-Jang, and Abdul-Aziz Mirakhur. Kannauj was given to Sultan-Muhammad Dulday. Also assigned to Etawah were troops under Firoz Khan, Mahmud Khan, Shaykh Bayazid, and Qazi Jia, all of whom had been greatly patronized and given parganas in the direction of Purab. [299]

Muhammad Zaytun was sitting in Dholpur and cunningly not coming. Dholpur was awarded to Sultan-Junayd Barlas, and we assigned troops under Adil Sultan, Muhammadi Kükäldash, Shah-Mansur Barlas, Qutlugh-Qadam, Abdullah, Wali, Jan Beg, Pir-Qulï, and Shah-Husayn Yaraki to take Dholpur by force, turn it over to Sultan-Junayd, and then attack Bayana.

After assigning the army, I summoned the Turk and India officers and consulted with them. We discussed the fact that the rebel officers in Purab, that is, Nasir Khan Nohani and Ma'ruf Farmuli, had crossed the Ganges with forty or fifty thousand soldiers, taken control of Kannauj, and were camped two or three marches this side of Kannauj. Rana Sanga the Infidel had taken Kandar and was sowing dissent. The end of the monsoon was near. It seemed to be necessary either to attack the rebels or to move against the infidel. The fortresses in the immediate area were easy. After eliminating these great enemies, where would they go? Rana Sanga was not imagined to be so difficult. All unanimously said that Rana Sanga was farther away. It was not known if he would be able to get any nearer. It was more important and imperative to repel the rebels who had come so close.

We were about to mount to ride against the rebels when [299b] Humayun said, "What necessity is there for the padishah to ride? Let me perform this service." Everyone was pleased by this, and the Turk and India officers alike approved his idea. Humayun was assigned Purab, and Kabuli Ahmad Qasim was dispatched at a gallop to the army that had been assigned to Dholpur to say, "Let the army come and join Humayun at Chandwar." An order was also sent to Mahdi Khwaja and Muhammad-Sultan Mirza's army, which had been assigned to attack Etawah, to join Humayun.

On Wednesday the thirteenth of Dhu'l-Qa'da [August 21], Humayun set forth and stopped in the village of Jalesar, three leagues from Agra. He stayed there one day and then proceeded march by march.

On Thursday the twentieth [August 28], Khwaja Kalan was given permission to go to Kabul.

BABUR PLANS A GARDEN

I always thought one of the chief faults of Hindustan was that there was no running water. Everywhere that was habitable it should be possible to construct waterwheels, create running water, and make planned, geometric spaces. A few days after coming to Agra, I crossed the Jumna with this plan in mind and scouted around for places to build gardens, but everywhere I looked was so unpleasant and desolate that I crossed back in great disgust. [300] Because the place was so ugly and disagreeable I abandoned my dream of making a charbagh (see illus. p. 157).

Although there was no really suitable place near Agra, there was nothing to do but work with the space we had. The foundation was the large well from which the water for the bathhouse came. Next, the patch of ground with tamarind trees and octagonal pond became the great pool and courtyard. Then came the pool in front of the stone building and the hall. After that came the private garden and its out-buildings, and after that the bathhouse. Thus, in unpleasant and inharmonious India, marvelously regular and geometric gardens were introduced. In every corner were beautiful plots, and in every plot were regularly laid out arrangements of roses and narcissus.

We suffered from three things in Hindustan. One was the heat, another the biting wind, and the third the dust. The bathhouse was a refuge from all three. Of course, a bathhouse has no dust or wind, and in the hot weather it is so cool that one almost feels chill. One chamber of the bath, the one in which the warm-water reservoir was, was finished completely in stone. The dado was of white stone; otherwise the floor and ceiling were of red stone from Bayana. Khalifa, Shaykh Zayn, Yunus Ali, and all who had acquired lands on the river [300b] also built geometric and beautifully planned gardens and ponds. As is done in Lahore and Dipalpur, they made running water with water-wheels. Since the people of India had never seen such planned or regular spaces, they nicknamed the side of the Jumna on which these structures stood, "Kabul."[105]

THE MAKING OF A WELL

Inside the fortress there was an open space between Ibrahim's building and the rampart. There I ordered a large stepwell made, ten by ten. In the parlance of Hindustan a large well with steps is called a stepwell. This one was begun before the charbagh. They began to dig in the middle of the monsoon, and it caved in several times, burying the workers. It was completed after the expedition against Rana Sanga,[106] as recorded on the date stone. It is a marvelous stepwell. Inside is a three-story structure, the lowest story of which has three porticos. The walkway leads down the steps to the well, and a path leads to each of the three porticos. Each portico is three steps higher than the last. The water level is one step lower than the lowest portico when the water is drawn off. Sometimes during the monsoon, when the water is at its highest level, water comes up to the highest portico. In the middle level is a carved portico, which echoes a dome in which an ox turns the waterwheel. [301] The upper level has one portico. From the courtyard outside and above the well a path leads straight to this portico on both sides down five or six steps. Directly opposite the path is the date stone. Next to this well another one was made. The bottom of the second well is a bit higher than the middle level of the first well. As was mentioned, oxen turn the waterwheel under the dome, and the water goes from the first well to the second. Another wheel was constructed for the second well, and it takes water up to the rampart to water the garden up on a level with the rampart. In the place where the steps to the well end a stone building was built. Outside the area of the well a stone mosque was built, but it was not well made. They built it in the Indian fashion.

HUMAYUN RIDES AGAINST THE REBELS

When Humayun rode out, the rebels under Nasir Khan Nohani and Ma'ruf Farmuli were gathered in Jajmau. From ten or fifteen kos away Humayun sent Mu'min Atäkä to gather intelligence while he proceeded on a raid. But Mu'min Atäkä was unable to bring back any worthwhile information. The rebels, catching wind of Mu'min Atäkä's movements, fled without bothering to make a stand. After him, Qïsïmtay, Baba Chuhra, and Böchkä were sent to reconnoiter, and they brought back news of the rebels' flight in confusion. Humayun took Jajmau and then went on to the Dalmau region, [301b] where Fath Khan Sarwani came to submit to him. He attached Fath Khan Sarwani to Mahdi Khwaja and Muhammad-Sultan Mirza and sent him to us.

IN KHURASAN THE UZBEKS
ATTACK MERV

That same year Ubayd Khan led his army from Bukhara against Merv. In the Merv citadel were ten to fifteen civilians, whom he killed. After reconstructing the dam at Merv in forty or fifty days, he proceeded against Sarakhs. In Sarakhs were forty to fifty Qïzïlbash (Savafids), who shut the gate and refused to give up the fortress. In confusion, the civilians opened the gates. The Uzbeks entered and killed these Qïzïlbash too. Taking Sarakhs, they went on to Tus and Mashhad. The inhabitants of Mashhad had no choice but to let them in. They besieged Tus for eight months and finally took it by truce, but instead of abiding by the terms, they slaughtered the men and took the women prisoner.

This same year Sultan Muzaffar of Gujarat's son, Bahadur Khan, who is now padishah in Gujarat in his father's stead, was estranged from his father and went to Sultan Ibrahim, who received him less than honorably. While I was in Panipat a petition came to me from him. I sent him encouraging and enticing decrees and invited him to join us. He was thinking about coming but then changed his mind, deserted Ibrahim's army, and set out for Gujarat. At that same time his father, Sultan Muzaffar, died, and his elder brother, [302] Sikandar Shah, Sultan Muzaffar's eldest son, became padishah of Gujarat in his father's stead. Because Sikandar's conduct was evil a slave of his named Imadulmulk conspired with a group of people, strangled Sikandar to death, and invited Bahadur Khan, who was still on his way, and en-

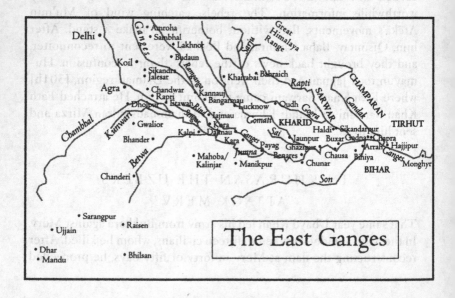

The East Ganges

throned him in his father's place. He became known as Bahadur Shah. Bahadur did one good thing: he had Imadulmulk, who had shown such ingratitude, killed and thereby wrought vengeance on him. He also killed many of the begs from his father's reign. These actions show him to be a bloodthirsty and audacious young man.

In the month of Muharram [October 1526], Beg Ways brought news of Faruq's birth. Although a runner had brought the news before this, Beg Ways arrived to give us the good news himself. The child was born on Thursday evening, the twenty-third of Shawwal [August 2], and was named Faruq.[108]

ALI-QULI CASTS A MORTAR

Master Ali-Qulï was ordered to cast a large mortar to be used on Bayana and some of the other fortresses that had not yet entered our domain. When he had the smelting furnace and all the implements ready, he sent someone to inform me. On Monday the fifteenth of Muharram [October 22] we went to watch Master Ali-Qulï cast the mortar. Around the place where it was to be cast he had constructed eight smelting furnaces and had already melted the metal. [302b] From the bottom of each furnace he had made a channel straight to the mortar mold. Just as we got there he was opening the holes in the furnaces. The molten metal was pouring like water into the mold, but after a while, before the mold was filled, one by one the streams of molten metal coming from the furnaces stopped. There was some flaw either in the furnace or in the metal. Master Ali-Qulï went into a strange depression and was about to throw himself into the mold of molten bronze, but I soothed him, gave him a robe of honor, and got him out of his black mood. A day or two later, when the mold had cooled, they opened it, and Master Ali-Qulï sent someone to announce with glee that the shaft was flawless. It was then easy to attach the powder chamber. He took out the shaft and assigned some men to fix it, and got to work connecting the chamber.

Mahdi Khwaja brought Fath Khan Sarwani from Humayun, whom he had left at Dalmau. I viewed Fath Khan favorably and gave him his father A'zam-Humayun's parganas and granted him a few more estates too. In all he was given parganas worth sixteen million tankas. In Hindustan greatly favored officers are given traditional titles. One of these is A'zam Humayun; others are Khanjahan [303] and Khankhanan. Fath Khan's father's title was A'zam-Humayun. Because of my own Humayun, it was considered inappropriate to invest anyone with such a title, so it was laid aside, and Fath Khan Sarwani was given the title Khanjahan.[109]

On Wednesday the eighth of Safar [November 14] marquees were set up beside the large pool on the upper side of the tamarind trees. A wine party was held there, and Fath Khan Sarwani was invited. Along with some wine, I presented him with a turban and a suit of clothing I had worn myself, and with this ennoblement he was given leave to return to his land. It was decided that his son, Mahmud Khan, would remain always in attendance on me.

THE SUBMISSION OF BAYANA

On Wednesday the twenty-fourth of Muharram [October 31], Muhammad-Ali Haydar Rikabdar was dispatched with an urgent message for Humayun. "The Purab rebel army has fled," the message said. "As soon as this envoy arrives assign a few appropriate begs to Jaunpur, take the army and come immediately to us. Rana Sanga the Infidel has drawn nigh and is at the gate. We will have to rethink our strategy for him." After the armies had gone to Purab, Qoch Beg's Turdï Beg and his younger brother Sherafkan, Muhammad Khalil Akhtabegi and his brothers and equerries, and Rustam the Turcoman and his brothers, together with Rao Ravi Sarwani of the Hindustanis, were assigned to go strike and plunder the Bayana area. [303b] If they could get the people in the fortress to come over to our side by means of promises and enticements, let them do so; otherwise, they were to strike and plunder and reduce the enemy to incapacity.

Alam Khan, one of the elder brothers of this Nizam Khan who was in Bayana, was in the fortress of Tahangarh.[110] His envoys came repeatedly to offer servitude and support. This Alam Khan took it upon himself to promise that if a troop were assigned by the padishah, he would win over the yeomen of Bayana and take possession of the Bayana fortress. The following order was issued to the warriors of the strike force led by Turdï Beg: "Since Alam Khan is landed, he has accepted such servitude and service of his own accord. Act therefore in accordance with his views and as he sees fit in the Bayana affair." Although some of the people of Hindustan know how to wield a sword, most have no idea of military manners or how to lead and command. This Alam Khan, who was put in charge of our strike force, listening to no one and never stopping to consider the good or bad outcome of any action, took the detachment near Bayana. The detachment we had sent was composed of 250 to three hundred Turks and a little more than two thousand soldiers from Hindustan and surrounding areas. Nizam Khan and the Afghans in Bayana had more than four thousand horsemen and more than ten thousand foot soldiers. [304] No sooner did they see our men and realize how few they were than all the above-mentioned cavalry and infantry charged us. As the attack party arrived, they spurred their horses at them and forced them to flee. Alam Khan of Tahangarh, Nizam Khan's elder brother, was unhorsed, and another five or six men were taken prisoner. Some of the baggage was lost too. Despite this action, promises and enticements were given, and decrees pardoning Nizam Khan's past and future offenses were sent.

When the news of Rana Sanga the Infidel's rapid approach was learned, Nizam Khan had no alternative. He summoned Sayyid Rafi', turned his fortresses over to our men through the mediation of Sayyid Rafi', and accompanied him to be ennobled by paying allegiance to us. I awarded him a twenty-lac pargana in the Doab. Dost Eshik-aqa was assigned temporarily to Bayana. A few days after, Mahdi Khwaja was awarded Bayana and seventy lacs of maintenance and salary and given leave to proceed to Bayana.

RAHIMDAD TAKES GWALIOR

Tatar Khan Sarangkhani was in Gwalior, and his envoy had come to offer submission and support. When the Infidel seized Kandar and approached Bayana, Dharmakant, one of the rajahs of Gwalior, and an infidel named Khan Jahan came to the vicinity of Gwalior and began to stir up trouble, with designs on the fortress. Tatar Khan was in dire straits and was about to turn over Gwalior. Our begs, ichkis, and most of our brave warriors were all with the army or on scouting parties scattered in all directions. [304b] A few men from Bhera and Lahore, as well as Hastichi Tünqatar and his brothers, were attached to Rahimdad, given estates in Gwalior, and dispatched to the abovementioned group. Mulla Apaq and Shaykh Ghuran were also sent to establish Rahimdad in Gwalior and then come back. When they approached Gwalior, Tatar Khan changed his mind and did not invite them into the fortress. At the same time, Shaykh Muhammad Ghaws, a dervish who was generally occupied with his many disciples and companions, sent a messenger to Rahimdad from inside the Gwalior fortress to say, "Get yourself inside the fortress however you may, for this fellow has changed his mind and has evil intentions." As soon as this news reached Rahimdad, he sent someone to say, "Outside there is danger from the infidels. Let me enter the fortress with a few men, and the others will remain outside." In the face of much insistence, Tatar Khan gave his consent. As soon as Rahimdad entered the fortress, he said, "Let our men stay at this gate." He stationed his men at the Hathi Pol,[111] through which he let his men in that night. The next morning there was nothing Tatar Khan could do. Willy-nilly he turned over the fortress and left, and then he came to Agra and paid homage. He was assigned a twenty-lac stipend from the pargana of Bianwan.

Muhammad Zaytun was also left with no choice, and he turned over Dholpur [305] and came to pay homage. He was awarded a pargana of a few lacs. Dholpur was made crown land, and Abu'l-Fath the Turcoman was made custodian and sent there. In the vicinity of Hissar Firoza, Hamid Khan Sarangkhani and a few Pani Afghans[112] and Afghans from surrounding areas amassed three or four thousand soldiers and rebelled.

On Wednesday the fifteenth of Safar [November 21], we attached Ahmadi Parwanachï, Abu'l-Fath the Turcoman, Malikdad of Kara,

A Reclining Prince, attributed to Aqa Mirak, Iran, ca. 1530. Album page; opaque watercolor and gold on paper. Arthur M. Sackler Gallery, Smithsonian Institution; Purchase—Smithsonian Unrestricted Trust Funds, Smithsonian Collections Acquisition Program, and Dr. Arthur M. Sackler, S1986.300.

and Mujahid Khan of Multan to Chïn Temür Sultan and assigned them to attack these Afghans. They charged from afar, defeated the Afghans, killed many of them, and sent back a good many heads.

ARRIVAL OF AN AMBASSADOR FROM PERSIA

Toward the end of Safar [November], Khwajagi Asad, who had been sent as ambassador to Prince Tahmasp in Iraq, came accompanied by a Turcoman called Sulayman and brought official gifts. Among them were two Circassian slave-girls.[113]

AN ATTEMPT ON BABUR'S LIFE

On Friday the sixteenth of Rabi' I [December 21] a strange incident took place. As it was written up in detail in a letter to Kabul, that letter is reproduced here without addition or deletion:

The details of the momentous incident that took place on Friday the sixteenth of Rabiʿ I 933 are as follows. The wretched Buwa, mother of Ibrahim, heard [305b] that I was eating foods prepared by Hindustani cooks. This came about because three or four months prior to this date, since I had never seen Hindustani food, I said that Ibrahim's cooks should be brought. Of fifty or sixty cooks I kept four. So, having heard of this, she sent a man to Etawah to obtain a tola of poison wrapped up in a piece of paper and then give it to an old woman servant, who would then pass it to Ahmad Chashnigir. (In Hindustan they call the taster *chashnigir,* and a tola is a measure slightly more than two mithcals, as has been described.) Ahmad gave it to the Hindustani cook in our kitchen, promising him four parganas to introduce it somehow into my food. After the first old woman, who gave Ahmad Chashnigir the poison, she sent another to see whether or not he had given me the poison. It is good that he put it on the plate and not in the pot, having done so because I had given the cooks strict instructions to supervise the Hindustanis and make them taste from the pot while the food was being prepared. When the meal was being dished out, however, our wretched cooks were negligent. The cook put a piece of thin bread on the porcelain plate and then sprinkled less than half of the poison from the paper on top of the bread. On top of the poison he put some meat dressed in oil. [306] If he had sprinkled the poison on the meat, or if he had thrown it into the pot, it would have been bad. In a fluster, he threw the rest into the stove.

Late Friday evening they served the food. I ate a lot of rabbit stew and had quite a bit of dressed saffroned meat. I also had one or two tidbits from the top of the poisoned Hindustani food. I took the dressed meat and ate it. There was no apparent bad taste. I had one or two pieces of dried meat. I felt sick. The day before, when I was eating dried meat, there had been an off-taste, so I thought that was the reason. Once again my stomach churned. While seated at the meal I felt sick two or three times and almost threw up. Finally I said to myself, "Enough of this." I got up and on my way to the toilet I almost threw up once. When I got to the toilet I vomited a lot. I never vomited after meals, not even when drinking. A cloud of suspicion came over my mind. I ordered the cook to be held while the vomit was given to a dog that was watched. Until near the end of the first watch the next morning the dog was pretty listless and its stomach was swollen. No matter how many stones they threw at it to try to get it to move, it refused to get up. It remained like that until midday, but then it got up and did not die. One or two pages had eaten the same food, and the next morning they too threw up a lot. [306b] One was very ill, but in the end they all recovered completely. "Calamity struck, but all's well that ends well." God gave me life anew; I had returned from the brink of death; I was born again. "Wounded, I died and came to life again. Now I have learned the value of life." I ordered Sultan-Muhammad Bakhshï to keep a close watch on the cook. When he was tortured he confessed the details given above.

On Monday I ordered the nobles, grandees, amirs, and ministers to attend court. The two men and two women were brought in for questioning. They confessed to all the details of the affair. I ordered the taster to be hacked to pieces and the cook to be skinned alive. One of the two women I had thrown under the elephants' feet, and the other I had shot. I had Buwa put under arrest. She will pay for what she has done.

On Saturday I drank a cup of milk. On Sunday I drank a cup of milk. I also drank some earth of Lemnos dissolved in spirits. On Monday, I mixed some earth of Lemnos and opiate in milk and drank it. The milk really shook up my insides. On Saturday, the first day of this medication, I excreted some pitch-black things like burnt bile. Thank goodness now everything is all right. I never knew how precious life was. There is a line of poetry that says, "He who reaches the point of death appreciates life." Every time I think of this dreadful incident I get angry. [307] It was by God's grace that I was given a new lease on life. How can I express my thanks?

Hoping that this will not occasion alarm, I have described in detail everything that happened. Although it was a dreadful incident that cannot be adequately described by words, thank God I have lived to see another day, and all's well that ends well. Do not worry.

Written on Tuesday the twentieth of Rabi' I [December 25] in the charbagh.

When I had finished writing the letter I sent it to Kabul.

Since such a monumental crime had been committed by the wretched Buwa, I had Yunus Ali and Khwajagi Asad hold her. After her money, property, and slaves were confiscated, she was turned over to Abdul-Rahim Shiqavul. Such an assassination attempt having been made by these people, it was not considered wise to keep Buwa's grandson, Ibrahim's son who had been maintained with great honor and dignity, so on Thursday the twenty-ninth of Rabi' I [January 3, 1527] he was sent to Kamran with Mulla Sarsan, who had come from there on some business.[114]

HUMAYUN'S CAMPAIGN

Humayun, who had gone against the rebels in Purab, had conquered Jaunpur [307b] and gone to attack Nasir Khan in Ghazipur, but Nasir Khan had learned of his approach and crossed the Ganges. From Ghazipur, Humayun went against Kharid. The Afghans there also learned of his approach and crossed the Sarju. The soldiers sacked Kharid and withdrew. As I had ordered, Shah Mir Husayn and Sultan-Junayd were assigned to Jaunpur with a troop of brave warriors, and Qazi Jia was assigned to them too. Shaykh Bayazid was stationed in Oudh. Having completed his tasks there, he crossed the Ganges in the vicinity of Kara and Manikpur and took the Kalpi road. A petition came from Alam Khan, son of Jalal Khan Jighat, who was in Kalpi, but he did not come himself. When Humayun reached opposite Kalpi, he sent an envoy to assuage his fears and bring him along.

On Sunday the third of Rabi' II [January 6], Humayun paid homage to me in the Hasht Bihisht garden. That same day Khwaja Dost Khawand arrived from Kabul.

RANA SANGA APPROACHES

During those days Mahdi Khwaja's men began to come continually to report that the Rana's approach had been confirmed. Hasan Khan of Mewat was also going to be able to join the Rana. It became necessary to deal with them above all else. If a contingent of the army were to go to Bayana as reinforcements, it would be to our advantage. [308] Having firmly resolved to mount the army, we dispatched Muhammad-Sultan Mirza, Yunus Ali, Shah-Mansur Barlas, Kätä Beg, Qïsïmtay, and Böchkä to Bayana ahead of ourselves. The son of Hasan Khan of Mewat, Nahar Khan, had been taken prisoner during the battle with Ibrahim, and we had kept him as a hostage. That is why Hasan Khan had kept up such obvious comings and goings and continually demanded his son back. It occurred to some that if the son were sent back, it would placate Hasan Khan and he would render better service, so Nahar Khan was dressed in a robe of honor and given leave to deliver enticements to his father. However, no sooner did this wretched fellow, who had spent so much time obtaining his son's release, have word of his son's departure than he left Alwar, without even waiting for his son to arrive, and joined Rana Sanga at Toda.[115] To have let the son go at such a time was a bad calculation.

At that time the rains came heavy. Parties were given continually, and Humayun attended them. Although he was loath, he drank a few times.

BALKH FALLS TO THE UZBEKS

About that time some strange incidents occurred. One is that while Humayun was coming to the Hindustan army from Zafar Fort, [308b] Mulla Baba of Pishagar and his younger brother Baba Shaykh deserted and went over to Kitin Qara Sultan. The men in Balkh were in dire straits, and Balkh fell to Kitin Qara Sultan. This worthless Mulla Baba and his brother took responsibility for affairs on this side and went to the vicinity of Aibak, Khuram, and Sarbagh. Shah Iskandar panicked when they entered Balkh and gave the Ghori fortress to the Uzbeks. Mulla Baba and Baba Shaykh then entered the Ghori fortress with a few Uzbeks.

Since Mir Hama's fortress was nearby, there was nothing he could do but submit to the Uzbeks. A few days later, Baba Shaykh and a few Uzbeks came to Mir Hama's fortress to drive out the mir and his troops and send them in the direction of Balkh. Mir Hama put Baba Shaykh up in the fortress and gave the others quarters here and there. Mir Hama struck Baba Shaykh with a sword, tied him up along with a few others, and sent a messenger at a gallop to Tengriberdi in Konduz, who sent Yar-Ali and Abdul-Latif with a few men. After they arrived, Mulla Baba and the Uzbeks went to Mir Hama's fortress intending to have a skirmish; however, unable to accomplish anything, the garrison joined Tengriberdi's men and set out for Konduz. Baba Shaykh's wound was bad, so Mir Hama cut off his head and brought it in at that time. [309] I rewarded him regally and promoted him over his peers. When Baqi Shiqavul left, I had promised a seer of gold each for the heads of those two old wretches. In addition to the promotions, I gave Mir Hama a seer of gold as I had promised.

Meanwhile, Qïsïmtay, who had attacked Bayana, brought back a few severed heads. When Qïsïmtay, Böchkä, and a few guerilla fighters went on a scouting expedition, they defeated two infidel raiding parties and took seventy or eighty men captive. Qïsïmtay brought back the confirmed news that Hasan Khan of Mewat had joined the Rana.

On Sunday the eighth of the month [February 10], I went out to watch Master Ali-Qulï shoot his great mortar, the barrel of which had come out perfect in the casting; the powder magazine he had cast later and then mounted. It was midafternoon. He shot a stone that went sixteen hundred paces. I rewarded him with a girth dagger, a robe of honor, and a fine horse.

BABUR MOVES AGAINST RANA SANGA

On Monday the ninth of Jumada I [February 11], I rode from the outskirts of the city[116] to make war on the infidels and camped in the plain, where we stayed for three or four days while the army was assembled and arranged. Since I had no great reliance upon the people of Hindustan, the Hindustani officers were given assignments in various directions. [309b] Alam Khan was designated to go to Gwalior and reinforce Rahimdad. Makkan, Qasim Beg of Sambhal, Muhammad Zaytun, and Hamid and his brothers were assigned to Sambhal. While camped there news came that Rana Sanga and his forces had struck up to near Bayana. The men on the scouting party were not able to get any news—they were unable even to enter the fortress. The defenders came out quite foolishly far from the fortress, and the enemy overwhelmed them and put them to flight. Sankar Khan Janjua was killed there. In the melee Kätä Beg charged into battle without armor. He had unhorsed an infidel and was about to take him when the man grabbed a sword from one of Kätä Beg's servants and hit Kätä Beg on the shoulder. He was so badly wounded he could not come on the Rana Sanga campaign. Later he recovered, but he was permanently disabled.

I don't know whether it was of their own fear or whether they were trying to scare the men, but in any case Qïsïmtay, Shah-Mansur Barlas, and all who came from Bayana could not say enough of the audacity and ferocity of the Infidel's army. Qasim Mirakhur and his shovelers were sent from the expeditionary camp to dig a lot of pits in the pargana of Madhakur,[117] where the army was to camp. On Saturday the fourteenth of Jumada I [February 16], we marched out of the Agra district and stopped where the pits had been dug. [310] At dawn the next day we marched from there. It occurred to me that in this vicinity the only place with enough water for the army camp was Sikri, and it was probable that the Infidel would take it and camp there. Therefore we moved forward in array—right flank, left flank, center. Darwesh Muhammad Sarban and Qïsïmtay, who had scouted out every direction on his way to Bayana and back, were sent forward to find a campsite on the banks of the Sikri reservoir. When we camped, an envoy was sent to Mahdi Khwaja and the men in Bayana to come straightaway and join us. Humayun's servant Beg Mirak Moghul was sent with a few warriors to get news of the Infidel. He left by night, and the next morning he brought back news that the enemy had camped one kos in front of Bhasawar. That same day Mahdi Khwaja, Muhammad-Sultan Mirza, and the group from Bayana joined us.

The begs were assigned to patrol by turns. During Abdul-Aziz's time, he went straight to Khanua, five kos from Sikri, without taking any precautions whatsoever. The Infidel was moving forward. When it was realized that our men were advancing unarmed, four or five thousand men loomed forth. Abdul-Aziz and Mulla Apaq had approximately a thousand to fifteen hundred men, [310b] and they grappled with the enemy without counting their numbers. In the confusion many were scattered. As soon as the news reached us, we dispatched Khalifa's Muhibb-Ali with Khalifa's liege men. Mulla Husayn and some others we dispatched "lickety-split" as reinforcements. Later Muhammad-Ali Jang-Jang was sent too. No sooner had the advance party assigned to Muhibb-Ali arrived than the enemy routed Abdul-Aziz, captured his yak tail, took prisoner Mulla Ni'mat, Mulla Daud, Mulla Apaq's younger brother, and some others and put them to death. As soon as they arrived, Tahir the Axman, Muhibb-Ali's uncle, charged. There was no one to help him. Tahir was captured right there. Muhibb-Ali was also felled during the battle, but Baltu came up from the rear and got him out. They were pursued for a kos, but when Muhammad-Ali Jang-Jang's troops could be seen in the distance, the pursuers halted.

News of the enemy's approach kept pouring in. We put on our armor, armored the horses, armed ourselves, and rode to the attack. I ordered the caissons brought forth. We went one kos. The enemy withdrew. Beside us was a large lake, for the sake of the water of which camp had been made here. The caissons were secured in front and tied together by chains. They were seven or eight yards apart, a space across which the chains were drawn. [311] Mustafa Rumi had made them in the Anatolian fashion,[118] so they were sleek and fast. Because Master Ali-Qulï was difficult to get along with, Mustafa was assigned to Humayun in the right wing. The Khurasani and Hindustani shovelers and pickax men were sent to dig trenches in the places where the caissons did not reach. It was evident that the soldiers were in trepidation resulting from the Infidel's rapid onslaught, from the battle he had done in Bayana, and from the praise and description of him given by Shah-Mansur, Qïsïmtay, and the men coming from Bayana. His defeat of Abdul-Aziz was merely the last straw. To reassure the men and to make a show of reinforcing the army in the places not reached by the caissons, devices like wooden tripods were set up, and between each two tripods, a distance of seven or eight yards, ox harness ropes were stretched and secured. It took twenty or twenty-five days to get all these preparations and implements ready.

Just at that time Sultan-Husayn Mirza's daughter's son, Qasim Husayn Sultan, and Ahmad Yusuf son of Sayyid Yusuf, Qiwam Ordushah, and others, altogether around five hundred men, dribbled in from Kabul, Muhammad Sharif the astrologer of gloom came with them. Baba Dost Suchï, who had gone to Kabul for wine, also came with them, [311b] bringing three camel trains loaded with superior Ghazni wine.

At such a time, when there was such hesitation and fear among the soldiers over past events and loose talk, as has been mentioned, Muhammad Sharif the doom-and-gloom astrologer, although he did not dare speak to me personally, with great exaggeration told everyone he met that Mars was presently in the west and anyone who fought from that direction would suffer defeat. The more these disheartened people consulted the prophet of doom, the more disheartened they became. Without lending an ear to his idle talk and without letting it affect what had to be done, we got ourselves ready to do battle in earnest.

On Sunday the twenty-second [February 24], Shaykh Jamali was sent to assemble as many yeomen from the Doab and Delhi as he could, strike and plunder the villages of Mewat, and do everything he could to harass the enemy from that direction. Mulla Turk Ali, who was coming from Kabul, was ordered to join Shaykh Jamali and do everything he could to wreak havoc in Mewat. Maghfur Divan was ordered to do the same. He went to Mewat, pillaged a few out-of-the-way villages, and took some prisoners. However, they were not much bothered by such maneuvers.

BABUR TAKES THE PLEDGE
OF TEMPERANCE

On Monday the twenty-third of Jumada I [February 25], [312] I mounted for a tour. During my excursion it occurred to me that the thought of repenting from drinking had long been on my mind, and that my heart had continually been clouded by committing this illegal act. I said, "O soul,

How long will you taste of sin? Temperance is not unpalatable. Have a taste! / How long will you be polluted by sin? How long will you stay comfortable in deprivation? / How long will you follow your lusts? How long will you waste your life? / When you march intent upon raiding the infidels you see your own death before you. / You know that he who is resolved to die will attain this state: / He throws off all these forbidden things from himself and cleanses himself of all sin! / I rid myself of this transgression and repented of wine drinking. / Gold and silver vessels and goblets, all the implements of the assembly / I had brought and broke them all. Abandoning wine, I gave my heart rest.

The broken pieces of the gold and silver vessels and implements were distributed among the deserving and the poor. The one who joined me in my repentance was Asas. He had also joined me in letting our beards grow.[119] That night and the next morning nearly three hundred [312b] begs and ichkis, soldiers and civilians, repented. All the wine on hand was poured out, and into the wine Baba Dost had brought we ordered salt put to turn it into vinegar. In the place where the wine was poured out a stepwell was dug, and I made an intention to have it finished in stone and a charitable building built next to it.

In Muharram of 935 [September 1528], when I went to tour

Gwalior, I returned from Dholpur to Sikri. The stepwell had been completed. Earlier I had made an intention that if I gained victory over Sanga the Infidel, I would exempt the Muslims from paying the tamgha tax. During my repentance Darwesh Muhammad Sarban and Shaykh Zayn reminded of my promise to repeal the tamgha. "It is good you reminded me," I said. "The Muslims in the provinces we hold are hereby exempted from the tamgha." I summoned the scribes and ordered them to write decrees informing of these two momentous events that had happened. The decree, of Shaykh Zayn's composition, was copied and dispatched to the entire realm, and it is as follows.

DECREE OF ZAHIRUDDIN MUHAMMAD BABUR
PADISHAH GHAZI

We praise the acceptor of repentance who loves the penitent and who loves the pure, and we thank the giver who guides the sinful and pardons those who seek pardon. And we pray for the best of his creation, Muhammad, and for his precious offspring and his pure companions.

The mirrors of the thoughts of the intelligent, which are manifestations of beautiful forms of things and treasuries of pearls of designs of truth and correctness, will reflect the jewels of flowers [313] of the notion that human nature is instinctively inclined to selfish pleasures and that the relinquishment of carnal desires is dependent upon divine help and heavenly assistance. The human soul is never far from an inclination to evil. "Neither do I justify myself, since every soul is prone unto evil."[120] And the avoidance of evil is accomplished solely through the loving-kindness of the all-pardoning king. "This is the bounty of God; he will give the same unto whom he pleaseth; and God is endued with great bounty."[121]

The reason for composing this treatise is that, in accordance with the exigencies of humanity, in keeping with the customs of kings and regal necessities, and in conformity with the custom of lords of high royal and military status, during the full bloom of youth some intemperances and a few indulgences were committed, but after a few days absolute regret and contrition occurred, and one by one those intemperances were abandoned and through true penance the gates of recourse to them were closed. However, repentance of wine, which is the most important goal and the most magnificent desire, remained hidden behind a veil—"Affairs are mortgaged to their times"—and did not appear until these felicitous times, when through earnest endeavor the garb of holy war was taken on and, with the forces of Islam, we combatted the infidels. Then, from an otherworldly inspiration and heavenly voice we heard the happy phrase, "Is not the time yet come unto those who believe that their hearts should humbly submit to the admonition of God?"[122] and to eradicate the instruments of sin we earnestly knocked on the gates of conversion. When the guide of divine assistance, in accordance with the words, "He who knocks on a door [313b] and perseveres will find," opened the door of fortune, I commanded an initiation of this holy war, which is the greatest endeavor, that is, opposition to the carnal soul. In short, I sincerely gave voice to the words, "O lord, we have dealt unjustly with our own souls,"[123] I inscribed upon the tablet of my heart the words, "I turn unto thee with repentance, and I am the first of the true believers,"[124] and I actualized the inner calling for repentance from wine, which is the sought-after pearl hidden in the treasure house of the breast.

My servants, in conformity with the felicitous command, broke to smithereens—like the idols that, God willing, we will soon succeed in breaking—the vessels and goblets and all the gold and silver implements and paraphernalia, which in their multiplicity and ornamentation beautified the assembly like heavenly bodies in the firmament, but which had reduced the glory of the holy law to the ground of humility and abasement, and cast every sherd to some unfortunate or poor person. By the felicity of this conversion, which will soon be rewarded, many of the elite of court were honored to repent—"People follow their kings' religion"—and totally renounced the drinking of intoxicants. Still droves of those obedient to the precepts of religion are flocking hour by hour to attain this felicity. It is hoped that, in accordance with the words, "He who shows the way to good is like him who does it," recompense for these actions will accrue during the fortunate days of the imperial lord and that through the blessing of this happiness victory and conquest will increase daily.

Upon the completion of this intention and the accomplishment of this hope, a decree obeyed by all the world was issued to the effect that within the protected realm (may God protect her from calamities and rebellions) [314] absolutely no creature would commit the sin of imbibing intoxicants or endeavor to acquire, produce, sell, purchase, possess, or transport same. "Avoid them that ye may prosper."[125]

In gratitude for this victory and in thanksgiving for the acceptance of this sincere repentance, the ocean of regal grace swelled and made manifest waves of generosity, which are the causes for the flourishing of the world and the honor of human beings, and issued a decree abolishing the tamgha throughout the realm for Muslims, the proceeds from which were beyond the limit of calculation, since, notwithstanding the continuance of former rulers in collecting it, it is outside the confines of the law of the Lord of Apostles. In no city, town, highway, byway, or port is the tamgha to be taken or exacted, nor is any change or mutation to be allowed in the foundation of this order. "But he who shall change it after he hath heard it, surely the sin thereof shall be on those who change it."[126]

The path of the legions of regal affection, Turks, Tajiks, Arabs, Iranians, Indians, and Persians, civilian and military, and all nations and classes of humanity is to seek succor and hope in the religion of him who is supported by all who know him. Let them occupy themselves with praying for eternal good fortune, and let them not transgress or deviate from orders. They must act in accordance with that which is commanded and rely upon the most noble, the most exalted for success. Written by majestic order on the twenty-fourth of Jumada I 933 [February 26, 1527]. **[314b]**

BABUR ENCOURAGES HIS TROOPS

During this same time, as has been mentioned before, great and small were suffering from trepidation and fear over past events. Manly words or courageous ideas were being heard from no one—neither from ministers who should have been speaking eloquently nor from amirs who should have been devouring provinces. Neither their strategies nor their tactics were noble. During this campaign Khalifa performed several outstanding feats, and there was no shortcoming in his earnestness or seriousness in maintaining order. Finally, having realized such fears and seen such weakness, I formulated a plan. I invited all the begs and warriors and said, "Begs and warriors,

> Whoever comes into the world is mortal; / he who remains forever is God.

Whoever enters the assembly of matter will, in the end, quaff the cup of death; and every person who comes to the way station of life will, in the end, pass from the abode of sorrow that is this world. It is better to die with a good name than to live with a bad one.

If I die with good repute, it is well. / I must have a good name, for the body belongs to death.

God has allotted us the happiness and has given us the good fortune that those who die are martyrs and those who kill are holy warriors. All must swear by God's Word [315] that they will not dream of turning their faces from this battle or leaving this contest and struggle while there is life left in their bodies."

Beg and liege man, great and small alike, all willingly took Korans in their hands and swore oaths to this effect. It was a really good plan, and it had favorable propagandistic effect on friend and foe.

REBELLION ON ALL FRONTS

Meanwhile, rebellion and strife broke out in all directions. Husayn Khan Nohani seized Rapri. Qutb Khan's men took Chandwar. A fellow called Rustam Khan gathered yeomen in the Doab and seized Koil, taking Kichik Ali captive. Zahid gave up Sambhal and left. Sultan-Muhammad Dulday gave up Kannauj. The infidels of Gwalior laid siege to Gwalior. Alam Khan, who had been sent as reinforcement to Gwalior, went instead to his own lands. Every day from some direction some piece of bad news arrived. Some of the Hindustanis began to desert from the army: Haybat Khan Kargandaz went to Sambhal, and Hasan Khan Bariwal went to the Infidel.

We paid no attention to those things, however, and concentrated on what had to be done. When the caissons, tripods on rollers, and other implements and tools were ready, we marched on Persian New Year's Day, Tuesday the ninth of Jumada II [March 13]. [315b] The right flank, left flank, and center were arrayed and the caissons and tripods with rollers were set in motion before us, and directly behind them Master Ali-Qulï and all his matchlockmen were ordered to march on foot in array. After the ranks came into their assigned places we rode swiftly through them to give heart to the begs, warriors, and soldiers of the left flank, right flank, and center, telling each group where it was to stand and how it was to march. In this way we advanced one kos and stopped. The Infidel's men had had news of us and drawn up their ranks. After camp was made, the camp and opposite it were made secure with caissons and trenches.

Since battle was not planned for that day, a few warriors went forward and engaged in hand-to-hand combat with the enemy for good luck. A few infidels were taken and their severed heads were brought back. Malik Qasim also brought in a few heads. Malik Qasim did well. With just this much the soldiers took heart and perked up, quite a different picture from before. Early the next morning we envisioned the begs marching and doing battle, but Khalifa and some of our supporters said that since [316] the selected campsite was far away, it would be better if we dug trenches and made fortifications before marching. Khalifa mounted and assigned the shovelers to the places for trenches, stationed commissars, and came back.

THE BATTLE OF KHANUA

On Saturday the thirteenth of Jumada II [March 17] we had the caissons drawn up before us, and the right wing, left wing, and center moved in array nearly a kos and camped in the site selected. Some tents had been pitched and others were in the process when news arrived that the enemy's array was in sight. Immediately we got to horse and commanded the right and left flanks to go to their places and the caissons and ranks to be drawn.

Since the following notice of victory, composed by Shaykh Zayn, describes the Army of Islam and the number of the enemy horde, and how the ranks and arrays encountered each other and how the Muslims and infidels fought, it is reproduced without addition or deletion.

DECREE OF ZAHIRUDDIN MUHAMMAD BABUR

PADISHAH GHAZI

Praise to God, who fulfills his promise, aids his servant, empowers his army, and routs the heathen. He alone exists, and beyond him is nothing. He has raised high the buttresses of Islam through the assistance of his rightly guided saints and laid low the foundations of idolatry through the defeat of his rebellious enemies. "And the utmost part of the people which had acted wickedly was cut off: praise be unto God, the Lord of all creatures."[127] May he pray for the best of his creation, Muhammad, lord of warriors and those who endeavor, and for his house and companions, the guides to righteousness until doomsday.

The continuum of divine blessings is cause for ever-increasing thanks and praise of the divine, and ever-increasing thanks and praise of the divine bequeaths a continuum of divine blessings. For every blessing there is an act of gratitude, and for every act of gratitude a blessing. However, it is beyond human power to give adequate thanks, and even those possessed of great puissance are incapable thereof, in particular the thanks that are due for that blessing, no greater fortune than which exists in this world and no more overwhelming felicity than which exists in the next, and this is none other than victory over unbelieving potentates and dominance over the wicked rich, regarding the likes of whom the verse, "These are the unbelievers, the wicked,"[128] was revealed, and in the view of the insightful there is no felicity greater than that. Thank God that this greatest felicity, this most splendid gift, which, from the cradle until now, has been the prime goal and true aim of right-thinking minds and sound intellects, has been manifested from the recesses of the emotions of the Omniscient King during these felicitous days. He who bestows victory without being entreated, he who sheds his grace without cause has once again opened with the key of victory the gates of grace to His Victorious Highness's hopes. The renowned names of our happy forces have been scriven in the register of great warriors for the faith, and the banner of Islam has reached the apex of sublimity with the help of our victorious soldiers. [317] How this felicity was gained and how this fortune was made manifest are as follows:

When the glint of the swords of our army, the refuge of Islam, lighted the land of India with flashes of the luminescence of conquest and victory, and, as has been reported in former notices of victory, the hands of success raised our victory-inscribed banners in the realms of Delhi, Agra, Jaunpur, Kharid, Bihar, and other places, most of the infidel tribes and Muslims elected obedience to our felicitous lord and trod the path of servitude with the feet of truth and sincerity. However, Sanga the Infidel, who in former days spoke of obedience to our felicitous lord, now acted in accordance with the verse, "He was puffed up with pride, and became of the number of unbelievers,"[129] devilishly rebelled and, at the head of the cavalry of the damned, caused an amassing of tribes, some of whom bore the accursed band of the *zunnar*[130] around their necks, and the skirts of others of whom were sullied with the brambles of apostasy. The domination of that cursed infidel— abandoned be he on doomsday—reached such an extent in the realm of India that before the rising of the sun of regal fortune and prior to the dawning of the luminary of the imperial caliphate, although the great rajahs and rays who obeyed his command in this confrontation and the apostate rulers [317b] and leaders whose reins he held during this conflict, had been too absorbed with their own greatness to follow him into any battle or accompany him on any expedition, all the ex- alted sultans of this vast realm, like the sultan of Delhi, the sultan of Gujarat, the sultan of Mandu, *et alii*, were incapable of resisting that maleficent on their own and used every ruse to placate him. In around two hundred cities within the realm of Islam he raised the banner of infidelity and undertook the destruction of mosques and places of worship, taking captive the wives and children of believers in those cities and towns. His power in truth reached such a degree that, taking into consideration the constant rule of India that a one-lac district suf- fices for a hundred cavalry and a one-crore district for ten thousand, the lands subdued by that leader of infidels reached ten crores, which would mean a lac of cavalry.[131] During these days many renowned in- fidels, not one of whom had ever helped him in any battle, joined his wretched forces out of enmity toward the Army of Islam, like the ten independent rulers, each of whom reared his head like smoke in rebel- lion and became the leader of a group of infidels in some region or other and attached himself like chains and bonds to that wicked infidel. [318] These infidel ten, like ten denouncers raising the banner of wretchedness—"denounce unto them a painful punishment"[132]—held many followers, soldiers, and districts broad in extent, like Silhadi, who possessed lands supporting thirty thousand cavalrymen. There were also Rawal Udai Singh of Nagaur with twelve thousand horsemen, Medini Rao with twelve thousand, Hasan Khan of Mewat with twelve thousand, Barmal Idari with four thousand, Nripat Hada with eight thousand, Sthirvi Kechi with six thousand, Dharm Deo with four thou- sand, and Nar Singh Deo with four thousand. Mahmud Khan son of Sultan Sikandar, although he possessed no estates or lands, had gath- ered approximately ten thousand cavalrymen in hopes of attaining leadership. The total of those deprived of the valley of well-being and security, in terms of estates and lands, was two lacs and one thousand.

In short, that infidel, blinded by his own conceit, convinced the hardened hearts of the star-crossed infidels to join forces, like "additions of darkness one over the other,"[133] and to take up a stance of rebellion and war against the people of Islam for the destruction of the foundation of the law of the Lord of Mankind, upon whom be peace. Like divine fate against the one-eyed Antichrist, the holy warriors of the royal army came forth and, fixing the gaze of their insight upon the words, "When the divine decree comes, sight is blinded," and bearing in mind the holy verse, "Whoever striveth to promote the true religion [318b] striveth for the advantage of his own soul,"[134] implemented the command that must be obeyed, "Wage war against the unbelievers and the hypocrites."[135] On Saturday the thirteenth of the month of Jumada II in the year 933 [March 17, 1527] a token of the blessedness of which are the words, "May God bless your sabbath," in the vicinity of the village of Khanua, a dependency of Bayana, near a mountain where the enemies of the true religion stretched for two kos, were pitched the victory-laden tents of the armies of Islam. When the sound of the Islamic hosts reached the ears of the enemies of true religion, those accursed infidel opponents of the Muhammadan nation, like the Elephanteers[136] intent upon the destruction of the Kaaba[137] they relied upon their elephants with bodies like mountains and countenances like demons and, all of one accord and of one intent, divided their wretched army into divisions.

With those elephants the vile Hindustani became as conceited as the Elephanteers. / All as hideous and gloomy as the evening of death, blacker than night, more numerous than the stars, / All like fire, but like smoke they raised their heads in spite to the blue celestial sphere. / Like ants they swarmed from left and right, mounted and on foot, thousands upon thousands.

They set forth for a martial confrontation with the Islamic horde. The holy warriors of the Islamic army, who are trees in the garden of bravery, formed their ranks as straight as pines, [319] their cone-shaped helmets, shining like the sun, reaching the apex of exaltedness like the hearts of God's holy warriors. Each rank was as ironlike as Alexander's dam, as firm in its straightness and force as the path of the prophet's holy law, "as though they were a well-compacted building,"[138] and slated for prosperity and victory in accordance with the verse, "These are directed by their Lord, and they shall prosper."[139]

No chink therein of cowardly natures, as firm as the emperor's determination and religion. / His banners all scraping against heaven, as straight as the *alifs* in *inna fatahna*.[140]

Maintaining their resolve, in the manner of the holy warriors of Anatolia they formed a row of caissons and bound them together with chains as cover for the matchlockmen and mortarmen, who were in front of the troops. In short, the sabaoth of Islam were so ordered and reinforced that ancient wisdom and the ethereal celestial sphere both cried bravo to its conceiver and organizer. In this tactical order Nizamuddin Ali Khalifa endeavored and strove, and all of his tactics were in accord with destiny, and all of his organization and management were approved by enlightened opinion.

The locus of imperial puissance was established in the center. [319b] To the right of the center Chïn Temür Sultan, Sulaymanshah, Khwaja Dost Khawand, Yunus-Ali, Shah-Mansur Barlas, Darwesh-Muhammad Sarban, Abdullah Kitabdar, and Dost Eshik-Aqa took up their positions.[141]

To the left of the center Sultan Alauddin Alam Khan son of Sultan Bahlul Lodi, the aforementioned Nizamuddin Ali Khalifa, Shaykh Zayn Khwafi, Muhibb-Ali son of the aforementioned Nizamuddin Ali Khalifa, Turdï Beg the brother of the late Qoch Beg, [320] Sherafkan son of the late Qoch Beg, Arayish Khan, Khwaja Husayn, and the great divanis all stood in their assigned positions.

In the right flank Muhammad Humayun Bahadur stood firm. To the right of that dear son were assigned Qasim Husayn Sultan, Ahmad Yusuf Oghlaqchï, Hindu Beg Qauchin, Khusraw Kükäldash, Qiwam Beg Ordushah, Wali Khazin Qaraquzi, Pir-Qulï Sistani, Khwaja Pahlawan Badakhshi, Abdul-Shakur, Sulayman Agha the ambassador of Iraq, and Husayn the ambassador of Seistan. [320b] To the left of that dear son were stationed Mir Hama, Muhammadi Kükäldash, and Khwajagi Asad Jandar. Of Indian officers in the right flank were Khankhanan Dilawar Khan, Malikdad of Kara, and Shaykh Ghuran, each standing in the position to which he had been ordered.

In the left flank of the Islamic forces were Sayyid Mahdi Khwaja, Muhammad-Sultan Mirza, Adil Sultan son of Mahdi Sultan, Abdul-

Aziz the stablemaster, Muhammad-Ali Jang-Jang, Qutlugh-Qadam Qaravul, Shah-Husayn Yaraki Moghul Ghanchï, and Jan-Muhammad Beg Atäkä. On this side were stationed the officers of India, Jalal Khan and Kamal Khan, [321] and the sons of the aforementioned Sultan Alauddin, Ali Khan Shaykhzada Farmuli, and Nizam Khan of Bayana.

For the rear assault Turdïka and Malik Qasim the brother of Baba Qashqa with a contingent of Moghuls were assigned to the left flank. Mu'min Atäkä and Rustam the Turcoman were appointed to the left flank with a troop from the royal tabin. Sultan-Muhammad Bakhshï positioned the nobles of the holy warriors of Islam in their assigned places and stations and then stood ready to hear our orders. The to-vachïs and *yasavuls*[142] he dispatched in all directions to deliver our orders for arraying the forces and soldiers to the magnificent sultans, noble officers, and all other respected holy warriors.

When the pillars of the army were established, everyone hastened to his place, and the order that must be obeyed was issued that no one was to move from his station of his own accord or begin to do battle without permission. Of the aforementioned day approximately two watches and two gharis had passed when the two opposing parties approached each other and began to fight and do battle. The two centers of the two armies, [321b] like light and darkness, faced each other, and in the left and right flanks there was such fierce battle that tremors occurred in the earth and quivers in the celestial sphere above. The wretched left wing of the infidel headed toward the lucky right wing of the forces of Islam and attacked Khusraw Kükäldash and Malik Qasim brother of Baba Qashqa. Our dearest elder brother, Chïn Temür Sultan, in accordance with orders, began to battle courageously in assistance of them and forced the infidels from their place almost to behind their center. For this a reward was assigned to him.

From the center of our dear eldest son, Muhammad Humayun, Mustafa Rumi brought forward the caissons, and with matchlocks and mortars broke not only the ranks of the infidel army but their hearts as well. In the pitch of battle Qasim Husayn Sultan, Ahmad Yusuf, and Qiwam Beg were ordered to hasten to their assistance. Since time and again the troops of the infidels came continuously and continually to the assistance of their own men, we too sent as reinforcements Hindu Beg Qauchin and after him Muhammadi Kükäldash and Khwajagi Asad, and after them [322] Yunus Ali, Shah-Mansur Barlas, and Abdullah Kitabdar, and after them Dost Eshik-Aqa and Muhammad Khalil Akhtabegi. Over and over again the infidels' right flank attacked the Army of Islam's left flank, but each time the great holy warriors dispatched some of them with their victorious lances to the house of perdition—"They shall be thrown to burn therein, and an unhappy dwelling shall it be"[143]—and others they drove back. Mu'min Atäkä and Rustam the Turcoman headed for the rear of the wretched infidels' dark forces, and we dispatched Mulla Mahmud and Nizamuddin Ali Khalifa's liege men led by Ali Atäkä to reinforce them. Our dear elder brother Muhammad-Sultan Mirza, Adil Sultan, Abdul-Aziz the stablemaster, Qutlugh-Qadam Qaravul, Muhammad-Ali Jang-Jang, and Shah-Husayn Yaraki Moghul Ghanchi began to fight and held their ground, and we dispatched Khwaja Kamaluddin Husayn with a troop of divanis to help them. [322b] All the forces of holy war came earnestly desirous of battle, and, thinking of the verse, "Say, do ye expect any other should befall us than one of the two most excellent things, victory, or martyrdom?"[144] and determined to give their all, they raised the banner of ferocity.

When the battle had raged for a long time, an order was issued that the warriors of the royal tabins and the lions of the jungle of fidelity, who were like lions in chains behind the caissons, should emerge from the right and left of the center and station the matchlockmen in the middle and fight from both sides. Like the rising of the lights of true dawn over the horizon, they charged from behind the caissons and spilled the dawn-red blood of the hapless infidels in the field of battle, which was like the spinning celestial sphere. Many rebellious heads winked out of existence, like stars from the firmament. Master Ali-Qulï, standing with his followers before the center and evincing many acts of bravery, shot toward the iron-clad citadel of the infidels' ranks rocks so huge that if they were placed in the scales of one's deeds, it could be said, "he whose balances shall be heavy with good works shall be happy,"[145] and if they were hurled upon the towering mountains and firm hills, they would bring them down "like carded wool,"[146] and by hurling stones and shooting matchlocks and mortars he reduced the foundations of the infidels' bodies. [323] The royal matchlockmen, as ordered, left the caissons for the midst of battle, and each one of them gave many of the infidels the poison of death to taste. The infantry, by rushing into great danger, caused their names to figure prominently among the lions of the jungle of courage and the chivalrous heroes of battle. At this same time the imperial command was issued to drive the caissons forward, and the royal personage himself, with victory and fortune to his right and luck and divine assistance to his left, moved toward the army of the infidels. On all sides, the victorious soldiers witnessed this, the churning sea of the divinely assisted army swelled mightily and brought forth from potentiality to actuality the courage of all the crocodiles of that sea. Clouds of dark dust rose up, like heaps of darkness, all over the battle, and streaks of glittering swords surpassed the lightning. The agitation of dust deprived the face of the sun of light, like the back of a mirror, and, victor and vanquished commingled, the title of advantage was lost to sight. The sorcerer Time brought into view such a night that the only heavenly bodies that appeared were arrows, and the only fixed stars that could be seen were firmly footed mounts.

On the day of battle down went wet blood to the nether regions and up went dust to the moon. / [323b] From the horses' hooves in that broad field the earth became six and the heavens eight.[147]

The holy warriors engaged in the lobbing off of heads and the taking of lives heard the good news from the voice of the unseen realm saying, "Be not dismayed, neither be ye grieved, for ye shall be superior."[148] And from the divine herald they heard the words, "Assistance from God, and a speedy victory," and, "Bear good tidings unto the faithful."[149] They battled so eagerly that the cry of bravo from the celestial holy ones reached them and the angels clustered like moths around their heads. Between the two prayers the fire of battle so blazed that its flames rose straight to the celestial sphere, and the left and right wings of the Army of Islam pushed into one place the hapless infidels' center and left and right wings. When signs of victory began to appear to the renowned warriors and the banner of Islam was raised high, immediately the accursed infidels and the evil heathen were struck dumb. Finally, in desperation, they attacked the right and left of the center and drove their advance much deeper into the left; however, the brave warriors, considering the fruits of heavenly recompense, planted saplings of arrows in the earth of the breast of each of them and turned them all around like their own untoward fortune. Just at this time the breezes of divine assistance and good luck blew over the meadow of our happy monarch's fortune to announce the good news, "Verily we have granted thee a manifest victory."[150] [324] The specter of victory, whose world-adorning beauty was enhanced by the tresses of the words, "God may assist thee with a glorious assistance,"[151] and whose full moon had been in eclipse, once again appeared. The vain Hindus, realizing that their position was untenable, scattered "like carded wool" and disappeared "like moths scattered abroad."[152] Many fell slain in battle. Many others lost their heads and headed off into the wilderness of aimlessness to become morsels for crows and ravens. There were piles of the slain, and towers of skulls were erected. Hasan Khan of Mewat entered the ranks of the slain from a gunshot wound, and so also came to an end through arrow and gunshot the days of the lives of many erroneous rebels who lead their people—among them the aforementioned Rawal Udai Singh, the ruler of Dungarpur who had twelve thousand cavalry; Ray Chandra Bhan Chauhan, who had four thousand cavalry; Nripat Rao, the son of the aforementioned Silhadi ruler of Chanderi district who had six thousand cavalry; Manik Chand Chauhan; Dilip Rao, the commander of four thousand cavalry; Gangu; Karam Singh; and Rao Bikrasi, who had three thousand cavalry; and many others, each of whom was the great leader of a magnificent troop—[324b] all took the road to hell and moved from this earthly abode to deepest perdition. The battlefield was as full of slain and wounded as hell, and the lowest depth of Hades was filled with hypocrites who had entrusted their souls to the warden of hell. In every direction the soldiers of Islam went, they found a slain rebel at every step, and as the renowned army camp moved in pursuit of the defeated it found no space devoid of obliterated retinue.

With stones and matchlocks the Hindus all were reduced as low as the Elephanteers. / Many mountains of bodies were created, and on every mountain running streams of blood. / From the lances of the splendid ranks the fighters fled into mountain and plain.

"They turned their backs, flying."[153] "The command of God is a determinate decree."[154] And praise be to God the all-hearing, all-knowing. Victory cometh from God alone, the powerful judge. Written on the twenty-fifth of the month of Jumada II in the year 933 [March 29, 1527].

AFTERMATH OF THE BATTLE
OF KHANUA

After this victory I had the title "Ghazi" added to my seal, and under
the seal on the proclamation of victory I wrote this quatrain:

> For the sake of Islam I became a wanderer; I battled infidels and Hin-
> dus. / I determined to become a martyr. [325] Thank God I became a
> holy warrior.

Shaykh Zayn found a chronogram in the phrase *Fath-i padishah-i
islam*.[155] Mir Gesu, one of those who came from Kabul, also found that
expression as a chronogram, incorporated it into a quatrain, and sent it
to me. It was a coincidence that both Shaykh Zayn and Mir Gesu invented the same chronogram. Another time, at the conquest of Dipalpur, Shaykh Zayn composed the chronogram *vasat-i shahr-i
Rabi'u'l-avval*,[156] and Mir Gesu came up with the exact same one.

Having conquered the enemy, we proceeded to bring them down.
The enemy's camp was two kos from ours. Muhammadi, Abdul-Aziz,
Ali Khan, and others were dispatched to pursue the enemy as far as
their camp, but they were rather slow. I should have gone myself rather
than trust in others. I had passed within a kos of the enemy's camp, but
since it was late in the day I returned to camp late that night. Muhammad Sharif, the astrologer who made such gloomy predictions, immediately showed up to congratulate me. I cursed him roundly and made
myself feel much better. Although he was heathenish and pessimistic,
terribly conceited, and very cold, he had a long service record, so I
gave him a lac with the proviso that he not remain in my realm. [325b]

The next morning we stayed at that campsite. Muhammad-Ali
Jang-Jang, Shaykh Ghuran, and Abdul-Malik Qorchï were dispatched
with a large force to attack Ilyas Khan, who had rebelled in the Doab,
seized Koil, and taken Kichik Ali prisoner. When they arrived, he was
not able to mount a battle and his men were dispersed pell-mell in all
directions. A few days after I came to Agra they captured him and
brought him in. I had him skinned alive. When the army was camped
at Koh Bachcha, they were ordered to erect a tower of infidel skulls on
the top of the mountain.

Marching two kos from this camp we came to Bayana. All the way there, indeed the road all the way to Alwar and Mewat, was strewn with innumerable infidel and apostate corpses. I made a tour of Bayana. When I came to the camp, I summoned the Turk and India officers and consulted them on the advisability of proceeding against the infidels' territories: the expedition was postponed due to the paucity of water along the way and the intense heat. However, the province of Mewat was near Delhi, with a total income of about three or four crores. Hasan Khan of Mewat and his forefathers had been ruling Mewat independently for a century or two, giving only halfhearted allegiance to the sultans of Delhi. The sultans of India, unable to consolidate the area further because of the vast extent of their territory, or for lack of opportunity or because the terrain in Mewat was mountainous, left them alone under nominal suzerainty. [326] After the conquest of India we too maintained this favor to Hasan Khan as had past rulers, but this heretical, heathen ingrate, in blatant disregard of our kindness and favor and expressing no gratitude for our patronage, was the instigator of all sedition and the cause of all evil, as has been mentioned.[157]

Since the expedition had been postponed, we set out to subdue Mewat. After stopping four times we camped on the banks of the Manasni River, six kos from the Alwar fortress, which was the seat of Mewat. Hasan Khan's fathers had dwelt in Tijara, but [in 1524,] the year I marched to Hindustan, defeated Pahar Khan, and took Lahore and Dipalpur, they set to work on this fortress, already apprehensive of my future plans. Hasan Khan's chief minister, Karam Chand, who had visited Hasan Khan's son in Agra, came on behalf of the son in Alwar and sought quarter. [326b] Abdul-Rahim Shiqavul was sent with him to deliver letters of safe conduct. He went and brought back Hasan Khan's son, Nahar Khan. Entering once more into favor, he was granted estates worth a few lacs.

Since I thought that Khusraw had performed an outstanding deed during the battle, he was awarded Alwar with a stipend of fifty lacs; but he was such a wretch that he whined and refused to accept. Later it was discovered that it was Chïn Temür Sultan who had done the deed, so the prize was given to him and he was rewarded with the city of Tijara, the capital of Mewat, and a stipend of fifty lacs. Turdika, who was in charge of the right-wing flank assault during the Sanga battle, had performed better than others, so he was rewarded with a stipend of fifteen lacs and given the Alwar fortress. The Alwar treasuries and their contents were awarded to Humayun.

HUMAYUN IS STATIONED IN KABUL

On Wednesday the first of Rajab [April 3] we marched from that camp and came within two kos of Alwar. I went to tour the Alwar fortress and stayed there that night. The next morning I returned to camp. As has been mentioned, before the raid on the Infidel, when all were sworn, [327] it was also stated that after this victory there would be no further duties and anyone who wanted to leave would be free to do so. Most of Humayun's liege men were Badakhshanis or from those parts, and they had never before suffered the rigors of an exhausting two-month campaign. They had reached the limits of their endurance even before the battle, and therefore such a promise had been made. Because Kabul was undermanned, the prevalent opinion was that Humayun should be sent to Kabul. It was so decided, and on Thursday the ninth of Rajab we marched four or five kos from Alwar and camped on the banks of the Manasni River. As Mahdi Khwaja was having great difficulty, he was permitted to return to Kabul, and the governorship of Bayana was given to Dost Eshik-aqa.

Since Etawah had previously been assigned to Mahdi Khwaja, in his stead his son Ja'far Khwaja was sent because Qutb Khan had fled Etawah. We stayed in this camp for two or three days in order to give Humayun permission to withdraw. While at the camp Mu'min Ali Tovachï was dispatched to Kabul with the victory proclamation.

AN EXCURSION TO FIROZPUR AND KOTLAH TANK

Great things had been heard of the spring at Firozpur and the big tank at Kotlah. In order both to escort Humayun and to tour these sites, I stationed the army at the camp on Sunday and rode out. [327b] That day I visited Firozpur and the spring there and also had some ma'jun. The whole valley into which the spring water flowed was full of oleanders in bloom. It was not a bad spot, even if it did not measure up to expectation. At one place in the valley, where the stream was a bit wider, I ordered stones cut to make a pool. That night I stayed in the valley, and the next morning rode out to inspect the tank at Kotlah. One side of the lake was against the skirt of the mountain. The Manasni River spills into the lake, which is huge—the far shore could scarcely be seen from this side. In the middle of the lake is a rise; all around the edges are small boats the village people on the shore use to save themselves when there is trouble. When we arrived a few of them got into their boats and went out into the lake. Having toured the lake, we returned to Humayun's camp, rested there, had some food, and presented the prince and his begs with robes of honor. Late that evening we bade Humayun farewell, got to horse, had a nap somewhere en route, remounted, and passed through the Kohri district at dawn, slept a bit again, and came to camp, which had been made in Toda.

We marched from Toda and camped at Sungarh. Hasan Khan [328] of Mewat's son, Nahar Khan, who had been entrusted to Abdul-Rahim, escaped. We stopped once for the night, at a spring located on an outcropping of a mountain between Bhasawar and Chausa. Here we had canopies erected, and indulged in some ma'jun. Turdï Beg Khaksar had praised this spring when the army had passed through, and this time we passed by on horseback and inspected it. It was excellent. What more could one want in Hindustan, where there is never any flowing water? Where the rare springs are, the water only oozes out of the ground—it does not gush out as it does in our country. The water of this spring, however, was nearly equivalent to a half-mill stream and came rushing out from the skirt of the mountain. All around was meadow—it was very nice. Above the spring I ordered an octagonal pool made of hewn stone. Seated next to the spring, Turdï Beg, high on ma'jun, kept repeating, "Since I like this place, it has to be given a name." Abdullah said, "It will have to be called the Imperial Spring-That-Turdï-Beg-Liked." This made us all laugh.

Dost Eshik-aqa came from Bayana and paid homage at the spring. [328b] From there I went to tour Bayana, then Sikri. I stopped two days next to the garden I had ordered, then tended to it, reaching Agra at dawn on Thursday, the twenty-third of Rajab [April 25].

As has been mentioned,[158] the rebels had occupied Chandwar and Rapri during this time of disturbance. Muhammad-Ali Jang-Jang, Qoch Beg's Turdï Beg, Abdul-Malik Qorchï, and Husayn Khan with his Daryakhanis were dispatched to attack Chandwar and Rapri. As they reached the vicinity of Chandwar, Qutb Khan's men, who were inside, discovered their approach and fled. Thus having gotten hold of Chandwar, they went on to Rapri. Husayn Khan Nohani's men block-aded the streets, planning to have a skirmish. Our men attacked with force, however, and the defenders, unable to hold their ground, took flight. Husayn Khan entered the river like a mad elephant with several of his men and was drowned in the Jumna. As soon as he received this news, Qutb Khan threw over Etawah and fled with a few men. Since Etawah had been assigned originally to Mahdi Khwaja, his son Ja'far Khwaja was sent in his stead.

MISCELLANEOUS ASSIGNMENTS

When Sanga the Infidel rebelled, as has been mentioned,[159] most of the Hindustanis and Afghans returned and regained control of all their es-tates and provinces. Sultan-Muhammad Dulday, who had abandoned Kannauj and come to me, [329] refused to go to Kannauj—either from fear or as a point of honor—and took Sirhind with fifteen lacs instead of the thirty lacs of Kannauj. Kannauj was then awarded to Muhammad-Sultan Mirza with a stipend of thirty lacs. Budaun was given to Qasim Husayn Sultan, and he was attached to Muhammad-Sultan Mirza, and of the Turk officers, Baba-Qashqa's Malik Qasim and his brethren and Mughuls, Abu'l-Muhammad Nayzabaz and Muayyad with his father's liege men, and Husayn Khan with his Daryakhanis and Sultan-Muhammad Dulday's liege men. Of the India officers: Ali Khan Far-muli, Malikdad of Kora, Shaykh-Muhammad, Shaykh Bhakkari, and Tatar Khan Khanjahan were attached to Muhammad-Sultan Mirza and dispatched against Biban, who had besieged and taken Lakhnor during the Sanga disturbance. When Biban learned that this battalion was cross-ing the Ganges, he abandoned his baggage and took flight. The battalion pursued him up to Khairabad, where they stopped for several days be-fore withdrawing.

The treasury had been distributed, but with attention turned to the affair of the Infidel, it had not been possible to assign provinces and es-tates. Once we were free of the raid on the Infidel, provinces and es-tates could be distributed. [329b] Since the rainy season was close at hand, it was decided that everyone should retire to his estate, see to his arms, and then present himself at Delhi when the monsoon had passed.

Meanwhile, news arrived that Humayun had gone to Delhi, opened several rooms in the Delhi treasury, and appropriated the contents. I would never have expected such a thing of him! It was difficult for me to believe. I wrote him some extremely harsh letters of reproach.

On Thursday the fifteenth of Sha'ban [May 16], Khwajagi Asad, who had gone to Persia[160] as ambassador and returned accompanied by Sulayman the Turcoman, was rejoined to Sulayman and sent back as ambassador with appropriate gifts for Prince Tahmasp.

Turdï Beg Khaksar, whom I had persuaded to leave off being a dervish and made a military man, had been in my service for several years. Once again, however, the call to be a dervish became overwhelming, and he requested leave. He was given permission to withdraw and was sent to Kamran as emissary. Three lacs of the treasury were sent to Kamran. The year before, I had composed a little poem appropriate to those who had left India. It was addressed to Mulla Ali Khan and sent to him with Turdï Beg. The poem is this:

O you who have gone from this country of India feeling pain and distress, [330] / You thought of Kabul and its wonderful climate and hotly left India. / There you have apparently found pleasure and joy, and many good things. / Yet we have not died, thank God, although we have suffered much pain and untold grief. / You have no more physical distress, but then neither do we.

We spent Ramadan in the Hasht Bihisht garden. Every *taravih*[161] was performed in a state of ritual purity. Ever since my eleventh year, I had never spent two successive Ramadan festivals in one place; and last year it had been celebrated in Agra. Lest this custom be broken, on Sunday, the eve of last day of the month, I went to Sikri for the festival. The stone platform I had ordered constructed on the northwest side of the Bagh-i-Fath[162] was ready. A felt tent was pitched on the platform, and there I celebrated. The evening I rode out of Agra, Mir Ali Qorchï was sent to Shah-Hasan in Tatta. Shah-Hasan was fond of *ganjafa*[163] and had requested a set, so one was sent. On Sunday the fifth of Dhu'l-Qa'da [August 4], I was taken ill. It lasted for seventeen days. On Friday the

Detail, Dervish, Iran or Central Asia, fifteenth century. Album page; opaque watercolor and gold on paper. Topkapi Palace Library, Istanbul, H.2160, fol. 67a.

twenty-fourth of the same month [August 23], I set out to make a tour of Dholpur. That night I slept somewhere along the way [330b] and stopped the next morning at Sultan Iskandar's dam. Below the dam, where the mountain ended, there was a mass of red building stone. I had Master Shah-Muhammad the stonemason brought and ordered him to carve a chamber from this single block, if possible. If it was too low for a building, he was to level it down into a pool.

From Dholpur we went to tour Bari. The next morning we mounted in Bari and rode via the mountain between Bari and Chambhal and inspected the Chambhal River before returning. We saw an ebony tree on that mountain. The fruit is called *tindu*. Most of the ebony trees on this mountain are white. Leaving Bari, we toured Sikri and reached Agra on Wednesday the twenty-ninth [August 28]. During these days disturbing news was heard of Shaykh Bayazid. Sultan-Ali Türk was dispatched to meet him and rendezvous in twenty days. On Friday the second of Dhu'l-Hijja [August 30], I began to recite a litany that was repeated forty-one times. At this same time I scanned the following lines of poetry 540 different ways:

Tell me, is it her eyes, her eyebrows, her mouth, or her tongue? / Tell me, is it her stature, her cheek, her hair, or her waist?

I wrote a treatise on the subject. I fell ill again on this day. [331] It lasted nine days. On Wednesday the twenty-ninth of Dhu'l-Hijja [September 25], I rode out to inspect Koil and Sambhal.

EVENTS OF THE YEAR 934
(1527-28)[164]

On Saturday the first of Muharram [September 28] we stopped in Koil. Darwesh and Ali Yusuf had been stationed in Sambhal by Humayun. They had crossed a river and defeated Qutb Sarwani and a group of rajahs in a skirmish. Many had been killed, and a few heads and an elephant were sent in while we were in Koil. We toured the area for two days and stopped in Shaykh Ghuran's house at his invitation. He put on an entertainment and presented gifts. From there we rode to Atrauli.

On Wednesday we crossed the Ganges and spent the night in some villages in the Sambhal district. On Thursday we stopped in Sambhal, where we spent two days touring before leaving at dawn on Saturday. On Sunday we went to Rao Sarwani's house in Sikandra. He performed good service in presenting a meal. We rode from there before dawn. Along the way I separated myself from the men on some pretext and galloped alone to within a kos of Agra. Thereafter the men caught up and joined me. We dismounted in Agra at noon.

On Sunday the sixteenth of Muharram [October 13], I came down with a fever and chills. The fever came and went intermittently for twenty-five or twenty-six days. I took purgatives and finally regained my health but was suffering from sleeplessness and dehydration. While down with this illness I composed three or four quatrains. [331b] One of them is the following:

By day fever rages in my body. Sleep flies from my eyes when it is night. These two are like my grief and patience: the more the one increases, the less the other becomes.

On Saturday the twenty-eighth of Safar [November 23] my aunts Fakhrijahan Begim and Khadija Sultan Begim arrived. I went by boat upstream from Sikandarabad to pay homage to them. On Sunday, Master Ali-Qulï fired a shot from his great mortar. Although the shot went far, the mortar shattered and pieces of it wounded some people. Eight of them died.

On Monday the seventh of Rabi' I [December 2], I rode out to tour Sikri. The octagonal platform I had ordered in the middle of the reservoir was ready. We went out by boat, had canopies erected, and indulged in some ma'jun. After returning from the tour of Sikri, we set out on the eve of Monday the fourteenth of Rabi' I on an expedition against the infidels in Chanderi, stopping in Jalisar after marching three kos.[165] We stayed here two days for the men to get their arms and equipment ready. On Thursday we marched to Anwar, whence we traveled by boat to Chandwar. Proceeding by forced march, we camped at the Kanar Ford on Monday the twenty-eighth. On Thursday the second of Rabi' II [December 26], I crossed the river. We halted on one side and the other for four or five days while the soldiers came over. [332] During these few days we continually went out in boats and had ma'jun. The confluence with the Chambhal River is a kos or two upstream from the Kanar Ford. On Friday we went up the Chambhal from the confluence and then returned to camp.

Although Shaykh Bayazid had not rebelled openly, it was clear from his actions and deeds that he was intent on rebelling. To deal with him Muhammad-Ali Jang-Jang was separated from the main body of the army and sent to gather a force made up of Muhammad-Sultan Mirza in Kannauj and the princes and officers of that region, such as Qasim Husayn Sultan, Beykhub Sultan, Malik Qasim of Koil, Abu'l-Muhammad Nayzabaz, and Minuchihr Khan and his Daryakhani brethren, and attack the rebel Afghans in Sarwar. They were also to invite Shaykh Bayazid. If he came with good grace and joined them, they were to proceed with him. If not, they were to deal with him first. Muhammad-Ali requested a few elephants and was given around ten of them. After he was dismissed, Baba Chuhra was ordered to go join them.

We proceeded by boat a march from Kanar. On Wednesday the eighth of Rabi' II [January 1, 1528], we stopped a kos from Kalpi. Baba Sultan, Sultan Sa'id Khan's younger brother and Sultan-Khalil Sultan's son, came to this camp and paid homage. The previous year he had fled from his elder brother [332b] but regretted his action when he reached the borders of Andarab. However, when he approached Kashghar on his way back, the Khan sent Haydar Mirza to intercept him and force him to turn back.

The next morning we stopped at Alam Khan's house in Kalpi. He presented a meal in the Hindustani fashion and gave us presents.

On Monday the thirteenth [January 6] we marched from Kalpi. On Friday we reached Iraj. Saturday camp was made in Bhander. Sunday the nineteenth, Chïn Temür Sultan was put in charge of six to seven thousand men and sent ahead of us to Chanderi. The officers who went on the expedition were Baqi Mingbegi, Qoch Beg's Turdï Beg, Ashiq Bökäül, Mulla Apaq, Muhsin Dulday, and Shaykh Ghuran of the Hindustani officers.

DESCRIPTION OF KACHWAHA

On Friday the twenty-fourth [January 17], camp was made near Kachwaha. The people of Kachwaha were given quarter, and the town was given to Badruddin's son. Kachwaha is a fine little place. All around it are little hillocks. Across the mountain to the southeast of Kachwaha is a dam, and behind it a large lake with a perimeter of five to six kos has formed. This lake surrounds Kachwaha on three sides. On the northwest side is a neck of dry land on which the town gate is located. On the lake are small boats that hold three or four people. Whenever the people need to flee, they get into the boats and go out into the middle of the water. [333] Before reaching Kachwaha, we saw two other places where dams were built across hills to form lakes, but the lakes were smaller than the one at Kachwaha. We stayed in Kachwaha two days, during which time overseers and many shovelers were assigned to repair the pits and potholes in the road and to cut the jungles so that the carts and artillery might pass without difficulty. The land between Kachwaha and Chanderi is forested. We spent the night in Kachwaha and camped within three kos of Chanderi, having crossed the river at Burhanpur.

THE CONQUEST OF CHANDERI

The citadel at Chanderi is on the top of a hill, with the outer fortress and town situated on the slope. The flat road over which a cart can go passes by the base of the fortress. Marching from Burhanpur, we proceeded a kos farther down from Chanderi because of the carts. I spent one night there and then, on Tuesday the twenty-eighth, camped atop the dam next to Bahjat Khan's pool. The next morning I mounted, and posts were distributed to the center, right, and left wings around the perimeter of the fortress. Master Ali-Qulï selected a flat place from which to fire. Overseers and shovelers were appointed to set up the batteries for firing the mortars. All the soldiers were ordered to make ready the shields, ladders, and *bükri tura*,[166] implements of siege.

Chanderi formerly belonged to the king of Mandu. [333b] After Sultan Nasiruddin died [in 1500], one of his sons, Sultan Mahmud, who is currently in Mandu, seized control of Mandu and that area. Another son, Muhammad Shah, got hold of Chanderi and took refuge with Sultan Iskandar, who sent a large army and took Muhammad Shah under his protection. After Sultan Iskandar, during the time of Sultan Ibrahim [ca. 1517–26], Muhammad Shah died, leaving an infant son, Ahmad Shah. Sultan Ibrahim deposed Ahmad Shah and installed his own man. When Rana Sanga led his forces to Dholpur against Ibrahim, Ibrahim's officers rebelled. It was then that Chanderi fell into Sanga's hands and he gave it to his high-ranking advisor, the infidel Medini Rao.

At this time Medini Rao was in the Chanderi fortress with four or five thousand infidels. Since Arayish Khan had some acquaintance with him, he and Shaykh Ghuran were sent to assure him of my favor and compassion toward him and promise him Shamsabad in lieu of Chanderi. One or two of his important men came over to us. I don't know whether he himself mistrusted us or whether he was overreliant on the fastness of his fort, but in any case the overture did not succeed. Intent upon taking the Chanderi fortress by force, on Tuesday morning, the sixth of Jumada I [January 28], we marched from Bahjat Khan's reservoir and camped next to the middle reservoir near the fortress. [334] This very morning while we were on the move, Khalifa brought a letter or two, the contents of which were: "The army that was assigned to Purab has gone ill prepared, engaged in battle, and

been defeated. They have abandoned Lucknow and gone to Kannauj."
I saw that for this reason Khalifa was greatly perturbed and fearful. I
said, "Alarm and fear are unreasonable. Nothing will happen that has
not been foreordained by God. Since this labor lies ahead of us, we
should not speak of it, but tomorrow we will bring force to bear upon
the fortress. After that we will face whatever happens." The foe was
making fast the citadel. Within the outer fortress people were moving
around one by one and two by two on various errands. That evening
my soldiers converged from all directions upon the outer fortress, in
which there were only a few men. Without putting up much resis-
tance, they fled into the citadel.

On Wednesday morning the seventh of Jumada I [January 29] the
soldiers were ordered to arm themselves, go to their stations, and prepare for an assault. As soon as I mounted with my drums and standards, they were to attack from all directions. I held the drums and
standards in abeyance until battle was engaged and went to watch
Master Ali-Quli's artillery fire. He fired three or four shots. Since he
was on a flat place and the ramparts [334b] were strong and completely of stone, it did not do any damage. It has been mentioned that
the Chanderi citadel is situated on a hill. On one side a water conduit
has been made to bring water in, and the rampart where the water conduit is is lower than the hill. This is the one place where an assault can
be made. The posts of the right and left flanks of the center and of the
royal tabin included this place. They were battling from all sides, but
they were focusing their strength more on this place than any other.
No matter how many stones the infidels threw or how much fire they
lit and hurled from above to drive them back, the warriors did not
withdraw. Finally Nur Beg's brother Shahïm got up at the spot where
the outer fortification rampart joined the water-conduit rampart.
Other warriors also scaled the walls in two or three other places. The
infidels on the water conduit turned and fled. The conduit was taken.
In the upper fortress they did not fight much but quickly ran away.
Many men climbed up and got into the upper fortress. After a short
time the infidels all came out stripped naked and began to fight. Many
people were put to flight and forced to jump over the ramparts. Several
men were struck with swords and killed. The reason so many were
hastening from atop the ramparts was that they had realized they were
going to lose and, having put their wives and womenfolk to the sword

and resigning themselves to death, came out stripped to fight. Our men pressed on, however, from all directions [335] and forced them to flee from the ramparts. Two to three hundred infidels entered Medini Rao's quarters, where they killed each other almost to the last by having one man hold a sword while the others willingly bent their necks. And thus most of them went to hell.

Through God's grace such a famous fortress was conquered within two or three gharis without standards or drums and without any fighting in earnest. A tower of infidels' skulls was erected on the hill on the northwest side of Chanderi. The chronogram for this victory was found to be *fath-i daru'l-harb*.[167] I versified it as follows:

> For a time Chanderi was full of infidels and the realm of war. I conquered the fortress in battle, the chronogram for which is "conquest of the infidel realm."

A DESCRIPTION OF CHANDERI

Chanderi is a superb place. All around the area are many flowing streams. The citadel is located atop a hill, and inside it a huge reservoir has been carved from rock. Another large reservoir was in the water conduit we captured. The houses of rich and poor alike are made of stone. Those of the grandees are elaborately carved, but the ordinary people's are not. The roofs are made of stone slabs instead of tile. [335b] In front of the fortress are three large reservoirs formed by dams built by former rulers. The land is elevated. The lake, called the Betwa, three kos from Chanderi, is renowned throughout Hindustan for its good, sweet water. It is truly a nice little lake, in which are many pieces of rock suitable for building. Chanderi lies ninety kos to the south of Agra. There the North Star is at twenty-five degrees elevation.

The next morning, Thursday, we marched from the vicinity of the fortress and camped next to Mallu Khan's reservoir. We had come to attack Raisen, Bhilsan, and Sarangpur, which were infidel regions held by Silhadi. Once these were taken we would proceed to Chitor against Sanga. Since distressing news was being received, however, we summoned the begs for consultation, during which it was realized that it was a priority to proceed to repel the sedition of those rebels. Chanderi was given to the above-mentioned Ahmad Shah,[168] the grandson of Sultan Nasiruddin. Fifty lacs from Chanderi were made royal demesne, and Mulla Apaq was made military governor with two or three thousand Turks and Hindustanis to assist Ahmad Shah.

When these affairs had been settled, [336] we marched back on Sunday the eleventh of Jumada I [February 2] to Mallu Khan's reservoir and camped next to the river at Burhanpur. Yaka Khwaja and Ja'far Khwaja were sent from Bhander to bring boats from Kalpi to the Kanar Ford. On Sunday the twenty-fourth we stopped at the ford, and the soldiers were ordered to begin crossing.

News arrived that the forward detachment had abandoned Kannauj and pulled back to Rapri. Abu'l-Muhammad Nayzabaz had made fast the Shamsabad fortress, but many men had come and taken it by force. During the three or four days it took the army to cross the river, halt was called on both sides. Once across, we proceeded toward Kannauj, having dispatched some guerilla warriors in advance to gather intelligence on the rebels. When we were two or three kos from Kannauj, they brought news that when our spies had been spotted, Ma'ruf's son had fled from Kannauj. Biban, Bayazid, and Ma'ruf had gotten wind of us and crossed the Ganges, halting on the eastern shore in hopes of being able to block our crossing.

On Thursday the sixth of Jumada II [February 27] we bypassed Kannauj and stopped on the western shore of the Ganges. Some of our warriors went and seized a few of the rebels' boats. [336b] From upstream and downstream thirty to forty boats, large and small, were brought. Mir-Muhammad Jalaban was sent to find a suitable place to make a bridge and find bridge-building materials. He found a place to his liking one kos downstream from camp. Overseers were appointed. Near the place where the bridge was to be made Master Ali-Quli found a place to set up his mortar and got busy firing shells. Downstream from the place where the bridge was to be made Mustafa Rumi had the artillery caissons taken out to an island and started firing. Upstream from the bridge, batteries were set up from which the matchlockmen fired their matchlocks. Once or twice Malik Qasim Moghul and some warriors crossed by boat and fought well, though they were few. One evening Baba Sultan, Darwesh, and ten to fifteen men crossed with nothing but audacity, returning without having engaged in battle or accomplishing anything. They were severely reprimanded for making such a crossing. Finally, in a heroic gesture, Malik

Qasim and a few men battled the enemy all the way to their camp. The rebels came out with many men and an elephant and fought furiously, forcing our men to withdraw. Before they could get into the boat and get it moving, [337] the elephant came up and sank it. Malik Qasim died in that encounter.

During these few days while the bridge was being built Master Ali-Qulï got off a few good shots. The first day he fired eight shots. The second day he fired sixteen, and so on for three or four days. The shots were made with the mortar "Ghazi," which was the mortar he fired during the battle with Sanga the Infidel, for which reason it was named Ghazi. He set up another rather large mortar, but it shattered the first time it was fired. The matchlockmen also fired a lot of shots and brought down many men and horses....[169] When the bridge was nearly finished, on Wednesday the nineteenth of Jumada II, we marched out onto it. The Afghans, who were quite skeptical about it, had been hooting and making fun of us.

On Thursday the bridge was completed. A few foot soldiers and Lahoris crossed, and a skirmish was held. On Friday the royal *tabin* from the center and the warriors from the right and left flanks crossed on foot with the matchlockmen. The Afghans, with their elephants, came forward in force, fully armed and mounted, and drove back the men of the left flank. The men of the center and right flank held their ground and fought the enemy back. [337b] Two men emerged quickly from the mass and slashed with their swords. One of them was felled and captured right there. The other man and his horse were both hit many times. The horse reared back and fell in the midst of the soldiers. That day seven or eight heads were brought in. Many received arrow and gun wounds. There was fighting until late that afternoon. That night all who had crossed were brought back.

If that very Friday evening men had been sent across, most of the enemy would probably have been taken captive. It occurred to me, however, that the previous year we had set out from Sikri on Nawroz, which fell on a Tuesday, to fight Sanga and we had defeated the enemy on a Saturday. This year we had set out to fight the enemy on Nawroz, which fell on a Wednesday. If we were victorious over the enemy on Sunday, it would be a remarkable coincidence. For this reason no one was sent across. On Saturday they did not come to fight but stood afar in formation. The same day, the caissons were taken across, and at dawn the order was given for the men to cross. When the drums were being sounded news came from the vanguard that the enemy had taken flight. Chïn Temür Sultan was ordered to take a contingent out in pursuit of the foe. Muhammad-Ali Jang-Jang, Husamuddin Ali Khalifa, Khalifa's Muhibb-Ali, Baba Qashqa's Kuki, [338] Baba Qashqa's Dost-Muhammad, Baqi Tashkandi, and Wali Qïzïl were assigned to lead the groups of the pursuing party with Sultan and not to disobey his orders. I myself crossed early in the morning. Orders were given for the camels to be taken across at the ford that had been found downstream. That day, Sunday, camp was made on the riverbank one kos from Bangarmau. Those assigned to the pursuit contingent had not proceeded well, and they too were halted at Bangarmau. That afternoon they were sent out from Bangarmau. The next morning camp was made next to the reservoir in front of Bangarmau.

This day Tokhta Buqa Sultan, my uncle Kichik Khan's son, came and paid me homage. On Saturday the twenty-ninth of Jumada II [March 21], I toured Lucknow, crossed the Gomati River, and halted. That same day I bathed in the Gomati. I don't know whether I got some water in my ear or whether it was the effect of the air, but my right ear got stopped up, although I had only a little pain for a few days. A march or two from Oudh, a man came with the following report from Chïn Temür Sultan: "The enemy is sitting on the other side of the Sarju. Send auxiliaries." Around a thousand warriors under Qaracha were dispatched from the center to reinforce him.

On Saturday the seventh of Rajab [March 28], camp was made two or three kos downstream from Oudh at the confluence of the Gogra and the Sarju. [338b] Until this day Shaykh Bayazid was supposed to be on the other side of the Sarju opposite Oudh.[170] He had sent a letter and held deliberations with Sultan. Realizing his deceit, Sultan sent a man to Qaracha at noon to get ready to cross the river. As soon as Qaracha joined Sultan they crossed. Bayazid had around fifty cavalrymen and three or four elephants. Unable to hold their ground, they fled. A few men were unhorsed, and their heads were sent in. Beykhub Sultan,[171] Turdï Beg, Baba Chuhra, Qoch Beg, and Baqi Shiqavul crossed after Sultan. Those who had crossed earlier pursued Shaykh Bayazid until evening. Shaykh Bayazid went into the jungle to escape. That night Chïn Temür Sultan camped on the banks of the still water and then mounted at midnight to make a drive in pursuit of the enemy.

After going forty kos they reached the place where the baggage train was, but the foe had fled. From here the posse spread out in all directions. Baqi Shiqavul and a few warriors went in pursuit of the enemy, reached their baggage train, and brought in some Afghans as prisoners.

Halt was called for a few days at this site in order to consolidate affairs in Oudh and that area. We had been told of a hunting ground seven or eight kos upstream from Oudh. Mir-Muhammad Jalaban was sent to inspect it. He looked at the fords on the Gogra and Sarju and returned. [339] On Thursday the twelfth [April 2] we rode out to hunt.[172]

EVENTS OF THE YEAR 935
(1528-29)[173]

Askari,[174] whom I had summoned before the Chanderi expedition to govern Multan, came on Friday the third of Muharram [September 18] and paid homage in my private quarters. The next morning Khwandamir the historian,[175] Mawlana Shihab the enigmatist,[176] and Mir Ibrahim the dulcimer player, a relative of Yunus Ali, all of whom had long ago left Herat wishing to enroll in my service, came and paid homage. On Sunday afternoon, the fifth of the month [September 20], I crossed the Jumna and entered the Agra fort, intending to make a tour of Gwalior, which is called Galior in books. I rode there to bid farewell to Fakhrijahan Begim and Khadija Sultan Begim, who were going to set out for Kabul within the next few days.

BABUR PROCEEDS TO GWALIOR
VIA DHOLPUR

Muhammad-Zaman Mirza requested permission to remain in Agra. That night we proceeded three or four kos, stopped beside a reservoir, and slept. We performed our prayers rather early and rode off. We spent the noon beside the Gambhir River and rode out in the afternoon. Along the way I mixed with barley flour some medicine Mulla Rafi' had made to raise our spirits and swallowed it. It tasted horrible.

A little before noon I halted at the garden and pavilion I had ordered a kos west of Dholpur. [339b] The place where the garden and pavilion are situated is at the end of a mountain spur, which is a solid piece of red building stone; I had ordered stone to be cut from the mountain and taken there. If a piece remained large enough to hew into a pavilion in one piece, then they were to do it. If not, they were to cut down the stone and make a pool in the courtyard. Since the stone broke and was not large enough, Master Shah-Muhammad the stonemason was ordered to design a scalloped octagonal pool on top of the solid rock that had been shaped into a courtyard. The stonecutters got to work in earnest. To the north of the spot where the pool of solid rock had been placed were many trees, mangoes, eugenias, and all sorts of trees. In the middle, I had a ten-by-ten well made, and it was nearly finished. The water from the well went to the pool. To the northwest of the pool, Sultan Sikandar had made a dam, on top of which he had built some structures. Behind the dam the monsoon rains collected and formed a large lake. On the eastern side of the lake was a garden. [340] To the east of the lake I ordered them to carve some things like benches from solid stone, and on the western side a mosque. Tuesday and Wednesday we stayed in Dholpur to tend to these affairs.

On Thursday we mounted and crossed the Chambhal River. We performed the afternoon prayer on the riverbank, left the Chambhal in the afternoon, and halted, having crossed the Kunwari River late in the evening. The water was so deep due to the rains that the horses had to be made to swim across. We crossed by boat. The next morning, Friday, which was Ashura,[177] we rode off, spent noon in a village, and then stopped one kos from Gwalior to the north of a charbagh I had ordered made the previous year. The next day, after the noon prayer, we mounted and made a tour of the hills to the north of Gwalior and inspected the namazgah before entering the city through the Hathi Pol, which was next to Rajah Man Singh's palace.[178] Late that afternoon we dismounted at Rajah Bikramajit's buildings, where Rahimdad was staying.[179]

That night I took some opium for the pain in my ear—the moonlight also induced me to take it. The next morning I really suffered from an opium hangover and vomited a lot. Nevertheless, I went out on a tour of all Man Singh's and Bikramajit's buildings. [340b]

A TOUR OF GWALIOR

The buildings are strange. In addition to being higgledy-piggledy and inharmonious, they are all of carved stone. Of all the rajahs' edifices, Man Singh's are the most beautiful and the best.

One side of the wall of Man Singh's palace is toward the east, and this side is more elaborate than the others.[180] It is approximately forty or fifty yards high. The entire face, which is of carved stone, has been covered with white stucco. In some places it is four stories tall. Inside, the two lower stories are extremely dark. After being inside for a while a bit of light can be perceived, but we toured them by candlelight anyway. On one side of the palace are five domes, between which are small, squarish domelets in the Hindustani style. To the tops of the five large domes have been attached plates of gilded copper. The outside of the walls are covered all around with green glazed tiles, which depict plantain trees. In the tower on the eastern side is the Hathi Pol. (*Hathi* means "elephant," and *pol* means "gate.") At the exit to the gate is a statue of an elephant with two keepers on its back. Since it has been made in the exact likeness of the animal, it is called Hathi Pol. [341] The lowest story of the four-story building has a window from which the elephant statue can be seen quite near. The upper story comprises the above-mentioned domes. The dwelling rooms are on the second story, which is below ground level. Although they have been decorated in the Hindustani style, they are rather airless.

The palace of Man Singh's son, Bikramajit, is located in an open space toward the northern fortification wall. The son's buildings are not equal to the father's. There is one large dome, in which it is very dark, although after a time some light can be perceived. Under it is another, smaller structure into which no light penetrates from any direction. Rahimdad had a small hall made on top of the large dome, and he stayed in Bikramajit's buildings. A passageway has been made leading from Bikramajit's to his father's buildings, but neither path is apparent from the outside nor can any trace of it be seen from the inside, although light gets in from somewhere. It is a fantastic passageway.

After touring the buildings we rode to the madrasa built by Rahimdad. We had a look at the garden he made next to the large reservoir on the southern side [341b] and came back late to the charbagh, where the army was camped. Many flowers had been planted there, with many lovely red oleanders. Generally the oleanders of these parts are like peach blossoms, but the Gwalior oleander is a beautiful bright red. I had some brought to Agra and planted in the gardens there. To the south of the garden is a large reservoir where the monsoon rainwater collects. To the west of the reservoir is a tall temple, next to which Sultan Iltutmish[181] had a congregational mosque built. The temple is extremely tall—the tallest structure in the fortress—and both the Gwalior fortress and the temple can be plainly seen from the hill in Dholpur. They say that the stones of this temple were cut and transported from the large reservoir. In the garden is a squat, inharmonious wooden hall, and at the garden gate are ugly porticos in the Hindustani style.

The next day at noon I mounted to tour the places in Gwalior I had not yet seen. I inspected the building called Badalgarh, which is outside the fortification walls, came back in through the Hathi Pol, and went to a valley called Urwahi.

The place called Urwahi is located to the west of the fortification wall. Although it lies outside the rampart built across the mountain, two high rampart walls are situated at the mouth of the valley, one inside the other. These ramparts are forty to fifty yards high. The inner rampart, the longer of the two, [342] is connected on both ends to the fortress rampart. In the open space it creates, another, lower rampart has been extended, but it does not go from end to end and was made solely for obtaining water. Inside it a stepwell has been made for drawing water. Ten or fifteen steps lead down to the water. Over the gate going from the large rampart to the stepwell rampart is a stone in which is carved Sultan Shamsuddin Iltutmish's name with the year 630 [1232–33]. At the base of the outer rampart, outside the fortification wall, is a large reservoir, which often dries up when the water is low. The water feeds the conduit. Inside Urwahi are two other large reservoirs. The people of the fortress prefer this water to any other.

Urwahi is surrounded on three sides by a single mountain, the stone of which is not so red as that of Bayana but somewhat paler. The solid rock outcroppings around Urwahi have been hewn into idols, large and small. On the southern side is a large idol, approximately twenty yards tall. They are shown stark naked with all their private parts exposed. [342b] Around the two large reservoirs inside Urwahi have been dug twenty to twenty-five wells, from which water is drawn to irrigate the vegetation, flowers, and trees planted there. Urwahi is not a bad place. In fact, it is rather nice. Its one drawback was the idols, so I ordered them destroyed. I observed the place of the Sultan Pol, which formerly led from Urwahi to the fortress but which had been shut up from the time of the infidels. At evening prayer time I returned to the garden made by Rahimdad and stayed there overnight.

On Tuesday the fourteenth of the month [September 29] emissaries came from Rana Sanga's second son, Bikramajit,[182] who was with his mother, Padmavati, in the Ranthambhor fort. Before I toured Gwalior, emissaries came from Bikramajit's chief minister, a Hindu named Asok, to assure me of Bikramajit's submission and fealty and to request a stipend of seventy lacs. It was decided to hand Ranthambhor over to him, and, having rewarded him with estates as he requested, we gave his men leave to withdraw.

As we were going to be touring Gwalior, we had given those men of his a date to return to Gwalior. It was now several days past the date. Asok, who was said to be a close relative of Bikramajit's mother, [343] explained the situation to the mother and son. They, in agreement with Asok, accepted fealty and suzerainty. In Bikramajit's possession were a headband and golden belt that Sultan Mahmud had been wearing when he was defeated and taken prisoner by Sanga. Bikramajit's elder brother, Ratansen, who was at that time the *rana*[183] in his father's stead and holder of Chitor, demanded the headband and belt from his younger brother. He refused. Through his men who had come he promised me the headband and belt and asked for Bayana in exchange for Ranthambhor. We dissuaded them from Bayana and promised Shamsabad in exchange for Ranthambhor. The same day, the emissaries were dressed in robes of honor and given leave with a rendezvous fixed at Bayana in nine days.

Riding out from this garden we made a tour of Gwalior's temples, some of which are two and three stories but are squat and in the ancient style with dadoes entirely of figures sculpted in stone. Other temples are like madrasas, with porches and large, tall domes and chambers like those of a madrasa. Atop the chambers are narrow, constricted domes carved of stone, [343b] and in the lower chambers are stone-carved idols. Having examined the edifices, we went out through the west gate of Gwalior, went around the south side of the fortress, and dismounted back at the charbagh that Rahimdad had made in front of the Hathi Pol.

There Rahimdad had a feast prepared. He served excellent food and presented many gifts of goods and cash worth four lacs. I left on horseback and went to my own garden late that night.

EXCURSION TO A WATERFALL

On Wednesday the fifteenth [September 30], I went out to make a tour of a waterfall six kos southeast of Gwalior. As we were rather late getting to horse, it was after noon when we reached our destination. From a cliff a cord[184] high a one-mill stream cascades down. Farther down from where the water falls is a large lake, and above the falls is a solid rock cliff. The bottom of the falls is also solid rock. Everywhere the water falls a lake is formed. On the banks of the stream are little pieces of rock one can sit on; the water, however, does not always flow. We sat down at the top of the falls and had some ma'jun. We then toured upstream as far as the source of the stream. We returned and went up on a rise, where we sat for a while. The musicians played their instruments, and the singers sang some songs. [344] Ebony trees, which the people of India call *tindu*, were shown to those who had not already seen them.

Coming down from the hill, we got to horse and rode off between the evening and bedtime prayers. At around the second watch we came to a place and slept. The first watch[185] of the day was almost over when we dismounted at the charbagh.

On Friday the seventeenth [October 2] I toured a village called Suhjana, Silhadi's birthplace,[186] and the lime and sadaphal orchard up from the village in a valley among the hills, returning to the charbagh at the first watch.

On Sunday the nineteenth [October 4], just before dawn, we rode out from the charbagh and crossed the Kunwari River and spent noon there. In the early afternoon we rode on, crossed the Chambhal River as the sun was setting, entered the Dholpur fortress between the evening and bedtime prayers, and toured by lamplight the bathhouse built by Abu'l-Fath.[187] Riding from there, we stopped on the top of the dam where a new garden was being made. The next morning I stayed to inspect the places that had been ordered. They had not yet raised the face of the scalloped pool I had ordered out of the solid rock, so I ordered more than a thousand stonecutters to come and cut down the base of the pool so that water could be put in and the edges leveled. Late that afternoon they got the face of the pool loose and filled it with water. [344b] Then they got to work leveling and smoothing the edges by means of the water. This time I ordered another cistern to be hewn of solid rock, with a small pool inside, also to be cut from solid rock.

On Monday [October 5] there was a ma'jun party. On Tuesday, I remained right there. That night, after breaking the fast and having something to eat, we rode out intending to go to Sikri. At around the second watch we dismounted somewhere to sleep. I don't know whether the cold had had some effect on my ear or what, but that evening it hurt a lot and I could not sleep. At dawn we moved out and at the first watch reached the garden I had built at Sikri. Because the garden wall and well buildings were not to my liking, the overseers were punished and threatened.

Between the afternoon and evening prayers we rode out of Sikri, passed Madhakur, dismounted somewhere, and slept. Riding on from there, we came to Agra at the first watch. In the Agra fortress I saw Khadija Sultan Begim, who had stayed to settle some business when Fakhrijahan Begim left. I crossed the Jumna and came to the Hasht Bihisht garden. On Saturday the third of Safar [October 17], three of my great lady aunts, Gawharshad Begim, Badi'uljamal Begim, and Aq Begim,[188] and, of the younger ladies, Khwanzada Begim (Sultan-Mas'ud Mirza's daughter), Sultan Bakht Begim's daughter, and my *yengächichä*'s[189] granddaughter, Zaynab Sultan Begim, came past Tota and camped beside the river at the edge of the suburbs. [345] I went to see them between the afternoon and evening prayers and returned by boat.

AN ENVOY IS SENT TO MONITOR THE SUBMISSION OF RANTHAMBHOR

On Monday the fifth of Safar [October 19], Hamusi son of Deva, an old Hindu retainer from Bhera, was attached to Bikramajit's earlier and later envoys and dispatched to take charge in his own manner and fashion of the handing over of Ranthambhor and the accepting of fealty. The man we were sending was to observe and, when he was satisfied, return. If Bikramajit stood by his word, I also promised that, God willing, I would make him rana in his father's stead and establish him in Chitor.

A DEFICIT IN THE TREASURY

Around this time Iskandar's and Ibrahim's treasuries in Delhi and Agra ran dry. To meet the requirements for the army's weapons, artillery, and gunpowder, on Thursday the eighth of Safar [October 22], an order was issued for stipend holders to remit to the divan 130 percent of their regular payments, to be spent on these accoutrements.

On Saturday the tenth [October 24], Sultan-Muhammad Bakhshi's footman named Shah Qasim, who once before had taken documents of protection to the people of Khurasan, was sent back to Herat taking documents, the contents of which were, in effect, that, thank God, our minds were at ease concerning the rebels in the east and west of Hindustan [345b] and the infidels. This coming summer, God willing, we would certainly get ourselves to Kabul somehow or other. Ahmad Afshar was also sent a document, and on the margin I wrote in my own hand asking for Faridun the *qopuz* player. At noon that day I began to take quicksilver.[190]

On Wednesday the twenty-first [November 4] a Hindustani runner brought letters from Kamran and Khwaja Dost Khawand. Khwaja Dost Khawand had reached Kabul on the tenth of Dhu'l-Hijja and gone on to see Humayun. At Hupian one of Kamran's men came to the khwaja, saying, "Let the khwaja come. Let him deliver whatever documents he has. Let him say what he has to say and then depart." Kamran arrived in Kabul on the seventeenth of Dhu'l-Hijja [September 2], and after speaking with the khwaja had him escorted to Zafar Fort on the twenty-eighth of Dhu'l-Hijja [September 13].

There was good news in the letters that came. Prince Tahmasp, determined to drive out the Uzbek, had captured Rinish the Uzbek at Damghan, killed him, and massacred his men. As soon as Ubayd Khan received confirmed intelligence on the Qïzïlbash's movements, he lifted the siege from Herat and went to Merv, where he summoned the Uzbek princes from Samarkand and that area. The princes in Transoxiana all went to Merv to help. [346] The same runner brought the news that a son had been born to Humayun by the daughter of Yadgar Taghayï.[191] Kamran was also about to get married in Kabul to the daughter of his uncle Sultan-Ali Mirza. This same day we had Sayyid Dakkani Shirazi the dowser clad in a robe of honor, gave him a reward, and ordered him to finish the fountain-well however he thought best.

VERSIFICATION OF A TREATISE BY KHWAJA UBAYDULLAH

On Friday the twenty-third [November 6] such an inflammation appeared in my bowels that I had difficulty performing the congregational prayer in the mosque. Some time later I reperformed the noon prayer in the library, but in great pain. Already on Sunday, I was having fever and chills. On the eve of Tuesday the twenty-seventh it occurred to me to make a versified rendering of Khwaja Ubaydullah's treatise, the *Walidiyya*.[192] I put my confidence in the saint's intercession and said to myself, "If this intention is acceptable to the saint, then too, just as the author of the *Burda*'s poem was accepted and he was cured of his paralysis,[193] if I am delivered of this illness it will be a sign of my poem's being accepted." With this intention I began to versify the treatise in the meter *Ramal musaddas makhbun*, with the final foot sometimes *abtar* and sometimes *makhbun*,[194] **[346b]** because Mawlana Abdul-Rahman Jami's *Subhat* is also in that meter.[195] That very night I composed thirteen lines. I stuck to it so assiduously that every day I wrote no less than ten lines, skipping one day at most. Last year—and every time—when such an illness had struck it had lasted at least a month to forty days. By the grace of God and the saint's powers, on Thursday the twenty-ninth of the month [November 12] it began to abate. Once more I was delivered of the sickness. On Saturday the eighth of Rabiʿ I [November 20], I completed the versification of the treatise. I had composed, on the average, fifty-two lines per day.

On Wednesday the twenty-eighth [November 11] orders were sent to the soldiers all around that since we would soon, God willing, be mounting a campaign, they should gather as quickly as possible with their arms. On Sunday the ninth of Rabiʿ I [November 21], Beg Muhammad Taʿliqchi came. He had gone at the end of Muharram last year to take Humayun a robe of honor and a horse.

MESSENGERS FROM HUMAYUN

On Monday the tenth, Begginä Ways Laghari and one of Humayun's servants named Buyan Shaykh came from Humayun. Begginä came to give the glad tidings of the birth of Humayun's son, who had been named al-Aman. For the birth, Shaykh Abu'l-Wajd had invented the chronogram [347] *Shah-i-sa'adatmand.*[196]

Buyan Shaykh had set out from Kabul long after Begginä. He had parted from Humayun on Friday the ninth of Safar [October 23] at a place called Dushanbe on the banks of the Kishm, and on Monday the tenth of Rabi' I [November 22] arrived in Agra. He certainly made good time. (Once before this same Buyan Shaykh had gone from Zafar Fort to Kandahar in eleven days.) Buyan Shaykh brought the news of the Prince of Persia's advance and the defeat of the Uzbeks, details of which follow.

REPORT OF THE QIZILBASH-UZBEK
BATTLE AT JAM[197]

Prince Tahmasp advanced rapidly from Persia with forty thousand men and matchlocks and artillery caissons arrayed in the Anatolian manner. In Bistam and Damghan he seized Rinish the Uzbek, put him and his men to death, and kept on proceeding rapidly. Köpäk Bey's son, Qambar-Ali, was also defeated by the Qïzïlbash, and returned to Ubayd Khan with only a few men. Ubayd Khan, seeing no use in staying in the vicinity of Herat, sent off urgent messages to all the khans and princes in Balkh, Hissar, Samarkand, and Tashkent and went himself to Merv. They quickly gathered. From Tashkent, Sevinchäk Khan's next to eldest son, Baraq Sultan; from Samarkand and Mian Kal, Köchüm Khan, Abu-Sa'id Sultan, Pulad Sultan, [347b] and Jani Beg Sultan and his sons; from Hissar, Hamza Sultan's and Mahdi Sultan's sons; from Balkh, Kitin Qara Sultan—all these princes went posthaste and joined Ubayd Khan in Merv. They were 105,000 strong. A spy reported that Prince Tahmasp, thinking that Ubayd Khan was sitting in the vicinity of Herat with only a few soldiers, had set out with forty thousand men. However, when he received word of the gathering in Merv, he had entrenched himself in Radkan Meadow.

The Uzbeks learned of this and, taking no notice of their foe, decided in council as follows: "Let all of us khans and sultans sit in Mashhad. We will assign twenty thousand men to a few princes to encircle the area of the Qïzïlbash's camp and not allow them to stick their heads out. When the sun enters Scorpio we will order the rainmakers to cause rain, and thus reducing them to inability, we will take them!" So saying, they marched out of Merv. The Prince of Persia left Mashhad and confronted the Uzbeks at Jam and Kharjerd, whereupon defeat was dealt to the Uzbeks. Many Uzbek princes were seized and put to death. In one letter it was written that [348] it had not been learned for certain whether any Uzbek prince other than Köchüm Khan had gotten out alive, for no one who had been with the army had come in as yet. The Uzbek princes in Hissar abandoned the fortress and fled. Ibrahim Jani's son Chalma, whose name was originally Isma'il, was said to have been in the Hissar fortress.

A LETTER TO HUMAYUN

I wrote letters to Humayun and Kamran. On Friday the fourteenth [November 27], when the letters and documents were ready, they were handed posthaste to Buyan Shaykh, and he was given leave to depart. On Saturday the fifteenth he was escorted out of Agra.

This is a copy of the letter to Humayun:

To Humayun. Thinking of you with much longing, I greet you. My words are these: On Monday the tenth of Rabi' I [November 23], Begginä and Buyan Shaykh came. From your letters and reports we have become acquainted with the situation on both sides of the Hindu Kush.

I give thanks for your son, a son to you and a beloved one to me.

May God ever grant me and you such joy. Amen, O Lord of the Universe. You have named him "al-Aman." May God bless him. However, although you yourself may write it thus, you have not considered the fact that frequently the common people will say either "Alaman" or "Ilaman." [348b] Moreover, names with "al-" are rare. Nonetheless, may God bless and keep both him and his name. For my sake and yours, may He keep al-Aman in fortune and happiness for many years, for many decades. God has ordered our affairs through his great grace and generosity. Such an event has not happened in how many decades?

Item: On Tuesday the eleventh rumors were heard to the effect that the people of Balkh had summoned Qurban and let him in.[198]

Item: Kamran and the Kabul begs were ordered to go join you, and you all will proceed to Hissar or Samarkand or whichever direction is in our best interests. Through God's grace you will defeat your enemies, take their territory, and make your friends happy by overthrowing the foe. God willing, this is your time to risk your life and wield your sword. Do not fail to make the most of an opportunity that presents itself. Indolence and luxury do not suit kingship.

Conquest tolerates not inaction; the world is his who hastens most. When one is master one may rest from everything—except being king.[199]

If, by God's grace and favor, Balkh and Hissar are won and subdued, let one of your men stay in Hissar and one of Kamran's in Balkh. If, by God's grace and favor, Samarkand is also subdued, you stay there yourself and, God willing, I will make Hissar royal demesne. [349] If Kamran thinks Balkh is small, write me. God willing, I will make up the deficiency to him out of those other territories.

Item: You know that this rule has always been observed: six parts to you and five to Kamran. Always observe this rule yourself and do not break it.

Item: Conduct yourself well with your younger brother. Elder brothers need to have restraint. It is my hope that you will get along well with him, for he has grown up to be a religiously observant and fine young man. Let him also display no deficiency in homage and respect for you.

Item: I have a few complaints of you. For two or three years now none of your men has come. The man I sent returned exactly a year later. Is this proper?

Item: In your letters you keep talking about being alone. Solitude is a flaw in kingship, as has been said, "If you are fettered, resign yourself; but if you are a lone rider, your reins are free."[200] There is no bondage like the bondage of kingship. In kingship it is improper to seek solitude.

Item: As I asked, you have written your letters, but you didn't read them over, for if you had had a mind to read them, you would have found that you could not. [349b] After reading them you certainly would have changed them. Although your writing can be read with difficulty, it is excessively obscure. Who has ever heard of prose designed to be an enigma? Your spelling is not bad, although it is not entirely correct either. You wrote *iltifat* with the wrong *t;* you wrote *qulinj* with a *y.*[201] Your handwriting can be made out somehow or other, but with all these obscure words of yours the meaning is not entirely clear. Probably your laziness in writing letters is due to the fact that you try to make it too fancy. From now on write with uncomplicated, clear, and plain words. This will cause less difficulty both for you and for your reader.

Item: You are going on a great mission. Consult the experienced begs for strategy and tactics and do what they say. If you want to make me happy, stop sitting by yourself and avoiding people. Don't leave the decision to your brother and your begs, but invite them in twice a day, consult with them on whatever has come up, and make your decisions with the agreement of these supporters of yours.

Item: Khwaja Kalan learned to be free and easy with me through constant contact. [350] So should you mingle with others as I did with him. If, through God's grace, the situation over there should demand less attention and you do not need Kamran, station trustworthy men in Balkh and let him come to me.

Item: There were such conquests and victories while we were in Kabul that I consider Kabul my lucky piece and have made it royal demesne. Let none of you covet it.

Item: Conduct yourself well. Make friends with Sultan Ways. Bring him in and act upon his opinion, for he is an experienced man. Keep the army disciplined and in training. Buyan Shaykh has had verbal instructions from me that he will communicate to you. With longing, peace. Written on Wednesday the thirteenth of Rabi' I [November 26].

In my own hand I wrote Kamran and Khwaja Kalan letters of similar content and sent them off.

ASKARI IS SENT TO THE EAST

On Wednesday the nineteenth [December 2], I summoned the mirzas, sultans, and Turk and India officers for consultation, during which the following was discussed. Since this year it was absolutely necessary for the army to advance in every direction, Askari was to continue to Purab. The sultans and officers who were on the other side of the Ganges with their armies would join him and then set out in whatever direction seemed in our best interests. These instructions were written, [350b] and Ghiyasuddin Qorchï was dispatched by post horse on Sunday the twenty-second of the month [December 5] to tell the Purab officers under the leadership of Sultan-Junayd Barlas to meet me within sixteen days. Oral instructions were given to the effect that the implements of war were to be culverins, caissons, and matchlocks. As soon as they were ready Askari was sent forward ahead of us. All the princes and officers on the other side of the Ganges were ordered to assemble with him and proceed under God's protection in whichever direction was thought in our best interests. "Consult our supporters there," I said. "If I am needed for any reason, I will ride straight there, God willing, as soon as the man who has gone for a meeting comes back. If the Bengali is in harmony with us and sincere in his support, and if there is nothing there that requires my presence, write and let me know. I'm not going to stand around idly watching: I'll go on a campaign in another direction. You take Askari, proceed after consultation with our supporters, and take care of affairs there with God's favor."

On Saturday the twenty-ninth of Rabi' I [December 12], Askari was clad in a regal robe of honor with a girth dagger and rewarded with a banner, yak-tail standard, drums, a set of fine horses, ten elephants, a string of camels, a string of mules, [351] and regal paraphernalia. An order was given that he should sit at court. Buttoned robes were awarded to his mulla and two atäkäs, and three sets of tunics to his other liege men.

On Sunday the last day of the month I went to Sultan-Muhammad Bakhshi's house. A *payandaz*[202] was spread and gifts were brought in. He presented goods and cash worth more than two lacs. After the meal and presentation of gifts, we went to another room and had ma'jun. I left there at the third watch, crossed the river, and came to my private quarters.

POST SYSTEM ESTABLISHED
BETWEEN AGRA AND KABUL

On Thursday the fourth of Rabi' II [December 17], it was decided that Chaqmaq Beg with Shahi Tamghachï as recorder should measure by cord the distance from Agra to Kabul. Every nine kos they were to raise a tower twelve yards high with a chardara on top. Every eighteen kos six post horses were to be kept, and maintenance for the post riders, grooms, and feed for the horses were to be assigned. It was ordered that if the place where the post horses were kept was a royal demesne, the above-mentioned items were to be taken care of therefrom. Otherwise, they were to make it the responsibility of the beg on whose estate it was. Chaqmaq and Shahi left Agra that same day. The kos assigned was made to conform to the mile as mentioned in the *Mubin*:[203] [351b]

Four thousand paces is one mile, and this the Indians call a kos. A cubit-and-a-half is this pace, they say; and every cubit is six spans. Every span is four fingers, and every finger is six barleycorns in width.

The measuring cord was to consist of forty cubits of the one-and-a-half-cubit measure mentioned above, which is nine spans, and a hundred of these cords made a mile.

A CELEBRATION IS HELD

On Saturday the sixth of the month [December 19] a feast was held, attended by the Qïzïlbash, Uzbek, and Hindu ambassadors. The Qïzïlbash ambassadors were seated under a canopy erected seventy or eighty yards to my right. Of the begs, Yunus Ali was ordered to sit with the Qïzïlbash. On my left, with the same arrangement, were the Uzbek ambassadors, and Abdullah was ordered to sit with them. I sat on the north side of the newly built octagonal hall hung with grass screens.[204] Five or six yards to my right sat Tokhta Buqa Sultan, Askari, His Eminence Khwaja Ubaydullah's descendants Khwaja Abdul-Shahid, Khwaja Kalan, and Khwaja Chishti; Khalifa; and the khwajas and their retinue, reciters, and mullas who had come from Samarkand. Five or six [352] yards to my left sat Muhammad-Zaman Mirza, Tang-Atmïsh Sultan, Sayyid Rafi', Sayyid Rumi, Shaykh Abu'l-Fath, Shaykh Jamali, Shaykh Shihabuddin Arab, and Sayyid Dakkani. Before the meal, all the princes, khans, grandees, and amirs brought in their gifts of gold, silver, and copper coins, textiles, and other goods. I ordered a mat spread in front of me, onto which the gold and silver coins were poured, while the textiles, brocades, and purses were piled up next to them. A little before the meal, while the presentations were being brought in, enraged camels and elephants were made to fight on an island opposite. A few rams were also, after which the wrestlers began to wrestle. After a large meal was served, Khwaja Abdul-Shahid and Khwaja Kalan were clad in sable jackets faced in light blue, along with robes of honor suitable to their station. Those who had come under Mulla Farrukh and Hafiz were clad in robes. Köchüm Khan's[205] ambassador and Hasan Chäläbi's younger brother were awarded sable jackets with silk buttons and robes of honor suitable to their rank. The ambassadors of Abu-Sa'id Sultan, Mihr Banu Khanïm and her son Pulad Sultan, and Shah Hasan's ambassador were given buttoned mantles and silk tunics. [352b] The two khwajas and the two great ambassadors, who were Köchüm Khan's liege man and Hasan Chäläbi's younger brother, were awarded gold measured by the silverstone and silver measured by the goldstone. (The goldstone is five hundred mithcals, which is a Kabul seer; the silverstone is 250 mithcals, or half a Kabul seer.) Khwaja Mir Sultan and his sons, Hafiz Tashkandi, Mulla Farrukh and his attendants, Mulla Zaman Khwaja, and other emissaries were awarded gold and silver by the quiverful. Yadgar Nasir was awarded a girth dagger. Mir-Muhammad Jalaban had earned a reward for making a fine bridge across the Ganges. He and the matchlockmen Pahlavan Hajji Muhammad, Pahlavan Bahlul, and Wali Parschï[206] were each awarded a dagger, as was Master Ali-Qulï's son. Sayyid Daud Garmseri was given gold and silver coins. My daughter Ma'suma's and my son Hindal's liege men were awarded buttoned mantles and silk robes of honor. Moreover, those who had come from Andizhan, those who had abandoned their homelands and followed us in exile, and those who had come from Sokh and Uchyar were awarded mantles, silk robes, gold and silver coins, textiles, and other goods. Qurban and his Shaykhi liege men and the citizens of Kahmard [353] were also similarly rewarded.

After the food was served I ordered the Hindustani acrobats to come and do tricks, which they did. Acrobats in Hindustan perform feats not seen in our country. One of them is to put seven rings, one on their foreheads, two around their knees, and the remaining four on two fingers and two toes, and to spin them around without cease. Another is to stand on one hand, which is spread on the ground like a peacock's foot, and then spin three rings on the other hand and two feet. Acrobats in our country tie two poles to their feet and walk on them as stilts, but those of Hindustan use only one pole and walk on it without even tying it. In another performance, two acrobats will hold onto each other, in our country cutting two somersaults but in Hindustan somersaulting three or four times. In yet another stunt, one acrobat puts the end of a pole six or seven yards long at his waist and stands holding the pole straight up; then a second acrobat climbs up the pole [353b] and performs tricks on top of it. Sometimes a little acrobat climbs on the head of a bigger one and stands straight; while the bottom person runs back and forth doing tricks, the little one on the other one's head stands ramrod straight without teetering and also performs tricks. Many dancing girls also came in and danced.

At around the evening prayer time many gold, silver, and copper coins were scattered, creating a huge ruckus and free-for-all. Between the evening and bedtime prayer times, five or six specially favored people were summoned to me. We sat past the first watch. The next morning at the second watch we got in a boat and went to the Hasht Bihisht garden.

On Monday, Askari, who was ready to set out on his campaign, came to me to take his leave while I was in the bath and then marched off to the east.

VISIT TO DHOLPUR

On Tuesday, I went to see the pool, well, and buildings I had ordered in Dholpur. I rode out of the garden at the first ghari of the first watch. It was the fifth ghari of the first watch of the night when we reached the Dholpur garden.

On Thursday the eleventh of the month [December 24] the stone well, the twenty-six stone waterspouts, the stone columns, and the water channels carved out of solid rock were ready, and at the third watch of this day water began to be drawn from the well. [354] The stonemasons, carpenters, and all the laborers working in Dholpur were rewarded like the masters and laborers in Agra. As a precaution against having any bad odor created from the well water, it was ordered that the waterwheels should be run and water drawn continuously for fifteen days and nights.

On Friday we rode out of Dholpur with one ghari left of the first watch. The sun had scarcely set when we crossed the river.

AN EYEWITNESS ACCOUNT OF THE QÏZÏLBASH-UZBEK BATTLE AT JAM

On Tuesday the sixteenth [December 29], Dev Sultan's liege man, who had been at the battle between the Qïzïlbash and the Uzbeks, came. He reported that the battle between the Turcomans and the Uzbeks took place in the vicinity of Jam and Kharjerd on Ashura[207] and was fought from sunup till noon. He said that the Uzbeks were three hundred thousand strong and the Turcomans forty to fifty thousand. He had estimated the mass at a hundred thousand, but the Uzbeks said their men were 105,000. The Qïzïlbash had made a defensive array of caissons, mortars, and matchlockmen in the Anatolian fashion and fought thus. They had two thousand caissons and six thousand matchlockmen. Prince Tahmasp and Joha Sultan[208] stood within the caissons with twenty thousand seasoned warriors. Other officers were arrayed outside the caissons in the right and left wings. [354b] When the Uzbeks arrived, they crushed the men outside, unhorsed them continually, and caused them to fall back. As they wheeled backward, the Uzbeks seized their camels and baggage as booty. Finally those inside the caissons opened the chains and poured out. Here there took place a pitched battle. Thrice the Uzbeks charged and forced them to retreat, but it was God's will that the Uzbeks be defeated. Nine princes under the leadership of Köchüm Khan, Ubayd Khan, and Abu-Sa'id Sultan were taken. Of these only Abu-Sa'id Sultan was left alive; the other eight princes were put to death.[209] Ubayd Khan's head was not found, although his body was. Fifty thousand Uzbeks and twenty thousand Turcomans were killed.

That same day Ghiyasuddin Qorchï, who had gone on a mission to Jaunpur to rendezvous in sixteen days,[210] came. Sultan-Junayd had led his men to Kharid, and for that reason he was unable to make the rendezvous. Sultan-Junayd had sent word orally, saying, "Thank God, no action has been seen in these parts that would occasion the emperor's setting out. If the prince comes, and if the sultans, khans, and amirs in these parts are ordered to proceed to meet the prince, it is hoped that everything will turn out to be easy." [355] Although such a response had come from Sultan-Junayd, since people were saying that Mulla Muhammad Muzahhib, who had been sent as an envoy to Bengal after the raid on Sanga the Infidel, would come today or tomorrow, we waited for news from him.

On Friday the nineteenth [January 1, 1529], I had some ma'jun and was sitting in my private quarters with a select few that evening, that is, the eve of Saturday, when Mulla Muhammad Muzahhib came and paid homage. We asked him about things one by one in those parts and found out that the Bengalis were in obeisance and agreement.

On Sunday [January 3] we summoned the Turk and India officers for consultation. The following items were discussed. The Bengali had sent an ambassador and was in obeisance and agreement with us. To go to Bengal would be improper, but if we did not, there was no other place in that vicinity that had a treasury from which the army could be provisioned. Some places to the west, however, were nearby and had treasuries.

Possessions plenty, the people infidels, the road short. If the east is far away, this is near.

It was finally decided that we would go west. Since the way was short, we halted a few days to set our minds at ease concerning the east, to which it was still possible to direct ourselves. [355b] Ghiyasuddin Qorchï set out once again, to rendezvous within twenty days, to carry urgent messages to the officers for all sultans, khans, and amirs who were on the other side of the Ganges to assemble with Askari and proceed against the rebels. He was to deliver these messages and come back for the rendezvous, bringing whatever information he learned while there.

AN EXPEDITION IS APPOINTED
AGAINST THE BALUCH

During these same days a letter came from Muhammadi Kükäldash saying that the Baluch had once more encroached and raided several places. To take care of this, Chïn Temür Sultan was appointed, and the begs on the other side of Sirhind and Samana, like Adil Sultan, Sultan-Muhammad Dulday, Khusraw Kükäldash, Muhammad-Ali Jang-Jang, Abdul-Aziz Mirakhur, Sayyid Ali, Wali Qïzïl, Qaracha, Halahil, Ashiq Bökäül, Shaykh Ali Kätä, Gajur Khan, and Hasan-Ali of Swat were ordered to assemble around Chïn Temür Sultan and proceed against the Baluch with enough armaments for six months. They were to present themselves for Sultan's muster and not disobey his command in any way. Abdul-Ghaffar Tovachï was assigned to deliver this order. It was also decided that first he should deliver the orders to Chïn Temür Sultan. [356] Thereafter he would cross the river and show the decree to the above-mentioned begs and assemble the whole army wherever Chïn Temür Sultan said. Abdul-Ghaffar himself was also to remain with this army and report anyone who exhibited sluggishness or indifference. Anyone who failed thus would be stripped of his rank and deprived of his lands and estates. Handing these decrees over and giving Abdul-Ghaffar verbal instructions, we gave him permission to leave.

On the eve of Sunday the twenty-eighth [January 8] we crossed the Jumna at the sixth ghari of the third watch, headed for the Bagh-i-Nilufar[211] in Dholpur. It was nearly the third watch when we arrived at the garden. Places were assigned on all sides of the garden for the begs and ichkis to build pavilions and gardens themselves.

On Thursday the third of Jumada I [January 14] a location for a bathhouse was chosen southeast of the garden, and the ground for the bath was made ready. I ordered that after raising the plinth for the bath in the place prepared they were to lay out the bath. In one of the rooms of the bath I ordered a ten-by-ten pool. This same day Khalifa sent Qazi Jia and Nar Singh Deo's petitions from Agra. [356b] Iskandar's son Mahmud was said to have taken Bihar. As soon as I received this news I determined to ride out the next morning at the sixth ghari from the Nilufar garden, and I reached Agra in the evening. Muhammad-Zaman Mirza was on his way to Dholpur, and I met him along the way. This same day Chïn Temür Sultan was said to be coming to Agra. The next morning, Saturday, I summoned the council begs, and on Thursday the tenth [January 21] a decision was made to ride to the Purab.

On this same Saturday a letter came from Kabul informing me that Humayun had assembled the army on that side, had attached Sultan Ways to himself, and set out against Samarkand with forty to fifty thousand men. Sultan Ways's younger brother Shah-Qulï had gone to Hissar and entered the fort. Tursun Muhammad Sultan had advanced from Termez, taken Kabadian, and was requesting assistance. Humayun had sent Tüläk Kükäldash and Mir Khurd with many men and what Moghuls there were as auxiliaries to Tursun Sultan, while he himself was going to set out after them.

BABUR SETS OUT FOR THE EAST

On Thursday the tenth of Jumada I [January 21], after the third ghari I marched out on an expedition to the Purab, crossed the Jumna by boat upstream from Jalisar village,[212] [357] and came to the Bagh-i-Zarafshan.[213] It was ordered that the yak-tail standard, drums, and royal stable, as well as all the soldiers, should camp on the other side of the river opposite the garden. People coming for *körünüsh*[214] might cross by boat.

On Saturday, Isma'il Mita, the ambassador of Bengal, brought the Bengali's gifts and rendered homage in the fashion of Hindustan. He approached within a bow shot, made an obeisance, and then withdrew. After being clad in the customary robe of honor, which they call a *sarmuina*, he was brought forward. In our manner he knelt thrice, approached, and submitted Nusrat Shah's petitions. Then, after having the gifts he had brought passed before us, he withdrew.

On Monday, Khwaja Abdul-Haqq came. I crossed the river by boat and went to pay a courtesy call on the khwaja in his tent.

On Tuesday, Hasan Chäläbi came to pay homage. Halt was made at the charbagh for several days to see to the army's equipage.

On Thursday the seventeenth [January 27] we marched after the third ghari. I got into a boat and went. Camp was made at Alwar village, seven kos from Agra.

On Sunday the Uzbek ambassadors were given permission to withdraw. Köchüm Khan's ambassador, Amir Mirza, [357b] was awarded a girth dagger, a gold-spun vest, and seventy thousand tankas. Abu-Sa'id Sultan's liege man Mulla Taghayï and the liege men of Mihri Khanïm and her son Pulad Sultan were clad in buttoned mantles and silk robes of honor. These too, in accordance with their rank, were awarded cash. The next morning Khwaja Abdul-Haqq was given permission to stay in Agra, and Khwaja Kalan, Khwaja Yahya's grandson, was given leave to go to Samarkand. These two had come as envoys from the Uzbek khan and princes.

Mirza Tabrizi and Mirza Beg Taghayï were dispatched with ten thousand shahrukhis as congratulatory gifts for Kamran's marriage and the birth of Humayun's son. A tunic and a belt I had worn myself were sent to the two princes. A jewel-studded girth dagger, a jewel-studded inkwell, a mother-of-pearl inlay box, a *nimcha* I myself had worn, a *takband*,[215] and a copy of the individual letters of the Baburi script were delivered to Hindal by Mulla Bihishti. Also, occasional poems written in the Baburi script were sent. Dispatched to Humayun were the translation and poems written after coming to India, and to Hindal and Khwaja Kalan the translation and some poems. By Mirza Beg Taghayï the translation and the poems I had composed since coming to India, as well as letters written in the Baburi script, were sent to Kamran.

On Tuesday, after letters were written, permission to leave was granted to the men to go to Kabul. Mulla Qasim, Master Shah-Muhammad the stonemason, Mirak [son of] Mir Ghiyas, [358] Mir Sangtarash, and Shah-Baba Beldar were given instructions concerning the buildings being done in Agra and Dholpur. Leaving these responsibilities to them, I gave them permission to withdraw.

It was nearly the first watch when we rode out of Anwar. After noon, camp was made one kos away from Chandwar in a village called Abapur.

Thursday evening Abdul-Malik Qorchï was attached to Hasan Chälabi as envoy to the Shah, while Chapuq was attached to the Uzbek ambassadors as envoy to the khans and sultans. Four gharis were left of the night when I marched from Abapur and got into a boat when I reached Chandwar at dawn. I disembarked that night at Rapri and went into camp, which had been pitched at Fatehpur.[216] We stayed there one day. At dawn on Saturday we made our ablutions and rode to perform the dawn prayer in congregation near Rapri. Mawlana Mahmud Farabi was the leader of the prayer. At sunrise we got into a boat downstream from the large rise at Rapri.

To write my translation in the *tarkib* script, today I made myself a *mistar* of eleven lines.[217] Also today an admonition appeared in my heart from the words of the Ahlullah.[218] We had the boats drawn up to shore that evening opposite a district of Rapri called Jhakan and spent the evening on board. [358b] Shortly before morning we had the boats move out from there and performed the dawn prayer along the way. I was on the boat when Sultan-Muhammad Bakhshï brought in Khwaja Kalan's liege man, Shamsuddin Muhammad, who brought letters and reports from which I ascertained the situation in Kabul. Mahdi Khwaja also came while I was on board. Before noon I got out at the garden on the other side of the Jumna at Etawah, performed my ablutions in the river, and discharged the noon prayer. From the place we performed the prayer we went a bit in the direction of Etawah, sat down on a hill overlooking the water in the shade of some trees in a garden, and set the young men to joking. The food Mahdi Khwaja had ordered was served here. That evening we crossed the river and came to the camp late that night. We halted at this site for two or three days to assemble the army and to write letters for Shamsuddin Muhammad to take to those in Kabul.

On Wednesday the last of Jumada I [February 9] we marched from Etawah, proceeded seven kos, camped at Muhuri and Adusa, and there wrote the remaining letters to go to Kabul. I wrote to Humayun that if nothing else was pressing he should take care of thieves and bandits lest the peace that was prevailing be broken. I also wrote that [359] I had made the province of Kabul royal demesne, and none of my sons should have any designs on it. I also summoned Hindal. To Kamran, I wrote that he should maintain good relations with Prince Tahmasp, that I was rewarding him with the province of Multan, that Kabul was royal demesne, and that my wives and household should come to me. Since several particulars are made known in the letter I wrote to Khwaja Kalan, it is reproduced here without change.

LETTER TO KHWAJA KALAN

To Khwaja Kalan, peace. Shamsuddin Muhammad arrived at Etawah. Affairs have been learned. Our concern for going thence is limitless and overwhelming. Affairs in Hindustan are getting into shape. It is hoped from God Almighty that soon, by God's grace, things will be consolidated. Immediately upon completion of this affair, if God brings it to fruition, I will set out. How can one forget the pleasures of that country? Especially when abstaining from drinking, how can one allow oneself to forget a licit pleasure like melons and grapes? Recently a melon was brought, and as I cut it and ate it I was oddly affected. I wept the whole time I was eating it.

The disarray of affairs in Kabul was written about. [359b] In that regard I have thought and finally decided that if there are seven or eight rulers in one province, how can things be in order and under control? For this reason I have summoned my sister and wives to Hindustan. I have made all of Kabul Province and appertaining villages royal demesne. To Humayun and Kamran, I have written of this explicitly. Let a trustworthy man carry the letters to the princes. Before now I had written and sent letters to the princes with similar contents. They may already have had word. Now let no excuse or plea remain for the control and flourishing of that province. Hereafter, if the fortress is in disarray or the subjects are not flourishing, or there is no treasury, or the treasury is not full, it will be attributed to the incompetence of your own exalted self. Orders have already gone for some necessary affairs that will be written of. One of these is to let the treasury increase. The things that must be done are as follows. First, repair of the fortress; item: the treasury; item: provisions and lodging for envoys coming and going; item: let money derived from taxes be made licit and spent on the congregational mosque building; item: repair of the caravanserai and bathhouse; item: completion of the half-finished building of baked brick made by Master Hasan Ali in the citadel. [360] After consultation with Master Sultan-Muhammad let it be ordered with an appropriate design. If the former design drawn by Master Hasan Ali is still there, let him finish it that way; if not, let them agree and make a building with a nice design such that its courtyard be as large as that of the divankhana. Item: the Khurd Kabul dam, which is to be built on the Butkhak river where the defile debouches toward Khurd Kabul. Item: repair of the Ghazni dam. Item: the Bagh-i-Khiaban and the Khiaban. The garden has little water; it is necessary to purchase a one-mill stream and route it there. Item: To the southwest of Khwaja Basta, I had routed the Tutumdara stream to atop a hill, made a pool, and planted saplings. Because it was opposite the ford and afforded an excellent view, it was named Nazargah.[219] Here too some nice saplings should be planted. It is necessary to make geometrical grass plots and plant some flowers with nice colors and scents and greenery around the edges of the grass. Item: Sayyid Qasim has been assigned as auxiliary. Item: do not neglect Master Muhammad-Amin Jebächi and the matchlockmen. Item: as soon as this letter arrives, send out my sister and wives right away and accompany them as far as Nilab. [360b] It is absolutely imperative that, however much they may tarry, as soon as this letter arrives they set out within the week because the soldiers who have gone out from Hindustan will be experiencing hardship in a tight spot, and the country will suffer. Item: it was written in the letter sent to Abdullah that my desire for success in the "valley of temperance" was great. This quatrain was somewhat dissuasive:

I am distraught to have given up wine. / I do not know what to do, and I am perplexed. / Everybody regrets drinking and then takes the oath, / But I have taken the oath and now regret it.

An anecdote about Banna'i comes to mind.[220] One day, in the presence of Ali-Sher, Banna'i made a joke. Ali-Sher Beg, who was wearing a mantle with buttons, said, "You have made a nice joke. I would give you my mantle, but the buttons prevent me from doing so." Banna'i retorted, "How are the buttons preventing you? It's the loops that prevent it."[221] And, of course, the guarantee of the veracity of this story is the responsibility of the one who told it. Forgive me, but that is how the joke goes. Please don't be offended. Moreover, that quatrain was composed last year. Actually two years ago the craving for a wine party was so overwhelming that many times out of longing for wine I was on the verge of weeping. This year, praise God, that desire has completely left my mind—it must be thanks to the blessing of versifying the translation of the *Walidiyya*.[222] [361] You too take the oath of temperance. Parties and wine are pleasant with comrades and drinking partners.

With whom do you hold parties? With whom do you drink wine?

But if your drinking partners are Sher Ahmad and Haydar-Quli, such an oath of temperance should not be too difficult. With best wishes, peace. Written on Thursday, the first of Jumada II [February 10].

While writing these words of advice I was much affected. The letters were handed to Shamsuddin Muhammad, who was also given verbal instructions, and he was given leave to depart on Thursday evening.

On Friday we went seven kos and camped at Jomandna. Kitin Qara Sultan's liege man arrived, whom Kitin Qara Sultan had sent to his liege man named Kamaluddin Qanaq, who had come as envoy. Kitin Qara Sultan had written to Qanaq complaining of the border begs' conduct and behavior and also complaining of outlaws and brigands. Qanaq had then brought the envoy here. Qanaq was given permission to withdraw, and orders were given to the border begs to control the outlaws and brigands and to conduct themselves well. The orders were turned over to the man who had come from Kitin Qara Sultan, and he was given permission to leave this campsite. A man called Shah-Qulï had come from Hasan Chäläbi and reported on the details of the battle. [361b] A letter to be delivered by this Shah-Qulï was written to the Shah excusing the late arrival of Hasan Chäläbi, and on Friday the second [February 11] he was given leave to withdraw.

On Saturday we proceeded eight kos and stopped in Kakora and Chachauli in the Kalpi district.

On Sunday the fourth [February 13] we went nine kos, and I shaved my head in a place called Derapur in Kalpi district. I had not had my head shaved for two months. I bathed in the Sengar River.

On Monday we went fourteen kos and stopped in Chaparghatta in the Kalpi district. The next morning, Tuesday the seventh [February 16], Qaracha's Hindustani servant brought me a letter written to Qaracha by Mahïm saying that she was coming. In a memorandum I might have written in my own hand she had summoned men from Lahore, Bhera, and those areas as escorts. She had written the letter from Kabul on the seventh of Jumada I [January 17].

On Wednesday we went seven kos and stopped in the Adampur district. On this day I mounted before dawn, spent the noon hour by myself, and proceeded as far as the Jumna. I proceeded down the bank of the Jumna. When I reached opposite Adampur, I had a canopy set up on an island near the campsite and had some ma'jun. [362] This same day we had Sadiq and Kulal wrestle. Kulal had come with great pretensions but in Agra had been given a respite for twenty days so as to shake off the dust of the road. Forty or fifty days had passed since then, so today was the day for the match. Sadiq wrestled well and easily threw his contender, for which he was rewarded with ten thousand tankas, a horse and saddle, a suit of clothes, and a buttoned mantle. Although Kulal had been thrown, lest he be discouraged he too was rewarded, with a suit of clothes and three thousand tankas. An order was given for the caissons and mortars to be taken off the boats. We halted for three or four days while that was being done, the road was made ready, and the emplacements were prepared.

On Monday the twelfth [February 21] we went twelve kos and stopped at Kora. I traveled by litter. From Kora we went twelve more kos and camped in Kurriah in the Kara district. From Kurriah we proceeded eight kos and stopped in Fatehpur Haswa, whence we proceeded eight more kos and stopped in Serai-Munda. While we were camped, Sultan Jalaluddin came late that night and rendered homage. He brought his two small sons with him. The next morning, Saturday the seventeenth [February 26], we went eight kos and stopped on the banks of the Ganges at Dugdugi in the Kara district.

On Sunday, Muhammad-Sultan Mirza, [362b] Qasim Husayn Sultan, Beykhub Sultan, and Turdïka came to the camp.

On Monday, Askari came and paid homage. They had all approached from the eastern side of the Ganges. It was ordered that Askari and the army should proceed on that side of the river. Wherever we camped, they should camp opposite.

While we were in those parts, news came continually from ahead that a hundred thousand Afghans had joined "Sultan Mahmud."[223] He had sent Shaykh Bayazid and Biban with a large army in the direction of Sarwar while he himself and Fath Khan Sarwani were proceeding down the riverbank to Chunar. Sher Khan Sur, whom I had patronized the year before and given large estates and stationed in this area, had joined the Afghans. They had had Sher Khan and a few other amirs cross the river. Sultan Jalaluddin's man was unable to hold Benares and fled. Their excuse was that they had left soldiers in the Benares fort and then come up the river to fight. We marched six kos from Dugdugi and stopped at Kusar, three or four kos from Kara. I went by boat. A halt was made for two or three days at the camp that we might be guests of Sultan Jalaluddin. [363]

On Friday we arrived in Sultan Jalaluddin's quarters in the Kara fortress. As host he served some food. After the meal he and his sons were clad in tunics and jerkins. In accordance with Sultan Jalaluddin's wish his elder son was given the title Sultan Mahmud. Riding out of Kara we went a kos and stopped on the bank of the Ganges. Shahrak Beg, who had come from Mahïm to the site at which we first came to the Ganges, was this day given leave to depart with letters we had written. Khwaja Yahya's grandson Khwaja Kalan had requested me to send him my journal of events, so I sent with Shahrak the copy I had had made.

The next morning, Saturday, we marched four kos and stopped. I went by boat. Since the site at which we were to stop was nearby, we reached it early. We sat in the boat for a long time and had ma'jun. Khwaja Abdul-Shahid was in Nur Beg's quarters, and we invited him.

We also had Mulla Mahmud summoned and brought from Mulla Ali Khan's quarters. We sat for a while and then crossed by boat to the other side and had the wrestlers wrestle. Dost Yasin Hiz was ordered to have a match, not with Pahlawan Sadiq but with the others. [363b] This was against custom, which was to wrestle with the strongest first. He wrestled well with eight men.

At noon Sultan-Muhammad Bakhshï came to that side by boat bringing news of the break-up of the army of Sultan Iskandar's son Mahmud Khan, whom the rebels styled "Sultan Mahmud." In the afternoon the spy who had gone from here brought the same news, and late that afternoon a report from Taj Khan Sarangkhani confirmed his account. Sultan-Muhammad came and reported the situation: The rebels had laid siege to Chunar and had provoked a little fighting. However, as soon as they received confirmed word of our approach they withdrew in a disorderly fashion. The Afghans who had crossed to Benares retreated in confusion and, while crossing the river, two boats had sunk and a few men were drowned.

The next morning we went six kos and stopped at Serauli in the Payag[224] district.[225]

That morning I went by boat. Esän Temür Sultan and Tokhta Buqa Sultan had dismounted and were waiting halfway there to perform a körünüsh. I invited the princes onto my boat. Tokhta Buqa Sultan worked the rain stone. A violent wind arose and it began to rain. It was terrible! The weather was so bad that some of us had ma'jun even though we had had some the day before. We arrived at the camp, and stayed there the next morning. Opposite the campsite there was a large island covered with greenery. We crossed over to it by boat and toured it on horseback. At the first watch we got back on the boat.

While there, we rode, oblivious, over a cracked precipice at the water's edge. As soon as I came out onto the cliff the fault cracked open and the cliff began to fall. Immediately I jumped from my horse and threw myself to safety. My horse did not fall either, but if I had stayed on, it was very likely that both of us would have.

The same day, I swam across the Ganges. I counted the strokes it took me to cross: thirty-three. Then, without pausing for breath I crossed back to the other side. I had swum all the rivers—only the Ganges had remained.

When we reached the confluence of the Ganges and the Jumna, I had the boat hauled toward Payag, reaching camp at the fourth ghari of the first watch.

On Wednesday the army began crossing the Jumna at the second watch. There were 420 boats.

On Friday the first of Rajab [March 11], I crossed the river. On Monday the fourth [March 14] we marched from the banks of the Jumna headed for Bihar. After going five kos we stopped in Lawayin.[226] I kept right on going by boat. Until this day the soldiers were crossing the river. It was ordered that the artillery caissons that had been brought by boat from Adampur should be reloaded at Payag and transported. When we stopped, we had the wrestlers wrestle. Dost Yasin Hiz was set against Skipper Pahlawan Lahori. Dost struggled a lot and threw his opponent only with great difficulty. Both were rewarded with suits of clothing.

Before us lay a muddy morass called the Tons River. We halted there for two days in order to find a ford and prepare the road. A crossing for the horses and camels was found farther upstream. Although it seemed that the loaded carts could not be taken that way because the rocks in the ford were uneven, it was ordered that they be taken across right there anyway. [364]

On Thursday we marched. I went by boat to the juncture with the Tons. I got out of the boat and walked up the Tons, returning in the late afternoon to the camp, which had been pitched on the other side of the river. We achieved six kos that day. The next day we remained at the campsite. On Saturday we marched twelve kos to Nilabar Gang, and from there proceeded six kos and stopped at a place overlooking a village. From there we went seven kos and came to Nanupur. Taj Khan and his sons came from Chunar to pay homage. Around that time a report arrived from Sultan-Muhammad Bakhshï confirming that the women and retinue were on their way from Kabul. On Wednesday we marched, toured the Chunar fort, and proceeded one kos before stopping.

While marching from Payag, I got an abscess on my body. An Anatolian gave me the treatment that is now common in Anatolia. He boiled pepper in an earthenware pot, and I held the abscess over the hot steam. When the steam died down, I bathed the abscess in the hot water for two hours. Someone said that lions and rhinoceroses had been seen on the island next to the camp. [364b] The next morning we formed a hunting circle around the island. Elephants were also brought in. Neither lion nor rhinoceros emerged, however. From the tip of the circle a wild ox came out. A fierce wind stirred up a lot of dust that gave us much difficulty. I returned to the boat and went to camp.

Camp had been made two kos above Benares. Many elephants are said to be in the jungles in the vicinity of Chunar. I went out of camp with an idea of hunting them. Taj Khan brought the news that Mahmud Khan was at the Son River. The begs were summoned, and the advisability of attacking the enemy was discussed. Finally it was decided that we would proceed as far as possible without delay. We marched out nine kos and stopped at the Ballooa ford. From that camp Tahir was sent to Agra on the eve of Monday the eighteenth [March 28]. He took a chit for money for lodging customarily allowed those coming from Kabul and left. That day I went by boat a little before dawn. I reached the confluence with the Gomati, which is the Jaunpur River, went a bit up the Gomati, and returned. Although it was a narrow little river, [365] there was nowhere to cross it. The soldiers on the other side had to cross by boat and raft and by making their horses swim.

Coming one kos below the confluence of the river I toured last year's campsite, from which we went to Jaunpur. Downstream was a fair breeze, so we had the sail hoisted on the Bengali ship and tied the large boat to it. It went very fast. Camp had been made a kos upstream from Madan-Benares. There were two gharis left of the day when we reached the campsite. By sailing fast and not stopping we reached our goal late that night, long before the boats coming behind us. At Chunar, Moghul Beg had been ordered to measure the straight road of every march with a cord, and whenever I went by boat Lutfi Beg was to measure the shore. By the straight road it was eleven kos and the riverbank was eighteen.

The next day we halted at that site. On Wednesday we went by boat and camped a kos above Ghazipur. On Thursday, Mahmud Khan Nohani came and paid homage. The same day, letters came from Jalal Khan son of Pahar Khan, Farid Khan son of Nasir Khan, Sher Khan Sur, Adil Khan Sur, and some other Afghan amirs. [365b] Also, a report written at Lahore on the twentieth of Jumada II [February 29] came from Abdul-Aziz Mirakhur. Qaracha's Hindustani servant, who had been sent from the Kalpi region, had arrived at Lahore the day it was written. The recount mentioned that he and the others assigned had gone to meet the womenfolk at Nilab on the ninth of Jumada II [February 18]. Abdul-Aziz had accompanied them as far as the Chenab and gone ahead to Lahore.

On Friday we moved out. I went by boat, got out, and toured the site opposite Chausa where we had camped the previous year when there was an eclipse and a fast was held.[227] Then I got back on the boat. Muhammad-Zaman Mirza also came from behind in a boat. At the mirza's instigation we had some ma'jun. Camp was made on the banks of the Karamnasa River. This river is scrupulously avoided by Hindus, and observant Hindus will not cross it. They must board boats and cross its mouth on the Ganges. They believe that the religious merit of anyone touched by its water is nullified. The etymology of its name is also said to be derived from this.[228] We went a little up the Karamnasa by boat and then returned, [366] crossed to the northern shore of the Ganges, and had the boats halt at the bank. Some of the warriors indulged in sport and others wrestled a bit. Saqi Muhsin claimed that he would wrestle four or five men. He grappled with one and was almost felled. The second man was Shadman, who threw Saqi Muhsin. Saqi was mortified. The professional wrestlers came and wrestled.

The next day, Saturday, we did not move out until nearly the first watch so that a man could be sent to inspect the river crossing. I mounted and went a kos up the Karamnasa toward the crossing. Since it was far, I returned and went back to the campsite by boat. Camp had been made a kos forward of Chausa. I repeated the pepper treatment. It was somewhat hotter and blistered my skin. I suffered greatly. Ahead of us was a smallish but swampy river. To prepare the way, we halted at the camp the next day.

On Sunday evening I wrote an answer to Abdul-Aziz's letter, which had been brought by the Hindustani runner, and sent it off. Monday morning I went by boat. On account of the wind the boats were hauled. We reached opposite the site where we had camped at Buxar the previous year,[229] [366b] crossed the river, and toured the site. Steps—probably between forty and fifty—had been made to the river, but only the top two remained. All the rest had been ruined by the water. We got back into the boat and had some ma'jun. We had the boat stop at an island a little upstream from camp and had the wrestlers wrestle, returning to camp late that night. The year before I had swum across the Ganges to the campsite where we were stopped now.[230] Some got on horses and others on camels, and we made a tour. I ate some opium that day.

The next day, Tuesday, Karimberdi, Muhammad-Ali Haydar Rikabdar, and Baba Shaykh were sent with some two hundred seasoned warriors to obtain news of the rebels. At the camp the ambassador of Bengal was ordered to present the three terms to his king.[231]

On Wednesday, Yunus Ali, who had been sent to sound out Muhammad-Zaman Mirza on Bihar, brought back a rather noncommittal reply. A report from the representative of the Shaykhzadas of Bihar gave news of the enemy's having abandoned Bihar and gone off.

On Thursday the Turk and India officers and two thousand of their yeomen were attached to Turdï Muhammad and Muhammad-Ali Jang-Jang and given leave after letters of conciliation had been written to the people of Bihar. [367] Khwaja Murshid Iraqi was made the divan of the province of Bihar and attached to Turdï Muhammad. The next day Muhammad-Zaman Mirza accepted to go to Bihar, reported a few items through Shaykh Zayn and Yunus Ali, and requested a few men as auxiliaries. Some warriors were assigned to Muhammad-Zaman Mirza as auxiliaries, others were made his liege men.

On Saturday the first of Sha'ban [April 9] we marched out of the site we had been camped in for three or four days. I rode out to tour Bhojpur and Bihiya and then returned, dismounting in camp. Muhammad-Ali's detachment, which had been sent to gather intelligence, had defeated a troop of infidels along the way before reaching the place where Sultan Mahmud was staying. Sultan Mahmud had two thousand men. Upon discovering this scouting party, his men had fallen into disarray and he had killed his two elephants before marching away. He had stationed one of his officers as a lookout. Around twenty of our scouts came up, but the officer fled without fighting. A few were taken captive, one's head was cut off, and one or two were brought in alive.

The next morning we moved out, I by boat. While at this site Muhammad-Zaman Mirza crossed the Gomati, and in order for the mirza to cross and get going we stayed there for two or three days. [367b] On Tuesday the fourth, Muhammad-Zaman Mirza was awarded a regal suit of clothing, a girth dagger, a fine horse, and a parasol,[232] and he was made to kneel in fealty for the province of Bihar. Of the Bihar district 12,500,000 was made royal demesne, and Murshid Iraqi was made responsible for the office of divan.

On Thursday, I went from that camp by boat. I had all the boats stop, and as soon as I arrived I ordered them to be linked together to form a circle. The resulting line would have been much wider than the river, so—although not all the boats could be included, since some places in the river were shallow and others deep, some places flowing and others not—it was not possible to go far in this fashion. A crocodile appeared within the circle of the boats. A fish, frightened by the crocodile, jumped so high that it landed inside one of the boats. It was caught and brought to me.

When we reached the campsite, names were given to the boats. The old boat *Baburi*, which had been finished at Agra shortly before the raid on Sanga, was renamed *Asayish*. This same year, just before the army mounted, [368] Arayish Khan had had a boat made and gave it to me as a present. During this trip I had added a deck to it. This boat was named *Arayish*. To the boat Sultan Jalaluddin had presented to me a rather large deck had been added, and yet another deck above that one. This one was named *Gunjayish*. Another, small skiff with a cabin, which was sent about on all sorts of errands, was named *Farmayish*.[233]

The next morning, Friday, we marched off. When all of Muhammad-Zaman Mirza's affairs were completed he moved off a kos or two from the camp headed for Bihar and stopped. This day he came and took leave of me. Two spies came from the army of Bengal and said that the Bengalis, led by Makhdum-i-Alam, had divided the banks of the Gandak River into twenty-four places and were raising rampart walls. They had prevented the Afghans under Sultan Mahmud from sending their women and families across and had joined these Afghans to themselves. As soon as this news came, since battle was probable, I detained Muhammad-Zaman Mirza and dispatched Shah Iskandar with three or four hundred men to Bihar.

On Saturday a man came from Dudu and her son [368b] Jalal Khan, son of Pahar Khan. The Bengalis must have been keeping them blindfolded. They opted for me, got loose from the Bengali by hard fighting, crossed the river, reached the vicinity of Bihar, and were headed to pay homage to me. The ambassador of Bengal, Isma'il Mita, was told that the answer to the three terms that had been written and sent was late in arriving. He was to write a letter and send it to the effect that if the Bengalis were in obedience and agreement with us, then an answer must come soon.

On Saturday evening a man came from Turdï Muhammad and Jang-Jang. When their scout came from this direction on Wednesday morning, the fifth of Sha'ban [April 13], the *shiqqdar*[234] of Bihar ran away through the gate on the other side.

On Sunday we marched from camp and stopped in the district of Arrah. News came that the Kharid army was stopped on the other side of the Sarju at the juncture with the Ganges with one hundred to 150 boats. Since there was peace with the Bengali—the affair of peace was always held forward during such affairs for the sake of auspiciousness—although he had breached etiquette by coming and blocking our way, nonetheless I maintained my perennial rule and attached Mulla Muhammad Muzahhib to the Bengali ambassador, [369] repeated the three terms from before, and decided to give him leave to withdraw. On Monday the ambassador came to pay homage. I had someone give him permission to withdraw. The following was also mentioned: "We will be proceeding on both sides of the river to repel the enemy. No harm will be done to the land and water belonging to you, as one of the three terms was to tell the army of Kharid to unblock the way and go to Kharid. Let us attach a few Turks to the army of Kharid, and let them give assurances of safety to the people of Kharid and take them to their place. If they do not withdraw from the ford and do not cease these unbecoming words, then let them consider whatever evil or unpleasantness comes upon their heads as coming from themselves and their words."

On Wednesday Isma'il Mita was clad in the customary robe of honor, rewarded, and given leave. On Thursday, Shaykh Jamali was dispatched with decrees of safe conduct and words of assurance for Dudu and her son Jalal Khan. This same day Mahïm's liege man arrived. He had left them on the other side of the Bagh-i-Safa at...[235] He brought letters. On Saturday the ambassador of Persia, Murad Qorchï Qajar, was seen. On Sunday, Mulla Muhammad Muzahhib was handed the usual mementoes and given leave. On Monday, Khalifa [369b] and some other begs were sent to inspect where we should cross the river. On Wednesday, Khalifa was again sent to inspect the area between the two rivers.

I mounted to tour the lotus field to the south near the district of Arrah. While touring it, Shaykh Ghuran brought me a newly formed lotus seedpod. It bore a striking resemblance to an almond. The pretty little flowerlike thing that would become a lotus is called *kanwal kukri* in Hindustani, and the seed is called *doda*. The Son River was said to be nearby. We went and had a look at it. Below it many trees could be seen. They said that it was Maner, where the tomb of Shaykh Yahya, the father of Shaykh Sharafuddin Maneri, was. Having reached this far, we crossed the Son, went two or three kos downriver, toured Maner, crossed its orchards, circumambulated the shrine, returned to the bank of the Son, made our ablutions, performed the noon prayer, and then went back toward camp.

The horses were so fat a few had fallen behind and a few others were worn out. Several men were stationed and ordered to gather the exhausted ones, water and rest them, and bring them without rushing them. If this had not been done many horses would have been lost. On the return from Maner, I ordered someone to count his horse's steps from the banks of the Son to the camp. [370] He counted 23,100 steps, which would be 46,200 paces, or eleven-and-a-half kos. From Maner to the Son is about half a kos. Therefore, the return was twelve. Going hither and yon during the tour we must have gone another fifteen or sixteen kos, so all told we had covered nearly thirty kos that day. There were six gharis left of the first watch of the night when we got to camp.

The next morning, Thursday, Sultan-Junayd Barlas from Jaunpur and the warriors stationed in Jaunpur came. Because they were late, I had them rebuked and did not allow them an interview. I summoned Qazi Jia and granted him an interview.

BATTLE PLANS

That same day, I summoned the Turk and India officers for consultation and held deliberations on crossing the river. It was decided that Master Ali-Quli should install the mortars, ballista, and culverin on high ground between the Ganges and Sarju rivers and provoke battle from there with lots of matchlockmen. A bit downstream from the confluence, on the Bihar side of the Ganges opposite the island where the Bengali had stationed an elephant and many boats, Mustafa was to make ready his implements and prepare for battle. He also was to have

many matchlockmen. Muhammad-Zaman Mirza and those so assigned would dismount behind Mustafa as reinforcements. Overseers
for the many shovelers and porters were assigned to Master Ali-Qulï
and Mustafa to raise emplacements and prepare the ground for shooting the culverins [370b] and placing the mortars. They all got busy
gathering and assembling their tools and implements. Askari, the sultans, the amirs, and the khans were to gallop off, cross the Sarju at the
Haldi ford, be ready from the other side at the appointed time, and
charge the enemy.

Meanwhile Sultan-Junayd and Qazi Jia reported that there was a
ford eight kos upstream. Ruyzard was appointed to take one of the
raftsmen, Sultan-Junayd, Mahmud Khan, and Qazi Jia's men and inspect the ford. If it was crossable, they would cross there. Among the
men word was that the Bengali was thinking of assigning someone to
the Haldi ford. A report came from Mahmud Khan's shiqqdar at
Sikandarpur, saying, "I have gathered around fifty boats at the Haldi
ford and have paid the boatmen, but they are afraid, having heard that
the Bengali is coming."

Since there was little time left for a way to be found across the Sarju
River, on Saturday, without waiting for the men who had gone to find
a ford to come back, I summoned the begs for consultation and said,
"As there are crossings all the way from Chaturmuk in Sikandarpur to
Oudh and Bahraich, while we are sitting here we will assign a large
contingent [371] to cross by boat at the Haldi ford and attack. While
they are going Master Ali-Qulï and Mustafa will get busy fighting
with mortars, matchlocks, culverin, and ballista. Let us cross the
Ganges, assign auxiliaries to Master Ali-Qulï, and stand ready. If the
contingent that has crossed at the ford gets close, let us too enjoin battle from here, press on, and cross. Muhammad-Zaman Mirza and
those who are nearby on the other side will fight with Mustafa from
the Bihar side of the Ganges."

Having made these decisions, we divided the army on the north of
the Ganges into four contingents, put Askari at their head, and sent
them off to the Haldi ford. One contingent was with Askari's own liege
man, the second was under Sultan Jalaluddin Sharqi, the third under the
Uzbek princes Qasim Husayn Sultan, Beykhub Sultan, and Tang-
Atmïsh Sultan, and Mahmud Khan Nohani of Ghazipur, Baba Qashqa's
Kuki, Qarïmïsh the Uzbek, Qurban Charkhi, and the Daryakhanis under

Husayn Khan, and to the fourth under Musa Sultan, Sultan-Junayd Barlas, and all the soldiers who were at Jaunpur—approximately twenty thousand men—were assigned overseers to get them to horse that very night, which was Saturday. [371b]

On Sunday morning the army began to cross the Ganges. I got into a boat at the first watch and crossed. It was the third watch when Ruyzard and his men, who had gone to inspect the crossing, arrived, without having found a crossing. They brought news of the meeting along the way of the boats and the division assigned.

On Tuesday we marched from the place we had crossed the river, proceeded, and dismounted a kos from the battlefield, which was at the junction of the two rivers. I went myself to watch Master Ali-Qulï fire the ballista and culverin. That day he had hit two boats with the ballista and sunk them. From the other side Mustafa had hit two boats with ballista shot and sunk them. The big gun had been transported to the battle site, and Mulla Ghulam was assigned as overseer to prepare the ground for it. We assigned a troop of yasavuls and nimble warriors to help him and then returned and had some ma'jun on an island opposite the camp. That evening, stoned on ma'jun, I had the boat brought near my tent and just laid back on it.

That night a strange thing happened. At around the third watch of the night an alarm broke out on the boat. All the pages had planks from the boat and were yelling to each other, "Strike! Strike!" A night watchman was on the boat *Farmayish,* which was beside the boat *Asayish,* on which I was lying down. [372] Opening his eyes, he saw a man with his hands on *Asayish,* about to get in. He hit him in the head with a rock. The man dove into the water and emerged to strike the night watchman on the head with a sword, wounding him slightly. Then he fled toward the water. This was the reason for the alarm. The night we came from Maner one or two night watchmen had driven away several Hindustanis from near the boat and brought in one or two of their swords and one of their daggers. God preserved us that time.

If the sword of the world moves from its place, it will not sever a vein unless God wills it.

The next morning, Wednesday, I got on the boat *Gunjayish,* went near the place where the stones were being shot, and assigned everyone a task.

A thousand warriors under Ughan Turdï Moghul were sent to get across, however they could, one, two, or three kos upstream. Meanwhile, the Bengalis were planning to cross in twenty to thirty boats opposite Askari's camp and emerge en masse on foot and strike a coup when these charged on their horses and sent them flying, capturing a few, severing some heads, shooting many with arrows, and seizing seven or eight boats. The same day, the Bengalis went in a few boats, got out on Muhammad-Zaman Mirza's side, [372b] and provoked a battle. Our men pressed hard, put the Bengalis to flight, and sank three boats with all hands aboard. They got hold of one boat and brought it to me. Here Baba Chuhra fought outstandingly. It was ordered that Muhammad Sultan, Yaka Khwaja, Yunus Ali, Ughanberdi, and the group that had previously been assigned to cross should haul upstream under the cover of darkness the seven or eight boats that Ughanberdi and his men had seized.

That very day a man came from Askari to say that they had crossed the river leaving nothing behind. The next morning, which was Thursday, they would attack the enemy. It was ordered that those who had crossed would join Askari and proceed to the battle. At noon a man came from Master Ali-Qulï to say that the stones were ready. An order was given to fire and to have another stone ready by the time I got there. Late that afternoon I got into a little Bengali skiff and went to the place where the emplacements had been raised. Master Ali-Qulï fired one large stone and then a few ballista shots. The Bengalis have a reputation for fireworks. This time we tried them well. They do not aim at a particular place and fire but simply shoot any way. That afternoon we ordered a few boats to be hauled across the Sarju opposite to where they were. [373] The boat pullers hauled a few boats across without fear and without cover. It was ordered that Esän Temür Sultan, Tokhta Buqa Sultan, Baba Sultan, Arayish Khan, and Shaykh Ghuran should position themselves at the place where the boats crossed to give them some protection.

I returned to camp at the first watch. At nearly midnight news came from the boats that were being hauled upstream: "The division assigned has gone forward. We were hauling the boats when the Bengalis discovered our position and attacked. A ball hit one of the boatmen in the leg and broke it. We could not cross."

On Thursday morning word came from the men of the emplacements: "All the boats from upstream have come. Their cavalry have all mounted and are headed straight for our division as they come." I too galloped to the boats that had been sent across by night. Someone was sent posthaste to tell the men assigned to cross under Muhammad-Sultan Mirza to ford immediately and join Askari. I ordered Esän Temür Sultan and Tokhta Buqa Sultan, who were above these boats, to get busy crossing. Baba Sultan had not come to his assigned place.

Immediately Esän Temür Sultan with a boat and thirty or forty of his liege men crossed, [373b] holding their horses by the manes next to the boat. After them another boat set out. Seeing them, a large troop of Bengali foot soldiers headed toward them. Seven or eight of Esän Temür Sultan's liege men mounted, rode to encounter the soldiers, and, while Sultan was getting mounted, battled and fought them in Sultan's direction. By this time Esän Temür Sultan had gotten to horse. The second boat had also crossed. With thirty or thirty-five horsemen he charged the many foot soldiers and easily put them to flight. It was a really outstanding feat he performed. First, he crossed nimbly and fearlessly before anyone else; and second, he charged a large body of foot soldiers with only a few men and put them to flight. Tokhta Buqa Sultan also crossed. The boats began to cross continuously. Lahoris and Hindustanis, each from where he was, began to cross, some swimming and others with bundles of reeds.

Seeing this situation, the mass of Bengalis opposite the batteries set their boats moving downstream to get away. Darwesh Muhammad Sarban, Dost Eshik-Aqa, Nur Beg, and some other warriors crossed opposite the batteries. I sent a man at a gallop to Sultan to say, "Assemble well those who have crossed and, when you reach near the opposing division, proceed around their flank and get to grips with the enemy." [374] The sultans attached those who had crossed to themselves, formed three or four groups, and set out in the direction of the enemy. As they approached, the enemy moved foot soldiers out front and began to move without breaking ranks. From the division assigned to Askari, Kuki arrived with his troop. From that side Kuki, and from this side the sultans arrived and began hand-to-hand combat. They unhorsed the enemy, seized them, and moved on. Kuki and his men unhorsed an important infidel named Basant Rao and cut off his head. Ten or fifteen of his men fell on them, but they were immediately cut to pieces. Tokhta Buqa Sultan went opposite the enemy and wielded his sword well. Moghul

Abdul-Wahhab and his younger brother also wielded their swords. Although Moghul did not know how to swim, he crossed the river in his armor holding on to his horse's mane. My boats were behind. I sent someone to the boats. The boat *Farmayish* came first. I got on, crossed, toured the Bengalis' campsites, got on *Gunjayish,* and asked if there was a place to cross farther up, where Mir-Muhammad Jalaban reported it was better to cross. An order was given for the soldiers to get busy crossing at the place he spoke of. While Muhammad Sultan Mirza and those commanders' troops were crossing as they had been ordered, [374b] Yaka Khwaja's boat sank and he perished. His liege men and estates were awarded to his younger brother, Qasim Khwaja.

While I was making my ablutions at noon, the sultans came. I praised them and made them hopeful of reward and promotion. Askari also came at that time. It was the first action Askari had seen, and it was taken as a good presage. That evening, since the camp had not crossed yet, I lay back on *Gunjayish* at an island.

On Friday we stopped in the Narhan district at a village named Godna, a dependency of Kharid on the northern side of the Sarju River. On Sunday, Kuki and his troop were sent to Hajjipur to gather intelligence. Shah-Muhammad, Ma'ruf's son, who had been greatly patronized when we came last year and given the district of Saran, performed a few outstanding feats, twice defeating and capturing his father, Ma'ruf. When Sultan Mahmud treacherously seized Bihar and was attacked by Biban and Shaykh Bayazid, Shah-Muhammad had been unable to do anything other than join them. This time too several reports had been received from him, even though among the men ridiculous things were being said about him. As soon as Askari crossed at the Haldi ford, Shah-Muhammad and his troop came to see Askari [375] and accompanied him against the Bengalis. While we were at this campsite he came and paid homage to me. At this same time, news was continually being received about Shaykh Bayazid and Biban, who were said to be thinking about crossing the Sarju.

At this time a strange piece of news came from Sambhal. Ali Yusuf, who had been doing an excellent job of consolidating Sambhal, and a young physician accompanying him had both died on the same day. To maintain order in Sambhal it was decided that Abdullah should go there on Friday the fifth of Ramadan [May 13]; Abdullah was given leave.

Around this same time a report came from Chïn Temür Sultan saying that several of the begs assigned had not been able to join him because of the womenfolk coming from Kabul. Muhammadi and some others had ridden straight with Sultan for around a hundred kos and crushed the Baluch decisively. Through Abdullah, orders were given to Chïn Temür Sultan, Sultan-Muhammad Dulday, Muhammadi, and some of the other begs and warriors there to assemble with Chïn Temür Sultan at Agra and stand at readiness to set out after the rebels wherever they might go.

On Monday the eighth [May 16], Jalal Khan, [375b] Darya Khan's grandson to whom Shaykh Jamali had gone, came with his high-ranking amirs to pay homage to me. This same day Yahya Nohani came to pay homage. Before he had sent his younger brother to advise us of his submission, and the brother had been sent back with notices of our good intentions. Since seven or eight thousand Nohanis and Afghans had come with great expectations, we, without discouraging them, made a crore of Bihar royal demesne, awarded fifty lacs to Mahmud Khan Nohani, and had the remainder held for Jalal Khan, who accepted to pay a crore as tribute. Mulla Ghulam Yasavul was sent to collect these monies. The district of Jaunpur was given to Muhammad-Zaman Mirza.

PEACE IS MADE WITH NUSRAT SHAH

On Thursday, Khalifa's liege man Ghulam-Ali, who had been dispatched with the prince of Monghyr's liege man Abu'l-Fath to deliver those three terms before Isma'il Mita was sent, arrived in the company of Abu'l-Fath bringing letters to Khalifa from the prince of Monghyr and Hasan Khan the Lashkar-Vazir in which he accepted the three terms and initiated peace talks on behalf of Nusrat Shah. Since this expedition was to repel the rebel Afghans, some of the rebels had gone off on their own and gotten lost, and others had come and accepted to submit to servitude. [376] The few that remained were being held by the Bengali, who took responsibility for them.

The monsoon was near. Therefore we wrote back words of peace in reply to the above-mentioned conditions.

On Saturday, Isma'il Jalwani, Alaul Khan Nohani, and Awliya Khan Ishraqi came with five or six amirs and paid homage. This same day

Esän Temür Sultan and Tokhta Buqa Sultan were awarded girth swords, girth daggers, armor, robes of honor, and fine horses. Esän Temür Sultan was awarded thirty lacs from the Narnaul district, and Tokhta Buqa Sultan was awarded thirty lacs from the district of Shamsabad and made to kneel in fealty.

On Monday the fifteenth [May 23], my mind at ease concerning Bihar and Bengal, we set out from camp in the vicinity of Godna, determined to repel the evil of the ingrates Biban and Shaykh Bayazid. Stopping twice for the night along the way, on Wednesday we stopped at a ford called Chaupara in Chaturmuk, Sikandarpur, and the men got busy crossing. News began to pour in continually that these ingrates had crossed the Sarju and Gogra and were headed in the direction of Lucknow.[236]

To block their way the Turk and India officers Sultan Jalaluddin Sharqi, Ali Khan Farmuli, Turdïka, Nizam Khan of Bayana, Tolmïsh the Uzbek, Qurban Charkhi, and the Daryakhanis under Hasan Khan [376b] were appointed and given leave to depart on Wednesday evening.

A MONSOON SQUALL

This same evening after taravih, it was the fifth ghari of the first watch when the monsoon clouds appeared, and within an instant such a storm brewed and fierce wind arose that few were the tents that did not blow down. I was in my tent writing. There was no time to gather my papers and notebooks. The wind brought down the tent and its *peshgah*[237] on my head. The smoke vent broke into pieces. God kept me safe, and no harm was done, but my books and papers were drenched. We gathered them together with difficulty, wrapped them up in a woolen bedspread, and put them under the cot and spread kilims on top. After two gharis the wind died down. We had the töshäkkhana tent erected, lit a candle, and with great difficulty got a fire going and then got busy drying out the papers and notebooks until dawn with no sleep.

On Thursday, I crossed the river. On Friday, I mounted and made a tour of Kharid and Sikandarpur. That same day, Abdullah and Baqi had written about the taking of Lucknow. On Saturday, Kuki and his troop were sent forward to join Baqi. On Sunday, Sultan-Junayd Barlas, Hasan Khalifa, [377] Mulla Apaq's troops, and Mu'min Atäkä's brethren were given permission to join Baqi and fail in nothing they might do before I arrived. This afternoon Shah-Muhammad, Ma'ruf's son, was awarded a regal robe of honor and a fine horse and given leave to withdraw. As last year, he was given Saran for his own stipend and Kandhla for the maintenance of his yeomen. That same day, Isma'il Jalwani was awarded a seventy-two-lac stipend from Sarwar, a regal robe of honor, and a fine horse and given leave. Stipends were assigned also to the men under Alaul Khan Nohani who had come with Isma'il Jalwani, and they were dismissed. It was decided that a brother or son of each of them should remain permanently in my service in Agra.

The Bengalis were made responsible to transport to Trimuhani and Ghazipur the boats *Gunjayish* and *Arayish* and another two Bengali boats selected from among those that had fallen to us this time. An order was given for *Asayish* and *Farmayish* to be transported up the Sarju River along with the camp. With my mind at ease concerning Bihar and Sarwar, on Monday we marched along the banks of the Sarju, across the Chaupara crossing of Chaturmuk toward Oudh. After going some ten kos we stopped on the banks of the Sarju beside a village called Kalira,[238] a dependency of Fatehpur. [377b] Those who had marched out early lost their way and went to the large lake at Fatehpur. A few men were sent out to get the nearby men to come back. Kichik Khwaja was dispatched to stay the night beside the lake and bring back to camp the next morning the soldiers who had bivouacked there.

We marched out early the next morning, and halfway along the way I got onto *Asayish* and had it hauled to the camp upstream. Along the way Khalifa brought Shah-Muhammad Dewana's son, who had come from Baqi with a report confirming the news of Lucknow: the assault was launched by Biban and Shaykh Bayazid on Saturday the thirteenth of Ramadan [May 21], but they were unable to accomplish anything. During the battle, fire broke out in the grass and straw huts that turned the inside of the fortress into an oven. They were not able to stay on top of the rampart. The fortress was taken. Two or three days later, having received word of our staying, they marched off to Dalmau. That day we made ten kos and stopped at the bank of the Sarju beside a village called Chaksar in the Sagri[239] district.

On Wednesday halt was made at that site to rest the animals. Some said that Shaykh Bayazid and Biban had crossed the Ganges [378] and were planning to get themselves to their baggage via Chunar and Chond.[240] The begs were summoned for consultation, and it was decided that Muhammad-Zaman Mirza and Sultan-Junayd Barlas, who had received Chunar and some other districts in exchange for Jaunpur, along with Mahmud Khan Nohani, Qazi Jia, and Taj Khan Sarangkhani should go and block the rebels' way at Chunar.

The next morning, Thursday, we marched out early, left the Sarju, proceeded eleven kos, crossed the Parsaru, and camped on its bank. I summoned the begs for consultation. Esän Temür Sultan, Muhammad Sultan Mirza, Tokhta Buqa Sultan, Qasim Husayn Sultan, Beykhub Sultan, Muzaffar-Husayn Sultan, Qasim Khwaja, Ja'far Khwaja, Zahid Khwaja, Jan Beg with Askari's liege men, and Kichik Khwaja, as well as those led by the India amirs Alam Khan of Kalpi, Malikdad of Kara, and Rao Sarwani, were assigned to detach themselves at Dalmau in pursuit of Bayazid and Biban and proceed swiftly.

While at Parsaru, I was making my ablutions at night when lots of fish gathered, drawn by the candlelight up to the surface of the water. I and others near me caught fish with our hands.

On Friday we camped at the beginning of a branch of the Parsaru. It was an extremely narrow river. Lest it be changed by the crossing of the soldiers I had it blocked upstream, [378b] and for ablutions I had a place made that would be ten by ten. On the eve of the twenty-seventh [June 3] we stayed in that camp. The next morning we left this river and camped after crossing the East Tons. On Sunday we camped beside this same river. On Monday the twenty-ninth [June 6] we also halted beside the Tons River. This evening, although the sky was not clear, a few men saw the moon and bore witness before the qadi to that effect, so the beginning of the month was established.[241] On Tuesday morning we performed the feast prayer and mounted. We made ten kos and camped beside the Gomati one kos from Maing.[242] At around noon we indulged in some ma'jun. Shaykh Zayn, Mulla Shihab, and Khwandamir were sent this little poem and summoned.

Shaykh, Mulla Shihab, and Khwandamir: come all three, or two, or one.

Darwesh Muhammad, Yunus Ali, and Abdullah also were there. That afternoon the wrestlers wrestled.

Detail, wrestlers, from a *Gulistan* (Rose Garden) of Saʿdi, Herat (?), dated A.H. 891 (A.D. 1486), fol. 21r. Album page; opaque watercolor, ink, and gold on paper. Art and History Trust Collection.

On Wednesday we stayed at that camp. Around midmorning we had some maʿjun. Malik Sharq, who had gone to get Taj Khan out of Chunar, arrived. Pahlawan of Oudh, who had come before, wrestled with a Hindustani wrestler who had come, and threw him. [379] Yahya Nohani was given a fifteen-lac stipend from Sarwar, clad in a suit of clothing, and given leave.

The next morning we made eleven kos, crossed the Gomati, and camped on the banks. News was received from the sultans and begs who had gone on expedition that they had gone to Dalmau but had not yet crossed the Ganges. Letters of rebuke[243] were sent, saying, "Quickly cross the Ganges and proceed after the enemy. Cross the Jumna also, attach Alam Khan to yourselves, and make every effort to engage the enemy." After two overnights crossing the Gomati we came to Dalmau. Most of the soldiers forded the Ganges that day. After getting the camp across we had some ma'jun on an island downstream. Since the camp had not completely crossed, we crossed the river and halted one day at the site at which we were camped. Baqi Tashkandi came with the Oudh army that day to pay homage. One night away from the Ganges camp was made beside the Rind River beside Kora, which is twenty-two kos from Dalmau. On Thursday we marched from there and stopped opposite the Adampur district.

In order to cross in pursuit of the rebels, [379b] one or two of the raftsmen had been sent before to Kalpi to fetch what boats were there. That night, while we were camped there, a few boats arrived. A crossing was also found on the river. I stayed on the island because the campsite was so dusty. Because no confirmed reports of the enemy had come, Baqi Shiqavul was sent across with the warriors who were around to gather intelligence. The next day, Friday afternoon, Baqi Beg's servant came with information that Shaykh Bayazid and Biban's outpost had been defeated, their major warrior, a man named Mubarak Khan Jalwani, and a few others had been killed, and a few heads and a few men alive were being sent. The next morning Shah-Husayn Bakhshï, who had gone with Baqi, came and reported in detail the defeat of the advance party and other news from there. That evening, which was the eve of Saturday the thirteenth, the Jumna swelled so much that by the next morning the island was completely covered with water. I went a bow shot downstream to another island and had my tent set up there.

On Monday, Jalal Tashkandi, who had gone with the sultans and begs who had gone on the expedition, came with news that Shaykh Bayazid and Biban had fled from the Mahoba district.[244] [380] Since the monsoon was near and the soldiers, horses, and pack animals were exhausted after a five- or six-month expedition, the sultans and begs were ordered to halt in the place they had reached until a fresh raiding party could come from Agra and those parts. That afternoon Baqi Shiqavul and the Oudh army were dismissed. Musa Ma'ruf Farmuli, who had come to pay homage when we crossed the Sarju returning from the expedition, was assigned a thirty-lac stipend from the district of Amroha, awarded a regal suit of clothing and a horse with saddle, and given leave to go to Amroha.

RETURN TO AGRA

With my mind at ease concerning these parts, on Monday night after the first ghari of the third watch we set out at a gallop for Agra. The next morning we made sixteen kos and by almost noon stopped to spend the midday in a district of Kalpi called Bilaur. After giving barley to the horses we rode out in the evening. That night we proceeded thirteen kos, stopped to sleep at Bahadur Khan Sarwani's tomb in Saugandpur in the Kalpi district, performed the dawn prayer, and moved on. After sixteen kos we reached Etawah at noon. Mahdi Khwaja came to meet us. We rode out at the first watch of the night, slept a bit along the way, and, after going sixteen kos, reached Rapri [380b] and spent midday in Fatehpur. The next noon we rode from Fatehpur, proceeded seventeen kos, and dismounted at the Hasht Bihisht garden in Agra at the second watch of the night. The next day, Friday, Muhammad Bakhshï and some others came to pay homage. Crossing the Jumna around noon and paying homage to Khwaja Abdul-Haqq, I went to the citadel to see the begims my aunts.

Balkhi the gardener had been left to plant melons, and he had kept a few, which he brought me. They were very nice little melons. I had had one or two vines planted in the Hasht Bihisht garden, and they too had turned out to be rather nice grapes. Shaykh Ghuran had also brought a basket of grapes. They were not bad. I was particularly happy that melons and grapes could turn out so well in Hindustan.

It was the second watch of Saturday night when Mahïm came. We had ridden out on expedition on the tenth of Jumada I [January 21]. By the strangest of coincidences they had also set out from Kabul on that same day. On Thursday the first of Dhu'l-Qa'da [July 7], when I sat in court in the large divankhana, Humayun's and Mahïm's presents were displayed. This day a servant of Maghfur the Divan was given 150 porters and sent to Kabul to bring melons, grapes, and fruit. [381] On Saturday the third, Hindu Beg, who had escorted the women from Kabul and who had been sent to Sambhal when Ali Yusuf died, came to pay homage. Husamuddin Ali Khalifa also came this day from Alwar to pay homage. The next morning, Sunday, Abdullah, who had been sent to Sambhal from Trimuhani when Ali Yusuf died, came.

SEDITION IN LAHORE

From those who had come from Kabul it was heard that Shaykh Sharif of Qarabagh, either instigated by Abdul-Aziz or out of loyalty to him, had attributed to me oppression I had not committed and outrages that had not taken place. Affidavits to that effect were written, the religious authorities of Lahore were forced to sign their names, and copies of the affidavit were sent to various towns in hopes of stirring up a controversy. Abdul-Aziz had also disobeyed a number of orders and had said and done a number of improper things. For this reason on Sunday the eleventh [July 17], Qambar-Ali Arghun was dispatched to bring to court Shaykh Sharif, the religious authorities and elders of Lahore, and Abdul-Aziz.

On Thursday the fifteenth [July 21], Chïn Temür Sultan came from Tijara to pay homage. That same day, Pahlawan Sadiq and the great wrestler from Oudh wrestled. [381b] Sadiq made a half-throw, and that only with great difficulty.

On Monday the nineteenth [July 25], the Qïzïlbash ambassador, Murad Qorchï, was given a girth dagger and clad in an appropriate robe of honor, awarded two lacs of tankas, and dismissed.

REBELLION IN GWALIOR

These days Sayyid Mashhadi came from Gwalior to report Rahimdad's instigation of rebellion. Khalifa's liege man Shah-Muhammad Muhrdar was sent to deliver some extremely harsh words of advice I had written. He went and returned a few days later with Rahimdad's son. Although the son had come, Rahimdad himself was not planning to. Nur Beg was dispatched to Gwalior on Tuesday the fifth of Dhu'l-Hijja [August 11] to allay his fears. A few days later Nur Beg returned and reported Rahimdad's requests. Decrees had been completed as he had asked and were at the point of being sent when one of Rahimdad's servants came and reported, "I have been sent to abduct his son. He is not planning to come." As soon as we heard this, we mounted to attack Gwalior, but just then Khalifa said, "I will write him another letter of advice and send it. Perhaps he will come 'round." For this purpose Shihabuddin Khusraw was sent.

On Thursday the seventh of the month [August 13], [382] Mahdi Khwaja came from Etawah. On the day of the feast [245] Hindu Beg was rewarded with a regal suit of clothing, a jewel-studded girth sword, and a fine horse. Hasan Ali, who was known among the Turcomans as "Chaghatay," was rewarded with a suit of clothing, a jewel-studded girth dagger, and an estate worth seven lacs.

EVENTS OF THE YEAR 936
(1529-30)[246]

On Tuesday the third of Muharram [September 7], Shihabuddin Khusraw came from Gwalior with Shaykh Muhammad Ghaws to intercede on behalf of Rahimdad. Since the shaykh was a dervish and a powerful spiritual man, I forgave Rahimdad's crime for his sake. Shaykh Ghuran and Nur Beg were sent to Gwalior so that Gwalior could be turned over to them...

NOTES

1. Babur's name has also appeared as Baber and Babar. There is not the slightest doubt, however, that the name is Babur (BAH-boor), which is ultimately derived from the Indo-European word for beaver. Although it has often been suggested that Babur means tiger, it has, in fact, nothing to do with the Persian word *babr*, "tiger." Mirza Muhammad Haydar explains how Babur was given his nickname: "At that time the Chaghatái were very rude and uncultured, and not refined as they are now; thus they found [his given name] Zahir-ud-Din Muhammad difficult to pronounce, and for this reason gave him the name of [Babur]" (Muhammad Haydar Dughlat, *A History of the Moghuls of Central Asia*, trans. E. Denison Ross, ed. and annot. Ney Elias [London: Sampson Low, Marston, 1898; reissue, New York: Praeger Publications, 1970], 173). For evidence of the reading Babur, see *Baburnama*, ed. W. M. Thackston, Sources of Oriental Languages and Literatures 18, Sources of Turkish Literature 16, part 1 (Cambridge, Mass.: Harvard University Department of Near Eastern Languages and Civilizations, 1993), xv, and E. Denison Ross, ed., "A Collection of Poems by the Emperor Babur," *Journal and Proceedings of the Asiatic Society of Bengal* 6 (1910): extra no., iv–vi.

2. Because he had a lifelong limp caused by a wound suffered during his youth, Amir Temür was known to his foes as Temür-i-Lang (Temür the Lame); that epithet, misunderstood as part of the name, has given a host of Western forms, such as Tamerlane, Tamburlaine, and Timurlink (via Arabic). Since there is no doubt that his real Turkish name was Temür (iron), there is no reason not to use it.

3. *Memoirs of Babar, Emperor of India, First of the Great Moghuls*, ed. F. G. Talbot (London: Arthur L. Humphreys, 1909), viii.

4. The "royal memoir" flourished around Babur's time. Somewhat earlier than Babur, Sultan-Husayn Mirza wrote in Chaghatay Turkish what has been called an apologia, but it is not autobiographical in any real sense (see Tourkhan Gandjeï, "Uno scritto apologetico di Husain Mirza, sultano del Khorasan," *Annali del' Istituto Orientale di Napoli*, n.s. 5 [1953]:

157–83. English translation by W. M. Thackston in *A Century of Princes* [Cambridge, Mass.: Aga Khan Program, 1989], 373–78). Babur's daughter, Gulbadan Begim, kept a diary of her own in which she recorded her brother Humayun's exploits (*The History of Humayun* [*Humayunnama*], trans. Annette Susannah Beveridge [London: Royal Asiatic Society, 1902]). Somewhat later the Safavid Shah Tahmasp (r. 1524–76) kept a diary for a few years of his reign, and he may have known of Babur's memoirs (Tahmasp 1, *Tadhkira-i Shah Tahmasp* [Berlin: Kaviani, 1343/1924]). The Mughal Emperor Jahangir (r. 1605–27) was certainly inspired by his great-grandfather Babur to keep a journal in which he recorded significant events of his reign and jotted down interesting tidbits and miscellaneous observations, but it lacks the focus, introspection, and analysis that makes Babur's work memorable (Jahangir, *Tuzuk-i-Jahangiri*, trans. A. Rogers, ed. Henry Beveridge [London, 1909–14]).

5. *Baburnama*, folio 201.

6. The type of Turkish that Babur spoke and wrote is now called Chaghatay Turkish because it was the dominant spoken language throughout the Ulus Chaghatay (see "Genghisid and Timurid Background," p. xxxv). Those who spoke it never called it anything other than Türki (Turkish), but now it needs to be distinguished from the modern Turkish of the Republic of Turkey, to which it is only distantly related, and from other forms of Turkish, such as Uzbek, Kirghiz, and Kazakh.

7. Since Babur never completed his memoirs, he did not give them a title. *Baburnama* (literally, Book of Babur) is a convenient title given to both the original Chaghatay Turkish text and the sixteenth-century Persian translation.

8. Samsam-ud-daula Shah Nawaz Khan, *The Maathir-ul-umara*, trans. Henry Beveridge (Calcutta: Royal Asiatic Society of Bengal, 1911–41), 1:368–78. Bayram Khan's great-grandfather was the Ali-Shukr Beg mentioned on folio 28 of the *Baburnama*. His grandfather, Yar Beg, had been in Khusrawshah's service in Badakhshan, where Bayram Khan was born.

9. Bayram Khan, *The Persian and Turki Divans of Bayram Khan*, ed. E. Denison Ross (Calcutta: Royal Asiatic Society of Bengal, 1910); for Abdul-Rahim Khankhanan's distinguished career see Abdul-Baqi Nihawandi, *Maathir-i-Rahimi*, ed. M. Hidayet Husain (Calcutta: Bibliotheca Indica, 1910–31).

10. Abu'l-Fazl, *Akbarnama*, trans. Henry Beveridge (Calcutta: Royal Asiatic Society of Bengal, 1897–1921), 3:862.

11. It is extremely unlikely, given the turmoil after Babur's death and Humayun's years of exile in Iran (1542–55), that there had ever been time to have many copies of the memoirs produced. The Persian translation

of the *Baburnama* incorporates into the text a marginal note Humayun made on Babur's mention of Humayun's first shave (fol. 263). The inclusion of Humayun's comment implies that Abdul-Rahim was working from the original manuscript, on which Humayun had made marginal notes.

12. Abdul-Hamid Lahawri, author of the *Badshahnama*, a history of Shahjahan's reign, writes:

    The auspicious career of the champion of blessed lineage, the ruler of heavenly temperament, adorner of the throne of might and majesty, solver of the knottiest problems of rule and reign, His Majesty Firdaws-Makani [Babur's posthumous title] Zahiruddin Muhammad Babur Padishah Ghazi, was recorded in the *Baburid Events*, which his majesty wrote in the Turki language in his own auspicious handwriting, and which, except for a few quires on the events of several years that have fallen away, is found in the imperial library (*Badshahnama*, ed. Kabir Al-Din and Abd Al-Rahim [Calcutta: Royal Asiatic Society of Bengal, 1867–68], 1:42, trans. mine).

13. See Ellen Smart, "Paintings from the *Baburnama:* A Study of Sixteenth-Century Mughal Historical Manuscript Illustrations" (Ph.D. diss., School of Oriental and African Studies, University of London, 1977), and John Seyller, "Scribal Notes on Mughal Manuscript Illustrations," *Artibus Asiae* 48 (1987): 247–77.

14. John Leyden and William Erskine, trans., *Memoirs of Zehir-ed-din Muhammed Baber, Emperor of Hindustan* (London: Longman, Rees, Orme, Brown, and Green, 1826). The Leyden-Erskine translation was abridged in 1909 (Talbot, *Memoirs of Babar*) and later revised and annotated by Sir Lucas King (Oxford: Oxford University Press, 1921). Sir Lucas's annotations on Indian geography are particularly valuable.

15. Leyden and Erskine, *Memoirs*, viii–ix.

16. Nikolai Ilminski, ed., *Baber-nameh Diagataice ad fidem codicis Petropolitani* (Kazan: Qazan Universityetining Tab'khanasi, 1857).

17. Abel Pavet de Courteille, trans., *Mémoires de Baber* (Paris: Maisonneuve, 1871).

18. *The Bábar-náma, Being the Autobiography of the Emperor Bábar, the Founder of the Moghul Dynasty in India, Written in Chaghatáy Turkish,* facsimile edited and indexed by Annette Susannah Beveridge (London: Luzac, 1905).

19. Annette Susannah Beveridge, trans., *The Babur-nama in English* (London: Luzac, 1921), 1:lix.

20. The translator into Persian was so intent upon reproducing Turkish syntax that he created forms that did not exist in Persian, such as *firod amada*

shud ("it was dismounted," an "impersonal passive" of an intransitive verb) for *tüshüldi*, a viable form in Turkish but not in Persian or English.

21. Muhammad Haydar Dughlat, *History of the Moghuls*, 173 f.

22. For examples of the florid style of these authors, see Thackston, *Century of Princes*, 363–78.

23. In several places it is obvious from the construction of the Turkish that what were originally marginal annotations have been incorporated "un-Turkically" into the text. Instead of the equivalent of "X's son Y, X being...," the text has "X's, who was..., son Y."

24. E. M. Forster, "The Emperor Babur," *Abinger Harvest* (New York: Harcourt, Brace and World, 1964), 303.

25. Forster, "Emperor Babur," 303.

26. Modern cartographers, particularly of the former Soviet Union, have fallen into the trap of thinking that all toponyms in the former Soviet Union are best represented by Cyrillic spelling; however, when Cyrillic is scrupulously transliterated into the Latin alphabet and the diacriticals for non-Slavic languages are ignored, Central Asian place-names can be severely distorted, as "Shakhrisyabz" for Shahrisabz, and "Gissar" for Hissar. Place-names that occur in the text are not translated even in the rare instance when they are still meaningful (e.g., Shahrisabz, Persian for Greenville). Translations for meaningful names of buildings, gardens, and so forth are generally provided (e.g., Kök Saray is Blue Palace).

27. Muhammad Haydar Dughlat, *A History of the Moghuls of Central Asia*, trans. E. Denison Ross, ed. and annot. Ney Elias (London: Sampson Low, Marston, 1898. Reissue: New York: Praeger Publications, 1970), 173.

28. Forster, "Emperor Babur," 304.

THE GENGHISID AND TIMURID: BACKGROUND OF IRAN
AND CENTRAL ASIA (P. XXXV)

1. From 1405, Shahrukh was recognized as the nominal ruler of Samarkand, although he remained in Herat. His son Ulughbeg Mirza was governor of Samarkand from 1411 until Shahrukh's death in 1447, when Ulughbeg became the effective ruler of Samarkand. Thereafter the two capitals were ruled separately until they were reunited in 1459 by Sultan-Abusa'id Mirza.

2. In Babur's time "Sart" referred more to settled peoples than to language or ethnic identification. Settled Turks were called Sarts even though they may have preserved their Turkish language, but since the vast majority of the settled population was Persian speaking, "Sart" most often referred to Persians. "Tajik" was closer to an ethnic term and designated the Iranian, Persian-speaking population specifically. Timurid adminis-

tration was divided into the *Türk dīvānī* (Turkish administration) and *Sart dīvānī* (Sart administration), and the phrase "Turk and Tajik" was used to include the entire population at large.

3. The exceptions to the Turkic military were high-ranking Sart bureaucrats, who accompanied the army on expeditions and also participated in battle. See Babur's comments (fol. 105b) on Khwaja Muhammad Ali, a Sart who got confused during a battle.

4. The name of Genghis Khan, also spelled Jenghis Khan and Jenghiz Khan, is synonymous in the West with butchery and slaughter, and since Mongolians have no effective lobbying power in our educational system, nothing has been done to rehabilitate Genghis Khan's centuries-old negative image. However, in fifteenth-century Central Asia, Genghisid descent was a powerful legitimizing factor. Where Genghisids reigned, their right to rule was unquestioned. Even where rulers were not descended from Genghis, as in Timurid Herat, Genghisid protocol was observed (see Babur's comments on fol. 186b).

5. René Grousset, *The Empire of the Steppes* (New Brunswick: Rutgers University Press, 1970), 326–28. Although the word *moghul,* employed in the *Baburnama* and elsewhere for the Turkicized descendants of Genghis Khan's Mongols, is originally the same as Mongol, and Moghulistan also means Mongolia proper, we have retained "Moghul" and "Moghulistan" in the translation to distinguish the Chaghatayid Turks of Moghulistan from the Mongols of today's Mongolia, who do not figure at all in Babur's writings.

6. Muhammad Haydar Dughlat, *History of the Moghuls,* 153.

7. When Babur says that Mongolian was spoken among some of the Hazaras and Negüdäris in the mountains of Ghazni (fol. 131b), he may mean a Mongolianized dialect of Turkish. It is quite possible, however, they they actually spoke a form of Mongolian.

8. Muhammad Haydar Dughlat, *History of the Moghuls,* 97.

9. Ibid., 83 f.

PART ONE: FERGANA AND TRANSOXIANA (P. 1)

1. In Ptolemaic geography the world is divided into seven climes south to north, the third through the fifth being the habitable climes.

2. For a description of the "Moghuls" see p. 26. The Uzbeks (Özbegs) were a tribal confederation formed by the Shiban khans ("arabicized" to Shayban), descendants of Genghis Khan's eldest son, Jöchi, through Jöchi's son Shiban, brother of the Qipchaq khans Batu and Berke. The Uzbek confederation that overwhelmed Transoxiana and threatened Khurasan in the early sixteenth century under the Shaybanids soon broke into nu-

merous khanates and successor states in Turkistan, but it has left its
name in modern Uzbekistan.

3. Babur uses the names Jaxartes (Syr Darya) and Khodzhent interchangeably.

4. Babur uses the names Kish and Shahrisabz interchangeably.

5. See folios 170b–171 for Babur's description of Mir Ali-Sher Nawa'i.

6. Khwaja Yusuf was a well-known singer contemporary with Baysunghur
Mirza (1397–1433). A passage concerning him occurs in Dawlatshah's
Tadhkirat al-shu'ara:

> It is related that during Baysunghur's time Khwaja Yusuf Andigani had
> no equal in all the world in recitation and singing. Khwaja Yusuf's Da-
> vidic voice pierced the heart, and his Chosroic melody augmented the
> agony of passion. Sultan-Ibrahim b. Shahrukh in Shiraz several times
> asked Baysunghur for Khwaja Yusuf, but he refused. Finally he sent one
> hundred thousand dinars in cash for Prince Baysunghur to send him
> Khwaja Yusuf. In reply Sultan Baysunghur sent this line: "We do not
> sell our Joseph [Yusuf]. You keep your black silver" (W. M. Thackston,
> *A Century of Princes* [Cambridge, Mass.: Aga Khan Program, 1989], 23.

7. The "league" (Turkish *yïghach,* Persian *farsang*) is a distance measured by
time: the distance a caravan can travel in one hour. Hence the distance of
a league varies over different terrains. As Annette Susannah Beveridge
has observed (*The Babur-nama in English* [London: Luzac, 1921], 1:4, n.5).
Babur's league ranges from about 4 to 8 miles, the lower figure being the
more normal equivalent. Once out of Transoxiana, Babur generally uses
the Indian *kos* for land measurement (though he first uses it in fol. 40,
outside of Samarkand).

8. Although "Sart" generally refers to the Persian populace (as opposed to
Turk), Babur may use the term to indicate settled peoples, without reference to language, as opposed to the transhumant and predominantly
but not exclusively Turkish tribesmen.

9. Shaykh Burhanuddin Ali Qilich al-Marghinani (ca. 1135–97) was the author of a famous compendium of Hanafi jurisprudence, *al-Hidaya fi furu'
al-hanafiyya* (Guidance in the Branches of Hanafism). An English translation of the Persian translation of this work commissioned by the gov-
ernor-general of India, Warren Hastings, was published by Charles
Hamilton in London in 1791. Hanafi is one of the four schools of jurisprudence of Sunni Islam and the one that is predominant in Central
Asia.

10. According to Khwandamir, the khans' expedition against Shaybani Khan
was mounted in 906, certainly a mistake, for by Babur's own account (fol.

103b ff.) it was in 908 (1502–3), most likely during the spring of 1503. Babur set out for Kabul in June 1504 after a year in the hills south of Fergana (the account of that year is missing from the memoirs, although he refers to it several times) (Khwandamir, *Habib al-siyar fi akhbar-i afrad-i bashar,* ed. Jalal Huma'i, vol. 4 [Tehran: Khayyam, 1333], 305).

11. Khwaja Kamaluddin Mas'ud Khujandi ("of Khodzhent") was a Persian poet who died around 1400.

12. Directly north of Khodzhent, and on the opposite side of the Syr Darya, is Mount Muzbek, with a summit of 1,245 meters (4,100 feet) above Khodzhent.

13. "Almond Town."

14. Asiruddin Akhsikati (d. ca. 1181) was one of the outstanding Persian poets of the twelfth century. His career began in Transoxiana, and he later served the Seljuq Sultan Arslan (1161–77) and several of the Atabegs of Azerbaijan.

15. Neither the correct form nor the meaning of this obscure expression has been ascertained with any degree of certainty. However, it may be *postin pesh-i-barra,* "the fleece before the lamb." Apparently, the sense is that the pleasant gardens lining the riverbank at Kassan are the "fleece" of the "lamb" that is at some remove, like Akhsi, where the gardens are at a distance from the town proper.

16. Yeti Kent probably refers to the district formerly called Haftdeh, the borderlands of eastern Fergana. See V. V. Bartold, *Turkistan Down to the Mongol Invasion.* E.J.W. Gibb Memorial Series, n.s. 5 (London: Luzac, 1928), 156.

17. That is, three to four thousand is the number of warriors the income of the province can support.

18. Padishah and other titles, such as amir, beg, begïm, khan, khanïm, khwaja, mawlana, mulla, mir, mirza, and sayyid, are explained in the Translator's Preface (pp. xxvi–xxvii) and the Glossary.

19. For the "Moghul nation," see pp. xli–xlii.

20. The "Chachi" (from Chach, another name for Tashkent) bow has been used in Persian since at least the beginning of the eleventh century (it is mentioned several times in Firdawsi's *Shahnama*). Often used as a metaphor for eyebrows, the Chachi bow was apparently a particularly fine type of bow, although the shape and material from which it was made are not known.

21. When Babur says "at that date" he means the time about which he is writing, that is, 899 (1493–94); "at this date" means the time he is writing.

22. It is impossible to reproduce the Turkish puns in this sentence, which reads, literally, he "flew from the ravine with his doves and dovecote and

became a falcon." "To become a falcon" is to die; "to fly" in both Turkish (*uchmaq*) and Persian (*paridan*) also means "to fall through the air."

23. *Beg atäkä:* a tutor to a prince.
24. *Dastarpech:* a peaked felt cap around which the turban was wound.
25. See note 160 below for Mongolian cap.
26. See note 9 above for Hanafi.
27. Khwaja Nasiruddin Ubaydullah, known as Khwaja Ahrar (1403–88), was a great shaykh of the Naqshbandi order. His life is the principal topic of the *Rashahat 'ayn al-hayat* (Effusions from the Spring of Life) by Mawlana Nuruddin Abdul-Rahman Jami (1414–92).
28. "[B]oth *Khamsas*" refers to the *Khamsa* (Quintet) of Ilyas b. Yusuf Nizami (1141–1209) and that of Amir Khusraw of Delhi (1253–1325). The first *Khamsa* was by Nizami of Ganja (later Kirovabad and now back to Ganja, but spelled Gyandzha) in Azerbaijan. The five poems that make up Nizami's Quintet are *Makhzan al-asrar* (Treasury of Secrets, a collection of aphorisms and good counsel), *Khusraw and Shirin, Layli and Majnun, Haft paykar* (Seven Beauties, tales narrated to Bahram Gor by the princesses of the seven climes), and the two-part *Sikandarnama* (the legendary exploits of Alexander the Great). The first, and greatest, imitation of Nizami's quintet was by Amir Khusraw, who wrote a *Khamsa* closely modeled on Nizami's.

The *Mathnawi* refers to the great opus of Persian mysticism, *Mathnawi-i-na'nawi* by Jalaluddin Rumi (1207–73).

29. The *Shahnama* (Book of Kings), completed in 1010 by Firdawsi, is the epic of Iranian kingship. In it are preserved the mythical, legendary, and quasihistorical exploits of the kings and heroes of Iran from creation to the Arab invasion.
30. *Ma'jun:* a mildly narcotic confection.
31. "Goat Jump."
32. Now called the Chirchik.
33. From *tümän* (literally, ten thousand; a military division) comes the title *tümän beg,* a leader of a military division of ten thousand.
34. "Black Eyes."
35. The date of the Diaspora of Erzän is given as 832 (1428–29) in the *Tarikh-i Rashidi* (Muhammad Haydar Dughlat, *History of the Moghuls,* 84).
36. Iraq encompassed Persian Iraq (the western part of modern Iran, Isfahan, Hamadan, and environs westward to the Zagros Mountains) and Arab Iraq, the other side of the Zagros, the southeastern portion of modern Iraq, including Baghdad and environs.
37. The name is given in Muhammad Haydar Dughlat, *History of the Moghuls* (p. 86), as "Mir Pir Haji Kunji."

38. The Moghul custom was to place the nominee to the khanate on a piece of felt and physically lift him.
39. The daughter was Habibi Sultan Khanïsh. See Muhammad Haydar Dughlat, *History of the Moghuls,* 207.
40. The wording here implies an embrace of piety after sowing the wild oats of youth.
41. Alexander the Great passed through Bactria in 329 B.C., leaving behind powerful Hellenicizing elements. According to legend, the shahs of Badakhshan were descended from Alexander:

> After he had conquered the regions of the world, [Alexander] consulted with his wise men, saying: "Find me a place which shall be out of the reach of the princes of the earth, in which I may place my descendants." The councillors chose Badakhshán, and they wrote a Book of Regulations; so that as long as the regulations were observed, no one prince could prevail in this country. From the time of [Alexander] down to the time of Sháh Sultán Muhammad, nobody had attacked Badakhshán. Thus they had ruled from generation to generation (Muhammad Haydar Dughlat, *History of the Moghuls,* 107).

42. In the 1450s and 1460s many clans formerly under the Uzbek khanate deserted the Uzbek Abu'l-Khayr Khan and joined Esän-Buqa II Khan Chaghatay (brother of Babur's grandfather, Yunus Khan), who settled them on the marches of Moghulistan. Known as Kazakhs (Qazaqs, "adventurers, brigands"), or Kirghiz-Kazakhs, they were constituted in three hordes. The territory of the Little Horde (*kishi jüz*) was between the Caspian and Aral seas in winter and the southern slopes of the Urals in summer; the Middle Horde (*orta jüz*) wintered on the Jaxartes and summered near the Tobol, Ishim, and Irtysh rivers; and the Great Horde (*ulu jüz*) wintered south of Lake Balkhash in what is now Semirechye and summered in the high valleys of the T'ien Shan and Altai mountains. One of their great leaders, Qasim Khan (ca. 1509–18), mentioned by Babur, attempted to unite the three hordes into a confederation. The Kazakh have given their name to the modern Kazakhstan, a Czarist and Soviet creation. See René Grousset, *The Empire of the Steppes* (New Brunswick: Rutgers University Press, 1970), 479 f.
43. In Temür's time the title Qauchin designated an elite band of royal bodyguards, and the title appears to have become hereditary. In time the Qauchins formed a class, but they do not seem to have ever formed a tribe. Their primary loyalty was to the ruler rather than to territory or a chieftain. See Beatrice F. Manz, *The Rise and Rule of Tamerlane* (Cambridge: Cambridge University Press, 1989), 161–63.

44. Taghayï, literally "maternal uncle," is a title applied to virtually all relatives on the maternal side.

45. *Nasta'liq* (originally called *naskh-ta'liq*) is a highly cursive form of Arabic script. Although it may have originated in Azerbaijan, this form of writing, which became the script par excellence of Persian, was developed as a refined art form in Herat during the reign of Shahrukh (1405–47). See calligraphy on p. 217.

46. "Butcher."

47. *Charbagh:* literally "four garden"; a garden, usually with a pool in the middle, divided into four sections by crosswalks. See illus. p. 157.

48. *Namazgah:* an area outside a city where festival prayers could be performed by the whole population together.

49. *Shaykhu'l-islam:* the chief religious official in a given region.

50. Jahangir Mirza was Babur's younger brother.

51. Darwesh Muhammad Tarkhan was amir to Sultan-Ahmad (*Mu'izz al-ansab fi shajarat al-ansab,* anonymous MS. Paris, Bibliothèque Nationale, Ancien Fonds Persan 67, fol. 154a).

52. See note 9 above for Hanafi.

53. *Ichki:* a member of a prince's inner circle; literally "insider."

54. "Black Eyes." See folios 9–9b.

55. The Turkish term is *qazaqliq,* a guerilla engagement. It refers to a claimant's battles and combats during an interregnum or before the claimant attains the throne. Here he means the period before he took Samarkand the second time—in 906 (1500–01).

56. The Arghuns were a Turco-Mongolian clan that rose to prominence with Zu'n-Nun Arghun. See note 87.

57. *Kükäldash:* "milk-brother/-sister"; in Turco-Iranian society, children nursed by the same woman were bonded as "milk-brothers" and "-sisters"; members of the opposite sex so related were forbidden to marry.

58. The *khwanzadas* (not to be confused with *khanzadas;* see Glossary) were the daughters of the Mir Khwands of Termez who married into the House of Timur.

59. *Divan:* a collection of a poet's works.

60. *Muhtasib:* the morals officer of a town or city.

61. To gain one's livelihood by producing copies of the Koran was considered an extremely pious act, particularly for a ruler.

62. *Qopuz:* a lutelike musical instrument.

63. *Saz:* also a lutelike musical instrument.

64. The Uyghurs, an ancient Turkic people, inhabited the eastern end of Lake Balkhash at the beginning of the eighth century. In 744 the khan of the Uyghurs took advantage of disturbances in Mongolia to set himself

up, with the approval of the T'ang court, as khaghan. This Uyghur kingdom, which adopted Manichaeism as its official religion, flourished for a century with its capital at Karabalgasun, then called Ordubaligh. The lasting contribution of the Uyghurs to Inner Asian civilization was the development of a script, derived from Syriac, by means of which they created a national literature. Later, after the destruction of the kingdom in 840 and the dispersal of the Uyghurs, they served as mentors to the unlettered peoples who succeeded them, including the Mongols, to whom they bequeathed their alphabet. The Uyghur alphabet was still used in eastern Turkistan and Moghulistan at the beginning of the Timurid period, and Uyghurs, like Ali-Sher Nawai's father, Kichikkinä, were often found in high bureaucratic positions throughout the Timurid period. See Grousset, *Empire,* 113 f., 120–26.

65. "Blue Palace." Babur describes the Kök Saray in folios 37 and 45b.
66. The year A.H. 900 corresponds to October 2, 1494–September 20, 1495.
67. A *ghazi* is a warrior for the faith. Rulers who made raids on non-Muslim territory could style themselves "ghazi."
68. After the death of the Qaraqoyunlu Jahanshah and the rise to power of the Aqqoyunlu Uzun Hasan in Persian Iraq and Azerbaijan, Jahanshah's eldest surviving son sent a request for assistance to Sultan-Abusa'id Mirza. In response, Sultan-Abusa'id made plans for an Iraq-Azerbaijan campaign and set out from Khurasan in February 1468. After negotiations failed and a defeat was dealt to Sultan-Abusa'id's forces, he was captured by Uzun Hasan's sons and executed in Qarabagh, Arran, on February 5, 1469.
69. Iron Gates, another name for Quhlugha (fol. 124), is south of Shahrisabz.
70. Folio 120b.
71. The Baharlu, also known as the Barani, were one of the premier Turcoman tribes of the Qaraqoyunlu confederation of Eastern Anatolia and Azerbaijan. Ali-Shukr Barani (Baharlu)'s son, Pir-Ali Beg, joined Sultan-Mahmud Mirza's service in Hisar Shadman. His son, Yar Beg, was with Khusrawshah in Badakhshan, and later he and his son, Sayf-Ali Beg, were in Babur's service. Sayf-Ali Beg's son, Bayram Khan, who was born in Badakhshan, became regent to the young Akbar Shah after Humayun's death. Bayram Khan's son, the khankhanan Abdul-Rahim, produced the Persian translation of the *Baburnama* that was presented to Akbar in 1589. See Samsam-ud-Daula Shah Nawaz Khan and Abdul-Hayy, *The Maathir-ul-umara,* trans. Henry Beveridge (Calcutta: Royal Asiatic Society of Bengal, 1911–52), 1:368–78.
72. Occasionally in Timurid histories persons with the tribal name Qipchaq are encountered; among them is Shaykh-Nuruddin Beg Qipchaq, an of-

ficer of Amir Temür's whose daughter was married to the Chaghatayid Ways Khan. The Qipchaqs were probably a minor tribe in the Ulus Chaghatay, without territory of their own (Manz, *Rise and Rule of Tamerlane,* 163). The original mass of the Qipchaqs had long since departed Central Asia and had headed in the direction of Europe. By the middle of the eleventh century they were in the steppe north of the Black Sea, where they remained masters until the Genghisid invasions of the thirteenth century. They bequeathed their name, however, to the entire steppe north of the Black Sea and the Caspian, practically the whole of modern Kazakhstan and the southern Ukraine, which was known in Persian sources throughout the medieval period as the Dasht-i-Qipchaq (Qipchaq Steppe). The Jöchid realm established there, the Golden and White Hordes, was also known as the khanate of Qipchaq. See Grousset, *Empire,* 185 f.

73. Amir Pir-Darwesh Hazaraspi and his brother Amir Ali were made governors of Balkh by Abu'l-Qasim Babur Mirza, and they were both felled at Andkhui in the spring of 1454 while attempting to stave off Sultan-Abusa'id Mirza's advance into Khurasan (Khwandamir, *Habib al-siyar,* 4:52).

74. The *khutba* is part of the Friday congregational prayer during which the name of the sovereign is announced. Mention of the ruler's name in the khutba and the issue of coinage in a ruler's name were the two methods of announcing de facto sovereignty and suzerainty in the medieval Islamic world.

75. The year A.H. 901 corresponds to September 21, 1495–September 8, 1496.

76. Babur's Kumrud, one of the sources of the Surkhandarya, is now known as the Karatag, which ends a short but treacherous distance from Sary-Tag across a 15,000-foot peak in the Gissarskiy (Hissar) Range (Bartold, *Turkistan,* 72).

77. This narrative is picked up again at folio 41.

78. "New Garden."

79. From its name, "Orchard Palace," it is apparent that the Bustan Saray was a pavilion or edifice either with an orchard attached, overlooking an orchard, or built on the site of an orchard. Babur's wording on folio 44b suggests that the Bustan Saray was inside the citadel.

80. This means that Khwaja Ubaydullah's elder son, Muhammad Ubaydullah Khwajaka Khwaja, supported Baysunghur Mirza, and the younger son, Khwaja Yahya, supported Sultan-Ali Mirza.

81. The year A.H. 902 corresponds to September 9, 1496–August 29, 1497.

82. Like the Chachi bow, the name of the Circassian sword may refer to a type and not to actual place of manufacture.
83. The Fitr holiday, which marks the end of the Ramadan fast, is held on the first of Shawwal.
84. *Kos:* an Indian measure of distance (*kuroh*), approximately 2 miles. See note 7 above for Babur's use of *kos.*
85. "Scarface."
86. An explanatory note is interpolated in the British Library manuscript of the Persian translation of the *Baburnama* (Add. 26,200): "That is, on account of the dispute between Muzaffar-Husayn and Muhammad-Mu'min, Muzaffar-Husayn's father Sultan-Husayn attacked Muhammad-Mu'min's father Badi'uzzaman Mirza in Balkh, and Sultan-Husayn's son Muzaffar-Husayn attacked Badi'uzzaman's son Muhammad-Mu'min in Astarabad."
87. A synoptic account of Zu'n-Nun Arghun's career is given by Khwandamir (*Habib al-siyar,* 4:170 f.), as follows:

> Amir Zu'n-Nun Arghun, son of Hasan Basri, was renowned for his valor and bravery among all the warriors of the Timurid ulus and was outstanding among ascetics for his orthodoxy and religiosity.... Without fear of exaggeration it can be said that this amir was totally brave and absolutely just, and in discharging his religious duties he made great endeavor. From dawn to dusk he dispensed justice, and from morn to evening he performed supererogatory acts and read the Koran. In battle the spirits of Isfandyar and Rustam would have cried bravo for his championlike daring, and in the prayer niche the spirit of Zu'n-Nun of Egypt and Ibrahim Adham would have applauded his perfect sincerity.

88. The year A.H. 903 corresponds to August 30, 1497–August 18, 1498.
89. "Playing-Field Garden."
90. In the Persian text (fols. 41a–42a) the continued narrative of the dispute between Sultan-Husayn and Badi'uzzaman is placed here.
91. These coordinates are by medieval reckoning. By modern standards Samarkand is at 67° longitude, 39° 40' latitude.
92. "Well-protected town."
93. The caliph Uthman ibn 'Affan ruled from 644–56.
94. Of the first generation of Muslims, those who actually knew the Prophet Muhammad (A.D. 570–632) are called the Companions (Sahaba). Many of them, such as Qutham b. Abbas, who died in Samarkand, went into the newly conquered territories to proselytize.
95. "King's Shrine."

96. Ruy González de Clavijo, the emissary to Temür from Don Henry III of Castile and Leon who arrived in Samarkand in 1404, has the following observation, which shows that the epithet of "Fat City" was already well known then:

    The richness and abundance of this great capital and its district is such as is indeed a wonder to behold: and it is for this reason that it bears the name of Samarqand: for this name would be more exactly written Semíz-kent, two words which signify "Rich-Town," for *Semíz* is fat or rich and *Kent* means city or township: in time these two words having been corrupted into the name Samarqand (Clavijo, *Embassy to Tamerlane, 1403–1406*. Trans. Guy Le Strange [New York and London: Harper and Bros., 1928], 287).

97. The Maturidites and Ash'arites were two schools of theological method that emerged around the end of the tenth century. Both used rational argumentation to defend their positions against more conservative groups, whose arguments were based on revelation and tradition; of the two the Maturidites, who were generally Hanafite, were more liberal than the Shafiite Ash'arites. From the middle of the twelfth century on, the Ash'arite school of thought was as close to an "orthodox" norm as Islam ever developed.

98. Khwaja Isma'il, or Muhammad b. Isma'il al-Bukhari (1407–66), was the author of one of the two standard compilations of prophetic *hadith*, known as the *Sahih Bukhari*. The hadith is the body of the Prophet Muhammad's sayings, a major source of precedent for Islamic law, and the study of the hadith confers religious merit.

99. See note 9 above for the *Hidaya* (Guidance).

100. If it is actually Persian and not a reflex of an older, non-Persian name, Kohak means "Little Mountain."

101. Dictionaries define the *sahibi* grape as a "large, thin-skinned red grape."

102. Koran 2:127.

103. Bagh-i-Dulday is "Dulday's Garden" and Bagh-i-Dilgusha is "Garden of Delight."

104. Amir Temür set out on his India Campaign in March 1398 and, after raiding as far as Delhi, returned to Samarkand in April 1399.

105. Bagh-i-Chanar is "Plane Tree Garden"; Bagh-i-Shimal, "Garden of the North Wind"; and Bagh-i-Bihisht, "Garden of Paradise."

106. *Madrasa:* an Islamic institution of higher learning.

107. *Khanaqah:* a Sufi hospice and chapterhouse.

108. "Muqatta'" means "piecework."

109. The kiblah is the direction of Mecca, toward which all Muslims turn

when they pray. This kiblah was determined by a great circle and not by simple compass direction.

110. A *zij* is an astronomical handbook that gives, among other things, the celestial locations of stars. Ulughbeg Mirza (1394–1449), eldest son of Shahrukh Mirza and grandson of Amir Temür, was a keen astronomer, and while he ruled in Samarkand he constructed an observatory on an enormous scale, some remnants of which can be seen today. The tables in the *Zij-i-Gurkani*, a reference to Ulughbeg's title Kürägän ("son-in-law," i.e., married to a Genghisid princess), begin in 1437.

111. Khwaja Nasiruddin Tusi (1201–74), great polymath of the thirteenth century, is known particularly for his work on astronomy, celestial mechanics, and ethics. The compilation of the tables in the *Zij-i-Ilkhani* was begun at the observatory in Maragha, Azerbaijan, by order of the Ilkhan Hülägü Khan (r. 1256–65) and completed under his successor, Abaqa Khan (r. 1265–82).

112. Claudius Ptolemy was an astronomer, mathematician, and geographer of second-century Alexandria; his *Mathematike syntaxis*, known to the West through its Arabic title, the *Almagest*, was a standard reference work on astronomy until modern times, although the tables were replaced by the measurements made during the Caliph Ma'mun's reign (813–33) and then by Ulughbeg's tables.

113. According to legend, Raja Vikramaditya was a king of Ujjain at whose court lived nine learned scholars, one of whom was the Kalidas who defeated the Sakas. The Vikrama era, dating from 58–57 B.C. (whence Babur's "1,584 years ago," i.e., from A.D. 1526–27, the time he was working on this section), is attributed to Raja Vikramaditya. See Sachchidananda Bhattacharya, *A Dictionary of Indian History* (New York: George Braziller, 1967), 840.

114. Chil Sutun, "forty columns," is a common name for many-columned pavilions.

115. Literally "four-door," a *chardara* is a roofed or domed pavilion open on all four sides; it may be a permanent or temporary structure or a tentlike, mobile pavilion.

116. "Clickety-Clack" Mosque.

117. *Abgir:* reservoir.

118. Babur describes the fruits of Fergana, including the mirtimuri, in folios 5–5b.

119. "Green City."

120. *Peshtaq:* an arched gatehouse leading to the forecourt of a building.

121. *Tovachi:* an officer of the muster.

122. *Divankhana:* an office of fiscal administration.

123. Chosroës' Arch refers to the great Sasanian (ca. 224–651) vaulted hall at Ctesiphon.

124. The chronogram *'Abbas kusht* gives 853 (1449). Abbas was the man Abdul-Latif Mirza hired to murder his father. See Khwandamir, *Habib al-siyar*, 4:33 f., translated in Thackston, *Century of Princes*, 166.

125. Six months after the murder of Ulughbeg, Abdul-Latif was ambushed and shot by a group of nobles. Apparently the man whose arrow hit the mark was named Baba Husayn, for the chronogram *Baba Husayn kusht* gives 854 (1450); see Khwandamir, *Habib al-siyar*, 4:42 f., translated in Thackston, *Century of Princes*, 173. Jamshed and Faridun are legendary great kings of Iran; Zoroaster is, of course, the eponymous founder of Zoroastrianism. The sense of the poetry is that Abdul-Latif, like Jamshed, was so splendid that Faridun and Zoroaster would have served in his retinue.

126. Babur describes the Tarkhan revolt beginning in folio 36.

127. The *fils* (pl. *fulus*) is a small copper coin, generally one twenty-fifth of a tanka. Salaries and grants were often stated in terms of *fulus* in order to inflate the face value.

128. The year A.H. 904 corresponds to August 19, 1498–August 7, 1499.

129. The year A.H. 905 corresponds to August 8, 1499–July 27, 1500.

130. A specimen of Baysunghur Mirza's calligraphy is preserved in Istanbul, Topkapi Palace Library, H.2154, folio 17a.

131. The boy's name, Baburi, is derived from Babur's own name.

132. In Ali-Sher Nawai's *Majalis al-nafayis*, Muhammad Salih is described thus:

> On account of his given name he adopted Salih as his pen name. He is the son of Amir Nur-i-Sa'id, who was factotum and majordomo in Sultan-Abusa'id Mirza's house but a maleficent and ill-tempered man. Muhammad Salih, however, is a mild-mannered youth whose conduct bears no resemblance to that of his father. In his poetic nature there is much precision and taste, and in calligraphy too he is not devoid of ability (*Majalis al-nafayis*, Persian trans. Sultan-Muhammad Fakhri Harati and Shah-Muhammad Qazwini, ed. Ali-Asghar Hikmat [Tehran: Bank-i Milli-i Iran, 1323/1944], 110).

> A later redactor has added: "The Mir [i.e., Ali-Sher] was too kind in his assessment of the aforementioned [Muhammad Salih]. Although he was good in his youth, he later took up his father's conduct. Maleficence in a man of good poetic nature is not good." Muhammad Salih joined Ubaydullah Khan's service after the occupation of Herat and accompanied the khan to Transoxiana, where he served at court and composed panegyrics on the Uzbeks.

133. A pun is involved. To share someone's salt supposedly creates a bond of gratitude and fidelity. *Kornamaklik,* literally "blind-saltedness," is the word used for an act of ingratitude, or infidelity. That is, his being "blind to the salt" was the cause of his being blinded, or having "salt poured into his eyes."

134. The year A.H. 906 corresponds to July 28, 1500–July 16, 1501.

135. *Toquz:* a set of nine; in Turkic custom, gifts are given in sets of nine.

136. "Shaykh Maslahat has bestowed."

137. Babur means that Fazil was not of the noble Tarkhan clan of Samarkand and Bukhara but was a merchant who had been dubbed "Tarkhan" by Shaybani Khan. Tarkhan was originally a title of rank that entitled the holder to commit with impunity nine "offenses" against a khan.

138. "Garden of the Ravens."

139. A *qasida* is a mono-rhymed Persian literary form used generally for encomiastic poetry. A *ghazal* is a Persian literary form, almost exclusively amorous in general tone and diction.

140. See part 2, note 144, for a description of the *nawâ* mode.

141. A hemistich is half a poetic line of verse usually divided by a caesura. Babur's quatrain rhymes in -*olghusïdur.* Banna'i took the whole rhyming word of the first hemistich (*bolghusïdur*), turned it into a *radif* (refrain), and added a new rhyme in -*ar.*

142. It was considered auspicious to have the Pleiades at one's back during battle. Babur did not want the constellation to move behind his opponent and thus be against himself.

143. Folios 66b, 67b, 74b, 77b, 88.

144. What Babur calls the Gazaristan Gate was also known as the Gazaran (Bleachers') Gate and Khwaja Ahrar's Gate (see Abu-Tahir Khwaja Samarqandi, *Samariyya,* ed. Iraj Afshar [Tehran: Mu'assasa-i Farhangi-i Jahangiri, 1367], 175). The name of this gate has often been conflated with karez (subterranean water channel) and misconstrued as Karezgah or Karizgah.

145. The year A.H. 907 corresponds to July 17, 1501–July 6, 1502.

146. Folio 51b.

147. In 904 (1498–99). See folio 59.

148. Folio 107.

149. The chronogram *fawt shud Noyan* gives 907 (1501–2).

150. One of the legendary "good kings" of Iran who figures prominently in the *Shahnama* (Book of Kings), Jamshed is credited with much wisdom and good counsel, as in this poetry. See also note 125 above.

151. Folio 39b.

152. The date in 907 was 10 Dhu'l-Hijja (June 16, 1502).

153. In the first two rhymes, *mihnatta* and *ghurbatta*, the final *-ta* is a Turkish suffix. The third rhyming word, *albatta*, is a single word without suffix. Babur probably wondered if it was legitimate to rhyme *albatta* with *mihnatta* and *ghurbatta*. Similarly the suffixes *-gha*, *-qa*, as well as *-kä* and *-gä*, may rhyme with each other.

154. Koumiss is a fermented beverage made originally by the nomadic peoples of Central Asia from mare's milk.

155. *Jergä:* a circle, both a hunting circle and advisory council.

156. The Persian translation says seven lines.

157. The year A.H. 908 corresponds to July 7, 1502–June 25, 1503.

158. Ata Ibrahim is Shaykh Abu-Ishaq Ibrahim (1132–1226), son of Shaykh Abdul-Qadir Gilani, the eponymous founder of the Qadiriyya dervish order (Ghulam Sarwar Lahawri, *Safinat al-asfiya* [Kanpur: Nawal Kishore, n.d.], 111).

159. The word "dismount" is used in the Persian translation; the Turkish text has "kneel." The khan would not kneel to a Timurid prince.

160. This paragraph has several difficulties. The Mongolian cap (*börk*) is described as *maftullugh/maftûldar*, perhaps meaning the high-peaked Mongolian cap decorated with a twisted appliqué or braid. The "stone" (*tash*, *sang*) that came with the Chinese quiver may possibly be a thumb-ring, not uncommonly made of agate, jade, and the like.

161. *Durdana* and *lulu* both mean pearl; the meaning of *tuqpay* is unknown.

162. *Tughchi:* a servant in charge of the *tugh*, the yak-tail standard attached to a ruler's horse.

163. *Goshagir:* an instrument for straightening arrows.

164. Folio 102b.

165. *Bakhshi:* originally the Inner Asian Buddhist term for teacher; during the Ilkhanid and Timurid periods, bakhshis were Turkish secretaries and scribes.

166. Qalmaqi armor is obviously derived from the Eastern Mongolian Qalmaq (or Oyrat) tribe, also known as the Kalmyks and the Kalpak. The exact configuration of the armor is not known.

167. The Persian text breaks off at this point and is picked up in the next section, with the year 910. The Turkish text continues, but the poetry is corrupt. See A. S. Beveridge, *Babur-nama in English*, vol. 2, Appendix D, for a lengthy discussion of whether or not the continuation is spurious.

PART TWO: KABUL (P. 141)

*Khwandamir, *Habib al-siyar*, 4:293.

1. The year A.H. 910 corresponds to June 14, 1504–June 3, 1505.

2. Folios 88–88b.

3. Lines from Saʿdi (b. ca. 1200), *Gulistan* (Rose Garden) in *Kulliyyat-i Saʿdi* (Collected Writings), 40.

4. There is a slight confusion in the names of two rivers now in Afghanistan, the Surkhab and the Surkhrud, both of which mean Red River. Babur uses sometimes one name and sometimes the other, and sometimes the Turkish "Qïzïl Su" (also "Red River"), to refer to both rivers, although it is always clear which one he means. Here he intends the Surkhab.

5. The *ghari* is an Indian measure of time equivalent to twenty-four minutes, the sixtieth part of a twenty-four-hour day, as Babur will explain much later (fol. 289). Babur introduces the ghari, like the kos, also an Indian measure, long before he gets to the Indian section of his memoirs. He obviously reworked this earlier section after he had gone to India and become accustomed to the Indian measures.

6. When Babur refers to the Afghans, he means a people from "Afghanistan" who were united by common ancestry and a common Indo-Iranian language, Pashto, a distant relative of Persian. Babur's "Afghanistan," generally mentioned together with Bangash, Bannu, and Dasht, is the area southeast of Kabul down to the Indus. Of the many various tribes that constituted the Afghan "nation," Babur mentions, at various times and in connection with various persons, the Abdurrahmani, Afridi, Dilazak, Farmuli, Gagiani (also Gugiani), Ghilji (also Ghilzai and Ghaljai), Givi, Isa Khel, Khirilji, Khizr-Khel, Khugiani, Kurani, Lodi, Lohani, Mohmand, Niazi, Orukzai, Shamu Khel, Sur, Tarklani, Waziri, and Yusufzai. See *A Dictionary of the Pathan Tribes in the North-West Frontier of India* (Delhi: Mittal Publications, 1983).

7. The star Canopus (*Suhayl*), renowned for its beauty and auspiciousness, has a celestial latitude of 75° south. At the summer solstice at terrestrial latitude 36° north, which runs through the passes of the Hindu Kush north of Kabul, Canopus is visible 3° above the horizon. Although this was September, the extremely high elevation at which Babur was would compensate for the altitude Canopus had lost since the solstice. Until then Babur had been entirely too far north ever to have seen this star. See Nasiruddin Tusi, *Hall-i mushkilat-i Muʿiniyya* (Tehran: Danishgah-i Tihran, 1335), 4.

8. Sinjit, "a kotal leading over the northern end of the Paghman range" (Ludwig W. Adamec, *Historical and Political Gazetteer of Afghanistan* [Graz: Akademische Druk- u. Verlagsanstalt, 1985], vol. 6, *Kabul*, 755).

9. *Uruq:* a family and household.

10. The meadow is described below, folio 130.

11. Babur speaks here of Qul-Bayazid Bökäül's tomb and below of Qutlugh-Qadam's tomb before they existed. Both men were alive in 1505–6, the

year he is reporting, although obviously they were dead when he was writing. The last mention of Qul-Bayazid is in the year 913 (1507–8); the last mention of Qutlugh-Qadam is at the Battle of Khanua in 1527.

12. "Garden Lane."

13. Yurt, "a plain situated on the crest of the Paghman range, fifty-six miles from Kabul" (Adamec, *Gazetteer*, 6:810).

14. The name Karnu is conjectural. The manuscripts vary considerably, and no such place or region has been located.

15. The Hazaras and Negüdäris are both Mongolian peoples, among some of whom, as Babur says (fol. 131b), Mongolian was spoken in his day. The Hazaras' name derives from the Persian *hazâr* "thousand," a translation of the Turco-Mongolian *tümän*, the term for a battalion. The Negüdäris were, according to Khwandamir, a Turco-Mongolian tribe that migrated from western Iran into Quhistan and the territory of the Kurt kings of Herat around 1300. By 1319 they were in Seristan, and much later, around 1480, when Amir Zu'n-Nun Arghun (see part one, note 87) was assigned by Sultan-Husayn Mirza to Ghur and Zamin Dawar, the entire territory was under the control of the Hazaras and the Negüdäris, whose combined tribal forces were also used by Zu'n-Nun's son, Muyammed-Muqim Beg, to seize Kabul. See Khwandamir, *Habib al-siyar*, 3:150, 276; 4:170, 293.

16. Ya'qub Deh, "a large village four miles southeast of Kabul" (Adamec, *Gazetteer*, 6:808).

17. Khwaja Shamsuddin Muhammad Hafiz of Shiraz (ca. 1325–90) was the premier poet of the ghazal in Persian.

18. A marginal note in the manuscript says: "He was called Ahmad Khwaja Shamsuddin Janbaz, but the common people have shortened it to Khwaja Shamu."

19. There are, throughout Iran and Afghanistan, shrines and holy places known as *qadamgâhs*, located where impressions of footprints, generally unusually large, can be seen impressed in rock. Khwaja Khizr is a legendary character who, having fallen into the Water of Life, roams the earth immortally and invisibly, although he appears from time to time as a deus ex machina figure.

20. "... Other bushes, which bear eatable berries, such as the *Umlook* [*amlûk*], the *Goorgooreh*, &c. are common in the hills" (Mountstuart Elphinstone, *An Account of the Kingdom of Caubul and Its Dependencies in Persia, Tartary, and India* [Graz: Akademische Druck- u. Verlagsanstalt, 1969], 1:194).

21. "The commonest trees in the mountains are pines of different kinds, one of which, the Jelgoozeh [*jalghoza*], is remarkable for cones larger than artochokes [*sic*], and containing seeds resembling pistachio nuts" (ibid., 193).

22. Apparently Babur means that at the time of writing, he was no longer in-dulging in strong drink. See below, folio 312.

23. The seven roads seems to consist of the three in Panjshir (Khawak, Tul, and Bazarak), the Parwan road, and the three in Ghorband (Yangï Yol, Qipchaq, and Shibartu).

24. "Elevation 11,650 feet. A pass leading over the Hindu Kush, crossed by the Kabul-Khanabad road; it is 115 miles from Kabul" (Adamec, *Gazetteer,* 6:422).

25. Bazarak, or Parandev, a "pass over the western Hindu Kush, leading from the Panjshir into the Andarab valley" (ibid., 6:636), is also known as Tul Dara (ibid., 6:793).

26. *Tûl* in Arabic means "length."

27. Parwan, now called Charikar, is the large village at the mouth of the Salang glen (Adamec, *Gazetteer,* 6:639).

28. "Seven Children."

29. Shibar, "elevation 9,800 feet. A pass leading from the head of the Ghor-band valley into the Bamian valley" (Adamec, *Gazetteer,* 6:728).

30. Ao Dara, "the rocky gorge through which the Bamian river flows from Shikari to Doab-i-Mekhzari" (ibid., 6:36).

31. Chaupara has not been identified or located. It should be on the Indus near the confluence of the Sohan.

32. The Aymaqs are Turco-Mongolian tribes and clans. The Arabs of Afghanistan were brought by Temür. They now speak only Persian and reside chiefly in the Jalalabad district (Adamec, *Gazetteer,* 6:37 f.).

33. According to Adamec (*Gazetteer,* 6:647) there are still a few Pashais left, "now obscure and nearly forgotten." The Paracha, now chiefly in Kabul, may be identical with the Paranchehs, a Hindustani-speaking people scattered in various parts (ibid., 6:635 f.). The Barakis are a "tribe of Tajiks who inhabit Logar and part of Butkhak" (ibid., 6:91).

34. In his classic study of Kafiristan in the late nineteenth century, Sir George Robertson gives as the main tribe of the Siyahposh Kafirs the Katir group, which includes the Katirs of Bashgul Valley, the Katwár Kafirs of the Kti Valley, and the Rámgulis, also known as Gabariks, the most numerous Katir division, who inhabited the most western part of Kafiristan. Gabarik is the name Babur gives as one of the Kafir groups, and his "Kator," a name also attested in earlier Persian sources like Yazdi's *Zafarnama* (Book of Triumph), may well be an earlier version of Robertson's Katir and Katwár. See Sir George Scott Robertson, *The Ká-firs of the Hindu-Kush* (London: Lawrence and Bullen, 1896), 75 f.

The area of Afghanistan that was historically known as Kafiristan (lately changed to Nuristan after forced conversion to Islam in the late nineteenth century) was assumed to be derived from the Arabic *kâfir* "infidel." Thus Kafiristan ostensibly meant a place of infidels, non-Muslims. The origin of the name Kafiristan probably has nothing at all to do with the Arabic *kâfir* but rather with Gabarik, the tribal name Babur gives. Over time and also because of the paganism of the region, "Gabar" could easily have been transformed into "Kafir."

35. The fourteen districts are the same as the subprovinces, or *tümän* (literally, ten thousand), the territory that would provide maintenance for such a division.

36. "Garden of Fidelity."

37. Babur measures the water flow in streams in mills (*tegirmän, âsyâ*), apparently one mill being the amount of water it took to turn one water mill.

38. *Charchaman:* a plot of lawn or garden, usually with a pool in the middle, divided into four sections by crosswalks. See illus. p. 157.

39. "White Mountain," also known by the Pashto name, Spin Ghar (Adamec, *Gazetteer,* 6:680 f.).

40. The Badpakht, or Badpash, pass is still "constantly traversed by kafilas [caravans] from Nijrao to Jalalabad" and "is the connecting pass between Mandrawar and Nagulu on the Kabul river" (Adamec, *Gazetteer,* 6:49).

41. Lam, Lamak, and Lamkan are the Islamic renderings of Noah's father's name, the Lamech of the Bible; and Mehter, or *mihtar,* is a Persian title, "master." Note also that since Babur's time the name of Lamghan province has undergone metathesis to Laghman. Babur speculates that Lamghan is a variant of Lamkan. He is quite mistaken in this, for the -ghan and -qan endings on so many toponyms in the area are of Iranian origin.

42. For *amlûk,* see note 20 above. *Qara yemish* means "black edible."

43. Mir Sayyid Ali Hamadani (1314–85) was a Sufi saint and apostle of Kashmir. Born to a noble family of sayyids in Hamadan, Sayyid Ali arrived in Kashmir first in 1372, again in 1379, and finally in 1383. He died near Kunar on January 18, 1385, and his body was taken to Khuttalan, where his mausoleum still exists in Kulab (see *Encyclopedia of Islam,* 2d ed., ed. J. H. Kramers, H.A.R. Gibb, and E. Levi Provençal [Leiden: E. J. Brill; London: Luzac, 1960], 1:392).

44. See note 21 above.

45. Babur's lucha may be the Himalayan snow-cock (*Tetraogallus himalayensis*).

46. Unidentified.

47. "Rose scent."

48. Although Babur says "Sind" (the Indus), he means the Kabul River, which eventually empties into the Indus.

49. Istalif, a "large village in the Koh Daman, twenty miles north-northwest of Kabul.... Every one agrees as to the beauty of Istalif. Masson says, 'Istalif is one of the most picturesque spots that can be conceived' " (Adamec, *Gazetteer,* 6:268). Istarghij, "two adjoining villages in the Koh Daman of Kabul, about six miles north of Istalif" (ibid., 269).

50. "Big Garden."

51. Seyaran is *seh yârân,* meaning "three saints."

52. Ten-by-ten cubits.

53. *Juy-i-khosh* (nice stream) is 925 (1519).

54. "Afghan-shu'ar" means something like "labeled as Afghan." The word Afghan occurs, even today, as Afghan, Avghan, and Awghan. Babur speculates, probably wrongly, that the name of the Awghan Shal of Logar is a corruption of Afghan-shu'ar. Most of Babur's etymological speculations are folk etymologies.

55. The *Tabaqat-i-Nasiri* (Nasirid Classes) is a history of dynasties written by Qazi Minhaj Siraj Juzjani in Delhi in 658 (1260). It has recently been edited by Abdul-Hayy Habibi ('Tehran: Dunya-yi Kitab, 1363 [1985]).

56. It is considered extremely pious to fast, in addition to the obligatory month of Ramadan, during the previous and following months as an act of supererogation. See part 1, note 9, for Hanafi.

57. "Garden."

58. The Ab-i-Istada is a seasonal lake sixty-five miles south-southwest of Ghazni. "Bounded by a gently shelving margin of naked clay; not a tree is in sight, nor a blade of grass; hardly a fort, and the blue of the distance makes it look more lonely" (Lt. J. S. Broadfoot, 1839, quoted in Adamec, *Gazetteer* [1980], *Kandahar and South-Central Afghanistan,* 5:13).

59. Sultan Mahmud, r. 998–1030.

60. Ala'uddin Jahansoz Ghuri, r. 1149–61.

61. The Ray of Hind (i.e., India) was "Ray Jaipal," identified as Gopala of the Rastrakuta dynasty, whose capital was at Badaon, and the event took place around A.D. 988. See Sir Henry Miers and Elliot and John Dowson, *The History of India as Told by Its Own Historians* (London: Trübner, 1867–77), 2:182 and 4:162, and C. E. Bosworth, *The Later Ghaznavids: Splendour and Decay* (New York: Columbia University Press, 1977), 66 f.

62. "The two Iraqs" (*'Iraqayn*) refer to Persian Iraq and Arab Iraq. See part 1, note 36.

63. For Awghan Shal, see note 54 above.

64. Shaykh Muhammad Musalman's dates are unknown.

65. Barmal and Birmal are modern variants of the name. The variant most often used in medieval times was Farmul.

66. Here ends the list of the fourteen districts of Kabul (Nangarhar, Alishang, Alingar, Mandrawar, Kunar and Nur Gul, Nijrao, Panjshir, Ghorband, Kohdaman, Logar, Ghazni, Zurmat, Barmal, and Bangash).

67. Eight hundred thousand shahrukhis.

68. "Clumps" is *bütä*, and "clump grass" *bütägä otï*.

69. For lucha, see note 45 above. The nilgai, also called the bluebull, is a large bluish gray antelope (*Boselaphus tragocamelus*) of India, the male of which has short horns, a black mane, and a bunch of long hair on the throat. Babur describes the *kutahpay* (hog deer) in folio 276.

70. *Qarqand* has not been identified. Perhaps it is the "stunted brush-wood, seldom exceeding three feet in height, and usually not so high ... scattered over the dreary waste" of Ghazni (1882 Intelligence Branch Compilations, in Adamec, *Gazetteer*, 6:200).

71. He means here the Surkhrud.

72. The word *bildürgä* has not been verified, as it does not occur in the dictionaries, although it is clear from the description that it is a stick that lends weight to the end of the throwing rope.

73. "Wild ass tail."

74. Annette Susannah Beveridge comments: "Much trouble would have been spared to himself and his translators, if Babur had known a lobster-pot" (*The Babur-nama in English* [London: Luzac, 1921], 1:226, n.2).

75. It is not known what type of script Babur invented, but it is likely that it was a cypher. It is mentioned again on folios 179 and 357b.

76. Perhaps China, although the reading is not definite. Several places in the vicinity are now named China, but none can be identified with this place with any certainty.

77. Modern Jamrud.

78. *Sangar* is a stone breastwork used in mountainous areas such as Afghanistan.

79. *Gosfand* means sheep in Persian. Gosfand Lyar is Sheep Road.

80. The directions in this paragraph are turned: for "north" read west, for "east" read north, etc.

81. See part 1, note 83.

82. Nawroz is the Iranian new year's festival, celebrated on the vernal equinox.

83. But it is not mentioned again.

84. At Sakhi Sarwar.

85. Folio 121.

86. The Logar.

87. A *qorchï* was originally a quiver bearer; by Babur's time it designated a personal guard or squire.

88. The year A.H. 911 corresponds to June 4, 1505–May 23, 1506.
89. "New Year's Garden."
90. An *ayvan* is an arched portico, characteristic of Timurid architecture.
91. He is mentioned above, folio 70.
92. *Naqara* refers to the drums traditionally sounded at a ruler's gate at dawn and dusk; this royal prerogative could be conferred upon a high-ranking officer.
93. A *tamgha* is a customs impost, a tax imposed by the Mongols that was always considered un-Islamic and was highly disapproved of by the ulema.
94. It was an old Turkic custom that a ruler would grant a beg immunity from nine future offenses.
95. The Jats are a tribe found particularly in the Punjab, Sind, Rajasthan, and western Uttar Pradesh. The Gujars are an ancient tribe akin to the Rajputs, and are believed to be descended from either the Scythians or the White Huns. Spread widely over the plains of Hindustan, they gave their name to Gujarat.
96. *Qor begi,* literally "lord of the quiver," was a fairly high field rank in the ruler's personal service.
97. *Pahar,* or *pahr,* is an Indian measure of time, the six-hour "watch," the fourth part of a twenty-four-hour day (see fol. 289 below for Babur's definition).
98. The text has an indecipherable phrase here.
99. Firoza Begim's father, Sultan-Husayn, was the son of Mir Temür's daughter Äkä Begim and Amir Muhammad Beg Taychiut, whose sister Tümän Agha was married to Temür. Firoza Begim's mother, Qutlugh Begim, was a daughter of Temür's son Miranshah and Urun Sultan, a daughter of the Chaghatayid Soyurghatmïsh Khan.
100. Her full name was Badi'uljamal. See *Mu'izz al-ansab fi shajarat al-ansab,* folio 111 (anonymous MS, Bibliothèque Nationale, Paris).
101. Sultan-Ahmad Mirza son of Sidi-Ahmad Mirza son of Miranshah Mirza son of Amir Temür.
102. The quatrain to which he refers, by Mawlana Nuruddin Abdul-Rahman Jami (1414–92), is found in *Diwan-i kamil-i Jami,* ed. Hashim Razi (n.p.: Piruz, 1341), 809, *ruba'i* 4: "My whole life I took great pains to be patient; / in longsuffering I showed myself to be outstanding. / When separation came, where did my longsuffering and patience go? / Thank God I tested myself." The term used for the similarity between the two quatrains (*tavârud*) can be a euphemism for plagiarism.
103. *Qalpaq:* a type of hat.
104. That is, to establish Shiism as the official state religion.
105. The Qaraqoyunlu (Black Sheep) Turcoman confederation (1380–1468)

rose to power in the vicinity of Lake Van in the late 1300s. Under Qara Yusuf (1389–1420) the Qaraqoyunlu occupied Tabriz, which they made their capital, and ended Jalayirid rule in Azerbaijan. At the height of their power under Jahanshah (1438–67) the Qaraqoyunlu controlled Azerbaijan, the Iraqs, Fars, and Kirman. The Qaraqoyunlu were succeeded by another Turcoman confederation, the Aqqoyunlu (White Sheep), who ruled eastern Anatolia and Azerbaijan from 1378 to 1508. By the "Qaraqoyunlu Turcomans who had come from Iraq" Babur means those Qaraqoyunlus who left Azerbaijan after the Aqqoyunlu defeat of Sultan-Abusa'id and the Qaraqoyunlu in 1469 and took refuge with Sultan-Husayn in Herat. See part 1, note 68, and Khwandamir, *Habib al-siyar*, 4:142.

106. The name Khushab is used interchangeably with Jhelum, the name of a town. See also note 222 below.

107. The *batman* is a Turkish unit of weight, generally equivalent to the maund (*man*). From the middle of the fourteen through the fifteenth century and later, the Tabrizi maund was around 3 kg. An English source of 1566 says, "The batman ... may be 6. pound and a halfe of English waight" (Walther Hinz, *Islamische Masse und Gewichte* [Leiden: E. J. Brill, 1955], 19). A "forty-batman" bow refers to the pull of the bow, not the weight.

108. Muhammad-Nasir Mirza was Babur's younger brother.

109. Sayyid Ata is Khwaja Ahmad Yasavi, eponymous founder of the Yasavi dervish order whose tomb in Turkestan City was patronized by Temür.

110. This is Yadgar Farrukh Mirza, son of Farrukhzad Mirza son of Sidi Ahmad son of Miranshah. This Yadgar Mirza was a first cousin to Muhammad-Sultan "Kichik Mirza."

111. Line from Sa'di, *Gulistan*, 88.

112. In the *Mu'izz al-ansab* (fol. 156b) she is listed as Tüläk Begim, "daughter of Husayn Sufi, sister of Amir Yusuf Sufi Jandar."

113. That is, Shahrbanu Begim relied on her younger brother Sultan-Mahmud Mirza, whom Sultan-Husayn was fighting, to protect her.

114. She was the daughter of Amir Muhammad Sarïq son of Amir Muhammad Khwaja (*Mu'izz al-ansab*, fol. 156b).

115. In the *Mu'izz al-ansab* (fol. 156b) she is said to be the daughter of Amir Hasan son of Amir Charkas (who is listed among Sultan-Husayn's amirs, fol. 156b).

116. In the *Mu'izz al-ansab* (fol. 157) she is listed as a wife, not a concubine, and was the daughter of Amir Sultan-Husayn Charshambai.

117. For mathnawis and the *Khamsa*, see part 1, note 28. *Mantiq al-tayr* (Discourse of the Birds) by the thirteenth-century poet Fariduddin Attar is one of the great classics of didactic Sufi poetry in Persian.

118. A *divan* is a collection of a poet's works (qasidas, ghazals, etc.). Particularly prolific poets often had multiple divans, issued periodically throughout their lives. The titles of Ali-Sher Beg's four divans are, in the order listed, Extraordinary Verse from Childhood, Rarities of Youth, Remarkable Verse from Middle Age, and Benefits of Old Age.

119. Jami's collected letters have been published. *Namaha-yi dastnivis-i Jami,* ed. Isam al-Din Uranbayef and Mayil Harawi (Tashkent: Uzbekistan Science Academy, Oriental Institute, n.d.).

120. Balance of Meters.

121. *Naqsh:* a type of musical composition. See note 144 below.

122. The "Miranshahid mirzas" refers to the Miranshahid branch of the Timurid House that included Babur's grandfather Sultan-Abusaʿid Mirza. Sultan-Husayn Mirza was descended from Temür's son Umar-Shaykh and represented a branch of the family that had not produced reigning sultans until Sultan-Husayn.

123. *Qabaq:* literally, "gourd"; the qabaq field was for mounted archery practice.

124. *Dar miyan,* "in the midst" or "in the way," appears from the context to mean something like "Johnny-on-the-spot." In *Muʿizz al-ansab* (fol. 158) the name is given as "Jan Dar-miyan."

125. Folios 171b–172.

126. The Battle of Gizhduvan between the Uzbek Ubaydullah Khan and the Safavid Shah Ismaʿil's general Najm II took place on November 12, 1512, at Gizhduvan, near Bukhara. Reinforced by Babur, who was still dreaming of the reconquest of Samarkand and had forged an alliance with the Safavids, the Safavids were dealt a disastrous defeat by the Uzbeks. Najm II was captured during the battle and later executed, and Babur beat a hasty retreat to Hissar. In the progression of the memoirs Babur is ahead of himself here, but the section for 1512 is missing.

127. Folios 57–57b.

128. He was the son of Muhammad-Baqir son of Sidi-Ahmad son of Miranshah.

129. Khwandamir's summary of Mir Sarbirahna's career is as follows:

> Sayyid Shamsuddin Muhammad of Andizhan was nicknamed Mir Sarbirahna (Bareheaded), and the reason for this nickname was as follows. During his youth, as you all know happens, he fell in love with a lad, and he turned out like and fell in behind the *qalandars* who were following that lad. Sometimes he would wander bareheaded with them through the lanes and markets and compose quatrains…. Mir Sarbirahna was superior to his contemporaries in good conduct, pleasing speech, quickness of understanding and sharpness of poetic tempera-

ment, and he constantly made nice jokes and amusing and comical stories. When he came from Turkistan to Herat he gained the Victorious
Khaqan [Sultan-Husayn Mirza]'s favor and was appointed to the custo-
dianship of the shrine of Shaykh Luqman Paranda [in Herat], where he
served for twenty years extending hospitality to all who came. Every
year he spent the nearly 150,000 Kebeki dinars of income of the shrine
from trusts and donations. Later some of the envious accused him of
waste and extravagance and slandered him before the Victorious
Khaqan, and that was the cause for his dismissal. Mir Sarbirahna imagined that [Mir Ali-Sher] had a hand in the slander of him and therefore
in answer to Ali-Sher's line of poetry, "Now that ashes of the furnace
are my resting place, / The madness of love combs my locks with black
dust," he composed this line: "That elegant cypress that allowed me in
its shade / Was fickle and sat me in the black dust." Mir Ali-Sher was
insulted by this allusion, and for a time the dust of rancor between the
two was flying. In the end Mir Ali-Sher forgave the sayyid, who was restored to the office of the Victorious Khaqan's comptroller. There was
a quarrel over precedence between him and Kamaluddin Husayn Ki-
rangi, and Mir Sarbirahna said to Mir Ali-Sher, "Despite my nobility as
a sayyid, my advanced age and my being a servant of this lofty thresh-
old, Khwaja Husayn claims precedence over me. I hope that through
your attention I will gain superiority over him." The mir remembered
the sayyid's days of being a beggar and said, "In a place where they give
the office of comptroller to beggars I expect you to be higher in status
than anyone." Mir Sarbirahna got his wish and was given precedence
over Khwaja Husayn. After serving in that post for a time thereafter, he
resigned and retired, spending the rest of his life, without the incum-
brance of office, in the company of Mir Nizamuddin Ali-Sher. He fell
ill in 898 [1492–93] and died (Khwandamir, *Habib al-siyar,* 4:322 f.).

130. Usually known as *Majalis al-'ushshaq* (Sessions on Lovers). See C. A.
Storey, *Persian Literature: A Bio-Bibliographical Survey* (London: Luzac,
1970–72), 1:ii, 960.
131. Ata'ullah son of Fazlullah, known as Jamal al-Husayni (d. 926/1520), was
the author of a popular history of the Prophet Muhammad, his companions, and his successors, *Rawzat al-ahbab.* See Hermann Ethé, *Catalogue of
Persian Manuscripts in the India Office Library* (London: India Office Library, 1903–37), 147 and 1081.
132. Mawlana Nuruddin Abdul-Rahman Jami (1414–92), the giant of the
"Herat florescence" of Persian letters and master of the Naqshbandiyya
dervish order. Jami's enormous output encompasses every genre of clas-

sical literary prose and poetry. He produced three divans of ghazals and qasidas and seven masnavis known collectively as the *Haft awrang* (Seven Thrones, also the name of the constellation Ursa Major). Three of the seven are recastings of the romances versified by Nizami, *Tuhfatu'l-ahrar* (Gift of the Free), adages and advice in imitation of Nizami's *Makhzanu'l-asrar, Layli and Majnun,* and *Khirudnamu-i Sikandari,* in imitation of the second part of Nizami's *Sikandarnama,* the philosophical counsels of Aristotle to Alexander. The other four parts to the Haft awrang are: (1) *Silsilatu'z-zahab* (Chain of Gold, a Naqshbandi doxology), (2) *Yusuf and Zulaykha,* the story of Joseph and Potiphar's wife, (3) *Subhatu'l-abrar* (Rosary of the Pious), a work on religion, mysticism, and ethics, and (4) *Salaman and Absal,* a mystical allegory based on a work of Avicenna's. In imitation of Sa'di's *Gulistan* Jami wrote his *Baharistan* in mixed prose and poetry, and his *Nafahatu'l-uns* (Breaths of Intimacy) consists of biographies of more than six hundred prominent Sufis.

133. Mawlana Shamsuddin Muhammad son of Mawlana Sharafuddin Usman, a teacher at the Sultaniyya and Ikhlasiyya madrasas in Herat, died in Rabi' I 901 [November 1495] (Khwandamir, *Habib al-siyar,* 4:340 f.). "Mulla Madarzad" means "Congenital Mulla."

134. The highest rank of Islamic jurisprudent is *mujtahid,* one who has reached the level at which he was empowered to issue legal decisions on his own personal initiative, independent of precedent. In Sunni Islam mujtahids had long ceased to exercise this option by Babur's time, but in Shiite Islam the institution still exists today.

135. *Murtâz* means one who practices rigorous asceticism.

136. This reference is to Jami's *Nafahatu'l-uns wa hazaratu'l-quds* (Breaths of Intimacy and Presences of Sanctity), a collection of biographies of important Sufis.

137. Remarkable Rhetorical Devices.

138. Jami is mentioned under "Learned Men" (fol. 177b), and Suhayli and Jalayir under "His Amirs" (fols. 174 and 174b).

139. The name is taken from Asaf ibn Barakhiya (Asaph ben Berechiah), Solomon's vizier in Islamic lore.

140. Born in Herat, Kamaluddin Ali Banna'i, or Bina'i (1453–1512), took his pen name from his father's occupation of master builder (*bannâ*). He served as poet at the court of Sultan Ya'qub Aqqoyunlu in Tabriz, returning to Herat after Ya'qub's death in 1491. He went to Samarkand around 1495 and joined Muhammad Khan Shaybani's service, with whose occupying army Banna'i entered Herat in 1507 (see below, fol. 206). Among Banna'i's numerous poetic compositions are his *Shaybani-nama* (Book of Shaybani)—and a later redaction of the same work titled

Futubat-i-khani (Khanid Conquests)—on Muhammad Khan Shaybani's life and exploits. See Jiří Becka, "Tajik Literature from the Sixteenth Century to the Present," in Jan Rypka, ed., *History of Iranian Literature* (Dordrecht: D. Reidel, 1968), 497–500.

141. The *mutaqarib* meter (˘— / ˘— / ˘— / ˘-) is the "heroic" meter of Persian.

142. The *khafif* meter is -˘— / —˘- / -˘— / —˘-.

143. "Nine Colors."

144. The theoretical underpinnings of Persian music are so unlike those of the modern Western tradition that it is almost impossible to describe composition and performance in Western terms. Fundamental to Asian music are the modal systems (*dastgâh*), set courses of development, and orders of succession of small melodic types. Babur mentions three modal systems, *râst, chârgâh*, and *nawâ*. (*Râst* and *nawâ* now form two of the standard six *maqâms* of Central Asian music.) Babur also mentions one of the smaller melodic types, *panjgâh*, now considered part of *râst*. Of the compositional types, he mentions *peshraw, naqsh*, and *ish*. A *peshraw* was "originally the general introduction for an instrumental piece consisting of several parts" (Angelika Jung, *Quellen der traditionellen Kunstmusik der Usbeken und Tadschiken Mittelasiens.* Beiträge zur Ethnomusikologie, no. 23 [Hamburg: Karl Dieter Wagner, 1989]), 199; an *ish* (assuming it is what became known in Ottoman music as *kâr*, which means the same as *ish*) is a complex composition linking several rhythmic cycles and modes through a series of sung texts; and in the fifteenth century a *naqsh* was the introduction to a vocal composition (Jung, *Kunstmusik*, 210).

145. See part 1, note 28, for the *Khamsa*.

146. The titles are, in the order listed, Seven Beauties, Seven Belvederes, The Story of Alexander the Great, and the Story of Temür.

147. The mathnawi by Muhammad Salih is the *Shaybaninama*, a poetical account of Muhammad Khan Shaybani's exploits. The meter *ramal* hexameter is -˘— / -˘— / -˘- /. The reference to the *Subhat* is to Jami's *Subhatu'l-abrar* (Rosary of the Pious; see note 132 above).

148. "Fat man" is *tambal*, so Tambalkhana is "fat man's house."

149. Sultan-Ali of Mashhadi (fl. 1453–1519) was a master calligrapher of nasta'liq. His calligraphy became so famous that the historian Mirza Muhammad Haydar Dughlat said of him: "In most countries of the world there are few connoisseurs of calligraphy who do not have specimens or books copied by [Sultan-Ali]. In the libraries of the emperors of the world, if there are not two or three books in the mulla's writing, it is not counted as a library" (Muhammad Haydar Dughlat, *Tarikh-i Rashidi,*

in W. M. Thackston, *A Century of Princes* [Cambridge, Mass.: Aga Khan Program, 1989], 360).

150. Kamaluddin Bihzad, by far the most famous of all Persian miniature painters in the literature, began his career in Herat and later joined the Safavid service in Tabriz. See Thomas W. Lentz and Glenn D. Lowry, *Timur and the Princely Vision: Persian Art and Culture in the Fifteenth Century* (Los Angeles: Los Angeles County Museum of Art, 1989), 285–92.

151. Of Shah-Muzaffar little is known. Mirza Haydar gives the following evaluation:

> Shah-Muzaffar, son of Master Mansur, than whom there was none better during the time of Sultan Abu-Sa'id.... However, Shah-Muzaffar surpassed [his father] many times over. His brush is extremely fine, pure and possesses such grace and maturity that the eye of the beholder is astonished. He passed away at the age of twenty-four; during his lifetime he finished seven or eight scenes. His pen-and-ink drawings are to be found in the possession of some people, [and] the masters of this art consider them very dear (Thackston, *Century of Princes,* 361).

152. For *naqsh, peshraw,* and *ish,* see note 144 above.

153. For Banna'i, see note 140 above.

154. For the *chârgâh* mode, see note 144 above.

155. Sa'di, *Gulistan,* 40.

156. The year A.H. 912 corresponds to May 24, 1506–May 12, 1507.

157. The word for deer is *keyik,* a generic term meaning "wild four-legged game animal." It encompasses deer, gazelle, antelope, wild goat, and the like.

158. A *tümän,* literally "ten thousand," is 10,000 dinars. The Kepeki, or Kebeki, tümän refers to the dinar standard established by Kebek Khan, who ruled in Transoxiana circa 1308–26. Three hundred Kepeki tümäns would be 3,000,000 dinars, a lot of money.

159. Throughout the post-Mongol period, the Genghisid Code (*Törä*) and the Genghisid Law (*Yasa*) are referred to, but, although it is clear that the writers have something particular in mind, there is no known written example of the *Törä.* Apparently it remained an unwritten code of conduct and protocol passed down over the generations.

160. The Bagh-i-Jahanara (World-Adoring Garden) was constructed in 1469 by Sultan-Husayn Mirza. See Khwandamir, *Habib al-siyar,* 4:136.

161. "White Garden."

162. The Tarabkhana, a pavilion for entertaining, was constructed by Abu'l-Qasim Babur (ruled in Herat, 1449–57) in the Bagh-i-Safed (see Terry Allen, *Timurid Herat* [Wiesbaden: Reichert, 1983], 22).

163. Neither Babur nor anyone else gives any hint as to the reason for these extraordinary creations.

164. A term of uncertain meaning, *chargab* probably refers to the embroidered "cloud collar" often represented in Timurid painting and associated with Central Asian Turkic rulers. For illustrations of such a cloud collar and collar-point designs, see Lentz and Lowry, *Timur and the Princely Vision*, p. 192, 194–96, 216 f.

165. "Belvedere Garden."

166. "Garden of the Avenue."

167. "Zubayda's Garden."

168. "City Garden."

169. For the monuments and sights of Herat, see Terry Allen, *Timurid Herat* (Weisbaden: Reichert, 1983).

170. In Chaghatay, äkä refers to any elder female relation. Payanda Sultan Begim was Babur's father Umar-Shaykh's sister.

171. *Yengä* is, among other things, the wife of a paternal uncle. Habiba Sultan Begim Arghun was the widow of Babur's uncle Sultan-Ahmad Mirza; Babur later married her daughter Ma'suma Sultan.

172. He is mentioned, among other places, in folios 216, 226b, 243, and 262.

173. The Ramadan feast is celebrated on the first of Shawwal, the month following Ramadan. The month-long fast from sunup to sundown during Ramadan ends when the new moon of Shawwal is spotted.

174. *Langar:* a hospice, often founded by a Sufi master or as a charitable institution by a ruler, at which travelers stayed and food was doled out to the needy.

175. Sa'di, *Gulistan,* 42.

176. Ala Qorghan means "Striped Fortress," doubtless a reference to the stripes of contrasting color and calligraphy on the outer walls of Ikhtiyaruddin fortress.

177. Sons of Sultan-Ahmad Khan.

178. *Töshäkkhana:* a tent in which textiles were stored.

179. Folio 142.

180. The year A.H. 913 corresponds to May 13, 1507–May 1, 1508.

181. For Mohmands, see note 6 above.

182. The tomb is unknown.

183. Neither the Turkish original nor the Persian translation is clear here.

184. Folios 198b–199.

185. That is, one hundred thousand sheep. A lac is one hundred thousand. See folio 272b.

186. Folios 172–173.

187. In Sufi belief the Qutb is the highest degree of sainthood. There is al-

ways one Qutb in the world to maintain the order of the cosmos, although his identity is never revealed.

188. For Banna'i, see note 140 above.

189. According to law, a widowed or divorced woman may not remarry until a certain interval has passed.

190. Both Qazi Ikhtiyar and Mir Muhammad Yusuf are mentioned in folio 179. Khwandamir gives more particulars on the life of Qazi Ikhtiyar:

> Qazi Ikhtiyaruddin Hasan, son of Qazi Ghiyasuddin of Turbat, was outstanding among judges. In his youth he went from Zawa to Herat for study. In a short time he had advanced greatly, specializing in the writing of legal opinions, writs and records. He was also expert in the art of epistolary stylistics, poetry and enigma. Toward the end of the Victorious Khaqan [Sultan-Husayn Mirza]'s reign he was promoted to chief justice, and in the discharge of the duties of that office he was renowned among all the judges of Herat for his honesty, and he deservedly enjoyed the emperor's favor. During Muhammad Khan Shaybani's occupation, Qazi Ikhtiyaruddin was reconfirmed in his office, and after Muhammad Khan was killed he returned to his native land and occupied himself with agriculture. He died of cachexy at the beginning of 928 [December 1521] and was buried in his ancestral tomb in Turbat. Among Qazi Ikhtiyaruddin's works *Iqtibasat* ("Borrowings") and *Mukhtaru'l-ikhtiyar* ("The Chosen of Choice") are well known among the literati of the age. The chronogram on the marble pulpit Amir Ali-Sher had made for the congregational mosque in Herat is as follows: "A pulpit was achieved through highmindedness, so lofty it vies with the divine throne. / No one has ever seen [such] a pulpit of marble, and its date is 'That which no one has ever seen' " (Khwandamir, *Habib al-siyar*, 4:355 f.).

Muhammad Mir Yusuf is Amir Ghiyasuddin Muhammad, son of Amir Jalaluddin Yusuf al-Razi, who is often mentioned in the histories as one of the most prominent religious figures of Herat. Babur mentions meeting him at folio 179. For Sultan-Ali of Mashhad and Bihzad, see notes 149 and 150 above.

191. For the Arghuns, see part 1, note 56. Shah Beg and Muhammad Muqim were sons of Zu'n-Nun Arghun.

192. Folios 191b–192.

193. Persian translation has "fortify."

194. By the Bayïndïr sultans, Babur means the ruling clan of the Aqqoyunlu. The Aqqoyunlu under Alvand Mirza were defeated by Shah Isma'il at the Battle of Sharur in Azerbaijan in 906/1500–1501 (see Khwandamir,

Habib al-siyar, 4:464–67), and after their fall from power many of the Bayïndïr and other Aqqoyunlu emigrated from Iraq and Azerbaijan to Khurasan.

195. Koran 2:249.

196. The name is missing from all manuscripts.

197. *Tanka:* a coin; the primary unit of currency under the Timurids.

198. Folio 212.

199. *Tabin:* the elite royal contingent.

200. Folio 211b.

201. Shah Sultan Begim was the daughter of the king of Badakhshan. Mirza Muhammad Haydar gives her words:

> Sháh Begum laid claim to Badakhshán, saying: "It has been our hereditary kingdom for three thousand years. Though I, being a woman, cannot myself attain to the sovereignty, yet my grandson Mirzá Khán can hold it. Males descended from me and my children will certainly not be rejected" (Muhammad Haydar Dughlat, *A History of the Moghuls of Central Asia,* 203).

202. The letters in the words "Sultan Humayun Khan" add up to 913, as do the letters in *shah-i firoz-qadr* (king mighty in victory).

203. The year A.H. 914 corresponds to May 2, 1508–April 20, 1509.

204. "Clover Garden."

205. The text breaks off abruptly here to be resumed after an eleven-year hiatus. For the major events of these years, see the Chronology, pp. xxxii–xxxiv.

206. The year A.H. 925 corresponds to January 3–December 22, 1519.

207. The form in which the word appears here, *gavsaru,* is not attested elsewhere; from the context it is clear that it is some sort of protective armor.

208. The phrase "by force" (*ba jaur*) forms a pun with Bajaur, where Khwaja Kalan had gone.

209. "Yellow bird" probably refers to a specific type of bird.

210. *Bürküt* means eagle, but here it seems to be the name of a particular falcon.

211. *Kamali,* like *ma'jun,* is a narcotic mixture.

212. For Hindal's birth, see folio 227.

213. Babur's wife Mahïm is asking him to give her Dildar's unborn child, who turned out to be Hindal.

214. *Peshkhana:* the canopy or awning that protrudes from the front of a trellis tent.

215. She was Babur's Afghan wife, Bibi Mubaraka, also known as Afghani Aghacha.

216. The *Zafarnama* (Book of Triumph) was written by Sharafuddin Ali Yazdi and completed around 1425 for the Timurid Shahrukh Mirza's son Ibrahim-Sultan, then governor of Shiraz. In its day the *Zafarnama* was considered the authoritative chronicle of Temür Beg's career and was taken as the perfect model of elegant, eloquent historiography.
217. These are the Salt Range mountains of northern Pakistan.
218. *Ray* is a variant of rajah, an Indian prince or chief, or bearer of a title of nobility among the Hindus. *Malik* is the title of a local ruler.
219. *Khabar:* "news."
220. "Garden of Purity."
221. But it is not described anywhere.
222. The Bahat River is also called the Jhelum, and Babur uses these names interchangeably. See also note 106 above.
223. Amir Temür set out on his India Campaign in March 1398 and, after raiding as far as Delhi, returned to Samarkand in April 1399.
224. Thirty million.
225. Babur's digression now ends and he returns to the narrative.
226. The name is undoubtedly derived from the common Sanskrit *Śankara,* more familiar in English as Shankar.
227. *Chaudhari:* village chieftains in the subcontinent.
228. The Baloch are a people whose traditional territory, Balochistan, is now divided among Iran, Afghanistan, and Pakistan.
229. *Hind* means India, and *al* is the Turkish root meaning to seize, to conquer. If Babur construed this unusual Turkish compound along the lines of a Persian compound, it would mean "conqueror of India."
230. For Jats and Gujars, see note 95 above. The Gakhars, or Gakkhars, known to the British as "Guckers," may be of Kushanic origin. An aristocratic clan in Babur's day as well as now, they inhabit mostly the Hazara district and parts of Rawalpindi, Attock, and Jhelum in modern Pakistan.
231. Folios 228 and 229.
232. Folio 228b.
233. *Jüldü:* an award, laurel.
234. But it does not occur in that section or anywhere else.
235. For Qalmaqi armor, see part 1, note 166.
236. Folio 145b.
237. Here Babur means the Surkhud.
238. "Violet Garden."
239. Folios 106b–107b.
240. Folios 114–114b.
241. *Dhek:* an adjutant.
242. Folio 280.

243. Babur puns on Pulad Sultan's name and *pulad*, which means steel.
244. The use of the toothpick (*miswak*) is a pious practice based on the example of the Prophet Muhammad. To gather toothpicks with one's own hand adds to the merit of the usage.
245. The name is doubtful; the manuscripts vary.
246. This sentence proves that the missing section (see note 126 above) once existed.
247. The Persian manuscript has Qutlugh-Qadam.
248. The colocynth is the bitter-apple (*Citrullus colocynthis*) of the gourd family, the fruit of which is extremely bitter and a well-known purgative.
249. Arafa night is the ninth of Dhu'l-Hijja (that year corresponding to December 2, 1519). As Erskine notes, he most likely meant the Ramadan feast, which had occurred several days before (*Memoirs of Zehir-ed-Din Muhammed Baber, Emperor of Hindustan*, trans. John Leyden and William Erskine [London: Longman, Rees, Orme, Brown, and Green, 1826]. Annot. and rev. Sir Lucas King [Oxford: Oxford University Press, 1921], 2:133, n. 4).
250. For the Khizr-Khel, see note 6 above.
251. On Thursday, September 13 (fol. 242).
252. Bishka Mirza was chief of the Itarji family. See Muhammad Haydar Dughlat, *History of the Moghuls*, 307.
253. It should be the seventeenth. The Persian translation has Thursday the sixteenth but leaves out the matter under the Turkish text's Thursday.
254. *Karez:* a subterranean water channel used to bring water from long distances to an agricultural area.
255. "Imperial Garden."
256. For Ali-Sher Beg's four divans, see note 118 above.
257. The year A.H. 926 corresponds to December 23, 1519–December 11, 1520.
258. The name is illegible; the Persian translation omits this sentence.
259. *Kotal:* a narrow mountain pass, specifically of the type encountered in the extremely high Hindu Kush and neighboring mountains.
260. The Turkish text has clearly "grasshopper, locust"; the Persian translation suspiciously retains the Turkish word. Beveridge's observation (*Baburnama in English*, 2:421, n.6) that January is not the time to be seeing locusts in the mountains above Kabul is apropos.
261. For the *panjgâh* mode see note 144 above; a *mukhammas* (pentad) is a strophic verse form containing five hemistiches.
262. The name varies considerably in the manuscripts. This is the best guess.
263. Folios 143–143b.

264. The text breaks off here and picks up again nearly six years later, in 932 (1525). The events of those years are summarized in the Chronology, pp. xxxiii–xxxiv.

PART THREE: HINDUSTAN (P. 307)

1. The year A.H. 932 corresponds to October 18, 1525–October 7, 1526.
2. *Ashrafi:* a coin.
3. Folios 132, 233, 242b, 245, 249–49b.
4. For Muhammad Salih, see part 1, note 132.
5. The *Risala-i mubin* (The Clarifying) is a treatise Babur composed in poetry for the instruction of his son Kamran in Islamic law. A large portion of it was published in Il'ya Nikolaevich Berezin's chrestomathy, *Biblioteka vostochnykh istorikov* (Kazan, 1849).
6. Babur's own poetry ("What am I to do with you,") is preceded and followed by verses from the Koran (48:10 and 7:23).
7. These names are conjectural. They are not clear in the manuscript.
8. Not the same Sultanpur as cited above, folio 252. This is in the Sultanpur southeast of Lahore.
9. The Baluch, who today inhabit Baluchistan (Iran and Pakistan), much as they did in Babur's time, were proverbial for leading a nomadic existence.
10. Note that this is a different Malot from the preceding and the following (fol. 260). This is the only mention of Malot in Bhera; all others are Malot in Hashiarpur.
11. The Sutlej.
12. Folio 257.
13. The name Karal is conjectural; it has not been verified.
14. April 20, 1526.
15. The name Chitar is conjectural; it has not been verified.
16. The Persian translation adds the following annotation by Humayun: " 'Since His Late Majesty has mentioned my shaving among these events, I follow him in mentioning it. At that date I was eighteen years old. Now I am in my forty-sixth year. Written by Muhammad Humayun.' Transcribed from the handwriting of His Blessed Majesty."
17. The Persian translation adds: "A *dim* is a method whereby soldiers are mounted and, with a bow or a crop in hand, they estimate the army according to the method established among them."
18. The defensive tactic known as the Anatolian method involved the hitching together of carts with chains in front of the camp as a sort of barrier, augmented with large shields and pylons. Infantry lines were in front of the carts, and matchlockmen could fire from behind. Similar

tactics were employed by the Aqqoyunlu Sultan-Murad in a battle with the Safavid Shah Isma'il (Khwandamir, *Habib al-siyar,* 4:471) and by the Ottoman Sultan Selim in the Battle of Chaldiran, again with Shah Isma'il (ibid., 546).

19. No satisfactory explanation of this term has been found.

20. All the sites Babur mentions in Delhi still stand: the tomb of Shaykh Nizam (uddin) Awliya (d. 1324), a well-known site in Delhi; Khwaja Qutbuddin's tomb, the Dargah of Khwaja Qutbuddin Bakhtyar Kaki (d. 1236), in Mehrauli; Sultan Ghiyasuddin Balban's tomb (d. 1286), situated in the southeast of Old Delhi and now in complete ruins; Sultan Alauddin Khalji's tombs, buildings, and minaret (the complex around the Quwwatu'l-Islam Mosque: the mausoleum was built in 1317 by Alauddin's son, Mubarakshah; by the minaret certainly must be meant the Qutb Minar, 238 feet tall, begun by Sultan Iltutmish in 1229 with subsequent extensions and repairs); the Shamsi pool, also known as the Tank of Qutb Sahib, built by Sultan Shamsuddin Iltutmish in 1229; the Khass pool, also known as the Hauz-i-Alai, built by Ala'uddin Khalji around 1295; the tomb of Sultan Bahlul Lodi (d. 1488), built by his son, Sultan Sikandar; Sultan Sikandar's tomb, built by his son, Sultan Ibrahim, in 1517, near Mauda Khairpur.

21. Gwalior was first taken by Muslim rulers under Qutbuddin Aybak in 1196. It was retaken by the Rajputs in 1210 and lost again to Sultan Shamsuddin Iltutmish in 1232. In 1398, Gwalior was recovered by the Tanwar Rajputs and held by them until it was taken from Rajah Bikramajit in 1518, during Sultan Ibrahim's reign.

22. Folios 223–38.

23. The Ghaznavid Empire established lasting rule in India under Sultan Mahmud (r. 998–1030), whose descendants ruled from the Punjab until 1186.

24. Shihabuddin (also known as Mu'izzuddin, r. 1173–1203) Ghuri's predecessor, Ghiyasuddin Muhammad, extinguished the Ghaznavid line in the Punjab in 1186. The Ghurid line ruled northern India until 1206.

25. For the *Tabaqat-i-Nasiri,* see part 2, note 55. The portion about Shihabuddin (Mu'izzuddin) Ghuri's campaign with 120,000 armored warriors occurs on page 400, where a campaign in 588 (1192) is described.

26. Husayn Shah, the last of the Sharqi sultans of Jaunpur, r. 1458–79.

27. Sultan Ala'uddin Alam Shah of the Sayyid dynasty ruled 1446–51.

28. Temür Beg took Dehli in December 1398. Bahlul Lodi ruled from 1451 to 1489, and his son, Nizam Khan Sikandar II, from 1489 to around 1517.

29. Muzaffar Shah II, r. 1512–26.

30. The Bahmanid dynasty ruled in the northern Deccan, 1347–1527.

31. Mahmud Shah II of the Khalji line in Malwa ruled from 1512 to 1531.
32. Nasiruddin Nusrat Shah, r. 1519–32.
33. Sayyid Ala'uddin Husayn Shah, r. 1494–1519.
34. The Abyssinian was Shamsuddin Muzaffar, r. 1494–97.
35. Vijayanagar (Bijanagar in Persian sources) was a kingdom in the Deccan founded around 1336. The kings of Vijayanagar ruled until 1565, when the kingdom of Vijayanagar was overthrown by the combined forces of the other Deccan kingdoms, Ahmadnagar, Bijapur, and Golconda, and the city of Vijayanagar was destroyed.
36. The Rajput Rana Sanga, also known as Sangramasinha, ruled Mewar from 1509 to 1529.
37. *Daru'l-harb:* "Abode of war," Islamic term for non-Islamicized countries.
38. Folios 333–335.
39. The modern Jhelum.
40. Throughout this section Babur compares the flora and fauna of India to those of "that country" and "our country" by which he means Kabul. The expression will be translated by "our country" throughout.
41. *Nîlgâu,* the Persian for "nilgai," means indigo cow. See part 2, note 69.
42. "Shortlegged."
43. For an illustration of the hog deer, see Mildred Archer, *Natural History Drawings in the India Office Library* (London: Her Majesty's Stationery Office, 1962), plate 18.
44. The black buck (*Antelope cervicapra*).
45. Probably the Indian gazelle (*Gazella benetti*).
46. Gynee, a "very diminutive kind of cow bred in Bengal. It is, when well cared for, a beautiful creature, is not more than three feet high, and affords excellent meat" (Henry Yule and A. C. Burnell, *Hobson-Jobson,* ed. William Crooke [London: John Murray, 1903], 407).
47. *Newal* is the common Hindustani word for mongoose, but that animal is not arboreal.
48. *Gilahri* is the common Hindustani word for squirrel.
49. Precise identification of all the birds that follow is impossible. The identifications given in the annotations are the best educated guesses.
50. For the Hanafite school of interpretation, see part 1, note 9.
51. May be the Indian loriquet (*Loriculus vernalis*).
52. The Himalayan starling (*Sturnus humii*).
53. The Indian grackle, or hill myna (*Eulabes intermedia*).
54. The glossy starling, or tree stare (*Calornis chalybeius*).
55. The pied myna (*Sturnopastor contra contra*).
56. The reading of this word, as well as the precise identification, is still a mystery.

57. *Buqalamun* is the modern Persian word for turkey, but its sense here is multicolored, iridescent.

58. Presumably because it has eaten too many grapes in the vineyard.

59. "I have milk and a little sugar" (Persian).

60. "Quick, they have seized me" (Turkish).

61. "With gratitude good things endure" (Arabic).

62. The horned monal (*Trapogon melanocephala*), a type of pheasant.

63. May be the red jungle fowl (*Gallus ferrugineus*).

64. May be the western bamboo partridge (*Bambusicola fytchii*) or a Himalayan pheasant (*Gallophasis albocristalus*).

65. May be another common Himalayan pheasant (*Pucrasia macrolopha*).

66. The gray quail (*Coturnix communis*).

67. The rock bush quail (*Perdicula argunda*).

68. The black-breasted or rain quail (*Coturnix coromandelica*).

69. This may be the lesser button quail (*Turnix dussumierii*).

70. The florican (*Sypheotis bengalensis* and *S. aurita*).

71. The Turkish *sar* means buzzard, but buzzards do not have red backs; in Persian, *sâr* means starling, but the starlings have already been dealt with. It has been suggested that the rose-colored starling (*Pastor roseus*) is meant here, although that identification is far from certain.

72. The crow pheasant, or Malabar pheasant (*Centropus sinensis*).

73. Perhaps some sort of green woodpecker.

74. *Sherabi.*

75. This is a *ghariyal*, a different type of alligator.

76. *Amba* (mango) without the second vowel would be *amb*, which must have sounded to Babur like the Turkish *am*, female genitalia.

77. Amir Khusraw of Delhi (1253–1325), from *Qiran al-sa'dayn* (Conjunction of the Two Auspicious Planets [Venus and Jupiter]).

78. The plant *aman qara*, apparently a Turkish name, has not been identified.

79. *Bassia latifolia.*

80. *Averrhoa carambola.*

81. Although the reading of the word is uncertain, it seems to be a sort of plum.

82. The Husayni grape is long and seedless.

83. Unidentified.

84. *Flaucortia cataphracta.*

85. For the making of mahua, see above, fol. 283.

86. Folio 330b.

87. Coconut is *nargil*. The vulgur pronunciation *naliyar* is metathesized from the common Hindi *nariyal*.

88. *Jawz-i-hindi* (Indian walnut) is the Persian name for coconut. Babur is

writing here for people who have seen objects made from the coconut husk but do not know what it comes from.

89. The liquor made from the palmyra (*tar*), called *tari* (with the retroflex Hindustani *r*), has given us the English word "toddy."

90. *Narang* is unmistakably Persian; *naranj* is the Arabicized form.

91. Galle-galle, a "mixture of lime and linseed oil, forming a kind of mortar impenetrable to water (Shakespeare)," is the Anglicized (Anglo-Indian) version of the Hindi word *galgal* (Henry Yule and A. C. Burnell, *Hobson-Jobson*, ed. William Crooke [London: John Murray, 1903])

92. This statement shows that this section of the memoirs was written in 935 (1528–29), the date given by Shaykh Zayn Khwafi.

93. The days Sanichar through Sukrawar correspond to Saturday through Friday.

94. The first chapter of the Koran is a brief prayer called Fatiha (Opening). The Basmala is the initiatory formula, *bi'smi 'llabi 'rrahmani 'rrahim* ("in the name of God, the compassionate, the merciful") with which all chapters of the Koran but one begin. According to Babur, six recitations of the Basmala and Fatiha can be accomplished in a minute—a feat that is possible only if the recitation is done at breakneck speed.

95. See part 2, note 5.

96. *Pas* and *pasman*, meaning watch and watchman, respectively.

97. Babur's calculation is correct.

98. The word *manyasa*, or *minasa*, is unidentified. Based on the definition that 1 masha equals 1.0042 grams (Walther Hinz, *Islamische Masse und Gewichte* [Leiden: E. J. Brill, 1955], 5, 23), the following can be extrapolated: 1 ratti equals 0.1255 gram; 1 tank equals 4.168 grams; 1 miscal equals 5 mashas equals 5.021 grams; 1 tola equals 12.0504 grams (in Akbar's time a tola was redefined as 8 masha 7 surkh, or 20.9628 grams); 1 seer equals 58.352 grams; 1 maund equals 2.334 kg; 1 mani equals 28 kg; 1 manyasa equals 2,800 kg. On folio 305b Babur says that the *tola* is "a measure slightly more than two miscals," which would be true based on his own definitions. For this period in Iran and India, Hinz (p. 6 f.) takes the miscal to be 4.6 grams, a slight discrepancy with Babur's definition.

99. Temür Beg's "stone mosque" is the large congregational mosque in Samarkand now known as the Bibi Khanïm Mosque (see illus. pp. 56 and 57). Babur's building in Agra is unknown.

100. Although we have no such figures for the income of Kabul, Babur speaks of it as a relatively poor province, and it is easy to imagine how impressed he must have been by the wealth of Hindustan, which was proverbial for the magnitude of its riches. Babur's descendants always

took great pride in their vast wealth, particularly when compared with the "paltry sums" their neighbors the Safavids realized from Iran.

101. That is, 1489–1517. See note 28 above.
102. See note 9 above.
103. The "Shawwal festival" refers to the feast for the end of the month of Ramadan (see part 2, note 173).
104. The word ("clarification") is *bayan,* a pun on Bayana.
105. That is, the locals named the new "suburb" after the place from which the conquerors had come.
106. That is, after March 1527.
107. The year A.H. 933 corresponds to October 8, 1526–September 26, 1527.
108. The child died in infancy. Faruq was Mahïm's son.
109. *A'zam* means "most magnificent" and *humâyûn* means "regal"; Khanjahan is a shortened form of *khân-i-jahân,* "lord of the world"; Khankhanan is an abbreviated form of *khân-i-khânân,* "khan of khans, lord of lords." Both Khanjahan and Khankhanan were retained as titles of investiture by Babur's descendants, such as, for example, the Khankhanan Abdul-Rahim, the translator of Babur's memoirs. The title Khanjahan was also regularly awarded to outstanding military leaders.
110. Tahangarh is at Karauli in Rajputana.
111. Hathi Pol or Hathiya Paur, meaning Elephant Gate, is one of several gates to Gwalior.
112. "... The Cauker [Kakar] clan of Punnee [Pani], who inhabit Seewee [Sibi] in the plains of Seestaun [Seistan].... It would be curious to ascertain the causes which have sent them to this spot, and which have filled the southern provinces of India with men of the Punnee clan, whose emigration...must have taken place some hundred years ago" (Mountstuart Elphinstone, *An Account of the Kingdom of Caubul and Its Dependencies in Persia, Tartary, and India* [Graz: Akademische Drucku. Verlagsanstalt, 1969], 2:164).
113. The two slaves were Gulnar Aghacha and Nargul Aghacha. See Gulbadan Begim, *The History of Humayun (Humayunnama),* trans. Annette Susannah Beveridge [London: Royal Asiatic Society, 1902].
114. Kamran Mirza (ca. 1508–27) was Babur's son by Gulrukh Begim.
115. Babur's "Toda" is Toda Bhim.
116. Probably Agra.
117. Madhakur is just north of Dholpur.
118. For the Anatolian fashion, see note 18 above.
119. A vow was commonly taken before a campaign against infidels not to clip the beard or shave the head until victory was attained.
120. Koran 12:53.

121. Koran 57:21.
122. Koran 57:16.
123. Koran 7:23.
124. Koran 7:143.
125. Koran 5:90.
126. Koran 2:181.
127. Koran 6:45.
128. Koran 80:42.
129. Koran 2:34.
130. *Zunnar*, which refers to the Zoroastrian and Christian girdle and the Brahmin thread, metaphorically indicates a non-Muslim.
131. That is, lands yielding a revenue of one hundred thousand tankas would support one hundred mounted soldiers. Rana Sanga's lands were worth one hundred million tankas, or support for one hundred thousand horsemen.
132. Koran 3:21.
133. Koran 24:40.
134. Koran 29:6.
135. Koran 9:73.
136. The Elephanteers, the Ashab al-Fil, were the Ethiopian invaders of Mecca in A.D. 570 whose miraculous defeat was taken as portentous of the birth of the Prophet, traditionally ascribed to that year.
137. The Kaaba (Ka'ba) in Mecca was originally a shrine that housed the deities of the pagan Arabs. Stripped of its idols, it was adopted by the Prophet Muhammad as the centerpiece of Islamic pilgrimage.
138. Koran 61:4.
139. Koran 2:5.
140. The letter *alif* is a straight vertical; the phrase *inna fatahna* ("we have conquered") begins and ends with *alifs*, which are seen as banner poles.
141. The lengthy titles and epithets of all the commanders have been deleted from the translation.
142. *Yasavul:* a messenger.
143. Koran 14:29.
144. Koran 9:52.
145. Koran 23:102.
146. Koran 101:5.
147. That is, so much dust was raised that one of the seven layers of the earth was added to the seven heavens. Poetry taken from Firdawsi, *Shahnama*, ed. A. E. Bertels, L. T. Gyuzalyan, et al. (Moscow: Nauk, 1966), 2:66, line 60 and note 3.
148. Koran 3:139.

149. Koran 61:13 and 9:112.
150. Koran 48:1.
151. Koran 48:3.
152. Koran 101:5 and 101:4.
153. Koran 17:46.
154. Koran 33:38.
155. "The padishah of Islam's victory." The chronogram has the numerological equivalence of 933, or 1526–27.
156. "The middle of the month of Rabi' I."
157. Folio 294.
158. Folio 315.
159. Folio 298.
160. In the original, Persia is referred to as "Iraq," meaning Persian Iraq, a common epithet for Persia.
161. *Taravih:* supererogatory prayers performed at night during Ramadan.
162. "Victory Garden."
163. *Ganjafa:* a type of card game.
164. The year A.H. 934 corresponds to October 27, 1527–September 14, 1528.
165. This is not the Jalesar that is northeast of Agra, the wrong direction. It is probably another small village in the vicinity of Agra.
166. *Bükri tura:* a form of shield.
167. "Conquest of the infidel realm," 934.
168. Folio 333b.
169. Incomprehensible sentence.
170. In modern terms the Sarju is an upper tributary of the Gogra. Babur uses the names Sarju and Gogra indiscriminately for the river down to its confluence with the Ganges. On folio 368b below, Babur speaks of that confluence.
171. "Beykhub" is only a guess at this name, which is garbled in all manuscripts and unidentifiable elsewhere.
172. An unexplained break of five-and-a-half months occurs in the text at this point.
173. The year A.H. 935 corresponds to September 15, 1528–September 4, 1529.
174. Babur's son, a younger sibling to Kamran. (1516–58)
175. Ghiyathuddin b. Humamuddin al-Husayni Khwandamir (ca. 1475–ca. 1535), author of *Habib al-siyar,* a large, universal history that is particularly rich in detail on the Timurid dynasty, was the grandson of Mir Khwand, author of *Rawzat al-safa,* also a general history. Khwandamir was in Ali-Sher Nawa'i's service and then joined Badi'uzzaman Mirza's retinue. After serving Shah Ismail for a time, he went to Babur in India

in 1528 and died on the return journey from Humayun's expedition to Bengal, around 1535. His accounts of Babur are particularly valuable for filling in some of the gaps in the text of Babur's memoirs.

176. Mulla Shihab the enigmatist is Mawlana Shihabuddin Ahmad al-Haqiri, of whom Khwandamir gives the following description: "Known for his good nature and purity of mind, and renowned for his expertise in the art of poetry and enigma, he has studied most of the curriculum and has composed an eloquent treatise on the art of the enigma. He is also expert at composing qasidas and ghazals, and at present [i.e., the time of writing, 1524] he composes in honor of Shah Ismail" (Khwandamir, *Habib al-siyar,* 4:361).

177. Ashura, the tenth of the month of Muharram, commemorates the day on which Husayn, the grandson of the Prophet Muhammad, was killed at Kerbela in 680.

178. Rajah Man Singh, r. 1486–1526.

179. Rahimdad, Mahdi Khwaja's nephew, had been put in charge of Gwalior (fol. 304b).

180. The impressive palace fortification built by Man Singh is called the Man Mandir.

181. Sultan Shamsuddin Iltutmish (or Iletmish) of the Delhi Sultanate, r. 1211–36.

182. Not to be confused with Man Singh's son Bikramajit (fols. 268, 340, 341), the Hindu rajah of Gwalior.

183. Rana, like rajah and ray, is a Hindu title of a ruler, particularly a Rajput. Rana is from the Hindustani; rajah (*râjâ*) goes back to the Prakrit and Sanskrit; and *rây,* or *râê,* goes back to the Prakrit *râyâ* and the Sanskrit *râjâ.* All are also ultimately derived from the Sanskrit root *râj*—"rule, dominion."

184. Erskine defines the "cord" (*arghamchi*) as a horse tether, 7–8 gaz, that is, 20–25 feet.

185. Although Babur has used the Indian ghari (24 minutes) many times in his memoirs, this is the first time he uses the watch (*pahar*) for the time of day.

186. Silhadi, Rajah of Raisen, was Rana Sanga's son-in-law.

187. This is Abu'l-Fath, the Turcoman mentioned above on folios 175b and 305.

188. All three were daughters of Sultan Abusa'id Mirza, Babur's paternal grandfather.

189. *Yengächichä:* an affectionate term for aunt in Chaghatay.

190. Quicksilver, or mercury, has long been considered a laxative in the east.

191. This is al-Aman (fol. 346b).

192. Babur's metrical translation of Khwaja Ubaydullah's treatise, the *Wa-lidiyya* (Parental), is preserved in the Rampur copy of Babur's divan and was published by E. Denison Ross, ed., "A Collection of Poems by the Emperor Babur," *Journal and Proceedings of the Asiatic Society of Bengal* 6 (1910): extra no., 1–13.

193. The reference is to the renowned *Qasidat al-burda* (Poem of the Cloak) by Sharafuddin Muhammad al-Busiri (1213–ca. 1295).

194. The meter *Ramal musaddas makhbun* is -˘— | ˘˘— | ˘˘-. When the final foot is abtar, it is one long syllable instead of two shorts and a long.

195. *Subhatu 'l-abrar* (Rosary of the Pious), one of the seven mathnawis that make up Jami's septet, *Haft awrang* (Seven Thrones). (See part 2, notes 132 and 147.)

196. *Shah-i-sa'adatmand*, numerically 934, or 1527–28, means "felicitous king."

197. Babur's "Jam" is Turbat-i-Jam.

198. Qurban is one of Babur's subjects (see below, fol. 352b).

199. Annette Susannah Beveridge (*Babur-nama in English*, 625, n.7) identifies these lines as being from Nizami, *Khusraw u Shirin*. I have not been able to locate them, however, in the printed edition.

200. Quoted from Sa'di, *Bustan*, in *Kulliyyat*, 211.

201. Writers of Persian and Chaghatay have spelling difficulties all too familiar to writers of English. Arabic words in Persian are spelled as they are in Arabic, although many discrete consonants in Arabic are pronounced alike in Persian. There are, for example, two *t*'s, three *s*'s, and four *z*'s. *Ilti-fat* means attention. *Qulinj* means cholic.

202. *Payandaz:* a carpet or cloth spread before a ruler for the presentation of gifts.

203. See note 5 above.

204. The screens spoken of are the loosely woven grass screens that are wet and hung up during the hot weather. Breezes blowing through the wet grass have a cooling effect and act as natural air-conditioning.

205. "Köchüm Khan" is Köchkünjü, successor to Muhammad Shaybani Khan. He ruled the Uzbeks from Samarkand from 916 (1510) until 937 (1531), when he was succeeded by his son, Muzaffaruddin Abusa'id.

206. "Cheetah keeper."

207. The tenth of Muharram. See note 177 above.

208. Joha Sultan Täkälü was a Safavid general. For a Safavid account of the battle of Kharjerd, see Iskandar Beg Turkman, *Tarikh-i alamara-yi 'Abbasi* (Tehran: Amir Kabir, 1350), 1:54–57. This was the Uzbeks' third attack on Khurasan.

209. Köchkünjü and Ubayd Khan both survived the battle. Ubayd Khan died

in Bukhara in 946 (1539), "yearning for Herat and longing to stroll along the banks of the Pul-i Malan" (Iskandar Beg, *Alam-ara*, 1:66).

210. See above, folio 350b.

211. "Water Lily Garden."

212. See above, note 165.

213. "Gold-Flecked Garden."

214. *Körünüsh* was a well-established Timurid ritual inherited from Turco-Mongolian custom. Literally meaning interview, the körünüsh was a face-to-face, or eye-to-eye, confrontation with the ruler, involving formal genuflection on the part of the person with less status. Babur uses the word of his formal interview with his uncle on folio 101b (beginning). Under the later Moghuls of India the word was domesticated in Persian as *kornish* and was the formal kowtow before the emperor.

215. A *nimcha* is a short upper garment, and a *takband* probably a belt or girdle, perhaps a sword belt.

216. There are several Fatehpurs today in the vicinity of Rapri. One, Fatehpur Chandarai, is seven-and-one-half miles northeast of Rapri at 26° 59' north, 78° 42' east; another, Fatehpur Karkha, is at 27° 0' north, 78° 36' east.

217. *Tarkib* script is unidentified; a *mistar* is a writing guide (see Glossary).

218. "Ahlullah" means literally "people of God." He must mean the saints, both living and dead, who were often said to be capable of casting an admonition into one's heart.

219. "View Place."

220. Kamaluddin Ali Banna'i (1453–1512). See folio 179b above.

221. The word for loop (*madagi*) is literally "female," the connotation that is certainly intended.

222. See note 192 above.

223. See folio 363b.

224. Payag, or Prayag, is the modern Allahabad at the confluence of the Ganges and the Jumna.

225. The following passage, down to "and prepare the road" (fol. 363b), is omitted from the Turkish text. Apparently several folios were lost before the Hyderabad text was copied.

226. The name Lawayin is uncertain and unidentified.

227. Not in the memoirs.

228. The folk etymology of the name Karamnasa is taken to mean "destroyed merit," compounded of *karm*, or *karam*, "religious merit" and *nâsnâ*, "to be destroyed."

229. Not in the memoirs.

230. This seems to contradict Babur's statement on folio 363b, which implies that he was swimming the Ganges for the first time only a few days prior to this.
231. The terms are nowhere stated explicitly; one is summarily referred to on folio 365.
232. In the Iranian tradition the parasol is a royal prerogative and is awarded to only the highest-ranking nobles. Badi'uzzaman Mirza's son, Muhammad-Zaman Mirza, was a Timurid royal prince.
233. Arayish (Decoration), Asayish (Comfort), Gunjayish (Capacity), Farmayish (Command).
234. *Shiqqdar:* a military governor.
235. Text is missing.
236. May be Lakhnor.
237. *Peshgah* is the same as *peshkhana,* the canopy or awning that protrudes from the front of a trellis tent.
238. Kalira is not located and the name is not verified.
239. Chaksar and the Sagri district are not located and the names are not verified.
240. Chond is not located and the name is not verified.
241. That is, the new moon of Shawwal had been sighted, signaling an end to the Ramadan fast.
242. Maing, a village in the Baraunsa pargana, Sultanpur tahsil (see H. R. Nevill, *Sultanpur: A Gazetteer* [Allahabad: Government Press, 1903], 192).
243. The phrase "of rebuke" is missing in the Turkish text, and the Persian is not entirely clear.
244. Mahoba was previously cited (fol. 292) as Kalinjar, the name of the fort in Mahoba.
245. The tenth of Dhu'l-Hijja (August 16, 1529).
246. The year A.H. 936 corresponds to September 5, 1529–August 24, 1530.

SELECTED GLOSSARY

KEY

A   Arabic
H   Hindustani
M   Mongolian
P   Persian (including Arabo-Persian)
T   Turkish

abgir (P) reservoir

äkä (T) any elder female relative

amir (P) commander (See *beg*, below.)

aqrab (P) "inflammation of the eyes"

arb (H) a unit of value equal to 100 crores

arghamchï (T) The "cord," a horse tether, 7–8 *gaz*, that is, 20–25 feet

ashrafi (P) a coin

atäkä (T) (See *beg atäkä*, below.)

aymaq a small Turco-Mongolian tribal grouping

ayvan (P) an arched portico, characteristic of Timurid architecture

bagh (P) garden

bakhshi (T) originally the Inner Asian Buddhist term for teacher; during the Timurid period, *bakhshi*s were Turkish secretaries and scribes

balda-i-mahfuza (P) well-protected town

bandar (H) in Hindustan, a monkey

baranghar (M) the right wing in a battle array

batman (T) a Turkish weight, usually corresponding to the maund. (See below.)

beg (T) a high-ranking officer, necessarily Turk, equivalent to *amir*

beg atäkä (T) a tutor to a prince

begim (T) the feminine form of *beg*; a lady of Timurid descent

bismillah (A) "in the name of God"

boy (T) a single unit in a battle array surrounding the ruler

buqalamun (P) the name for the brilliantly colored *lucha* bird, or Hindustani partridge, found in the Nijrao district, Laghman region, northeast of Kabul

cadi a Muslim judge who interprets and administers the religious laws of Islam; from the Arabic, *qadi*

charbagh (P) a garden, usually with a pool in the middle, divided into four sections by crosswalks

charchaman (P) a division of a garden; a section divided into four plots

chardara (P) an open pavilion, belvedere

chargah (P) a musical mode

charqab (P) possibly the typically Central Asian "cloud collar"

chaudhari (H) a village chieftain in the subcontinent

crore a unit of value equal to 100 lacs, or ten million

daru'l-harb (A) literally, "abode of war," Islamic term for non-Islamicized countries

dastarpech (P) a peaked felt cap around which the turban was wound

deoti (H) in Hindustan, a person who carries the lamps for kings and noblemen

divan (P) both the fiscal administration and a fiscal administrator; also, a collection of a poet's works, such as *qasidas*, *ghazals*, and the like

divankhana (P) an office of fiscal administration

eshik-aqasi (T) literally "lord of the gate," the officer who controlled

access to a prince, one of the highest positions at a princely court

ghari (H) an Indian measure of time (24 minutes)

ghariyal (H) alligator; also, a disc of brass used in Hindustan for keeping track of time

ghariyali (H) in Hindustan, a group of men appointed to keep track of time

ghazal (P) a Persian literary form, almost exclusively amorous in general tone

ghazi (P) a warrior for the faith

ghichak (P) a small, bowed stringed instrument

goshagir (P) an instrument for straightening arrows

hadith (A) the body of the Prophet Muhammad's sayings, a major source of precedent for Islamic law; the study of the hadith confers religious merit

hathi (H) in Hindustan, an elephant

ichki (T) a member of a prince's inner circle, literally "insider"

ish (T) a type of musical composition

jalghoza (P) a type of pine tree with large cones containing edible seeds

jamdhar (H) an Indian dagger. (See illus. p. 361.)

javanghar (M) the left wing of a battle array

jergä (T) a circle, both a hunting circle and advisory council

jüldü (T/M) an award, laurel

kamali (P) a narcotic mixture

karez (P) a subterranean water channel used to bring water from long distances to an agricultural area

kattar (H) an Indian dagger. (See illus. p. 361.)

khan (T) a lineal descendant of Genghis Khan

khanaqah (P) a Sufi hospice and chapterhouse

khanïm (T) a female descendant of Genghis Khan

khanzada (P) literally "offspring of a khan," *khanzada* was often applied as a proper name to the daughters of Genghisid khans who married into the Timurid family (not to be confused with *khwanzada*, below)

kharb (H) a unit of value equal to 100 arbs

khutba (A) the section of the Friday prayer in which the ruler's name is mentioned

khwaja (P) a title of learning, generally accorded to Sufi masters

khwanzada (P) derived from *khwând* ("lord"), the *khwanzada*s were the daughters of the Mir Khwands of Termez who married into the House of Timur (not to be confused with *khanzada*, above)

kiblah (A) the direction of Mecca, toward which all Muslims turn when they pray

körünüsh (T) the formal Turco-Mongolian salute (literally "interview"); in Moghal India the word became *kornish*, the formal genuflection before the emperor

kos (H) an Indian measure of distance (*kuroh*) (approximately 2 miles)

kotal a narrow pass in the high mountains around Kabul

kükäldash (T) "milk-brother/-sister"; in Turco-Iranian society, children nursed by the same woman were bonded as "milk-brothers" and "-sisters"; members of the opposite sex so related were forbidden to marry

kutahpay (P) literally, "shortlegged," the Indian hog deer

lac (H) the Hindustani *lak*, a unit of value equal to one hundred thousand

langar (P) a charitable institution at which food was doled out to the poor; langars were often located on heavily traveled routes

lucha (See *buqalamun*, above.)

ma'jun (P) a mild narcotic concoction made into a chewable pellet

madrasa (P) an Islamic institution of higher learning

malik (P) the title of a local ruler

mathnawi (P) a Persian literary form, similar to rhymed couplets in English

maund (*man*) (P) a Persian measure of weight

mawlana (A) a title of respect accorded to the learned

mir (P) Sayyids (descendants of the Prophet Muhammad) may have the title Amir, sometimes shortened to Mir, before their names instead of Sayyid

mirza (P) a shortened form of *amirzada*, "offspring of the Amir," the courtesy title of all male descendants of Amir Temür; in the Turkish fashion, the title follows the proper name

mithcal an Islamic measure of weight (4.6 grams); from the Arabic, *mithqal*

muhtasib (P) the morals officer of a town or city

mukhammas (P) a strophic verse form consisting of five hemistiches

mulla (P) shortened form of *mawlana*. (See above.)

mujtahid (P) a level of religious learning in Shiite Islam at which one is entitled to issue independently derived legal opinions

namazgah (P) an area outside a city where festival prayers could be performed by the whole population together

naqara (P) drums traditionally sounded at a ruler's gate at dawn and dusk; this royal prerogative could be conferred upon a high-ranking officer

naqsh (P) a type of musical composition

nasta'liq (P) a Persianate calligraphic style, originally called *naskh-ta'liq*

naskh-ta'liq (P) (See *nasta'liq*.)

nawa (P) a musical mode

nilgau (P/H) indigo cow, or blue bull (nilgai)

nimcha (P) a short upper garment

nökär (T) a liege man; retainer

orchin (T) an administrative district in Andizhan and Kashghar, similar to the *pargana* in Hindustan

padam (H) a unit of value equal to 100 nils

padishah (P) an independent, autonomous ruler of an area

pahar (H) a watch, for the time of day

panjgah (P) a musical mode

parschï (T) cheetah keeper

pargana (H) an administrative district or estate in Hindustan, similar to the *orchin* in Andizhan and Kashghar

pas (P) the Indian *pahar*, or watch

pasban (P) watchman

peshgah (P) same as *peshkhana*. (See below.)

peshkhana (P) the canopy or awning that protrudes from the front of a trellis tent

peshraw (P) a type of musical composition

peshtaq (P) an arched gatehouse leading to the forecourt of a building

pulad (P) steel

qalpaq (M) a type of broad-brimmed hat named for the Qalpaqs (Kalmyks)

qasida (P) a monorhymed Persian literary form used generally for encomiastic poetry

qïzïbash (T) literally "red-head," the nickname for the Safavids of Iran, from the tall red felt cap they wore, visible in the figure on p. 372

qol (T/M) the center in a battle array

qopuz (T) a lutelike musical instrument

qor begi (T) literally "lord of the quiver," a fairly high field rank in the ruler's personal service; a chief arms bearer

qorchï (T) originally a quiver bearer; by Babur's time it probably indicated a squire

radif (P) a refrain

rajah (H) a Rajput title of rule; same as *ray*. (See below.)

rana (H) a Rajput title of rule; same as *ray*. (See below.)

ray (H) an alternate form of rajah, an Indian prince or chief, or the bearer of a title of nobility among the Hindus

rubâb (P) a rebec, a lutelike musical instrument

sangar (P) stone breastwork used in mountainous areas such as Afghanistan

saqirlât (P) dictionaries define the term as "fine woolen stuff of European manufacture"; since it is doubtful that European textiles had made their way to the Orient in Babur's time, it must mean some finely woven cloth; tents were also made of *saqirlât*

sarkob (P) a war engine, siege machine like a rolling tower

sayyid (A) a descendant of the Prophet Muhammad

saz (P) a lutelike musical instrument

seer (P) a Persian measure of weight

shah (P) (See *padishah*, above.)

shahnishin (P) a dais, or bench, often with three raised sides. (See illus. p. 227.)

shahrukhi (P) a gold coin left from the reign of Shahrukh. (See *tanka*, below.)

shaykh (P) a title of respect accorded to Sufi masters

shaykhu'l-islam (A) the chief religious official in a given region

shaykhzada (P) in the subcontinent, the *shaykhzada*s, descendants of the Companions of the Prophet Muhammad, formed a distinct class. Babur mentions in particular the descendants of Shaykh Muhammad Musalman of Barmal (Farmul)

shibä (T) a type of arrow

ta'liq (P) a chancery script

tabin (T) the elite royal contingent

takband (P) a belt or girdle, perhaps a sword belt

tamgha (T/M) a customs impost, a tax imposed by the Mongols that was always considered un-Islamic

tank (H) an Indian measure of weight

tanka (H/P) a coin; the primary unit of currency under the Timurids; under Temür it weighed 5.38 grams of silver; under Shahrukh the weight was reduced to 4.72 grams, and the coin became known as the *shahrukhi*

taravih (A) supererogatory prayers customarily performed at night during Ramadan

tola (H) an Indian measure of weight, slightly more than two *mithcals*

toquz (T) a set of nine; in Turkic custom, gifts are given in sets of nine

töshäkkhana (T/P) a tent in which textiles were stored

tovachï (T) a officer of the muster

tughchï (T) a servant in charge of the *tugh*, the yak-tail standard attached to a ruler's horse

tümän (T) literally, "ten thousand"; a military division; the territory that would provide maintenance for such a division

tümän begi (T) a leader of a military division of ten thousand

ulus (T) nation, tribal confederation

ülüsh (T/M) a champion's portion, a Mongolian custom

uruq (T) a family and household

üy-el (T) literally "house-people," all the members of a household, wives, children, and servants

yasavul (T) a messenger

yengä (T) a wife of a paternal uncle

yengächichä (T) an affectionate term for aunt in Chaghatay

zunnar (P) applied to various articles of clothing, the term implies that the wearer is non-Muslim

REFERENCES

Abdul-Baqi Nihawandi. *Maathir-i-Rahimi.* Edited by M. Hidayet Husain. Calcutta: Bibliotheca Indica, 1910–31.

Abdul-Hamîd Lahawrî. *Bâdshâhnâma.* Edited by Kabír Al-Dín and Abd Al-Rahím. 2 vols. Calcutta: Royal Asiatic Society of Bengal, 1867–68.

Abu'l-Fazl. *Ain-i-Akbari.* Vol. 2. Translated by Col. H. S. Jarrett. 2d ed. Annotated by Sir Jadu-Nath Sarkar. Calcutta: Royal Asiatic Society of Bengal, 1949.

————. *Akbarnama.* Translated by Henry Beveridge. 3 vols. Calcutta: Royal Asiatic Society of Bengal, 1897–1921.

Abû-Tâhir Khwâja Samarqandî. *Samariyya.* Edited by Iraj Afshâr. Tehran: Mu'assasa-i Farhangî-i Jahângîrî, 1367.

Adamec, Ludwig W. *Historical and Political Gazetteer of Afghanistan.* 6 vols. Graz: Akademische Druk- u. Verlagsanstalt, 1972–85.

Ali-Sher Nawâ'i. *Majâlis al-nafâyis.* Persian translation by Sultân-Muhammad Fakhrî Harâtî and Shah-Muhammad Qazwînî. Edited by Ali-Asghar Hikmat. Tehran: Bank-i Millî-i Irân, 1323 [1944].

Allen, Terry. *A Catalogue of the Toponyms and Monuments of Timurid Herat.* Cambridge, Mass.: Aga Khan Program, 1981. Reprint. Wiesbaden: Reichert, 1983.

Ansari, A. S. Bazmee. "Djat." *Encyclopedia of Islam,* 2d ed., 2:488 f.

————. "Gakkhar." *Encyclopedia of Islam,* 2d ed., 2:972–74.

————. "Gudjar." *Encyclopedia of Islam,* 2d ed., 2:1122 f.

Archer, Mildred. *Natural History Drawings in the India Office Library.* London: Her Majesty's Stationery Office, 1962.

Azimdzhanova, S. A. *Gosudarstvo Babura v Kabule i v Indii.* Moscow, 1977.

Babur, Zahîr al-Dîn Muhammad. *Baber-nameh Diagataice ad fidem codicis Petropolitani.* Edited by Nikolai Ilminski. Kazan: Qazân Universityetînîng Tab'khânasî, 1857.

————. *Bâburnâma.* Chaghatay text and Persian translation edited by W. M. Thackston. Sources of Oriental Languages and Literatures 18, Sources of Turkish Literature 16. Parts 1–3. Cambridge, Mass.: Harvard University Department of Near Eastern Languages and Civilizations, 1993.

————. Dîvân. In E. Denison Ross, ed. "A Collection of Poems by the Emperor Babur." Journal and Proceedings of the Asiatic Society of Bengal 6 (1910): extra no.

————. Le livre de Babur: Mémoires de Zahiruddin Muhammad Babur de 1494 à 1529. Translated by J.-L. Bacqué Grammont. Paris: Imprimerie Nationale, 1986.

————. Memoirs of Babar, Emperor of India, First of the Great Moghuls. Edited by F. G. Talbot. London: Arthur L. Humphreys, 1909.

————. Memoirs of Zehir-ed-Din Muhammed Baber, Emperor of Hindustan. Translated by John Leyden and William Erskine. London: Longman, Rees, Orme, Brown, and Green, 1826. Annotated and revised by Sir Lucas King. 2 vols. Oxford: Oxford University Press, 1921.

————. Mémoires de Baber. Translated by Abel Pavet de Courteille. Paris: Maisonneuve, 1871.

————. Risâla-i mubîn. In Il'ya Nikolaevich Berezin, ed. Biblioteka vostochnykh istorikov. Kazan, 1849.

————. The Bâbar-náma, Being the Autobiography of the Emperor Bábar, the Founder of the Moghul Dynasty in India, Written in Chaghatáy Turkish. Facsimile of the Hyderabad manuscript. Edited by Annette Susannah Beveridge. E.J.W. Gibb Memorial Series, 1. London: Luzac, 1905. Reissue, 1971.

————. The Bâbur-nâma in English. Translated by Annette Susannah Beveridge, 2 vols. London: Luzac, 1921.

————. Vekayi: Babur'un Hâtirati. Translated by Re‚sit Rahmeti Arat. Türk Tarih Kurumu Yayinlari, vol. 2. Seri, 5. 2 vols. Ankara: Türk Tarih Kurumu Basimevi, 1943–46.

————. Zapiski Babura. Edited by S. A. Azimdzhanova. Tashkent, 1958.

Barger, Evert, and Philip Wright. Excavations in Swat and Explorations in the Oxus Territories of Afghanistan. Calcutta, 1941. Reprint. Delhi: Sri Satguru, 1985.

Bartold, V. V. Abyârî dar Turkistân. Translated by Karîm Kishâwarz. Intishârât-i Mu'assasa-i Mutâla'ât u Tahqîqât-i Ijtimâ'î 76. Tehran: Dânishgâh-i Tihrân, 1350.

————. Turkistan Down to the Mongol Invasion. E.J.W. Gibb Memorial Series, n.s. 5. London: Luzac, 1928.

Bayram Khan. The Persian and Turki Divans of Bayram Khan. Edited by E. Denison Ross. Calcutta: Royal Asiatic Society of Bengal, 1910.

Becka, Jirí. "Tajik Literature from the Sixteenth Century to the Present." In History of Iranian Literature, edited by Jan Rypka, 485–605. Dordrecht: D. Reidel, 1968.

Bhargava, Visheshwar Sarup. Marwar and the Mughal Emperors (A.D. 1526–1748). Delhi: Munshiram Manoharlal, 1966.

Bhattacharya, Sachchidananda. *A Dictionary of Indian History.* New York: George Braziller, 1967.

Blagova, G. F. "K istorii izucheniya 'Babur-name' v Rosii." *Tyurkologicheskiy sbornik k shestidesyatiletiyu Andreya Nikolaevicha Kononova* [Moscow] (1966): 168–76.

———. "K voprosu o podlinnosti teksta 'Babur-name' po kerovskomu spisku." *Kratkie Soobshcheniya Instituta Narodov Azii AnSSR* 44 (1961): 89–105.

Blochet, Edgar. *Catalogue des manuscrits persans.* Vol. 1. Paris: Imprimerie Nationale, 1905.

Bosworth, C. E. "Kafiristan." *Encyclopedia of Islam,* 2d ed., 4:409–11.

———. *The Later Ghaznavids: Splendour and Decay.* New York: Columbia University Press, 1977.

Brandenburg, Dietrich. *Samarkand: Studien zur islamischen Baukunst in Uzbekistan Zentralasien.* Berlin: Bruno Hersling, 1972.

Burhân, Muhammad Husayn b. Khalaf Tabrîzî. *Burhân-i Qâti'.* Edited by Muhammad Mu'în. 5 vols. Tehran: Zuwwâr, 1330.

Chakravarty, Kalyan Kumar. *Gwalior Fort: Art, Culture and History.* New Delhi: Arnold-Heinemann, 1984.

Clauson, Sir Gerard. *An Etymological Dictionary of Pre-Thirteenth-Century Turkish.* Oxford: Clarendon Press, 1972.

Clavijo, Ruy González de. *Embassy to Tamerlane, 1403–1406.* Translated by Guy Le Strange. New York and London: Harper and Bros., 1928.

A Dictionary of the Pathan Tribes in the North-West Frontier of India. Calcutta, 1910. Reprint. Delhi: Mittal Publications, 1983.

Doerfer, G. *Türkische und mongolische Elemente im Neupersischen.* 4 vols. Akademie der Wissenschaften und der Literatur, Veröffentlichungen der Orientalischen Kommission, 16, 19–21. Wiesbaden: Harrassowitz, 1963–75.

Drury, Heber. *Hand-book of the Indian Flora.* 3 vols. Dehra Dun: Bishen Singh Mahendra Pal Singh, 1982–83.

During, Jean, et al. *The Art of Persian Music.* Washington, D.C.: Mage, 1991.

Elliot, Sir Henry Miers, and John Dowson. *The History of India as Told by Its Own Historians.* 8 vols. London: Trübner, 1867–77.

Elphinstone, Mountstuart. *An Account of the Kingdom of Caubul and Its Dependencies in Persia, Tartary, and India.* London: Longman, Hurst, Rees, Orme, and Brown, 1815. Reprint. 2 vols. Graz: Akademische Druck- u. Verlagsanstalt, 1969.

Encyclopedia of Islam, 2d ed. Edited by J. H. Kramers, H. A. R. Gibb, and E. Levi Provencal. Leiden: E. J. Brill; London: Luzac, 1954–.

Ethé, Hermann. *Catalogue of Persian Manuscripts in the India Office Library.* 2 vols. London: India Office Library, 1903–37.

Faris, Nabih Amin, and Robert Potter Elmer. *Arab Archery.* Princeton: Princeton University Press, 1945.

Firdawsi. *Shâhnâma.* Edited by A. E. Bertels, L. T. Gyuzalyan, et al. 9 vols. Moscow: Nauk, 1966–71.

Fletcher, T. Bainbrigge, and C. M. Inglis. *Birds of an Indian Garden.* Calcutta and Simla: Thacker, Spink, 1924.

Forster, E. M. "The Emperor Babur." In *Abinger Harvest,* 283–87. New York: Meridian Books, 1955. Reprint. New York: Harcourt, Brace and World, 1964.

Frey, Wolfgang. *Vegetation und Flora des Zentralen Hindükuš (Afghanistan).* Wiesbaden: Reichert, 1978.

Gandjeï, Tourkhan. "Uno scritto apologetico di Husain Mirza, sultano del Khorasan." In *Annali del' Istituto Orientale di Napoli,* n.s. 5 (1953): 157–83.

Garren, W. R., and Carl R. Page. *Gazetteer of Pakistan.* 3d ed. Washington, D.C.: Defense Mapping Agency, 1983.

Geographic Names Division, U.S. Army Topographic Command. *U.S.S.R. Official Standard Names Approved by the U.S. Board on Geographic Names.* June 1970.

Ghulâm Sarwar Lâhawrî. *Safînat al-asfiyâ.* Kanpur: Nawal Kishore, n.d.

Golombek, Lisa, and Donald Wilbur. *The Timurid Architecture of Iran and Turan.* 2 vols. Princeton: Princeton University Press, 1988.

Grousset, René. *The Empire of the Steppes.* New Brunswick: Rutgers University Press, 1970.

Gulbadan Begim. *The History of Humâyûn (Humâyûnnâma).* Translated by Annette Susannah Beveridge. London: Royal Asiatic Society, 1902.

Hâfiz-i Abrû, Nûr al-Dîn 'Abdullâh Khwâfî. *Târîkh-i Hâfiz-i Abrû.* Vol. 2. Edited by Dorothea Krawulsky. Wiesbaden: Reichert, 1982.

Hâfiz. *Dîwân-i Khwâja Hâfiz-i Shîrâzî.* Edited by Sayyid Abû'l-Qâsim Injuwî Shîrâzî. N.p.: 'Ilmî, n.d.

Hinz, Walther. *Islamische Masse und Gewichte.* Leiden: E. J. Brill, 1955.

Imperial Gazetteer of India. 25 vols. Oxford: Clarendon Press, 1907–9.

Iskandar Beg Turkmân. *Târîkh-i 'âlamârâ-yi 'Abbâsî.* 2 vols. Tehran: Amîr Kabîr, 1350.

Jahangir. *Tuzuk-i-Jahangiri.* Translated by A. Rogers. Edited by Henry Beveridge. London, 1909–14.

Jami, Nuruddin Abdul-Rahman. *Dîwân-i kâmil-i Jâmî.* Edited by Hâshim Razî. N.p.: Pîrûz, 1341.

———. *Nafahât al-uns wa hazarât al-quds.* Edited by Mahdî Tawhîdîpûr. Tehran: Mahmûdî, 1337.

———. *Nâmahâ-yi dastniwîs-i Jâmî.* Edited by Isâm al-Dîn Uranbâyef and Mâyil Harawî. Tashkent: Uzbekistan Science Academy, Oriental Institute, n.d.

Jung, Angelika. *Quellen der traditionellen Kunstmusik der Usbeken und Tadschiken Mittelasiens.* Beiträge zur Ethnomusikologie, no. 23. Hamburg: Karl Dieter Wagner, 1989.

Kâshgharî, Mahmûd al-. *Compendium of the Turkic Dialects.* Translated by Robert Dankoff and James Kelly. 3 parts. Sources of Oriental Languages and Literatures 7, Turkish Sources 7. Cambridge: Harvard University, 1982–85.

Kâshifî, Kamâl al-Dîn Husayn Wâ'iz. *Anwâr-i Suhaylî.* Tehran: Amîr Kabîr, 1362.

Khwândamîr, Ghiyâth al-Dîn b. Humâm al-Dîn al-Husaynî. *Habîb al-siyar fî akhbâr-i afrâd-i bashar.* Edited by Jalâl Humâ'î. 4 vols. Tehran: Khayyâm, 1333.

Kitamura, Shiro. *Flora of Afghanistan.* Kyoto: Committee of the Kyoto University Scientific Expedition to the Karakoram and Hindukush, 1968.

Latham, J. D., and W. F. Paterson. *Saracen Archery.* London: Holland Press, 1970.

Lentz, Thomas W., and Glenn D. Lowry. *Timur and the Princely Vision: Persian Art and Culture in the Fifteenth Century.* Los Angeles: Los Angeles County Museum of Art, 1989.

Mano, Eiji. "A Study of *Bâbur-nâma* (III). Annette Susannah Beveridge and the Hyderabad Codex" (in Japanese). *Memoirs of the Faculty of Letters,* Kyoto University 24 (1985): 1–58.

———. "The Weeping-willows Passage in the Babur-nama." *Proceedings of the 27th Meeting of Haneda Memorial Hall Symposium on Central Asia and Iran, August 30, 1993.* Kyoto: Kyoto University, 1993. pp. 28–35.

Manz, Beatrice F. *The Rise and Rule of Tamerlane.* Cambridge: Cambridge University Press, 1989.

Marquart, Joseph. *Erânšahr nach der Geographie des Ps. Moses Xorenac'i.* Abhandlungen der Königlichen Gesellschaft der Wissenschaften zu Göttingen. Berlin: Weidmannsche Buchhandlung, 1901.

Marsh, Lawrence K. *Gazetteer of Afghanistan: Names Approved by the United States Board of Geographic Names.* Washington, D.C.: Defense Mapping Agency, 1983.

Masson, Charles. *Narratives of Various Journeys in Beluchistan, Afghanistan, the Panjab and Kalát.* London: R. Bentley, 1844.

Minhâj Sirâj Jûzjânî, Qâzî. *Tabaqât-i Nâsirî.* Edited by Abdul-Hayy Habîbî. Tehran: Dunyâ-yi Kitâb, 1363 [1985].

Morgenstierne, G. "Afghan." *Encyclopedia of Islam,* 2d ed., 1:216–21.

Moynihan, Elizabeth. "The Lotus Garden: Babur the First Mughal Architect." *India Magazine* 6 (1986): 10–16.

Mu'izz al-ansâb fî shajarat al-ansâb. Anonymous MS. Paris, Bibliothèque Nationale. Ancien Fonds Persan 67.

Mu'în, Muhammad. *Farhang-i fârsî.* 6 vols. Tehran: Amîr Kabîr, 1364.

Muhammad Haydar Dughlat, Mirza. *A History of the Moghuls of Central Asia.* Translated by E. Denison Ross. Edited and annotated by Ney Elias. London: Sampson Low, Marston, 1898. Reissue. New York: Praeger Publications, 1970.

————. *Tarikh-i Rashidi.* Extract in Persian edited by Muhammad Shafi', "Iqtibas az Tarikh-i Rashidi." In *Oriental College Magazine* 10, no. 3 (1934): 150–72.

Muhammad ibn 'Abd al-Jalîl Samarqandî. *Qandiyya.* Edited by Iraj Afshâr. Tehran: Mu'assasa-i Farhangî-i Jahângîrî, 1367.

Nasîruddîn Tûsî. *Hall-i mushkilât-i Mu'îniyya.* Tehran: Dânishgâh-i Tihrân, 1335.

Nath, R. *Monuments of Delhi: Historical Study.* New Delhi: Ambika Publications, Indian Institute of Islamic Studies, 1979.

Nâdir Khân, Muhammad. *Râhnumâ-yi Qataghan u Badakhshân.* Tehran: Mu'assasa-i Farhangî-i Jahângîrî. 1367.

Nevill, H. R. *District Gazetteers of the United Provinces of Agra and Audh.* Allahabad: Government Press. Vol. 30, *Ballia: A Gazetteer,* 1907. Vol. 46, *Sultanpur: A Gazetteer,* 1903.

Pant, G. N. *Mughal Weapons in the Baburnama.* Delhi: Agam Kala Prakashan, 1989.

Parpagliolo, Maria Teresa S. *Kabul: The Bagh-i Babur.* Rome: IsMEO, 1972.

Payne-Gallwey, Sir Ralph. *Projectile Throwing Engines with a Treatise on the Turkish and Other Oriental Bows.* London, 1907.

Platts, John T. *A Dictionary of Urdû, Classical Hindî and English.* Oxford: Oxford University Press, 1968.

Pougatchenkova, Galina A. *Chefs-d'oeuvre d'architecture de l'Asia Centrale, XIVe–XVe siècle.* Paris: UNESCO, 1981.

Radloff, Wilhelm. *Versuch eines Wörterbuches der Türk-Dialecte.* 4 vols. Saint Petersburg, 1893–1911. Reprint. The Hague: Moutin, 1960.

Randhawa, M. S. *Paintings of the Bâburnâmâ.* New Delhi: National Museum, 1983.

Raverty, Henry George. *Notes on Afghanistan and Baluchistan.* Reprint of 1878 ed. Lahore: Sang-e-Meel Publications, 1976.

Robertson, Sir George Scott. *The Káfirs of the Hindu-Kush.* London: Lawrence and Bullen, 1896.

Ross, E. Denison. "A Collection of Poems by the Emperor Babur." *Journal and Proceedings of the Asiatic Society of Bengal* 6 (1910): extra no.

Roux, Jean-Paul. *Histoire des grands moghols: Babur.* Paris: Fayard, 1986.

Rypka, Jan. *History of Iranian Literature.* Edited by Karl Jahn. Dordrecht: D. Reidel, 1968.

Sa'dî. *Kulliyyât-i Sa'dî*. Edited by Muhammad-'Alî Furûghî. Tehran: Amîr Kabîr, 1363.

Saljûqî, Fikrî, ed. *Risâla-i mazârât-i Harât*. Kabul: Publishing Institute, 1967.

Seyller, John. "Scribal Notes on Mughal Manuscript Illustrations." *Artibus Asiae* 48 (1987): 247–77.

Shah Nawaz Khan, Samsam-ud-daula, and Abdul-Hayy. *The Maathir-ul-umara*. Translated by Henry Beveridge. 2 vols. Calcutta: Royal Asiatic Society of Bengal, 1911–52.

Sharp, H. *Delhi: Its Story and Buildings*. London: Oxford University Press, 1921.

Smart, Ellen. "Paintings from the *Bâburnâma:* A Study of Sixteenth-Century Mughal Historical Manuscript Illustrations." Ph.D. diss., School of Oriental and African Studies, University of London, 1977.

Steingass, Francis Joseph. *A Comprehensive Persian-English Dictionary.* London: Routledge and Kegan Paul, 1963.

Stone, George Cameron. *A Glossary of the Construction, Decoration and Use of Arms and Armor*. Portland, Maine: Southworth Press, 1934.

Storey, C. A. *Persian Literature: A Bio-Bibliographical Survey.* Vol. 1. London: Luzac, 1970–72.

Stuart, C. M. Villiers. *Gardens of the Great Mughals*. London: Adam and Charles Black, 1913.

Subtelny, Maria. "Art and Politics in the Sixteenth Century." *Central Asiatic Journal* 27 (1983): 121–48.

———. "Bâbur's Rival Relations: A Study of Kinship and Conflict in Fifteenth–Sixteenth Century Central Asia." *Der Islam* 66/1 (1989): 102–18.

———. "Socioeconomic Bases of Cultural Patronage under the Later Timurids." *International Journal of Middle Eastern Studies* 20 (1988): 479–505.

Sulaymân Efendî Bukhârî, Shaykh. *Lughât-i chaghatay va turkî-i 'uthmânî*. Istanbul, 1297.

Suleiman, Hamid, ed. *Miniatures of Babur-Nama*. Tashkent: Fan, 1970.

Sultanov, T. I. " 'Zapiski' Babura kak istochnik po istorii mogolov Vostochnogo Turkestana i Sredney Azii." In *Turcologica* [Leningrad] (1986): 253–67.

Tahmasp I. *Tadhkira-i Shah Tahmasp*. Berlin: Kaviani, 1343/1924.

Thackston, W. M. *A Century of Princes*. Cambridge, Mass.: Aga Khan Program, 1989.

Tyulyayev, S., ed. *Miniatyury rukopisi "Babur-name."* Moscow: Gosudarstvennoe Izdatel'stvo Izobrazitel'nogo Iskusstva, 1960.

Vullers, Johann August. *Lexicon persicolatinum etymologicum*. 2 vols. Bonn: A. Marci, 1855–67.

Wescoat, James L., Jr. "Early Water Systems in Mughal India." *Environmental Design: Journal of the Islamic Environmental Design Research Centre* 2 (1985): 50–57.

———. "Picturing an Early Mughal Garden." *Asian Art* 2, no. 4 (1989): 59–79.

Yule, Henry, and A. C. Burnell. *Hobson-Jobson.* Edited by William Crooke. London: John Murray, 1903.

Zamchî Isfizârî, Mu'în al-Dîn Muhammad. *Rawdât al-jannât fî awsâf madînat Harât.* Edited by Muhammad-Kâzim Imâm. 2 vols. Tehran: Dânishgâh, 1338–39.

Zayn al-Dîn Khwâfî. *Zain Khan's Tabaqat-i Baburi.* Translated by Sayed Hasan Askari. Annotation by B. P. Ambastha. Delhi: Idarah-i Adabiyat-i Delli, 1982.

INDEX OF PERSONS

INDEX OF PLACES

A NOTE ON THE TYPE

The principal text of this Modern Library edition
was set in a digitized version of Janson, a typeface that
dates from about 1690 and was cut by Nicholas Kis,
a Hungarian working in Amsterdam. The original matrices have
survived and are held by the Stempel foundry in Germany.
Hermann Zapf redesigned some of the weights and sizes for
Stempel, basing his revisions on the original design.

MODERN LIBRARY IS ONLINE AT
WWW.MODERNLIBRARY.COM

MODERN LIBRARY ONLINE IS YOUR GUIDE TO CLASSIC LITERATURE ON THE WEB

THE MODERN LIBRARY E-NEWSLETTER

Our free e-mail newsletter is sent to subscribers, and features sample chapters, interviews with and essays by our authors, upcoming books, special promotions, announcements, and news.

To subscribe to the Modern Library e-newsletter, send a blank e-mail to: sub_modernlibrary@info.randomhouse.com or visit www.modernlibrary.com

THE MODERN LIBRARY WEBSITE

Check out the Modern Library website at
www.modernlibrary.com for:

- The Modern Library e-newsletter
- A list of our current and upcoming titles and series
- Reading Group Guides and exclusive author spotlights
- Special features with information on the classics and other paperback series
- Excerpts from new releases and other titles
- A list of our e-books and information on where to buy them
- The Modern Library Editorial Board's 100 Best Novels and 100 Best Nonfiction Books of the Twentieth Century written in the English language
- News and announcements

Questions? E-mail us at **modernlibrary@randomhouse.com**
For questions about examination or desk copies, please visit the Random House Academic Resources site at
www.randomhouse.com/academic